GOLF
RECORD FILE

ALUN EVANS

First published in Great Britain in 2000 by
Virgin Books
an imprint of Virgin Publishing Ltd
Thames Wharf Studios
Rainville Road
London W6 9HA

ISBN 0 7535 0471 5

Designed by Roger Kohn
Typeset by Mark Webb
Printed and bound in Great Britain by
Mackays of Chatham plc, Chatham, Kent

CONTENTS

INTRODUCTION 5

MAJOR CHAMPIONSHIPS 7

RYDER CUP 231

GOLF IN THE USA 305
US PGA Tour 306; Buy.Com (Nike) Tour 337;
PGA Seniors Tour 338; US Amateur
Championships 341; LPGA Tour 344

GOLF IN BRITAIN AND EUROPE 347
PGA European Tour 349; Challenge Tour 383;
European Seniors Tour 386; British Amateur
Championship 389; European Ladies
PGA Tour 392

OTHER WORLD GOLF 395
World Golf Championships 397; Presidents Cup
400; Alfred Dunhill Cup 402; World Cup of Golf
403; Walker Cup 407; Solheim Cup 410;
Curtis Cup 413

THE OFFICIAL WORLD GOLF RANKING 415

Golf Record File

Golf is a sport of long traditions, diverse and sometimes complex. What I have attempted to do, therefore, while including, subjectively of course, all the major facts along the way, is to cover all those relevant strands from their origins; and, where interrelations with other strands exist, point them out. This is particularly so in the sections on the various Tours, where an event may have begun under a completely different name from the one that is running today.

I have also sectionalised the book so that those areas of greatest interest to the majority of readers are at the beginning, and are accorded the most space. I apologise therefore for those followers of amateur or ladies golf, therefore, if you seem to be getting a harsh deal, but I hope I have included the statistics that matter even there. All data is accurate (please tell me if it isn't!) up to 31 December 1999, an obvious point to cut off.

ACKNOWLEDGEMENTS AND BIBLIOGRAPHY

The sheer breadth of politics in golf means that anyone attempting to put together such a comprehensive volume has to seek the assistance of so many different sporting bodies, and the pioneering work of not a few individuals. The Majors section owes much to the support I've been given over the years from Peter Lewis and Elinor Clark of the British Golf Museum in St Andrews (for the Open); Nancy Stulack of the USGA (US Open); Terry McSweeney and Bob Denney of the PGA of America (US PGA Championship); and Glenn Greenspan at Augusta National (Masters). For the various other sections thanks go to the (US) PGA Tour and Senior Tour; European Tour and Senior and Challenge Tours; the LGU (Jane Fleming) and the Ladies European Tour (Tilly Thomson and Fay Wilson).

Alan F. Jackson, through his engrossing *The British Professional Golfers, 1887-1930*, Alex Hay and Sal Johnson (whose *Official US Open Almanac* is without doubt the best book on any one aspect of golf history ever compiled) helped me improve the (sometimes very poor) raw data, with full names, nationalities, etc. I am grateful also for the assistance of the PGAs of Argentina, South Africa and Australia in that matter. *Golf Weekly* magazine has been a constant goldmine of information.

For background, Peter Alliss' *Who's Who of Golf* is still unbeatable, but badly in need of an update, and Derek Lawrenson's *The Complete Encyclopedia of Golf* is spoiled only by inaccurate statistics. Finally I am indebted to Tony Greer of IMG for his permission to quote on a previously unheard-of scale from his Official World Ranking, which I hope you see as a most suitable summation of this book. On a personal note, Jonathan Taylor at Virgin has the patience of Job; and I am grateful to my wife Caryl, yet again, for being there, particularly at the end when everything and everyone gets a bit ragged. I hope I haven't missed anyone out – if so, please forgive me.

ABBREVIATIONS USED IN THIS BOOK

a	Amateur
ARG	Argentina
AUS	Australia
BEL	Belgium
BOP	British Open
BRA	Brazil
CAN	Canada
EGY	Egypt
ELPGA	European Ladies PGA
ENG	England
FIJ	Fiji
FRA	France
GER	Germany (including former West Germany)
HOL	Holland
IRE	Ireland (including Northern Ireland and the former Irish Free State)
IT	Italy
JAP	Japan
LGU	Ladies Golf Union
MAS	US Masters
MEX	Mexico
NZ	New Zealand
PAR	Paraguay
PGA	US PGA Championship, or Professional Golfers' Association
PR	Puerto Rico
R&A	Royal and Ancient Club of St Andrews
SA	South Africa
SCO	Scotland
SP	Spain
SWE	Sweden
TAI	Taiwan (including former Formosa)
TRI	Trinidad and Tobago
URU	Uruguay
US	United States
USGA	US Golf Association
USO	US Open
WAL	Wales
ZIM	Zimbabwe (including former Southern Rhodesia and Rhodesia)

THE DEVELOPMENT OF THE MAJORS

Excepting perhaps Ryder Cup glory, what is it about the Open Championship, the US Open, the US PGA and Masters that has held golfers and golf followers so enthralled throughout history and, seemingly, increasingly more so over recent decades? These pages deal with the development of each of the 'Major' Championships, the reasons for their coming to be and some of the characters who have influenced or have been associated with them. Much is drawn from the author's own *The Golf Majors – Records and Yearbook*, which first appeared in 1997, after combining my own research with that of others (like Sal Johnson on the US Open): a book which came together partly because golf has had no world-wide governing body to pull together, through common archives, a total history of all four Majors. As a result, therefore, the section on the Majors, particularly the year-by-year results and commentaries, cannot be found anywhere else in print apart from the above-mentioned title. With some exceptions, excellent records and anecdotal histories are to be found across a range of publications – but only pertain to one Championship or another. These volumes, quite naturally, promote the credentials of the Championship of subject – in short, every Major Championship claims to be the best in one way or another! There has never been the perceived necessity from within the structure of the game to cross-fertilise records for the benefit of the tradition of golf as a whole, as other sports do. This is an attempt to set that right.

This story begins in Scotland, sometime in the middle of the nineteenth century...

THE OPEN CHAMPIONSHIP (THE BRITISH OPEN)

Allan Robertson was the subject of many legends. Some say he was never beaten in a singles match, and the pairing of Robertson with his assistant at St Andrews, Tom Morris (Senior, that is), over many years was probably also undefeated – and very lucrative for a time when professional sportsmen were usually only found in the ring, or on the turf, or playing cricket. Whatever the veracity of the stories, it is uniformly regarded that Robertson was the best player of his day in Scotland, which in the mid-eighteenth Century meant the world. When he died in 1859, aged just 44, could it be that a new golf tournament was arranged to discover who was to be the new king of golf? Certainly few other valid reasons

have been given for the 'Championship' which was organised for the following year; and single medal strokeplay at that. Robertson was known in his later life to play less and less singles golf; and his objections may even have been responsible for such a Championship not taking place any earlier.

During the 1850s a founder member of the Prestwick Club (1851), local squire Col James Ogilvy Fairlie, was the prime mover in setting up a tournament for professionals, based on the less familiar concept of medal play; but it didn't get off the ground until after Robertson's death. Was that because Robertson was so against the idea, and would there be any credibility in the event if it proceeded without him? It is maybe more than coincidence, therefore, despite having no support from other Clubs or Societies, that Prestwick went ahead with the competition just one year after Allan Robertson died.

On 16 October 1860, just eight professional golfers went out to play three rounds of Prestwick's 12 holes. Records of scoring are patchy, to say the least, and would be for many years to come; but there is no argument that Tom Morris was beaten into second place by life-long rival Willie Park. Park's reward was a belt of Moroccan leather, buckled in silver, but no winner's prize money was to be awarded for a few years yet. The following year, encouraged by the inaugural success, James Fairlie played himself as an amateur, thus creating the term 'Open' Championship for the first time. The term 'Open' may just have drifted into sporting parlance for the first time without anyone giving its historical importance any real significance. This time 'Old' Tom Morris won the Championship ahead of Park. Morris had become professional at Prestwick some years before, after falling out with Allan Robertson. In 1848, the gutta-percha ball, or 'guttie', was introduced. It flew further, had a longer life, and it was very much cheaper to produce than the old 'feathery' ball. 'Old' Tom wanted to employ the new technology, but as Robertson was famed for his making of featheries, a rift ensued and Morris moved away; he only returned to St Andrews in 1864 after Robertson's death.

The older Morris and Parks dominated the Championship until 1868 when the all-to-brief but brilliant career of Tom Morris, Jr began. Just 17 when he won in 1868, this tragic figure came and went like a comet. He was to shine like a brilliant light which illuminated the golf world for the next eight years, before burning out before the age of 25. He won the Open for three years running (1868-70) and the Belt was awarded to him for posterity. Partly because of this, and much off-course politicking, no Championship was held in 1871. When it was re-launched in 1872, Prestwick shared the organisation of the event with the prestigious east coast Societies; the Royal and Ancient Club and the Honourable Company of Edinburgh Golfers. It also shared in the outlay for a new trophy – the famous silver claret jug, still presented today. The first winner was inevitably 'Young' Tom Morris, but, instead of dominating the world of golf for the next decade and more, this was to be his last Open victory. Commonplace among Scottish professionals of the time, Morris was a heavy whisky drinker, and his health began to suffer. In 1874, he was reputedly heart-broken when his wife died in childbirth and a combination of grief and the resultant need for succour from the bottle killed him. He was found dead by his father on Christmas morning, 1874.

The Open Championship consolidated its development over the following two decades by rotating Prestwick with the other Clubs' courses at St Andrews and Musselburgh. The longevity of Messrs Morris and Parks Senior was matched by very few players. The short, spectacular careers of Jamie Anderson and Bob Ferguson, both of whom won three successive Opens, ended in poverty and obscurity. But by the 1890s a great sea change in the game was about to occur.

Golf had been exported from Scotland throughout the world during the nineteenth century: it had taken root in England even earlier, following the influence of the Stuart kings who inherited the throne of England in 1603. Indeed, it is claimed that the Blackheath Club was founded in 1608, encouraged by King James I (James VI of Scotland). The British Empire was the catalyst for the world-wide playing of many British sports in the nineteenth century; but a certain contretemps with some colonials which ended badly for the British in 1781, finished – or changed, through evolution – many sports in the new United States of America. Golf was played in the Carolinas, according to some records, in the mid eighteenth century, but it wasn't until the 1880s that the sport was to be re-established.

The 1890s saw a huge exodus of Scots, and some English, to work as professionals (which also included greenkeeping, club-making and the like) in the newly, rapidly-forming golf hierarchies of the eastern seaboard and Great Lakes cities. The emigrations, and the spreading

south of the game in Britain, meant that the Open took on a less-parochial feel from 1890. Indeed that year it was won by an Englishman, John Ball, for the first time. Ball became the youngest ever competitor in any Major Championship when he competed in the 1878 Open at the tender age of 14; and he was, after the event had run for 30 years, the first amateur to win. In 1892, when Harold Hilton became the second English amateur winner, the competition was extended to four rounds over two days; and the Honourable Company left their nine-hole course at Musselburgh to host the Championship a few miles further along the Firth of Forth, at Muirfield, for the first time. The rota of courses acknowledged the importance of the English improvement in the game when the Open took in English courses at (Royal) St George's, Sandwich (1894) and Royal Liverpool, Hoylake (1897). And the first world stars of golf appeared.

When JH Taylor won at Sandwich in 1894 and 1895, he was to unwittingly start the age of the so-called 'Great Triumvirate'. Between then and 1914, he (five times), Harry Vardon (six) and James Braid (five) won all but five of the Opens played. Vardon and Taylor toured the US in 1900, competed in the US Open and finished first and second. At the end of their reign, however, the faster development of all aspects of the game in the US, from administration, golf courses, ball and club technology and players, meant America became the totally dominant force in world golf; and the Open Championship. Few Britons have won the Open since Vardon's last win, and within 25 years, total Scottish dominance of the Championship they spawned had evaporated completely. George Duncan won the first post-World war Open in 1920, being one of only three Scotsmen, émigrés Jock Hutchison and Tommy Armour apart, after Braid's last title in 1910 to win the Open again in the twentieth century (Sandy Lyle in 1985, then Paul Lawrie, as if in defiance, in 1999, being the others).

The Royal and Ancient Club (the R&A) had been at the forefront of British golf developments in the nineteenth century; and particularly so in the area of Rules, which they had based on the Honourable Company's original template. By 1897, all the host clubs for the Open had adopted 'St Andrews' Rules, thus giving the Club unique hegemony over the sport as a whole, somewhat like the Marylebone Club (MCC) in cricket. Although other countries developed national bodies to monitor the game (including the USGA in America), with one or two local amendments, all looked to the R&A on the question of rules. After World War I, the British clubs were still organising the Open Championship as a cartel, and as such differences and inconsistencies occurred. Looking to the US where the War had not exacted so much cost, and golf was only suspended for two years, the clubs saw the success the USGA had made of the US Open and the birth of the powerful PGA of America; and decided that some form of rationalisation was required if the British national championship was to remain competitive. In 1920, therefore, instead of setting up a national authority for golf, they vested further powers in the R&A, who took over the running of the Open Championship totally, and still does so today.

The 1920s saw the first phase of American dominance. The flashy Walter Hagen coincided with the Hollywood boom and he became the world's first superstar of golf. He won four Opens in a period when only Arthur Havers was a home winner. When Hagen didn't win, it seemed that Bobby Jones must be playing. Inspired by Francis Ouimet's epoch-ending victory over Vardon and Ted Ray in the 1913 US Open, Jones (after tearing up his card in a fit of pique in 1921) won three Open titles in just three further attempts, in a run which also included four US Open wins, and ended with his amazing year of 1930.

The decades leading up to the next War and immediately after it were the bleakest in the history of the Open. Because of the inability of the R&A to match the purses on offer across the Atlantic; the sea crossing taking up the time an American professional could be lucratively employed in another tournament or two; the difference in the size of the balls (US 1.68" diameter v. GB 1.62"); and the overall strength in depth of the American tournament player against his counterpart in Britain (by 1955 the US team was leading the Great Britain & Ireland team 9-2 in the Ryder Cup series); little was remembered of the tradition which started in 1860, and even less was cared. Used to fast, manicured greens, firm, lush fairways, why should the American pro give up all that to play on links courses completely alien to him – and for comparatively little reward? Sam Snead won the 1946 Open at St Andrews, and with little grace criticised the state of the Old Course, pocketed the obviously unsatisfactory cheque and didn't return until 1962. Ben Hogan competed just once, famously in 1953, slammed Carnoustie's greens, and took the old Claret Jug. Many others didn't come at all.

Unfortunately, lessons were either not learned, or if they were understood, there was nothing the R&A could do to reverse the trend. It was hoped that at least without US opposition there would be home victories to celebrate. This was the case in the thirties when American interest dwindled, and there were wins for Cotton, Perry, Padgham, Reg Whitcombe and Burton – but to the concerned onlooker, the Championship paled into comparison with the 1920s heyday of Hagen and Jones, and even the days of the 'Triumvirate'. As a world event it became second division fare.

Immediately after the War, Snead's visit apart, Fred Daly won a low-key affair at Hoylake, and Henry Cotton won his third Open. Maddeningly, Cotton, the best British player of his generation, didn't persevere with his promising early US visits, and thus was not to be the home Champion who might have inspired a new spate of British world-beaters. Then in 1949, a rotund South African, Arthur D'Arcy Locke, whom all knew as Bobby, brought some colour back to the Championship. He went on to win three more times in the 1950s, when even if the Americans stayed away, the new Commonwealth was well represented. If Locke was eclipsed at all during the fifties, it was by Australia's Peter Thomson, who won four times in five years to Locke's four in eight. However, it was to be another South African, globe-trotting Gary Player, who was to herald a new dawn for the Open with a win in 1959; while Thomson's compatriot, Kel Nagle, made it 10 wins for the Commonwealth in 12 years. The only home winner during this time was Max Faulkner, ironically the only time the Championship was not held in Great Britain – at Portrush in 1951. The only American winner from a Stars and Stripes starved decade was Ben Hogan, who in 1953 did the unique treble of Masters, US and British Opens – but was denied any potential Grand Slam as the US PGA frustratingly clashed with Carnoustie.

Meanwhile across the Atlantic the US Tour professional was, through the efforts of the PGA of America, becoming one of the world's most affluent sportsmen. Prize money, sponsorship and royalties were booming thanks mainly to the shrewd marketing of the game to the burgeoning TV networks. At the end of the fifties, the sport found the ideal hero for the television age: Arnold Daniel Palmer. A cigarette-smoking cavalier, with a devil-may-care approach whilst possessing that human touch, Palmer almost single-handedly helped to elevate the sport into a media business. The effect was not just restricted to America. Golf, through Palmer, the dashing black-clad figure of Player and the chubby young Golden Bear, Jack Nicklaus, assumed a major world-wide audience for the first time. Television relays and jet aircraft transported the stars across the globe: and the biggest beneficiary of all was to be the increasingly-moribund British Open Championship.

Palmer came to St Andrews in 1960 and finished second behind Kel Nagle. Two years later at Troon, he had become a double Champion, posting a record 276 and beating the Australian by six shots. The R&A, witnessing the huge galleries following Palmer, realised they had to make provision for this new-style golf fan in future Opens. The sixties saw Arnie finally superseded by Nicklaus, but not before Player had won again; Thomson added his fifth title to match Braid and Taylor; and the Open had its oldest winner in an Argentinian faithful of two decades, Roberto de Vicenzo.

If Palmer had re-ignited the spark, the man who set the Open ablaze for home supporters was Tony Jacklin. Young, good-looking, a symbol of British confidence in the 1960s, he captured the hearts of the nation at Lytham in 1969. Together with his memorable half in the singles with an over-generous Jack Nicklaus which tied the Ryder Cup at Birkdale later that year; and the win, at Hazeltine in the US Open – all within 12 months – Lytham established him as the standard-bearer for the British golfing fightback against American rule. Whether we would have seen world-class golfers like Faldo, Lyle, Woosnam, Montgomerie and Westwood if there had been no Tony Jacklin, we will never know. His success in the all-important eyes of America, closely followed, if not so spectacularly, in the seventies by Peter Oosterhuis, was, without doubt, the first sign of improving standards since the days of Dai Rees; and going further back, Henry Cotton and Abe Mitchell. It may be that the Open had been saved forever by Palmer and the rest of the 'Big Three' a decade earlier. Conversely, if there had been no Jacklin, would there have been any resurgence in British, then European golf, to maintain that re-born US interest in the Open? It, by now, may have been regarded by a super-dominant America only as an anachronistic curiosity. Also, would the R&A still be holding its position today, along with the USGA, as the sport's law-makers? One thing I believe is certain: the eventual loss of US interest in the Ryder Cup would have killed that competition.

Jacklin's presence, however seminal, was, in real performance terms, relatively short-lived. The Americans' new love affair with the Open carried on apace in the 1970s. Lee Trevino won twice, both times at Jacklin's expense: his chips-in at the 15th and 18th at Muirfield in 1972 are said to have unnerved the Englishman so much, that his game would never be the same again. Tony was never the same player after 1973, whatever the cause. Stylish newcomers Weiskopf and Miller also won, spelling the end of the Nicklaus-Player era and ushering in the tremendous Open run of Tom Watson. Watson won the first of his five titles at Carnoustie; and all his first four were on different Scottish courses.

In 1979, to make the competition more meaningful, the Ryder Cup allowed the British and Irish team to become one representative of Europe. Not that this first selection was too different in composition. Apart from Antonio Garrido, there was only one non-Great Britain & Ireland player; another Spaniard, and current Open Champion, Severiano Ballesteros. When Ballesteros won at Lytham, the reception was like that afforded to Jacklin ten years before. The British golf fans had taken a 19 year-old Seve to heart three years earlier when he led the field for 54 holes and chased the ball, and, finally in vain, Johnny Miller, all over the splendid Birkdale links, for a famous second place tie with demi-god Nicklaus. Whereas Jacklin's applause was based on national pride, the young Spaniard's was a result of his wonderful cavalier performances. From a perspective of European golf, if Jacklin was the standard-bearer, Seve Ballesteros was his bravest captain; as he was to prove with some exciting wins in the Open and the Masters, and for Jacklin in the ensuing Ryder Cups; before memorably taking over the Cup mantle himself at Valderrama in 1997.

The Open Championships since 1980 have been much more evenly-spread, with popular British wins for Nick Faldo (three times), Sandy Lyle and most recently Paul Lawrie; two more for Seve; two for Australian Greg Norman; and one for fellow countryman Ian Baker-Finch. The Zimbabwean with the English father and Welsh mother, Nick Price, won at Turnberry (the most recent course added to the rota). The other wins have gone to America. Bill Rogers was a surprise winner at Sandwich in 1981; Tom Watson picked titles three, four and five; and Mark Calcavecchia collected his only Major at Troon. Significantly perhaps, with wins in recent years from John

Daly, Tom Lehman, Justin Leonard and Mark O'Meara, the balance is swinging back to the US. Fittingly, it was the Open that closed the Majors of the twentieth century with the most historic of Championships. Held at a Carnoustie with teeth-like rough to put any US Open to shame, local lad and qualifier Paul Lawrie overturned a ten-stroke overnight lead held by another qualifier, Frenchman Jean Van de Velde. Van de Velde, still leading by three on the 18th tee, thereafter committed golfing suicide in a sporting tragedy without rival.

The British Open is without doubt one of the most important of the Majors, if only for its venerable traditions. All the Majors, as we shall see, have their own customs and characteristics, levels of prize money and qualifying rigmaroles. However, the Open has the richest history as befits the home of golf, and it is unique as a Major in that it is the only one played over links courses. These semi-natural, semi-man-made amalgams of sand, gorse, marram grass and bare lies, often criss-crossed by deeply-cut burns and dykes, are the antipathy of the lush, tree-lined parkland courses associated with the US Open; and in more-recent years the US PGA Championship. They bear no resemblance at all to the relatively rough-free, easy fairways and lightning-fast greens of Augusta National – home of the Masters. The exposed tracts, open to the winds of the Firth of Clyde, the Irish Sea, the Channel or the North Sea in an unpredictable British summer, can result in different conditions, and a different golf course, every day, sometimes twice or three times a day. As much for the tradition then, the playing conditions make the Open Championship one of the greatest – if not, in some eyes, the greatest – challenges in golf, and, as such, still worthy to be called a Major.

The lessons of the thirties, forties and fifties though, must tell the R&A there is no room for complacency. Then, reliant only on its historic inertia, it was being by-passed by a more vibrant, more commercially-aware society 3000 miles away. If it wasn't for the kick-start given by the likes of Palmer and Nicklaus there would not have been famous victories for Jacklin, Seve and Faldo, and Britain and Europe could have remained a golfing backwater. The Open must never be allowed to lose its position again.

THE US OPEN

When John Reid, a Scottish immigrant to the US, asked his friend Bob Lockhart to bring back some golf equipment

from a trip home to Scotland, it (indirectly and spontaneously) led to the formation of the St Andrews Club at Yonkers, NY, in 1888. We have seen that golf may have been played in America as much as a century earlier, but most golf historians agree that 1888 and St Andrews were the defining moment and location for US golf's amazing explosion.

Six years later the St Andrews Club broke new ground by devising a tournament for the professionals to go along with the events that were being organised for amateurs in some of the other infant east coast clubs. The professionals were (self-?)regarded as the best from the army of Scots and more than a sprinkling of English golfers that had taken to crossing the Atlantic to seek their golfing fortunes over the previous few years. By the turn of the century, the proliferation of golf courses in the US, which took the estimated number beyond 1000, gives an indication of just how many Old World pros had come to the States. The 1894 'Championship' at St Andrews was contested in a matchplay format by Willies Dunn, Campbell and Davis; and Sam Tucker – with Dunn winning the first, and unofficial, national title. Willie Dunn had appeared in the Top 10 at the 1883 British Open, and his father (also Willie!) played in the second British Open in 1861. Willie Campbell was runner-up to David Brown in the 1886 Open at Musselburgh, while Davis had been the pro at Carnoustie and Hoylake before coming to the Newport, RI Club in 1892. Tucker was the sole Englishman.

Dunn's win was not ratified among the other clubs, however, and through the efforts of leading amateur, Charles Blair Macdonald, a meeting was called for 22 December 1894, to reach a degree of uniformity over such matters as rules and equipment; and to set up an authority recognised by all the clubs to organise a national championship. The clubs at St Andrews, Newport, Chicago, Brookline and Shinnecock Hills met in New York City, and the United States Golf Association (USGA) was formed. In October 1895 at Newport, running concurrently with the first US Amateur Championship over the same course, the US Open Championship came into being.

The first winner, Horace Rawlins, is a bit of a mystery man. Born on the Isle of Wight in 1874, he was professional at the Mid Herts Club from 1893 to 1894, moving back to the Isle of Wight Ladies Club briefly, before arriving at Newport in January 1895. He did not compete in the British Open before emigrating, so was an unknown quantity. His four-round, 36-hole total (it didn't become a 72-hole championship until 1898) of 173, suggested that the field was short of quality as well as quantity (only 11 competed). Certainly Rawlins would never win again.

In 1896, at Shinnecock Hills, the infant Championship nearly didn't take place. The professionals objected strongly when caddies, John Shippen and Oscar Bunn, filed for entry. Shippen was (according to differing reports) either an African-American, or half African-American and half Shinnecock, and Bunn was reported to be a full native American of the same tribe. A stand-off ensued as Theodore Havermayer, the USGA President, ruled that the Open would go on – even if Shippen and Bunn were the only two competitors. The professionals mutinously fell into line.

For the first fifteen years the pattern remained broadly the same, with various Smiths, Rosses and Macs dominating the Championship; although Willie Anderson was individually the star of the period, collecting four wins in five years. The dominance of the hired professional who had learned his golf from generations of British experience was the major feature of the early years. The American golfer was still predominantly the gentleman amateur; but slowly, as the new century wore on, a new breed of player, the home-grown caddie/professional, was starting to appear. Standards of play were undoubtedly lower than in Britain, as even the best of the émigrés, such as Alex Smith, performed only moderately when they ventured back across the Atlantic to take part in the British Open. This differential was cruelly exposed in 1900 when Harry Vardon and JH Taylor led home the US Open at Chicago by nine and seven strokes respectively.

Then, however, the period of British success came to an abrupt end. Over the next decade, facilitated partly because of America's coming out of the Great War less damaged than Britain, and partly because of there being no line of succession in Britain when the time of the 'Triumvirate' came to a close, the whole emphasis in the golf world swung – permanently – to the other side of the Atlantic. The catalysts for this turnabout were to be found in the next five years of the US Open.

In 1911, John J McDermott, two months short of his 20th birthday, erased the memory of his runner-up disappointment from the previous year; and become the

first American-born winner of the US Open. The following year, proving this was no flash in the pan, he won again at the Buffalo Club. Home-grown talents, Mike Brady and Tom McNamara, were second on each occasion respectively, suggesting that the dam was about to burst. Then, in 1913, came another twist, and a huge symbolic breakthrough. Francis Ouimet, hanging on to the coat-tails of Harry Vardon (back for the first time since his 1900 success) and Ted Ray – arguably the two best players in the world at the time – to force a three-way play-off, had the temerity to go on to outplay these icons, and make it three US wins in a row. Now the Americans had proved they could beat the very best of British, and no-one saw this more clearly than the confident young man who tied for fourth, just behind the joint leaders: his name was Walter Hagen.

But Ouimet was also an amateur; the first to win the US Open. The heyday of the British Amateur had flickered briefly during the 1890s when John Ball and Harold Hilton won the British Open. When Hilton won his second title in 1897, no-one would ever have thought that he would be the last British amateur to win a Major championship. In America, however, with the sport developing so rapidly across all fronts, the style of amateur was different. Unlike the British type of landowner, army officer or socialite, the socio-economic growth of America in the early decades of the twentieth century meant that the successful amateur could equally spring from the ranks of the Ivy League colleges, and be the heir of some industrial magnate, or have learned his golf as a caddie and be holding down a regular job. Francis Ouimet was one of the latter. While Hagen was contemplating the end of British dominance and the lot of the American professional, Ouimet's victory was stirring the amateur golfing ambitions of a young Atlanta schoolboy – one Robert Tyre Jones, Jr.

Hagen was fast off the mark, winning the first of his two US Opens in the following year. In 1915 and 1916, while all Championship golf was suspended in Europe, two more amateurs – Jerome Travers and Chuck Evans – had their names inscribed on the trophy. This made it five American wins in a row and three amateur champions in four years. Apart from Ted Ray (1920) and various émigrés during the twenties, and on the back of sixteen straight wins between 1895 and 1910, the disappointing statistic for British fans was that the next Briton (and the only one since) to win the US Open would be Tony Jacklin in 1970.

Thereafter, along with the PGA Championship, the US Open would be viewed as an American preserve. Overseas players did enter from time to time, but they were few and far between until Gary Player's emergence in the sixties hinted at a small but strong Southern Hemisphere presence thereafter, and the re-emergence of European players in the eighties and nineties.

Walter Hagen didn't win a US Open during his purple patch in the 1920s. Despite picking up 5 PGAs and 4 British Opens, the colourful first superstar of golf' won his last US Open in 1919. It was more than a coincidence that he never won a Major when Bobby Jones competed. This was not because Jones won every time, but the mere appearance of the man seemed to jinx Hagen. During the period 1920-30, Jones' US Open performances read: 8, 5, 2, W, 2, 2, W, 11, 2, W, W. Jones, along with Hagen, and to a slightly lesser extent, Gene Sarazen (who won the US Open in 1922 and 1932), were the outstanding golfers of the decade; but, with the exception of Jones' four wins, the US Open remained true to its name with an even spread of one- and two-time winners during the twenties, and, indeed, the thirties.

In 1933, Johnny Goodman became the fifth and last amateur US Open Champion. Of the 19 US Opens beginning with Ouimet's win in 1913, and ending with Goodman's triumph at North Shore, amateurs had claimed eight. The brief explosion on to the scene of Ralph Guldahl produced two wins (1937 and 1938) and ushered in the dawn of Hogan, Nelson and Snead – and World War II.

During the thirties and even more so after the War, there had been a gradual defining of the type of course required for the national championship. Partly because of historical reasons, and partly due to geography, the typical Open course was built in the early part of the century for clubs who bought up large tracts of (usually well-wooded) land close to the industrial conurbations of the east, mid-west and California. Early golf-course architects often took Scottish links characteristics, such as varying grades of rough and narrow fairways, and adapted them to the parkland environment. Liberal use of water and dog-legging, and ubiquitous sand, were employed to increase the hazards. As the century developed the US Open-style of course made it a demanding trial of any aspiring Champion's skills. In the view of architect AW Tillinghast (Baltusrol, Fresh Meadow, Inverness, Winged Foot), '...a controlled shot to a closely-guarded green is the surest test of any man's golf'.

In conjunction with this tightening of course criteria, the overwhelming prowess of the American golfer, and the sad decline of the British game helped to erode the importance of the British Open – at least in American eyes – and promote the US Open as the world's premier championship of golf. It was certainly true that the inauguration of the Masters in 1934 had polarised the British Championship even further; and fewer and fewer US golfers saw the need to support what must have seemed like an outmoded and under-funded competition thousands of miles away. There was a strong argument for the US Open's hegemony over the other Majors for the next two decades.

In 1947, Lew Worsham beat Sam Snead (already 1942 PGA and 1946 British Open Champion) in a play-off. Sam was never to come as close to the Open title again: the only Major he was destined never to win, and which, in time, was to gnaw away at him. The next few years belonged to Snead's arch rival, Ben Hogan, whose courage and incredible talent were to make him probably the biggest hero in the annals of the US Open. If Bobby Jones had dominated the event in the 1920s, even by playing a minimum of golf in between, then Hogan matched Jones now, although his limited appearances on a golf course were for other reasons.

In 1948, at the Riviera Country Club, Hogan set one of the golf Majors' landmark low scores, when he scorched the course in an eight-under par 276. Then, in February of the following year, courtesy of a head-on collision with a Greyhound bus, Hogan was badly injured. It was felt he may not be able to walk any more, but throughout 1949 he battled against the odds and played again in January 1950. He competed at the US Open at Merion, proving that he still had enormous golfing talent; but faded badly when exhaustion took over. He somehow hung on to force a play-off, and limped to a famous victory over Lloyd Mangrum and George Fazio. Thereafter, he declined to play too much golf – saving himself for the Majors. He only played one British Open, however, which he won in 1953; and he eschewed the PGA completely because of the potential six or seven days round-by-round grind of qualifying strokeplay, followed by matchplay. He effectively only played in the Masters and the US Open, then; and he won them both in 1951 and again in 1953. With the British Open win as well in 1953, he still remains the only golfer to win three Grand Slam tournaments in one season.

In 1960, the new order took over when Arnold Palmer won from the still amateur Jack Nicklaus. Nicklaus went on to equal the record of four wins between 1962 and 1980 and tie with Willie Anderson, Jones and Hogan. Americans continued to dominate during the sixties and seventies with two wins each by Billy Casper and Lee Trevino, but overseas players got a glimpse of success for the first time for many years with wins from Player, Jacklin and David Graham. In the eighties, there was no dominant force, although Curtis Strange did win back-to-back in 1988 and 1989, and there was a popular second win for 'all-time old Champion', Hale Irwin: he was 45 when he claimed the title in 1990. Lee Janzen and the late Payne Stewart had a penchant for doing well with two wins each between 1989 and 1999, while Ernie Els, winning for the second time at Congressional in 1997, could continue to be a contender for many championships to come.

Since the sixties, the perceived No. 1 status of the US Open among the Majors may be called into question. The charisma of the Masters, and the Americans re-found love affair with the traditions of the British Open, have tended to level out the Majors. Add to that the change in the US PGA Championship from matchplay to strokeplay; its mirroring the US Open philosophy on the type of course it should be played on; and the more-cosmopolitan fields since the mid-eighties, the PGA has also come of age. There is no doubting the claim, however, that the US Open, year-in, year-out, is the toughest test set for the players of all the Majors: apart from the golf course set-up, it also comes at the end of the first half of the season, an ideal time for many golfers; it allows players time to develop some form, to reach a peak, unlike the Masters in April which can be too early for many. The competition when it meets, therefore, is potentially at its strongest, both physically and mentally. The US Open, also, as it is the only totally national (both professional and amateur) championship in the US, has the support, respect and affection, and thus the considerable influence, of the American golfer, commentator and fan alike.

THE PGA CHAMPIONSHIP

The excitement created by the exploits of John McDermott, Francis Ouimet and Walter Hagen led to an enormous growth in the game of golf in America. The spread of the sport affected both recreational and professional, competitive ranks. The birth of the tour professional, a player who could devote as much time to tournaments as his members lessons, his greenkeeping and club-repairing duties, introduced a new stratum of golfer; and with it came the need to protect his interests.

The British PGA was founded in 1901 and as part of its role it identified sponsors who would support special golfing events. The *News of the World* Sunday newspaper was asked to sponsor the Association's own Championship and by 1916 it was a well-run, well-established 36-hole matchplay competition. On 16 January of that year, a mixture of professionals, amateurs, course architects and golf industry representatives met in New York City at the invitation of department store entrepreneur, Rodman Wanamaker. Wanamaker could see the potential the new craze for golf could have commercially, and the upshot of the meeting was the creation of the PGA of America (ratified in April 1916) and the Wanamaker-sponsored PGA Championship.

The basis for the competition was matchplay, like its British counterpart, and was only open to professional golfers. The matchplay aspect also complemented the US Amateur Championship and provided a balance to the medal play of the British and US Opens.

Jim Barnes won the first PGA Championship, held in October 1916 at the Siwanoy Country Club, beating Scot Jock Hutchison, 1up in the final. Barnes also won the second Championship, but had to wait three years to defend it due to World War I. During the 1920s, Walter Hagen, who had attended that historic January 1916 meeting, won five titles, including four in a row. Before Leo Diegel beat him to go on to win the 1928 Championship, Hagen had gone 22 straight round matches without defeat. Gene Sarazen and Diegel won two PGAs in the twenties, and Sarazen went on to win a third in 1933. Sarazen's second victory – when defending his title in 1923 – featured one of the famous finals. He played a magical shot close to the pin to beat Hagen at the second extra hole. At this time, the 32 qualifiers each year had to endure 36 holes of strokeplay before the matchplay sessions. In 1935, 64 qualifiers went forward to matchplay.

Denny Shute, in 1936 and 1937, became the last player to win back-to-back Championships, and Paul Runyan also won two titles in the thirties. With war-time approaching, Byron Nelson was in devastating form, while Sam Snead won the Championship in 1942, the day before he joined the navy. Nelson won in 1940 and was runner-up to Vic Ghezzi in 1941: he was also runner-up (to Bob Hamilton) when the Championship resumed after a break due to hostilities in 1944. In 1945 he won the PGA for the second time when the event at the Moraine Country Club was his ninth in a sequence of 11 straight tournament wins that season – one of those records in sport that surely will never ever be beaten (at the time of writing, after the first Tour event of the new millennium, a certain T Woods, Esq was standing at five in a row; hence the slight equivocation!).

The PGA Championship, perhaps because of its format of week-long qualifying strokeplay and matchplay, was not as popular as the US Open with spectators. It may have been something to do also with course selection – some venues were not particularly good; and because a certain number of non-Tour, work-a-day club pros were guaranteed entry, this may have reduced the glamour of the event. What it didn't want was any defection from the top pros, however, and as a result the prize money was kept competitive with the Open and the new-fangled Tournament down South for amateurs and fancy dans, now called the Masters. A major blow, however, was the enforced withdrawal, during the 1950s, of just about its greatest star: Ben Hogan. Having won the Championship in 1946 and 1948, Hogan's terrible road accident precluded his playing in the stamina-sapping week-long event. After his 1948 triumph, he stayed away until he was in semi-retirement and the Championship had switched to strokeplay. He would never win again, but finished as high as ninth in 1964, at the age of 52.

The years leading up to and immediately after the dropping of matchplay were fairly nondescript in that no golfer or group of golfers dominated the Championship. In fact, between 1950 and 1970, even after strokeplay was introduced, the PGA was won by a different player each year. The end of matchplay finally came about when the PGA of America sensed permanent harm to the Championship because of the time involved and poor spectator-aspect previously alluded to, and that the needs of the new pervasive and persuasive TV phenomenon

would have to be met. A proposal by Horton Smith, who was the then President of the PGA of America, to limit matchplay to just the top seven qualifiers from the strokeplay session plus the defending champion, was superseded by one which did away with matchplay altogether. This was certainly not a happy period for the Championship. Having to overhaul its format comprehensively in order to make it attractive to those outside golf, it was also being criticised from within, with the type and location of courses usually top of the agenda. That the PGA Championship, up to 1999, should have been played on 67 different courses over 25 states in its 81 years says it all. In fairness, it was previous policy for the PGA of America to expand the frontiers of its flagship event, but commercially it was awry. Moreover, the Masters had become a big hit with American TV audiences; and from a player's perspective, the PGA's July timing clashed with the British Open too frequently, as well as proving unpopular when the Championship was played in the steamier South.

Arnold Palmer failed to leave his mark on the PGA, surprisingly never winning. Typically, however, he couldn't be kept out of the record books. When Bobby Nichols won in 1964, Arnie became the first player to shoot sub-70 rounds throughout without winning. He tied second with Jack Nicklaus. Nicklaus didn't have it all his own way in the sixties, winning just once, in the Dallas heat; not for the first time in a Major at the expense of Bruce Crampton. In 1968, at the age of 48, Julius Boros won, also in Texas (San Antonio), to become the oldest winner of any Major Championship.

Since the 1970s, however, when Nicklaus started to stitch together regular wins, the PGA Championship has made up lost ground. Firstly, there has been some rationalisation of the courses. The use of more courses employed by the US Open – Oakland Hills, Inverness, Pebble Beach and Winged Foot, for instance – reduced the rota and made the test as difficult as the Open. It also, finally, took its spot in August, as the finale to the Major Championship season. Over the last 25 years or so the Championship has had a base to move forward and to develop its own style. Before that, constant change, dubious quality of both course and player, almost reduced the PGA to a non-Major.

Nicklaus went on to emulate Hagen's five wins, and for a while between 1972 and 1974, Sam Snead was having something of an Indian Summer. Then in his sixties, he collected fourth, ninth, then third positions, respectively. He finally called it a day, aged 69, in 1981. He was not the oldest participant, though. Back in 1972, Gene Sarazen (who else?) had appeared at the age of 70 years and 5 months, and shot two 79s to miss the cut. He thus had the distinction, and still does, of being the PGA's oldest competitor and youngest winner (20 years 5 months in 1922). Lee Trevino won twice, in 1974 and 1984, and Tom Watson came as close as he has got to winning the Championship in 1978 when he tied for first with John Mahaffey and Jerry Pate; but Mahaffey it was that emerged victorious from the sudden-death play-off. Mahaffey's win was improbable to say the least. After a first round 75, he was never in the hunt. At the start of the last round he was still seven behind Watson, but a series of brilliant putts put together a score of 66 while Tom folded to a 73; and the chance of his joining Sarazen, Hogan, Player and Nicklaus as the only players to have lifted all four Major titles had gone, never to return.

As the PGA Championship has always been an event for the US Tour and Club professional, first and foremost, it was not until the breakthrough of Gary Player in 1962 that a true overseas player won the Championship. He repeated the victory in 1972, and since 1979, when Australia's David Graham won, there has been a veritable surge of foreign winners. Whereas the Masters was a favourite event for Europeans in the eighties and nineties, the golfers of the Southern Hemisphere took to the PGA. Following Player and Graham, there have been wins for Australians Wayne Grady and Steve Elkington, and two for Nick Price of Zimbabwe. In between, Larry Nelson picked up two titles and when Ray Floyd won for the second time in 1982, he set a record of the longest span between wins of any one Major Championship (13 years). John Daly's fairytale success in 1991 heralded a new breed of super-hitter and paved the way for a certain Tiger Woods, who after stuttering slightly following his first success, won the last Major of the century, the 1999 PGA Championship at Medinah.

The PGA Championship today has every right to be thought of as a Major. Whereas the purist might pine for the days of matchplay, no-one can doubt the progress the Championship has made over the last two decades or so. Once dubbed as a second-rate parochial competition, the PGA of America quoted that in 1998 at Sahalee there were 36 overseas players representing 16 countries. Not exactly the breakdown for the British Open, but a great improvement than on just a few years before. The PGA Championship now proudly signs off the Majors season, attracting a better and better field every year as the Holy Grail of a Major Championship taunts the players who have never won – and those who have won, but want to win again – to effect one last try for immortality, before next year. A more important statistic from 1998, perhaps, cited that Vijay Singh (another Southern Hemisphere golfer) finished ahead of a field made up of 85 of the Official World Ranking Top 100, the classiest field for any golf tournament, Major Championship or not, since the World Ranking was launched in 1986.

THE MASTERS

After such an extraordinary year as 1930, Robert Tyre Jones, Jr – Bobby Jones – retired from competitive golf. He had nothing else to prove; he had done it all. Being amateur, he played his golf in the spare time he allowed himself from his law firm. Being amateur, he couldn't compete with the professional golfers in their own tournament, the PGA Championship. By 1930 then, he had achieved all that his status would allow him, but in doing so left a series of golfing records unsurpassed by any amateur in the history of the game; records that even the hugely-talented Tiger Woods, if he had remained amateur at the end of 1996, I'm sure would admit may even have been beyond him.

The 'Grand Slam' is made up of the four Majors as we know them today: the British and US Opens, the US PGA and the Masters. Only four players – Sarazen, Hogan, Nicklaus and Player – have won every championship. However, no golfer has ever achieved all four in one season. Back in 1930, the Amateur Championships of America and Britain were also considered 'Majors', and the Grand Slam consisted of these plus both Opens. As an amateur, Jones won the US Amateur title five times and the British equivalent once. He took on and beat the professionals more often than not; winning the first of his four US Open titles in 1923. He also won three British Opens. His main professional rival, Walter Hagen – undoubtedly one of golf's all-time greats himself – despite winning 11 Major Championships, never won one when Jones was in the same field. These feats were achieved in just eight incredible years.

And so to Bobby Jones' *annus mirabilis*: 1930. He appeared in the American Walker Cup side at Sandwich and stayed on to take the British Amateur. In June he went to Hoylake and beat the best of the British, and no small number of American, professionals, to lift the Open Championship. The following month at Interlachen he beat an even stronger field for the US Open; before rounding off his competitive career at the Merion Cricket Club in Pennsylvania, by winning his fifth US Amateur title. At the end of the year he returned to the law full-time.

During his brief but intensive career, Jones had played golf on most of the famous courses on either side of the Atlantic. No longer playing, in 1931 he switched his golfing mind to course construction, and he knew exactly what he wanted to achieve. A resident of Atlanta, Georgia, he was made aware of a 365-acre piece of land a hundred miles or so away at Augusta. It had once been a plant nursery but had gone to the wall during the Depression. Jones, with the backing of financier Clifford Roberts, and Scottish golf course designer, Dr Alister Mackenzie, bought it and planned out a course that would encompass all that was best (in Jones' view) from the courses he'd known. Jones saw his course as a private member's club: open only to his closest associates, business colleagues and clients. It was, however, intended to be exclusive on a wide geographic front; hence the name it was given – Augusta National. It was also meant to provide a fitting climax to the professionals' winter tour, by invitation (from Jones) to a special tournament. The winter tour was a small offshoot of the professionals' regular summer tour, allowing them to play the Southern States 'out of season' thus avoiding the heat and humidity of other times. Like many clubs in the region, Augusta National closed down for the summer – and still does.

Augusta National was designed so that it wouldn't be too intimidating for Jones' members, yet it would require meticulous planning from the pros to score well. The fairways were wide and accommodating; anything a touch off-line not being penalised too severely. Bobby Jones knew how excruciating the rough could be at the Opens, but he wanted his members to continue to play the course and not be humbled by it. A hook or a slice here would probably result in nothing more punitive than the ball nestling among pine needles, and the members' sense of well-being would remain intact. Moreover, he wanted to make the playing of golf the greatest possible pleasure.

No-one who has seen, even photographs of, Augusta in spring can fail to be uplifted by the beauty of the course, fringed as it is with all manner of flowering shrubs.

In order to beat the par of 72 at Augusta, however, a strategy has to be planned hole-by-hole. Assuming that the green is reached in regulation, it depends here (more than almost anywhere else) where the ball has landed as to whether a player gets his par, better – or much, much worse. The greens are often huge; always undulating, with several different levels. The approach shot has to be aimed at the 'right' side of the pin. Reading the contours is difficult, and the putting surfaces are lightning-fast. For example, a four foot putt from the wrong side of the hole, not hit with exactly the right speed and borrow, can easily trundle past and roll on 15 feet or a lot more.

Mackenzie and Jones completed the course for Jones' first invitation event, simply called 'The Augusta National Invitational', in March 1934. Mackenzie unfortunately died that year, so he was unaware of the impact the tournament made. By the following year the tournament was being dubbed the Championship of Champions, and the easier-off-the-tongue sobriquet 'Masters' was not long in driving that out. Horton Smith won in 1934, beating one of golf's perennial bridesmaids, Craig Wood, into second place. Bob Jones came out of retirement to tie 13th with arch rival of old, Walter Hagen. But it was not regarded yet as a Major.

To become a Major Championship, the competition has to be the best; the course has to be one of the toughest; there should at least be tradition in the organisation running it. Augusta National was lacking in all three. There was no qualifying – entry was by invitation only; this was no Carnoustie or Olympia Fields; and the club was only formed in 1934. However, to misquote the Bard: 'Some events are born great; some events achieve greatness; and some events have greatness thrust upon them'. The Opens can be thought of as the first; the PGA achieved its status through a workmanlike progress; and the Masters can thank Gene Sarazen, TV and Arnold Palmer for the third!

'Probably the best-known shot in all golf Tournament history', states Augusta National's own *Records of the Masters Tournament*. It alludes to a shot holed from all of 220 yards with fairway spoon (four wood) by a desperate Sarazen on the 15th hole of the final round of the 1935 Tournament. Sarazen was three behind the ever-unlucky Craig Wood, and his double-eagle or albatross (three under par) on this par-five hole enabled him to tie, and force a play-off which he was to win. In doing so, Sarazen became the first player to win all four Majors as we now know them. The news story was probably blown up out of all proportion, but 'that shot' did take the infant Masters tournament on to the front page. Its real popularity, however, and therefore credibility as a Major, came in the late fifties with TV coverage and, in centre-screen, the man of the people, the risk-taker, the mould-breaking Arnold Palmer. Being shown on television, the early-season heady combination backdrop of sunshine and Southern flowers for Arnie's incredible escapades made for compulsive viewing. His first win, in 1958, merely set the scene. In 1960 Palmer, one behind the leader Ken Venturi with two to play, improbably birdied both holes to win. Then, in the 1962 three-way play-off, Palmer, three shots behind Gary Player at the turn, scorched the back nine in 31 to win. Comic-hero stuff, but the Masters had arrived.

Since the sixties, coming as it does early in the season, and being the smallest of all Major Championship fields, the Masters rapidly became a favourite and much-coveted tournament amongst the world's leading golfers. With his great advantage of extra length without compromising on control, Jack Nicklaus was to win an unprecedented and unsurpassed six times, the last occasion in 1986. By that time, the newly-emerging European force in golf was starting to take a fancy to Augusta in April. Seve Ballesteros had already won twice in the eighties and Bernhard Langer won the first of his two titles the previous year. Sandy Lyle, Nick Faldo (three times), Ian Woosnam and Jose-Maria Olazabal (twice) would all go on to win over the next few years. American favourite Ben Crenshaw, whose 1984 win was one of the most popular of all time, delighted his supporters with a belated second Green Jacket in 1995. Greg Norman – a runner-up in 1985 and 1986 – had the field at his mercy starting out on the last round of the 1996 Tournament. His six-shot lead was turned into a five shot deficit by partner Nick Faldo, who ground out a 67 to Greg's 78 to collect a most unlikely third Masters, after the most incredible last round in Majors history.

Then, in 1997, a new star was born. Child prodigy and reigning US Amateur Champion, Eldrick 'Tiger' Woods, took the course and the competition apart, breaking all sorts of records along the way. A new era seemed to be dawning as Woods' power play was seen as much of a quantum leap in the sport as was Nicklaus' nearly 40 years before. The much-vaunted Woods, the World No. 1 for much of the remainder of the twentieth century following his 97 win, was clear favourite to win again in 1998 and 1999. It was his old pal and mentor, 41 year-old Mark O'Meara, who won in 1998, though, after almost two decades of trying: whilst a popular second Masters was claimed in 1999, on his return to the game after a career-threatening back injury, by Jose-Maria Olazabal.

The Masters may be the fourth Major historically, but such is its charm and attraction that every golfer wants to play in it. It may, therefore, be held by many in higher regard than fourth most-important among the Majors. It certainly can argue that because it is so different to the others, it merits being a Major. At the time of the creation of the Masters, the British Open was different from the other Majors in that it was always played on seaside links and had the longest history; the US Open was arguably the sternest test of golf with narrow fairways, bunkers galore and jungle-like rough; the PGA was matchplay with tough qualifying rounds. At that time it was argued that Augusta National was too easy to be a venue for a Major Championship. Why then did so many of the game's top players fail to beat par? It was said that the Masters was a glorified putting contest: far from it. What sorts out the men from the boys at Augusta is how and where the approach shot is played .

The Masters is different in several ways, some of which we've already seen. It is also unique in that it is always held at Augusta National. It has a trophy like the others, but it is not a cup. Instead the Masters trophy is a silver replica of the Clubhouse at Augusta, itself a replica of a fine *ante bellum*-style Southern homestead. It is different in that the winner is presented with the traditional Green Jacket as a member of the Augusta club – presented and held for him by the previous-year's champion (the first ceremony being conferred upon Sam Snead in 1949). It is different because it calls itself a tournament, not a championship. It is just different, and it is that difference that justifies the Masters' claim to be one of the four Major Championships of golf. Who would argue?

With holes which have names like Tea Olive, Yellow Jasmine, Magnolia, Azalea, Redbud and the rest, the Masters oozes sheer style and class. This so much reflects on Robert Tyre Jones, Jr – the gentleman – and the Master golfer.

THE MAJOR CHAMPIONSHIPS CALENDAR

A YEAR-BY-YEAR LOOK AT THE MAJORS

Highlighting the individual Major Championships played to date, the following pages take events year-by-year; starting, of course, when there was only the Open Championship, back in the bleak days of 1860.

COURSE:	Prestwick GC
LOCATION:	Prestwick, Ayrshire, Scotland
DATE:	17 October
DISTANCE:	3799 yards
PAR:	n/a
WINNER:	£nil

Pos	Player	1st	2nd	3rd	Total
1	**WILLIE PARK, Sr**	55	59	60	174
2	Tom Morris, Sr	58	59	59	176
3	Andrew Strath				180
4	Robert Andrew				191
5	George Brown				192
6	Charlie Hunter				195
	Alexander Smith				
	William Steel				232?

Prestwick was a 12-hole course which went "...dodging in and out among lofty sandhills" and "The holes were, for the most part, out of sight..." Eight men embarked on this inauspicious first occasion.

1861/2 BRITISH OPEN

BRITISH OPEN

COURSE:	Prestwick GC			
LOCATION:	Prestwick, Ayrshire, Scotland			
DATE:	26 September			
DISTANCE:	3799 yards			
PAR:	n/a			
WINNER:	£nil			

Pos	Player	1st	2nd	3rd	Total
1	**TOM MORRIS, Sr**	54	56	53	163
2	Willie Park, Sr	54	54	59	167
3	William Dow	59	58	54	171
4	David Park	58	57	57	172
5	Robert Andrew	58	61	56	175
6	Peter McEwan	56	60	62	178
7	Willie Dunn, Sr	61	59	60	180
8	James Fairlie (a)				184
9	George Brown	60	65	60	185
10	Robert Chambers, Jr (a)				187
11	Jamie Dunn	63	62	63	188
12	Charlie Hunter	67	64	59	190

Organiser, Col JO Fairlie, set the scene for the involvement of amateurs by taking part himself. The term 'Open' Championship may have originated from this date.

COURSE:	Prestwick GC			
LOCATION:	Prestwick, Ayrshire, Scotland			
DATE:	17 October			
DISTANCE:	3799 yards			
PAR:	n/a			
WINNER:	£nil			

Pos	Player	1st	2nd	3rd	Total
1	**TOM MORRIS, Sr**	52	55	56	163
2	Willie Park, Sr	59	59	58	176
3	Charlie Hunter	60	60	58	178
4	William Dow	60	58	63	181
5	James Knight (a)	62	61	63	186
6	J F Johnston (a)	64	69	75	208
	William Mitchell (a)				
	R Pollock (a)				

The last year that no monetary prize was offered. The winning margin of 13 shots still stands as the all-time record for the Open, or any other Major.

COURSE:	Prestwick GC
LOCATION:	Prestwick, Ayrshire, Scotland
DATE:	18 September
DISTANCE:	3799 yards
PAR:	n/a
WINNER:	£10 (shared out)

Pos	Player	1st	2nd	3rd	Total
1	**WILLIE PARK, Sr**	56	54	58	168
2	Tom Morris, Sr	56	58	56	170
3	David Park	55	63	54	172
4	Andrew Strath	61	55	58	174
5	George Brown	58	61	57	176
6	Robert Andrew	62	57	59	178
7	Charlie Hunter	61	61	62	184
8	James Knight (a)	66	65	59	190
9	James Miller (a)	63	63	66	192
10	James Paxton	65	65	66	196
11 =	Peter Chalmers (a)	65	67	65	197
	J F Johnston (a)	66	66	65	197
13	William Mitchell (a)	70	70	66	206
14	William Moffat (a)	75	78	80	233

A £10 purse was shared by the professionals.

COURSE:	Prestwick GC
LOCATION:	Prestwick, Ayrshire, Scotland
DATE:	16 September
DISTANCE:	3799 yards
PAR:	n/a
WINNER:	£6

Pos	Player	1st	2nd	3rd	Total
1	**TOM MORRIS, Sr**	54	58	55	167
2	Andrew Strath	56	57	56	169
3	Robert Andrew	57	58	60	175
4	Willie Park, Sr	55	67	55	177
5	William Dow	56	58	67	181
6	William Strath	60	62	60	182

'Old' Tom Morris squared his private battle with Willie Park. He returned to St Andrews as pro, having been at Prestwick previously.

1865/6 ■ BRITISH OPEN

COURSE:	Prestwick GC
LOCATION:	Prestwick, Ayrshire, Scotland
DATE:	14 September
DISTANCE:	3799 yards
PAR:	n/a
WINNER:	£8

Pos	Player	1st	2nd	3rd	Total
1	**ANDREW STRATH**	55	54	53	162
2	Willie Park, Sr	56	52	56	164
3	William Dow				171
4	Bob Kirk	64	54	55	173
5	Tom Morris, Sr	57	61	56	174
6	William Doleman (a)	62	57	59	178
7	Robert Andrew	61	59	59	179
8	William Strath	60	60	62	182
9	William Miller	63	60	66	189
10	Tom Hood (a)	66	66	66	198

Official printed scorecards were introduced for the first time.

BRITISH OPEN

COURSE:	Prestwick GC
LOCATION:	Prestwick, Ayrshire, Scotland
DATE:	16 September
DISTANCE:	3799 yards
PAR:	n/a
WINNER:	£6

Pos	Player	1st	2nd	3rd	Total
1	**WILLIE PARK, Sr**	54	56	59	169
2	David Park	58	57	56	171
3	Robert Andrew	58	59	59	176
4	Tom Morris, Sr	61	58	59	178
5	Bob Kirk	60	62	58	180
6 =	William Doleman (a)	60	60	62	182
	Andrew Strath	61	61	60	182
8	John Allan	60	63	60	183
9	Tom Morris, Jr	63	60	64	187
10	Willie Dunn, Sr	64	63	62	189
11	Tom Hood (a)	61	69	61	191
12	James Hutchison	63	67	64	194

How many competitors made up the field at the start? As the *Ayrshire Express* conceded, '...cards were not given to the secretary and cannot consequently be recorded'.

COURSE:	Prestwick GC
LOCATION:	Prestwick, Ayrshire, Scotland
DATE:	n/k
DISTANCE:	3799 yards
PAR:	n/a
WINNER:	£n/k

Pos	Player	1st	2nd	3rd	Total
1	**TOM MORRIS, Sr**	58	54	58	170
2	Willie Park, Sr	58	56	58	172
3	Andrew Strath	61	57	56	174
4	Tom Morris, Jr	58	59	58	175
5	Bob Kirk	57	60	60	177
6	William Doleman (a)	55	66	57	178
7	Robert Andrew	56	58	65	179
8 =	William Dow	62	57	65	184
	T Hunter (a)	62	60	62	184
10	Willie Dunn, Sr	64	63	62	189

'Old' Tom became, at 46 years 99 days, the oldest ever winner of the Open and any Major until Julius Boros' US PGA title in 1968.

COURSE:	Prestwick GC
LOCATION:	Prestwick, Ayrshire, Scotland
DATE:	23 September
DISTANCE:	3799 yards
PAR:	n/a
WINNER:	£6

Pos	Player	1st	2nd	3rd	Total
1	**TOM MORRIS, Jr**	50	55	52	157
2	Robert Andrew	53	54	52	159
3	Willie Park, Sr	58	50	54	162
4	Bob Kirk	56	59	56	171
5	John Allan	54	55	63	172
6	Tom Morris, Sr	56	62	58	176
7	William Dow	61	58	60	179
8	William Doleman (a)	57	63	61	181
9	Charlie Hunter	60	64	58	182
10	Willie Dunn, Sr	60	63	60	183

The Son of the Father. Enter 'Young' Tom Morris to dominate the Championship for several years and create new scoring records year-by-year. He recorded the Open's first hole-in-one on the 166(?)-yard 8th hole. At 17 yrs 5 mths 8 days, he is the youngest winner of the Championship – and of any of the Majors.

BRITISH OPEN

COURSE:	Prestwick GC
LOCATION:	Prestwick, Ayrshire, Scotland
DATE:	16 September
DISTANCE:	3799 yards
PAR:	n/a
WINNER:	£6

Pos	Player	1st	2nd	3rd	Total
1	**TOM MORRIS, Jr**	51	54	49	154
2	Tom Morris, Sr	54	50	53	157
3	S Mure Fergusson (a)	57	54	54	165
4	Bob Kirk	53	58	57	168
5	Davie Strath	53	56	60	169
6	Jamie Anderson	60	56	57	173
7	William Doleman (a)	60	56	59	175
8	G Mitchell-Innes (a)	64	58	58	180

Morris, Jr shot the Open's first sub-50 round at Prestwick to steal the title from his Dad.

BRITISH OPEN

COURSE:	Prestwick GC
LOCATION:	Prestwick, Ayrshire, Scotland
DATE:	15 September
DISTANCE:	3799 yards
PAR:	n/a
WINNER:	£6

Pos	Player	1st	2nd	3rd	Total
1	**TOM MORRIS, Jr**	47	51	51	149
2 =	Bob Kirk	52	52	57	161
	Davie Strath	54	49	58	161
4	Tom Morris, Sr	56	52	54	162
5	William Doleman (a)	57	56	58	171
6	Willie Park, Sr	60	55	58	173
7	Jamie Anderson	59	57	58	174
8	John Allan	61	58	57	176
9 =	A Doleman (a)	61	59	58	178
	Charlie Hunter	58	56	64	178
11	J Brown	66	55	59	180
12	J Millar	66	62	54	182
13	T Hunter (a)	62	63	60	185
14	F Doleman	65	64	60	189
15 =	W Boyd	65	59	67	191
	J Hunter	62	65	64	191
17	William Dow	68	64	66	198

Young Tom's third win gave him the Belt outright.

No Championship

COURSE:	Prestwick GC
LOCATION:	Prestwick, Ayrshire, Scotland
DATE:	13 September
DISTANCE:	3799 yards
PAR:	n/a
WINNER:	£8

Pos	Player	1st	2nd	3rd	Total
1	**TOM MORRIS, Jr**	57	56	53	166
2	Davie Strath	56	52	61	169
3	William Doleman (a)	63	60	54	177
4 =	Tom Morris, Sr	62	60	57	179
	David Park	61	57	61	179
6	Charlie Hunter	60	60	69	189
7	Hugh Brown	65	73	61	199
8	William Hunter (a)	65	63	74	202

Tom Morris Jr won his fourth and last Open at 21: his is
the first name on the new trophy – the famous Claret Jug.
From this year rotation began between Prestwick, the Royal
& Ancient Club (St Andrews) and the Hon Co of Edinburgh
Golfers (Musselburgh).

BRITISH OPEN

COURSE: Royal & Ancient GC
LOCATION: St Andrews, Fife, Scotland
DATE: 4 October
DISTANCE: n/k
PAR: n/a
WINNER: £11

Pos	Player	1st	2nd	Total
1	**TOM KIDD**	91	88	179
2	Jamie Anderson	91	89	180
3 =	Bob Kirk	91	92	183
	Tom Morris, Jr	94	89	183
5	Davie Strath	97	90	187
6	Walter Gourlay	92	96	188
7	Tom Morris, Sr	93	96	189
9	Henry Lamb (a)	96	96	192
10 =	Willie Fernie	101	93	194
	Bob Martin	97	97	194
12 =	R Armitage (a)	96	99	195
	Jas Fenton	94	101	195
	JOF Morris	96	99	195
15	S Mure Fergusson (a)	98	101	199
16	R Manzie	96	104	200
17	Jack Morris	106	100	206
18 =	David Ayton	111	96	207
	R Thomson	98	109	207
20	John Chisholm	103	105	208

The first Open Championship to be held at the Old Course was dominated by local St Andrews golfers, of which, Kidd, the winner, was one. Another, David Ayton, was the forerunner of various Aytons' appearances in different Majors spread over the next 80 years or so.

BRITISH OPEN

COURSE: Honourable Company of
Edinburgh Golfers
LOCATION: Musselburgh, Midlothian, Scotland
DATE: 10 April
DISTANCE: n/k
PAR: n/a
WINNER: £8

Pos	Player	1st	2nd	Total
1	**MUNGO PARK**	75	84	159
2	Tom Morris, Jr	83	78	161
3	George Paxton	80	82	162
4	Bob Martin	85	79	164
5	Jamie Anderson	82	83	165
6 =	David Park	83	83	166
	William Thomson	84	82	166
8 =	Bob Ferguson	83	84	167
	Tom Kidd	84	83	167
10 =	J Fergusson	87	82	169
	G M'Cachnie	79	90	169
	JOF Morris	88	81	169
13	Willie Park, Sr	83	87	170
14 =	Tom Hood	83	88	171
	Bob Pringle	85	86	171
16	T Hunter (a)	88	86	174
17	T Brown	87	88	175
18 =	Tom Morris, Sr	90	86	176
	Davie Strath	86	90	176
20 =	William Cosgrove	88	89	177
	William Doleman (a)	89	88	177

Mungo Park (probably related to the famous late-eighteenth Century explorer) beat 'Young' Tom, whose health was now starting to decline. Mungo was the brother of Willie, and his son, also Mungo, became a pioneer of golf and course architecture in the United States. His first round 75 was the record low score for any 18 holes; and was only lowered by Harold Hilton, who shot 72 on the much-criticised Muirfield Links in 1892; and by Willie Smith (71), George Duncan (71), James Braid (73&74), and others, on the Old Course as late as 1910.

COURSE:	Prestwick GC
LOCATION:	Prestwick, Ayrshire, Scotland
DATE:	10 September
DISTANCE:	n/k
PAR:	n/a
WINNER:	£8

COURSE:	Royal & Ancient GC
LOCATION:	St Andrews, Fife, Scotland
DATE:	30 September
DISTANCE:	n/k
PAR:	n/a
WINNER:	£10

Pos	Player	1st	2nd	3rd	Total
1	**WILLIE PARK, Sr**	56	59	51	166
2	Bob Martin	56	58	54	168
3	Mungo Park	59	57	55	171
4	Bob Ferguson	58	56	58	172
5	James Rennie	61	59	57	177
6	Davie Strath	59	61	58	178
7	Bob Pringle	62	58	61	181
8 =	William Doleman (a)	65	59	59	183
	Hugh Morrison	62	59	62	183
10	John Campbell	57	66	63	186
11	Neil Boon	67	60	62	189
12	James Guthrie	63	64	66	193
13	Matthew Allan	67	65	62	194
14	James Boyd	67	65	63	195

Pos	Player	1st	2nd	3rd	Total
1	**BOB MARTIN***		86	90	176
2	Davie Strath		86	90	176
3	Willie Park, Sr		94	89	183
4 =	Tom Morris, Sr		90	95	185
	Mungo Park		95	90	185
	William Thomson		90	95	185
7	Henry Lamb (a)		94	92	186
8 =	Walter Gourlay		98	89	187
	Bob Kirk		95	92	187
	George Paxton		95	92	187
11	Robert Kinsman		88	100	188
12=	Jamie Anderson		96	93	189
	David Lamb (a)		95	94	189
14=	David Anderson, Sr		93	97	190
	John Thompson		89	101	190

Play-off: see below

Willie Park picked up his 4th and last title after a few years of indifferent form. It is thought that the Morris's did not compete due the death of 'Young' Tom's wife in childbirth – a factor, coupled with the consequent heavy drinking, that led to the discovery by 'Old' Tom of his son's body on Christmas morning, 1874. The greatest golfer of his generation was dead at 24.

The first-ever play-off in the Open – except that it never took place. Strath protested about a claim against him for disqualification. The decision was that he and Martin should play off, but Strath refused on the basis that his protest had not been properly decided upon.

BRITISH OPEN

BRITISH OPEN

COURSE:	Honourable Company of Edinburgh Golfers
LOCATION:	Musselburgh, Midlothian, Scotland
DATE:	6 April
DISTANCE:	n/k
PAR:	n/a
WINNER:	£8

Pos	Player	1st	2nd	3rd	4th	Total
1	**JAMIE ANDERSON**	40	42	37	41	160
2	Bob Pringle	44	38	40	40	162
3 =	William Cosgrove	41	39	44	40	164
	Bob Ferguson	40	40	40	44	164
5 =	William Brown	39	41	45	41	166
	Davie Strath	45	40	38	43	166
7	Mungo Park					167

The Hon Co continued experimenting with an early-season Championship. Anderson's first of three wins, 'back-to-back', was over four rounds of Musselburgh's nine holes.

COURSE:	Prestwick GC
LOCATION:	Prestwick, Ayrshire, Scotland
DATE:	4 October
DISTANCE:	n/k
PAR:	n/a
WINNER:	£8

Pos	Player	1st	2nd	3rd	Total
1	**JAMIE ANDERSON**	53	53	51	157
2	Bob Kirk	53	55	51	159
3	JOF Morris	50	56	55	161
4 =	John Ball, Jr (a)	53	57	55	165
	Bob Martin	57	53	55	165
6 =	William Cosgrove	55	56	55	166
	Willie Park, Sr	53	56	57	166
8	Jamie Allan	62	53	52	167
9 =	John Allan	55	55	58	168
	Tom Dunn	54	60	54	168
11	Tom Morris, Sr	55	53	63	171
12	Ben Sayers	56	59	58	173
13	Edwin Paxton	58	59	58	175
14	George Strath	63	62	51	176
15	Alex Patrick	62	56	60	178
16	Jack Morris	58	57	64	179
17	Mungo Park	60	58	62	180
18	George Low	57	61	63	181
19	Neil Boon	63	54	66	183
20	William Hunter (a)	67	65	55	187

Jamie Anderson recorded the second 'hole-in-one' in the Championship, following Morris Jr's effort in 1868. Amateur John Ball finished 4th in his first Open: he was also the highest-placed non-Scot to date. He was aged just 14! Ten years later Ball won the embryonic British Amateur Championship for the first of eight occasions (he won it as late as 1912), and in 1890 broke the stranglehold of the Scottish professional in the Open. They had previously won every Open since the first in 1860.

COURSE: Royal & Ancient GC
LOCATION: St Andrews, Fife, Scotland
DATE: 27 September
DISTANCE: n/k yards
PAR: n/a
WINNER: £10

Pos	Player	1st	2nd	Total
1	**JAMIE ANDERSON**	84	85	169
2 =	Jamie Allan	88	84	172
	Andrew Kirkaldy	86	86	172
4	George Paxton			174
5	Tom Kidd			175
6	Bob Ferguson			176
7	David Anderson, Sr			178
8 =	Tom Dunn			179
	Walter Gourlay			179
	JOF Morris	92	87	179
11	AW Smith (a)			180
12 =	Willie Fernie			181
	John Kirkaldy			181
	James Rennie			181
15 =	Thomas Arundel			184
	David Ayton			184
	Henry Lamb (a)			184
18 =	William Doleman (a)			185
	Robert Kinsman			185
	Tom Morris, Sr			185

Anderson's 'Hat trick' had the the lowest total of all 36-hole Opens on this, his home course, until Hugh Kirkaldy's 166 in the very last one, in 1891. Joint runner-up, Andrew Kirkaldy, would never win the Open (with four second places, including losing a play-off, surely one of the most unlucky) but went on to become one of the most influential people in the game. Despite a wonderful record at a time when the 'Great Triumvirate' seemed to be winning everything, it was as professional at the R&A, following Tom Morris in 1910, until his death in 1934, that he will always be remembered.

COURSE: Honourable Company of Edinburgh Golfers
LOCATION: Musselburgh, Midlothian, Scotland
DATE: 9 April
DISTANCE: n/k
PAR: n/a
WINNER: £8

Pos	Player	1st	2nd	Total
1	**BOB FERGUSON**	81	81	162
2	Peter Paxton	81	86	167
3	Ned Cosgrove	82	86	168
4 =	David Brown	86	83	169
	George Paxton	85	84	169
	Bob Pringle	90	79	169
7	Andrew Kirkaldy	85	85	170
8 =	William Brown	87	84	171
	David Grant	87	84	171
10 =	Thomas Arundel	86	93	179
	T Brown	90	89	179
	Willie Campbell	88	91	179
	J Foreman	92	87	179
14	Willie Park, Sr	89	92	181
15	Willie Park, Jr	92	90	182
16 =	A Brown	91	92	183
	D Corstorphine	93	90	183
	George Strath	87	96	183
19	Ben Sayers	91	93	184
20	Mungo Park	95	92	187

The early date of the Championship was inconvenient for Jamie Anderson, and he was unable to compete. This left Bob Ferguson the chance to secure the first of his three wins in a row. Anderson, although featuring strongly over the next few years, never won again, and died in a Poor House in Perth in 1905. So much for the rich pickings of the nineteenth Century professional golfer.

1881/2 BRITISH OPEN

COURSE:	Prestwick GC
LOCATION:	Prestwick, Ayrshire, Scotland
DATE:	14 October
DISTANCE:	n/k
PAR:	n/a
WINNER:	£8

Pos	Player	1st	2nd	3rd	Total
1	**BOB FERGUSON**	53	60	57	170
2	Jamie Anderson	57	60	56	173
3	Ned Cosgrove	61	59	57	177
4	Bob Martin	57	62	59	178
5 =	Willie Campbell	60	56	65	181
	Tom Morris, Sr	58	65	58	181
	Willie Park, Jr	66	57	58	181
8	Willie Fernie	65	62	56	183

A violent storm reduced the field to 22 starters, of whom only eight finished. The conditions were so bad that Ferguson's winning total was the highest for Prestwick's 36 holes since 'Old' Tom's last win in 1867; and only exceeded by Willie Park's 174 in the inaugural year. About 180 fishermen were drowned in Scottish waters due to the storms.

BRITISH OPEN

COURSE:	Royal & Ancient GC
LOCATION:	St Andrews, Fife, Scotland
DATE:	30 September
DISTANCE:	n/k
PAR:	n/a
WINNER:	£12

Pos	Player	1st	2nd	Total
1	**BOB FERGUSON**	83	88	171
2	Willie Fernie	88	86	174
3 =	Jamie Anderson	87	88	175
	Fitz Boothby (a)	86	89	175
	John Kirkcaldy	86	89	175
	Bob Martin	89	86	175
7 =	David Ayton	90	88	178
	James Mansfield (a)	91	87	178
	Willie Park, Sr	89	89	178
	James Rennie	90	88	178
11 =	Tom Kidd	87	93	180
	Henry Lamb (a)	88	92	180
13 =	Andrew Alexander	93	88	181
	George Low	95	86	181
	Douglas Rolland	88	93	181
16 =	W Honeyman	93	89	182
	William Thomson	95	87	182
18 =	Tom Dunn	93	90	183
	Willie Park, Jr	90	93	183
	Ben Sayers	92	91	183

Ferguson held his three-stroke R1 lead to pick up his third consecutive Open. Like Anderson before him, obscurity was to follow in a few years, and he resorted to greenkeeping and caddying thereafter at his home club of Musselburgh.

COURSE:	Honourable Company of Edinburgh Golfers
LOCATION:	Musselburgh, Midlothian, Scotland
DATE:	16 November
DISTANCE:	n/k
PAR:	n/a
WINNER:	£n/k

Pos	Player	1st	2nd	Total
1	**WILLIE FERNIE***	75	84	159
2	Bob Ferguson	78	81	159
3	William Brown	83	77	160
4	Bob Pringle	79	82	161
5 =	Willie Campbell	80	83	163
	George Paxton	80	83	163
7	Ben Sayers	81	83	164
8	Willie Park, Jr	77	88	165
9	Willie Dunn, Jr	85	81	166
10 =	Ben Campbell	81	86	167
	Tom Morris, Sr	86	81	167
	Peter Paxton	85	82	167
	Douglas Rolland (a)	82	85	167
14	T Grossart	82	86	168
15	F Park	84	85	169
16	William Cosgrove	79	91	170
17 =	Tom Dunn	87	84	171
	Jack Simpson (a)	90	81	171
19	G Miller (a)	80	92	172
20	D Leitch (a)	88	86	174

* Willie Fernie (158) beat Bob Ferguson (159) in the 36-Hole Play-off

Willie Fernie, despite shooting the only 10 to appear on any Major winner's card in history, tied with Ferguson and denied him from making four wins in as many years – by one shot in the first contested play-off. Fernie, although St Andrews born, was then of Dumfries, thus becoming the first winner from outside the host clubs. This just sums up the parochial nature of the Championship to date. Musselburgh played host to the Open in November for the first time, seemingly not happy with its previous equally-eccentric habit of April Championships.

COURSE:	Prestwick GC
LOCATION:	Prestwick, Ayrshire, Scotland
DATE:	n/k
DISTANCE:	n/k
PAR:	n/a
WINNER:	£n/k

Pos	Player	1st	2nd	Total
1	**JACK SIMPSON**	78	82	160
2 =	Willie Fernie	80	84	164
	Douglas Rolland	81	83	164
4 =	Willie Campbell	84	85	169
	Willie Park, Jr	86	83	169
6	Ben Sayers	83	87	170
7 =	Tom Dunn			171
	George Fernie			171
9 =	Peter Fernie			172
	John Kirkaldy			172
11 =	Matthew Allan			173
	Willie Dunn, Jr			173
13 =	JOF Morris			174
	Tom Morris, Sr			174
15	Jamie Anderson			175
16 =	William Cosgrove			178
	William Doleman (a)			178
18	James Hunter (a)			179
19	David Grant			180
20	G Smith			183

Just about the only thing known about the 1884 Prestwick Championship is that Jack Simpson was the only one of several golfing brothers to win the Open. His brother Archie was runner-up in 1885 and 1890 – something that was to happen to this year's joint-second, Willie Fernie, on more than one occasion in future Championships.

BRITISH OPEN

COURSE: Royal & Ancient GC
LOCATION: St Andrews, Fife, Scotland
DATE: 3 October
DISTANCE: n/k
PAR: n/a
WINNER: £10

Pos	Player	1st	2nd	Total
1	**BOB MARTIN**	84	87	171
2	Archie Simpson	83	89	172
3	David Ayton	89	84	173
4 =	Willie Fernie	89	85	174
	Willie Park, Jr	86	88	174
	Bob Simpson	85	89	174
7	Jack Burns	88	87	175
8	Peter Paxton	85	91	176
9 =	Willie Campbell	86	91	177
	JOF Morris	91	86	177
11 =	Horace Hutchinson (a)	87	91	178
	John Kirkaldy	94	84	178
13 =	Johnny Laidlay (a)	87	92	179
	Jack Simpson	87	92	179
15	Ben Sayers	94	86	180
16 =	Leslie Balfour (a)	90	91	181
	William Greig (a)	89	92	181
18 =	HSC Everard (a)	90	92	182
	George Fernie	87	95	182
	James Rennie	90	92	182

During the 1880s a minor exodus of Scottish pros moved to clubs south of the border; but only a handful of English golfers, all amateur, had ventured north for the Championship. One of the most influential of these, Horace Hutchinson, made his debut this year. Through his playing, and writing about golf, over the ensuing few years he had much to do with encouraging the burgeoning English talent of the 1890s to participate in the Open.

BRITISH OPEN

COURSE: Honourable Company of
Edinburgh Golfers
LOCATION: Musselburgh, Midlothian, Scotland
DATE: 5 November
DISTANCE: n/k
PAR: n/a
WINNER: £8

Pos	Player	1st	2nd	Total
1	**DAVID BROWN**	79	78	157
2	Willie Campbell	78	81	159
3	Ben Campbell	79	81	160
4 =	Bob Ferguson	82	79	161
	Thomas Gossett	80	81	161
	Willie Park, Jr	84	77	161
	Archie Simpson	82	79	161
8 =	Willie Fernie	79	83	162
	David Grant	86	76	162
	Johnny Laidlay (a)	80	82	162
11	JOF Morris	81	82	163
12 =	John Lambert	78	86	164
	Thomas McWatt	81	83	164
	Jack Simpson	83	81	164
15	Bob Simpson	84	81	165
16 =	Tom Dunn	83	83	166
	Horace Hutchinson (a)	81	85	166
	Bob Pringle	80	86	166
	Ben Sayers	84	82	166
20 =	William Cosgrove	84	83	167
	Bob Tait	84	83	167

An unsung champion, David Brown emigrated to America where he tied with Willie Anderson for the US Open as late as 1903 – losing the play-off by two strokes. The Championship could have drifted away in the 1880s; it hadn't really developed beyond a regional event. Despite the Scots traditional antipathy to the Sassenach, it would take a particularly introspective one not to acknowledge the shot in the arm the English were to give the Championship in the next decade.

COURSE:	Prestwick GC			COURSE:	Royal & Ancient GC			
LOCATION:	Prestwick, Ayrshire, Scotland			LOCATION:	St Andrews, Fife, Scotland			
DATE:	16 September			DATE:	6 October			
DISTANCE:	n/k			DISTANCE:	n/k			
PAR:	n/a			PAR:	n/a			
WINNER:	£8			WINNER:	£8			

Pos	Player	1st	2nd	Total
1	**WILLIE PARK, Jr**	82	79	161
2	Bob Martin	81	81	162
3	Willie Campbell	77	87	164
4	Johnny Laidlay (a)	86	80	166
5 =	Ben Sayers	83	85	168
	Archie Simpson	81	87	168
7 =	Willie Fernie	86	87	173
	David Grant	89	84	173
9	David Brown	82	92	174
10 =	Ben Campbell	88	87	175
	Horace Hutchinson (a)	87	88	175
12 =	David Ayton	89	87	176
	James Kay	89	87	176
	John Kirkaldy	89	87	176
	Jack Simpson	85	91	176
16	Bob Simpson	90	89	179
17 =	George Fernie	92	88	180
	A Monaghan	90	90	180
19	Hugh Kirkaldy	89	92	181
20 =	James Boyd	95	87	182
	P Wilson (a)	90	92	182

Pos	Player	1st	2nd	Total
1	**JACK BURNS**	86	85	171
2 =	David Anderson, Jr	86	86	172
	Ben Sayers	85	87	172
4	Willie Campbell	84	90	174
5	Leslie Balfour (a)	86	89	175
6 =	David Grant	88	88	176
	Andrew Kirkaldy	87	89	176
8	Sandy Herd	93	84	177
9	David Ayton	87	91	178
10	Johnny Laidlay (a)	93	87	180
11 =	HSC Everard (a)	93	89	182
	Hugh Kirkaldy	98	84	182
	Willie Park, Jr	90	92	182
14 =	Laurie Auchterlonie	91	92	183
	Willie Fernie	91	92	183
16 =	Bob Martin	86	98	184
	Archie Simpson	91	93	184
18 =	Jamie Allan	95	90	185
	Willie Auchterlonie	92	93	185
	John Kirkaldy	92	93	185
	Allan Macfie (a)	94	91	185
	Bob Tait	95	90	185

Willie Jr's win completed the second set of father-son victories. Fittingly it should be the Parks and the Morrises, the fathers having carved up the first five Championships between them. After winning again in 1889, Willie Park, Jr increasingly turned his mind to club and ball development; and has been called the father of modern golf course architectutre – the classic Sunningdale being his greatest achievement. He was also the first professional to write on the game: his The *Game of Golf* was published in 1896.

Jack Burns's win was one of great surprise. He only contested the Championship with any great seriousness during the 1880s, and had just one Top Ten finish before he collected the Claret Jug. Immediately afterwards he moved as pro to the English Midlands; before eventually returning to St Andrews, the place of his birth, to retire from all golf in 1897 – not yet 40. Alex 'Sandy' Herd made the Top 10 for the first time, in his fourth year of a 54-year span in the Open Championship. His remarkable run included a win in 1902, and 2nds in 1892, 1895, 1910 and 1920. He competed in his last Open in 1939, aged 71. His brother Fred won the 1898 US Open.

COURSE: Honourable Company of
Edinburgh Golfers
LOCATION: Musselburgh, Midlothian, Scotland
DATE: 8 November
DISTANCE: n/k
PAR: n/a
WINNER: £8

Pos	Player	1st	2nd	3rd	4th	Total
1	WILLIE PARK, Jr*	39	39	39	38	155
2	Andrew Kirkaldy	39	38	39	39	155
3	Ben Sayers	39	40	41	39	159
4 =	David Brown	43	39	41	39	162
	Johnny Laidlay (a)	42	39	40	41	162
6	Willie Fernie	45	39	40	40	164
7 =	Willie Brown	44	43	41	37	165
	Willie Campbell	44	40	42	39	165
	David Grant	41	41	41	42	165
10 =	High Kirkaldy	44	39	43	40	166
	William Thomson	43	42	40	41	166
12	Archie Simpson	44	45	37	41	167
13	AM Ross (a)	42	45	42	40	169
14	Jack Burns	47	39	42	42	170

*Willie Park Jr (158) beat Andrew Kirkaldy (163) in the 18-Hole Play-off

The last Championship held at Musselburgh produced a course record low winning total in the tie between Willie Jr and Andrew Kirkaldy – the lowest at any venue since the heyday of 'Young' Tom in 1869 and 1870. The Honourable Company, in order to stay involved with the Open, forsook their 9-hole home for Muirfield, further along the southern shores of the Firth of Forth, some 15 miles east of Edinburgh. The fact that the end of the second round was played in a November gloom so deep that final pairs had to be guided by street lights, triggered the move to earlier calendar dates.

COURSE: Prestwick GC
LOCATION: Prestwick, Ayrshire, Scotland
DATE: 11 September
DISTANCE: n/k
PAR: n/a
WINNER: £nil–Amateur

Pos	Player	1st	2nd	Total
1	JOHN BALL, Jr (a)	82	82	164
2 =	Willie Fernie	85	82	167
	Archie Simpson	85	82	167
4 =	Andrew Kirkaldy	81	89	170
	Willie Park, Jr	90	80	170
6	Horace Hutchinson (a)	87	85	172
7 =	David Grant	86	87	173
	Hugh Kirkaldy	82	91	173
9	W McEwan	87	87	174
10	David Brown	85	90	175
11 =	James Kay	86	91	177
	Johnny Laidlay (a)	89	88	177
13	D Leitch (a)	86	93	179
14	David Anderson, Jr	90	90	180
15 =	John Allan	93	88	181
	Ben Campbell	93	88	181
17 =	D Anderson (a)	91	91	182
	David Ayton	97	85	182
19	Ben Sayers	90	93	183
20	A Wright	92	92	184

With the change of decade, a new wind was starting to blow around the fading Championship. John Ball, returning to the event that he graced as a 14 year-old in 1878, became the first Englishman, and the first amateur, to win the Open Championship in all the 30 years of its existence. He also pre-empted the great Bobby Jones in doing the 'double' – both the Open and The Amateur Championships in the same year. The invasion had not quite started though – he was the only Englishman out of 31 to finish.

COURSE: Royal & Ancient GC
LOCATION: St Andrews, Fife, Scotland
DATE: 6 October
DISTANCE: n/k
PAR: n/a
WINNER: £10

Pos	Player	1st	2nd	Total
1	**HUGH KIRKALDY**	83	83	166
2 =	Willie Fernie	84	84	168
	Andrew Kirkaldy	84	84	168
4	R Mure Fergusson (a)	86	84	170
5	WD More	84	87	171
6	Willie Park, Jr	88	85	173
7	David Brown	88	86	174
8	Willie Auchterlonie	85	90	175
9 =	Ben Sayers	91	85	176
	Tom Vardon	89	87	176
11 =	John Ball, Jr (a)	94	83	177
	Archie Simpson	86	91	177
13	Sandy Herd	87	91	178
14 =	David Grant	84	95	179
	James Kay	93	86	179
	John Kirkaldy	90	89	179
	Bob Mearns	88	91	179
18 =	Laurie Auchterlonie	87	93	180
	Charles Hutchings (a)	89	91	180
	Johnny Laidlay (a)	90	90	180
	David Simpson	91	89	180

Hugh was the only Kirkaldy brother to pick up the title although John, and particularly Andrew, as we have already seen, featured prominently. When Andrew became pro at the R&A in 1910 he was in direct succession, not just to Tom Morris, Sr; but before him, the legendary Allan Robertson. The three held sway at St Andrews in a dynasty unbroken for over 80 years.

COURSE: Honourable Company of Endinburgh Golfers
LOCATION: Muirfield, East Lothian, Scotland
DATE: 22-23 September
DISTANCE: n/k
PAR: n/a
WINNER: £nil–Amateur

Pos	Player	1st	2nd	3rd	4th	Total
1	**HAROLD HILTON** (a)	78	81	72	74	305
2 =	John Ball, Jr (a)	75	80	74	79	308
	Sandy Herd	77	78	77	76	308
	Hugh Kirkaldy	77	83	73	75	308
5 =	James Kay	82	78	74	78	312
	Ben Sayers	80	76	81	75	312
7	Willie Park, Jr	78	77	80	80	315
8	Willie Fernie	79	83	76	78	316
9	Archie Simpson	81	81	76	79	317
10	Horace Hutchinson (a)	74	78	86	80	318
11	Jack White	82	78	78	81	319
12	Tom Vardon	83	75	80	82	320
13 =	Edward BH Blackwell (a)	81	82	82	76	321
	Andrew Kirkaldy	84	82	80	75	321
15	S Mure Fergusson (a)	78	82	80	82	322
16 =	David Anderson, Jr	76	82	79	87	324
	RT Boothby (a)	81	81	80	82	324
	Ben Campbell	86	83	79	76	324
19 =	FA Fairlie (a)	83	87	79	76	325
	William McEwan	79	83	84	79	325

The first championship to be spread over two days and 72 holes resulted in the second win for an amateur (and an English one at that) in three years. For the only time in the history of the Major Championships, amateurs finished first and second. The Honourable Company of Edinburgh Golfers were hosts at Muirfield, where the Championship was held for the first time. Many critics thought that the course was not a sufficient challenge for the Championship and alterations were made for future Opens there. Entry fees, to deter mere hopefuls, were introduced.

BRITISH OPEN

COURSE:	Prestwick GC					
LOCATION:	Prestwick, Ayrshire, Scotland					
DATE:	31 August - 1 September					
DISTANCE:	n/k					
PAR:	n/a					
WINNER:	£30					

Pos	Player	1st	2nd	3rd	4th	Total
1	**WILLIE AUCHTERLONIE**	78	81	81	82	322
2	Johnny Laidlay (a)	80	83	80	81	324
3	Sandy Herd	82	81	78	84	325
4 =	Andrew Kirkaldy	85	82	82	77	326
	Hugh Kirkaldy	83	79	82	82	326
6 =	James Kay	81	81	80	85	327
	Bob Simpson	81	81	80	85	327
8 =	John Ball, Jr (a)	83	79	84	86	332
	Harold Hilton (a)	88	81	82	81	332
10 =	JH Taylor	75	89	86	83	333
	Jack White	81	86	80	86	333
12	Ben Sayers	87	88	84	76	335
13	C Hutchings (a)	81	92	80	84	337
14	Archie Simpson	84	86	84	85	339
15 =	S Mure Fergusson (a)	83	85	85	87	340
	John Hunter	87	85	83	85	340
17 =	David Grant	86	86	85	84	341
	Joe Lloyd	85	91	84	81	341
19 =	LS Anderson (a)	89	83	86	84	342
	PC Anderson (a)	93	84	83	82	342
	Willie Park, Jr	82	89	86	85	342

'Old' Tom Morris – winner of four of the first eight Opens, and playing in the Championship for the 33rd consecutive time, told *The Field* magazine that conditions on the first day were the worst he had ever experienced. The magazine's correspondent was more flowery: '...it rained in the most pitiless fashion from morn to eve...'. Willie Auchterlonie's brother, Laurie, made it a family double when he picked up the US Open in 1902. Willie's winning purse was £1.10.0 more than the total prizemoney two years earlier. With JH Taylor leading after the first round, and Harry Vardon also finishing in the Top 30, things were starting to happen to the Open.

BRITISH OPEN

COURSE:	St George's GC					
LOCATION:	Sandwich, Kent, England					
DATE:	11-12 June					
DISTANCE:	n/k					
PAR:	n/a					
WINNER:	£30					

Pos	Player	1st	2nd	3rd	4th	Total
1	**JH TAYLOR**	84	80	81	81	326
2	Douglas Rolland	86	79	84	82	331
3	Andrew Kirkaldy	86	79	83	84	332
4	AH Toogood	84	85	82	82	333
5 =	Willie Fernie	84	84	86	80	334
	Ben Sayers	85	81	84	84	334
	Harry Vardon	86	86	82	80	334
8	Sandy Herd	83	85	82	88	338
9	Freddie Tait (a)	90	83	83	84	340
10 =	AD Blyth (a)	91	84	84	82	341
	James Braid	91	84	82	84	341
12	Willie Park, Jr	88	86	82	87	343
13 =	John Ball, Jr (a)	84	89	87	84	344
	David Brown	93	83	81	87	344
	Hugh Kirkaldy	90	85	80	89	344
	Archie Simpson	90	86	86	82	344
17	Joe Lloyd	95	81	86	83	345
18	S Mure Fergusson (a)	87	88	84	87	346
19	Tom Vardon	87	88	82	91	348
20 =	CE Dick (a)	85	89	89	90	353
	David Grant	91	84	87	91	353
	David Herd	92	93	84	84	353

The English influence in the Open Championship really started to kick in in 1894. The event left Scotland for the first time in an expanded rotation which would also take in Royal Liverpool at Hoylake in 1897. This was the first win for one of the 'Great Triumvirate' of JH Taylor, Harry Vardon and James Braid, who between 1894 and 1914 collected 16 Open Championships – with Vardon also raiding the US Open successfully in 1900. Joe Lloyd, in 17th place, was to achieve greater glory after emigrating, by winning the 1897 US Open.

COURSE:	Royal & Ancient GC
LOCATION:	St Andrews, Fife, Scotland
DATE:	12-13 June
DISTANCE:	n/k
PAR:	n/a
WINNER:	£30

COURSE:	Newport GC
LOCATION:	Newport, Rhode Island
DATE:	4 October
DISTANCE:	n/k
PAR:	n/a
WINNER:	$150

Pos	Player	1st	2nd	3rd	4th	Total
1	**JH TAYLOR**	86	78	80	78	322
2	Sandy Herd	82	77	82	85	326
3	Andrew Kirkaldy	81	83	84	84	332
4	George Pulford	84	81	83	86	334
5	Archie Simpson	88	85	78	85	336
6 =	David Anderson, Jr	86	83	84	84	337
	David Brown	81	89	83	84	337
	Willie Fernie	86	79	86	86	337
9 =	Ben Sayers	84	87	85	82	338
	AH Toogood	85	84	83	86	338
	Harry Vardon	80	85	85	88	338
	Tom Vardon	82	83	84	89	338
13 =	Laurie Auchterlonie	84	84	85	87	340
	J Robb	89	88	81	82	340
15 =	Hugh Kirkaldy	87	87	83	84	341
	Freddie Tait (a)	87	86	82	86	341
17	Johnny Laidlay (a)	91	83	82	86	342
18 =	John Ball, Jr (a)	85	85	88	86	344
	L Waters	86	83	85	90	344
20	David Herd	85	85	84	91	345

Pos	Player	1st	2nd	3rd	4th	Total
1	**HORACE RAWLINS**	45	46	41	41	173
2	Willie Dunn, Jr	43	46	44	42	175
3 =	James Foulis	46	43	44	43	176
	AW Smith (a)	47	43	44	42	176
5	Willie Davis	45	49	42	42	178
6	Willie Campbell	41	48	42	48	179
7 =	John Harland	45	48	43	47	183
	John Patrick	46	48	46	43	183
9	Samuel Tucker	49	48	45	43	185
10	John Reid	49	51	55	51	206

Taylor, three behind Herd going into the last round, shot a 78 – four strokes better than anyone in the field – to overhaul the Scotsman over the last 18 holes. Many Brits had left the country by now to seek their fortunes in America, and professional golfers were soon to find out that, at least to begin with, there were some rich pickings for them among the thriving new clubs.

From one island to another – Rawlins left Isle of Wight, England for Rhode Island; where he became pro at the Newport club. The field was made up of British professionals plus Scottish amateur, AW Smith. Runner-up Dunn, whose father had finished 7th in the second-ever British Open, had won the unofficial US national championship in the previous year, but like his father was never destined to win either Major. For the first three years the Championship was held over 36 holes, then followed the 72-hole example of its British counterpart. Just like with its elder brother, the US Open calendar was all over the place in the early years; but, at least, the prizemoney was realistic from the start.

1896

COURSE:	Honourable Company of Edinburgh Golfers
LOCATION:	Muirfield, East Lothian, Scotland
DATE:	10-11 June
DISTANCE:	n/k
PAR:	n/a
WINNER:	£30

COURSE:	Shinnecock Hills GC
LOCATION:	Southampton, New York
DATE:	18 July
DISTANCE:	4423 yards
PAR:	n/a
WINNER:	$150

Pos	Player	1st	2nd	3rd	4th	Total
1	HARRY VARDON*	83	78	78	77	316
2	JH Taylor	77	78	81	80	316
3 =	Willie Fernie	78	79	82	80	319
	Freddie Tait (a)	83	75	84	77	319
5	Sandy Herd	72	84	79	85	320
6	James Braid	83	81	79	80	323
7 =	David Brown	80	77	81	86	324
	Ben Sayers	83	76	79	86	324
	Andrew Scott	83	84	77	80	324
10	Tom Vardon	83	82	77	83	325
11	Peter McEwan	83	81	80	84	328
12 =	Willie Auchterlonie	80	86	81	82	329
	Archie Simpson	85	79	78	87	329
14 =	James Kay	77	88	83	82	330
	Andrew Kirkaldy	84	85	79	82	330
	Willie Park, Jr	79	80	83	88	330
17	AH Toogood	81	85	84	84	334
18 =	John Hunter	85	79	83	88	335
	Johnny Laidlay (a)	85	82	82	86	335
	David McEwan	83	89	81	82	335
	Jack Ross	83	87	84	81	335

Pos	Player	1st	2nd	Total
1	JAMES FOULIS	78	74	152
2	Horace Rawlins	79	76	155
3	Joe Lloyd	76	81	157
4 =	George Douglas	79	79	158
	AW Smith (a)	78	80	158
6 =	John Shippen	78	81	159
	HJ Wigham (a)	82	77	159
8	Willie Tucker	78	82	160
9	Robert Wilson	82	80	162
10	Alfred Ricketts	80	83	163
11	WH Way	83	81	164
12	Willie Dunn, Jr	78	87	165
13	Willie Davis	83	84	167
14	Willie Campbell	85	85	170
15	WT Hoare	90	81	171
16 =	JN Mackrell	89	83	172
	Alex Patrick	86	86	172
	John Reid	88	84	172
19 =	Tom Gourley	82	91	173
	John Patrick	88	85	173

* Harry Vardon (157) beat JH Taylor (161) in the 36-Hole Play-off

Harry Vardon was to eclipse his famous Triumvirate cohorts by winning six Opens (and a US Open) to Taylor's and Braid's five. This, his first, followed a marathon play-off after a tie with Taylor at the toughened-up Muirfield course – now reputedly four strokes more difficult than in 1892. Vardon's and Taylor's total was 11 shots poorer than Hilton's four years earlier. 'Old' Tom Morris competed in his last Open, aged 75.

The Foulis family emigrated to America *en bloc* and featured strongly in early Opens. Jim Foulis, part of the next generation, reached the Quarter-final of the PGA Championship in 1938 and was 11th in the 1946 Masters. John Shippen and Oscar Bunn (who finished 21st) were the first golfers to suffer racial discrimination in a Major. Indeed, they almost were refused entry to the Championship.

COURSE:	Royal Liverpool GC
LOCATION:	Hoylake, Cheshire, England
DATE:	19-20 May
DISTANCE:	6150 yards
PAR:	n/a
WINNER:	£nil-Amateur

COURSE:	Chicago GC
LOCATION:	Wheaton, Illinois
DATE:	17 September
DISTANCE:	6682 yards
PAR:	n/a
WINNER:	$150

Pos	Player	1st	2nd	3rd	4th	Total
1	**HAROLD HILTON** (a)	80	75	84	75	314
2	James Braid	80	74	82	79	315
3 =	George Pulford	80	79	79	79	317
	Freddie Tait (a)	79	79	80	79	317
5	Sandy Herd	78	81	79	80	318
6	Harry Vardon	84	80	80	76	320
7 =	David Brown	79	82	80	83	324
	Archie Simpson	83	81	81	79	324
	Tom Vardon	81	81	79	83	324
10 =	Andrew Kirkaldy	83	83	82	82	330
	JH Taylor	82	80	82	86	330
12 =	Ben Sayers	84	78	85	84	331
	S Mure Fergusson (a)	87	83	79	82	331
14 =	Peter McEwan	86	79	85	82	332
	TG Renouf	86	79	83	84	332
16	Andrew Scott	83	83	84	83	333
17	John Ball, Jr (a)	78	81	88	87	334
18 =	Willie Auchterlonie	84	85	85	81	335
	Jack Graham, (a)	85	80	87	83	335
20 =	James Kinnell	82	83	78	93	336
	Joe Lloyd	86	84	82	84	336

Pos	Player	1st	2nd	Total
1	**JOE LLOYD**	83	79	162
2	Willie Anderson, Jr	79	84	163
3 =	Willie Dunn, Jr	87	81	168
	James Foulis	80	88	168
5	WT Hoare	82	87	169
6 =	Bernard Nicholls	87	85	172
	Alfred Ricketts	91	81	172
8 =	David Foulis	86	87	173
	Horace Rawlins	91	82	173
	HJ Wigham (a)	87	86	173
11 =	Charles Macdonald (a)	85	89	174
	William Marshall	87	87	174
	Robert Wilson	83	91	174
14	Harry Turpie	85	90	175
15 =	Willie Davis	88	89	177
	Robert Foulis	88	89	177
	Willie Tucker	90	87	177
	JA Tyng (a)	86	91	177
19	Findlay Douglas (a)	89	91	180
20	WG Stewart (a)	91	90	181

Hoylake's debut. Hilton's second victory made him the only amateur multiple winner of the Open until the advent of Bobby Jones in the 1920s. Joe Lloyd became the first golfer to play both British and US Opens in the same year.

Lloyd's decision to move to the US in 1897 paid immediate dividends for this much-travelled golfer for his time: he was a summer pro in the US, and spent his winters at the Pau club in South-West France. He collected the US title five months after finishing 20th in the British Open.

BRITISH OPEN

COURSE:	Prestwick GC
LOCATION:	Prestwick, Ayrshire, Scotland
DATE:	8-9 June
DISTANCE:	5732 yards
PAR:	n/a
WINNER:	£30

Pos	Player	1st	2nd	3rd	4th	Total
1	**HARRY VARDON**	79	75	77	76	307
2	Willie Park, Jr	76	75	78	79	308
3	Harold Hilton (a)	76	81	77	75	309
4	JH Taylor	78	78	77	79	312
5	Freddie Tait (a)	81	77	75	82	315
6	David Kinnell	80	77	79	80	316
7	Willie Fernie	79	85	77	77	318
8	John Hunter	82	79	81	77	319
9	TG Renouf	77	79	81	83	320
10 =	James Braid	80	82	84	75	321
	Philip Wynn	83	79	81	78	321
12	James Kay	81	81	77	83	322
13 =	George Pulford	83	81	78	81	323
	Jack White	82	81	77	83	323
15 =	James Kinnell	77	81	78	88	324
	Archie Simpson	83	80	82	79	324
17 =	Sandy Herd	80	79	84	82	325
	Peter McEwan	83	83	77	82	325
19 =	Ben Sayers	85	78	79	85	327
	Walter Toogood	82	84	83	78	327

New restrictions on players' performances were introduced. Competitors who were 20 or more strokes behind the leader at the halfway stage were excluded from the final two rounds. The 'cut' was born. One victim was the last winner at Prestwick, Willie Auchterlonie.

US OPEN

COURSE:	Myopia Hunt Club
LOCATION:	South Hamilton, Massachusetts
DATE:	17-18 June
DISTANCE:	6236 yards
PAR:	n/a
WINNER:	$150

Pos	Player	1st	2nd	3rd	4th	Total
1	**FRED HERD**	84	85	75	84	328
2	Alex Smith	78	86	86	85	335
3	Willie Anderson, Jr	81	82	87	86	336
4	Joe Lloyd	87	80	86	86	339
5	Willie Smith	82	91	85	82	340
6	WV Hoare	84	84	87	87	342
7	Willie Dunn, Jr	85	87	87	84	343
8 =	John Jones	83	84	90	90	347
	HC Leeds (a)	81	84	93	89	347
	RG McAndrews	85	90	86	86	347
	Bernard Nicholls	86	87	88	86	347
12	Harry Turpie	85	87	86	91	349
13	Alex Findlay	89	88	84	89	350
14 =	John Lister	92	88	90	85	355
	Willie Tucker	90	89	87	89	355
16	JF Curtis (a)	87	88	88	93	356
17	John Harland	84	93	93	87	357
18	Willie Davis	91	88	95	85	359
19 =	Horace Rawlins	91	90	92	88	361
	JA Tyng (a)	92	91	88	90	361

The first 72-hole US Open, which meant circumnavigating Myopia's nine holes eight times. While elder brother Sandy was to stay in Scotland and be successful in the British Open over many years, Fred Herd arrived in the US in 1898, and promptly picked up the Open Championship. However, he never came close again.

COURSE:	St George's GC	
LOCATION:	Sandwich, Kent, England	
DATE:	7-8 June	
DISTANCE:	6012 yards	
PAR:	n/a	
WINNER:	£30	

Pos	Player	1st	2nd	3rd	4th	Total
1	**HARRY VARDON**	76	76	81	77	310
2	Jack White	79	79	82	75	315
3	Andrew Kirkaldy	81	79	82	77	319
4	JH Taylor	77	76	83	84	320
5 =	James Braid	78	78	85	81	322
	Willie Fernie	79	83	82	78	322
7 =	James Kinnell	76	84	80	84	324
	Freddie Tait (a)	81	82	79	82	324
9 =	Albert Tingey, Sr	81	81	79	85	326
	Tom Williamson	76	84	80	86	326
11	Ben Sayers	81	79	82	86	328
12 =	Harold Hilton (a)	86	80	80	83	329
	TG Renouf	79	82	84	84	329
14	Willie Park, Jr	77	79	85	89	330
15	Willie Aveston	77	86	82	86	331
16 =	Sandy Herd	82	81	80	89	332
	Peter Rainford	79	83	83	87	332
	Ted Ray	84	80	84	84	332
	Archie Simpson	84	84	81	83	332
20	Walter Toogood	82	86	81	84	333

Although 101 entered, so many withdrew after the first round, only 28 finished. Vardon's third win in four years was based on his early rounds (152 – easily the best opening 18 holes since the Open went to a 72-hole format). This was the first occasion where the winner led from start-to-finish over four rounds. It was also Freddie Tait's last Open. He was killed the following year leading a unit of the Black Watch into battle in the Boer War.

COURSE:	Baltimore CC	
LOCATION:	Baltimore, Maryland	
DATE:	14-18 September	
DISTANCE:	n/k	
PAR:	n/a	
WINNER:	$150	

Pos	Player	1st	2nd	3rd	4th	Total
1	**WILLIE SMITH**	77	82	79	77	315
2 =	Val Fitzjohn	85	80	79	82	326
	George Low	82	79	89	76	326
	WH Way	80	85	80	81	326
5	Willie Anderson, Jr	77	81	85	84	327
6	Jack Park	88	80	75	85	328
7	Alex Smith	82	81	82	85	330
8	Henry Gullane	81	86	80	84	331
9 =	Laurie Auchterlonie	86	87	82	78	333
	Peter Walker	84	86	77	86	333
11	AH Findlay	88	86	79	81	334
12	Alex Campbell	83	80	79	94	336
13 =	HM Harriman (a)	87	88	85	79	339
	Alex Patrick	82	83	84	90	339
	Horace Rawlins	81	85	86	87	339
16	Alfred Ricketts	87	85	88	80	340
17	Bernard Nicholls	86	88	85	84	343
18 =	David Foulis	83	86	91	85	345
	Harry Turpie	91	88	83	83	345
20 =	James Foulis	94	84	88	80	346
	Gilbert Nicholls	90	83	86	87	346

Willie Smith was one of five brothers from Carnoustie – two of whom won the US Open Championship. Alex was to win in 1906 and 1910. A third brother, Macdonald, had a few close misses in both US and British Opens and was one of the outstanding players in an era to be dominated by Walter Hagen and Bobby Jones. The winning margin is still the biggest in the US Open and only falls behind Morris Sr (13 in 1862 British Open), Morris Jr (12 in 1870) and Tiger Woods (12 in 1997 Masters) in any Major. Willie went on to become pro at Mexico City where he was killed during the Revolution in 1915.

1900

COURSE: Royal & Ancient GC
LOCATION: St Andrews, Fife, Scotland
DATE: 6-7 June
DISTANCE: 6323 yards
PAR: n/a
WINNER: £50

Pos	Player	1st	2nd	3rd	4th	Total
1	**JH TAYLOR**	79	77	78	75	309
2	Harry Vardon	79	81	80	77	317
3	James Braid	82	81	80	79	322
4	Jack White	80	81	82	80	323
5	Willie Auchterlonie	81	85	80	80	326
6	Willie Park, Jr	80	83	81	84	328
7 =	Robert Maxwell (a)	81	81	86	81	329
	Archie Simpson	82	85	83	79	329
9	Ben Sayers	81	83	85	81	330
10 =	Sandy Herd	81	85	81	84	331
	Andrew Kirkaldy	87	83	82	79	331
	Tom Vardon	81	85	84	81	331
13	Ted Ray	88	80	85	81	334
14 =	David Anderson, Jr	81	87	85	84	337
	Tom Simpson	84	86	83	84	337
16 =	William Greig (a)	93	84	80	81	338
	Harold Hilton (a)	83	87	87	81	338
18	JW Taylor	91	81	84	83	339
19 =	John Kirkaldy	86	85	87	82	340
	Peter Paxton	87	87	79	87	340

Taylor's third win was comprehensive and stopped Vardon's amazing run – at least temporarily. 'JH' led 'wire-to-wire' as did Vardon in the previous year, but Taylor also produced the lowest score in every round – a feat never repeated in any Major Championship.

COURSE: Chicago GC
LOCATION: Wheaton, Illinois
DATE: 4-5 October
DISTANCE: 6032 yards
PAR: n/a
WINNER: $200

Pos	Player	1st	2nd	3rd	4th	Total
1	**HARRY VARDON**	79	78	76	80	313
2	JH Taylor	76	82	79	78	315
3	David Bell	78	83	83	78	322
4 =	Laurie Auchterlonie	84	82	80	81	327
	Willie Smith	82	83	79	83	327
6	George Low	84	80	85	82	331
7	Tom Hutchinson	81	87	81	84	333
8	Harry Turpie	84	87	79	84	334
9	Stewart Gardner	85	78	84	89	336
10	Val Fitzjohn	84	83	89	82	338
11 =	Willie Anderson, Jr	83	88	79	89	339
	Alex Campbell	86	77	93	83	339
13	Alex Smith	90	84	82	84	340
14 =	James Foulis	86	88	87	82	343
	Robert Simpson	84	84	88	87	343
16 =	Fred Herd	85	89	84	86	344
	Arthur Smith	89	85	85	85	344
	WH Way	88	85	84	87	344
19 =	Willie Norton	87	87	84	87	345
	Harry Rawlins	86	84	90	85	345

The roles were reversed a few months later when Vardon, on an exhibition tour of the States, won in Chicago with Taylor second. Vardon became the first player to win two different Majors. A look at the respective Top 20s this year shows the Herd and Auchterlonie Brothers represented on both sides of the Atlantic.

BRITISH OPEN

COURSE: Honourable Company of Edinburgh Golfers
LOCATION: Muirfield, East Lothian, Scotland
DATE: 5-6 June
DISTANCE: 5810 yards
PAR: n/a
WINNER: £50

Pos	Player	1st	2nd	3rd	4th	Total
1	**JAMES BRAID**	79	76	74	80	309
2	Harry Vardon	77	78	79	78	312
3	JH Taylor	79	83	74	77	313
4	Harold Hilton (a)	89	80	75	76	320
5	Sandy Herd	87	81	81	76	325
6	Jack White	82	82	80	82	326
7 =	James Kinnell	79	85	86	78	328
	Johnny Laidlay (a)	84	82	82	80	328
9 =	PJ Gaudin	86	81	86	76	329
	Jack Graham (a)	82	83	81	83	329
11	Rowland Jones	85	82	81	83	331
12 =	Ted Ray	87	84	74	87	332
	TG Renouf	83	86	81	82	332
	Tom Yeoman	85	83	82	82	332
15 =	Fred Collins	89	80	81	84	334
	S Mure Fergusson (a)	84	86	82	82	334
	JH Oke	91	83	80	80	334
18 =	Andrew Kirkaldy	82	87	86	81	336
	Alf Lewis	85	82	83	86	336
	Willie Park, Jr	78	87	81	90	336
	Andrew Scott	85	80	81	90	336

Braid established enough of a lead to withstand attacks from Vardon and Taylor over the last round. Just how good this threesome were can be understood from the scoring, all being at least seven shots clear of the rest of field. Braid was due the title after several good finishes in previous years, including second on the same course in 1897. His great years were to come towards the end of the decade though, when he truly (in terms of Open victories) became part of the Triumvirate.

US OPEN

COURSE: Myopia Hunt Club
LOCATION: South Hamilton, Massachusetts
DATE: 14-16 June
DISTANCE: 6032 yards
PAR: n/a
WINNER: $200

Pos	Player	1st	2nd	3rd	4th	Total
1	**WILLIE ANDERSON, Jr***	84	83	83	81	331
2	Alex Smith	82	82	87	80	331
3	Willie Smith	84	86	82	81	333
4	Stewart Gardner	86	82	81	85	334
5 =	Laurie Auchterlonie	81	85	86	83	335
	Bernard Nicholls	84	85	83	83	335
7	David Brown	86	83	83	84	336
8	Alex Campbell	84	91	82	82	339
9 =	George Low	82	89	85	85	341
	Jack Park	87	84	85	85	341
11	James Foulis	88	85	85	89	347
12 =	Val Fitzjohn	86	86	89	87	348
	John Jones	87	84	87	80	348
14 =	Gilbert Nicholls	87	87	88	87	349
	Robert Simpson	88	87	87	87	349
16	Isaac Mackie	87	88	85	90	350
17 =	AH Fenn	87	90	87	87	351
	AG Lockwood (a)	82	89	89	91	351
	Horace Rawlins	90	84	88	89	351
20	Joe Lloyd	90	87	86	89	352

*Willie Anderson Jr beat Alex Smith in the 18-Hole Play-off

No such pond-hopping this year as the Opens virtually clashed, leaving anyone with the ambition to participate in both thwarted by the week-long sea passage. Willie Anderson from North Berwick, Scotland, won the first of his four wins in five years, after beating Alex Smith in the Open's first play-off, and his brother Willie by two. After emigrating in 1897, David Brown, the 1886 British Open winner, participated in his first US Open.

1902

COURSE:	Royal Liverpool GC
LOCATION:	Hoylake, Cheshire, England
DATE:	4-5 June
DISTANCE:	6335 yards
PAR:	n/a
WINNER:	£50

COURSE:	Garden City GC
LOCATION:	Garden City, New York
DATE:	10-11 October
DISTANCE:	6170 yards
PAR:	n/a
WINNER:	$200

Pos	Player	1st	2nd	3rd	4th	Total
1	**SANDY HERD**	77	76	73	81	307
2 =	James Braid	78	76	80	74	308
	Harry Vardon	72	77	80	79	308
4	Robert Maxwell (a)	79	77	79	74	309
5	Tom Vardon	80	76	78	79	313
6 =	Harold Hilton (a)	79	76	81	78	314
	James Kinnell	78	80	79	77	314
	JH Taylor	81	76	77	80	314
9	Ted Ray	79	74	85	80	318
10 =	Andrew Kirkaldy	77	78	83	82	320
	Arnaud Massy	77	81	78	84	320
12 =	Willie Fernie	76	82	84	79	321
	Rowland Jones	79	78	85	79	321
14	SH Fry (a)	78	79	80	85	322
15 =	John Ball, Jr (a)	79	79	84	81	323
	John Rowe	79	78	85	81	323
17	James Sherlock	79	84	80	81	324
18	Jack White	82	75	82	86	325
19	Ben Sayers	84	80	80	82	326
20 =	TG Renouf	84	82	77	84	327
	Walter Toogood	83	83	80	81	327

Pos	Player	1st	2nd	3rd	4th	Total
1	**LAURIE AUCHTERLONIE**	78	78	74	77	307
2 =	Stewart Gardner	82	76	77	78	313
	Walter Travis (a)	82	82	75	74	313
4	Willie Smith	82	79	80	75	316
5 =	Willie Anderson, Jr	79	82	76	81	318
	John Shippen	83	81	75	79	318
7	Charles Thom	80	82	80	77	319
8	Harry Turpie	79	85	78	78	320
9	Donald Ross	80	83	78	81	322
10	Alex Ross	83	77	84	79	323
11	Willie Norton	83	82	79	81	325
12 =	David Brown	80	88	82	76	326
	George Low	83	84	78	81	326
14 =	Jack Campbell	77	87	79	85	328
	Jack Hobens	85	82	80	81	328
16 =	AS Griffiths	79	86	82	83	330
	Horace Rawlins	89	83	79	79	330
18 =	Gilbert Nicholls	88	86	73	84	331
	Alex Smith	79	86	80	86	331
20 =	Alex Campbell	88	82	83	79	332
	James Foulis	81	88	82	81	332
	John Harland	82	82	83	85	332
	Willie Hunter	82	82	81	87	332

Herd won his only Open in a long and distinguished career. He was the first winner to use a rubber-cored Haskell ball and beat Vardon and Braid, who were still using the 'gutty', by one stroke. Braid pulled back seven shots over the last round – not quite enough. Vardon's first round 72 equalled Herd's own record of 1896 and his halfway score of 149 was the first below 150.

Another brotherly double. Laurie emulated Willie Auchterlonie's British Open win at Prestwick in 1893, scoring sub-80 in every round for the first time in these Championships. (As visitors to St Andrews will vouch, the family club-making and repair shop started by Willie, who succeeded Andrew Kirkaldy as R&A pro in 1935, still snuggles in the corner of the old grey building which runs parallel to the 18th on the Old Course.) Following the British Open, the Haskell ball was used, but even more widely. The result was a greater improvement in all-round scoring over previous Championships.

COURSE:	Prestwick GC
LOCATION:	Prestwick, Ayrshire, Scotland
DATE:	9-10 June
DISTANCE:	5948 yards
PAR:	n/a
WINNER:	£50

Pos	Player	1st	2nd	3rd	4th	Total
1	**HARRY VARDON**	73	77	72	78	300
2	Tom Vardon	76	81	75	74	306
3	Jack White	77	78	74	79	308
4	Sandy Herd	73	83	76	77	309
5	James Braid	77	79	79	75	310
6 =	Andrew Scott	77	77	83	77	314
	Robert Thomson	83	78	77	76	314
8	William Leaver	79	79	77	80	315
9 =	George Cawsey	80	78	76	82	316
	JH Taylor	80	82	78	76	316
11	Andrew Kirkaldy	82	79	78	78	317
	Tom Williamson	76	80	79	82	317
13 =	Willie Hunter, Sr	81	74	79	84	318
	Robert Maxwell (a)	82	84	76	76	318
15 =	Ernest Gray	77	83	79	80	319
	James Kinnell	78	86	76	79	319
	Willie Park, Jr	78	86	80	75	319
18 =	David Kinnell	82	78	80	80	320
	George Pulford	79	86	79	76	320
	AH Toogood	86	77	80	77	320

Vardon joined the Morrises and Willie Park, Sr on four Open wins as he coasted home – courtesy of a seven-stroke lead after three rounds. His third round 72 was a record, as were his 54- and 72-hole totals. Brother Tom finished runner-up, his highest-ever Open position.

COURSE:	Baltusrol GC
LOCATION:	Springfield, New Jersey
DATE:	8-9 July
DISTANCE:	6003 yards
PAR:	n/a
WINNER:	$200

Pos	Player	1st	2nd	3rd	4th	Total
1	**WILLIE ANDERSON, Jr***	73	76	76	82	307
2	David Brown	79	77	75	76	307
3	Stewart Gardner	77	77	82	79	315
4	Alex Smith	77	77	81	81	316
5	Donald Ross	79	79	78	82	318
6	Jack Campbell	76	83	83	77	319
7	Laurie Auchterlonie	75	79	84	83	321
8	Findlay Douglas (a)	77	79	82	84	322
9 =	Jack Hobens	76	81	82	84	323
	Alex Ross	83	82	78	80	323
	Willie Smith	80	81	83	79	323
12	Horace Rawlins	82	77	78	87	324
13 =	Isaac Mackie	83	80	78	84	325
	FO Reinhart (a)	81	75	89	80	325
15 =	Alex Campbell	79	84	80	83	326
	Gilbert Nicholls	86	82	78	80	326
	Walter Travis (a)	83	80	81	82	326
	WH Way	84	79	82	81	326
19	Bernard Nicholls	85	78	82	83	328
20 =	Willie Norton	78	81	83	87	329
	David Ogilvie	81	86	81	81	329

*Willie Anderson, Jr (82) beat David Brown (84) in the 18-Hole Play-off

The Open's first visit to Baltusrol (pre-Tillinghast). Anderson's second win in three years and the first of three back-to-back wins may have had something to do with his settling at the Apawamis Club. Prior to 1903 he had been changing clubs annually. He was caught by 1886 British Open Champion, David Brown, in the final round, conceding a six-stroke lead (not helped by an eight at the 9th), before steeling himself to win the play-off by two.

1904

COURSE: St George's GC
LOCATION: Sandwich, Kent, England
DATE: 8-10 June
DISTANCE: 6223 yards
PAR: n/a
WINNER: £50

COURSE: Glen View GC
LOCATION: Golf, Illinois
DATE: 8-9 July
DISTANCE: 6003 yards
PAR: n/a
WINNER: $200

Pos	Player	1st	2nd	3rd	4th	Total
1	**JACK WHITE**	80	75	72	69	296
2 =	James Braid	77	80	69	71	297
	JH Taylor	77	78	74	68	297
4	Tom Vardon	77	77	75	72	301
5	Harry Vardon	76	73	79	74	302
6	James Sherlock	83	71	78	77	309
7 =	Jack Graham (a)	76	76	78	80	310
	Andrew Kirkaldy	78	79	74	79	310
9	Sandy Herd	84	76	76	75	311
10 =	Robert Maxwell (a)	80	80	76	77	313
	Ben Sayers	80	80	76	77	313
12 =	Willie Park, Jr	84	72	81	78	315
	Ted Ray	81	81	77	76	315
	Robert Thomson	75	76	80	84	315
	AH Toogood	88	76	74	77	315
16 =	George Coburn	79	82	75	80	316
	John Rowe	86	82	75	73	316
17	John Ball, Jr (a)	83	78	79	78	318
18 =	George Cawsey	82	80	78	79	319
	Frederick Collins	88	77	75	79	319
	Ernest Gray	84	77	74	84	319

Pos	Player	1st	2nd	3rd	4th	Total
1	**WILLIE ANDERSON, Jr**	75	78	78	72	303
2	Gilbert Nicholls	80	76	79	73	308
3	Fred MacKenzie	76	79	74	80	309
4 =	Laurie Auchterlonie	80	81	75	78	314
	Bernard Nicholls	80	77	79	78	314
6 =	Percy Barrett	78	79	79	80	316
	Stewart Gardner	75	76	80	85	316
	Robert Simpson	82	82	76	76	316
9	James Foulis	83	84	78	82	317
10	Donald Ross	80	82	78	78	318
11 =	Jack Hobens	77	82	80	80	319
	Charles Murray	84	81	76	78	319
13	Alex Campbell	81	87	80	82	320
14	Horace Rawlins	79	76	86	81	322
15 =	George Braid	82	76	85	81	324
	Alex Ross	87	78	80	79	324
	George Thomson	78	87	81	78	324
18	Alex Smith	78	81	82	85	326
19	David Robertson	82	78	80	88	328
20 =	Jack Campbell	80	88	79	82	329
	H Chandler Egan (a)	84	79	83	83	329
	Harry Turpie	81	82	86	80	329

A nephew of Ben Sayers from North Berwick, Jack White held off the Triumvirate by significantly lowering his numbers each round. He became the first man to break the 300 barrier, and, along with Taylor and Braid, was the first to record a score in the 60s at any Major. To alleviate congestion with a field of 144, play was taken into a third day for the first time.

Following the British example, the half-way cut was introduced – excluding those players not within 15 strokes of the lead from further participation. Anderson's scoring, as in the previous year, set new records; with lows of 72 for any round, and 303 for 72 holes. Fred MacKenzie led by two going into the last round, but his 80, coupled with Anderson's record, saw him finish third – six strokes off the winner.

BRITISH OPEN

COURSE:	Royal & Ancient GC					
LOCATION:	St Andrews, Fife, Scotland					
DATE:	7-9 June					
DISTANCE:	6333 yards					
PAR:	n/a					
WINNER:	£50					

Pos	Player	1st	2nd	3rd	4th	Total
1	**JAMES BRAID**	81	78	78	81	318
2 =	Rowland Jones	81	77	87	78	323
	JH Taylor	80	85	78	80	323
4	James Kinnell	82	79	82	81	324
5 =	Ernest Gray	82	81	84	78	325
	Arnaud Massy	81	80	82	82	325
7	Robert Thomson	81	81	82	83	327
8	James Sherlock	81	84	80	83	328
9 =	Tom Simpson	82	88	78	81	329
	Harry Vardon	80	82	84	83	329
11 =	Ted Ray	85	82	81	82	330
	John Rowe	87	81	80	82	330
13 =	Willie Park, Jr	84	81	85	81	331
	Tom Williamson	84	81	79	87	331
15	Sandy Herd	80	82	83	87	332
16 =	TG Renouf	81	85	84	83	333
	Alex Smith	81	88	86	78	333
18 =	JC Johnstone	85	86	84	80	335
	Archie Simpson	87	84	81	83	335
	Tom Watt	86	85	79	85	335
	Jack White	86	83	83	83	335

Braid's four wins over the next six years were to put him above Vardon *et al* on five Open victories. His record for the decade 1901-10 was something special: W, 2, 5, 2, W, W, 5, W, 2, W. The cut was drawn, as in the previous year's US Open, at 15 behind the leader. The Old Course took its toll on scoring, with only 10 rounds under 80 being recorded in the whole Championship.

US OPEN

COURSE:	Myopia Hunt Club					
LOCATION:	South Hamilton, Massachusetts					
DATE:	21-22 September					
DISTANCE:	6300 yards					
PAR:	n/a					
WINNER:	$200					

Pos	Player	1st	2nd	3rd	4th	Total
1	**WILLIE ANDERSON, Jr**	81	80	76	77	314
2	Alex Smith	76	80	80	80	316
3 =	Percy Barrett	81	80	77	79	317
	Peter Robertson	79	80	81	77	317
5	Stewart Gardner	78	78	85	77	318
6	Alex Campbell	82	76	80	81	319
7 =	Jack Hobens	82	80	81	78	321
	Gilbert Nicholls	82	76	84	79	321
9	George Cummings	85	82	75	81	323
10	Arthur Smith	81	77	80	86	324
11 =	AG Lockwood (a)	84	85	76	80	325
	Walter Travis (a)	81	80	80	84	325
13 =	Alex Ross	79	86	78	83	326
	Willie Smith	86	81	76	83	326
15	George Low	83	82	81	81	327
16 =	Joe Lloyd	75	86	83	84	328
	Fred McKenzie	81	85	80	82	328
18	Walter Clark	86	81	82	80	329
19	Fred McLeod	80	84	80	86	330
20 =	Tom McNamara	81	79	82	89	331
	Bernard Nicholls	80	82	85	84	331
	George Turnbull	81	88	81	81	331
	WH Way	81	89	84	77	331

Willie Anderson secured a place in US Open history when he won his fourth title at Myopia. His feat has only been matched by Bobby Jones, Ben Hogan and Jack Nicklaus – exalted company indeed. Alex Smith became the second golfer to try his luck at both Opens in one year – finishing 16th at St Andrews and second for the third time in the US Championship.

BRITISH OPEN

COURSE: Honourable Company of Edinburgh Golfers
LOCATION: Muirfield, East Lothian, Scotland
DATE: 13-15 June
DISTANCE: 5934 yards
PAR: n/a
WINNER: £50

Pos	Player	1st	2nd	3rd	4th	Total
1	**JAMES BRAID**	77	76	74	73	300
2	JH Taylor	77	72	75	80	304
3	Harry Vardon	77	73	77	78	305
4	Jack Graham (a)	71	79	78	78	306
5	Rowland Jones	74	78	73	83	308
6	Arnaud Massy	76	80	76	78	310
7	Robert Maxwell (a)	73	78	77	83	311
8 =	George Duncan	73	78	83	78	312
	Ted Ray	80	75	79	78	312
	TG Renouf	76	77	76	83	312
11	David Kinnell	78	76	80	79	313
12 =	William Hunter	79	76	80	80	315
	WJ Leaver	80	76	78	81	315
	Tom Vardon	76	81	81	77	315
15 =	George Cawsey	79	80	79	78	316
	Thomas Simpson	78	78	81	79	316
	Walter Toogood	83	79	83	71	316
	RW Whitecross (a)	74	83	80	79	316
19 =	PJ Gaudin	77	77	80	83	317
	Harry Hamill	83	78	79	77	317
	Sandy Herd	81	79	77	80	317
	David McEwan	79	79	81	78	317
	Tom Williamson	77	77	78	85	317

Progressively better scoring gave Braid his second win in a row. Both Taylor and Vardon were in the hunt at the end of R3, but fell away over the last 18. This was the third occasion in seven years when Braid, Taylor and Vardon had finished 1-2-3 in the Open, although not always in that order. Triumvirate indeed. Muirfield, despite being 'toughened'-up was still the shortest course on the rota, and comparatively the easiest.

US OPEN

COURSE: Onwentsia Club
LOCATION: Lake Forest, Illinois
DATE: 28-29 June
DISTANCE: 6107 yards
PAR: n/a
WINNER: $300

Pos	Player	1st	2nd	3rd	4th	Total
1	**ALEX SMITH**	73	74	73	75	295
2	Willie Smith	73	81	74	74	302
3 =	Laurie Auchterlonie	76	78	75	76	305
	James Maiden	80	73	77	75	305
5	Willie Anderson, Jr	73	76	74	84	307
6	Alex Ross	76	79	75	80	310
7	Stewart Gardner	80	76	77	78	311
8 =	H Chandler Egan (a)	79	78	76	80	313
	Gilbert Nicholls	76	81	77	79	313
10	Jack Hobens	75	84	76	79	314
11 =	George Low	79	82	76	79	316
	Bernard Nicholls	79	77	79	81	316
13	Harry Turpie	80	80	76	83	319
14 =	Walter Fovargue	77	84	78	81	320
	Jack Jolly	78	82	79	81	320
	Peter Robertson	79	78	80	83	320
17	Alex Baxter	83	81	81	86	321
18 =	Fred Brand	78	78	85	81	322
	Alex Campbell	76	84	76	86	322
	George Cummings	79	76	84	83	322
	George Smith	79	76	82	85	322

Alex Smith led all the way to pick up the first of two Open titles; and set a new low total score of 295, bettering the 1903 total by eight shots, and a stroke better than Jack White's British Open record. Three of the Smith brothers finished in the Top 18.

BRITISH OPEN	
COURSE:	Royal Liverpool GC
LOCATION:	Hoylake, Cheshire, England
DATE:	20-21 June
DISTANCE:	6355 yards
PAR:	n/a
WINNER:	£50

US OPEN	
COURSE:	Philadelphia Cricket Club
LOCATION:	Chestnut Hill, Pennsylvania
DATE:	28-29 June
DISTANCE:	5952 yards
PAR:	n/a
WINNER:	$300

Pos	Player	1st	2nd	3rd	4th	Total
1	**ARNAUD MASSY**	76	81	78	77	312
2	JH Taylor	79	79	76	80	314
3 =	George Pulford	81	78	80	78	317
	Tom Vardon	81	81	80	75	317
5 =	James Braid	82	85	75	76	318
	Ted Ray	83	80	79	76	318
7 =	George Duncan	83	78	81	77	319
	Harry Vardon	84	81	74	80	319
	Tom Williamson	82	77	82	78	319
10	Tom Ball	80	78	81	81	320
11	PJ Gaudin	83	84	80	76	323
12	Sandy Herd	83	81	83	77	324
13 =	Jack Graham (a)	83	81	80	82	326
	Walter Toogood	76	86	82	82	326
15 =	John Ball, Jr (a)	88	83	79	77	327
	Frederick Collins	83	83	79	82	327
17 =	Alf Matthews	82	80	84	82	328
	Charles Mayo	86	78	82	82	328
	TG Renouf	83	80	82	83	328
20	Reg Gray	83	85	81	80	329

Pos	Player	1st	2nd	3rd	4th	Total
1	**ALEX ROSS**	76	74	76	76	302
2	Gilbert Nicholls	80	73	72	79	304
3	Alex Campbell	78	74	78	75	305
4	Jack Hobens	76	75	73	85	309
5 =	George Low	78	76	79	77	310
	Fred McLeod	79	77	79	75	310
	Peter Robertson	81	77	78	74	310
8 =	David Brown	75	80	78	78	311
	Bernard Nicholls	76	76	81	78	311
10	Donald Ross	78	80	76	78	312
11 =	Laurie Auchterlonie	77	77	83	76	313
	Fred Brand	78	80	73	82	313
13	David Robertson	80	78	75	81	314
14	Tom McNamara	82	79	78	76	315
15	Willie Anderson, Jr	81	77	81	77	316
16 =	Mike Brady	76	77	84	80	317
	David Hunter	77	75	85	80	317
	Martin O'Loughlin	81	81	77	78	317
19	Jack Campbell	78	79	82	80	319
20	GJ Bouse	78	78	86	78	320

Arnaud Massy, from La Boulie, France, became the first overseas winner when he outplayed JH Taylor over the final holes. He is the only winner from France and continental Europe had to wait until 1979, and Severiano Ballesteros, for its next winner. France should have collected their second Open in 1999, but the story of the unfortunate Jean Van de Velde is too recent – and still too painful – to recall here!

Yet another Scot, Alex Ross, added the US Open title to his portfolio. Alex was the brother of the famous golf-course designer, Donald, who also finished in 10th place in the Championship this year.

1908

COURSE:	Prestwick GC
LOCATION:	Prestwick, Ayrshire, Scotland
DATE:	18-19 June
DISTANCE:	5948 yards
PAR:	n/a
WINNER:	£50

COURSE:	Myopia Hunt Club
LOCATION:	South Hamilton, Massachusetts
DATE:	27-29 August
DISTANCE:	6335 yards
PAR:	n/a
WINNER:	$300

Pos	Player	1st	2nd	3rd	4th	Total
1	**JAMES BRAID**	70	72	77	72	291
2	Tom Ball	76	73	76	74	299
3	Ted Ray	79	71	75	76	301
4	Sandy Herd	74	74	79	75	302
5 =	David Kinnell	75	73	80	78	306
	Harry Vardon	79	78	74	75	306
7 =	Thomas Simpson	75	77	76	79	307
	JH Taylor	79	77	76	75	307
9 =	PJ Gaudin	77	76	75	80	308
	Arnaud Massy	76	75	76	81	308
11 =	James Edmundson	80	72	76	82	310
	Tom Watt	81	73	78	78	310
13 =	John Ball, Jr (a)	74	78	78	81	311
	Fred Collins	78	77	77	79	311
	Ernest Gray	68	79	83	81	311
	William Leaver	79	79	75	78	311
	Tom Vardon	77	79	76	79	311
18 =	George Duncan	79	77	80	76	312
	Jack Graham (a)	76	82	76	78	312
	George Pulford	81	77	74	80	312
	Fred Robson	72	79	83	78	312
	AH Toogood	82	76	77	77	312
	Walter Toogood	80	75	78	79	312

Pos	Player	1st	2nd	3rd	4th	Total
1	**FRED McLEOD***	82	82	81	77	322
2	Willie Smith	77	82	85	78	322
3	Alex Smith	80	83	83	81	327
4	Willie Anderson, Jr	85	86	80	79	330
5	John Jones	81	81	87	82	331
6 =	Jack Hobens	86	81	85	81	333
	Peter Robertson	89	84	77	83	333
8 =	Percy Barrett	94	80	86	78	338
	Jock Hutchison	82	84	87	85	338
10 =	Richard Kimball	84	86	83	86	339
	Tom McNamara	85	82	86	86	339
12 =	Donald Ball	90	81	86	83	340
	Alex Campbell	85	83	89	83	340
	George Low	92	80	84	84	340
	Robert Peebles	85	85	85	85	340
16	David Hunter	87	87	84	83	341
17 =	HH Barker	84	85	88	86	343
	Mike Brady	86	87	87	83	343
	Orrin Terry	86	87	83	87	343
20	David Robertson	89	83	86	86	344

*Fred McLeod (77) beat Willie Smith (83) in the 18-Hole Play-off

Leading all the way, Braid lowered the Open (and Majors) record total even further, adding a lowest-to-date 18-hole score of 70; 36-hole total of 144; and 54-holes at 221. He took a six-shot lead into the last round and stretched it to eight.

The players must have been glad see the back of the Myopia Hunt Club; host to the US Open for the fourth and last time. The course has the dubious distiction of holding the three highest winning totals in US Open history – 331 (1901), 328 (1898) and now 322. Wind created the havoc in 1908, as much as the golf course itself, though – only Gilbert Nicholls broke 80 twice; and he was disqualified! How 5'4", 108 lbs Fred McLeod withstood it we'll never know. He did, though, to tie with Willie Smith; then went on to win the play-off.

BRITISH OPEN

COURSE: Royal Cinque Ports GC
LOCATION: Deal, Kent, England
DATE: 10-11 June
DISTANCE: 6495 yards
PAR: n/a
WINNER: £50

Pos	Player	1st	2nd	3rd	4th	Total
1	**JH TAYLOR**	74	73	74	74	295
2 =	Tom Ball	74	75	76	76	301
	James Braid	79	75	73	74	301
4	Charles Johns	72	76	79	75	302
5	TG Renouf	76	78	76	73	303
6	Ted Ray	77	76	76	75	304
7	William Horne	77	78	77	74	306
8 =	James Hepburn	78	77	76	76	307
	Sandy Herd	76	75	80	76	307
10 =	Bertie Lassen (a)	82	74	74	78	308
	Bernard Nicholls	78	76	77	77	308
	George Pulford	81	76	76	75	308
13	Robert Maxwell (a)	75	80	80	74	309
14 =	EP Gaudin	76	77	77	80	310
	Peter Rainford	78	76	76	80	310
16	George Cawsey	79	76	78	78	311
17 =	Ben Sayers	79	77	79	77	312
	Robert Thomson	81	79	75	77	312
19 =	CK Hutchison (a)	75	81	78	79	313
	Tom Vardon	80	75	80	78	313

In one of only two visits to Deal, The Open fell into the hands of JH Taylor for the first time since 1900. It was his fourth victory overall, and a triumph for consistently solid scoring. After a few years in America, when he featured in the US Open, Bernard Nicholls returned home to gain a Top 10 place.

US OPEN

COURSE: Englewood Golf Club
LOCATION: Englewood, New Jersey
DATE: 24-25 June
DISTANCE: 6205 yards
PAR: 72 (288)
WINNER: $300

Pos	Player	1st	2nd	3rd	4th	Total
1	**GEORGE SARGENT**	75	72	72	71	290
2	Tom McNamara	73	69	75	77	294
3	Alex Smith	76	73	74	72	295
4 =	Willie Anderson, Jr	79	74	76	70	299
	Jack Hobens	75	78	72	74	299
	Isaac Mackie	77	75	74	73	299
7 =	Tom Anderson, Jr	78	74	75	73	300
	HH Barker	75	79	73	73	300
	Andrew Campbell	71	75	77	77	300
	Tom Peebles	76	73	73	78	300
	Walter Travis (a)	72	78	77	73	300
12	Mike Brady	76	77	74	75	302
13 =	Alex Campbell	75	73	81	74	303
	Fred McLeod	78	76	74	75	303
15 =	Orrin Terry	78	80	73	73	304
	FR Upton, Jr (a)	72	79	78	75	304
17	Gilbert Nicholls	73	75	79	79	306
18 =	Walter Fovargue	80	76	77	74	307
	David Ogilvie	76	78	79	74	307
20 =	Peter Robertson	79	72	78	79	308
	Charles Rowe	74	77	76	81	308

Sargent, after Rawlins and Lloyd, became the third Englishman to win the US Open in its 15 year existence. In something like 50 years, only four Englishmen had won the British Open – accepting that Hilton, Taylor and Vardon were multi-winners – which indicates how great a straglehold the Scots had, and were, to a lesser degree, still having on the Majors, and golf in general. Sargent shot a new low total for either Open, and McNamara, the first home-grown American talent to lead the US Open, set a record for both Championships at 36 and 54 holes. David Hunter led after the first round with an exceptional 68, only to shoot 84, 84 and 77, to finish tied for 30th.

1910

COURSE:	Philadelphia Cricket Club	
LOCATION:	Chestnut Hill, Pennsylvania	
DATE:	17-18, 20 June	
DISTANCE:	5956 yards	
PAR:	n/a	
WINNER:	$300	

Pos	Player	1st	2nd	3rd	4th	Total
1	**ALEX SMITH***	73	73	79	73	298
2	John McDermott	74	74	75	75	298
3	Macdonald Smith	74	78	75	71	298
4	Fred McLeod	78	70	78	73	299
5 =	Tom McNamara	73	78	73	76	300
	Gilbert Nicholls	73	75	77	75	300
7	Jack Hobens	74	77	74	76	301
8 =	Tom Anderson, Jr	72	76	81	73	302
	HH Barker	75	78	77	72	302
	Jock Hutchison	77	76	75	74	302
11	Willie Anderson, Jr	74	78	76	75	303
12 =	George Low	75	77	79	74	305
	Charles Thom	80	72	78	75	305
14 =	Tom Bonnar	78	78	71	80	307
	George Cummings	78	73	79	77	307
16 =	Alex Campbell	79	76	80	74	309
	George Sargent	77	81	74	77	309
18 =	Jack Campbell	77	77	81	75	310
	James Thomson	74	80	80	76	310
20	Fred Herreshoff (a)	76	77	79	79	311

*Alex Smith (71) beat John McDermott (75) and
Macdonald Smith (77) in the 18-Hole Play-off

The US Open preceeded the British Open for the first time
this year – the last day at Philadephia Cricket Club was the
day before the first at the R&A Club. Alex Smith collected
his second Open, in a Monday play-off, after brother
MacDonald and Champion-to-be, McDermott, finished in
the first-ever three-way tie. Brother Willie was to lead the
British Open after 36 holes later that week. Four-time
champion Willie Anderson, aged just 30, died (probably
due to a drink-related condition) several months later.

COURSE:	Royal & Ancient GC	
LOCATION:	St Andrews, Fife, Scotland	
DATE:	21(rain), 22-24 June	
DISTANCE:	6487 yards	
PAR:	n/a	
WINNER:	£50	

Pos	Player	1st	2nd	3rd	4th	Total
1	**JAMES BRAID**	76	73	74	76	299
2	Sandy Herd	78	74	75	76	303
3	George Duncan	73	77	71	83	304
4	Laurie Ayton, Sr	78	76	75	77	306
5 =	Ted Ray	76	77	74	81	308
	Fred Robson	75	80	77	76	308
	Willie Smith	77	71	80	80	308
8 =	EP Gaudin	78	74	76	81	309
	James Kinnell	79	74	77	79	309
	TG Renouf	77	76	75	81	309
	Donald Ross	78	79	75	77	309
12 =	Tom Ball	81	77	75	78	311
	PJ Gaudin	80	79	74	78	311
14 =	Michael Moran	77	75	79	81	312
	JH Taylor	76	80	78	78	312
16 =	Fred MacKenzie	78	80	75	80	313
	William Ritchie	78	74	82	79	313
	Harry Vardon	77	81	75	80	313
19 =	John Ball, Jr (a)	79	75	78	82	314
	James Hepburn	78	82	76	78	314
	Tom Williamson	78	80	78	78	314

Braid's magical decade was capped with his fifth Open win
– then a record – beating the previous St Andrews low
score by ten, and Sandy Herd by four. Only the 60 lowest
scorers (and ties) were allowed to proceed to R3. Fred
MacKenzie, third in the 1904 US Open, had returned
(permanently) to his home course to finish 16th; while
Willie Smith and Donald Ross were just visiting.

COURSE:	Chicago GC			
LOCATION:	Wheaton, Illinois			
DATE:	23-24 June			
DISTANCE:	6605 yards			
PAR:	n/a			
WINNER:	$300			

COURSE:	St George's GC			
LOCATION:	Sandwich, Kent, England			
DATE:	26-29 June			
DISTANCE:	6594 yards			
PAR:	n/a			
WINNER:	£50			

Pos	Player	1st	2nd	3rd	4th	Total
1	**JOHN McDERMOTT***	81	72	75	79	307
2	Mike Brady	76	77	79	75	307
3	George Simpson	76	77	79	75	307
4	Fred McLeod	77	72	76	83	308
5 =	Jock Hutchison	80	77	73	79	309
	Gilbert Nicholls	76	78	74	81	309
7 =	HH Barker	75	81	77	78	311
	George Sargent	76	77	84	74	311
9 =	Peter Robertson	79	76	78	79	312
	Alex Ross	74	75	81	82	312
11	Albert Seckel (a)	78	80	80	75	313
12 =	Alex Campbell	81	77	72	84	314
	Harry Turpie	77	76	82	79	314
14	CP Nelson	79	85	74	77	315
15 =	James Donaldson	78	81	83	74	316
	George Low	80	78	82	76	316
17	RL Simpson	81	82	75	79	317
18 =	John Burke	79	77	78	85	319
	DE Sawyer (a)	84	79	77	79	319
20 =	Grange Alves	82	80	73	85	320
	George Cummings	82	80	79	79	320
	Mason Phelps (a)	78	78	78	86	320

1	**HARRY VARDON***	74	74	75	80	303
2	Arnaud Massy	75	78	74	76	303
3 =	Sandy Herd	77	73	76	78	304
	Horace Hilton (a)	76	74	78	76	304
5 =	James Braid	78	75	74	78	305
	Ted Ray	76	72	79	78	305
	JH Taylor	72	76	78	79	305
8	George Duncan	73	71	83	79	306
9	Laurie Ayton, Sr	75	77	77	78	307
10 =	James Hepburn	74	77	83	75	309
	Fred Robson	78	74	79	78	309
12	Fred Collins	77	76	83	74	310
13 =	J Piper	78	79	80	74	311
	TG Renouf	75	76	79	81	311
15	Tom Ball	76	77	79	80	312
16 =	Rowland Jones	80	76	85	72	313
	Charles Mayo	78	78	79	78	313
	Wilfred Reid	78	79	80	76	313
	James Sherlock	73	80	76	84	313
	HE Taylor (a)	83	73	76	81	313

* Harry Vardon (143 after 35 holes) beat Arnaud Massy (148 after 34 holes) when Massy conceded at the 35th hole of the 36-Hole Play-off

*John McDermott (80) beat Mike Brady (82) and George Simpson (86) in the 18-Hole Play-off

The much-awaited first US Open (and Major championship) win by a native-born American. The unlucky Mike Brady could have entered US golfing folklore, but he was always to be the nearly-man. Born in Philadelphia and not yet 20, McDermott tied with Brady and Scot George Simpson, before easing out Brady in the play-off after Simpson's game was plagued by an attack of rheumatism.

James Braid's record of five victories was short-lived when arch-rival Vardon equalled his mark at Sandwich. Arnaud Massy, the 1907 champion, took him to the 35th extra hole, however, for the privilege.

BRITISH OPEN

COURSE:	Honourable Company of Edinburgh Golfers	
LOCATION:	Muirfield, East Lothian, Scotland	
DATE:	24-25 June	
DISTANCE:	6194 yards	
PAR:	n/a	
WINNER:	£50	

Pos	Player	1st	2nd	3rd	4th	Total
1	**TED RAY**	71	73	76	75	295
2	Harry Vardon	75	72	81	71	299
3	James Braid	77	71	77	78	303
4	George Duncan	72	77	78	78	305
5 =	Laurie Ayton, Sr	74	80	75	80	309
	Sandy Herd	76	81	76	76	309
7 =	Fred Collins	76	79	81	74	310
	Jean Gassiat	76	80	78	76	310
	Reg Wilson	82	75	75	78	310
10	Arnaud Massy	74	77	82	78	311
11 =	Charles Mayo	76	77	78	81	312
	JH Taylor	75	76	77	84	312
13 =	George Fotheringham	75	78	79	81	313
	Robert Thomson	73	77	80	83	313
15 =	Hughie McNeill	76	78	82	78	314
	Michael Moran	76	79	80	79	314
17 =	Fred Leach	75	82	81	77	315
	Tom Williamson	80	77	79	79	315
19	TG Renouf	77	80	80	79	316
20 =	Douglas Edgar	77	81	80	79	317
	William Horne	73	85	82	77	317
	Wilfred Reid	80	79	79	79	317

Ted Ray was the heir apparent to the Great Triumvirate – except that they were at the top so long, he was usurped before he could properly wear the crown. Ray would surely have won more Opens (British, or US – which he collected in 1920) if Braid, Vardon and Taylor had been mere mortals; and if there wasn't an enforced sabbatical in the middle of his career, courtesy of Kaiser Wilhelm II. Leading all the way, Ray set a new 54-hole low for the Open of 220.

US OPEN

COURSE:	Country Club of Buffalo	
LOCATION:	Buffalo, New York	
DATE:	1-2 August	
DISTANCE:	6326 yards	
PAR:	74 (296)	
WINNER:	$300	

Pos	Player	1st	2nd	3rd	4th	Total
1	**JOHN McDERMOTT**	74	75	74	71	294
2	Tom McNamara	74	80	73	69	296
3 =	Mike Brady	72	75	73	79	299
	Alex Smith	77	70	77	75	299
5	Alex Campbell	74	77	80	71	302
6	George Sargent	72	78	76	77	303
7 =	Jack Dowling	76	79	76	74	305
	Otto Hackbarth	77	77	75	76	305
9	Charles Murray	75	78	77	76	306
10 =	Tom Anderson, Jr	75	76	81	75	307
	Frank Peebles	73	76	83	75	307
	Walter Travis (a)	73	79	78	77	307
13 =	Fred McLeod	79	77	75	77	308
	George Simpson	79	73	77	79	308
15	Percy Barrett	74	73	83	79	309
16 =	John G Anderson (a)	80	79	78	73	310
	David Ogilvie	74	83	73	80	310
18 =	Jim Barnes	77	73	79	82	311
	John Dingwall	77	77	78	79	311
	Willie MacFarlane	77	81	73	80	311

Proving that his 2nd in 1910 and win of the previous year were not flukes, McDermott made it back-to-back victories. He shot an impressive 294 total to lead home fellow 'home-breds', Tom McNamara and Mike Brady. Only Alex Smith of the British imports scored within eight strokes of the winner. In 1911, the USGA officially defined the term 'par'; which meant that McDermott was two 'under' for the Championship.

BRITISH OPEN

COURSE:	Royal Liverpool GC	
LOCATION:	Hoylake, Cheshire, England	
DATE:	23-24 June	
DISTANCE:	6455 yards	
PAR:	n/a	
WINNER:	£50	

Pos	Player	1st	2nd	3rd	4th	Total
1	**JH TAYLOR**	73	75	77	79	304
2	Ted Ray	73	74	81	84	312
3 =	Michael Moran	76	74	89	74	313
	Harry Vardon	79	75	79	80	313
5 =	John McDermott	75	80	77	83	315
	TG Renouf	75	78	84	78	315
7 =	James Bradbeer	78	79	81	79	317
	Arnaud Massy	77	80	81	79	317
	James Sherlock	77	86	79	75	317
	Tom Williamson	77	80	80	80	317
11 =	Fred Collins	77	85	79	77	318
	Jack Graham (a)	77	79	81	81	318
	Sandy Herd	73	81	84	80	318
14 =	Bertie Lassen (a)	79	78	80	82	319
	Charles Roberts	78	79	84	78	319
	Josh Taylor	80	75	85	79	319
17	Philip Taylor	78	81	83	78	320
18 =	James Braid	80	79	82	80	321
	Claude Gray	80	81	79	81	321
	Ernest Jones	75	85	81	80	321
	Hughie McNeill	80	81	81	79	321

Taylor joined Vardon and Braid on five Open wins, 19 years after his first success. His margin of eight strokes matched his win of 1900 and Braid's of 1908 – the widest margins of victory in the Open in the twentieth century. Double US Open Champion, John McDermott, became the first US-born professional to compete in the Championship, finishing tied-5th.

US OPEN

COURSE:	The Country Club	
LOCATION:	Brookline, Massachusetts	
DATE:	18-20 September	
DISTANCE:	6245 yards	
PAR:	71 (284)	
WINNER:	$nil-Amateur	

Pos	Player	1st	2nd	3rd	4th	Total
1	**FRANCIS OUIMET*** (a)	77	74	74	79	304
2	Harry Vardon	75	72	78	79	304
3	Ted Ray	79	70	76	79	304
4 =	Jim Barnes	74	76	78	79	307
	Walter Hagen	73	78	76	80	307
	Macdonald Smith	71	79	80	77	307
	Louis Tellier	76	76	79	76	307
8	John McDermott	74	79	77	78	308
9	Herbert Strong	75	74	82	79	310
10	Pat Doyle	78	80	73	80	311
11 =	WC Fownes, Jr (a)	79	75	78	80	312
	Elmer Loving	76	80	75	81	312
13	Alex Campbell	77	80	76	80	313
14	Mike Brady	83	74	78	80	315
15	Matt Campbell	83	80	77	76	316
16 =	Fred Herreshoff (a)	75	78	83	82	318
	Jock Hutchison	77	76	80	85	318
	Tom McNamara	73	86	75	84	318
	Wilfred Reid	75	72	85	86	318
	Alex Smith	82	75	82	79	318

*Francis Ouimet (72) beat Harry Vardon (77) and Ted Ray (78) in the 18-Hole Play-off

If the Opens of 1911 and 1912 were seminal in that they witnessed the birth of the hitherto embryonic American professional, the Open Championship of 1913 showed how the golf and golfers of the New World would soon outgrow their Old World teachers. Not only did it point to the crumbling hegemony of Britain with Vardon's and Ray's defeat in a play-off – it took US golf on to the front pages; and it heralded a golden era for the successful amateur. Francis Ouimet's destruction of arguably the world's two best players of the time is one of golf's biggest upsets – and turning points. Already the USGA had improved on the British administration of such a championship: qualifying rounds were held for the first time, reducing the first round starters starters to 64, for instance. Now America had the players to lead with as well.

1914

COURSE:	Prestwick GC
LOCATION:	Prestwick, Ayrshire, Scotland
DATE:	18-19 June
DISTANCE:	6122 yards
PAR:	n/a
WINNER:	£50

COURSE:	Midlothian CC
LOCATION:	Blue Island, Illinois
DATE:	20-21 August
DISTANCE:	6355 yards
PAR:	72 (288)
WINNER:	$300

Pos	Player	1st	2nd	3rd	4th	Total
1	**HARRY VARDON**	73	77	78	78	306
2	JH Taylor	74	78	74	83	309
3	Harry Simpson	77	80	78	75	310
4 =	Abe Mitchell	76	78	79	79	312
	Tom Williamson	75	79	79	79	312
6	Reg Wilson	76	77	80	80	313
7	James Ockenden	75	76	83	80	314
8 =	PJ Gaudin	78	83	80	74	315
	JLC Jenkins (a)	79	80	73	83	315
10 =	James Braid	74	82	78	82	316
	George Duncan	77	79	80	80	316
	Arnaud Massy	77	82	75	82	316
	Ted Ray	77	82	76	81	316
14 =	James Bradbeer	77	80	80	80	317
	Douglas Edgar	79	75	84	79	317
	Jean Gassiat	76	81	80	80	317
17 =	William Hunter	82	77	77	83	319
	Bertie Lassen (a)	85	78	79	77	319
19 =	Ernest Foord	82	81	82	76	321
	Cyril Hughes	80	81	80	80	321

Pos	Player	1st	2nd	3rd	4th	Total
1	**WALTER HAGEN**	68	74	75	73	290
2	Charles Evans, Jr (a)	76	74	71	70	291
3 =	Fred McLeod	78	73	75	71	297
	George Sargent	74	77	74	72	297
5 =	Mike Brady	78	72	74	74	298
	James Donaldson	72	79	74	73	298
	Francis Ouimet (a)	69	76	75	78	298
8	Louis Tellier	72	75	74	78	299
9 =	John McDermott	77	74	74	75	300
	Arthur Smith	79	73	76	72	300
11 =	WM Rautenbusch (a)	76	75	75	75	301
	James Simpson	76	71	77	77	301
13 =	Jim Barnes	73	76	80	73	302
	Charles Hoffner	77	76	77	72	302
	Tom McNamara	72	71	76	83	302
	Joe Mitchell	77	69	77	79	302
	JJ O'Brien	74	72	77	79	302
	Robert Peebles	78	75	74	75	302
	George Simpson	73	76	76	77	302
20 =	Dan Kenny	76	75	76	76	303
	Tom Kerrigan	76	73	77	77	303

Vardon's last Open win, his sixth, was a record, and is still unsurpassed. It was the end of an era: the Great War caused a five-year vacuum in the Open Championship, at the end of which the Triumvirate had reached the age of 50. Vardon was to challenge for both Opens in 1920, but that was his parting shot. American hero, Francis Ouimet, who was to add the 1914 US Amateur title to his 1913 US Open, came to Prestwick, but finished well down the field on 332.

It didn't take long for the infant US golfer to grow up. As if the outbreak of war in Europe signalled the end of the old and the start of the new, 1914 heralded a different order of all things golf. Leading this movement was one Walter Hagen. Finishing fourth behind all the excitement the previous year, Hagen burst on to the scene with a record R1 score of 68; stayed ahead of the field, and won by one stroke from fast-finishing Chick Evans, another emerging amateur. The winning score tied George Sargent's record low total of 1909. Hagen was to go to become the first worldwide superstar of golf – in fact, he probably invented the role, with his brash but charming manner and lavish lifestyle.

No Championship

COURSE:	Baltusrol GC
LOCATION:	Springfield, New Jersey
DATE:	17-18 June
DISTANCE:	6212 yards
PAR:	72 (288)
WINNER:	$nil-Amateur

Pos	Player	1st	2nd	3rd	4th	Total
1	**JEROME TRAVERS** (a)	76	72	73	76	297
2	Tom McNamara	78	71	74	75	298
3	Bob MacDonald	72	77	73	78	300
4 =	Jim Barnes	71	75	76	79	301
	Louis Tellier	75	71	76	79	301
6	Mike Brady	76	71	75	80	302
7	George Low	78	74	76	75	303
8 =	Jock Hutchison	74	79	76	76	305
	Fred McLeod	74	76	76	79	305
10 =	Alex Campbell	76	75	74	81	306
	Emmett French	77	79	75	75	306
	Walter Hagen	78	73	76	79	306
	Tom Kerrigan	78	75	76	77	306
	Gilbert Nicholls	78	81	73	74	306
	Jack Park	77	77	75	77	306
	Wilfred Reid	77	78	75	76	306
	George Sargent	75	77	79	75	306
18	Charles Evans, Jr (a)	71	81	80	75	307
19 =	James Donaldson	83	79	76	70	308
	Max Marston (a)	77	77	80	74	308

Returning to the original Baltusrol course. The US Open produced its second amateur winner. Jerome Travers had won the matchplay US Amateur title four times. He gave up competitive golf shortly afterwards to concentrate on his Wall St career.

1916

BRITISH OPEN

No Championship

US OPEN

COURSE:	Minikahda Club	
LOCATION:	Minneapolis, Minnesota	
DATE:	29-30 June	
DISTANCE:	6130 yards	
PAR:	72 (288)	
WINNER:	$nil-Amateur	

Pos	Player	1st	2nd	3rd	4th	Total
1	**CHARLES EVANS, Jr** (a)	70	69	74	73	286
2	Jock Hutchison	73	75	72	68	288
3	Jim Barnes	71	74	71	74	290
4 =	Gilbert Nicholls	73	76	71	73	293
	Wilfred Reid	70	72	79	72	293
	George Sargent	75	71	72	75	293
7	Walter Hagen	73	76	75	71	295
8	Bob MacDonald	74	72	77	73	296
9 =	Mike Brady	75	73	75	74	297
	JJ O'Brien	76	72	73	76	297
	Tom Vardon	76	72	75	74	297
12	Jack Dowling	71	76	75	76	298
13 =	Walter Fovargue	76	74	74	75	299
	Louis Tellier	74	75	72	78	299
15 =	Herbert Lagerblade	77	78	72	73	300
	Tom McNamara	75	79	73	73	300
	Robert Peebles	73	72	76	79	300
	JB Simpson	75	76	76	73	300
19 =	Otto Hackbarth	77	80	69	75	301
	George McLean	77	76	74	74	301

Chick Evans became the third amateur in four years to win. In doing so he shattered the record for 36 and 54 holes. There is no truth in the rumour that the then recently-formed PGA of America was inaugurated as a protectionist society, and that it wanted the upcoming PGA Championship closed to the pros in order to keep the amateurs out! Tom Vardon, brother of the illustrious Harry, attained his highest US Open position this year after several less-successful visits; and Wilfred Reid finished fourth in his first US Open – much higher than in any British Open.

COURSE:	Siwanoy GC
LOCATION:	Bronxville, New York
DATE:	9-14 October
QUALIFYING:	32 qualify to matchplay after 36 holes strokeplay
ROUNDS/HOLES:	All rounds 36 holes
WINNER:	$500

Final

JIM BARNES beat Jock Hutchison, 1up

Round 1 (Last 32)

Tom Kerrigan beat Charles Adams 6&4; George McLean beat Tom NacNamara 6&5; Alex Smith beat James Ferguson 4&2; JIM BARNES beat George Fotheringham 8&7; Willie MacFarlane beat Robert McNulty 10&9; Mike Brady beat James West 7&6; Emmett French beat Eddie Towns 3&1; Jack Dowling (bye); JJ O'Brien beat Wilfred Reid 1up; George Simpson beat Walter Fovargue 6&5; Bob MacDonald beat Jimmie Donaldson 3&2; Walter Hagen beat JR Thomson 7&6; JOCK HUTCHISON beat Joe Mitchell 11&9; W Brown beat F Clarkson (default); Cyril Walker beat Louis Tellier 4&2; Jack Hobens beat Mike Sherman (default)

Round 2 (Last 16)

Kerrigan beat McLean 2&1; BARNES beat Smith 8&7; MacFarlane beat Brady 3&2; Dowling beat French 1up (after 37); O'Brien beat Simpson 3&2; Hagen beat MacDonald 3&2; HUTCHISON beat Brown 11&9; Walker beat Hobens 5&4

Quarter Final

BARNES beat Kerrigan 3&1
MacFarlane beat Dowling 2&1
Hagen beat O'Brien 10&9
HUTCHISON beat Walker 5&4

Semi Final

BARNES beat MacFarlane 6&5
HUTCHISON beat Hagen 2up

Jim Barnes, originally from Cornwall, England, became the first winner of the Rodman Wanamaker Trophy. The competition was based on the British PGA Championship sponsored by the *News of the World* newspaper, 36-hole matchplay, providing an alternative format for the pros, already successfully operating in the British and US Amateur Championships. Jock Hutchison had the dubious honour of finishing second in both the year's Majors.

1917/18 ■ BRITISH OPEN

No Championships

■ US OPEN

No Championships

■ US PGA

No Championships

1919

No Championship

COURSE:	Brae Burn CC
LOCATION:	West Newton, Massachusetts
DATE:	9-12 June
DISTANCE:	6375 yards
PAR:	71 (284)
WINNER:	$500

Pos	Player	1st	2nd	3rd	4th	Total
1	**WALTER HAGEN***	78	73	75	75	301
2	Mike Brady	74	74	73	80	301
3 =	Jock Hutchison	78	76	76	76	306
	Tom McNamara	80	73	79	74	306
5 =	George McLean	81	75	76	76	308
	Louis Tellier	73	78	82	75	308
7	John Cowan	79	74	75	81	309
8	George Bowden	73	78	75	86	312
	Fred McLeod	78	77	79	78	312
10	Charles Evans, Jr (a)	77	76	82	78	313
11 =	Jim Barnes	77	78	79	81	315
	Harry Hampton	79	81	77	78	315
13 =	Clarence Hackney	83	78	81	74	316
	Charles Hoffner	72	78	77	89	316
	Isaac Mackie	82	75	78	81	316
16 =	Gilbert Nicholls	81	78	82	77	318
	Alex Ross	77	78	77	86	318
18 =	Pat Doyle	78	82	76	83	319
	Francis Ouimet (a)	76	79	79	85	319
	James West	79	82	80	78	319

* Walter Hagen (77) beat Mike Brady (78)
in the 18-Hole Play-off

The resurrection of the Majors after World War I saw many
familiar faces returning to the golfing fray. Mike Brady,
who lost in a play-off against John McDermott in 1911,
suffered a similar fate at the hands of Walter Hagen this
year. The 'Haig' closed a five-shot gap over the last round
to tie.

COURSE:	Engineers CC
LOCATION:	Long Island, New York
DATE:	15-10 September
QUALIFYING:	32 qualify to matchplay after 36 holes strokeplay
ROUNDS/HOLES:	All rounds 36 holes
WINNER:	$500

Final

JIM BARNES beat Fred McLeod, 6&5

Round 1 (Last 32)

JIM BARNES beat Carl Anderson 8&6; Otto Hackbarth beat Joe Sylvester 5&4; Tom Kerrigan beat Bill Mehlhorn 3&2; Emmett French beat Clarence Hackney 7&6; Bob MacDonald beat Tom Boyd 1up; George Fotheringham beat Eddie Loos 8&6; Tom MacNamara beat Louis Martucci 7&6; Jock Hutchison beat John Bredemus 6&5; Harry Hampton beat Jack Hobens 7&6; Douglas Edgar beat Joe Rosman (default); FRED McLEOD beat James Rose 9&7; George Gordon beat Dave Wilson 3&2; Wilfred Reid beat Pat Doyle 1up; Jimmy West beat Willie Kidd (default); Mike Brady beat Louis Tellier 7&6; George McLean beat Johnny Farrell 7&6

Round 2 (Last 16)

BARNES beat Hackbarth 3&2; French beat Kerrigan 2up; MacDonald beat Fotheringham 2&1; Hutchison beat MacNamara 8&6; Edgar beat Hampton 5&4; McLEOD beat Gordon 2up; West beat Reid 2&1; McLean beat Brady 6&5

Quarter Final

BARNES beat French 3&2
MacDonald beat Hutchison 3&2
McLeod beat Edgar 8&6
McLean beat West 9&7

Semi Final

BARNES beat MacDonald 5&4
McLEOD beat McLean 3&2

The hiatus caused by the War didn't stop Barnes from winning his second PGA title. He demolished 1908 US Open Champion Fred McLeod in the final. Apart from Tom Morris, Jr (1870 & 1872) he is the only champion in any Major to have won 'back-to-back' titles but not in successive years. 'Young' Tom did manage three in a row, though, before the British Open break in 1871.

1920

COURSE:	Royal Cinque Ports GC
LOCATION:	Deal, Kent, England
DATE:	30 June-1 July
DISTANCE:	6653 yards
PAR:	n/a
WINNER:	£75

COURSE:	Inverness Club
LOCATION:	Toledo, Ohio
DATE:	12-13 August
DISTANCE:	6569 yards
PAR:	72 (288)
WINNER:	$500

Pos	Player	1st	2nd	3rd	4th	Total
1	**GEORGE DUNCAN**	80	80	71	72	303
2	Sandy Herd	72	81	77	75	305
3	Ted Ray	72	83	78	73	306
4	Abe Mitchell	74	73	84	76	307
5	Len Holland	80	78	71	79	308
6	Jim Barnes	79	74	77	79	309
7 =	Arthur Havers	80	78	81	74	313
	Sydney Wingate	81	74	76	82	313
9 =	GR Buckle	80	80	77	78	315
	Archie Compston	79	83	75	78	315
	William Horne	80	81	73	81	315
12	JH Taylor	78	79	80	79	316
13	L Lafitte	75	85	84	73	317
14 =	Eric Bannister	78	84	80	76	318
	Harry Vardon	78	81	81	78	318
16 =	A Gaudin	81	82	77	79	319
	Charles Johns	82	78	81	78	319
	James Sherlock	82	81	80	76	319
	Philip Taylor	78	84	77	80	319
	Angel de la Torre	84	78	78	79	319

Pos	Player	1st	2nd	3rd	4th	Total
1	**TED RAY**	74	73	73	75	295
2 =	Jack Burke, Sr	75	77	72	72	296
	Leo Diegel	72	74	73	77	296
	Jock Hutchison	69	76	74	77	296
	Harry Vardon	74	73	71	78	296
6 =	Jim Barnes	76	70	76	76	298
	Charles Evans, Jr (a)	74	76	73	75	298
8 =	Bobby Jones (a)	78	74	70	77	299
	Willie MacFarlane	76	75	74	74	299
10	Bob MacDonald	73	78	71	78	300
11	Walter Hagen	74	73	77	77	301
12	Clarence Hackney	78	74	74	76	302
13	Fred McLeod	75	77	73	79	304
14 =	Mike Brady	77	76	74	78	305
	Frank McNamara	78	77	76	74	305
	Charles Rowe	76	78	77	74	305
17 =	Laurie Ayton, Sr	75	78	76	77	306
	John Golden	77	80	74	75	306
	Eddie Loos	75	74	73	84	306
20 =	Douglas Edgar	73	82	74	78	307
	James West	80	77	75	75	307

George Duncan's only Open win was extraordinary in its scoring. After shooting two successive 80s, he was 13 behind half-way leader Abe Mitchell, but then his final 36-holes took only 143, which had only previously been bettered by Jack White and James Braid at Sandwich in 1904. This was the second, but also the last, visit to Deal. Many of the pros found it geographically remote (SE England, when the centre of the British golfing universe was still north of the border) and too close to Sandwich. The R&A took over the running of the Open from the host clubs and some rationalisation ensued.

Having a chastening experience in 1913 did not deter Ted Ray from trying his luck in the US Open one more time. He was 43 in 1920 and was to be the oldest winner of this championship until Ray Floyd in 1986, then Hale Irwin, four years later, lifted the trophy. In his two visits he tied the lead and was outright winner. His travelling companion, Harry Vardon, was aged 50, and his three visits, spanning 21 years, saw this sequence of results: W, 2, 2. Reigning double PGA Champion, Jim Barnes matched his sixth place in the British Open. In one of those classic era-spanning fields, the likes of Vardon and Alex Ross (tied-27) upheld the honour of the older generation against Jones, Hagen and Sarazen (tied-30).

COURSE:	Flossmoor CC
LOCATION:	Chicago, Illinois
DATE:	17-21 August
QUALIFYING:	32 qualify to matchplay after 36 holes strokeplay
ROUNDS/HOLES:	All rounds 36 holes
WINNER:	$500

Final

JOCK HUTCHISON beat Douglas Edgar, 1up

Round 1 (Last 32)

Alex Cunningham beat Willie MacFarlane 2&1; Peter O'Hara beat Pat Doyle 1up; George McLean beat George Sayers 6&5; Tom Kennett beat Otto Hackbarth 3&1; DOUGLAS EDGAR beat Pat O'Hara 1up; Joe Sylvester beat Tom Boyd 4&3; Bob MacDonald beat Leo Diegel 4&3; Bill Mehlhorn beat Wallie Nelson 3&2; Harry Hampton beat Jack Gordon 6&5; George Thompson beat Isaac Mackie 3&2; Clarence Hackney beat Phil Hesler 3&2; Jim Barnes beat George Bowden 4&3; Charles Mayo beat Lloyd Gullickson 2&1; Louis Tellier beat Joe Rosman 10&9; Laurie Ayton, Sr beat Charles Hoffner 1up (after 39); JOCK HUTCHISON beat Eddie Loos 5&3

Round 2 (Last 16)

Peter O'Hara beat Cunningham 5&4; Mclean beat Kennett 2&1; EDGAR beat Sylvester 11&9; MacDonald beat Mehlhorn 1up; Hampton beat Thompson 5&4; Hackney beat Barnes 5&4; Tellier beat Mayo 4&2; HUTCHISON beat Ayton 5&3

Quarter Final

McLean beat O'Hara 1up (after 38); EDGAR beat MacDonald 5&4; Hampton beat Hackney 4&3; HUTCHISON beat Tellier 6&5

Semi Final

EDGAR beat McLean 8&7; HUTCHISON beat Hampton 4&3

Jim Barnes crashed out in R2, ending a streak of 11 wins. The final was fought between St Andrews-born Jock Hutchison and JD (Douglas) Edgar of Northumberland, England. Hutchison won to make up for his defeat in the 1916 final. Edgar had taken America by storm when he emigrated in 1918. He beat a high-class field by 16 strokes to win the Canadian Open (still a record), and was ahead of his time in preaching golfing techniques. He died, in mysterious circumstances, the following year in Atlanta, aged 37.

1921

COURSE:	Royal & Ancient GC
LOCATION:	St Andrews, Fife, Scotland
DATE:	23-25 June
DISTANCE:	6487 yards
PAR:	n/a
WINNER:	£75

COURSE:	Columbia CC
LOCATION:	Chevy Chase, Maryland
DATE:	21-22 July
DISTANCE:	6380 yards
PAR:	70 (280)
WINNER:	$500

Pos	Player	1st	2nd	3rd	4th	Total
1	**JOCK HUTCHISON***	72	75	79	70	296
2	Roger Wethered (a)	78	75	72	71	296
3	Tom Kerrigan	74	80	72	72	298
4	Arthur Havers	76	74	77	72	299
5	George Duncan	74	75	78	74	301
6 =	Jim Barnes	74	74	74	80	302
	Walter Hagen	74	79	72	77	302
	Sandy Herd	75	74	73	80	302
	Joe Kirkwood, Sr	76	74	73	79	302
	Fred Leach	78	75	76	73	302
	Arnaud Massy	74	75	74	79	302
	Tom Williamson	79	71	74	78	302
13 =	Abe Mitchell	78	79	76	71	304
	W Pursey	74	82	74	74	304
15	J W Gaudin	78	76	75	76	305
16 =	James Braid	77	75	78	76	306
	Len Holland	78	78	76	74	306
	Bill Mehlhorn	75	77	76	78	306
19 =	Frank Ball	79	78	74	76	307
	P Hunter (a)	75	78	76	78	307
	Ted Ray	76	72	81	78	307
	William Watt	81	77	75	74	307

Pos	Player	1st	2nd	3rd	4th	Total
1	**JIM BARNES**	69	75	73	72	289
2 =	Walter Hagen	79	73	72	74	298
	Fred McLeod	74	74	76	74	298
4	Charles Evans, Jr (a)	73	78	76	75	302
5 =	Emmett French	75	77	74	77	303
	Bobby Jones (a)	78	71	77	77	303
	Alex Smith	75	75	79	74	303
8 =	George Duncan	72	78	78	77	305
	Clarence Hackney	74	76	78	77	305
10	Emil Loeffler	74	77	74	81	306
11	Alfred Hackbarth	80	76	82	69	307
12	Eddie Loos	76	79	75	78	308
13	Cyril Walker	78	76	76	79	309
14 =	Mike Brady	77	80	78	75	310
	Jess Sweetser (a)	78	78	77	77	310
	Louis Tellier	76	74	78	82	310
17	Gene Sarazen	83	74	77	77	311
18 =	Laurie Ayton, Sr	81	74	74	83	312
	Jock Hutchison	75	83	77	77	312
	Peter O'Hara	81	82	76	73	312

* Jock Hutchison (150) beat Roger Wethered (159) in the 36-Hole Play-off

Jock Hutchison won the Open on the back of the 1920 US PGA Championship. His homecoming resulted in the first win for an American golfer – albeit one who was Scottish born. Hutchison, the amateur Wethered, and Kerrigan, were all inside James Braid's 1910 St Andrews record, with Hutchison's last round 70 also a record course low in the Championship. Four Americans in the Top 10 signified that the invasion was about to begin.

Jim Barnes won his third Major in collecting the Open Championship for the only time. He increased his lead with every round and stretched away to win by nine shots – but still two short of Willie Smith's 1899 record. It was still the greatest margin of victory in the Open in the twentieth century; and, in any Major, it has only been matched by Jack Nicklaus at the 1965 Masters, and bettered by Tiger Woods (12 strokes) at Augusta in 1997, during the same timespan.

COURSE:	Inwood CC
LOCATION:	Far Rockaway, New York
DATE:	17-21 August
QUALIFYING:	Field selected from the Top 31 PGA available finishers in the 1921 US Open, plus the defending champion (Jock Hutchison)
ROUNDS/HOLES:	All rounds 36 holes
WINNER:	$500

Final
WALTER HAGEN beat Jim Barnes, 3&2

Round 1 (Last 32)
Fred McLeod beat Fred Canausa 1up (after 37); Jack Gordon beat Bill Leach 8&7; Bobby Cruickshank beat Charlie Thom 4&3; JIM BARNES beat Clarence Hackney 3&2; George McLean beat Tom Kerrigan 2&1; Jimmy West beat Jack Pirie 1up (after 37); Charles Clarke beat Peter O'Hara 1up; Emmett French beat Joe Sylvester 8&7; Cyril Walker beat Emil Loeffler 1up (after 37); Charles Mothersole beat Johnny Farrell 1up (after 40); Gene Sarazen beat Harry Hampton 4&3; Jock Hutchison beat Pat O'Hara 1up (after 39); Tom Boyd beat Eddie Towns (default); WALTER HAGEN beat Jack Forrester 6&4; Laurie Ayton, Sr beat TJ Rajoppi 7&6; John Golden beat Robert Barnett 5&3

Round 2 (Last 16)
McLeod beat Gordon 4&2; BARNES beat Cruickshank 8&7; McLean beat West 8&7; French beat Clarke 8&7; Walker beat Mothersole 4&2; Sarazen beat Hutchison 8&7; HAGEN beat Boyd 6&5; Golden beat Ayton 1up

Quarter Final
BARNES beat McLeod 11&9
French beat McLean 5&3
Walker beat Sarazen 5&4
HAGEN beat Golden 8&7

Semi Final
BARNES beat French 5&4
HAGEN beat Walker 5&4

Inwood CC was to become the first host to two different Majors when it also welcomed the US Open in 1923. Hagen's first matchplay Major win prefaced a phenomenal run in the middle of the decade. British Open Champion and defending PGA Champion, Jock Hutchison, was beaten by a 19 year-old – one Gene Sarazen.

1922

COURSE: Royal St St George's GC
LOCATION: Sandwich, Kent, England
DATE: 22-23 June
DISTANCE: 6616 yards
PAR: n/a
WINNER: £75

COURSE: Skokie CC
LOCATION: Glencoe, Illinois
DATE: 14-15 July
DISTANCE: 6563 yards
PAR: 70 (280)
WINNER: $500

Pos	Player	1st	2nd	3rd	4th	Total
1	**WALTER HAGEN**	76	73	79	72	300
2 =	Jim Barnes	75	76	77	73	301
	George Duncan	76	75	81	69	301
4	Jock Hutchison	79	74	73	76	302
5	Charles Whitcombe	77	79	72	75	303
6	JH Taylor	73	78	76	77	304
7	Jean Gassiat	75	78	74	79	306
8 =	Harry Vardon	79	79	74	75	307
	Thomas Walton	75	78	77	77	307
10	Percy Alliss	75	78	78	77	308
11	Charles Johns	78	76	80	75	309
12 =	George Gadd	76	81	76	77	310
	Arthur Havers	78	80	78	74	310
	Len Holland	79	81	74	76	310
	FC Jewell	75	80	78	77	310
	Ernest R Whitcombe	77	78	77	78	310
17 =	Aubrey Boomer	75	80	76	80	311
	Dick Wheildon	80	80	76	75	311
18	Abe Mitchell	79	79	78	76	312
19 =	Joe Kirkwood, Sr	79	76	80	78	313
	Herbert Osborne	80	81	76	76	313
	Michael Scott (a)	77	83	79	74	313

Pos	Player	1st	2nd	3rd	4th	Total
1	**GENE SARAZEN**	72	73	75	68	288
2 =	John Black	71	71	75	72	289
	Bobby Jones (a)	74	72	70	73	289
4	Bill Mehlhorn	73	71	72	74	290
5	Walter Hagen	68	77	74	72	291
6	George Duncan	76	73	75	72	296
7	Leo Diegel	77	76	73	71	297
8 =	Mike Brady	73	75	74	76	298
	John Golden	73	77	77	71	298
	Jock Hutchison	78	74	71	75	298
11 =	Laurie Ayton, Sr	72	76	78	73	299
	Johnny Farrell	73	76	75	75	299
13 =	Joe Kirkwood, Sr	77	74	75	74	300
	Bob MacDonald	73	76	75	76	300
15	Eddie Loos	75	76	73	77	301
16	Charles Evans, Jr (a)	72	76	74	80	302
17 =	George Hackney	74	78	74	77	303
	Abe Mitchell	79	75	76	73	303
19 =	Emmett French	76	74	77	78	305
	Jesse Guilford (a)	74	77	76	78	305
	Harry Hampton	76	75	77	77	305
	Charles Hoffner	79	76	77	73	305
	Willie Ogg	79	72	78	76	305

Hagen's win meant he became the first person to take all three Majors. The Open at Sandwich was his fourth Major in a career haul of 11 – second only in the all-time lists after Jack Nicklaus – and all were achieved in the pre-Masters era.

Gene Sarazen's long and glittering Majors career really began here at Skokie CC. His final round 68 took him from fifth place and four shots adrift after R3, to his first Open title. Little-known Scottish emigrant, John Black, needed two pars to tie and didn't get them. British Open Champion, Walter Hagen, threatened with a record-equalling 68 in R1 and was in the hunt until the last few holes. Admission was charged for the first time.

US PGA

COURSE:	Oakmont CC
LOCATION:	Oakmont, Pennsylvania
DATE:	12-18 August
QUALIFYING:	64 qualify to matchplay after 36 holes strokeplay
ROUNDS/HOLES:	Rs 1&2 -18 holes; QF, SF, F – 36 holes
WINNER:	$500

Final
GENE SARAZEN beat Emmett French, 1up

Round 2 (Last 32)
Francis Gallett beat Fred Brand 5&4; Bobby Cruickshank beat Al Watrous 3&2; Jack Burgess beat Peter Walsh 3&2; Charles Rowe beat Tom Boyd 3&1; Frank Sprogell beat Dan Kenny 4&3; GENE SARAZEN beat Willie Ogg 2&1; Jock Hutchison beat Dan Goss 6&4; Harry Hampton beat Charles Hoffner 3&2; Tom Kerrigan beat Charles Hilgendorf 5&4; Johnny Farrell beat Jim Barnes 1up; John Golden beat PJ Gaudin 8&7; Al Ciuci beat George Stark 4&2; Emil Loeffler beat Dave Robertson 4&3; Eddie Towns beat Matt Duffy 1up; RS Miner beat Fred Baroni 1up (after 19); EMMETT FRENCH beat Mike Brady 3&1

Round 3 (Last 16)
Cruickshank beat Gallett 7&6
Rowe beat Burgess 6&5
SARAZEN beat Sprogell 9&7
Hutchison beat Hampton 4&3
Kerrigan beat Farrell 4&3
Golden beat Ciuci 3&2
Loeffler beat Towns 3&1
FRENCH by Miner 8&7

Quarter Final
Cruickshank beat Rowe 3&2
SARAZEN beat Hutchison 3&1
Golden beat Kerrigan 4&3
FRENCH beat Loeffler 4&2

Semi Final
SARAZEN beat Cruickshank 3&2
FRENCH beat Golden 8&7

Although both Jock Hutchison and Walter Hagen had been reigning PGA Champions when they respectively won the 1921 and 1922 British Opens, Gene Sarazen was the first to win two Majors in the same season. He was made US Open Champion only a month earlier. Hagen missed his opportunity due to other engagements.

1923

COURSE:	Troon GC
LOCATION:	Troon, Ayrshire, Scotland
DATE:	14-15 June
DISTANCE:	6415 yards
PAR:	n/a
WINNER:	£75

COURSE:	Inwood CC
LOCATION:	Inwood, New York
DATE:	13-15 July
DISTANCE:	6532 yards
PAR:	72 (288)
WINNER:	$nil-Amateur

Pos	Player	1st	2nd	3rd	4th	Total
1	**ARTHUR HAVERS**	73	73	73	76	295
2	Walter Hagen	76	71	74	75	296
3	Macdonald Smith	80	73	69	75	297
4	Joe Kirkwood, Sr	72	79	69	78	298
5	Tom Fernie	73	78	74	75	300
6 =	George Duncan	79	75	74	74	302
	Charles Whitcombe	70	76	74	82	302
8 =	Herbert Jolly	79	75	75	74	303
	JH Mackenzie	76	78	74	75	303
	Abe Mitchell	77	77	72	77	303
	William Watt	76	77	72	78	303
12 =	Gordon Lockhart	78	71	76	79	304
	Ted Ray	79	75	73	77	304
	Tom Williamson	79	78	73	74	304
	Sydney Wingate	80	75	74	75	304
16 =	Frank Ball	76	77	77	75	305
	Tom Barber	78	80	76	71	305
	Fred Collins	76	78	72	79	305
19 =	Johnny Farrell	79	73	75	79	306
	Angel de la Torre	78	80	74	74	306
	Thomas Walton	77	74	78	77	306

Pos	Player	1st	2nd	3rd	4th	Total
1	**BOBBY JONES*** (a)	71	73	76	76	296
2	Bobby Cruickshank	73	72	78	73	296
3	Jock Hutchison	70	72	82	78	302
4	Jack Forrester	75	73	77	78	303
5 =	Johnny Farrell	76	77	75	76	304
	Francis Gallett	76	72	77	79	304
	WM Reekie (a)	80	74	75	75	304
8 =	Leo Diegel	77	77	76	76	306
	Bill Mehlhorn	73	79	75	79	306
	Al Watrous	74	75	76	81	306
11	Cyril Hughes	74	76	80	77	307
12 =	Jim Barnes	78	81	74	75	308
	Joe Kirkwood, Sr	77	77	79	75	308
14 =	Charles Evans, Jr (a)	79	80	76	74	309
	Joe Turnesa	76	81	74	78	309
16 =	Charles Mothersole	77	80	71	82	310
	Gene Sarazen	79	78	73	80	310
18 =	Walter Hagen	77	75	73	86	311
	Willie Ogg	74	76	80	81	311
20 =	Mike Brady	74	81	76	81	312
	Macdonald Smith	77	76	81	78	312

For Royal Cinque Ports, read the-not-yet 'Royal' Troon. Troon, along with Royal Lytham in 1925 and Carnoustie in 1931 pulled the Open's centre of gravity further north again, with Sandwich henceforward being the only Open host site in southern England. 20 year-old Arthur Havers held off a clutch of mighty Americans to be the last English winner until Henry Cotton's first win in 1934.

*Bobby Jones (76) beat Bobby Cruickshank (78) in the 18-Hole Play-off

Robert Tyre Jones, Jr – Bobby Jones – one of the very few immortals of golf, won the first of his seven (professional) Majors at Inwood. He was virtually retired before the Masters era he was instrumental in creating, and was, as an amateur, excluded from the PGA; so all his Majors were Opens (four US and three British). At that time, the Amateur Championships were considered 'Majors' too, and Jones collected five US and one British. Some archivists therefore have Jones with 13 Majors: and all this between 1923 and 1930. Wee Bobby Cruickshank was one of the greatest players never to win a Major – so there is some irony in his losing to Jones in a play-off for the latter's first of many titles.

COURSE:	Pelham GC
LOCATION:	Pelham Manor, New York
DATE:	12-18 August
QUALIFYING:	64 qualify to matchplay after 36 holes strokeplay
ROUNDS/HOLES:	All Rounds 36 holes
WINNER:	$n/k

Final

GENE SARAZEN beat Walter Hagen, 1up (after 38)

Round 2 (Last 32)

Bobby Cruickshank beat Herbert Obendorf 7&5; Ray Derr beat Frank Coltart 5&4; Willie MacFarlane beat Wilfred Reid 3&2; Jack Stait beat Jack Forrester 1up; Jim Barnes beat John Cowan 12&11; Cyril Walker beat Harry Cooper 2&1; Alex Campbell beat Willie Klein 4&3; GENE SARAZEN beat DK White 11&10; Clarence Hackney beat RS Miner 7&6; Fred McLeod beat James Meehan 4&3; WALTER HAGEN beat Jack Elplick 10&9; John Golden beat Robert Barnett 1up; Joe Kirkwood, Sr beat Jimmy West 2up; Johnny Farrell beat Willie Hunter, Jr 4&3; George McLean beat Jimmie Donaldson 6&4; Willie Ogg beat Carl Anderson 12&11

Round 3 (Last 16)

Cruickshank beat Derr 1up; MacFarlane beat Stait 5&4; Barnes beat Walker 8&7; SARAZEN beat Campbell 3&2; McLeod beat Hackney 1up; HAGEN beat Golden 4&3; Kirkwood beat Farrell 1up; McLean beat Ogg 1up (after 38)

Quarter Final

Cruickshank beat MacFarlane 1up (after 39)
SARAZEN beat Barnes 1up
HAGEN beat Mcleod 5&4
McLean beat Kirkwood 5&4

Semi Final

SARAZEN beat Cruickshank 6&5
HAGEN beat McLean 12&11

Sarazen made it two PGAs in a row, but this time Hagen was there to compete. The two met in the final, and their gargantuan battle only ended at the second extra hole. Hagen had clawed back three strokes on the final back nine to take it to sudden-death and must have thought he'd won when Sarazen's tee-shot at the 38th ended up in thick rough. Sarazen, however, hacked out to within two feet of the pin, while an amazed Hagen bunkered his approach.

1924

COURSE:	Oakland Hills CC
LOCATION:	Birmingham, Michigan
DATE:	5-6 June
DISTANCE:	6880 yards
PAR:	72 (288)
WINNER:	$500

Pos	Player	1st	2nd	3rd	4th	Total
1	**CYRIL WALKER**	74	74	74	75	297
2	Bobby Jones (a)	74	73	75	78	300
3	Bill Mehlhorn	72	75	76	78	301
4 =	Bobby Cruickshank	77	72	76	78	303
	Walter Hagen	75	75	76	77	303
	Macdonald Smith	78	72	77	76	303
7 =	Abe Espinosa	80	71	77	77	305
	Peter O'Hara	76	79	74	76	305
9	Mike Brady	75	77	77	77	306
10 =	Charles Evans, Jr (a)	77	77	76	77	307
	Eddie Loos	73	81	75	78	307
	Dave Robertson	73	76	77	81	307
13 =	Tommy Armour	78	76	75	80	309
	Clarence Hackney	81	72	78	78	309
15 =	Willie Ogg	75	80	76	79	310
	Joe Turnesa	76	78	78	78	310
17 =	Walter Bourne	78	76	79	80	313
	Gene Sarazen	74	80	80	79	313
19 =	Johnny Farrell	79	76	77	82	314
	Tom Kerrigan	77	74	89	74	314
	Jock Rogers	82	77	77	78	314

Regional qualifying (East and West) took place for the first time with the lowest 40 and ties making it to R1. Another 'first' was that steel-shafted putters were allowed. Oakland Hills, at nearly 6900 yards, was the longest course yet used for a Major, and not far short of some of the modern-day monsters. Cyril Walker was the rather surprising winner, his past form in the British Open before he emigrated not suggesting he could best a field which included the likes of Hagen, Jones, Sarazen and Macdonald Smith.

COURSE:	Royal Liverpool GC
LOCATION:	Hoylake, Cheshire, England
DATE:	23-24 June
DISTANCE:	6750 yards
PAR:	n/a
WINNER:	£75

Pos	Player	1st	2nd	3rd	4th	Total
1	**WALTER HAGEN**	77	73	74	77	301
2	Ernest R Whitcombe	77	70	77	78	302
3 =	Frank Ball	78	75	74	77	304
	Macdonald Smith	76	74	77	77	304
5	JH Taylor	75	74	79	79	307
6 =	Aubrey Boomer	75	78	76	79	308
	George Duncan	74	79	74	81	308
	Len Holland	74	78	78	78	308
9 =	JM Barber	78	77	79	75	309
	George Gadd	79	75	78	77	309
	James Sherlock	76	75	78	80	309
	Percy Weston	76	77	77	79	309
13 =	Sandy Herd	76	79	76	79	310
	Gilbert Nicholls	75	78	79	78	310
	Tom Williamson	79	76	80	75	310
16 =	JW Gaudin	79	78	80	76	313
	Charles Johns	77	77	78	81	313
18 =	James Braid	80	80	78	76	314
	Albert Tingey, Jr	82	81	76	75	314
	Cyril Tolley (a)	73	82	80	79	314

Hagen's second Open out of four he was to claim during the twenties was a tight affair. In a high-scoring last round he edged out Ernest Whitcombe – one of the three famous golfing brothers. Bobby Jones didn't compete – and it is worth considering, that for all Hagen's successes in the Opens, he never once won when Jones was in the field.

US PGA

COURSE:	French Springs GC
LOCATION:	French Lick, Indiana
DATE:	15-20 September
QUALIFYING:	32 qualify to matchplay after 36 holes strokeplay (Low – Johnny Farrell, 140)
ROUNDS/HOLES:	All Rounds 36 holes
WINNER:	$n/k

Final

WALTER HAGEN beat Jim Barnes, 2up

Round 1 (Last 32)

Willie MacFarlane beat George Dow 5&4; Johnny Farrell beat Neil Christian 2&1; Al Watrous beat George Aulbach 3&1; WALTER HAGEN beat Tom Harmon, Jr 6&5; Al Espinosa beat Arthur Ham 4&2; Francis Gallett beat Bill Mehlhorn 4&3; Bobby Cruickshank beat Willie Ogg 7&5; Ray Derr beat Harry Hampton 2up; Henry Ciuci beat Charles Hoffner 4&2; Dan Williams beat Fred Baroni 4&2; Gene Sarazen beat Fred McLeod 5&4; Larry Nabholtz beat Jack Forrester 1up; Mortie Dutra beat Leo Diegel 3&1; Emmett French beat Jock Robertson 6&4; Jim Barnes beat Mike Brady 1up (after 39); Eddie Towns beat Jock Hutchison 4&3

Round 2 (Last 16)

Farrell beat MacFarlane 2&1; HAGEN beat Watrous 4&3; Espinosa beat Gallett 4&3; Derr br Cruickshank 2&1; Ciuci beat Williams 4&3; Nabholtz beat Sarazen 2&1; French beat Dutra 3&1; BARNES beat Towns 10&9

Quarter Final

HAGEN beat Farrell 3&2
Derr beat Espinosa 2&1
Nabholtz beat Ciuci 5&4
BARNES beat French 6&4

Semi Final

HAGEN beat Derr 8&7
BARNES beat Nabholtz 1up

It was Hagen's turn again, in a repeat of the 1921 final. He became the first golfer to hold the British Open and one other Major in the same season, and his win record in Majors between 1919 and 1929 is formidable: 1919, US Open; 1921, PGA; 1922, B Open; 1924, B Open & PGA; 1925, PGA; 1926, PGA; 1927, PGA; 1928, B Open; 1929, B Open.

1925

COURSE: Worcester CC
LOCATION: Worcester, Massachusetts
DATE: 3-5 June
DISTANCE: 6430 yards
PAR: 71 (284)
WINNER: $500

Pos	Player	1st	2nd	3rd	4th	Total
1	**WILLIE MACFARLANE***	74	67	72	78	291
2	Bobby Jones (a)	77	70	70	74	291
=3	Johnny Farrell	71	74	69	78	292
	Francis Ouimet (a)	70	73	73	76	292
5 =	Walter Hagen	72	76	71	74	293
	Gene Sarazen	72	72	75	74	293
7	Mike Brady	74	72	74	74	294
8	Leo Diegel	73	68	77	78	296
9 =	Laurie Ayton, Sr	75	71	73	78	297
	Al Espinosa	72	71	74	80	297
11 =	Macdonald Smith	73	79	72	75	299
	Joe Turnesa	76	74	71	78	299
13 =	Willie Hunter, Jr	75	77	75	73	300
	Al Watrous	78	73	74	75	300
15 =	Bob MacDonald	75	77	77	72	301
	Bill Mehlhorn	78	72	75	76	301
17	Clarence Hackney	78	72	73	79	302
18 =	John Golden	76	75	82	70	303
	Tom Kerrigan	75	79	74	75	303
20 =	Tom Boyd	73	79	75	77	304
	Jack Forrester	71	76	76	81	304
	Emmett French	77	74	77	76	304
	Francis Gallett	73	70	84	77	304
	Harry Hampton	79	75	76	74	304
	Bob Shave	81	72	77	74	304

*Willie MacFarlane (75,72) beat Bobby Jones (75,73) after the Second 18-Hole Play-off

The era of Scottish-born US Open Champions, and indeed Major winners in general, was just coming to an end. Willie MacFarlane, from Aberdeen, tied with Bob Jones – and tied again on 75 the first 18-hole play-off. Jones uncharacteristically threw away a four-stroke lead in the second play-off, to allow MacFarlane to come home in 72, and beat him by one. Earlier, in R2, MacFarlane set a new low score of 67.

COURSE: Prestwick GC
LOCATION: Prestwick, Ayrshire, Scotland
DATE: 25-26 June
DISTANCE: 6444 yards
PAR: n/a
WINNER: £75

Pos	Player	1st	2nd	3rd	4th	Total
1	**JIM BARNES**	70	77	79	74	300
2 =	Archie Compston	76	75	75	75	301
	Ted Ray	77	76	75	73	301
3	Macdonald Smith	76	69	76	82	303
4	Abe Mitchell	77	76	75	77	305
5 =	Percy Alliss	77	80	77	76	310
	Bill Davies	76	76	80	78	310
	JW Gaudin	78	81	77	74	310
	JH Taylor	74	79	80	77	310
	Sydney Wingate	74	78	80	78	310
10 =	Robert Harris (a)	75	81	78	77	311
	Fred Robson	80	77	78	76	311
12	HA Gaudin	76	79	77	80	312
13 =	Tom Fernie	78	74	77	85	314
	Sandy Herd	76	79	82	77	314
	Joe Kirkwood, Sr	83	79	76	76	314
16 =	JI Cruickshank (a)	80	78	82	75	315
	Jack Smith	75	78	82	80	315
	Harry Vardon	79	80	77	79	315
19 =	Arthur Havers	77	80	80	79	316
	Duncan McCulloch	76	77	84	79	316
	James Ockenden	80	78	80	78	316
	Reg Whitcombe	81	80	79	76	316

Jim Barnes took his fourth Major title – he had already won the first two PGAs (1916 & 1919) and collected the US Open in 1921. He thus followed Walter Hagen's feat of winning all the contemporary Major Championships. Barnes' win, ahead of 48 year-old Ted Ray and rising British hope, Compston, was in the 23rd and last Open to be played at historic Prestwick. Of the 13 Championships held there between 1860 and 1875, the Morrisses and Willie Park had won a dozen. By 1925, the Ayrshire links, having far too many blind shots for the sophisticated modern golfer, had become a Majors dinosaur.

COURSE:	Olympia Fields CC
LOCATION:	Olympia Fields, Illinois
DATE:	21-26 September
QUALIFYING:	32 qualify to matchplay after 36 holes strokeplay (Low – Al Watrous, 140)
ROUNDS/HOLES:	All Rounds 36 holes
WINNER:	$n/k

Final
WALTER HAGEN beat Bill Mehlhorn, 6&5

Round 1 (Last 32)
WALTER HAGEN beat Al Watrous 1up (after 39); Mike Brady beat JS Collins 10&9; Leo Diegel beat Laurie Ayton, Sr 2&1; Bobby Cruickshank beat Bill Leach 4&3; Harry Cooper beat Jack Blakeslee 7&6; Jack Burke, Sr beat Gene Sarazen 8&7; Johnny Farrell beat William Creavy 6&4; Ray Derr beat Abe Espinosa 4&3; BILL MEHLHORN beat Emmett French 5&4; Al Espinosa beat George Howard 5&3; Tom Kerrigan beat George Smith 5&3; Dan Williams beat Charles Hoffner 4&3; Motrie Dutra beat Willie Ogg 2&1; Ed Dudley beat Mike Patton 3&2; Tommy Armour beat George Griffin 3&1; John Golden beat Dave Robertson 9&8

Round 2 (Last 16)
HAGEN beat Brady 7&6
Diegel beat Cruickshank 2&1
Cooper beat Burke 2&1
Farrell beat Derr 1up (after 37)
MEHLHORN beat Al Espinosa 1up
Kerrigan beat Williams 2up
Dutra beat Dudley 6&5
Armour beat Golden 6&5

Quarter Final
HAGEN beat Diegel 1up (after 40)
Cooper beat Farrell 2&1
MEHLHORN beat Kerrigan 7&6
Dutra beat Armour 2up

Semi Final
HAGEN beat Cooper 3&1
MEHLHORN beat Dutra 8&6

Walter Hagen's third PGA win was not without a fright or two: he was taken into extra holes by Al Watrous and Leo Diegel. Having seen Jim Barnes match a record of his at the British Open in June, Hagen now equalled Barnes' (and Sarazen's) feat of back-to-back PGA titles.

1926

COURSE: Royal Lytham and St Anne's GC
LOCATION: St Annes, Lancashire, England
DATE: 22-24 June
DISTANCE: 6456 yards
PAR: n/a
WINNER: £nil-Amateur

Pos	Player	1st	2nd	3rd	4th	Total
1	**BOBBY JONES** (a)	72	72	73	74	291
2	Al Watrous	71	75	69	78	293
3=	Walter Hagen	68	77	74	76	295
	George Von Elm (a)	75	72	76	72	295
5=	Tom Barber	77	73	78	71	299
	Abe Mitchell	78	78	72	71	299
7	Fred McLeod	71	75	76	79	301
8=	Emmett French	76	75	74	78	303
	Jose Jurado	77	76	74	76	303
	Bill Mehlhorn	70	74	79	80	303
10=	HA Gaudin	78	78	71	77	304
	JH Taylor	75	78	71	80	304
12	Tommy Armour	74	76	75	80	305
13=	WL Hartley (a)	74	77	79	76	306
	H Walker	74	77	78	77	306
	Reg Whitcombe	73	82	76	75	306
	Tom Williamson	78	76	76	76	306
17=	Jim Barnes	77	80	72	78	307
	Fred Robson	79	76	77	75	307
	Cyril Walker	79	71	80	77	307
20=	George Duncan	75	79	80	74	308
	Sandy Herd	81	76	75	76	308

With sectional qualifying and expanding the competition over three days, the Opens were beginning to think in unison – except on the question of the calendar. This year, the British Open preceded its US counterpart once more. The Lancashire links of Royal Lytham were hosting the Championship for the first time; and Bobby Jones won for the first time. He was the first amateur to win since Harold Hilton in 1897.

COURSE: Scioto CC
LOCATION: Columbus, Ohio
DATE: 8-10 July
DISTANCE: 6675 yards
PAR: 72 (288)
WINNER: $nil-Amateur

Pos	Player	1st	2nd	3rd	4th	Total
1	**BOBBY JONES** (a)	70	79	71	73	293
2	Joe Turnesa	71	74	72	77	294
3=	Leo Diegel	72	76	75	74	297
	Johnny Farrell	76	79	69	73	297
	Bill Mehlhorn	68	75	76	78	297
	Gene Sarazen	78	77	72	70	297
7	Walter Hagen	73	77	74	74	298
8	Willie Hunter, Jr	75	77	69	79	300
9=	Tommy Armour	76	76	74	75	301
	Willie Klein	76	74	75	76	301
	Macdonald Smith	82	76	68	75	301
	Dan Williams	72	74	80	75	301
13=	Al Espinosa	71	79	78	74	302
	Charles Evans, Jr (a)	75	75	73	79	302
	Jack Forrester	76	73	77	76	302
16=	Laurie Ayton, Sr	76	78	76	76	306
	Mike Brady	77	82	76	71	306
	George McLean	74	74	79	79	306
	Jimmy Thomson	77	82	73	74	306
20=	Willie MacFarlane	72	79	75	81	307
	JE Rogers	80	79	75	73	307

Returning to the States, Jones picked up his second Major in succession, and became the first player to win both Opens in the same year. Joe Turnesa's second place was to start a runner's-up jinx in the Majors over many years – on him and his brothers, Mike and Jim; until Jim broke it by picking up the 1952 PGA title.

COURSE:	Salisbury GL
LOCATION:	Westbury, Long Island, New York
DATE:	20-25 September
QUALIFYING:	32 qualify to matchplay after 36 holes strokeplay (Low – Walter Hagen, 140)
ROUNDS/HOLES:	All Rounds 36 holes
WINNER:	$n/k

Final
WALTER HAGEN beat Leo Diegel, 5&3

Round 1 (Last 32)
Marshall Crichton beat Francis Gallett 1up; Pat Doyle beat Willie Maguire 2&1; Dick Grout beat Jock Hendry 4&3; WALTER HAGEN beat Joe Turnesa 3&2; Dick Linnars beat Fred McLeod 5&4; Johnny Farrell beat Al Watrous 6&5; Harry Hampton beat Larry Nabholtz 6&5; Tom Harmon, Jr beat Al Espinosa 6&4; Abe Espinosa beat Gunnar Nelson 7&6; Mike Brady beat George Aulbach 1up (after 37); LEO DIEGEL beat Mike Patton 8&7; Neal McIntyre beat Bobby Cruickshank 4&2; John Golden beat Harry Cooper 5&3; Gene Sarazen beat Jim Barnes 5&4; Bill Leach beat Laurie Ayton, Sr 3&2; George Christ beat Leo Shea 3&2

Round 2 (Last 16)
Doyle by Crichton 3&2; HAGEN beat Grout 7&6; Farrell beat Linnars 6&5; Hampton beat Harmon 6&5; Abe Espinosa beat Brady 1up; DIEGEL beat McIntyre 6&5; Golden beat Sarazen 4&3; Christ beat Leach 1up (after 38)

Quarter Final
HAGEN beat Doyle 6&5
Farrell beat Hampton 3&1
DIEGEL beat Abe Espinosa 3&2
Golden beat Christ 7&6

Semi Final
HAGEN beat Farrell 6&5
DIEGEL beat Golden 1up

Bobby Jones may have been having all his own way in the Opens, but in matchplay, Walter Hagen was peerless during the mid-twenties. If Jones was elegible to compete in the PGA, it would have been a very mouth-watering prospect to contemplate he and Hagen head-to-head. As it was, in 1926, the 'Haig' demolished the opposition round-by-round to take his fourth PGA – and the third in succession

US OPEN

COURSE:	Oakmont CC
LOCATION:	Oakmont, Pennsylvania
DATE:	14-17 June
DISTANCE:	6965 yards
PAR:	72 (288)
WINNER:	$500

Pos	Player	1st	2nd	3rd	4th	Total
1	**TOMMY ARMOUR***	78	71	76	76	301
2	Harry Cooper	74	76	74	77	301
3	Gene Sarazen	74	74	80	74	302
4	Emmett French	75	79	77	73	304
5	Bill Mehlhorn	75	77	80	73	305
6	Walter Hagen	77	73	76	81	307
7 =	Archie Compston	79	74	76	79	308
	Johnny Farrell	81	73	78	76	308
	John Golden	83	77	75	73	308
	Harry Hampton	73	78	80	77	308
11 =	Bobby Cruickshank	77	78	76	78	309
	Leo Diegel	78	74	80	77	309
	Bobby Jones (a)	76	77	79	77	309
	Eddie Loos	78	75	79	77	309
15 =	Fred Baroni	80	72	79	79	310
	Perry Del Vecchio	79	79	76	76	310
	Arthur Havers	79	77	74	80	310
18 =	Al Espinosa	83	80	79	69	311
	Harrison Johnston (a)	73	74	87	77	311
	Willie MacFarlane	82	76	80	73	311
	Macdonald Smith	78	76	81	76	311
	Al Watrous	82	74	78	77	311

*Tommy Armour (76) beat Harry Cooper (79) in the 18-Hole Play-off

Tommy Armour won the first of his three Majors over the classic Oakmont parkland course. He tied 'Light Horse' Harry Cooper – another for whom a Major Championship was just beyond the grasp – and comfortably won the play-off. Armour was the last Scots-born player to win the US Open. Ted Ray, the Champion of 1920, finished tied-27th, and said farewell to America at the age of 50.

BRITISH OPEN

COURSE:	Royal & Ancient GC
LOCATION:	St Andrews, Fife, Scotland
DATE:	13-15 July
DISTANCE:	6572 yards
PAR:	n/a
WINNER:	£nil-Amateur

Pos	Player	1st	2nd	3rd	4th	Total
1	**BOBBY JONES** (a)	68	72	73	72	285
2 =	Aubrey Boomer	76	70	73	72	291
	Fred Robson	76	72	69	74	291
4 =	Joe Kirkwood, Sr	72	72	75	74	293
	Ernest R Whitcombe	74	73	73	73	293
6	Charles Whitcombe	74	76	71	75	296
7 =	Arthur Havers	80	74	73	70	297
	Bert Hodson	72	70	81	74	297
8	Henry Cotton	73	72	77	76	298
9 =	Percy Alliss	73	74	73	80	300
	Sandy Herd	76	75	78	71	300
	Phil Perkins (a)	76	78	70	76	300
	Phillip H Rodgers	76	73	74	77	300
	WB Torrance	72	80	74	74	300
	RD Vickers	75	75	77	73	300
	Tom Williamson	75	76	78	71	300
16 =	Jim Barnes	76	76	72	77	301
	GR Buckle	77	69	77	78	301
	O Johns	74	78	73	76	301
19 =	Donald Curtis	73	76	79	74	302
	Jean Gassiat	76	77	73	76	302
	Tom Stevens	76	73	74	79	302

Bobby Jones continued to re-write the record books: record low score for either Open; first back-to-back British Open win for an amateur; third win in row in eligible Championships (he won both Opens in 1926); and so on. St Andrews introduced a larger scoreboard for spectators – the precursor of the modern leaderboard.

COURSE:	Cedar Crest CC
LOCATION:	Dallas, Texas
DATE:	31October-5 November
QUALIFYING:	32 qualify to matchplay after 36 holes strokeplay (Low – Walter Hagen, 141)
ROUNDS/HOLES:	All Rounds 36 holes
WINNER:	$n/k

Final

WALTER HAGEN beat Joe Turnesa, 1up

Round 1 (Last 32)

Tommy Armour beat Johnny Farrell 4&3; Tom Harmon, Jr beat Johnny Perelli 4&3; Tony Manero beat Bobby Cruickshank 4&3; WALTER HAGEN beat Jack Farrell 3&2; Mortie Dutra beat Albert Alcroft 12&11; Charles Guest beat Roland Hancock 3&2; Al Espinosa beat Mel Smith 5&4; Harry Cooper beat Eddie Murphy 7&6; Ed Dudley beat James Gullane 8&7; Gene Sarazen by Jack Curley 1up (after 37); Willie Klein beat Bill Mehlhorn 1up; JOE TURNESA beat Charles McKenna 5&3; John Golden beat Charles Koontz 2&1; Harold Long beat Willie Kidd 4&3; Francis Gallett beat Bob Shave 4&3; Ralph Beach beat Fred Baroni 1up

Round 2 (Last 16)

Armour beat Harmon, Jr 7&6; HAGEN beat Manero 11&10; Dutra beat Guest 2up; Espinosa beat Cooper 5&4; Sarazen beat Dudley 4&3; TURNESA beat Klein 1up; Golden beat Long 1up (after 37); Gallett beat Beach 2up

Quarter Final

HAGEN beat Armour 4&3; Espinosa beat Dutra 1up; TURNESA beat Sarazen 3&2; Golden beat Gallett 4&2

Semi Final

HAGEN beat Espinosa 1up (after 37); TURNESA beat Golden 7&6

Hagen set his remarkable record of four consecutive wins in the PGA. He joined Tom Morris, Jr as the only player in history to win the same Major Championship four times in succession – and the only one to do it four years in a row ('Young' Tom won four British Opens between 1868 and 1872, but there was no Championship in 1871).

BRITISH OPEN

COURSE:	Royal St St George's GC
LOCATION:	Sandwich, Kent, England
DATE:	9-11 June
DISTANCE:	6751 yards
PAR:	n/a
WINNER:	£75

Pos	Player	1st	2nd	3rd	4th	Total
1	**WALTER HAGEN**	75	73	72	72	292
2	Gene Sarazen	72	76	73	73	294
3	Archie Compston	75	74	73	73	295
4 =	Percy Alliss	75	76	75	72	298
	Fred Robson	79	73	73	73	298
6 =	Jim Barnes	81	73	76	71	301
	Aubrey Boomer	79	73	77	72	301
	Jose Jurado	74	71	76	80	301
9	Bill Mehlhorn	71	78	76	77	302
10	Bill Davies	78	74	79	73	304
11 =	Fred Taggart	76	74	77	78	305
	Albert Whiting	78	76	76	75	305
13	Jack Smith	79	77	76	74	306
14 =	Phil Perkins (a)	80	79	76	72	307
	William Twine	75	79	77	76	307
16	Stewart Burns	76	74	75	83	308
17	CO Hezlet (a)	79	76	78	76	309
18 =	Henry Cotton	77	75	83	75	310
	Duncan McCulloch	78	78	78	76	310
	George Duncan	75	77	78	80	310

Walter Hagen edged away from his arch-rival pro, Gene Sarazen, over the second 36 holes to win his second Open, both at Sandwich. He lowered his own 1922 record there by eight strokes. In the last appearance of members of the Triumvirate among the finishers, James Braid shot a 316 to finish tied-41st and Harry Vardon tied-47th (317).

US OPEN

COURSE:	Olympia Fields CC
LOCATION:	Matteson, Illinois
DATE:	21-23 June
DISTANCE:	6725 yards
PAR:	71 (284)
WINNER:	$500

Pos	Player	1st	2nd	3rd	4th	Total
1	**JOHNNY FARRELL***	77	74	71	72	294
2	Bobby Jones (a)	73	71	73	77	294
3	Roland Hancock	74	77	72	72	295
4 =	Walter Hagen	75	72	73	76	296
	George Von Elm (a)	74	72	76	74	296
6 =	Henry Ciuci	70	77	72	80	299
	Waldo Crowder	74	74	76	75	299
	Ed Dudley	77	79	68	75	299
	Bill Leach	72	74	73	80	299
	Gene Sarazen	78	76	73	72	299
	Denny Shute	75	73	79	72	299
	Macdonald Smith	75	77	75	72	299
	Joe Turnesa	74	77	74	74	299
14 =	Al Espinosa	74	74	77	75	300
	Willie MacFarlane	73	74	73	80	300
16	Tommy Armour	76	75	77	73	301
17	Jack Forrester	77	76	75	74	302
18 =	Billy Burke	74	79	73	77	303
	Neil Christian	80	78	74	71	303
	Leo Diegel	72	79	75	77	303
	Charles Hilgendorf	76	77	79	71	303

*Johnny Farrell (143) beat Bobby Jones (144) in the 36-Hole Play-off

The number of entries had been steadily rising in all Majors, but in 1928, the 1000 mark was passed, here, at Olympia Fields near Chicago, for the first time. The Championship went to a tie once more, and although he was to win the fourth of his five US Amateur titles in the coming September, did Jones, as in 1925, give a glimpse of a slight weakness in matchplay golf? Willie MacFarlane beat him then: this year it was Johnny Farrell.

US PGA

COURSE:	Five Farms CC
LOCATION:	Baltimore, Maryland
DATE:	1-6 October
QUALIFYING:	32 qualify to matchplay after 36 holes strokeplay (Low – Al Espinosa,142)
ROUNDS/HOLES:	All Rounds 36 holes
WINNER:	$n/k

Final
LEO DIEGEL beat Al Espinosa, 6&5

Round 1 (Last 32)
Willie McFarlane beat Jim Foulis 9&7; Horton Smith beat Billy Burke 2&1; Glen Spencer beat Fred McDermott 8&6; Perry Del Vecchio beat Jack Burke, Sr 1up (after 37); AL ESPINOSA beat John Golden 8&7; Bob MacDonald beat Willie Kidd 2up; Jock Hutchison beat Willie Klein 3&2; Pat Doyle beat Mortie Dutra 6&4; Jim Barnes beat Tommy Armour 3&2; Gene Sarazen beat Bill Mehlhorn 3&2; Al Watrous beat Olin Dutra 2&1; Ed Dudley beat Wiffy Cox 3&2; George Christ beat Albert Alcroft 1up (after 38); LEO DIEGEL beat Tony Manero 10&8; Walter Hagen beat Willie Ogg 4&3; Julian Blanton beat Ed McElligott 9&8

Round 2 (Last 16)
Smith beat MacFarlane 1up
Del Vecchio beat Spencer 1up (after 37)
ESPINOSA by MacDonald 1up (after 37)
Hutchison beat Doyle 1up
Sarazen beat Barnes 3&2
Dudley beat Watrous 3&2
DIEGEL beat Christ 6&4
Hagen beat Blanton 2up

Quarter Final
Smith beat Del Vecchio 2up
ESPINOSA beat Hutchison 5&4
Sarazen beat Dudley 7&6
DIEGEL beat Hagen 2&1

Semi Final
ESPINOSA beat Smith 6&5
DIEGEL beat Sarazen 9&8

Leo Diegel broke Walter Hagen's four-year run and 22 consecutive match wins in the PGA when he won at the 35th hole in the quarter final. Only Gene Sarazen before that had beaten Hagen in PGA Championship matches going back to 1921. Diegel then demolished Sarazen before beating top-qualifier, Al Espinosa, in the one-sided final.

BRITISH OPEN

COURSE:	Honourable Company of Edinburgh Golfers
LOCATION:	Muirfield, East Lothian, Scotland
DATE:	8-10 May
DISTANCE:	6738 yards
PAR:	n/a
WINNER:	£75

Pos	Player	1st	2nd	3rd	4th	Total
1	**WALTER HAGEN**	75	67	75	75	292
2	Johnny Farrell	72	75	76	75	298
3	Leo Diegel	71	69	82	77	299
4 =	Percy Alliss	69	76	76	79	300
	Abe Mitchell	72	72	78	78	300
6	Bobby Cruickshank	73	74	78	76	301
7	Jim Barnes	71	80	78	74	303
8 =	Gene Sarazen	73	74	81	76	304
	Al Watrous	73	79	75	77	304
10	Tommy Armour	75	73	79	78	305
11	Arthur Havers	80	74	76	76	306
12	Archie Compston	76	73	77	81	307
13 =	Johnny Golden	74	73	86	75	308
	Jimmy Thomson	78	78	75	77	308
15 =	Aubrey Boomer	74	74	80	81	309
	Herbert Jolly	72	80	78	79	309
	Macdonald Smith	73	78	78	80	309
18 =	Sid Brews	76	77	78	79	310
	Bill Davies	79	76	81	74	310
	Ed Dudley	72	80	80	78	310
	Mark Seymour	75	74	78	83	310

US OPEN

COURSE:	Winged Foot GC
LOCATION:	Mamaroneck, New York
DATE:	27-30 June
DISTANCE:	6786 yards
PAR:	72 (288)
WINNER:	$nil-Amateur

Pos	Player	1st	2nd	3rd	4th	Total
1	**BOBBY JONES*** (a)	69	75	71	79	294
2	Al Espinosa	70	72	77	75	294
3 =	Gene Sarazen	71	71	76	78	296
	Denny Shute	73	71	76	76	296
5 =	Tommy Armour	74	71	76	76	297
	George Von Elm (a)	79	70	74	74	297
7	Henry Ciuci	78	74	72	75	299
8 =	Leo Diegel	74	74	76	77	301
	Peter O'Hara	74	76	73	78	301
10	Horton Smith	76	77	74	75	302
11 =	Wiffy Cox	74	76	80	75	305
	JE Rogers	78	76	77	74	305
13 =	PO Hart	76	78	75	77	306
	Charles Hilgendorf	72	79	75	80	306
15	Billy Burke	75	80	78	74	307
16 =	Louis Chiapetta	78	79	72	79	308
	George Smith	77	77	77	77	308
	Craig Wood	79	71	80	78	308
19 =	Walter Hagen	76	81	74	78	309
	Joe Kirkwood, Sr	75	82	76	76	309

* Bobby Jones (141) beat Al Espinosa (164) in the 36-Hole Play-off

Hagen repeated his 1928 victory when the first three on the leaderboard were the three reigning Majors champions from 1928. A startling record-equalling 67 in R2, and a bad third round from Diegel made the difference; Hagen only having to play solid golf over the last 18 holes to win his fourth – and last – Open. He stands, with a group of players; one behind Taylor, Braid, Peter Thomson and Tom Watson; and two behind Vardon – in the list of most wins.

Al Espinosa may have wished he hadn't bothered to tie with Bobby Jones. Jones had two 7s in his last round 79 and only made the play-off courtesy of a 12-foot putt on the last green. In his fourth Open play-off though, Jones played golf as majestic as Espinosa's was abject, winning by 23 shots, and landed his third US Open.

COURSE:	Hillcrest CC
LOCATION:	Los Angeles, California
DATE:	2-7 December
QUALIFYING:	32 qualify to matchplay after 36 holes strokeplay (Low – Fred Morrison, 136)
ROUNDS/HOLES:	All Rounds 36 holes
WINNER:	$n/k

Final

LEO DIEGEL beat Johnny Farrell, 6&4

Round 1 (Last 32)

Larry Nabholtz beat Albert Alcroft 1up; Al Watrous beat Neal McIntyre 4&3; Al Espinosa beat Dave Hackney 5&4; Bill Mehlhorn beat Guy Paulsen 7&6; Neil Christian beat Frank Walsh 7&6; Craig Wood beat Horton Smith 1up (after 37); Henry Ciuci beat Clarence Clark 3&2; JOHNNY FARRELL beat John Golden 1up; Tony Manero by Denny Shute 6&5; Eddie Schultz beat Wiffy Cox 5&4; Walter Hagen beat Bob Shave 9&8; Charles Guest beat Mortie Dutra 1up; LEO DIEGEL beat PO Hart 10&9; Herman Barron beat Clarence Doser 5&4; Gene Sarazen beat Jock Hendry 3&2; Fred Morrison beat Joe Kirkwood, Sr 5&4

Round 2 (Last 16)

Watrous beat Nabholtz 9&7

Espinosa beat Mehlhorn 1up (after 40)

Wood beat Christian 3&2

FARRELL by Ciuci 3&1

Manero beat Schultz 6&5

Hagen beat Guest 5&4

DIEGEL beat Barron 10&9

Sarazen beat Morrison 3&2

Quarter Final

Watrous beat Espinosa 2up

FARRELL beat Wood 1up (after 37)

Hagen beat Manero 6&5

DIEGEL beat Sarazen 3&2

Semi Final

FARRELL beat Watrous 6&5

DIEGEL beat Hagen 3&2

Leo Diegel not only repeated his 1928 win, he had to negotiate prevous multiple Champions – Sarazen in the quarter final; then Hagen in the semis – in doing it. In his fourth meeting with Hagen in five years, Diegel squared the series. He went on to beat 1928 US Open winner, Johnny Farrell.

BRITISH OPEN

	COURSE:	Royal Liverpool GC
	LOCATION:	Hoylake, Cheshire, England
	DATE:	18-20 June
	DISTANCE:	6750 yards
	PAR:	n/a
	WINNER:	£75

Pos	Player	1st	2nd	3rd	4th	Total
1	**BOBBY JONES** (a)	70	72	74	75	291
2 =	Leo Diegel	74	73	71	75	293
	Macdonald Smith	70	77	75	71	293
4 =	Fred Robson	71	72	78	75	296
	Horton Smith	72	73	78	73	296
6 =	Jim Barnes	71	77	72	77	297
	Archie Compston	74	73	68	82	297
8	Henry Cotton	70	79	77	73	299
9 =	Tom Barber	75	76	72	77	300
	Auguste Boyer	73	77	70	80	300
	Charles Whitcombe	74	75	72	79	300
12	Bert Hodson	74	77	76	74	301
13 =	Abe Mitchell	75	78	77	72	302
	Reg Whitcombe	78	72	73	79	302
15 =	Donald Moe (a)	74	73	76	80	303
	Phillip H Rodgers	74	73	76	80	303
17 =	Percy Alliss	75	74	77	79	305
	William Large	78	74	77	76	305
	Ernest R Whitcombe	80	72	76	77	305
	Arthur Young	75	78	78	74	305

This was Bobby Jones' year. As if his performances as an amateur over the previous eight years – against amateurs and pros – were not enough, his feats in 1930 will never be repeated. Jones played steady golf to win by two from a clutch of outstanding Americans, and the best of British – who, Compston and Cotton apart, were not of the best vintage.

US OPEN

	COURSE:	Interlachen CC
	LOCATION:	Minneapolis, Minnesota
	DATE:	10-12 July
	DISTANCE:	6609 yards
	PAR:	72 (288)
	WINNER:	$nil-Amateur

Pos	Player	1st	2nd	3rd	4th	Total
1	**BOBBY JONES** (a)	71	73	68	75	287
2	Macdonald Smith	70	75	74	70	289
3	Horton Smith	72	70	76	74	292
4	Harry Cooper	72	72	73	76	293
5	Johnny Golden	74	73	71	76	294
6	Tommy Armour	70	76	75	76	297
7	Charles Lacey	74	70	77	77	298
8	Johnny Farrell	74	72	73	80	299
9 =	Bill Mehlhorn	76	74	75	75	300
	Craig Wood	73	75	72	80	300
11 =	Leo Diegel	75	75	76	75	301
	Johnny Goodman (a)	74	80	72	75	301
	Al Heron (a)	76	78	74	73	301
	Peter O'Hara	75	77	73	76	301
	George Smith	72	81	74	74	301
	George Von Elm (a)	80	74	73	74	301
17 =	Ed Dudley	74	75	78	76	303
	Mortie Dutra	76	80	69	78	303
	Charles Guest	76	73	77	77	303
	Walter Hagen	72	75	76	80	303
	Willie Hunter, Jr	76	76	78	73	303
	Bob Shave	76	72	78	77	303
	Joe Turnesa	73	78	78	74	303
	Al Watrous	79	73	73	78	303

The Jones Bandwagon rolled on. Already possessing the British Amateur and Open titles, he won the US Open at Interlachen by two from British Open runner-up Macdonald Smith. In doing so he was the only player under par for the four rounds; he notched up his fourth US Open; and the third leg of the never-to-be-repeated Grand Slam. When he picked up the US Amateur title the following September his challenge was complete, and he retired to practise law full-time at the age of 28.

COURSE:	Fresh Meadows CC
LOCATION:	Flushing, New York
DATE:	8-13 September
QUALIFYING:	32 qualify to matchplay after 36 holes strokeplay (Low – Johnny Farrell, Horton Smith, 145)
ROUNDS/HOLES:	All Rounds 36 holes
WINNER:	$n/k

Final
TOMMY ARMOUR beat Gene Sarazen, 1up

Round 1 (Last 32)
Al Watrous beat Eric Seavall 3&1; Charles Lacey beat Charles Guest 3&2; Harold Sampson beat Clarence Ehresman 4&3; Leo Diegel beat Henry Ciuci 8&7; TOMMY ARMOUR beat Clarence Hackney 11&10; Bob Shave beat Joseph Kenny 1up; Denny Shute beat Joe Frank 8&6; Johnny Farrell beat Norman Smith 7&5; GENE SARAZEN beat Charles Schneider 1up; Bob Crowley beat Wiffy Cox 4&3; Harry Cooper beat Bill Mehlhorn 2&1; Al Espinosa beat Mark Fry 2&1; Joe Kirkwood, Sr beat Gunnar Johnson 8&7; JS Collins beat John Golden 5&4; Horton Smith beat Billy Burke 2&1; Laurie Ayton, Sr beat Earl Fry 4&3)

Round 2 (Last 16)
Lacey beat Watrous 5&4
Sampson beat Diegel 1up (after 38)
ARMOUR beat Shave 7&5
Farrell beat Shute 1up
SARAZEN beat Crowley 7&6
Espinosa beat Cooper 4&3
Kirkwood beat Collins 1up (after 37)
Horton Smith beat Ayton 5&4

Quarter Final
Lacey beat Sampson 4&3
ARMOUR beat Farrell 2&1
SARAZEN beat Espinosa 2&1
Kirkwood beat Horton Smith 1up

Semi Final
ARMOUR beat Lacey 1up
SARAZEN beat Kirkwood 5&4

The 'Silver Scot', Tommy Armour, became the last British-born golfer to win the PGA and it was not until Gary Player in 1962 that the American stranglehold on the Championship was next broken. Ex-champions Hagen and Barnes didn't make it to the matchplay stage, but, another, finalist Gene Sarazen, had his best PGA since winning in 1923.

BRITISH OPEN

COURSE:	Carnoustie GC				
LOCATION:	Carnoustie, Angus, Scotland				
DATE:	3-5 June				
DISTANCE:	6900 yards				
PAR:	n/a				
WINNER:	£100				

Pos	Player	1st	2nd	3rd	4th	Total
1	**TOMMY ARMOUR**	73	75	77	71	296
2	Jose Jurado	76	71	73	77	297
3 =	Percy Alliss	74	78	73	73	298
	Gene Sarazen	74	76	75	73	298
5 =	Johnny Farrell	72	77	75	75	299
	Macdonald Smith	75	77	71	76	299
7 =	Marcos Churio	76	75	78	71	300
	Bill Davies	76	78	71	75	300
8	Arthur Lacey	74	80	74	73	301
9 =	Henry Cotton	72	75	79	76	302
	Arthur Havers	75	76	72	79	302
11 =	Gus Faulkner	77	76	76	74	303
	Tomas Genta	75	78	75	75	303
	Abe Mitchell	77	74	77	75	303
	Horton Smith	77	79	75	72	303
	Tom Williamson	77	76	73	77	303
16 =	Marcel Dallemagne	74	77	78	75	304
	William I Hunter	76	75	74	79	304
	William Oke	74	80	75	75	304
	Reg Whitcombe	75	78	71	80	304
20 =	Aubrey Boomer	76	77	80	73	306
	Fred Robson	80	76	76	74	306

Reigning US PGA Champion, Tommy Armour, won his third different Major on the Open's first visit to mighty Carnoustie – the longest golf course of any to date for the Majors. This is also the most-northerly site of any Major Championship course, and, curiously, Argentina (with apologies to Chile!) – the southernmost stronghold of world golf – was well represented, with three players in the first 11 places. In fact Jurado was leading, five better than the winner, going into the last round. Although a naturalised American, Armour was the last Scot to win the Open before Sandy Lyle 54 years later; and the last born in Scotland before the 1999 Champion, Paul Lawrie.

US OPEN

COURSE:	Inverness GC				
LOCATION:	Toledo, Ohio				
DATE:	2-6 July				
DISTANCE:	6529 yards				
PAR:	71 (284)				
WINNER:	$1000				

Pos	Player	1st	2nd	3rd	4th	Total
1	**BILLY BURKE***	73	72	74	73	292
2	George Von Elm	75	69	73	75	292
3	Leo Diegel	75	73	74	72	294
4 =	Wiffy Cox	75	74	74	72	295
	Bill Mehlhorn	77	73	75	71	296
	Gene Sarazen	74	78	74	80	296
7 =	Mortie Dutra	71	77	73	76	297
	Walter Hagen	74	74	73	76	297
	Phil Perkins (a)	78	76	73	70	297
10 =	Al Espinosa	72	78	75	74	299
	Johnny Farrell	78	70	79	72	299
	Macdonald Smith	73	73	75	78	299
13 =	Guy Paulsen	74	72	74	80	300
	Frank Walsh	73	77	75	75	300
15 =	Herman Barron	71	75	78	77	301
	Harry Cooper	76	75	75	75	301
	Ed Dudley	75	76	76	74	301
	Al Watrous	74	78	76	73	301
19 =	Charles Guest	71	75	76	80	302
	Tony Manero	74	75	80	73	302

* Billy Burke beat George Von Elm after two 36-Hole Play-offs:

5 July – Burke (149) tied with Von Elm (149)
6 July – Burke (148) beat Von Elm (149)

It took the sixth play-off in nine years to decide who was to fill the vaccum left by Bobby Jones. The play-off had the effect of doubling the amount of golf the protagonists had to play as the result was only known at the 72nd extra hole. Perhaps surprisingly, Billy Burke, and recently-turned pro, Von Elm, tied for the lead ahead of a more-fancied Top 10, with Burke winning by one shot.

COURSE:	Wannamoisett CC
LOCATION:	Rumford, Rhode Island
DATE:	7-14 September
QUALIFYING:	31 plus the defending champion (Tommy Armour), qualify to matchplay after 36 holes strokeplay (Low – Gene Sarazen, 145)
ROUNDS/HOLES:	All Rounds 36 holes
WINNER:	$1000

Final
TOM CREAVY beat Denny Shute, 2&1

Round 1 (Last 32)
Paul Runyan beat Arthur Gusa 3&2; Gene Sarazen beat Al Espinosa 9&8; Willie MacFarlane beat Henry Ciuci 3&2; Horton Smith beat Walter Bemish 7&6; Cyril Walker beat Ed Dudley 3&2; John Golden beat Alfred Sargent 3&2; Peter O'Hara beat Walter Hagen 4&3; TOM CREAVY beat Jack Collins 5&4; Bob Crowley beat Pat Circelli 1up; Billy Burke beat Dave Hackney 5&3; Abe Espinosa by Vincent Eldred 4&3; Bill Mehlhorn beat Leo Diegel 3&2; DENNY SHUTE beat Tony Butler 1up (after 38); Jim Foulis beat Johnny Farrell 2up; Tommy Armour beat Joe Kirkwood, Sr 2&1; Walter Murray beat Eddie Schultz 6&5

Round 2 (Last 16)
Sarazen beat Runyan 7&6; Smith beat McaFarlane 6&5; Walker beat Golden 5&4; CREAVY beat O'Hara 2up; Burke beat Crowley 5&4; Abe Espinosa beat Mehlhorn 2&1; SHUTE beat Foulis 2&1; Armour beat Murray 5&3

Quarter Final
Sarazen beat Smith 5&4
CREAVY beat Walker 3&1
Burke beat Abe Espinosa 5&3
SHUTE beat Armour 3&1

Semi Final
CREAVY beat Sarazen 5&3
SHUTE beat Burke 1up

Tom Creavy beat former US Open Champions, Cyril Walker and Gene Sarazen on his way to a Major at the age of 20. After featuring quite well for the next year or two in the PGA and appearing in the US Open Top 10 of 1934, Creavy was struck down by a debilitating illness and faded into obscurity.

BRITISH OPEN

COURSE:	Prince's GC
LOCATION:	Sandwich, Kent, England
DATE:	8-10 June
DISTANCE:	6983 yards
PAR:	71 (284)
WINNER:	£100

Pos	Player	1st	2nd	3rd	4th	Total
1	**GENE SARAZEN**	70	69	70	74	283
2	Macdonald Smith	71	76	71	70	288
3	Arthur Havers	74	71	68	76	289
4 =	Percy Alliss	71	71	78	72	292
	Alf Padgham	76	72	74	70	292
	Charles Whitcombe	71	73	75	73	292
7 =	Bill Davies	71	73	74	75	293
	Arthur Lacey	73	73	71	76	293
9	Fred Robson	74	71	78	71	294
10 =	Archie Compston	74	70	75	76	295
	Henry Cotton	74	72	77	72	295
	Abe Mitchell	77	71	75	72	295
13 =	Syd Easterbrook	74	75	72	77	298
	H Prowse	75	75	75	73	298
15 =	CS Denny	73	81	72	73	299
	WL Hope (a)	74	79	75	71	299
17 =	Tommy Armour	75	70	74	81	300
	Bert Hodson	77	73	77	73	300
	Alf Perry	73	76	77	74	300
	Charlie Ward	73	77	77	73	300
	Reg Whitcombe	75	74	75	76	300

Sarazen joined Hagen, Barnes and Armour in a select band who had won all three Majors. A record 36- and 54-hole total for either Open set the scene for a comfortable victory. The Prince's Club, adjacent to Royal St George's, was host to the Open for the one and only time.

US OPEN

COURSE:	Fresh Meadow CC
LOCATION:	Flushing, New York
DATE:	23-25 June
DISTANCE:	6815 yards
PAR:	70 (280)
WINNER:	$1000

Pos	Player	1st	2nd	3rd	4th	Total
1	**GENE SARAZEN**	74	76	70	66	286
2 =	Bobby Cruickshank	78	74	69	68	289
	Phil Perkins	76	69	74	70	289
4	Leo Diegel	73	74	73	74	294
5	Wiffy Cox	80	73	70	72	295
6	Jose Jurado	74	71	75	76	296
7 =	Billy Burke	75	77	74	71	297
	Harry Cooper	77	73	73	74	297
	Olin Dutra	69	77	75	76	297
10	Walter Hagen	75	73	79	71	298
11	Clarence Clark	79	72	74	75	300
12 =	Vincent Eldred	78	73	77	73	301
	Paul Runyan	79	77	69	76	301
14 =	Henry Ciuci	77	74	77	74	302
	Ed Dudley	80	74	71	77	302
	Johnny Goodman (a)	79	78	77	68	302
	Fred Morrison	77	80	69	76	302
	Denny Shute	78	76	76	72	302
	Macdonald Smith	80	76	74	72	302
	Craig Wood	79	71	79	73	302

After setting records at the British Open the previous month, Gene Sarazen became the second man after Bobby Jones to lift both Opens in the same season. If the earlier rounds were his strength at Sandwich, it was his final 36-hole low of 136 (including a record for both Opens with his last round of 66) which provided the victory at Fresh Meadow. English amateur Phil Perkins (runner-up to Bob Jones in the 1928 US Amateur) had just turned professional and led after 54 holes, eventually tying second. His game was somewhat hampered in future after picking up a gun-shot wound to the thigh later that year.

COURSE:	Keller GC
LOCATION:	St Paul, Minnesota
DATE:	31 August–4 September
QUALIFYING:	31 plus the defending champion (Tom Creavy), qualify to matchplay after 36 holes strokeplay (Low – Olin Dutra, 140)
ROUNDS/HOLES:	All Rounds 36 holes
WINNER:	$1000

Final
OLIN DUTRA beat Frank Walsh, 4&3

Round 1 (Last 32)
OLIN DUTRA beat George Smith 9&8; Reggie Myles beat Horton Smith 1up (after 37); Herman Barron beat Neal McIntyre 8&7; Abe Espinosa beat Eddie Schultz 4&3; Henry Picard beat Charles Lacey 6&4; Ed Dudley beat Joe Turnesa 8&7; Al Collins beat Gunnar Nelson 5&4; John Golden beat Walter Hagen 1up (after 43); Vincent Eldred beat Paul Runyan 1up (after 38); Bobby Cruickshank beat Al Watrous 1up (after 41 holes); Gene Kunes beat Craig Wood 3&2; FRANK WALSH beat Ted Longworth 7&6; Ralph Stonehouse beat Vic Ghezzi 6&5; John Kinder beat Joe Kirkwood, Sr 1up; Johnny Perelli beat Denny Shute 3&2; Tom Creavy beat Jimmy Hines 7&6

Round 2 (Last 16)
DUTRA by Myles 5&3; Barron beat Espinosa 1up (after 38); Dudley beat Picard 10&9; Collins beat Golden 1up; Cruickshank beat Eldred 3&1; WALSH beat Kunes 9&8; Stonehouse beat Kinder 3&2; Creavy beat Perelli 1up

Quarter Final
DUTRA beat Barron 5&4
Dudley beat Collins 1up (after 38)
WALSH beat Cruickshank 8&7
Creavy beat Stonehouse 3&2

Semi Final
DUTRA beat Dudley 3&2
WALSH beat Creavy 1up (after 38)

Olin Dutra proved that his qualifying score was no fluke. However, he was helped by notables such as Armour, Cooper and Billy Burke not making the matchplay 32, and the early round exits of Horton Smith and Walter Hagen. In Round One, a generous act by Al Watrous backfired. Nine-up with just 12 to play, he conceded a testing two-footer to Cruickshank. The match result tells the story.

1933

COURSE:	Royal & Ancient GC
LOCATION:	St Andrews, Fife, Scotland
DATE:	5-7 July
DISTANCE:	6500 yards
PAR:	n/a
WINNER:	£100

COURSE:	North Shore CC
LOCATION:	Glenview, Illinois
DATE:	1-2 August
DISTANCE:	6927 yards
PAR:	72 (288)
WINNER:	$nil-Amateur

Pos	Player	1st	2nd	3rd	4th	Total
1	**DENNY SHUTE***	73	73	73	73	292
2	Craig Wood	77	72	68	75	292
3 =	Leo Diegel	75	70	71	77	293
	Syd Easterbrook	73	72	71	77	293
	Gene Sarazen	72	73	73	75	293
6	Olin Dutra	76	76	70	72	294
7 =	Henry Cotton	73	71	72	79	295
	Ed Dudley	70	71	76	78	295
	Abe Mitchell	74	68	74	79	295
	Alf Padgham	74	73	74	74	295
	Reg Whitcombe	76	75	72	72	295
12 =	Archie Compston	72	74	77	73	296
	Ernest R Whitcombe	73	73	75	75	296
14 =	Auguste Boyer	76	72	70	79	297
	Arthur Havers	80	72	71	74	297
	Joe Kirkwood, Sr	72	73	71	81	297
	Horton Smith	73	73	75	76	297
18 =	Aubrey Boomer	74	70	76	78	298
	Jack M'Lean (a)	75	74	75	74	298
	Cyril Tolley (a)	70	73	76	79	298

Pos	Player	1st	2nd	3rd	4th	Total
1	**JOHNNY GOODMAN** (a)	75	66	70	76	287
2	Ralph Guldahl	76	71	70	71	288
3	Craig Wood	73	74	71	72	290
4 =	Tommy Armour	68	75	76	73	292
	Walter Hagen	73	76	77	66	292
6	Mortie Dutra	75	73	72	74	294
7 =	Olin Dutra	75	71	75	74	295
	Gus Moreland (a)	76	76	71	72	295
9 =	Clarence Clark	80	72	72	72	296
	Johnny Farrell	75	77	72	72	296
	Willie Goggin	79	73	73	71	296
	Joe Kirkwood, Sr	74	70	79	73	296
13 =	Herman Barron	77	77	74	69	297
	Al Watrous	74	76	77	70	297
15 =	Henry Ciuci	73	79	74	72	298
	Johnny Revolta	73	76	75	74	298
17 =	George Dawson (a)	78	74	71	76	299
	Leo Diegel	78	71	75	75	299
19 =	Lester Bolstad (a)	76	74	73	77	300
	Macdonald Smith	77	72	77	74	300

* Denny Shute (149) beat Craig Wood (154) in the 36-Hole Play-off

Always listed in British records and newspapers as 'Densmore', Denny Shute won his first Major, and only British Open, at the Home of Golf. In one of the tightest-ever finishes, only three shots covered the first 11 home. Craig Wood tied Shute on 292, but, as was to be his fashion for some years to come it seems, he lost the play-off. Shute's regulation four rounds all took 73 strokes; the consistency of which has never been equalled in a Major Championship, before or since.

Johnny Goodman was the last amateur to win any Major. He equalled Sarazen's Open low of 66 in R2 and was never headed after that. Like Ouimet, Evans and Jones previously, he won the Open before taking the Amateur Championship (in 1937). Hagen, aged 41, also shot a 66 – in R4 – his best strokeplay score in the Majors. From this year on (apart from peculiar changes around, and just after, the War with the PGA Championship) the present order of Majors in the golfing calendar was to prevail.

US PGA

COURSE:	Blue Mound CC
LOCATION:	Milwaukee, Wisconsin
DATE:	8-13 August
QUALIFYING:	31 plus the defending champion (Olin Dutra), qualify to matchplay after 36 holes strokeplay (Low – Mortie Dutra, Jimmy Hines, 138)
ROUNDS/HOLES:	All Rounds 36 holes
WINNER:	$1000

Final

GENE SARAZEN beat Willie Goggin, 5&4

Round 1 (Last 32)

Jimmy Hines beat Mortie Dutra 3&2; Henry Picard beat Willie Klein 2&1; Frank Walsh beat Jack Curley 3&2; Tom Creavy beat Dick Metz 3&2; Al Espinosa beat Charles Schneider 3&2; WILLIE GOGGIN beat Leo Diegel 4&3; Paul Runyan beat Al Houghton 6&5; Johnny Revolta beat Alex Gerlak 12&11; Clarence Clark beat Horton Smith 6&5; Ed Dudley beat Ben Pautke 2&1; GENE SARAZEN beat Vincent Eldred 8&7; Harry Cooper beat Dave Hackney 6&5; John Golden beat Gunnar Johnson 4&3; Bobby Cruickshank beat Bunny Torpey 3&2; Johnny Farrell beat Vic Ghezzi 1up; Olin Dutra beat Reggie Myles 4&3

Round 2 (Last 16)

Hines beat Picard 5&3; Creavy beat Walsh 2&1; GOGGIN beat Espinosa 9&7; Runyan beat Revolta 2&1; Dudley beat Clark 3&1; SARAZEN beat Cooper 4&3; Golden beat Cruickshank 2&1; Farrell beat Olin Dutra 1up

Quarter Final

Hines beat Creavy 4&3
GOGGIN beat Runyan 6&5
SARAZEN beat Dudley 675
Farrell beat Golden 5&4

Semi Final

GOGGIN beat Hines 1up
SARAZEN beat Farrell 5&4

'Pretty good for a washed up golfer', commented Gene Sarazen, when he collected his third PGA title – countering a jibe from Tommy Armour that the little man was past his best. Hagen, along with the pair who tied for the British Open a month earlier, Shute and Wood, declined to enter the Championship. I don't think Sarazen minded too much as Major Number Six went into the record books.

1934

COURSE:	Augusta National GC
LOCATION:	Augusta, Georgia
DATE:	22-25 March
DISTANCE:	6925 yards
PAR:	72 (288)
WINNER:	$1500

COURSE:	Merion Cricket Club
LOCATION:	Ardmore, Pennsylvania
DATE:	7-9 June
DISTANCE:	6694 yards
PAR:	70 (280)
WINNER:	$1000

Pos	Player	1st	2nd	3rd	4th	Total
1	**HORTON SMITH**	70	72	70	72	284
2	Craig Wood	71	74	69	71	285
3 =	Billy Burke	72	71	70	73	286
	Paul Runyan	74	71	70	71	286
5	Ed Dudley	74	69	71	74	288
6	Willie MacFarlane	74	73	70	74	291
7 =	Al Espinosa	75	70	75	72	292
	Jimmy Hines	70	74	74	74	292
	Harold McSpaden	77	74	72	69	292
	MacDonald Smith	74	70	74	74	292
11 =	Mortie Dutra	74	75	71	73	293
	Al Watrous	74	74	71	74	293
13 =	Walter Hagen	71	76	70	77	294
	Bobby Jones (a)	76	74	72	72	294
	Denny Shute	73	73	76	72	294
16 =	Leo Diegel	73	72	74	76	295
	Ralph Stonehouse	74	70	75	76	295
18 =	Ky Laffoon	72	79	72	73	296
	Johnny Revolta	75	72	75	74	296
	WJ Schwartz	75	72	71	78	296

Pos	Player	1st	2nd	3rd	4th	Total
1	**OLIN DUTRA**	76	74	71	72	293
2	Gene Sarazen	73	72	73	76	294
3 =	Harry Cooper	76	74	74	71	295
	Wiffy Cox	71	75	74	75	295
	Bobby Cruickshank	71	71	77	76	295
6 =	Billy Burke	76	71	77	72	296
	Macdonald Smith	75	73	78	70	296
8 =	Tom Creavy	79	76	78	76	299
	Ralph Guldahl	78	73	70	78	299
	Jimmy Hines	80	70	77	72	299
	Johnny Revolta	76	73	77	73	299
12 =	Joe Kirkwood, Sr	75	73	78	74	300
	Ted Luther	78	71	78	73	300
14 =	Willie Hunter, Jr	75	74	80	72	301
	Alvin Krueger	76	75	75	75	301
16	Mark Fry	79	75	74	74	302
17 =	Henry Ciuci	74	74	79	76	303
	Leo Diegel	76	71	78	78	303
	Johnny Golden	75	76	74	78	303
	Horton Smith	74	73	79	77	303

At the inaugural 'Masters' – properly called at the time, the Augusta National Invitational – Horton Smith's 20-foot putt for a birdie at 17 sealed the fate of Craig Wood once again. Bobby Jones came out of retirement to play in this, the tournament he devised, on a course he helped design; and finished in a tie for 13th with his erstwhile adversary, Walter Hagen.

Olin Dutra made up eight strokes on the 36-hole leader, Bobby Cruickshank to add a second Major to his 1932 PGA triumph. Despite not having played golf for ten days due to a crippling dysentery, he picked up two birdies on the last nine holes to overhaul Cruickshank, Cox and Sarazen – the last shooting a three over par seven at the 11th hole.

BRITISH OPEN

	COURSE:	Royal St George's GC
	LOCATION:	Sandwich, Kent, England
	DATE:	27-29 June
	DISTANCE:	6776 yards
	PAR:	n/k
	WINNER:	£100

Pos	Player	1st	2nd	3rd	4th	Total
1	**HENRY COTTON**	67	65	72	79	283
2	Sid Brews	76	71	70	71	288
3	Alf Padgham	71	70	75	74	290
4 =	Marcel Dallemagne	71	73	71	77	292
	Joe Kirkwood, Sr	74	69	71	78	292
	Macdonald Smith	77	71	72	72	292
7 =	Bert Hodson	71	74	74	76	295
	Charles Whitcombe	71	72	74	78	295
9 =	Percy Alliss	73	75	71	77	296
	Ernest R Whitcombe	72	77	73	74	296
11	William Twine	72	76	75	74	297
12	John Burton	80	72	72	74	298
13 =	Bill Davies	76	68	73	82	299
	Edward Jarman	74	76	74	75	299
	Charlie Ward	76	71	72	70	299
16 =	Allan Dailey	74	73	78	75	300
	James McDowall	73	74	76	77	300
	Jack M'Lean (a)	77	76	69	78	300
	Reg Whitcombe	75	76	74	75	300
20	Denny Shute	71	72	80	78	301

After ten years of American dominance, there was a British winner at Sandwich. Henry Cotton's second round score of 65 was not beaten in the Open until 1977. His 36- and 54-hole totals smashed all existing Majors records.

Macdonald Smith was the leading American – nine behind Cotton – but it is fair to say that the trans-Atlantic presence was not as numerous as in previous years.

US PGA

	COURSE:	Park Club of Buffalo
	LOCATION:	Williamsville, New York
	DATE:	24-29 July
	QUALIFYING:	31 plus the defending champion (Gene Sarazen), qualify to matchplay after 36 holes strokeplay (Low – Bob Crowley, 138)
	ROUNDS/HOLES:	All Rounds 36 holes
	WINNER:	$1000

Final
PAUL RUNYAN beat Craig Wood, 1up (after 38)

Round 1 (Last 32)
Gene Sarazen beat Herman Barron 3&2; Al Watrous beat Errie Ball 8&7; Harry Cooper beat Bill Mehlhorn 4&2; CRAIG WOOD beat Leo Fraser 6&5; Ky Laffoon beat George Smith 12&10; Denny Shute beat Walter Hagen 4&3; Al Houghton beat George Christ 7&6; Fay Coleman beat Leo Diegel 4&2; Dick Metz beat Joe Paletti 6&5; Tommy Armour beat Byron Nelson 4&3; Vic Ghezzi beat Eddie Burke 2&1; PAUL RUNYAN beat Johnny Farrell 8&6; Johnny Revolta beat Jim Foulis 7&6; Gene Kunes beat Orville White 3&2; Ted Turner beat Willie Goggin 1up (after 37); Bob Crowley beat Eddie Loos 3&2

Round 2 (Last 16)
Watrous beat Sarazen 4&3; WOOD beat Cooper 4&3; Shute beat Laffoon 3&2; Houghton beat Coleman 4&3; Metz beat Armour 3&2; RUNYAN beat Ghezzi 2&1; Kunes beat Revolta 2&1; Crowley beat Turner 1up

Quarter Final
WOOD beat Watrous 2&1
Shute beat Houghton 6&5
RUNYAN beat Metz 1up
Kunes beat Crowley 4&3

Semi Final
WOOD beat Shute 2&1
RUNYAN beat Kunes 4&2

Craig Wood wreaked revenge on Denny Shute for his 1933 British Open play-off defeat. Victory was still not to be for Wood, though, as he missed out again; after extra holes to leading money-winner, Paul Runyan.

THE MASTERS

COURSE:	Augusta National GC
LOCATION:	Augusta, Georgia
DATE:	4-8 April
DISTANCE:	6925 yards
PAR:	72 (288)
WINNER:	$1500

COURSE:	Oakmont CC
LOCATION:	Oakmont, Pennsylvania
DATE:	6-8 June
DISTANCE:	6981 yards
PAR:	72 (288)
WINNER:	$1000

Pos	Player	1st	2nd	3rd	4th	Total
1	**GENE SARAZEN***	68	71	73	70	282
2	Craig Wood	69	72	68	73	282
3	Olin Dutra	70	70	70	74	284
4	Henry Picard	67	68	76	75	286
5	Denny Shute	73	71	70	73	287
6	Lawson Little (a)	74	72	70	72	288
7	Paul Runyan	70	72	75	72	289
8	Vic Ghezzi	73	71	73	73	290
9 =	Bobby Cruickshank	76	70	73	72	291
	Jimmy Hines	70	70	77	74	291
	Byron Nelson	71	74	72	74	291
	Joe Turnesa	73	71	74	73	291
13 =	Ray Mangrum	68	71	76	77	292
	Johnny Revolta	70	74	73	75	292
15 =	Walter Hagen	73	69	72	79	293
	Sam Parks Jr	74	70	74	75	293
17 =	John Dawson (a)	75	72	72	75	294
	Al Espinosa	76	72	73	73	294
19 =	Clarence Clark	77	75	73	71	296
	Leo Diegel	72	73	74	77	296
	Ed Dudley	73	73	74	76	296
	Harold McSpaden	75	72	75	74	296
	Horton Smith	74	75	74	73	296
	Charlie Yates (a)	75	70	76	75	296

Pos	Player	1st	2nd	3rd	4th	Total
1	**SAM PARKS, Jr**	77	73	73	76	299
2	Jimmy Thomson	73	73	77	78	301
3	Walter Hagen	77	76	73	76	302
4 =	Ray Mangrum	76	76	72	79	303
	Denny Shute	78	73	76	76	303
6 =	Alvin Krueger	71	77	78	80	306
	Henry Picard	79	78	70	79	306
	Gene Sarazen	75	74	78	79	306
	Horton Smith	73	79	79	75	306
10 =	Dick Metz	77	76	76	78	307
	Paul Runyan	76	77	79	75	307
12 =	Olin Dutra	77	76	78	77	308
	Vincent Eldred	75	77	77	79	308
14 =	Herman Barron	73	79	78	79	309
	Bobby Cruickshank	78	76	77	78	309
	Mortie Dutra	75	77	80	77	309
	Macdonald Smith	74	82	76	77	309
	Ted Turner	80	71	81	77	309
	Al Watrous	75	80	79	75	309
20	Vic Ghezzi	75	78	81	77	311

* Gene Sarazen (144) beat Craig Wood (149) in the 36-Hole Play-off

The Masters reputation was forever set, back in 1935, with just one golf shot. Gene Sarazen's double-eagle on the par 15th, achieved by a miraculous fairway wood approach from 220 yards, did for poor Craig Wood yet again. The ensuing newspaper hype brought national attention to this Southern off-season tournament – and the rest became history. Sarazen also made history of another kind. He became the first of only four players (Hogan, Nicklaus and Player, the others) to win all four Majors – the first modern Grand Slam. This was his last Majors win.

The 11-over par winning total was a testimony to the Oakmont trial. A look at the final round scores says more than any words can. Sam Parks, fresh out of college, was a surprise winner. He was pro at the nearby South Hills CC, though, and was certainly helped by his local knowledge of Oakmont.

COURSE:	Honourable Company of Edinburgh Golfers
LOCATION:	Muirfield, East Lothian, Scotland
DATE:	26-28 June
DISTANCE:	6806 yards
PAR:	n/k
WINNER:	£100

Pos	Player	1st	2nd	3rd	4th	Total
1	**ALF PERRY**	69	75	67	72	283
2	Alf Padgham	70	72	74	71	287
3	Charles Whitcombe	71	68	73	76	288
4 =	Bert Gadd	72	75	71	71	289
	Lawson Little (a)	75	71	74	69	289
6	Henry Picard	72	73	72	75	292
7 =	Henry Cotton	68	74	76	75	293
	Syd Easterbrook	75	73	74	71	293
8	William Branch	71	73	76	74	294
9	Laurie Ayton, Sr	74	73	77	71	295
10	Auguste Boyer	74	75	76	71	296
11 =	Aubrey Boomer	76	69	75	77	297
	JJ Busson	75	76	70	76	297
	Bill Cox	76	69	77	75	297
	Ernest WH Kenyon	70	74	74	79	297
15 =	Percy Alliss	72	76	75	75	298
	JA Jacobs	78	74	75	71	298
17 =	W Laidlaw	74	71	75	79	299
	Philip H Rodgers	74	76	74	75	299
	Mark Seymour	75	76	75	73	299
	Macdonald Smith	69	77	75	78	299
	Ernest R Whitcombe	75	72	74	78	299

Once again a light assault from the Americans facilitated another home victory. Alf Perry's only win owed much to an excellent start and a record-equalling third round. With Fred (no relation) also winning at Wimbledon, it was a good year for the Perrys! Double-double Amateur Champion in the making (US & British, 1934-35), Lawson Little was the best-placed overseas player.

COURSE:	Twin Hills CC
LOCATION:	Oklahoma City, Oklahoma
DATE:	18-23 October
QUALIFYING:	63 plus the defending champion (Paul Runyan), qualify to matchplay after 36 holes strokeplay (Low – Walter Hagen, 139)
ROUNDS/HOLES:	Rs1&2, 18 holes: R3,QF,SF&F, 36
WINNER:	$1000

Final

JOHNNY REVOLTA beat Tommy Armour, 5&4

Round 2 (Last 32)

Paul Runyan beat Mortie Dutra 3&2; Tony Manero beat Clarence Doser 1up; Levi Lynch beat Art Bell 4&2; Al Zimmerman beat Vic Ghezzi 2&1; Pat Cicelli beat Orville White 3&2; JOHNNY REVOLTA beat Jimmy Hines 1up; Alvin Krueger beat Gene Sarazen 2&1; Eddie Schultz beat G Slingerland 2&1; Al Watrous beat Harold Sampson 2&1; Sam Parks, Jr beat Francis Scheider 1up; Horton Smith beat Ray Mangrum 1up; Denny Shute beat Henry Bontempo 4&3; Jimmy Thomson beat JG Collins 6&4; Ed Dudley beat Dick Metz 3&1; Ky Laffoon beat Eddie Loos 1up (after 21); TOMMY ARMOUR beat Charles Schneider 3&2

Round 3 (Last 16)

Runyan beat Manero 9&8; Zimmerman beat Lynch 7&6; REVOLTA beat Circelli 4&2; Schultz beat Krueger 1up (after 37); Watrous beat Parks, Jr 4&3; Smith beat Shute 2&1; Dudley beat Thomson 6&4; ARMOUR beat Laffoon 3&2

Quarter Final

Zimmerman beat Runyan 3&2; REVOLTA beat Schultz 4&2; Watrous beat Smith 1up; ARMOUR beat Dudley 1up (after 39)

Semi Final

REVOLTA beat Zimmerman 4&3
ARMOUR beat Watrous 2&1

The Championship format was changed from this year to allow more players into the matchplay stage. It was to remain in this format for most of the remaining years until it gave way to medal play totally in 1958. Johnny Revolta stopped Tommy Armour claiming his second PGA with a comfortable win in a final which was played in quite wintry conditions.

THE MASTERS

COURSE:	Augusta National GC
LOCATION:	Augusta, Georgia
DATE:	2-5 April
DISTANCE:	6925 yards
PAR:	72 (288)
WINNER:	$1500

Pos	Player	1st	2nd	3rd	4th	Total
1	**HORTON SMITH**	74	71	68	72	285
2	Harry Cooper	70	69	71	76	286
3	Gene Sarazen	78	67	72	70	287
4 =	Bobby Cruickshank	75	69	74	72	290
	Paul Runyan	76	69	70	75	290
6 =	Ed Dudley	75	75	70	73	293
	Ky Laffoon	75	70	75	73	293
	Ray Mangrum	76	73	68	76	293
9 =	John Dawson (a)	77	70	70	77	294
	Henry Picard	75	72	74	73	294
11 =	Walter Hagen	77	74	73	72	296
	Denny Shute	76	68	75	77	296
13 =	Wiffy Cox	82	69	75	72	298
	Byron Nelson	76	71	77	74	298
15 =	Al Espinosa	72	73	75	79	299
	Vic Ghezzi	77	70	77	75	299
	Harold McSpaden	77	75	71	76	299
	Jimmy Thomson	76	78	71	74	299
	Orville White	78	73	77	71	299
20 =	Tommy Armour	79	74	72	75	300
	Chick Chin	76	74	71	79	300
	Lawson Little	75	75	73	77	300
	Sam Parks, Jr	76	75	72	77	300
	Craig Wood	88	67	69	76	300

Within the course of three years, Horton Smith won his second and last Masters, and second and last Major. He overcame Harry Cooper – another with the regular propensity to lose Majors when in contention – to turn a three-shot deficit into a one-stroke victory. Smith chipped in from 50 feet at the 14th and came home under par from there.

US OPEN

COURSE:	Baltusrol GC
LOCATION:	Springfield, New Jersey
DATE:	4-6 June
DISTANCE:	6866 yards
PAR:	72 (288)
WINNER:	$1000

Pos	Player	1st	2nd	3rd	4th	Total
1	**TONY MANERO**	73	69	73	67	282
2	Harry Cooper	71	70	70	73	284
3	Clarence Clark	69	75	71	72	287
4	Macdonald Smith	73	73	72	70	288
5 =	Wiffy Cox	74	74	69	72	289
	Ky Laffoon	71	74	70	74	289
	Henry Picard	70	71	74	74	289
8 =	Ralph Guldahl	73	70	73	74	290
	Paul Runyan	69	75	73	73	290
10	Denny Shute	72	69	73	77	291
11 =	Herman Barron	73	74	69	76	292
	Tom Kerrigan	70	75	72	75	292
	Ray Mangrum	69	71	76	76	292
14 =	Charles Kocsis (a)	72	71	73	77	293
	Frank Moore	70	74	75	74	293
	Johnny Revolta	70	71	77	75	293
	Jimmy Thomson	74	73	71	75	293
18 =	Billy Burke	72	76	72	74	294
	Vic Ghezzi	70	70	73	81	294
	Willie Goggin	73	73	72	76	294
	Harold McSpaden	75	71	78	70	294

Just to prove he could do it again, just two months after the Masters, Cooper, five strokes clear over the field, saw Tony Manero charge past with a brilliant 67 to win by two. Chick Evans' 20-year low score of 286 for the US Open had been finally beaten, as had the 283 set (successively) by Sarazen, Cotton and Perry in the British Open. Manero was relatively unknown, and although would be around for a few years, he never won another Major.

COURSE:	Royal Liverpool GC
LOCATION:	Hoylake, Cheshire, England
DATE:	24-26 June
DISTANCE:	7078 yards
PAR:	n/k
WINNER:	£100

Pos	Player	1st	2nd	3rd	4th	Total
1	**ALF PADGHAM**	73	72	71	71	287
2	Jimmy Adams	71	73	71	73	288
3 =	Henry Cotton	73	72	70	74	289
	Marcel Dallemagne	73	72	75	69	289
5 =	Percy Alliss	74	72	74	71	291
	Tom Green	74	72	70	75	291
	Gene Sarazen	73	75	70	73	291
8 =	Arthur Lacey	76	74	72	72	294
	Bobby Locke (a)	75	73	72	74	294
	Reg Whitcombe	72	77	71	74	294
11	Dai Rees	77	71	72	75	295
12 =	Dick Burton	74	71	75	76	296
	Bill Cox	70	74	79	73	296
14	Bill Davies	72	76	73	77	298
15 =	Aubrey Boomer	74	75	75	75	299
	Wally Smithers	75	73	77	74	299
	Hector Thomson (a)	76	76	73	74	299
	Ted Turner	75	74	76	74	299
19 =	Gordon Good	75	73	79	73	300
	Charles Whitcombe	73	76	79	72	300

Consistent solid golf gave Alf Padgham his only Open win.
Gene Sarazen was there, but precious few other US stars.
Although no official par figures are available for the Open
Championship courses via the R&A at this time, where
figures do appear they are courtesy of the clubs or
contemporary newspaper reports. Over the first 7000+ yard
course prepared for any Major, Hoylake's Scratch score
was 76 in 1936.

COURSE:	Pinehurst CC
LOCATION:	Pinehurst, North Carolina
DATE:	17-22 November
QUALIFYING:	63 plus the defending champion (Johnny Revolta), qualify to matchplay after 36 holes strokeplay (Low – Fay Coleman, 143)
ROUNDS/HOLES:	Rs1&2, 18holes: R3,QF,SF&F, 36
WINNER:	$1000

Final
DENNY SHUTE beat Jimmy Thompson, 3&2

Round 2 (Last 32)
Harold McSpaden beat Johnny Revolta 1up (after 19); Leo
Walper beat Clarence Hackney 2&1; JIMMY THOMSON
beat Willie Klein 3&2; Henry Picard beat Alvin Krueger
5&4; Harry Cooper beat Clarence Doser 3&2; Craig Wood
beat Frank Walsh 1up; Bobby Cruickshank beat Errie Ball
2&1; Tony Manero beat Mortie Dutra 6&5; Horton Smith
beat Jack Patroni 6&5; Willie Goggin beat Les Madison
5&4; DENNY SHUTE beat Al Zimmerman 3&2; Billy Burke
beat Ky Laffoon 4&3; Bill Mehlhorn beat Dick Metz 1up
(after 23); Ed Dudley beat Tom LoPresti 2&1; Jimmy Hines
beat Ray Mangrum 2&1; Vic Ghezzi beat Fay Coleman 1up

Round 3 (Last 16)
McSpaden beat Walper 4&3; THOMSON beat Picard 4&2;
Wood beat Cooper 2&1; Manero beat Cruickshank 4&2;
Smith beat Goggin 2&1; SHUTE beat Burke 2&1; Mehlhorn
beat Dudley 6&4; Hines beat Ghezzi 4&3

Quarter Final
THOMSON beat McSpaden 1up
Wood beat Manero 5&4
SHUTE beat Smith 3&2
Mehlhorn beat Hines 4&2

Semi Final
THOMSON beat Wood 5&4
SHUTE beat Mehlhorn 1up

Shute beat Jimmy Thomson to add a PGA title to his 1933
British Open. It was a bad event for former Champions.
Hagen and Diegel didn't qualify and Sarazen, Armour and
Runyan were eliminated in R1. Defending Champion,
Revolta, also went out early. Pinehurst's belated first Major,
and even more surprisingly, its only one until it gained
USGA recognition finally for the 1999 US Open.

THE MASTERS

US PGA

COURSE:	Augusta National GC			
LOCATION:	Augusta, Georgia			
DATE:	1-4 April			
DISTANCE:	6925 yards			
PAR:	72 (288)			
WINNER:	$1500			

Pos	Player	1st	2nd	3rd	4th	Total
1	**BYRON NELSON**	66	72	75	70	283
2	Ralph Guldahl	69	72	68	76	285
3	Ed Dudley	70	71	71	74	286
4	Harry Cooper	73	69	71	74	287
5	Ky Laffoon	73	70	74	73	290
6	Jimmy Thomson	71	73	74	73	291
7	Al Watrous	74	72	71	75	292
8 =	Tommy Armour	73	75	73	72	293
	Vic Ghezzi	72	72	72	77	293
10 =	Leonard Dodson	71	75	71	77	294
	Jimmy Hines	77	72	68	77	294
12	Wiffy Cox	70	72	77	76	295
13 =	Clarence Clark	77	75	70	74	296
	Tony Manero	71	72	78	75	296
	Johnny Revolta	71	72	72	81	296
	Denny Shute	74	75	71	76	296
17	Bobby Cruickshank	79	69	71	78	297
18	Sam Snead	76	72	71	79	298
19 =	Lawson Little	70	79	74	76	299
	Willie MacFarlane	73	76	73	77	299
	Paul Runyan	74	77	72	76	299
	Felix Serafin	75	76	71	77	299
	Horton Smith	75	72	77	75	299

Byron Nelson burst on to the scene. After a faltering start to his career, the 1937 Masters was his big breakthrough. He set a new low of 66 for the Tournament and led at half-way. Then a bad third round let in Ralph Guldahl for a four-stroke lead going into the last round. A combination of the latter's bad figures thereafter, and Nelson's two-under par last round, turned it all round.

COURSE:	Pittsburgh Field Club			
LOCATION:	Aspinwall, Pennsylvania			
DATE:	26-30 May			
QUALIFYING:	63 plus the defending champion (Denny Shute), qualify to matchplay after 36 holes strokeplay (Low – Byron Nelson, 139)			
ROUNDS/HOLES:	Rs1&2, 18holes: R3,QF,SF&F, 36			
WINNER:	$1000			

Final
DENNY SHUTE beat Harold McSpaden, 1up (after 37)

Round 2 (Last 32)
DENNY SHUTE beat Olin Dutra 3&2; Ed Dudley beat Pat Wilcox 4&3; Paul Runyan beat Willie Goggin 2&1; Jimmy Hines beat Al Espinosa 1up; Harry Cooper beat Johnny Revolta 1up; Jim Foulis beat Gene Sarazen 1up; Vic Ghezzi beat Sam Parks, Jr 1up; Tony Manero beat Willie MacFarlane 4&3; Byron Nelson beat Craig Wood 4&2; Johnny Farrell beat Charles Schneider 1up; Ky Laffoon beat Billy Burke 2&1; Jimmy Thomson beat Ralph Guldahl 2&1; HAROLD McSPADEN beat Bunny Torpey 1up (after 20); Sam Snead beat Alvin Krueger 2up; Henry Picard beat Sam Bernardi 1up; Horton Smith beat Al Watrous 1up (after 19)

Round 3 (Last 16)
SHUTE beat Dudley 3&2; Hines beat Runyan 2&1; Cooper beat Foulis 5&4; Manero by Ghezzi 3&1; Nelson beat Farrell 5&4; Laffoon beat Thomson 4&3; McSPADEN beat Snead 3&2; Picard beat Smith 4&3

Quarter Final
SHUTE beat Hines 4&3; Manero beat Cooper 1up; Laffoon beat Nelson 2up; McSPADEN beat Picard 1up (after 39)

Semi Final
SHUTE beat Manero 1up
McSPADEN beat Laffoon 2&1

Denny Shute's back-to-back PGA titles took his Majors wins to three, and no-one has regained a title in such rapid time – the PGA's spring re-scheduling resulted in the 1936 and 1937 Championships being just six months apart. Shute also became the fifth multiple winner of the Championship. He beat Harold 'Jug' McSpaden over extra holes – something that McSpaden had experienced against Bunny Torpey and Henry Picard in earlier rounds.

COURSE:	Oakland Hills CC	
LOCATION:	Birmingham, Michigan	
DATE:	10-12 June	
DISTANCE:	7037 yards	
PAR:	72 (288)	
WINNER:	$1000	

COURSE:	Carnoustie GC	
LOCATION:	Carnoustie, Angus, Scotland	
DATE:	7-9 July	
DISTANCE:	7135 yards	
PAR:	n/k	
WINNER:	£100	

Pos	Player	1st	2nd	3rd	4th	Total
1	**RALPH GULDAHL**	71	69	72	69	281
2	Sam Snead	69	73	70	71	283
3	Bobby Cruickshank	73	73	67	72	285
4	Harry Cooper	72	70	73	71	286
5	Ed Dudley	70	70	71	76	287
6	Al Brosch	74	73	68	73	288
7	Clarence Clark	72	75	73	69	289
8	Johnny Goodman (a)	70	73	72	75	290
9	Frank Strafaci (a)	70	72	77	72	291
10 =	Charles Kocsis (a)	72	73	76	71	292
	Henry Picard	71	75	72	74	292
	Gene Sarazen	78	69	71	74	292
	Denny Shute	69	76	75	72	292
14 =	Ray Mangrum	75	75	71	72	293
	Paul Runyan	76	72	73	72	293
16 =	Billy Burke	75	73	71	75	294
	Jimmy Demaret	72	74	76	72	294
	Sam Parks, Jr	74	74	72	74	294
	Pat Sawyer	72	70	75	77	294
20 =	Vic Ghezzi	72	71	78	74	295
	Jimmy Hines	75	72	76	72	295
	Ky Laffoon	74	74	74	73	295
	Harold McSpaden	74	75	73	73	295
	Fred Morrison	71	76	74	74	295
	Byron Nelson	73	78	71	73	295
	Bob Stupple	73	73	73	76	295
	Frank Walsh	70	70	78	77	295

Pos	Player	1st	2nd	3rd	4th	Total
1	**HENRY COTTON**	74	73	72	71	290
2	Reg Whitcombe	72	70	74	76	292
3	Charles Lacey	76	75	70	72	293
4	Charles Whitcombe	73	71	74	76	294
5	Byron Nelson	75	76	71	74	296
6	Ed Dudley	70	74	78	75	297
7 =	Arthur Lacey	75	73	75	75	298
	W Laidlaw	77	72	73	76	298
	Alf Padgham	72	74	76	76	298
10	Horton Smith	77	71	79	72	299
11 =	Ralph Guldahl	77	72	74	77	300
	Sam Snead	75	74	75	76	300
13	Bill Branch	72	75	73	81	301
14	Denny Shute	73	73	76	80	302
15 =	Percy Alliss	75	76	75	77	303
	Henry Picard	76	77	70	80	303
17 =	Jimmy Adams	74	78	76	76	304
	Arthur Havers	77	75	76	76	304
	Bobby Locke (a)	74	74	77	79	304
	Fred Robertson	73	75	78	78	304

Nelson's good form continued on his only visit to the Open Championship – but he still finished six behind Henry Cotton. Many Americans now saw the British Open as less relevant than their domestic Majors. There were several reasons for this in the thirties. Post-Depression USA was commercially more lucrative for a professional golfer; and the time taken by sea would mean two extra tournaments sacrificed. Also, the US golfers saw themselves Post-Vardon, *et al*, as in the ascendancy (the Ryder Cup wins, started in 1927, were going their way). Perhaps Cotton might have been the British champion to throw down the gauntlet in the USA – but it wasn't to be.

Guldahl made up for his Masters disappointment with a stunning win, lowering Manero's US Open record of the previous year. The win was the dawn of Guldahl's great but brief reign at the top of world golf. A new era was coming in, with Nelson's Masters win, and the entry of Sam Snead into the record books as runner-up in the 1937 US Open. This started a 38-year span of Majors Top 10s for Snead – he finished tied for third in the PGA as late as 1974 – but this was as close as he would come in the US Open: he would never lift his own national title, despite being runner-up on three further occasions.

THE MASTERS

COURSE:	Augusta National GC	
LOCATION:	Augusta, Georgia	
DATE:	1-4 April	
DISTANCE:	6925 yards	
PAR:	72 (288)	
WINNER:	$1500	

Pos	Player	1st	2nd	3rd	4th	Total
1	**HENRY PICARD**	71	72	72	70	285
2 =	Harry Cooper	68	77	71	71	287
	Ralph Guldahl	73	70	73	71	287
4	Paul Runyan	71	73	74	70	288
5	Byron Nelson	73	74	70	73	290
6 =	Ed Dudley	70	69	77	75	291
	Felix Serafin	72	71	78	70	291
8 =	Dick Metz	70	77	74	71	292
	Jimmy Thomson	74	70	76	72	292
10 =	Vic Ghezzi	75	74	70	74	293
	Jimmy Hines	75	71	75	72	293
	Lawson Little	72	75	74	72	293
13 =	Billy Burke	73	73	76	73	295
	Gene Sarazen	78	70	68	79	295
15	Stanley Horne	74	74	77	71	296
16 =	Bobby Jones (a)	76	74	72	75	297
	Harold McSpaden	72	75	77	73	297
18 =	Bobby Cruickshank	72	75	77	74	298
	Johnny Revolta	73	72	76	77	298
	Tommy Taller	74	69	75	80	298

Harry Cooper again came in second (tied this time), once again failing to capitalise on a good start. Henry Picard's first Major was compensation for his 1935 disappointment in the Masters. Leading by four after 36 holes, he fell away badly then, but this time a solid final 36 holes saw him home.

US OPEN

COURSE:	Cherry Hills CC	
LOCATION:	Denver, Colorado	
DATE:	9-11 June	
DISTANCE:	6888 yards	
PAR:	71 (284)	
WINNER:	$1000	

Pos	Player	1st	2nd	3rd	4th	Total
1	**RALPH GULDAHL**	74	70	71	69	284
2	Dick Metz	73	68	70	79	290
3 =	Harry Cooper	76	69	76	71	292
	Toney Penna	78	72	74	68	292
5 =	Byron Nelson	77	71	74	72	294
	Emery Zimmerman	72	71	73	78	294
7 =	Frank Moore	79	73	72	71	295
	Henry Picard	70	70	77	78	295
	Paul Runyan	78	72	71	74	295
10	Gene Sarazen	74	74	75	73	296
11 =	Vic Ghezzi	79	71	75	72	297
	Jimmy Hines	70	75	69	83	297
	Denny Shute	77	71	72	77	297
	George Von Elm	78	72	71	76	297
15	Willie Hunter, Jr	73	72	78	75	298
16 =	Olin Dutra	74	71	77	77	299
	Harold McSpaden	76	67	74	82	299
	Johnny Revolta	74	72	77	76	299
19 =	Jim Foulis	74	74	75	77	300
	Horton Smith	80	73	73	74	300
	Al Zimmerman	76	77	75	72	300

Guldahl's easy back-to-back win was only the fourth time it had happened in the Open: Willie Anderson, John McDermott and Bobby Jones were the other successful defending champions. Ray Ainsley set a record which he would never crow about. He took 19 at the par-four 16th in R2 and unsurprisingly missed the cut.

COURSE:	Royal St George's GC	
LOCATION:	Sandwich, Kent, England	
DATE:	6-8 July	
DISTANCE:	6728 yards	
PAR:	n/k	
WINNER:	£100	

Pos	Player	1st	2nd	3rd	4th	Total
1	**REG WHITCOMBE**	71	71	75	78	295
2	Jimmy Adams	70	71	78	78	297
3	Henry Cotton	74	73	77	74	298
4 =	Dick Burton	71	69	78	85	303
	Jack (JJ) Busson	71	69	83	80	303
	Allan Dailey	73	72	80	78	303
	Alf Padgham	74	72	75	82	303
8 =	Fred Bullock	73	74	77	80	304
	Bill Cox	70	70	84	80	304
10 =	Bert Gadd	71	70	84	80	305
	Bobby Locke	73	72	81	79	305
	Charles Whitcombe	71	75	79	80	305
13 =	Sid Brews	76	70	84	77	307
	Dai Rees	73	72	79	83	307
15 =	JH Ballingall	76	72	83	77	308
	Alf Perry	71	74	77	86	308
17	Arthur Lacey	74	72	82	81	309
18	Bill Shankland	74	72	84	81	311
19	Ernest R Whitcombe	70	77	83	82	312
20 =	JL Black	72	72	83	86	313
	PJ Mahon	73	74	83	83	313

Reg Whitcombe, the youngest of the family after Ernest (R) and Charles, improved on his previous-year's runner-up position to take the Open at Sandwich. The winds on the last day were the strongest since Muirfield in 1929, and the Exhibition Tent collapsed. Padgham drove the green on the 384-yard 11th for an eagle-two, while the opposite happened to tied-30th placed Cyril Tolley who, on the 14th, saw his one iron clear water only for it to blow back in. He'd already hit a driver off the tee.

COURSE:	Shawnee CC	
LOCATION:	Shawnee-on-Delaware, Pennsylvania	
DATE:	10-16 July	
QUALIFYING:	63 plus the defending champion (Denny Shute), qualify to matchplay after 36 holes strokeplay (Low – Frank Moore, 136)	
ROUNDS/HOLES:	Rs1&2, 18holes: R3, QF, SF&F, 36	
WINNER:	$1100	

Final

PAUL RUNYAN beat Sam Snead, 8&7

Round 2 (Last 32)

Denny Shute beat John Thoren 7&6; Jimmy Hines beat Frank Walsh 2&1; Byron Nelson beat Alvin Krueger 1up (after 20); Harry Bassler beat Ed Dudley 4&3; Marvin Stahl beat George Whitehead 6&5; Jim Foulis beat Jimmy Thomson 1up; SAM SNEAD beat Terl Johnson 4&3; Felix Serafin beat Ky Laffoon 3&2; Billy Burke beat Frank Moore 1up (after 19); Horton Smith beat Leo Diegel 2&1; Ray Mangrum beat Harold McSpaden 1up (after 20); PAUL RUNYAN beat Tony Manero 3&2; Gene Sarazen beat Harry Nettlebladt 6&5; Jimmy Demaret beat Johnny Revolta 2up; Henry Picard beat Bob Shave 3&2; Dick Metz beat Ralph Guldahl 1up

Round 3 (Last 16)

Hines beat Shute 2&1; Nelson beat Bassler 11&10; Foulis beat Stahl 6&5; SNEAD beat Serafin 4&3; Smith beat Burke 3&2; RUNYAN beat Mangrum 1up (after 37); Sarazen beat Demaret 1up (after 38); Picard beat Metz 4&3

Quarter Final

Hines by Nelson 2&1; SNEAD beat Foulis 8&7
RUNYAN beat Smith 4&3; Picard beat Sarazen 3&2

Semi Final

SNEAD beat Hines 1up
RUNYAN beat Picard 4&3

Paul Runyan immediately followed Denny Shute into the record books as a two-time winner of the PGA. He joined Shute, Jim Barnes, Walter Hagen, Gene Sarazen and Leo Diegel as the only golfers to have won the Championship more than once. Runan had a reasonably trouble-free ride to the final where he defeated the young Sam Snead.

THE MASTERS

	COURSE:	Augusta National GC
	LOCATION:	Augusta, Georgia
	DATE:	30-31 March & 2 April
	DISTANCE:	6925 yards
	PAR:	72 (288)
	WINNER:	$1500

Pos	Player	1st	2nd	3rd	4th	Total
1	**RALPH GULDAHL**	72	68	70	69	279
2	Sam Snead	70	70	72	68	280
3 =	Billy Burke	69	72	71	70	282
	Lawson Little	72	72	68	70	282
5	Gene Sarazen	73	66	72	72	283
6	Craig Wood	72	73	71	68	284
7	Byron Nelson	71	69	72	75	287
8	Henry Picard	71	71	76	71	289
9	Ben Hogan	75	71	72	72	290
10 =	Ed Dudley	75	75	69	72	291
	Toney Penna	72	75	72	72	291
12 =	Tommy Armour	71	74	76	72	293
	Vic Ghezzi	73	76	72	72	293
	Harold McSpaden	75	72	74	72	293
15	Denny Shute	78	71	73	72	294
16 =	Paul Runyan	73	71	75	76	295
	Felix Serafin	74	76	73	72	295
18 =	Chick Harbert	74	73	75	74	296
	Jimmy Thomson	75	71	73	77	296
	Charlie Yates (a)	74	73	74	75	296

After the trauma of his 8&7 drubbing at the hands of Paul Runyan in the last Major of 1938, Sam Snead may have been forgiven for turning his back on golf after the first Major of 1939. He had already set a new low for all Majors and looked a certainty to win the Masters; then Ralph Guldahl came home in 33 to set the first-ever sub-280 total. This also established a record of eight-under par for Major Championships.

US OPEN

	COURSE:	Philadelphia CC
	LOCATION:	Philadelphia, Pennsylvania
	DATE:	8-12 June
	DISTANCE:	6786 yards
	PAR:	69 (276)
	WINNER:	$1000

Pos	Player	1st	2nd	3rd	4th	Total
1	**BYRON NELSON***	72	73	71	68	284
2	Craig Wood	70	71	71	72	284
3	Denny Shute	70	72	70	72	284
4	Bud Ward (a)	69	73	71	72	285
5	Sam Snead	68	71	73	74	286
6	Johnny Bulla	72	71	68	76	287
7 =	Ralph Guldahl	71	73	72	72	288
	Dick Metz	76	72	71	69	288
9 =	Ky Laffoon	76	70	73	70	289
	Harold McSpaden	70	73	71	75	289
	Paul Runyan	76	70	71	72	289
12 =	Harry Cooper	71	72	75	72	290
	Ed Dudley	76	72	73	69	290
	Henry Picard	72	72	72	74	290
15	Horton Smith	72	68	75	76	291
16 =	Sam Byrd	75	71	72	74	292
	Olin Dutra	70	74	70	78	292
	Clayton Heafner	73	73	66	80	292
	Wilford Wehrle (a)	71	77	69	75	292
20 =	Jimmy Hines	73	74	77	69	293
	Johnny Rogers	75	70	69	79	293

* Byron Nelson beat Craig Wood and Denny Shute after two 18-Hole Play-offs:
11 June: Nelson (68) tied with Wood (68) – Shute (76) eliminated;
12 June: Nelson (70) beat Wood (73)

Byron Nelson's second Major, after a triple-tie, should also have belonged to the seemingly luckless Sam Snead. Building on a good start, Snead led, or had a share of the lead, throughout. Arriving at the 18th tee he needed a par five to win; shot eight, and didn't even make the play-off. Old hand at being bridesmaid, Craig Wood has the dubious honour of being the first man to finish second in every Major. He holds the equally-undesirable record of having been beaten in a play-off (extra holes in the PGA) in every Major.

	COURSE:	Royal & Ancient GC
	LOCATION:	St Andrews, Fife, Scotland
	DATE:	5-7 July
	DISTANCE:	6842 yards
	PAR:	n/k
	WINNER:	£100

Pos	Player	1st	2nd	3rd	4th	Total
1	**DICK BURTON**	70	72	77	71	290
2	Johnny Bulla	77	71	71	73	292
3 =	Johnny Fallon	71	73	71	79	294
	Sam King	74	72	75	73	294
	Alf Perry	71	74	73	76	294
	Bill Shankland	72	73	72	77	294
	Reg Whitcombe	71	75	74	74	294
8	Martin Pose	71	72	76	76	295
9 =	Percy Alliss	75	73	74	74	296
	Ernest WH Kenyon	73	75	74	74	296
	Bobby Locke	70	75	76	75	296
12	Dai Rees	71	74	75	77	297
13 =	Jimmy Adams	73	74	75	76	298
	Enrique Bertolino	73	75	75	75	298
	Jimmy Bruen (a)	72	75	75	76	298
	Henry Cotton	74	72	76	76	298
17 =	Bill Anderson	73	74	77	75	299
	Enrique Serra	77	72	73	77	299
19	WH Green	75	75	72	78	300
20 =	Bill Davies	71	79	74	77	301
	Syd Easterbrook	74	71	80	76	301
	Alex Kyle (a)	74	76	75	76	301

The last Open Championship before the second great war in Europe was to intervene, was won for the only time by Dick Burton. It was the end of an era in more ways than one. The 1902 Champion, Sandy Herd, concluded his 54-year relationship with The Open at the age of 71. In his first Open, in 1885, he was in a field that included one of the originals, 'Old' Tom Morris; and his younger brother Fred won the US Open as long ago as 1898. He is undoubtedly *the* stepping stone linking the origins of Major Championships in 1860 to modern times. And, as if to underline the continuity of past and present, both Laurie Aytons, Sr and Jr, members of a particularly elastic St Andrews family, fittingly finished in the 1939 Top 30; whilst Dai Rees would grace the Championship for many years yet, coming second as late as 1961, a century after it all began.

	COURSE:	Pomonock CC
	LOCATION:	Flushing, New York
	DATE:	9-15 July
	QUALIFYING:	64 qualify to matchplay after 36 holes strokeplay
		(Low – Dutch Harrison, Ben Hogan, Emerick Kocsis, Ky Laffoon, 138)
	ROUNDS/HOLES:	Rs1&2, 18holes: R3,QF,SF&F, 36
	WINNER:	$1100

Final

HENRY PICARD beat Byron Nelson, 1up (after 37)

Round 2 (Last 32)

Paul Runyan beat Frank Champ 3&2; Ben Hogan beat Abe Espinosa 5&4; Billy Burke beat Herman Barron 2&1; Dick Metz beat Al Brosch 1up; Tom O'Connor beat Ky Laffoon 2up; Rod Munday beat Jack Ryan 2up; HENRY PICARD v Joe Zarhardt 2up; Al Watrous beat Ken Tucker 5&3; Dutch Harrison beat Johnny Farrell 3&2; Bruce Coltart beat Mike Turnesa 1up (after 21); Clarence Doser beat Ralph Guldahl 2up; Horton Smith beat Ray Mangrum 3&2; Emerick Kocsis beat Vic Ghezzi 3&1; Denny Shute beat Leo Diegel 3&1; Johnny Revolta beat Tony Manero 3&2; BYRON NELSON beat William Francis 3&1

Round 3 (Last 16)

Runyan beat Hogan 3&2; Metz beat Burke 6&4; Munday beat O'Connor 2up; PICARD beat Watrous 8&7; Harrison beat Coltart 10&9; Smith beat Doser 4&2; Kocsis beat Shute 3&1; NELSON beat Revolta 6&4

Quarter Final

Metz beat Runyan 2&1; PICARD beat Munday 2&1; Harrison beat Smith 4&3; NELSON beat Kocsis 10&9

Semi Final

PICARD beat Metz 1up
NELSON beat Harrison 9&8

Byron Nelson was denied consecutive Majors victories when Henry Picard birdied the 36th to take the final into overtime – and repeated the dose on the 37th. This was Picard's second Major (he collected the Masters in the previous year) but he was not destined to add to them. Poor health was shortly to curtail his career; but his driver lived for many years and did great things. He gave it to Sam Snead.

THE MASTERS

	COURSE:	Augusta National GC
	LOCATION:	Augusta, Georgia
	DATE:	4-7 April
	DISTANCE:	6925 yards
	PAR:	72 (288)
	WINNER:	$1500

Pos	Player	1st	2nd	3rd	4th	Total
1	**JIMMY DEMARET**	67	72	70	71	280
2	Lloyd Mangrum	64	75	71	74	284
3	Byron Nelson	69	72	74	70	285
4 =	Harry Cooper	69	75	73	70	287
	Ed Dudley	73	72	71	71	287
	Willie Goggin	71	72	73	71	287
7 =	Henry Picard	71	71	71	75	288
	Sam Snead	71	72	69	76	288
	Craig Wood	70	75	67	76	288
10 =	Ben Hogan	73	74	69	74	290
	Toney Penna	73	73	72	72	290
12 =	Paul Runyan	72	73	72	74	291
	Frank Walsh	73	75	69	74	291
14 =	Sam Byrd	73	74	72	73	292
	Johnny Farrell	76	72	70	74	292
	Ralph Guldahl	74	73	71	74	292
17 =	Harold McSpaden	73	71	74	75	293
	Charlie Yates (a)	72	75	71	75	293
19 =	Lawson Little	70	77	75	72	294
	Ed Oliver	73	75	74	72	294

Records fell to Jimmy Demaret, who posted 30 on the back nine; and Lloyd Mangrum, whose low of 64 beat the previous record for any Major. Demaret gradually clawed his way back into the Tournament and eventually won by a then Masters record margin of four. He was to become a feature in a few Masters to come and went on to regain the title in 1947. He was less lucky in the other Majors, though.

US OPEN

	COURSE:	Canterbury GC
	LOCATION:	Cleveland, Ohio
	DATE:	6-9 June
	DISTANCE:	6894 yards
	PAR:	72 (288)
	WINNER:	$1000

Pos	Player	1st	2nd	3rd	4th	Total
1	**LAWSON LITTLE***	72	69	73	73	287
2	Gene Sarazen	71	74	70	72	287
3	Horton Smith	69	72	78	69	288
4	Craig Wood	72	73	72	72	289
5 =	Ralph Guldahl	73	71	76	70	290
	Ben Hogan	70	73	74	73	290
	Lloyd Mangrum	75	70	71	74	290
	Byron Nelson	72	74	70	74	290
9	Dick Metz	75	72	72	72	291
10 =	Ed Dudley	73	75	71	73	292
	Frank Walsh	73	69	71	79	292
12 =	Tommy Armour	73	74	75	71	293
	Harold McSpaden	74	72	70	77	293
	Henry Picard	73	73	71	76	293
15	Vic Ghezzi	70	74	75	75	294
16 =	Jim Foulis	73	73	77	72	295
	Gene Kunes	76	72	73	74	295
	Johnny Revolta	73	74	72	76	295
	Sam Snead	67	74	73	81	295
20 =	Andrew Gibson	71	75	77	73	296
	Jimmy Hines	73	74	77	72	296
	Felix Serafin	77	74	71	74	296

* Lawson Little (70) beat Gene Sarazen (73) in the 18-Hole Play-off

Former multiple Amateur Champion, Lawson Little, beat Gene Sarazen after a play-off. Sarazen had pulled back three shots over the final holes to tie. Ed Oliver scored 287, but was disqualified for starting his last round earlier than scheduled due to the threat of a storm. Lawson became the sixth player to have won both US Amateur and Open Championships, but only the first of them to win the Open as a professional.

No Championship

COURSE:	Hershey CC
LOCATION:	Hershey, Pennsylvania
DATE:	26 August-2 September
QUALIFYING:	64 qualify to matchplay after 36 holes strokeplay
	(Low – Dick Metz, 140)
ROUNDS/HOLES:	Rs1,2&3, 18holes: QF,SF&F, 36
WINNER:	$1100

Final

BYRON NELSON beat Sam Snead, 1up

Round 2 (Last 32)

Henry Picard beat Alex Gerlak 4&3; Gene Sarazen beat Ray Mangrum 2&1; Jimmy Hines beat Ray Hill 2&1; SAM SNEAD beat Charles Sheppard 3&2; Ed Dudley beat John Gibson 2&1; Paul Runyan beat Al Watrous 3&2; Walter Hagen beat Vic Ghezzi 2&1; Harold McSpaden beat Herman Keiser 2&1; Dick Metz beat Ky Laffoon 3&2; BYRON NELSON beat Frank Walsh 1up (after 20); Arthur Clark beat Billy Burke 1up; Eddie Kirk beat Jimmy Demaret 2&1; Al Brosch beat Red Francis 5&4; Ben Hogan beat Harry Nettlebladt 5&4; Ralph Guldahl beat John Kinder 6&5; Jim Foulis beat Craig Wood 1up (after 19)

Round 3 (Last 16)

Sarazen beat Picard 1up; SNEAD beat Hines 2&1; Runyan beat Dudley 4&3; McSpaden beat Hagen 1up; NELSON beat Metz 2&1; Kirk beat Clark 5&4; Hogan beat Brosch 5&4; Guldahl beat Foulis 5&3

Quarter Final

SNEAD by Sarazen 1up
McSpaden beat Runyan 8&6
NELSON beat Kirk 6&5
Guldahl beat Hogan 3&2

Semi Final

SNEAD beat McSpaden 5&4
NELSON beat Guldahl 3&2

Byron Nelson matched Hagen, Sarazen, Barnes and Armour by winning his third different Major. Sam Snead was still searching for his first title when he when down to Nelson at the 36th hole. Hagen's victory was his 40th and last match win in the PGA, while rival Sarazen, in beating Ray Mangrum, notched up win No. 43 – and still had some years to go.

THE MASTERS

COURSE:	Augusta National GC
LOCATION:	Augusta, Georgia
DATE:	3-6 April
DISTANCE:	6925 yards
PAR:	72 (288)
WINNER:	$1500

Pos	Player	1st	2nd	3rd	4th	Total
1	**CRAIG WOOD**	66	71	71	72	280
2	Byron Nelson	71	69	73	70	283
3	Sam Byrd	73	70	68	74	285
4	Ben Hogan	71	72	75	68	286
5	Ed Dudley	73	72	75	68	288
6 =	Vic Ghezzi	77	71	71	70	289
	Sam Snead	73	75	72	69	289
8	Lawson Little	71	70	74	75	290
9 =	Willie Goggin	71	72	72	76	291
	Harold McSpaden	75	74	72	70	291
	Lloyd Mangrum	71	72	72	76	291
12 =	Jimmy Demaret	77	69	71	75	292
	Clayton Heafner	73	70	76	73	292
14 =	Harry Cooper	72	73	75	73	293
	Ralph Guldahl	76	71	75	71	293
17	Jack Ryan	73	74	74	74	295
18	Denny Shute	77	75	74	70	296
19 =	Dick Chapman (a)	76	73	70	78	297
	Jimmy Hines	76	74	75	72	297
	Gene Kunes	76	74	76	71	297
	Dick Metz	74	72	75	76	297
	Sam Parks, Jr	75	76	75	71	297
	Toney Penna	73	74	80	70	297
	Gene Sarazen	76	72	74	75	297
	Felix Serafin	72	79	74	72	297
	Horton Smith	74	72	77	74	297

Craig Wood's luck had changed. After a decade and more of disappointment he won his first Major. The US entered the War before the end of the year, so Wood's success seemed to arrive just in time. His win equalled the record under par score – eight – and set a new first 36-hole low for the Masters.

US OPEN

COURSE:	Colonial CC
LOCATION:	Fort Worth, Texas
DATE:	5-7 June
DISTANCE:	7005 yards
PAR:	70 (280)
WINNER:	$1000

Pos	Player	1st	2nd	3rd	4th	Total
1	**CRAIG WOOD**	73	71	70	70	284
2	Denny Shute	69	75	72	71	287
3 =	Johnny Bulla	75	71	72	71	289
	Ben Hogan	74	77	68	70	289
5 =	Herman Barron	75	71	74	71	291
	Paul Runyan	73	72	71	75	291
7 =	Dutch Harrison	70	82	71	71	294
	Harold McSpaden	71	75	74	74	294
	Gene Sarazen	74	73	72	75	294
10 =	Ed Dudley	74	74	74	73	295
	Lloyd Mangrum	73	74	72	76	295
	Dick Metz	71	74	76	74	295
13 =	Henry Ransom	72	74	75	75	296
	Horton Smith	73	75	73	75	296
	Sam Snead	76	70	77	73	296
	Harry Todd (a)	72	77	76	71	296
17 =	Lawson Little	71	73	79	74	297
	Byron Nelson	73	73	74	77	297
19	Vic Ghezzi	70	79	77	72	298
20	Gene Kunes	71	79	74	75	299

As if to make up for all his previous failures, Craig Wood made it two in a row when he won the Open at Colonial in June. Just as sweet as the win was being able to turn the tables on Denny Shute – something of a *bête noir* to Wood over the years. Par golf over the second 36 holes kept him ahead of the field.

No Championship

COURSE:	Cherry Hills CC
LOCATION:	Denver, Colorado
DATE:	7-13 July
QUALIFYING:	63 qualify to matchplay, plus the defending champion (Byron Nelson), after 36 holes strokeplay. (Low – Sam Snead, 138)
ROUNDS/HOLES:	Rs1&2, 18holes: R3,QF,SF&F, 36
WINNER:	$1100

Final
VIC GHEZZI beat Byron Nelson, 1up (after 38)

Round 2 (Last 32)
BYRON NELSON beat William Heinlein 1up; Ralph Guldahl beat Gene Kunes 2&1; Ben Hogan beat Bud Oakley 2up; Horton Smith beat Ralph Stonehouse 3&2; Denny Shute beat Jim Foulis 1up; Leonard Ott beat Jack Ryan (default); Bruce Coltart beat George Fazio 1up (after 19); Gene Sarazen beat Toney Penna 1up (after 19); Sam Snead beat Phil Greenwaldt 7&6; Mike Turnesa beat Harry Bassler 4&2; Mark Fry beat Craig Wood 6&5; Lloyd Mangrum beat Charles Sheppard 3&1; Jack Grout beat Fay Coleman 1up; VIC GHEZZI beat Augie Nordone 1up; Harold McSpaden beat George Schneiter 3&2; Jimmy Hines beat Ed Dudley 3&2

Round 3 (Last 16)
NELSON beat Guldahl 4&3; Hogan beat Smith 2&1; Shute beat Ott 5&3; Sarazen beat Coltart9&7; Snead beat Turnesa 1up; Mangrum beat Fry 1up; GHEZZI beat Grout 1up; Hines beat McSpaden 6&4

Quarter Final
NELSON beat Hogan 2&1
Sarazen beat Shute 7&6
Mangrum beat Snead 6&4
GHEZZI beat Hines 6&4

Semi Final
NELSON beat Sarazen 2up
GHEZZI beat Mangrum 1up

Wood's bid to win all three US Majors in one season failed at the second fence in the PGA, when he was hammered 6&5 by little-known Mark Fry. Vic Ghezzi had been competing in the PGA for some years without proceeding to the later stages. Now wins over Lloyd Mangrum in the semi final and an overtime win in the final over Byron Nelson made him a worthy Champion.

THE MASTERS

BRITISH OPEN

COURSE:	Augusta National GC
LOCATION:	Augusta, Georgia
DATE:	9-13 April
DISTANCE:	6925 yards
PAR:	72 (288)
WINNER:	$1500

No Championship

Pos	Player	1st	2nd	3rd	4th	Total
1	**BYRON NELSON***	68	67	72	73	280
2	Ben Hogan	73	70	67	70	280
3	Paul Runyan	67	73	72	71	283
4	Sam Byrd	68	68	75	74	285
5	Horton Smith	67	73	74	73	287
6	Jimmy Demaret	70	70	75	75	290
7 =	Dutch Harrison	74	70	71	77	292
	Lawson Little	71	74	72	75	292
	Sam Snead	78	69	72	73	292
10 =	Chick Harbert	73	73	72	75	293
	Gene Kunes	74	74	74	71	293
12	Jimmy Thomson	73	70	74	77	294
13	Chandler Harper	75	75	76	69	295
14	Willie Goggin	74	70	78	74	296
15 =	Bobby Cruickshank	72	79	71	75	297
	Jim Ferrier	71	76	80	70	297
	Henry Picard	75	72	75	75	297
18 =	Harry Cooper	74	77	76	72	299
	Harold McSpaden	74	72	79	74	299
	Felix Serafin	75	74	77	73	299

* Byron Nelson (69) beat Ben Hogan (70) in the 18-Hole
Play-off

The Clash of the Titans. The two biggest names in the
game at that time went to an historic play-off. Hogan had
reduced Nelson's 36-hole lead of eight to tie on a record-
equalling 280 after the latter's 135 – another Masters low.
In the play-off, Hogan raced away to lead by three, but
starting at the sixth, Nelson started to reel him in and pass
him to win by one. Three greats from the previous
generation, Tommy Armour, Bobby Jones and Gene
Sarazen, were in a bunch tied 28th.

No Championship

COURSE:	Seaview CC
LOCATION:	Atlantic City, New Jersey
DATE:	23-31 May
QUALIFYING:	31 qualify to matchplay, plus the defending champion (Vic Ghezzi), after 36 holes strokeplay. (Low – Harry Cooper, 138)
ROUNDS/HOLES:	All Rounds 36 holes
WINNER:	$1100

Final
SAM SNEAD beat Jim Turnesa, 2&1

Round 1 (Last 32)
Jimmy Demaret beat Vic Ghezzi 4&3; Tom Harmon, Jr beat Bruce Coltart 3&2; Craig Wood beat Rod Munday 5&4; Leland Gibson beat Jimmy Gauntt 10&9; SAM SNEAD beat Sam Byrd 7&6; Willie Goggin beat Eddie Burke 2&1; Ed Dudley beat Denny Shute 3&2; Toney Penna beat Jimmy Hines 3&2; Harry Cooper beat Mike Turnesa 3&1; Lloyd Mangrum beat Dick Metz 6&5; Byron Nelson beat Harry Nettlebladt 5&3; Joe Kirkwood, Sr beat Jimmy Thomson 4&2; JIM TURNESA beat Dutch Harrison 6&5; Harold McSpaden beat Sam Parks, Jr 7&5; Ben Hogan beat Ben Loving 7&6; Ky Laffoon beat Vic Bass 12&11

Round 2 (Last 16)
Demaret beat Harmon 3&2; Wood beat Gibson 7&6; SNEAD beat Goggin 9&8; Dudley beat Penna 4&2; Cooper beat Mangrum 1up; Nelson beat Kirkwood 2&1; JIM TURNESA beat McSpaden 1up; Hogan beat Laffoon 9&8

Quarter Final
Demaret beat Wood 7&6; SNEAD beat Dudley 1up; Nelson beat Cooper 1up (after 39); JIM TURNESA beat Hogan 2&1

Semi Final
SNEAD beat Demaret 3&2
JIM TURNESA beat Nelson 1up (after 37)

World War II was less disruptive for the PGAs than the other Majors. Some pros had volunteered, others conscripted, but in 1942 the PGA still attracted a strong field. There was a military feel to the final, all the same, when Jim Turnesa (shortly to become Sergeant) lost out to Sam Snead, due to join the US Navy the following day; in a closer match than most people predicted. Snead made his Majors breakthrough at last …and went to war.

1943

THE MASTERS

No Championship

BRITISH OPEN

No Championship

US OPEN

No Championship

US PGA

No Championship

No Championship

No Championship

No Championship

US PGA

1944

COURSE:	Manito G&CC
LOCATION:	Spokane, Washington
DATE:	14-20 August
QUALIFYING:	32 qualify to matchplay after 36 holes strokeplay. (Low – Byron Nelson, 138)
ROUNDS/HOLES:	All Rounds 36 holes
WINNER:	$3500

Final
BOB HAMILTON beat Byron Nelson, 1up

Round 1 (Last 32)
BYRON NELSON beat Mike DeMassey 5&4; Mark Fry beat Neil Christian 2&1; Willie Goggin beat Purvis Ferree 8&7; Tony Manero beat Clayton Aleridge 1up (after 38); Sam Byrd beat WA Stackhouse 4&3; Chuck Congdon beat Henry Williams, Jr 7&6; Ed Dudley beat Steve Savel 7&6; Jimmy Hines beat Thurman Edwards 7&6; Harold McSpaden beat Bruce Coltart 7&5; Fred Annon beat Harry Nettlebladt 5&4; BOB HAMILTON beat Gene Kunes 6&5; Harry Bassler beat Joe Mozel 6&5; Art Bell beat Joe Zarhardt 1up (after 37); Craig Wood beat Jimmy D'Angelo 5&4; Toney Penna beat Morrie Gravatt 3&2; George Schneiter beat Ted Longworth 7&6

Round 2 (Last 16)
NELSON beat Fry 7&6; Goggin beat Manero 4&3; Congdon beat Byrd 2&1; Dudley beat Hines 1up (after 37); McSpaden beat Annon 8&7; HAMILTON beat Bassler 6&5; Bell beat Wood 3&2; Schneiter beat Penna 4&3

Quarter Final
NELSON beat Goggin 4&3; Congdon beat Dudley 6&5; HAMILTON beat McSpaden 2&1; Schneiter beat Bell 2&1

Semi Final
NELSON beat Congdon 8&7
HAMILTON beat Schneiter 1up

There was a less-familiar look to the competitors when the Championship resumed in 1944. It looked to be a foregone conclusion for Byron Nelson as he coasted through an under-strength field to meet little-known Bob Hamilton. Hamilton was 10-1 to beat Nelson, but in one of golf's biggest upsets, he did just that. Hamilton did less well in future – hampered as he was with burns from an aircraft accident, although he contested the 1946 Masters.

THE MASTERS

No Championship

BRITISH OPEN

No Championship

US OPEN

No Championship

US PGA

COURSE:	Moraine CC
LOCATION:	Dayton, Ohio
DATE:	9-15 July
QUALIFYING:	31 qualify to matchplay, plus the defending champion (Bob Hamilton), after 36 holes strokeplay. (Low – Byron Nelson, Johnny Revolta, 138)
ROUNDS/HOLES:	All Rounds 36 holes
WINNER:	$3750

Final
BYRON NELSON beat Sam Byrd, 4&3

Round 1 (Last 32)
Jack Grout beat Bob Hamilton 5&4; Ky Laffoon beat Felix Serafin 4&3; Clarence Doser beat Harold McSpaden 5&4; Toney Penna beat Wayne Timberman 2up; Johnny Revolta beat Frank Kringle 10&9; SAM BYRD beat Augie Nordone 4&3; Herman Barron beat Harry Nettlebladt 5&3; Vic Ghezzi beat Ed Dudley 7&6; BYRON NELSON beat Gene Sarazen 4&3; Mike Turnesa beat John Gibson 5&4; Denny Shute beat Barney Clark 4&3; Bob Kepler beat George Schneiter 2&1; Terl Johnson beat Dutch Harrison 1up; Ralph Hutchison beat Ted Huge 6&5; Jim Turnesa beat Byron Harcke 6&5; Claude Harmon beat Verl Stinchcomb 2&1

Round 2 (Last 16)
Laffoon beat Grout 5&4; Doser beat Penna 1up; BYRD beat Revolta 2&1; Ghezzi beat Barron 2up; NELSON beat Mike Turnesa 1up; Shute beat Kepler 5&4; Hutchison beat Johnson 6&5; Harmon beat Jim Turnesa 8&7

Quarter Final
Doser beat Laffoon 2&1; BYRD beat Ghezzi 7&6; NELSON beat Shute 3&2; Harmon beat Hutchison 4&3

Semi Final
BYRD beat Doser 7&6; NELSON beat Harmon 5&4

If 1930 was the year of Bobby Jones, then surely 1945 was to be Byron Nelson's year. Although no other Major was played, the PGA Championship was part of the Players' Tour which restarted the previous year. From March to August 1945, he won every tournament he entered, to put together a sequence of wins, which just like Jones' achievement in 1930, will surely never be beaten (although Tiger Woods may have something to say about that). He won 11 altogether, including the PGA in July.

1946

THE MASTERS

COURSE:	Augusta National GC				
LOCATION:	Augusta, Georgia				
DATE:	4-7 April				
DISTANCE:	6925 yards				
PAR:	72 (288)				
WINNER:	$2500				

Pos	Player	1st	2nd	3rd	4th	Total
1	**HERMAN KEISER**	69	68	71	74	282
2	Ben Hogan	74	70	69	70	283
3	Bob Hamilton	75	69	71	72	287
4 =	Jimmy Demaret	75	70	71	73	289
	Jim Ferrier	74	72	68	75	289
	Ky Laffoon	74	73	70	72	289
7 =	Chick Harbert	69	75	76	70	290
	Clayton Heafner	74	69	71	76	290
	Byron Nelson	72	73	71	74	290
	Sam Snead	74	75	70	71	290
11	Jim Foulis	75	70	72	74	291
12	Cary Middlecoff (a)	72	76	70	74	292
13 =	Vic Ghezzi	71	79	67	76	293
	George Schneiter	73	73	72	75	293
15	Fred Haas	71	75	68	80	294
16 =	Johnny Bulla	72	76	73	74	295
	Lloyd Mangrum	76	75	72	72	295
18	Claude Harmon	76	75	74	71	296
19	Chandler Harper	74	76	73	74	297
20	Frank Stranahan (a)	76	74	73	75	298

Normal service was resumed in 1946 with all Majors taking place. Herman Keiser surprisingly won the first post-war Masters, leaving Ben Hogan then with the longest reign of any golfer as runner-up in a Major – at least for a few months. Keiser's excellent start meant that Hogan had to charge the last round. This he duly did and had the chance to tie on the 18th when Keiser three-putted. That Hogan did precisely the same was somewhat of an anti-climax.

US OPEN

COURSE:	Canterbury GC				
LOCATION:	Cleveland, Ohio				
DATE:	13-16 June				
DISTANCE:	6926 yards				
PAR:	72 (288)				
WINNER:	$1500				

Pos	Player	1st	2nd	3rd	4th	Total
1	**LLOYD MANGRUM***	74	70	68	72	284
2 =	Vic Ghezzi	71	69	72	72	284
	Byron Nelson	71	71	69	73	284
4 =	Herman Barron	72	72	72	69	285
	Ben Hogan	72	68	73	72	285
6 =	Jimmy Demaret	71	74	73	68	286
	Ed Oliver	71	71	74	70	286
8 =	Chick Harbert	72	78	67	70	287
	Dick Metz	76	70	72	69	287
10 =	Dutch Harrison	75	71	72	70	288
	Lawson Little	72	69	76	71	288
12 =	Ed Furgol	77	69	74	69	289
	Clayton Heafner	75	72	71	71	289
	Henry Picard	71	73	71	74	289
15 =	Claude Harmon	72	77	70	72	291
	Chandler Harper	76	74	67	74	291
	Steve Kovach	71	72	73	75	291
	Toney Penna	69	77	74	71	291
19 =	Gene Kunes	74	73	73	72	292
	Sam Snead	69	75	74	74	292

* Lloyd Mangrum beat Vic Ghezzi and Byron Nelson after two 18-Hole Play-offs:
(am): Mangrum (72) tied with Ghezzi (72) and Nelson (72)
(pm): Mangrum (72) beat Ghezzi (73) and Nelson (73)

Vic Ghezzi was denied his second Major and Nelson his sixth, when Lloyd Mangrum won the three-way play-off at Cleveland. The first play-off was indecisive, and in the repeat, with Mangrum three down on Ghezzi and two on Hogan with six to play, all look lost. Three successive birdies changed all that, and Mangrum's second 72 was too good for the others.

	BRITISH OPEN			US PGA	
COURSE:	Royal & Ancient GC		COURSE:	Portland GC	
LOCATION:	St Andrews, Fife, Scotland		LOCATION:	Portland, Oregon	
DATE:	3-5 July		DATE:	19-25 August	
DISTANCE:	6923 yards		QUALIFYING:	63 qualify to matchplay, plus the	
PAR:	n/k			defending champion (Byron	
WINNER:	£150			Nelson), after 36 holes strokeplay.	
				(Low – Jim Ferrier, 134)	

Pos	Player	1st	2nd	3rd	4th	Total
1	**SAM SNEAD**	71	70	74	75	290
2 =	Johnny Bulla	71	72	72	79	294
	Bobby Locke	69	74	75	76	294
4 =	Henry Cotton	70	70	76	79	295
	Norman von Nida	70	76	74	75	295
	Dai Rees	75	67	73	80	295
	Charlie Ward	73	73	73	76	295
8 =	Fred Daly	77	71	76	74	298
	Joe Kirkwood, Sr	71	75	78	74	298
10	Lawson Little	78	75	72	74	299
11	Harry Bradshaw	76	75	76	73	300
12	Dick Burton	74	76	76	76	302
13	Bill Shankland	76	76	77	75	304
14 =	Bill Anderson	76	76	78	75	305
	Reg Whitcombe	71	76	82	76	305
16	Laurie Ayton, Jr	77	74	80	75	306
17	Percy Alliss	74	72	82	79	307
18 =	Archie Compston	77	74	77	80	308
	Frank Jowle	78	74	76	80	308
	Arthur Lees	77	71	78	82	308

	US PGA
ROUNDS/HOLES:	Rs1&2, 18holes: R3,QF,SF&F, 36
WINNER:	$3500

Final

BEN HOGAN beat Ed Oliver, 6&4

Round 2 (Last 32)

Byron Nelson beat Larry Lamberger 3&2; Herman Barron beat Fay Coleman 3&2; ED OLIVER beat Dick Metz 3&1; Chandler Harper beat Jimmy Thomson 2&1; Dutch Harrison beat Toney Penna 1up; Harold McSpaden beat Bob Hamilton 4&3; Chuck Congdon beat Newton Bassler 1up (after 19); George Schneiter beat Sam Snead 6&5; Jim Ferrier beat Lawson Little 3&2; Jimmy Demaret beat Dave Tinsley 3&2; Jim Turnesa beat Henry Ransom 1up; Dick Shoemaker beat Vic Ghezzi 1up; BEN HOGAN beat William Heinlein 4&3; Art Bell beat Al Nelson 4&3; Frank Moore beat George Fazio 2&1; Harry Bassler beat Lew Worsham 1up

Round 3 (Last 16)

Nelson beat Barron 3&2 ; OLIVER beat Harper 5&4; McSpaden beat Harrison 4&3; Congdon beat Schneiter 2&1; Demaret beat Ferrier 3&2; Turnesa beat Shoemaker 5&4; HOGAN beat Bell 5&4; Moore beat Harry Bassler 4&3

Quarter Final

OLIVER beat Nelson 1up; McSpaden beat Congdon 5&3; Demaret beat Turnesa 6&5; HOGAN beat Moore 5&4

Semi Final

OLIVER beat McSpaden 6&5; HOGAN beat Demaret 10&9

It was fitting for the the first post-war Open Championship, just like the last pre-war one, should be held over the Old Course at St Andrews. Unfortunately, Sam Snead did not consider his second Major all that important (compare the respective prize money, for one thing); and the Americans stayed away in their droves for another decade and more. All but one, that is: Johnny Bulla remained faithful to the British Open for several years to come – and it was he that relieved Ben Hogan of his longevity crown for a Majors runner-up, set the previous April at Augusta.

The PGA reverted to the 1941 set-up once more. Australian Jim Ferrier shot a round of 63 in his record qualifying score, and although the field was back to strength, no-one could stop Ben Hogan ripping it apart. Big defeats of Art Bell and Frank Moore preceded the semi final demolition of ex-Masters Champion, Jimmy Demaret. Hogan then blasted away Ed Oliver in the final. Byron Nelson, after his amazing year previously, and with a haul of five Majors, dramatically and prematurely retired from tournament golf. He did, however, play in a dwindling number of Major Championships for another 20 years.

THE MASTERS

COURSE:	Augusta National GC				
LOCATION:	Augusta, Georgia				
DATE:	3-6 April				
DISTANCE:	6925 yards				
PAR:	72 (288)				
WINNER:	$2500				

Pos	Player	1st	2nd	3rd	4th	Total
1	**JIMMY DEMARET**	69	71	70	71	281
2 =	Byron Nelson	69	72	72	70	283
	Frank Stranahan (a)	73	72	70	68	283
4 =	Ben Hogan	75	68	71	70	284
	Harold McSpaden	74	69	70	71	284
6 =	Jim Ferrier	70	71	73	72	286
	Henry Picard	73	70	72	71	286
8 =	Chandler Harper	77	72	68	70	287
	Lloyd Mangrum	76	73	68	70	287
	Dick Metz	72	72	72	71	287
	Ed Oliver	70	72	74	71	287
	Toney Penna	71	70	75	71	287
13	Johnny Bulla	70	75	74	69	288
14 =	Dick Chapman (a)	72	71	74	72	289
	Lawson Little	71	71	76	71	289
	Bobby Locke	74	74	71	70	289
17 =	Herman Barron	71	71	74	74	290
	Fred Haas	70	74	73	73	290
	Johnny Palmer	70	73	74	73	290
20	Denny Shute	73	75	72	71	291

Jimmy Demaret, badly beaten finalist in the PGA of 1946, was on much more familiar territory in the first Major of 1947 at Augusta National. Charged with a R1 69, he led from start to finish to win his second Masters. The outstanding amateur of the next decade, Frank Stranahan, finished tied-second with recent retiree Nelson.

US OPEN

COURSE:	St Louis CC				
LOCATION:	St Louis, Missouri				
DATE:	12-15 June				
DISTANCE:	6532 yards				
PAR:	71 (284)				
WINNER:	$2000				

Pos	Player	1st	2nd	3rd	4th	Total
1	**LEW WORSHAM***	70	70	71	71	282
2	Sam Snead	72	70	70	70	282
3 =	Bobby Locke	68	74	70	73	285
	Ed Oliver	73	70	71	71	285
5	Bud Ward (a)	69	72	73	73	287
6 =	Jim Ferrier	71	70	74	74	289
	Vic Ghezzi	74	73	73	69	289
	Leland Gibson	69	76	73	71	289
	Ben Hogan	70	75	70	74	289
	Johnny Palmer	72	70	75	72	289
	Paul Runyan	71	74	72	72	289
12	Chick Harbert	67	72	81	70	290
13 =	Ed Furgol	70	75	72	74	291
	Dutch Harrison	76	72	70	73	291
	Dick Metz	69	70	78	74	291
	Bill Nary	77	71	70	73	291
	Frank Stranahan (a)	73	74	72	72	291
	Harry Todd	67	75	77	72	291
19 =	Claude Harmon	74	72	74	72	292
	Gene Kunes	71	77	72	72	292
	George Payton	71	75	75	71	292
	Alfred Smith	70	73	76	73	292

* Lew Worsham (69) beat Sam Snead (70) in the 18-Hole Play-off

Sam Snead never won the US Open – the only jewel missing from the crown. In the previous September the original trophy was destroyed by fire. Old trophy or new, Snead was never to get as close as 1947, when he and Lew Worsham tied. Worsham won the play-off on the last green in controversial circumstances. He asked for a measure after Snead had addressed his 2.5 foot putt. The measure still meant that Snead was first to putt. He missed, but Worsham made his to win.

COURSE:	Plum Hollow CC
LOCATION:	Detroit, Michigan
DATE:	18-24 June
QUALIFYING:	63 qualify to matchplay, plus the defending champion (Ben Hogan), after 36 holes strokeplay. (Low – Jimmy Demaret, 137)
ROUNDS/HOLES:	Rs1&2, 18holes: R3,QF,SF&F, 36
WINNER:	$3500

COURSE:	Royal Liverpool GC
LOCATION:	Hoylake, Cheshire, England
DATE:	2-4 July
DISTANCE:	c7000 yards
PAR:	n/k
WINNER:	£150

Final

JIM FERRIER beat Chick Harbert, 5&4

Round 2 (Last 32)

Ky Laffoon beat Toney Penna 1up; Gene Sarazen beat Sam Snead 2&1; Dick Metz beat Henry Ransom 1up; Art Bell beat Johnny Bulla 4&3; Claude Harmon beat Jim Milward 5&3; JIM FERRIER beat Herman Barron 3&2; Mike Turnesa beat Chandler Harper 1up (after 22); Lloyd Mangrum beat Ed Dudley 4&3; Vic Ghezzi beat Earl Martin 6&5; Jim Turnesa beat Walter Ambo 4&3; Lew Worsham beat Clarence Doser 5&4; Reggie Myles beat George Schneiter 1up; CHICK HARBERT beat Clayton Heafner 1up (after 20); Ed Oliver beat Harry Bassler 4&3; Eddie Joseph beat Lloyd Wadkins 1up; Leland Gibson beat Jack Smith 3&2

Round 3 (Last 16)

Laffoon beat Sarazen 4&3 ; Bell beat Metz 1up (after 37); FERRIER beat Harmon 1up (after 37); Mangrum beat Mike Turnesa 1up; Ghezzi beat Jim Turnesa 4&3; Worsham beat Myles 7&6; HARBERT beat Oliver 3&2; Gibson beat Joseph 1up (after 37)

Quarter Final

Bell beat Laffoon 2up
FERRIER beat Mangrum 4&3
Ghezzi beat Worsham 3&2
HARBERT beat Gibson 2up

Semi Final

FERRIER beat Bell 10&9
HARBERT beat Ghezzi 6&5

Jim Ferrier became the first non-American born winner of the PGA since Tommy Armour in 1930. It was also the first final since 1937 without Hogan, Nelson or Snead. Good putting (just 52 over the 35 holes played) was Ferrier's secret. It was just as well, as his driving off the tee and approach play were erratic. It is reported that he struck seven spectators during the course of the final!

Pos	Player	1st	2nd	3rd	4th	Total
1	**FRED DALY**	73	70	78	72	293
2 =	Reg Horne	77	74	72	71	294
	Frank Stranahan (a)	71	79	72	72	294
4	Bill Shankland	76	74	75	70	295
5	Dick Burton	77	71	77	71	296
6 =	Johnny Bulla	80	72	74	71	297
	Henry Cotton	69	78	74	76	297
	Sam King	75	72	77	73	297
	Arthur Lees	75	74	72	76	297
	Norman von Nida	74	76	71	76	297
	Charlie Ward	76	73	76	72	297
12	Jimmy Adams	73	80	71	75	299
13 =	Alf Padgham	75	75	74	76	300
	Reg Whitcombe	75	77	71	77	300
15 =	Laurie Ayton, Jr	69	80	74	79	302
	Fred Bullock	74	78	78	72	302
17	Norman Sutton	77	76	73	77	303
18 =	Vic Ghezzi	75	78	72	79	304
	Alf Perry	76	77	70	81	304
	Ernest E Whitcombe	77	76	74	77	304

Ulsterman Fred Daly became the only player, to date, from the island of Ireland to win a Major. As Liverpool is often considered as a cultural extension of the Emerald Isle, I suppose the win at Hoylake was apposite. Laurie Ayton is the third generation of that family to feature in Major Championships, although sadly, none ever threatened to win.

1948

COURSE:	Augusta National GC
LOCATION:	Augusta, Georgia
DATE:	8-11 April
DISTANCE:	6925 yards
PAR:	72 (288)
WINNER:	$2500

Pos	Player	1st	2nd	3rd	4th	Total
1	**CLAUDE HARMON**	70	70	69	70	279
2	Cary Middlecoff	74	71	69	70	284
3	Chick Harbert	71	70	70	76	287
4 =	Jim Ferrier	71	71	75	71	288
	Lloyd Mangrum	69	73	75	71	288
6 =	Ed Furgol	70	72	73	74	289
	Ben Hogan	70	71	77	71	289
8 =	Byron Nelson	71	73	72	74	290
	Harry Todd	72	67	80	71	290
10 =	Herman Keiser	70	72	76	73	291
	Bobby Locke	71	71	74	75	291
	Dick Metz	71	72	75	73	291
13 =	Johnny Bulla	74	72	76	71	293
	Dutch Harrison	73	77	73	70	293
	Skee Riegel (a)	71	74	73	75	293
16 =	Al Smith	73	73	74	74	294
	Sam Snead	74	75	72	73	294
18 =	Jimmy Demaret	73	72	78	72	295
	Ed Dudley	73	76	75	71	295
	Vic Ghezzi	75	73	73	74	295
	Fred Haas	75	75	76	69	295
	Bob Hamilton	72	72	76	75	295

Claude Harmon was the first non-tournament playing professional to win the Masters. No-one would have noticed – he equalled Ralph Guldahl's low score set in 1939 and won by the biggest margin to date.

COURSE:	Norwood Hills CC
LOCATION:	St Louis, Missouri
DATE:	19-25 May
QUALIFYING:	63 qualify to matchplay, plus the defending champion (Jim Ferrier) after 36 holes strokeplay. (Low – Skip Alexander, 134)
ROUNDS/HOLES:	Rs1&2, 18holes: R3,QF,SF&F, 36
WINNER:	$3500

Final
BEN HOGAN beat Mike Turnesa, 7&6

Round 2 (Last 32)
Claude Harmon beat Jim Ferrier 1up; Henry Ransom beat Lloyd Mangrum 3&2; Sam Snead beat Frank Moore 4&3; Leland Gibson beat Pete Cooper 1up; Johnny Bulla beat Armand Farina 4&3; Ky Laffoon beat Chandler Harper 3&2; MIKE TURNESA beat Zell Eaton 1up (after 21); Al Smith beat Jimmy Hines 4&3; Skip Alexander beat Al Brosch 2up; Chick Harbert beat Eddie Burke 1up (after 26); BEN HOGAN beat Johnny Palmer 1up; Gene Sarazen beat Jackson Bradley 2&1; Jimmy Demaret beat George Getchell 3&1; Lew Worsham beat Errie Ball 7&6; Ed Oliver beat Sherman Elworthy 3&2; George Fazio beat Henry Williams Jr 7&6

Round 3 (Last 16)
Harmon beat Ransom 2&1; Snead beat Gibson 5&3; Bulla beat Laffoon 6&5; TURNESA beat Smith 3&2; Harbert beat Alexander 11&10; HOGAN beat Sarazen 1up; Demaret beat Worsham 3&2; Fazio beat Oliver 1up

Quarter Final
Harmon beat Snead 1up (after 42); TURNESA beat Bulla 6&5; HOGAN beat Harbert 2&1; Demaret beat Fazio 5&4

Semi Final
TURNESA beat Harmon 1up (after 37); HOGAN beat Demaret 2&1

While the Masters and both Open Championship dates remained quite static, the PGA didn't settle into its August slot until 1969 and, rather eccentrically, it took place in 1971 in February! The Hogan era was well and truly here as he added a second PGA to his 1946 title, with a third Turnesa brother experiencing the anguish of runner-up in a Major. An accident involving a Greyhound bus on 2 February 1949 was to cut short Hogan's PGA career. He was to return to it again only in 1960.

US OPEN

COURSE:	Riviera CC	
LOCATION:	Pacific Palisades, California	
DATE:	10-12 June	
DISTANCE:	7020 yards	
PAR:	71 (284)	
WINNER:	$2000	

Pos	Player	1st	2nd	3rd	4th	Total
1	**BEN HOGAN**	67	72	68	69	276
2	Jimmy Demaret	71	70	68	69	278
3	Jim Turnesa	71	69	70	70	280
4	Bobby Locke	70	69	73	70	282
5	Sam Snead	69	69	73	72	283
6	Lew Worsham	67	74	71	73	285
7	Herman Barron	73	70	71	72	286
8 =	Johnny Bulla	73	72	75	67	287
	Toney Penna	70	72	73	72	287
	Smiley Quick	73	71	69	74	287
11	Skip Alexander	71	73	71	73	288
12 =	Charles Congdon	71	70	71	77	289
	Harold McSpaden	74	69	69	77	289
14 =	Vic Ghezzi	72	74	74	70	290
	Leland Gibson	71	76	69	74	290
	Otto Greiner	74	73	71	72	290
	Herman Keiser	71	71	73	75	290
	George Schneiter	73	68	75	74	290
	Herschel Spears	72	71	76	71	290
	Ellsworth Vines	75	72	69	74	290

Ben Hogan's first US Open win was his second Major in successive events, and third in total. His 276 was a landmark record in the US Open. It was not lowered until Jack Nicklaus' 275 at Baltusrol in 1967. In fact, up until 1964 only one total bettered this in any Major – 274 in the 1954 Masters by Hogan himself.

BRITISH OPEN

COURSE:	Honourable Company of Edinburgh Golfers	
LOCATION:	Muirfield, East Lothian, Scotland	
DATE:	30 June-2 July	
DISTANCE:	6806 yards	
PAR:	n/k	
WINNER:	£150	

Pos	Player	1st	2nd	3rd	4th	Total
1	**HENRY COTTON**	71	66	75	72	284
2	Fred Daly	72	71	73	73	289
3 =	Roberto de Vicenzo	70	73	72	75	290
	Jack Hargreaves	76	68	73	73	290
	Norman von Nida	71	72	76	71	290
	Charlie Ward	69	72	75	74	290
7 =	Johnny Bulla	74	72	73	72	291
	Sam King	69	72	74	76	291
	Alf Padgham	73	70	71	77	291
	Flory van Donck	69	73	73	76	291
11 =	Mario Gonzales	76	72	70	75	293
	EC Kingsley (a)	77	69	77	70	293
	Arthur Lees	73	79	73	78	293
	Alan Waters	75	71	70	77	293
15 =	Max Faulkner	75	71	74	74	294
	Dai Rees	73	71	76	74	294
	Ernest E Whitcombe	74	73	73	74	294
18 =	Dick Burton	74	70	74	77	295
	Frank Jowle	70	78	74	73	295
	Reg Whitcombe	77	67	77	74	295

Cotton won his third Open at the age of 41, courtesy of a second round of 66 – a score only beaten by his own 65 at Sandwich, 14 years before. This gave him enough of a cushion to hold off defending champion Daly. US veteran, Bobby Cruickshank, 54, finished down the field on 302.

THE MASTERS

US PGA

COURSE:	Augusta National GC
LOCATION:	Augusta, Georgia
DATE:	7-10 April
DISTANCE:	6925 yards
PAR:	72 (288)
WINNER:	$2750

Pos	Player	1st	2nd	3rd	4th	Total
1	**SAM SNEAD**	73	75	67	67	282
2 =	Johnny Bulla	74	73	69	69	285
	Lloyd Mangrum	69	74	72	70	285
4 =	Johnny Palmer	73	71	70	72	286
	Jim Turnesa	73	72	71	70	286
6	Lew Worsham	76	75	70	68	289
7	Joe Kirkwood, Jr	73	72	70	75	290
8 =	Jimmy Demaret	76	72	73	71	292
	Clayton Heafner	71	74	72	75	292
	Byron Nelson	75	70	74	73	292
11 =	Claude Harmon	73	75	73	72	293
	Herman Keiser	75	68	78	72	293
13 =	Herman Barron	73	75	71	75	294
	Leland Gibson	71	77	74	72	294
	Bobby Locke	74	74	74	72	294
16 =	Charles R Coe (a)	77	72	72	74	295
	John Dawson (a)	78	72	72	73	295
	Jim Ferrier	77	72	67	79	295
19 =	Tony Holguin	81	70	71	74	296
	Frank Stranahan (a)	70	77	75	74	296

Snead's first Masters was down to a superb last 36 holes. The final round 67 included eight birdies. This was his second Major, but another was just around the corner. Bulla, after two experiences in the British Open, became a runner-up for the third time. He was also third in the 1941 US Open, and must be considered unlucky not to have become a Majors winner. This was the first occasion upon which the famous winner's Green Jacket was awarded by the Augusta National Club.

COURSE:	Hermitage CC
LOCATION:	Richmond, Virginia
DATE:	25-31 May
QUALIFYING:	64 qualify to matchplay (the defending champion, Ben Hogan, was unable to compete), after 36 holes strokeplay. (Low – Ray Hill, 136)
ROUNDS/HOLES:	Rs1&2, 18holes: R3,QF,SF&F, 36
WINNER:	$3500

Final
SAM SNEAD beat Johnny Palmer, 3&2

Round 2 (Last 32)
Ray Hill beat Jack Isaacs 3&2; Walter Romans beat Frank Moore 4&2; Herman Barron beat Jimmy Thomson 2&1; LLoyd Mangrum beat Bob Hamilton 3&2; JOHNNY PALMER beat Clay Gaddie 8&6; Lew Worsham by George Schneiter 5&4; Henry Williams Jr beat Jack Harden 1up; Al Brosch beat Horton Smith 5&4; SAM SNEAD beat Henry Ransom 3&1; Dave Douglas beat Mike DeMassey 3&2; Jimmy Demaret by George Fazio 3&1; Jim Turnesa beat Johnny Bulla 1up; Clyton Heafner beat Claude Harmon 2&1; Jack Patroni beat Jimmy Johnson 1up; Jim Ferrier beat Skip Alexander 1up; Marty Furgol beat Eddie Burke 2&1

Round 3 (Last 16)
Hill beat Romans 5&4; Mangrum beat Barron 4&3; PALMER beat Worsham 2&1; Williams Jr beat Brosch 7&6; SNEAD beat Douglas 1up; Demaret beat Turnesa 5&3; Heafner beat Patroni 5&4; Ferrier beat Furgol 8&6

Quarter Final
Mangrum beat Hill 7&6; PALMER beat Williams Jr 7&6; SNEAD beat Demaret 4&3; Ferrier beat Heafner 3&2

Semi Final
PALMER beat Mangrum 6&5
SNEAD beat Ferrier 3&2

It is very difficult to win a Masters and a PGA in the same season. They are usually at the opposite ends of the calendar, which requires the sustaining of form in a notoriously fickle sport over several months, or the ability to 'peak' twice in the same year. Sam Snead's feat was no doubt facilitated by another springtime PGA – and the absence of Ben Hogan due to his horrendous road accident.

	US OPEN		BRITISH OPEN
COURSE:	Medinah CC	COURSE:	Royal St George's GC
LOCATION:	Medinah, Illinois	LOCATION:	Sandwich, Kent, England
DATE:	9-11 June	DATE:	6-8 July
DISTANCE:	6936 yards	DISTANCE:	6728 yards
PAR:	71 (284)	PAR:	n/k
WINNER:	$2000	WINNER:	£300

Pos	Player	1st	2nd	3rd	4th	Total
1	**CARY MIDDLECOFF**	75	67	69	75	286
2 =	Clayton Heafner	72	71	71	73	287
	Sam Snead	73	73	71	70	287
4 =	Bobby Locke	74	71	73	71	289
	Jim Turnesa	78	69	70	72	289
6 =	Dave Douglas	74	73	70	73	290
	Buck White	74	68	70	78	290
8 =	Pete Cooper	71	73	74	73	291
	Claude Harmon	71	72	74	74	291
	Johnny Palmer	71	75	72	73	291
11 =	Eric Monti	75	72	70	75	292
	Herschel Spears	76	71	71	74	292
13	Al Brosch	70	71	73	79	293
14 =	Johnny Bulla	73	75	72	74	294
	Lloyd Mangrum	74	74	70	76	294
	Skee Riegel (a)	72	75	73	74	294
	Harry Todd	76	72	73	73	294
	Ellsworth Vines	73	72	71	78	294
19 =	Fred Haas	74	73	73	75	295
	Les Kennedy	69	74	79	73	295
	Gene Webb	73	77	70	75	295

Pos	Player	1st	2nd	3rd	4th	Total
1	**BOBBY LOCKE***	69	76	68	70	283
2	Harry Bradshaw	68	77	68	70	283
3	Roberto de Vicenzo	68	75	73	69	285
4 =	Sam King	71	69	74	72	286
	Charlie Ward	73	71	70	72	286
6 =	Max Faulkner	71	71	71	74	287
	Arthur Lees	74	70	72	71	287
8 =	Jimmy Adams	67	77	72	72	288
	Johnny Fallon	69	75	72	72	288
	WD Smithers	72	75	70	71	288
11 =	Ken Bousfield	69	77	76	67	289
	Bill Shankland	69	73	74	73	289
13	Frank Stranahan (a)	71	73	74	72	290
14 =	Bill Branch	71	75	74	71	291
	Dick Burton	73	70	74	74	291
	J Knipe	76	71	72	72	291
17	Walter Lees	74	72	69	78	293
18	Alan Waters	70	76	75	73	294
19	Norman Sutton	69	78	75	73	295
20 =	Reg Horne	73	74	75	74	296
	Arthur Lacey	72	73	73	78	296
	Gregor McIntosh	70	77	76	73	296
	William McMinn	70	75	78	73	296
	EA Southerden	69	76	74	77	296

Hogan was crippled for 12 months and played no part in any of the 1949 Majors. Cary Middlecoff won the first of his two Opens, winning at Medinah by just holding off late challenges by Heafner, and especially Snead.

* Bobby Locke (135) beat Harry Bradshaw (147) in the 36-Hole Play-off

In 1949, Bobby Locke of South Africa was undoubtedly the best non-American golfer in the world. He had already won several times on the US tour and featured well in the US Open; and was about to embark on an orgy of British Open Championships. He had to endure a second 36-hole dogfight with Harry Bradshaw first – then an easier head-to-head in the play-off. Bradshaw's R2 77 was not helped by his having to play one shot out of a broken beer bottle. In an attempt to attract a more international field, the R&A doubled the winner's prize money. The Americans were still not interested.

THE MASTERS

COURSE:	Augusta National GC
LOCATION:	Augusta, Georgia
DATE:	6-9 April
DISTANCE:	6925 yards
PAR:	72 (288)
WINNER:	$2400

Pos	Player	1st	2nd	3rd	4th	Total
1	**JIMMY DEMARET**	70	72	72	69	283
2	Jim Ferrier	70	67	73	75	285
3	Sam Snead	71	74	70	72	287
4 =	Ben Hogan	73	68	71	67	288
	Byron Nelson	75	70	69	74	288
6	Lloyd Mangrum	76	74	73	68	291
7 =	Clayton Heafner	74	77	69	72	292
	Cary Middlecoff	75	76	68	73	292
9	Lawson Little	70	73	75	75	293
10 =	Fred Haas	74	76	73	71	294
	Gene Sarazen	80	70	72	72	294
12 =	Roberto de Vicenzo	76	76	73	71	296
	Horton Smith	70	79	75	72	296
14 =	Skip Alexander	78	74	73	72	297
	Vic Ghezzi	78	75	70	74	297
	Leland Gibson	78	73	72	74	297
	Herman Keiser	75	72	75	75	297
	Joe Kirkwood, Jr	75	74	77	71	297
	Henry Picard	74	71	77	75	297
	Frank Stranahan (a)	74	79	73	71	297

Jim Ferrier conceded seven strokes over the final six holes to lose to Jimmy Demaret. Although Demaret kept up the pressure by playing these holes in two under par, Ferrier's game collapsed as he dropped five shots. Demaret's win was his third – the first to achieve this number in the Masters. After 12 months, when to walk again was considered optimistic, Ben Hogan finished in par to tie for fourth place, with part-timer Nelson in fifth.

US OPEN

COURSE:	Merion GC
LOCATION:	Ardmore, Pennsylvania
DATE:	8-11 June
DISTANCE:	6694 yards
PAR:	70 (280)
WINNER:	$4000

Pos	Player	1st	2nd	3rd	4th	Total
1	**BEN HOGAN***	72	69	72	74	287
2	Lloyd Mangrum	72	70	69	76	287
3	George Fazio	73	72	72	70	287
4	Dutch Harrison	72	67	73	76	288
5 =	Jim Ferrier	71	69	74	75	289
	Joe Kirkwood, Jr	71	74	74	70	289
	Henry Ransom	72	71	73	73	289
8	Bill Nary	73	70	74	73	290
9	Julius Boros	68	72	77	74	291
10 =	Cary Middlecoff	71	71	71	79	292
	Johnny Palmer	73	70	70	79	292
12 =	Al Besselink	71	72	76	75	294
	Johnny Bulla	74	66	78	76	294
	Dick Mayer	73	76	73	72	294
	Henry Picard	71	71	79	73	294
	Skee Riegel	73	69	79	73	294
	Sam Snead	73	75	72	74	294
18 =	Skip Alexander	68	74	77	76	295
	Fred Haas	73	74	76	72	295
20 =	Jimmy Demaret	72	77	71	76	296
	Marty Furgol	75	71	72	78	296
	Dick Metz	76	71	71	78	296
	Bob Toski	73	69	80	74	296
	Harold Williams	69	75	75	77	296

*Ben Hogan (69) beat Lloyd Mangrum (73) and George Fazio (75) in the 18-Hole Play-off

Lee Mackey's R1 record score of 64 was the lowest for any round in any Major to date. Hogan's comeback was complete when he repeated his 1948 Open win at the Riviera CC here at Merion. He was to achieve it the hard way, however, with the three-way tie taking him to the physical limit. The 36-holes on the final day proved almost too much for him, but, refreshed for the Sunday play-off, he shot a 69 to win comfortably. This lesson was to dissuade Hogan from playing too much golf.

US PGA

COURSE:	Scioto CC
LOCATION:	Columbus, Ohio
DATE:	21-27 June
QUALIFYING:	63 qualify to matchplay, plus the defending champion (Sam Snead) after 36 holes strokeplay. (Low – Sam Snead, 140)
ROUNDS/HOLES:	Rs1&2, 18holes: R3,QF,SF&F, 36
WINNER:	$3500

Final
CHANDLER HARPER beat Henry Williams Jr, 4&3

Round 2 (Last 32)
Eddie Burke beat Sam Snead 1up; Ray Gafford by Leonard Schmutte 1up; Denny Shute beat Elsworth Vines 4&3; Jimmy Demaret beat Rod Munday 5&3; Lloyd Mangrum beat Skip Alexander 1up; Chick Harbert beat Harold Williams 5&3; Bob Toski beat George Fazio 1up; CHANDLER HARPER beat Dick Metz 1up; Claude Harmon beat Al Brosch 2&1; HENRY WILLIAMS Jr by Emery Thomas 6&5; Elmer Reed beat Jim Ferrier 5&4; Dave Douglas beat Jimmy Hines 5&4; Jackson Bradley by George Shafer 4&3; Henry Picard beat Clarence Doser 4&2; Johnny Palmer beat Lew Worsham 4&2; Ted Kroll beat Al Watrous 2&1

Round 3 (Last 16)
Gafford beat Burke 4&3; Demaret beat Shute 4&3; Mangrum beat Harbert 6&5; HARPER beat Toski 2&1; WILLIAMS Jr beat Harmon 1up (after 38); Douglas beat Reed 3&2; Picard beat Bradley 1up; Palmer beat Kroll 1up

Quarter Final
Demaret beat Gafford 5&4; HARPER beat Mangrum 1up; WILLIAMS Jr beat Douglas 1up; Picard beat Palmer 10&8

Semi Final
HARPER beat Demaret 2&1
WILLIAMS Jr beat Picard 1up (after 38)

Hogan's absence, and the defeat of Sam Snead in R2, made for a very open PGA Championship at Scioto. Experienced campaigners like Jimmy Demaret and Lloyd Mangrum were then favourites; but it was 36-year old Chandler Harper who defeated Demaret in the semi final to go on and gain his only Major. The final was played between two men who's best PGA record previously was Harper's making the third round in 1946.

BRITISH OPEN

COURSE:	Troon GC
LOCATION:	Troon, Ayrshire, Scotland
DATE:	5-7 July
DISTANCE:	6583 yards
PAR:	n/k
WINNER:	£300

Pos	Player	1st	2nd	3rd	4th	Total
1	**BOBBY LOCKE**	69	72	70	68	279
2	Roberto de Vicenzo	72	71	68	70	281
3 =	Fred Daly	75	72	69	66	282
	Dai Rees	71	68	72	71	282
5 =	Max Faulkner	72	70	70	71	283
	Eric Moore	74	68	73	68	283
7 =	Fred Bullock	71	71	71	71	284
	Arthur Lees	68	76	68	72	284
9 =	Sam King	70	75	68	73	286
	Frank Stranahan (a)	77	70	73	66	286
	Flory van Donck	73	71	72	70	286
12 =	Jimmy Adams	73	75	69	70	287
	Wally Smithers	74	70	73	70	287
14 =	Johnny Bulla	73	70	71	74	288
	Hector Thomson	71	72	73	72	288
16	Harry Bradshaw	73	71	75	70	289
17 =	Reg Horne	73	75	71	71	290
	JB McHale (a)	73	73	74	70	290
	Ernest E Whitcombe	69	76	72	73	290
20 =	Alf Padgham	77	71	74	69	291
	John Panton	76	69	70	76	291
	Norman von Nida	74	72	76	69	291

From this year onward, apart from the odd US Open, Bobby Locke concentrated his time more in Europe and his native South Africa – after 15 wins on the US Tour. He collected the first back-to-back Open Championship win since Hagen's in 1929. In doing so he set a new low of 279. Johnny Bulla apart, the American professional interest waned even further, as the PGA only finished eight days before the Open started; and there was still some disparity in the respective purses.

THE MASTERS

COURSE:	Augusta National GC
LOCATION:	Augusta, Georgia
DATE:	5-8 April
DISTANCE:	6925 yards
PAR:	72 (288)
WINNER:	$3000

Pos	Player	1st	2nd	3rd	4th	Total
1	**BEN HOGAN**	70	72	70	68	280
2	Skee Riegel	73	68	70	71	282
3 =	Lloyd Mangrum	69	74	70	73	286
	Lew Worsham	71	71	72	72	286
5	Dave Douglas	74	69	72	73	288
6	Lawson Little	72	73	72	72	289
7	Jim Ferrier	74	70	74	72	290
8 =	Johnny Bulla	71	72	73	75	291
	Byron Nelson	71	73	73	74	291
	Sam Snead	69	74	68	80	291
11	Jack Burke, Jr	73	72	74	73	292
12 =	Charles R Coe (a)	76	71	73	73	293
	Cary Middlecoff	73	73	69	78	293
	Gene Sarazen	75	74	73	71	293
15 =	Ed Furgol	80	71	72	71	294
	Dutch Harrison	76	71	76	71	294
17	Julius Boros	76	72	74	73	295
18 =	George Fazio	68	74	74	80	296
	Bob Toski	75	73	73	75	296
20 =	Al Besselink	76	73	71	77	297
	Dick Chapman (a)	72	76	72	77	297
	Clayton Heafner	74	72	73	78	297
	Joe Kirkwood, Jr	73	71	78	75	297
	Roberto de Vicenzo	75	74	74	74	297

Ben Hogan won his first Masters to keep his incredible comeback going. It was his seventh Major title, and second since his accident. Recently-turned professional, 1947 US Amateur Champion, Skee Riegel, finished at six under par for the Tournament, but he succumbed to the power and experience of Hogan in R4.

US OPEN

COURSE:	Oakland Hills CC
LOCATION:	Birmingham, Michigan
DATE:	14-16 June
DISTANCE:	6927 yards
PAR:	70 (280)
WINNER:	$4000

Pos	Player	1st	2nd	3rd	4th	Total
1	**BEN HOGAN**	76	73	71	67	287
2	Clayton Heafner	72	75	73	69	289
3	Bobby Locke	73	71	74	73	291
4 =	Julius Boros	74	74	71	74	293
	Lloyd Mangrum	75	74	74	70	293
6 =	Al Besselink	72	77	72	73	294
	Dave Douglas	75	70	75	74	294
	Fred Hawkins	76	72	75	71	294
	Paul Runyan	73	74	72	75	294
10 =	Al Brosch	73	74	76	72	295
	Smiley Quick	73	76	74	72	295
	Skee Riegel	75	76	71	73	295
	Sam Snead	71	78	72	74	295
14 =	Jimmy Demaret	74	74	70	78	296
	Lew Worsham	76	71	76	73	296
16 =	Charles Kocsis (a)	75	74	76	72	297
	Henry Ransom	74	74	76	73	297
	Buck White	76	75	74	72	297
19 =	Raymond Gafford	76	74	74	74	298
	Johnny Revolta	78	72	72	76	298

Hogan made it two US Opens in a row – and wins in the last three consecutive Major Championships he had entered. Still playing a modicum of golf to conserve his strength, but enough to stay sharp, Hogan made it a last round special performance once again, burning up Oakland Hills in 67 – 32 for the back nine. He considered this his best-ever round of golf.

COURSE:	Oakmont CC
LOCATION:	Oakmont, Pennsylvania
DATE:	27 June-3 July
QUALIFYING:	63 qualify to matchplay, plus the defending champion (Chandler Harper), after 36 holes strokeplay. (Low – Pete Cooper, Claude Harmon, Lloyd Mangrum, 142)
ROUNDS/HOLES:	Rs1&2, 18holes: R3,QF,SF&F, 36 holes
WINNER:	$3500

Final

SAM SNEAD beat Walter Burkemo 7&6

Round 2 (Last 32)

Charles Bassler beat Jim Turnesa 5&4; George Bolesta beat Ed Oliver 2&1; Al Brosch beat Lew Worsham 5&4; Jack Harden beat Toney Penna 5&3; Lloyd Mangrum beat Buck White 2&1; SAM SNEAD beat Marty Furgol 1up (after 21); Jack Burke, Jr beat Gene Sarazen 5&3; Gene Kunes beat Ray Gafford 2&1; Dick Shoemaker beat Lawson Little 2&1; WALTER BURKEMO beat Chick Harbert 1up (after 19); Vic Ghezzi beat Rod Munday 4&3; Reggie Myles by Mike Pavella 1up (after 20); Jackson Bradley beat Denny Shute 2&1; Elsworth Vines beat Henry Picard 1up; Jim Ferrier beat Milon Marusic 3&2; Johnny Bulla beat Bob Hamilton 5&3

Round 3 (Last 16)

Bassler beat Bolesta 1up (after 37); Brosch beat Harden 6&5; SNEAD beat Mangrum 3&2; Burke Jr beat Kunes 4&3; BURKEMO by Shoemaker 2&1; Myles beat Ghezzi 1up; Vines beat Bradley 2&1; Bulla beat Ferrier 9&8

Quarter Final

Bassler beat Brosch 1up; SNEAD beat Burke Jr 2&1; BURKEMO beat Myles 1up; Vines beat Bulla 1up

Semi Final

SNEAD beat Bassler 9&8
BURKEMO beat Vines 1up (after 37)

After squeaking past Fred Haas in R1, and needing three extra holes before disposing of Marty Furgol, Sam Snead really came to life in the semi final. From there he annihilated Charles Bassler and Walter Burkemo to become the last multiple PGA Champion until Nicklaus repeated his own first win in 1971 – making it 19 different winners in succession.

COURSE:	Royal Portrush GC
LOCATION:	Portrush, Co Antrim, Northern Ireland
DATE:	4-6 July
DISTANCE:	6802 yards
PAR:	n/k
WINNER:	£300

Pos	Player	1st	2nd	3rd	4th	Total
1	**MAX FAULKNER**	71	70	70	74	285
2	Antonio Cerda	74	72	71	70	287
3	Charlie Ward	75	73	74	68	290
4 =	Jimmy Adams	68	77	75	72	292
	Fred Daly	74	70	75	73	292
6 =	Bobby Locke	71	74	74	74	293
	Bill Shankland	73	76	72	72	293
	Norman Sutton	73	70	74	76	293
	Peter Thomson	70	75	73	75	293
	Harry Weetman	73	71	75	74	293
11	John Panton	73	72	74	75	294
12 =	Dick Burton	74	77	71	73	295
	Dai Rees	70	77	76	72	295
	Frank Stranahan (a)	75	75	72	73	295
15	Harry Bradshaw	80	71	74	71	296
16	Eric Cremin	73	75	75	74	297
17 =	Kep Enderby (a)	76	74	75	73	298
	Alan Waters	74	75	78	71	298
19 =	Ugo Grappasoni	73	73	77	76	299
	Jack Hargreaves	73	78	79	69	299
	WJ Henderson	77	73	76	73	299
	Kel Nagle	76	76	72	75	299
	Christy O'Connor, Sr	79	74	72	74	299

The Open left the shores of Great Britain for the one and only time and visited picturesque Royal Portrush. Max Faulkner interrupted Bobby Locke's recent stranglehold, building up enough of any early lead to hold off fast-finishing Argentinian, Antonio Cerda. This year, the US PGA and the British Open effectively overlapped, with the finals of the former held on the day before the first round in Ulster. The Open and the US Majors were never further apart.

THE MASTERS

COURSE:	Augusta National GC					
LOCATION:	Augusta, Georgia					
DATE:	3-6 April					
DISTANCE:	6925 yards					
PAR:	72 (288)					
WINNER:	$4000					

Pos	Player	1st	2nd	3rd	4th	Total
1	**SAM SNEAD**	70	67	77	72	286
2	Jack Burke, Jr	76	67	78	69	290
3 =	Al Besselink	70	76	71	74	291
	Tommy Bolt	71	71	75	74	291
	Jim Ferrier	72	70	77	72	291
6	Lloyd Mangrum	71	74	75	72	292
7 =	Julius Boros	73	73	76	71	293
	Fred Hawkins	71	73	78	71	293
	Ben Hogan	70	70	74	79	293
	Lew Worsham	71	75	73	74	293
11	Cary Middlecoff	72	72	72	78	294
12	Johnny Palmer	69	74	75	77	295
13	Johnny Revolta	71	71	77	77	296
14 =	George Fazio	72	71	78	76	297
	Claude Harmon	73	74	77	73	297
	Chuck Kocsis (a)	75	78	71	73	297
	Ted Kroll	74	74	76	73	297
	Skee Riegel	75	71	78	73	297
19 =	Joe Kirkwood, Jr	71	77	74	76	298
	Frank Stranahan (a)	72	74	76	76	298

Sam Snead overcame high winds, which affected scoring generally over the last two rounds, to post 286; the only score better than par in the Tournament. It was his second Masters and sixth Major. Ray Gafford tied for the lead after R1 with a 69 – then followed it with an 80 and eventual 49th place.

US OPEN

COURSE:	Northwood GC					
LOCATION:	Dallas, Texas					
DATE:	12-14 June					
DISTANCE:	6782 yards					
PAR:	70 (280)					
WINNER:	$4000					

Pos	Player	1st	2nd	3rd	4th	Total
1	**JULIUS BOROS**	71	71	68	71	281
2	Ed Oliver	71	72	70	72	285
3	Ben Hogan	69	69	74	74	286
4	Johnny Bulla	73	68	73	73	287
5	George Fazio	71	69	75	75	290
6	Dick Metz	70	74	76	71	291
7 =	Tommy Bolt	72	76	71	73	292
	Ted Kroll	71	75	76	70	292
	Lew Worsham	72	71	74	75	292
10 =	Lloyd Mangrum	75	74	72	72	293
	Sam Snead	70	75	76	72	293
	Earl Stewart	76	75	70	72	293
13 =	Clarence Doser	71	73	73	77	294
	Harry Todd	71	76	74	73	294
15 =	Al Brosch	68	79	77	71	295
	Jimmy Demaret	74	77	73	71	295
	Milon Marusic	73	76	74	72	295
	Horton Smith	70	73	76	76	295
19 =	Doug Ford	74	74	74	74	296
	James Jackson (a)	74	76	75	71	296
	Bill Trombley	72	73	81	70	296

Julius Boros didn't turn professional until 1950, when he was already 30 years old. This was his first of three Majors – the other two occurred in the next decade, when he was to set records for his age. The odds were in favour of Hogan winning again when he equalled the Open 36-hole low score. The heat and 36 holes on the last day were too much for him this time though.

COURSE:	Big Spring CC
LOCATION:	Louisville, Kentucky
DATE:	18-25 June
QUALIFYING:	63 qualify to matchplay, plus the defending champion (Sam Snead), after 36 holes strokeplay. (Low – Dutch Harrison, 136)
ROUNDS/HOLES:	Rs1&2, 18holes: R3,QF,SF&F, 36 holes
WINNER:	$3500

Final
JIM TURNESA beat Chick Harbert, 1up

Round 2 (Last 32)
Ray Honsberger beat Jim Ferrier 1up; Ted Kroll beat Lloyd Mangrum 2up; Cary Middlecoff beat Charles Harter 3&2; Al Smith beat Labron Harris 1up (after 19); JIM TURNESA beat Chandler Harper 3&1; Roberto de Vicenzo beat Jack Burke Jr 1up; Clarence Doser beat Bob Gajda 3&2; Jack Isaacs beat Marty Furgol 3&2; Fred Haas beat Lew Worsham 1up; Milon Marusic beat Zell Eaton (default); Henry Williams Jr beat Jack Jones 1up; CHICK HARBERT beat Leonard Schmutte 3&2; Frank Champ beat John Trish 2&1; Walter Burkemo beat Dave Douglas 1up; Vic Ghezzi beat Mel Carpenter 5&3; Bob Hamilton beat Sam Bernardi 3&1

Round 3 (Last 16)
Kroll beat Honsberger 1up (after 38); Middlecoff beat Smith 4&2; TURNESA beat de Vicenzo 5&4; Doser beat Isaacs 1up; Haas beat Marusic 1up (after 38); HARBERT beat Williams Jr 6&5; Champ beat Burkemo 3&1; Hamilton beat Ghezzi 9&8

Quarter Final
Kroll beat Middlecoff 1up (after 38); TURNESA beat Doser 2&1; HARBERT beat Haas 2&1; Hamilton beat Champ 2&1

SEMI FINAL
TURNESA beat Kroll 4&2
HARBERT beat Hamilton 2&1

At the age of 40, and after 26 years and four Major Championship second places for him and his brothers (Joe and Mike), Jim Turnesa finally buried the family jinx at Big Spring. The youngest of the seven Turnesa brothers to make a mark was Willie – he won the US Amateur title in 1938 and 1948, but he never turned pro. Sam Snead, the defending champion, went out in R1 to Lew Worsham.

COURSE:	Royal Lytham and St Anne's GC
LOCATION:	St Annes, Lancashire, England
DATE:	9-11 July
DISTANCE:	6657 yards
PAR:	n/k
WINNER:	£300

Pos	Player	1st	2nd	3rd	4th	Total
1	**BOBBY LOCKE**	69	71	74	73	287
2	Peter Thomson	68	73	77	70	288
3	Fred Daly	67	69	77	76	289
4	Henry Cotton	75	74	74	71	294
5 =	Antonio Cerda	73	73	76	73	295
	Sam King	71	74	74	76	295
7	Flory van Donck	74	75	71	76	296
8	Fred Bullock	76	72	72	77	297
9 =	Harry Bradshaw	70	74	75	79	298
	Eric Brown	71	72	78	77	298
	Willie Goggin	71	74	75	78	298
	Arthur Lees	76	72	76	74	298
	Syd Scott	75	69	76	78	298
	Norman von Nida	77	70	74	77	298
15 =	John Panton	72	72	78	77	299
	Harry Weetman	74	77	71	77	299
17 =	Max Faulkner	72	76	79	73	300
	Gene Sarazen	74	73	77	76	300
	Wally Smithers	73	74	76	77	300
20	Norman Sutton	72	74	79	76	301

Emulating Harry Vardon and James Braid, Locke won his third Open in four years. He held firm in the last round under the challenge of young Australian, Peter Thomson. Gene Sarazen, at the age of 50, made a creditable 17th place, 18 years after his success at Prince's, Sandwich. Otherwise the field was almost bereft of an American challenge.

1953

COURSE:	Augusta National GC
LOCATION:	Augusta, Georgia
DATE:	9-12 April
DISTANCE:	6925 yards
PAR:	72 (288)
WINNER:	$4000

Pos	Player	1st	2nd	3rd	4th	Total
1	**BEN HOGAN**	70	69	66	69	274
2	Ed Oliver	69	73	67	70	279
3	Lloyd Mangrum	74	68	71	69	282
4	Bob Hamilton	71	69	70	73	283
5 =	Tommy Bolt	71	75	68	71	285
	Chick Harbert	68	73	70	74	285
7	Ted Kroll	71	70	73	72	286
8	Jack Burke, Jr	78	69	69	71	287
9	Al Besselink	69	75	70	74	288
10 =	Julius Boros	73	71	75	70	289
	Chandler Harper	74	72	69	74	289
	Fred Hawkins	75	70	74	70	289
13	Johnny Palmer	74	73	72	71	290
14 =	Frank Stranahan (a)	72	75	69	75	291
	E Harvie Ward, Jr (a)	73	74	69	75	291
16 =	Charles R Coe (a)	75	74	72	71	292
	Jim Ferrier	74	71	76	71	292
	Dick Mayer	73	72	71	76	292
	Sam Snead	71	75	71	75	292
	Earl Stewart, Jr	75	72	70	75	292

Ben Hogan, in winning his second Masters title, lowered the Masters' and all Majors' low score to 274; trimming the Augusta National Tournament's record, and beating the field, by five shots. Conditions were benign, but Hogan played what was reported as 'the best 72-hole stretch of golf played by anyone anywhere'. The Masters' record low was to stand until taken by Nicklaus in 1965, and equalled by Ray Floyd 11 years later. It was then reduced to 270 by Tiger Woods in 1997. Porky Oliver added another runner-up spot to his 1946 PGA and previous year's US Open.

COURSE:	Oakmont CC
LOCATION:	Oakmont, Pennsylvania
DATE:	11-13 June
DISTANCE:	6916 yards
PAR:	72 (288)
WINNER:	$5000

Pos	Player	1st	2nd	3rd	4th	Total
1	**BEN HOGAN**	67	72	73	71	283
2	Sam Snead	72	69	72	76	289
3	Lloyd Mangrum	73	70	74	75	292
4 =	Pete Cooper	78	75	71	70	294
	Jimmy Demaret	71	76	71	76	294
	George Fazio	70	71	77	76	294
7 =	Ted Kroll	76	71	74	74	295
	Dick Metz	75	70	74	76	295
9 =	Marty Furgol	73	74	76	73	296
	Jay Hebert	72	72	74	78	296
	Frank Souchak (a)	70	76	76	74	296
12 =	Fred Haas	74	73	72	78	297
	Bill Ogden	71	78	75	73	297
14 =	Jack Burke, Jr	76	73	72	77	298
	Dutch Harrison	77	75	70	76	298
	Bobby Locke	78	70	74	76	298
17 =	Julius Boros	75	72	76	76	299
	Clarence Doser	74	76	78	71	299
	Bill Nary	76	74	73	76	299
	Jim Turnesa	75	78	72	74	299

Returning to Oakmont for the first time since 1935 (although the course was host site to the PGA two years earlier), the Open saw Hogan rewriting the record books once again. In beating top rival Snead by six strokes, Hogan drew level with Willie Anderson's and Bobby Jones' four US Opens; and it was the first wire-to-wire win since Jim Barnes in 1921. He also repeated his 1951 feat of lifting the Masters and US Open in the same year.

COURSE:	Birmingham CC
LOCATION:	Birmingham, Michigan
DATE:	1-7 July
QUALIFYING:	63 qualify to matchplay, plus the defending champion (Jim Turnesa) after 36 holes strokeplay. (Low – Johnny Palmer, 134)
ROUNDS/HOLES:	Rs1&2, 18holes: R3,QF,SF&F, 36 holes
WINNER:	$3500

Final

WALTER BURKEMO beat Felice Torza, 2&1

Round 2 (Last 32)

FELICE TORZA beat Jim Turnesa 4&3; Wally Ulrich beat Buck White 2&1; Jimmy Clark beat Cary Middlecoff 5&4; Henry Williams Jr beat Charles Bassler 3&1; Jack Isaacs beat Fred Haas 1up; Labron Harris beat Marty Furgol 1up; Al Smith beat Iverson Martin 3&2; Henry Ransom beat Bob Toski 3&2; Jackson Bradley beat Tommy Bolt 1up; Dave Douglas beat Sam Snead 1up (after 19); WALTER BURKEMO beat Mike Turnesa 3&1; Pete Cooper beat Leonard Dodson 6&5; Bill Nary beat Dutch Harrison 1up; Jim Browning beat Broyles Plemmons 3&1; Ed Furgol beat Jim Ferrier 3&1; Claude Harmon beat Jack Grout 4&2

Round 3 (Last 16)

TORZA beat Ulrich 1up (after 38); Clark beat Williams Jr 4&3; Isaacs beat Harris 5&4; Ransom beat Smith 1up; Douglas beat Bradley 1up (after 37); BURKEMO beat Cooper 3&2; Nary beat Browning 6&5; Harmon beat Furgol 5&3

Quarter Final

TORZA beat Clark 1up; Isaacs beat Ransom 1up; BURKEMO beat Douglas 2up; Harmon beat Nary 6&5

Semi Final

TORZA beat Isaacs 1up (after 39)
BURKEMO beat Harmon 1up

Once more the PGA clashed with the British Open, so even if Ben Hogan did contemplate a Grand Slam in 1953, he would have been denied it. He was persuaded to try the British Open instead. Walter Burkemo was a local boy and his match wins were cheered on by a partisan crowd. His one and only Major win, and his second place in the PGA in 1951, picked him out as a match-player and he was selected for the 1953 Ryder Cup. He lost his only match.

COURSE:	Carnoustie GC
LOCATION:	Carnoustie, Angus, Scotland
DATE:	8-10 July
DISTANCE:	7103 yards
PAR:	n/k
WINNER:	£500

Pos	Player	1st	2nd	3rd	4th	Total
1	**BEN HOGAN**	73	71	70	68	282
2 =	Antonio Cerda	75	71	69	71	286
	Dai Rees	72	70	73	71	286
	Frank Stranahan (a)	70	74	73	69	286
	Peter Thomson	72	72	71	71	286
6	Roberto de Vicenzo	72	71	71	73	287
7	Sam King	74	73	72	71	290
8	Bobby Locke	72	73	74	72	291
9 =	Peter Alliss	75	72	74	71	292
	Eric Brown	71	71	75	75	292
11	Fred Daly	73	75	71	75	294
12	Max Faulkner	74	71	73	77	295
13	Arthur Lees	76	76	72	72	296
14 =	THT Fairbairn	74	71	73	79	297
	John Jacobs	79	74	71	73	297
	Harry Weetman	80	73	72	72	297
17 =	H Hassanein	78	71	73	76	298
	EG Lester	83	70	72	73	298
	Charlie Ward	78	71	76	73	298
20 =	Reg Horne	76	74	75	74	299
	Flory van Donck	77	71	78	73	299

Ben Hogan paid his one and only visit to the Open Championship, adapted very quickly to conditions and the size of the ball – the British still used the 1.62" small ball, whereas the American big ball (1.68") had been in operation since 1932 – and won the title. His reducing round-by-round score of 282 meant he was the first, and only, golfer to win three modern Majors in one season. In doing so he joined Sarazen as the second man to achieve the Grand Slam. This was his last Major title (his ninth, two behind Walter Hagen). He had played in few other tournaments apart from Majors since the accident in 1949, but his sequence in those Majors played between 1950 and 1953, inclusive, was: 4, W, W, W, 7, 3, W, W, W.

THE MASTERS

COURSE:	Augusta National GC
LOCATION:	Augusta, Georgia
DATE:	8-12 April
DISTANCE:	6925 yards
PAR:	72 (288)
WINNER:	$5000

Pos	Player	1st	2nd	3rd	4th	Total
1	**SAM SNEAD***	74	73	70	72	289
2	Ben Hogan	72	73	69	75	289
3	Billy Joe Patton (a)	70	74	75	71	290
4 =	Dutch Harrison	70	79	74	68	291
	Lloyd Mangrum	71	75	76	69	291
6 =	Jerry Barber	74	76	71	71	292
	Jack Burke, Jr	71	77	73	71	292
	Bob Rosburg	73	73	76	70	292
9 =	Al Besselink	74	74	74	72	294
	Cary Middlecoff	73	76	70	75	294
11	Dick Chapman (a)	75	75	75	70	294
12 =	Tommy Bolt	73	74	72	77	296
	Chick Harbert	73	75	75	73	296
	Byron Nelson	73	76	74	73	296
	Lew Worsham	74	74	74	74	296
16 =	Julius Boros	76	79	68	74	297
	Jay Hebert	79	74	74	70	297
	Peter Thomson	76	72	76	73	297
	Ken Venturi (a)	76	74	73	74	297
20 =	Charles R Coe (a)	76	75	73	74	298
	E Harvie Ward, Jr (a)	78	75	74	71	298

* Sam Snead (70) beat Ben Hogan (71) in the 18-Hole Play-off

Hogan could have made that famous sequence four in a row had not Sam Snead chipped away at the great man's lead in R4. Hogan slipped to three over for the round, allowing Snead to force a tie through his solid par play. Snead then won the head-to-head between the world's two greatest players of the time, and two of the very best of all-time, to become a three-time Masters Champion.

US OPEN

COURSE:	Baltusrol GC
LOCATION:	Springfield, New Jersey
DATE:	17-19 June
DISTANCE:	7027 yards
PAR:	70 (280)
WINNER:	$6000

Pos	Player	1st	2nd	3rd	4th	Total
1	**ED FURGOL**	71	70	71	72	284
2	Gene Littler	70	69	76	70	285
3 =	Lloyd Mangrum	72	71	72	71	286
	Dick Mayer	72	71	70	73	286
5	Bobby Locke	74	70	74	70	288
6 =	Tommy Bolt	72	72	73	72	289
	Fred Haas	73	73	71	72	289
	Ben Hogan	71	70	76	72	289
	Shelley Mayfield	73	75	72	69	289
	Billy Joe Patton (a)	69	76	71	73	289
11 =	Cary Middlecoff	72	71	72	75	290
	Sam Snead	72	73	72	73	290
13 =	Rudy Horvath	75	72	71	73	291
	Al Mengert	71	72	73	75	291
15 =	Jack Burke, Jr	73	73	72	75	293
	Claude Harmon	75	72	72	74	293
17	Jay Hebert	77	70	70	77	294
18 =	Marty Furgol	73	74	73	75	295
	Leland Gibson	72	77	69	77	295
	Bob Toski	70	74	78	73	295

National TV covered the 1954 Open to witness Ed Furgol just hold off 1953 US Amateur Champion, now professional, Gene Littler, to win his only Major. The human interest story here was that Furgol had a withered left arm after a childhood accident. Amateur, Billy Joe Patton, after leading and almost tying the Masters, took the lead again here, at Baltusrol, after 18 holes.

BRITISH OPEN

COURSE: Birkdale GC
LOCATION: Southport, Lancashire, England
DATE: 7-9 July
DISTANCE: 6867 yards
PAR: n/k
WINNER: £750

Pos	Player	1st	2nd	3rd	4th	Total
1	**PETER THOMSON**	72	71	69	71	283
2 =	Bobby Locke	74	71	69	70	284
	Dai Rees	72	71	69	72	284
	Syd Scott	76	67	69	72	284
5 =	Jimmy Adams	73	75	69	69	286
	Antonio Cerda	71	71	73	71	286
	Jim Turnesa	72	72	71	71	286
8 =	Peter Alliss	72	74	71	70	287
	Sam King	69	74	74	70	287
10 =	Jimmy Demaret	73	71	74	71	289
	Flory van Donck	77	71	70	71	289
12 =	Alfonso Angelini	76	70	73	71	290
	Harry Bradshaw	72	72	73	73	290
	JW Spence	69	72	74	75	290
15 =	Bobby Halsall	72	73	73	73	291
	Peter Toogood (a)	72	75	73	71	291
17 =	Ugo Grappasoni	72	75	74	71	292
	C Kane	74	72	74	72	292
	Gene Sarazen	75	74	73	70	292
20 =	Norman Drew	76	71	74	72	293
	Max Faulkner	73	78	69	73	293
	Jack Hargreaves	77	72	77	67	293
	John Jacobs	71	73	80	69	293
	Eric Lester	72	75	73	73	293
	Christy O'Connor, Sr	74	72	72	75	293
	Lambert Topping	75	76	69	73	293

Following Ben Hogan's famous interruption the previous year, Bobby Locke must have wondered what had happened to his Open hegemony when Peter Thomson converted his two previous runner-up spots into his first Open; to put the South African into joint-second place. Sarazen again belied his age, and there were Top 10 performances from other US veterans, Jim Turnesa and Jimmy Demaret. To put British golf of this era in perspective, the US won six of the seven Ryder Cups in the period 1949-61 and the British would have to wait until Tony Jacklin in 1969 for their next home success. Classic Birkdale, scheduled for use when World war Two arrived, finally got on the roster for the Open.

US PGA

COURSE: Keller GC
LOCATION: St Paul, Minnesota
DATE: 21-27 July
QUALIFYING: 63 qualify to matchplay, plus the defending champion (Walter Burkemo), after 36 holes strokeplay. (Low – Ed Oliver, 136)
ROUNDS/HOLES: Rs1&2, 18holes: R3,QF,SF&F, 36 holes
WINNER: $5000

Final
CHICK HARBERT beat Walter Burkemo, 4&3

Round 2 (Last 32)
Tommy Bolt beat Arthur Doering 2&1; Jim Browning beat Ed Furgol 1up; Sam Snead beat Jin Milward 4&3; Dutch Harrison beat Johnny Palmer 4&3; Charles Bassler beat Bill Trombley 5&4; Jerry Barber beat Fred Haas 1up (after 19); CHICK HARBERT beat John O'Donnell 3&1; Ed Oliver beat Bill Nary (1up); WALTER BURKEMO beat Claude Harmon 2&1; Johnny Revolta beat Toby Lyons 5&4; Roberto de Vicenzo beat Henry Ransom; 4&3; Elroy Marti beat Henry Williams Jr 2up; Cary Middlecoff beat Bob Toski 2&1; Ted Kroll beat Max Evans 1up (after 24); Shelley Mayfield beat Wally Ulrich 5&4; Horton Smith beat Jack Isaacs 3&2

Round 3 (Last 16)
Bolt beat Browning 2&1; Snead beat Harrison 4&3; Barber beat Bassler 1up (after 38); HARBERT beat Oliver 3&1; BURKEMO beat Revolta 4&3; de Vicenzo beat Marti 8&6; Middlecoff beat Kroll 5&4; Mayfield beat Smith 3&2

Quarter Final
Bolt beat Snead 1up (after 39)
HARBERT beat Barber 1up
BURKEMO beat de Vicenzo 5&4
Middlecoff beat Mayfield 3&1

Semi Final
HARBERT beat Bolt 1up
BURKEMO beat Middlecoff 1up (after 37)

Settling finally (give or take a year) for its position in the Majors calendar, the 1954 PGA Championship was won by 1952 runner-up Chick Harbert. Burkemo again confirmed his reputation in matchplay, but was no match in this instance for Harbert, who took control of the final early into the second 18 holes.

1955

COURSE: Augusta National GC
LOCATION: Augusta, Georgia
DATE: 7-10 April
DISTANCE: 6925 yards
PAR: 72 (288)
WINNER: $5000

COURSE: Olympic CC
LOCATION: San Fransisco, California
DATE: 16-19 June
DISTANCE: 6700 yards
PAR: 70 (280)
WINNER: $6000

Pos	Player	1st	2nd	3rd	4th	Total
1	**CARY MIDDLECOFF**	72	65	72	70	279
2	Ben Hogan	73	68	72	73	286
3	Sam Snead	72	71	74	70	287
4 =	Julius Boros	71	75	72	71	289
	Bob Rosburg	72	72	72	73	289
	Mike Souchak	71	74	72	72	289
7	Lloyd Mangrum	74	73	72	72	291
8 =	E Harvie Ward, Jr (a)	77	69	75	71	292
	Stan Leonard	77	73	68	74	292
10 =	Dick Mayer	78	72	72	71	293
	Byron Nelson	72	75	74	72	293
	Arnold Palmer	76	76	72	69	293
13 =	Jack Burke, Jr	67	76	71	80	294
	Skee Riegel	73	73	73	75	294
15 =	Walter Burkemo	73	73	72	77	295
	Jay Hebert	75	74	74	72	295
	Frank Stranahan	77	76	71	71	295
18 =	Joe Conrad (a)	77	71	74	75	297
	Billy Maxwell (a)	77	72	77	71	297
	Johnny Palmer	77	73	72	75	297
	Peter Thomson	74	73	74	76	297

Pos	Player	1st	2nd	3rd	4th	Total
1	**JACK FLECK***	76	69	75	67	287
2	Ben Hogan	72	73	72	70	287
3 =	Tommy Bolt	67	77	75	73	292
	Sam Snead	79	69	70	74	292
5 =	Julius Boros	76	69	73	77	295
	Bob Rosburg	78	74	67	76	295
7 =	Doug Ford	74	77	74	71	296
	Bud Holscher	77	75	71	73	296
	E Harvie Ward, Jr (a)	74	70	76	76	296
10 =	Jack Burke, Jr	71	77	72	77	297
	Mike Souchak	73	79	72	73	297
12 =	Shelley Mayfield	75	76	75	72	298
	Frank Stranahan	80	71	76	71	298
14	Walker Inman, Jr	70	75	76	78	299
15	Gene Littler	76	73	73	78	300
16 =	Al Mengert	76	76	72	77	301
	Smiley Quick	76	74	74	77	301
	Art Wall	77	78	72	74	301
19 =	Fred Hawkins	73	78	75	76	302
	George Schneiter	78	74	77	73	302

* Jack Fleck (69) beat Ben Hogan (72) in the 18-Hole Play-off

Thanks to a blistering 65 in R2, Cary Middlecoff finished a remarkable seven shots clear of Hogan, and eight of Snead. This was the second Major victory for trained dentist, 'Doc' Middlecoff, having beaten Snead into second place earlier, in the 1949 US Open at Medinah. 1954 US Amateur Champion, 26 year-old Arnold Daniel Palmer, finished tenth.

Jack Fleck, in his first full year on the Tour, sensationally held his nerve to beat 43 year-old Ben Hogan in a play-off. He had arrived there after birdying two of the last four holes to tie. With a par of 70 the difficult Olympic CC course took its toll, with only seven rounds beating par throughout the Championship – including the play-off. Fittingly, Fleck achieved three of them. After his momentous year in 1953, Hogan's Majors sequence read: 2, 6, 2, 2. He was never to get any higher again.

BRITISH OPEN

COURSE:	Royal & Ancient GC				
LOCATION:	St Andrews, Fife, Scotland				
DATE:	6-8 July				
DISTANCE:	6526 yards				
PAR:	n/k				
WINNER:	£1000				

Pos	Player	1st	2nd	3rd	4th	Total
1	**PETER THOMSON**	71	68	70	72	281
2	Johnny Fallon	73	67	73	70	283
3	Frank Jowle	70	71	69	74	284
4	Bobby Locke	74	69	70	72	285
5 =	Ken Bousfield	71	75	70	70	286
	Antonio Cerda	73	71	71	71	286
	Bernard Hunt	70	71	74	71	286
	Flory van Donck	71	72	71	72	286
	Harry Weetman	71	71	70	74	286
10 =	Romualdo Barbieri	71	71	73	72	287
	Christy O'Connor, Sr	71	75	70	71	287
12 =	Eric Brown	69	70	73	76	288
	Fred Daly	75	72	70	71	288
	John Jacobs	71	70	71	76	288
15 =	Iain Anderson	71	72	77	69	289
	Willie John Henderson	74	71	72	72	289
17 =	DF Smalldon	70	69	78	73	290
	Arturo Soto	72	73	72	73	290
20 =	Ed Furgol	71	76	72	73	292
	Kel Nagle	72	72	74	74	292
	Syd Scott	69	77	73	73	292

Despite never winning a tournament, Johnny Fallon came close to the Open Championship twice – both times at St Andrews. In 1939 he finished third, and went one better in 1955. Peter Thomson won his second Open in a row, but the aficionados gathered around the Old Course more to see the legend that was Byron Nelson. Effectively retired for almost a decade, he decided to take a golfing 'holiday' in Europe. Aged 43, he won the French Open, but his last British Open placing was 33rd, after shooting 296.

US PGA

COURSE:	Meadowbrook CC
LOCATION:	Northville, Michigan
DATE:	20-26 July
QUALIFYING:	64 qualify to matchplay, after 36 holes strokeplay. (Low – Doug Ford, 136)
ROUNDS/HOLES:	Rs1&2, 18holes: R3,QF,SF&F, 36 holes
WINNER:	$5000

Final

DOUG FORD beat Cary Middlecoff, 4&3

Round 2 (Last 32)

Brien Charter beat Lionel Hebert 1up; Don Fairfield beat Vic Ghezzi 1up (after 23); Shelley Mayfield by Gene Sarazen 4&3; Claude Harmon beat Eldon Briggs 2&1; Ed Furgol beat Gus Salerno 1up (after 20); Fred Hawkins beat Fred Haas 2up; Wally Ulrich beat Leonard Wagner 2up; DOUG FORD beat Ted Kroll 2&1; Johnny Palmer beat Chick Harbert 1up; Lew Worsham beat Ray Hill 2&1; Tommy Bolt beat Sam Snead 3&2; Jack Fleck beat Jay Hebert 2&1; CARY MIDDLECOFF beat Bill Nary 3&2; Mike Pavella beat Jim Browning 4&3; Marty Furgol beat Tony Holguin 1up; Jack Burke Jr beat Dave Douglas 8&6

Round 3 (Last 16)

Fairfield beat Charter 2&1; Mayfield beat Harmon 1up; Hawkins beat E Furgol 6&5; FORD beat Ulrich 12&10; Worsham beat Palmer 6&5; Bolt beat Fleck 3&1; MIDDLECOFF beat Pavella 8&6; Burke Jr beat M Furgol 2&1

Quarter Final

Mayfield beat Fairfield 3&2; FORD beat Hawkins 5&4; Bolt beat Worsham 8&7; MIDDLECOFF beat Burke Jr 1up (after 40)

Semi Final

FORD beat Mayfield 4&3
MIDDLECOFF beat Bolt 4&3

Doug Ford became only the fourth player, after Walter Hagen, in 1926 and 1927; Olin Dutra in 1932; and, inevitably in 1945, Byron Nelson, to shoot the lowest qualifying score and then go on to win the matchplay series. He overcame reigning Masters Champion, Cary Middlecoff, in a final that could have gone either way until he picked up birdies at 29, 30 and 32, for a three shot lead he was not going to give away.

THE MASTERS

COURSE:	Augusta National GC
LOCATION:	Augusta, Georgia
DATE:	5-8 April
DISTANCE:	6925 yards
PAR:	72 (288)
WINNER:	$6000

Pos	Player	1st	2nd	3rd	4th	Total
1	**JACK BURKE, Jr**	72	71	75	71	289
2	Ken Venturi (a)	66	69	75	80	290
3	Cary Middlecoff	67	72	75	77	291
4 =	Lloyd Mangrum	72	74	72	74	292
	Sam Snead	73	76	72	71	292
6 =	Jerry Barber	71	72	76	75	294
	Doug Ford	70	72	75	77	294
8 =	Tommy Bolt	68	74	78	76	296
	Ben Hogan	69	78	74	75	296
	Shelley Mayfield	68	74	80	74	296
11	Johnny Palmer	76	74	74	73	297
12 =	Pete Cooper	72	70	77	79	298
	Gene Littler	73	77	74	74	298
	Billy Joe Patton (a)	70	76	79	73	298
	Sam Urzetta	73	75	76	74	298
16	Bob Rosberg	70	74	81	74	299
17 =	Walter Burkemo	72	74	78	76	300
	Roberto de Vicenzo	75	72	78	75	300
	Hillman Robbins, Jr (a)	73	73	78	76	300
	Mike Souchak	73	73	74	80	300

Jack Burke achieved what his father never could when he won a Major Championship, and in the most dramatic fashion at Augusta. Amateur Ken Venturi led Cary Middlecoff by four going into the last round, with Burke back in the pack, eight off the leader. The young Venturi crumbled in a generally high-scoring round, allowing Burke to come through on the rails to win by one.

US OPEN

COURSE:	Oak Hill CC
LOCATION:	Rochester, New York
DATE:	14-16 June
DISTANCE:	6902 yards
PAR:	70 (280)
WINNER:	$6000

Pos	Player	1st	2nd	3rd	4th	Total
1	**CARY MIDDLECOFF**	71	70	70	70	281
2 =	Julius Boros	71	71	71	69	282
	Ben Hogan	72	68	72	70	282
4 =	Ed Furgol	71	70	73	71	285
	Ted Kroll	72	70	70	73	285
	Peter Thomson	70	69	75	71	285
7	Arnold Palmer	72	70	72	73	287
8	Ken Venturi (a)	77	71	68	73	289
9 =	Jerry Barber	72	69	74	75	290
	Wes Ellis, Jr	71	70	71	78	290
	Doug Ford	71	75	70	74	290
12	Billy Maxwell	72	71	76	72	291
13	Billy Joe Patton (a)	75	73	70	74	292
14 =	Billy Casper	75	71	71	76	293
	Pete Cooper	73	74	76	70	293
	Fred Haas	72	71	72	78	293
17 =	Henry Cotton	74	72	73	75	294
	Dutch Harrison	72	76	72	74	294
	Jay Hebert	71	76	73	74	294
	Bill Ogden	76	73	76	69	294
	Bob Toski	76	71	74	73	294

Middlecoff's second US Open and third Major came after a nail-biting few minutes watching his pursuers. To tie, first Hogan (for a par) missed a 2.5 foot putt on the 17th; then Boros (for birdie) rattled the cup on the final hole. Peter Thomson, in the middle of his unassailable period in the British Open, finished in his highest position in a US Major.

COURSE:	Royal Liverpool GC
LOCATION:	Hoylake, Cheshire, England
DATE:	4-6 July
DISTANCE:	6960 yards
PAR:	n/k
WINNER:	£1000

Pos	Player	1st	2nd	3rd	4th	Total
1	**PETER THOMSON**	70	70	72	74	286
2	Flory van Donck	71	74	70	74	289
3	Roberto de Vicenzo	71	70	79	70	290
4	Gary Player	71	76	73	71	291
5	John Panton	74	76	72	70	292
6 =	Enrique Bertolino	69	72	76	76	293
	Henry Cotton	72	76	71	74	293
8 =	Antonio Cerda	72	81	68	73	294
	Mike Souchak	74	74	74	72	294
10 =	Christy O'Connor, Sr	73	78	74	70	295
	Harry Weetman	72	76	75	72	295
12	Frank Stranahan	72	76	72	76	296
13 =	Bruce Crampton	76	77	72	72	297
	Angel Miguel	71	74	75	77	297
	Dai Rees	75	74	75	73	297
16	John Jacobs	73	77	76	72	298
17 =	Al Balding	70	81	76	73	300
	Jack Hargreaves	72	80	75	73	300
	Ricardo Rossi	75	77	72	76	300
	Dave Thomas	70	78	77	75	300
	Charlie Ward	73	75	78	74	300

Peter Thomson achieved something that had not happened since Bob Ferguson did it in 1882; that is, win the Open Championship three times in succession. Only Jamie Anderson and Tom Morris Jr, moving progressively backwards from Ferguson, had managed the same: and only Willie Anderson (US Open) and Walter Hagen (PGA) – in the history of the other Major Championships – had achieved it. No-one has done it since.

COURSE:	Blue Hill G&CC
LOCATION:	Canton, Massachusetts
DATE:	20-24 July
QUALIFYING:	128 players matchplay
ROUNDS/HOLES:	Rs1,2,3&4, 18holes: QF,SF&F, 36 holes
WINNER:	$5000

Final
JACK BURKE Jr beat Ted Kroll, 3&2

Round 3 (Last 32)
Walter Burkemo beat Doug Ford 5&3; Bill Johnston beat Tony Fortino 4&3; Henry Ransom beat Claude Harmon 1up (after 23); Lew Worsham beat Shelley Mayfield 5&4; Sam Snead beat Bob Toski 4&3; Gene Sarazen beat Mike Krak 3&2; TED KROLL beat Michael Rooney 3&2; Jim Turnesa beat Jack Fleck 1up; Charles Harper Jr beat Babe Lichardus 1up; JACK BURKE Jr beat Fred Haas 1up (after 20); Fred Hawkins beat Art Wall 1up (after 19); Lionel Hebert beat Skee Riegel 3&1; Toby Lyons beat Charles Lepre 3&2; Terl Johnson beat Charles DuPree 4&2; Robert Kay beat Mike Fetchick 1up; Ed Furgol beat Jerry Barber 2&1

ROUND 4 (Last 16)
Johnston beat Burkemo 1up; Ransom beat Worsham 2up; Snead beat Sarazen 5&4; KROLL beat Turnesa 1up; BURKE Jr beat Harper Jr 3&2; Hawkins beat Hebert 4&3; Johnson beat Lyons 1up (after 19); Furgol beat Kay 4&3

Quarter Final
Johnston beat Ransom 3&2; KROLL beat Snead 2&1; BURKE Jr beat Hawkins 4&2; Furgol beat Johnson 1up

Semi Final
KROLL beat Johnston 10&8
BURKE Jr beat Furgol 1up (after 37)

In the penultimate year of matchplay, the format was changed again to allow matchplay for 128 competitors and cut down on two days of qualifying. Jack Burke became the 11th player to win two or more Majors in the same season – by doing the difficult Masters-PGA double. He beat Ted Kroll, who had finished well up in the US Open, in the final. Kroll strolled to the final after a semi final which saw Bill Johnston commit golfing suicide with a morning 81.

THE MASTERS

COURSE:	Augusta National GC				
LOCATION:	Augusta, Georgia				
DATE:	4-7 April				
DISTANCE:	6925 yards				
PAR:	72 (288)				
WINNER:	$8750				

Pos	Player	1st	2nd	3rd	4th	Total
1	**DOUG FORD**	72	73	72	66	283
2	Sam Snead	72	68	74	72	286
3	Jimmy Demaret	72	70	75	70	287
4	E Harvie Ward, Jr (a)	73	71	71	73	288
5	Peter Thomson	72	73	73	71	289
6	Ed Furgol	73	71	72	74	290
7 =	Jack Burke, Jr	71	72	74	74	291
	Dow Finsterwald	74	74	73	70	291
	Arnold Palmer	73	73	69	76	291
10	Jay Hebert	74	72	76	70	292
11 =	Marty Furgol	73	74	73	73	293
	Stan Leonard	75	72	68	78	293
13 =	Henry Cotton	73	73	72	76	294
	Frank M Taylor, Jr (a)	74	74	77	69	294
	Ken Venturi	74	76	74	70	294
16 =	Al Balding	73	73	73	76	295
	Billy Casper	75	75	75	70	295
	Mike Fetchick	74	73	72	76	295
	Fred Hawkins	75	74	72	74	295
	Byron Nelson	74	72	73	76	295

A 36-hole cut was applied for the first time in the 1957 Masters. Doug Ford added to his 1955 PGA title thanks to a six-shot swing over the last 18 holes. R3 leader Sam Snead shot par, but Ford's record last round 66 took him from three behind to three in front. Snead, at 45 was second, and Masters expert Jimmy Demaret who finished third, was 47. Henry Cotton, making a rare visit to the US was 13th at the age of 50; Byron Nelson 16th at 45.

US OPEN

COURSE:	Inverness GC				
LOCATION:	Toledo, Ohio				
DATE:	13-15 June				
DISTANCE:	6919 yards				
PAR:	70 (280)				
WINNER:	$7200				

Pos	Player	1st	2nd	3rd	4th	Total
1	**DICK MAYER***	70	68	74	70	282
2	Cary Middlecoff	71	75	68	68	282
3	Jimmy Demaret	68	73	70	72	283
4 =	Julius Boros	69	75	70	70	284
	Walter Burkemo	74	73	72	65	284
6 =	Fred Hawkins	72	72	71	71	286
	Ken Venturi	69	71	75	71	286
8 =	Roberto de Vicenzo	72	70	72	76	290
	Chick Harbert	68	79	71	72	290
	Billy Maxwell	70	76	72	72	290
	Billy Joe Patton (a)	70	68	76	76	290
	Sam Snead	74	74	69	73	290
13 =	Mike Fetchick	74	71	71	75	291
	Dow Finsterwald	74	72	72	73	291
	William Hyndman III (a)	77	73	72	69	291
	Frank Stranahan	72	76	69	74	291
17 =	Don Fairfield	78	72	73	69	292
	Jim Ferree	74	74	73	71	292
	Doug Ford	69	71	80	72	292
	Bud Ward	70	74	70	78	292

* Dick Mayer (72) beat Cary Middlecoff (79) in the 18-Hole Play-off

Dick Mayer won his only Major and stopped a Middlecoff double when he outplayed him in the play-off. A tie had resulted after 72 holes when Mayer's 138 over the first 36 holes (shared with Billy Joe Patton) was compensated by Middlecoff's 136 over the last 36 (this equalled a 25 year-old record set by Gene Sarazen at Fresh Meadow). Demaret was again in the hunt and was leading going into R4.

COURSE:	Royal & Ancient GC	
LOCATION:	St Andrews, Fife, Scotland	
DATE:	3-5 July	
DISTANCE:	6936 yards	
PAR:	n/k	
WINNER:	£1000	

Pos	Player	1st	2nd	3rd	4th	Total
1	**BOBBY LOCKE**	69	72	68	70	279
2	Peter Thomson	73	69	70	70	282
3	Eric Brown	67	72	73	71	283
4	Angel Miguel	72	72	69	72	285
5 =	Tom Haliburton	72	73	68	73	286
	Dick Smith (a)	71	72	72	71	286
	Dave Thomas	72	74	70	70	286
	Flory van Donck	72	68	74	72	286
9 =	Antonio Cerda	71	71	72	73	287
	Henry Cotton	74	72	69	72	287
	Max Faulkner	74	70	71	72	287
12 =	Peter Alliss	72	74	74	68	288
	Harry Weetman	75	71	71	71	288
14	Cary Middlecoff	72	71	74	72	289
15 =	Norman Drew	70	75	71	74	290
	Eric Lester	71	76	70	73	290
	Sebastian Miguel	71	75	76	68	290
	John Panton	71	72	74	73	290
19 =	Harry Bradshaw	73	74	69	75	291
	Johnny Fallon	75	67	73	76	291
	Christy O'Connor, Sr	77	69	72	73	291
	Frank Stranahan	74	71	74	72	291

TV cameras caught the finish 'live' for the first time, as Bobby Locke regained the crown after four years from Peter Thomson. This was Locke's fourth and last Open (and Major) win, to put him level with Willie Park Sr and Tom Morris (Sr and Jr); but one behind Taylor and Braid, and two behind Vardon (who also, of course, was US Open Champion in 1900). Token American interest came in the form of current US Open runner-up, Cary Middlecoff, and the now professional Frank Stranahan.

COURSE:	Miami Valley GC	
LOCATION:	Dayton, Ohio	
DATE:	17-21 July	
QUALIFYING:	128 players matchplay	
ROUNDS/HOLES:	Rs1,2,3&4, 18holes: QF,SF&F, 36 holes	
WINNER:	$8000	

Final

LIONEL HEBERT beat Dow Finsterwald, 3&1

Round 3 (Last 32)

Milon Marusic beat Mike Krak 2&1; Donald Whitt beat Ellsworth Vines 4&3; Ted Kroll beat Ewing Pomeroy 4&3; Dick Mayer beat Al Smith 5&3; Warren Smith beat Skee Riegel 3&2; Charles Sheppard beat Buck White 1up; Sam Snead beat John Thoren 3&2; DOW FINSTERWALD beat Joe Kirkwood Jr 2&1; Mike Souchak beat Brien Charter 4&3; LIONEL HEBERT beat Charles Farlow 3&1; Claude Harmon beat Charles Bassler 4&3; Tommy Bolt beat Eldon Briggs 7&6; Henry Ransom beat Herman Keiser 5&3; Walter Burkemo beat Tony Holguin 1up; Jay Hebert beat Charles Harper Jr 1up; Doug Ford beat Bob Gajda 3&2

ROUND 4 (Last 16)

Whitt beat Marusic 2&1; Mayer beat Kroll 1up; Sheppard beat Smith 4&3; FINSTERWALD beat Snead 2&1; L HEBERT beat Souchak 2&1; Harmon beat Bolt 1up; Burkemo beat Ransom 5&4; J Hebert beat Ford 3&2

Quarter Final

Whitt beat Mayer 2&1; FINSTERWALD beat Sheppard 2up; L HEBERT beat Harmon 2&1; Burkemo beat J Hebert 3&2

Semi Final

FINSTERWALD beat Whitt 2up; L HEBERT beat Burkemo 3&1

Due to commercial demands brought on by the burgeoning TV era, and not altogether approved of by the professionals, matchplay in the PGA was brought to a close in 1957. To be fair, the Championship still took five days as against three for the other Majors – so it was perhaps a little unwieldy. Medal play ensued thereafter. Lionel Hebert beat Dow Finsterwald in the last final.

THE MASTERS

COURSE:	Augusta National GC
LOCATION:	Augusta, Georgia
DATE:	3-6 April
DISTANCE:	6925 yards
PAR:	72 (288)
WINNER:	$11250

Pos	Player	1st	2nd	3rd	4th	Total
1	**ARNOLD PALMER**	70	73	68	73	284
2 =	Doug Ford	74	71	70	70	285
	Fred Hawkins	71	75	68	71	285
4 =	Stan Leonard	72	70	73	71	286
	Ken Venturi	68	72	74	72	286
6 =	Cary Middlecoff	70	73	69	75	287
	Art Wall	71	72	70	74	287
8	Billy Joe Patton (a)	72	69	73	74	288
9 =	Claude Harmon	71	76	72	70	289
	Jay Hebert	72	73	73	71	289
	Billy Maxwell (a)	71	70	72	76	289
	Al Mengert	73	71	69	76	289
13	Sam Snead	72	71	68	79	290
14 =	Jimmy Demaret	69	79	70	73	291
	Ben Hogan	72	77	69	73	291
	Mike Souchak	72	75	73	71	291
17 =	Dow Finsterwald	72	71	74	75	292
	Chick Harbert	69	74	73	76	292
	Bo Winninger	69	73	71	79	292
20 =	Billy Casper	76	71	72	74	293
	Byron Nelson	71	77	74	71	293

It was somehow appropriate that the first five-figure winner's purse in a Major Championship should go to Arnold Palmer. Over the next two decades he, more than anyone else, is associated with the commercial revolution that took place in golf. Arnie's first win made him, at 28, the youngest winner of the Masters since Byron Nelson in 1938. He was almost caught by Ford and Hawkins over the last holes, but they both missed holeable birdie putts on the 18th. The aforementioned Nelson, along with fellow veterans Snead, Demaret and Hogan, gave the Top 20 a nostalgic glow.

US OPEN

COURSE:	Southern Hills CC
LOCATION:	Tulsa, Oklahoma
DATE:	12-14 June
DISTANCE:	6907 yards
PAR:	70 (280)
WINNER:	$8000

Pos	Player	1st	2nd	3rd	4th	Total
1	**TOMMY BOLT**	71	71	69	72	283
2	Gary Player	75	68	73	71	287
3	Julius Boros	71	75	72	71	289
4	Gene Littler	74	73	67	76	290
5 =	Walter Burkemo	75	74	70	72	291
	Bob Rosburg	75	74	72	70	291
7 =	Jay Hebert	77	76	71	69	293
	Don January	79	73	68	73	293
	Dick Metz	71	78	73	71	293
10 =	Ben Hogan	75	73	75	71	294
	Tommy Jacobs	76	75	71	72	294
	Frank Stranahan	72	72	75	75	294
13 =	Billy Casper	79	70	75	71	295
	Chalrles R Coe (a)	75	71	75	74	295
	Marty Furgol	75	74	74	72	295
16	Bob Goetz	75	75	77	69	296
17 =	Tom Nieporte	75	73	74	75	297
	Jerry Pittman	75	77	71	74	297
19 =	Jerry Barber	79	73	73	73	298
	Bruce Crampton	73	75	74	76	298
	Jim Ferree	76	74	73	75	298
	Jerry Magee	76	77	75	70	298

The number of entries topped 2000 for the first time; and Sam Snead, after 18 consecutive years of making the final day, missed the cut. Irascible Tommy Bolt's humour was tempered by his leading all the way to collect his solitary Major Championship victory. A second Top 5 placing in two years for Walter Burkemo belied the myth he was just a matchplay golfer. Despite a wrist injury, Ben Hogan still finished tenth: and the younger generation was represented, almost emulating Palmer in the Masters, by a young South African, one Gary Jim Player.

BRITISH OPEN	
COURSE:	Royal Lytham and St Anne's GC
LOCATION:	St Annes, Lancashire, England
DATE:	2-4 July
DISTANCE:	6635 yards
PAR:	n/k
WINNER:	£1000

US PGA	
COURSE:	Llanerch CC
LOCATION:	Havertown, Pennsylvania
DATE:	17-20 July
DISTANCE:	6710 yards
PAR:	70 (280)
WINNER:	$5500

Pos	Player	1st	2nd	3rd	4th	Total
1	**PETER THOMSON***	66	72	67	73	278
2	Dave Thomas	70	68	69	71	278
3 =	Eric Brown	73	70	65	71	279
	Christy O'Connor, Sr	67	68	73	71	279
5 =	Leopoldo Ruiz	71	65	72	73	281
	Flory van Donck	70	70	67	74	281
7	Gary Player	68	74	70	71	283
8 =	Henry Cotton	68	75	69	72	284
	Eeic Lester	73	66	71	74	284
	Harry Weetman	73	67	73	71	284
11 =	Peter Alliss	72	70	70	73	285
	Don Swaelens	74	67	74	70	285
13	Harold Henning	70	71	72	73	286
14 =	Jean Garaialde	69	74	72	72	287
	Dai Rees	77	69	71	70	287
16 =	Max Faulkner	68	71	71	78	288
	Bobby Locke	76	70	72	70	288
	Eric Moore	72	72	70	74	288
	Gene Sarazen	73	73	70	72	288
20 =	AB Coop	69	71	75	75	290
	Fred Daly	71	74	72	73	290
	Norman Drew	69	72	75	74	290
	Christy Greene	75	71	72	72	290

Pos	Player	1st	2nd	3rd	4th	Total
1	**DOW FINSTERWALD**	67	72	70	67	276
2	Billy Casper	73	67	68	70	278
3	Sam Snead	73	67	67	73	280
4	Jack Burke, Jr	70	72	69	70	281
5 =	Tommy Bolt	72	70	73	70	285
	Julius Boros	72	68	73	72	285
	Jay Hebert	68	71	73	73	285
8 =	Buster Cupit	71	74	69	73	287
	Ed Oliver	74	73	71	69	287
	Mike Souchak	75	69	69	74	287
11 =	Doug Ford	72	70	70	76	288
	Bob Rosburg	71	73	76	68	288
	Art Wall	71	78	67	72	288
14 =	Fred Hawkins	72	75	70	73	290
	Dick Mayer	69	76	69	76	290
16 =	John Barnum	75	69	74	73	291
	Walter Burkemo	76	73	66	76	291
	Lionel Hebert	69	73	74	75	291
	Bo Wininger	76	73	69	73	291
20 =	Ted Kroll	69	74	75	74	292
	Cary Middlecoff	71	73	76	72	292
	Eric Monti	73	71	73	75	292
	Bob Toski	79	70	71	72	292
	Ken Venturi	72	73	74	73	292

* Peter Thomson (139) beat Dave Thomas (143) in the 36-Hole Play-off

The game of musical chairs between Locke and Thomson continued at Lytham. Between them they had claimed the Open eight times since 1949. Only Max Faulkner (1951) and Ben Hogan (1953) disturbed their party game. Thomson's fourth win placed him alongside Locke in the all-time lists, and only James Braid had more wins in the century to date. Thomson's incredible sequence in the event since 1952 read: 2, 2, W, W, W, 2, W! In 1958, he was taken to the wire – and beyond – though, by Dave Thomas. Good finishes from a couple of much-loved ancients, Cotton and Sarazen.

Dow Finsterwald became the first strokeplay winner of the PGA – atoning for his defeat in the last matchplay final the previous year, by Lionel Hebert. It was Lionel's brother, Jay, who was the early threat this time. For Sam Snead, the scenario was not too dissimilar from the Masters of the previous year. Again he led into the final round, but was once more overhauled by a superb round. This time, for Doug Ford's 66 read Finsterwald's 67.

1959

COURSE:	Augusta National GC
LOCATION:	Augusta, Georgia
DATE:	2-5 April
DISTANCE:	6925 yards
PAR:	72 (288)
WINNER:	$15000

Pos	Player	1st	2nd	3rd	4th	Total
1	**ART WALL**	73	74	71	66	284
2	Cary Middlecoff	74	71	68	72	285
3	Arnold Palmer	71	70	71	74	286
4 =	Stan Leonard	69	74	69	75	287
	Dick Mayer	73	75	71	68	287
6	Charles R Coe (a)	74	74	67	73	288
7	Fred Hawkins	77	71	68	73	289
8 =	Julius Boros	75	69	74	72	290
	Jay Hebert	72	73	72	73	290
	Gene Littler	72	75	72	71	290
	Billy Maxwell (a)	73	71	72	74	290
	Billy Joe Patton (a)	75	70	71	74	290
	Gary Player	73	75	71	71	290
14 =	Chick Harbert	74	72	74	71	291
	Chandler Harper	71	74	74	72	291
	Ted Kroll	76	71	73	71	291
	Ed Oliver	75	69	73	74	291
18 =	Dow Finsterwald	79	68	73	72	292
	Jack Fleck	74	71	71	76	292
	William Hyndman III (a)	73	72	76	71	292
	Bo Wininger	75	70	72	75	292

Art Wall was to be the leading money winner on the Tour in 1959 – set up by the biggest-ever first prize in a Major to date. His 66 in R4 to squeeze out Middlecoff was remarkable in its five-under-par sequence over the last four holes. Wall was a remarkable golfer in many ways. He won a Tour tournament aged 51 as late as 1975; he also claims the world record for holes-in-one – an astonishing 42! This was to be his only Major win, though.

COURSE:	Winged Foot GC
LOCATION:	Mamaroneck, New York
DATE:	11-13 June
DISTANCE:	6873 yards
PAR:	70 (280)
WINNER:	$12000

Pos	Player	1st	2nd	3rd	4th	Total
1	**BILLY CASPER**	71	68	69	74	282
2	Bob Rosburg	75	70	67	71	283
3 =	Claude Harmon	72	71	70	71	284
	Mike Souchak	71	70	72	71	284
5 =	Doug Ford	72	69	72	73	286
	Arnold Palmer	71	69	72	74	286
	Ernie Vossler	72	70	72	72	286
8 =	Ben Hogan	69	71	71	76	287
	Sam Snead	73	72	67	75	287
10	Dick Knight	69	75	73	73	290
11 =	Dow Finsterwald	69	73	75	74	291
	Fred Hawkins	76	72	69	74	291
	Ted Kroll	71	73	73	74	291
	Gene Littler	69	74	75	73	291
15 =	Dave Marr	75	73	69	75	292
	Gary Player	71	69	76	76	292
17 =	Gardner Dickinson	77	70	71	75	293
	Jay Hebert	73	70	78	72	293
19 =	Jack Fleck	74	74	69	77	294
	Mac Hunter	75	74	73	72	294
	Don January	71	73	73	77	294
	Cary Middlecoff	71	73	73	77	294
	Johnny Pott	77	72	70	75	294
	Bo Wininger	71	73	72	78	294

The increasing number of entrants forced the introduction of local and final qualifying sessions. Billy Casper hung on to his halfway lead to head up an unfancied Top 4. Disappointing last rounds for Palmer, Hogan and Snead reduced the pressure on him in a Championship where – which was to be his trademark – his putting had kept his scores together.

COURSE: Honourable Company of
Edinburgh Golfers
LOCATION: Muirfield, East Lothian, Scotland
DATE: 1-3 July
DISTANCE: 6806 yards
PAR: n/k
WINNER: £1000

COURSE: Minneapolis GC
LOCATION: St Louis Park, Minnesota
DATE: 20 July-2 August
DISTANCE: 6850 yards
PAR: 70 (280)
WINNER: $8250

Pos	Player	1st	2nd	3rd	4th	Total
1	**GARY PLAYER**	75	71	70	68	284
2 =	Fred Bullock	68	70	74	74	286
	Flory van Donck	70	70	73	73	286
4	Syd Scott	73	70	73	71	287
5 =	Reid Jack (a)	71	75	68	74	288
	Sam King	70	74	68	76	288
	Christy O'Connor, Sr	73	74	72	69	288
	John Panton	72	72	71	73	288
9 =	Dai Rees	73	73	69	74	289
	Leopoldo Ruiz	72	74	69	74	289
11 =	Michael Bonallack (a)	70	72	72	76	290
	Ken Bousfield	73	73	71	73	290
	Jimmy Hitchcock	75	68	70	77	290
	Bernard Hunt	73	75	71	71	290
	AF Stickley	68	74	77	71	290
16 =	Peter Alliss	76	72	76	67	291
	Harry Bradshaw	71	76	72	72	291
	Antonio Cerda	69	74	73	75	291
	Harry Weetman	72	73	76	70	291
	Guy Wolstenholme (a)	78	70	73	70	291
21 =	Neil Coles	72	74	71	75	292
	Jean Garaialde	75	70	74	73	292

Pos	Player	1st	2nd	3rd	4th	Total
1	**BOB ROSBURG**	71	72	68	66	277
2 =	Jerry Barber	69	65	71	73	278
	Doug Sanders	72	66	68	72	278
4	Dow Finsterwald	71	68	71	70	280
5 =	Bob Goalby	72	69	72	68	281
	Mike Souchak	69	67	71	74	281
	Ken Venturi	70	72	70	69	281
8 =	Cary Middlecoff	72	68	70	72	282
	Sam Snead	71	73	68	70	282
10	Gene Littler	69	70	72	73	284
11 =	Doug Ford	71	73	71	70	285
	Billy Maxwell	70	76	70	69	285
	Ed Oliver	75	70	69	71	285
14 =	Paul Harney	74	71	71	70	286
	Tommy Jacobs	73	71	68	74	286
	Arnold Palmer	72	72	71	71	286
17 =	Tommy Bolt	76	69	68	74	287
	Jack Burke, Jr	70	73	72	72	287
	Walter Burkemo	69	72	73	73	287
	Billy Casper	69	71	73	74	287
	Pete Cooper	78	70	68	71	287
	Buster Cupit	70	72	72	73	287
	Babe Lichardus	71	73	72	71	287
	Ernie Vossler	75	71	72	69	287

Gary Player had announced his arrival when he finished fourth in the British Open in 1956 and second in the US Open in 1958. The South African's first Major Championship win of an illustrious career coincided with the nadir of the Open's gradual decline in comparative importance with the US Open. A glance at the comparative prizemoney is enough on its own to suggest why. The influx of top-class American challengers had dwindled to a trickle since the mid-thirties until, by 1959, there were none. It was to change very quickly indeed.

Rosburg made up for his second place disappointment in the US Open by taking his one and only Major at Minneapolis. Nine people (three of whom, Dick Hart, Chuck Klein and Mike Krak, would miss the cut: Jackson Bradley would finish in 31st place) tied at the end of R1, on 69 – the largest leadership grouping for any Major. Rosburg, nine behind Barber at halfway, and six shots adrift after 54 holes, blasted a final round 66 to win by one.

THE MASTERS

COURSE:	Augusta National GC
LOCATION:	Augusta, Georgia
DATE:	7-10 April
DISTANCE:	6925 yards
PAR:	72 (288)
WINNER:	$17500

Pos	Player	1st	2nd	3rd	4th	Total
1	**ARNOLD PALMER**	67	73	72	70	282
2	Ken Venturi	73	69	71	70	283
3	Dow Finsterwald	71	70	72	71	284
4	Billy Casper	71	71	71	74	287
5	Julius Boros	72	71	70	75	288
6 =	Walter Burkemo	72	69	75	73	289
	Ben Hogan	73	68	72	76	289
	Gary Player	72	71	72	74	289
9 =	Lionel Hebert	74	70	73	73	290
	Stan Leonard	72	72	72	74	290
11 =	Jack Burke, Jr	72	72	74	74	292
	Sam Snead	73	74	72	73	292
13 =	Ted Kroll	72	76	71	74	293
	Jack Nicklaus (a)	75	71	72	75	293
	Billy Joe Patton	75	72	74	72	293
16 =	Bruce Crampton	74	73	75	72	294
	Claude Harmon	69	72	75	78	294
	Fred Hawkins	69	78	72	75	294
	Mike Souchak	72	75	72	75	294
20 =	Tommy Bolt	73	74	75	73	295
	Don January	70	72	74	79	295
	Ed Oliver	74	75	73	73	295
	Bob Rosburg	74	74	71	76	295
	Frank M Taylor, Jr (a)	70	74	73	78	295

Palmer's second Masters triumph swept in the new decade like the breath of fresh air the sixties was to become on many fronts. Post-War colourless austerity, and cloying formalities and conventions gave way to new freedoms of expression; none freer than in golf, personified by the phenomenon of Arnold Palmer. The people's man, he took the playing of golf into a new dimension through his vision and daring. He almost single-handedly, through the media of press and, particularly, TV, popularised the sport for spectators; and created a surge in new players like no time before. At Augusta in 1960, in front of a TV audience sitting on the edge of their seats, he dramatically birdied 17 and 18 to beat the disbelieving Ken Venturi by one.

US OPEN

COURSE:	Cherry Hills CC
LOCATION:	Denver, Colorado
DATE:	16-18 June
DISTANCE:	7004 yards
PAR:	71 (284)
WINNER:	$14400

Pos	Player	1st	2nd	3rd	4th	Total
1	**ARNOLD PALMER**	72	71	72	65	280
2	Jack Nicklaus (a)	71	71	69	71	282
3 =	Julius Boros	73	69	68	73	283
	Dow Finsterwald	71	69	70	73	283
	Jack Fleck	70	70	72	71	283
	Dutch Harrison	74	70	70	69	283
	Ted Kroll	72	69	75	67	283
	Mike Souchak	68	67	73	75	283
9 =	Jerry Barber	69	71	70	74	284
	Don Cherry (a)	70	71	71	72	284
	Ben Hogan	75	67	69	73	284
12 =	George Bayer	72	72	73	69	286
	Billy Casper	71	70	73	72	286
	Paul Harney	73	70	72	71	286
15 =	Bob Harris	73	71	71	72	287
	Johnny Pott	75	68	69	75	287
17 =	Dave Marr	72	73	70	73	288
	Donald Whitt	75	69	72	72	288
19 =	Jackson Bradley	73	73	69	74	289
	Bob Goalby	73	70	72	74	289
	Gary Player	70	72	71	76	289
	Sam Snead	72	69	73	75	289

Two months later Palmer was still rolling on. Once more, he saved his heroics until R4; when trailing leader Mike Souchak, he went out in a record-equalling 30, to make 65 and leapfrog the leading pack. With a proper sense of the occasion, Jack William Nicklaus also entered the scene, when he took the highest place claimed by an amateur since Goodman's win in 1933. Along with Palmer and British Open Champion, Player, the emergence of the 'Golden Bear' heralded the modern version of the Great Triumvirate. From Arnie's 1958 Masters win to Jack's in 1986, they were to scoop 34 Major titles between them.

BRITISH OPEN

COURSE:	Royal & Ancient GC
LOCATION:	St Andrews, Fife, Scotland
DATE:	6-8 July
DISTANCE:	6936 yards
PAR:	n/k
WINNER:	£1250

Pos	Player	1st	2nd	3rd	4th	Total
1	**KEL NAGLE**	69	67	71	71	278
2	Arnold Palmer	70	71	70	68	279
3 =	Roberto de Vicenzo	67	67	75	73	282
	Harold Henning	72	72	69	69	282
	Bernard Hunt	72	73	71	66	282
6	Guy Wolstenholme (a)	74	70	71	68	283
7	Gary Player	72	71	72	69	284
8	Joe Carr (a)	72	73	67	73	285
9 =	David Blair (a)	70	73	71	72	286
	Eric Brown	75	68	72	71	286
	Dai Rees	73	71	73	69	286
	Syd Scott	73	71	67	75	286
	Peter Thomson	72	69	75	70	286
	Harry Weetman	74	70	71	71	286
15	Ramon Sota	74	72	71	70	287
16 =	Fidel de Luca	69	73	75	71	288
	Reid Jack (a)	74	71	70	73	288
	Angel Miguel	72	73	72	71	288
	Ian Smith	74	70	73	71	288
20	Peter Mills	71	74	70	74	289

Another final round Palmer charge just failed to net him the Centenary Open Championship on his first visit, and thus emulate the great Ben Hogan's triple in 1953. The Commonwealth succession continued in the person of Australian Kel Nagle. Palmer's presence, however, and the introduction of a new style of play – and player – had a two-pronged effect. It blew new life into an increasingly-parochial Championship: it also re-introduced the British Open to a new generation of US golfers.

US PGA

COURSE:	Firestone CC
LOCATION:	Akron, Ohio
DATE:	21-24 July
DISTANCE:	7165 yards
PAR:	70 (280)
WINNER:	$11000

Pos	Player	1st	2nd	3rd	4th	Total
1	**JAY HEBERT**	72	67	72	70	281
2	Jim Ferrier	71	74	66	71	282
3 =	Doug Sanders	70	71	69	73	283
	Sam Snead	68	73	70	72	283
5	Don January	70	70	72	72	284
6	Wes Ellis, Jr	72	72	72	69	285
7 =	Doug Ford	75	70	69	72	286
	Arnold Palmer	67	74	75	70	286
9	Ken Venturi	70	72	73	72	287
10 =	Fred Hawkins	73	69	72	74	288
	Dave Marr	75	71	69	73	288
12 =	Bill Collins	71	75	71	73	290
	Ted Kroll	73	71	72	74	290
	Mike Souchak	73	73	70	74	290
15 =	Pete Cooper	73	74	70	74	291
	Dow Finsterwald	73	73	69	76	291
	Johnny Pott	75	72	72	72	291
18 =	Paul Harney	69	78	73	72	292
	Lionel Hebert	75	72	70	75	292
	Gene Littler	74	70	75	73	292
	Tom Nieporte	72	74	74	72	292

Jay Hebert followed younger brother Lionel as PGA Champion; the only brothers to achieve this (albeit one matchplay, one medal play). He pipped 1947 winner, Jim Ferrier, for the 1960 title. The only other sets of brothers to win Majors are: the Parks, Sr – Willie & Mungo (British Open); the Auchterlonies – Willie (British Open) and Laurie (US Open); the Herds – Fred (US Open) and Sandy (British Open); and the Smiths – Willie and Alex (both US Open). Palmer's outstanding year looked set to continue when he led after R1, but two poor rounds dropped him to seventh.

THE MASTERS

COURSE:	Augusta National GC					
LOCATION:	Augusta, Georgia					
DATE:	6-10 April (Sun play washed out)					
DISTANCE:	6925 yards					
PAR:	72 (288)					
WINNER:	$20000					

Pos	Player	1st	2nd	3rd	4th	Total
1	**GARY PLAYER**	69	68	69	74	280
2 =	Charles R Coe, Jr (a)	72	71	69	69	281
	Arnold Palmer	68	69	73	71	281
4 =	Tommy Bolt	72	71	74	68	285
	Don January	74	68	72	71	285
6	Paul Harney	71	73	68	74	286
7 =	Jack Burke, Jr	76	70	68	73	287
	Billy Casper	72	77	69	69	287
	Bill Collins	74	72	67	74	287
	Jack Nicklaus (a)	70	75	70	72	287
11 =	Walter Burkemo	74	69	73	72	288
	Robert Gardner (a)	74	71	72	71	288
	Doug Sanders	76	71	68	73	288
	Ken Venturi	72	71	72	73	288
15 =	Stan Leonard	72	74	72	74	289
	Gene Littler	72	73	72	72	289
	Bob Rosburg	68	73	73	75	289
	Sam Snead	74	73	69	73	289
19 =	Dick Mayer	76	72	70	73	291
	Johnny Pott	71	75	72	73	291
	Peter Thomson	73	76	68	74	291

In a Masters of 'firsts', Gary Player's first Masters and second Major came after an extra day was required due to the weather. He collected golf's first $20000 winning purse and was the first non-American to win the Masters (and the first since Jim Ferrier in the 1947 PGA to win any US Major). His victory was built on a 54 hole-total of 206, allowing him a cushion of four strokes over Palmer and six over Coe (emulating Nicklaus' feat as an amateur at the previous year's US Open) going into R4. He was to need every one.

US OPEN

COURSE:	Oakland Hills CC					
LOCATION:	Birmingham, Michigan					
DATE:	15-17 June					
DISTANCE:	6907 yards					
PAR:	70 (280)					
WINNER:	$14000					

Pos	Player	1st	2nd	3rd	4th	Total
1	**GENE LITTLER**	73	68	72	68	281
2 =	Bob Goalby	70	72	69	71	282
	Doug Sanders	72	67	71	72	282
4 =	Jack Nicklaus (a)	75	69	70	70	284
	Mike Souchak	73	70	68	73	284
6 =	Dow Finsterwald	72	71	71	72	286
	Doug Ford	72	69	71	74	286
	Eric Monti	74	67	72	73	286
9 =	Jacky Cupit	72	72	67	76	287
	Gardner Dickinson	72	69	71	75	287
	Gary Player	75	72	69	71	287
12 =	Deane Beman (a)	74	72	72	70	288
	Al Geiberger	71	70	73	74	288
14 =	Dave Douglas	72	72	75	70	289
	Ben Hogan	71	72	73	73	289
	Arnold Palmer	74	75	70	70	289
17 =	Billy Casper	74	71	73	72	290
	Dutch Harrison	74	71	76	69	290
	Kel Nagle	71	71	74	74	290
	Sam Snead	73	70	74	73	290

Gene Littler's Open win, after a fine closing round took him past Sanders, Goalby and Souchak, came relatively early in a long career. After winning the US Amateur in 1953 (thereby becoming the eighth player to pick up the Amateur-Open double), much was expected; but perhaps he just missed that dedicated edge which is required to get to the very top, and remain there, in any field. Ben Hogan missed a Top 10 finish for the first time in any Open he competed in since 1940.

COURSE:	Birkdale GC	
LOCATION:	Southport, Lancashire, England	
DATE:	12-14 July	
DISTANCE:	6844 yards	
PAR:	n/k	
WINNER:	£1400	

COURSE:	Olympia Fields CC	
LOCATION:	Olympia Fields, Illinois	
DATE:	27-31 July	
DISTANCE:	6722 yards	
PAR:	70 (280)	
WINNER:	$11000	

Pos	Player	1st	2nd	3rd	4th	Total
1	**ARNOLD PALMER**	70	73	69	72	284
2	Dai Rees	68	74	71	72	285
3 =	Neil Coles	70	77	69	72	288
	Christy O'Connor, Sr	71	77	67	73	288
5 =	Eric Brown	73	76	70	70	289
	Kel Nagle	68	75	75	71	289
7	Peter Thomson	75	72	70	73	290
8 =	Peter Alliss	73	75	72	71	291
	Ken Bousfield	71	77	75	68	291
10 =	Harold Henning	68	74	75	76	293
	Syd Scott	76	75	71	71	293
12	Ramon Sota	71	76	72	76	295
13	AB Coop	71	79	73	74	297
14 =	Norman Johnson	69	80	70	79	298
	Reg Knight	71	80	73	74	298
	Angel Miguel	73	79	74	72	298
	Sebastian Miguel	71	80	70	77	298
18 =	Dennis Hutchinson	72	80	74	73	299
	Paul Runyan	75	77	75	72	299
20 =	Harry Bradshaw	73	75	78	74	300
	Peter Butler	72	76	78	74	300
	John Jacobs	71	79	76	74	300
	Lionel Platts	70	80	71	79	300

Pos	Player	1st	2nd	3rd	4th	Total
1	**JERRY BARBER***	69	67	71	70	277
2	Don January	72	66	67	72	277
3	Doug Sanders	70	68	74	68	280
4	Ted Kroll	72	68	70	71	281
5 =	Wes Ellis, Jr	71	71	68	72	282
	Doug Ford	69	73	74	66	282
	Gene Littler	71	70	72	69	282
	Arnold Palmer	73	72	69	68	282
	Johnny Pott	71	73	67	71	282
	Art Wall	67	72	73	70	282
11 =	Paul Harney	70	73	69	71	283
	Cary Middlecoff	74	69	71	69	283
13	Jay Hebert	68	72	72	72	284
14	Walter Burkemo	71	71	73	70	285
15 =	Billy Casper	74	72	69	71	286
	Bob Goalby	73	72	68	73	286
	Ernie Vossler	68	72	71	75	286
	Don Whitt	76	72	70	68	286
19 =	Gardner Jackson	71	71	71	74	287
	Jack Fleck	70	74	73	70	287
	Bob Rosburg	70	71	73	73	287

* Jerry Barber (67) beat Don January (68) in the 18-Hole Play-off

Dai Rees, according to Peter Alliss and others, was probably the best British player never to win his native Championship. He was undoubtedly the best golfer to come out of Wales until Ian Woosnam appeared on the scene; and was captain of the victorious British Ryder Cup team of 1957, when he beat Ed Furgol in the Singles, 7&6. His third runner-up place in the Open after a tooth-and-nail struggle with the best player in the world, was to be his last serious challenge. Palmer's first win in the Open seemed inevitable after his runner's-up place the previous year, and the spectacle did even more to encourage his compatriots to return, despite the prizemoney.

With three holes to play, Don January led Jerry Barber by four strokes. Thanks to two dropped shots and three big putts by Barber (two for birdie), the latter drew level; and after a few traumas, went on to win the play-off. At 45, Barber was the oldest man to win the PGA, and he overtook Ted Ray's 1920 record to become the oldest player of the century to win a Major – at least for a few years, until Julius Boros took both records away from him.

THE MASTERS

	COURSE:	Augusta National GC
	LOCATION:	Augusta, Georgia
	DATE:	5-9 April
	DISTANCE:	6925 yards
	PAR:	72 (288)
	WINNER:	$20000

Pos	Player	1st	2nd	3rd	4th	Total
1	**ARNOLD PALMER***	70	66	69	75	280
2	Gary Player	67	71	71	71	280
3	Dow Finsterwald	74	68	65	73	280
4	Gene Littler	71	68	71	72	282
5 =	Jerry Barber	72	72	69	74	287
	Jimmy Demaret	73	73	71	70	287
	Billy Maxwell (a)	71	73	72	71	287
	Mike Souchak	70	72	74	71	287
9 =	Charles R Coe (a)	72	74	71	71	288
	Ken Venturi	75	70	71	72	288
11 =	Julius Boros	69	73	72	76	290
	Gay Brewer	74	71	70	75	290
	Jack Fleck	72	75	74	69	290
	Harold Henning	75	73	72	70	290
15 =	Billy Casper	73	73	73	72	291
	Gardner Dickinson	70	71	72	78	291
	Paul Harney	74	71	74	72	291
	Jack Nicklaus	74	75	70	72	291
	Sam Snead	72	75	70	74	291
20 =	Jacky Cupit	73	73	72	74	292
	Lionel Hebert	72	73	71	76	292
	Don January	71	73	74	74	292
	Johnny Pott	77	71	75	69	292

*Arnold Palmer (68) beat Gary Player (71) and Dow Finsterwald (77) in the 18-Hole Play-off

There could be no quibbling about quality at Augusta in 1962. All the 1961 Major Champions featured in the Top 5 in the spring Major; two of them, along with Dow Finsterwald, in the three-way play-off. Palmer's supremacy was maintained, however, when he reeled in Gary Player – the pretender to his crown (?) – pulling back three shots to win with a blistering home nine score of 31.

US OPEN

	COURSE:	Oakmont CC
	LOCATION:	Oakmont, Pennsylvania
	DATE:	14-17 June
	DISTANCE:	6894 yards
	PAR:	72 (288)
	WINNER:	$17500

Pos	Player	1st	2nd	3rd	4th	Total
1	**JACK NICKLAUS***	72	70	72	69	283
2	Arnold Palmer	71	68	73	71	283
3 =	Bobby Nichols	70	72	70	73	285
	Phil Rodgers	74	70	69	72	285
5	Gay Brewer	73	72	73	69	287
6 =	Tommy Jacobs	74	71	73	70	288
	Gary Player	71	71	72	74	288
8 =	Doug Ford	74	75	71	70	290
	Gene Littler	69	74	72	75	290
	Billy Maxwell	71	70	75	74	290
11 =	Doug Sanders	74	74	74	69	291
	Art Wall	73	72	72	74	291
13	Bob Rosburg	70	69	74	79	292
14 =	Deane Beman (a)	74	72	80	67	293
	Bob Goalby	73	74	73	73	293
	Mike Souchak	75	73	72	73	293
17 =	Jacky Cupit	73	72	72	77	294
	Jay Hebert	75	72	73	74	294
	Earl Stewart	75	73	75	71	294
	Donald Whitt	73	71	75	75	294
	Bo Wininger	73	74	69	78	294

* Jack Nicklaus (71) beat Arnold Palmer (74) in the 18-Hole Play-off

Two months later Palmer was not so lucky in the play-off. He succumbed to 22 year-old Jack Nicklaus, who was in his first year as a professional. Nicklaus was the first player since Bobby Jones to hold the US Amateur and US Open titles at the same time. The balance of power was changing again. Although Palmer would remain at the very top for some years yet, this was definitely the start of the Jack Nicklaus era. Between 1962 and 1986 – a record span – a blend of power and precision never before witnessed on a golf course was to reap him a harvest of 18 Majors: seven more than the next man, Walter Hagen.

BRITISH OPEN

COURSE: Troon GC
LOCATION: Troon, Ayrshire, Scotland
DATE: 11-13 July
DISTANCE: 7045 yards
PAR: n/k
WINNER: £1400

Pos	Player	1st	2nd	3rd	4th	Total
1	**ARNOLD PALMER**	71	69	67	69	276
2	Kel Nagle	71	71	70	70	282
3 =	Brian Huggett	75	71	74	69	289
	Phil Rodgers	75	70	72	72	289
5	Bob Charles	75	70	70	75	290
6 =	Sam Snead	76	73	72	71	292
	Peter Thomson	70	77	75	70	292
8 =	Peter Alliss	77	69	74	73	293
	Dave Thomas	77	70	71	75	293
10	Syd Scott	77	74	75	68	294
11	Ralph Moffitt	75	70	74	76	295
12 =	Jean Garaialde	76	73	76	71	296
	Sebastian Miguel	72	79	73	72	296
	Harry Weetman	75	73	73	75	296
	Ross Whitehead	74	75	72	75	296
16 =	Roger Foreman	77	73	72	75	297
	Bernard Hunt	74	75	75	73	297
	Dennis Hutchinson	78	73	76	70	297
	Jimmy Martin	73	72	76	76	297
	Christy O'Connor, Sr	74	78	73	72	297
	John Panton	74	73	79	71	297

Nicklaus was not to get all his own way yet. He wouldn't forget his first visit to Troon, where rounds of 80 and 79 contributed to a humbling score of 305, and a tie for 34th place. Palmer, on the other hand, found the links much to his liking; setting a new record low for the Championship and tying Hogan's famous score in the 1948 US Open. His lead from the end of the second round increased from two, to four, to six, over Kel Nagle.

US PGA

COURSE: Aronimink GC
LOCATION: Newtown Square, Pennsylvania
DATE: 19-22 July
DISTANCE: 7045 yards
PAR: 70 (280)
WINNER: $12000

Pos	Player	1st	2nd	3rd	4th	Total
1	**GARY PLAYER**	72	67	69	70	278
2	Bob Goalby	69	72	71	67	279
3 =	George Bayer	69	70	71	71	281
	Jack Nicklaus	71	75	69	67	281
5	Doug Ford	69	69	73	71	282
6	Bobby Nichols	72	70	71	70	283
7 =	Jack Fleck	74	69	70	71	284
	Paul Harney	70	73	72	69	284
	Dave Ragan	72	74	70	68	284
10	Jay Hebert	73	72	70	70	285
11 =	Julius Boros	73	69	74	70	286
	Dow Finsterwald	73	70	70	73	286
	Chick Harbert	68	76	69	73	286
	Bob McCallister	74	66	70	76	286
15 =	Cary Middlecoff	73	66	74	74	287
	Doug Sanders	76	69	73	69	287
17 =	Jack Burke, Jr	73	69	71	75	288
	Bruce Crampton	76	73	67	72	288
	Billy Farrell	73	71	73	71	288
	Arnold Palmer	71	72	73	72	288
	Sam Snead	75	70	71	72	288
	Frank Stranahan	69	73	72	74	288

Gary Player – in just four years – won his third different Major. He was the tenth player to achieve it, and the first non-American since Tommy Armour in 1931. Two others, Snead and Palmer, were also in the Top 20. Scoring was tough on this 7000+ yard, par 70 course.

THE MASTERS

COURSE:	Augusta National GC				
LOCATION:	Augusta, Georgia				
DATE:	4-7 April				
DISTANCE:	6925 yards				
PAR:	72 (288)				
WINNER:	$20000				

Pos	Player	1st	2nd	3rd	4th	Total
1	**JACK NICKLAUS**	74	66	74	72	286
2	Tony Lema	74	69	74	70	287
3 =	Julius Boros	76	69	71	72	288
	Sam Snead	70	73	74	71	288
5 =	Dow Finsterwald	74	73	73	69	289
	Ed Furgol	70	71	74	74	289
	Gary Player	71	74	74	70	289
8	Bo Wininger	69	72	77	72	290
9 =	Don January	73	75	72	71	291
	Arnold Palmer	74	73	73	71	291
11 =	Billy Casper	79	72	71	70	292
	Bruce Crampton	74	74	72	72	292
	Doug Ford	75	73	75	69	292
	Mike Souchak	69	70	79	74	292
15 =	Bob Charles	74	72	76	71	293
	Chen Ching-po	76	71	71	75	293
	Billy Maxwell (a)	72	75	76	70	293
	Dick Mayer	73	70	80	70	293
	Mason Rudolph	75	72	72	74	293
	Dan Sikes	74	76	72	71	293

Nicklaus' second Major was gained when confronting Augusta National at its most difficult. Weather conditions accounted for the relatively high scoring, but Nicklaus made the best of it when it relented during R2. At 23, he was the youngest winner of the Masters to that date.

US OPEN

COURSE:	The Country Club				
LOCATION:	Brookline, Massachusetts				
DATE:	20-23 June				
DISTANCE:	6870 yards				
PAR:	71 (284)				
WINNER:	$17500				

Pos	Player	1st	2nd	3rd	4th	Total
1	**JULIUS BOROS***	71	74	76	72	293
2	Jacky Cupit	70	72	76	75	293
3	Arnold Palmer	73	69	77	74	293
4	Paul Harney	78	70	73	73	294
5 =	Bruce Crampton	74	72	75	74	295
	Tony Lema	71	74	74	76	295
	Billy Maxwell	73	73	75	74	295
8 =	Walter Burkemo	72	71	76	77	296
	Gary Player	74	75	75	72	296
10	Dan Sikes	77	73	73	74	297
11	Don January	72	74	78	75	299
12 =	Dow Finsterwald	73	69	79	79	300
	Dave Ragan	78	74	74	74	300
14 =	Mike Fetchick	74	76	75	77	302
	Lionel Hebert	71	79	76	76	302
	Davis Love, Jr	71	74	78	79	302
	Bobby Nichols	74	75	75	78	302
	Dean Refram	72	71	80	79	302
19 =	Bob Charles	74	76	76	77	303
	Ken Still	76	75	78	74	303

* Julius Boros (70) beat Jacky Cupit (73) and Arnold Palmer (76) in the 18-Hole Play-off

From the youngest winner of the Masters we come to the oldest American winner of the US Open. Julius Boros, in adding to his 1952 Open title, was just 26 days younger than Ted Ray when the Englishman won at Inverness in 1920. A three-way play-off resulted when Boros caught Palmer, who missed a two-footer at the 17th; and Jackie Cupit, who dropped three shots over 17 and 18. Paul Harney also bogeyed the last to miss the play-off.

BRITISH OPEN

COURSE: Royal Lytham and St Anne's GC
LOCATION: St Annes, Lancashire, England
DATE: 10-12 July
DISTANCE: 6836 yards
PAR: n/k
WINNER: £1500

Pos	Player	1st	2nd	3rd	4th	Total
1	**BOB CHARLES***	68	72	66	71	277
2	Phil Rodgers	67	68	73	69	277
3	Jack Nicklaus	71	67	70	70	278
4	Kel Nagle	69	70	73	71	283
5	Peter Thomson	67	69	71	78	285
6	Christy O'Connor, Sr	74	68	76	68	286
7 =	Gary Player	75	70	72	70	287
	Ramon Sota	69	73	73	72	287
9 =	Jean Garaialde	72	69	72	75	288
	Sebastian Miguel	73	69	73	73	288
11 =	Bernard Hunt	72	71	73	73	289
	Alex King	71	73	73	72	289
13	Sewsunker Sewgolum	71	74	73	72	290
14 =	Brian Allen	75	71	71	74	291
	Brian Huggett	73	74	70	74	291
	Hugh Lewis	71	77	69	74	291
	Ian MacDonald	71	71	74	75	291
18 =	Peter Alliss	74	71	77	80	292
	Frank Phillips	70	73	75	74	292
20 =	Neil Coles	73	75	72	73	293
	Max Faulkner	77	71	71	74	293
	Harold Henning	76	68	71	78	293
	Malcolm Leeder	76	73	74	70	293
	John MacDonald	73	75	75	70	293
	Brian Wilkes	70	77	74	72	293

* Bob Charles (140) beat Phil Rodgers (148) in the 36-Hole Play-off

So far, the only left-handed player to win a Major, and the first from New Zealand, Bob Charles, tied with Phil Rodgers before comfortably winning the play-off. They both, along with third-placed Nicklaus, beat the Lytham links scratch score of 70 (280), playing off Championship tees, which accumulatively added 79 yards to the members' course.

US PGA

COURSE: Dallas Athletic Club
LOCATION: Dallas, Texas
DATE: 18-21 July
DISTANCE: 7046 yards
PAR: 71 (284)
WINNER: $13000

Pos	Player	1st	2nd	3rd	4th	Total
1	**JACK NICKLAUS**	69	73	69	68	279
2	Dave Ragan	75	70	67	69	281
3 =	Bruce Crampton	70	73	65	74	282
	Dow Finsterwald	72	72	66	72	282
5 =	Al Geiberger	72	73	69	70	284
	Billy Maxwell	73	71	69	71	284
7	Jim Ferrier	73	73	70	69	285
8 =	Gardner Dickinson	72	74	74	66	286
	Tommy Jacobs	74	72	70	70	286
	Bill Johnson	71	72	72	71	286
	Gary Player	74	75	67	70	286
	Art Wall	73	76	66	71	286
13 =	Julius Boros	69	72	73	73	287
	Bob Charles	69	76	72	70	287
	Tony Lema	70	71	77	69	287
	Jack Sellman	75	70	74	68	287
17 =	Manuel de la Torre	71	71	74	72	288
	Wes Ellis, Jr	71	74	71	72	288
	Bob Goalby	74	70	74	70	288
	Dick Hart	66	72	76	74	288
	Dave Hill	73	72	69	74	288
	Doug Sanders	74	69	70	75	288

Nicklaus emulated Gary Player's feat of the previous year – except Jack's third different Major was achieved in just a two-year span. He also became only the fourth player, after Sarazen, Nelson and Hogan to lift all the US Majors; the fourth player after Snead, Hogan and Jack Burke, Jr to do the Masters-PGA double in the same year; and the eighth to have won two Majors in one season. And this was only his second full year as a pro!

1964

THE MASTERS

COURSE:	Augusta National GC					
LOCATION:	Augusta, Georgia					
DATE:	9-12 April					
DISTANCE:	6925 yards					
PAR:	72 (288)					
WINNER:	$20000					

Pos	Player	1st	2nd	3rd	4th	Total
1	**ARNOLD PALMER**	69	68	69	70	276
2 =	Dave Marr	70	73	69	70	282
	Jack Nicklaus	71	73	71	67	282
4	Bruce Devlin	72	72	67	73	284
5 =	Billy Casper	76	72	69	69	286
	Jim Ferrier	71	73	69	73	286
	Paul Harney	73	72	71	70	286
	Gary Player	69	72	72	73	286
9 =	Dow Finsterwald	71	72	75	69	287
	Ben Hogan	73	75	67	72	287
	Tony Lema	75	68	74	70	287
	Mike Souchak	73	74	70	70	287
13 =	Peter Butler	72	72	69	75	288
	Al Geiberger	75	73	70	70	288
	Gene Littler	70	72	78	68	288
	Johnny Pott	74	70	71	73	288
	Dan Sikes	76	68	71	73	288
18 =	Don January	70	72	75	72	289
	Billy Maxwell (a)	73	73	69	74	289
	Mason Rudolph	75	72	69	73	289

Arnold Palmer led all the way to win an unprecedented fourth Masters; putting him above Sam Snead and Jimmy Demaret. His victory by six from Dave Marr was his seventh and last Major, and he joined a stellar band of golfers on this mark: Vardon, Jones, Sarazen and Snead. 49 year-old former PGA Champion, Jim Ferrier, was a surprising Top 10 finisher.

US OPEN

COURSE:	Congressional CC					
LOCATION:	Bethesda, Maryland					
DATE:	18-20 June					
DISTANCE:	7053 yards					
PAR:	70 (280)					
WINNER:	$17500					

Pos	Player	1st	2nd	3rd	4th	Total
1	**KEN VENTURI**	72	70	66	70	278
2	Tommy Jacobs	72	64	70	76	282
3	Bob Charles	72	72	71	68	283
4	Billy Casper	71	74	69	71	285
5 =	Gay Brewer	76	69	73	68	286
	Arnold Palmer	68	69	75	74	286
7	Bill Collins	70	71	74	72	287
8	Dow Finsterwald	73	72	71	72	288
9 =	Johnny Pott	71	73	73	72	289
	Bob Rosburg	73	73	70	73	289
11 =	George Bayer	75	73	72	71	291
	Don January	75	73	74	69	291
	Gene Littler	73	71	74	73	291
14 =	Bruce Crampton	72	71	75	74	292
	Terry Dill	73	73	75	71	292
	Ray Floyd	73	70	72	77	292
	Ed Furgol	72	74	72	74	292
	Al Geiberger	74	70	75	73	292
	Bobby Nichols	72	72	76	72	292
20	Tony Lema	71	72	75	75	293

After two momentous failures in the Masters, Ken Venturi put his past behind him to take a Major Championship. In 1956, as an amateur, he blew up and shot a last-round 80 to concede nine strokes to Jack Burke, and the Tournament. Then in the 1960 Masters, the nightmare returned, this time in the guise of Arnold Palmer's birdie-birdie finish, to pip him at the last. At Congressional Venturi, however, came from behind in R4 to overtake the collapsing Tommy Jacobs, who in the second round had equalled Lee Mackey's 14 year-old low.

BRTISH OPEN

COURSE:	Royal & Ancient GC
LOCATION:	St Andrews, Fife, Scotland
DATE:	8-10 July
DISTANCE:	6926 yards
PAR:	72 (288)
WINNER:	£1500

Pos	Player	1st	2nd	3rd	4th	Total
1	**TONY LEMA**	73	68	68	70	279
2	Jack Nicklaus	76	74	66	68	284
3	Roberto de Vicenzo	76	72	70	67	285
4	Bernard Hunt	73	74	70	70	287
5	Bruce Devlin	72	72	73	73	290
6 =	Christy O'Connor, Sr	71	73	74	73	291
	Harry Weetman	72	71	75	73	291
8 =	Harold Henning	78	73	71	70	292
	Angel Miguel	73	76	72	71	292
	Gary Player	78	71	73	70	292
11	Doug Sanders	78	73	74	68	293
12	Frank Phillips	77	75	72	70	294
13 =	Jean Garaialde	71	74	79	72	296
	Christy Greene	74	76	73	73	296
	Ralph Moffitt	76	72	74	74	296
	Dave Thomas	75	74	75	72	296
17 =	Alex Caygill	77	74	71	75	297
	Bob Charles	79	71	69	78	297
19 =	Malcolm Gregson	78	70	74	76	298
	John MacDonald	78	74	74	72	298
	A Murray	77	73	76	72	298
	Phil Rodgers	74	79	74	71	298
	Syd Scott	75	74	73	76	298

'Champagne' Tony Lema won the Open Championship at his first attempt. His nine-under-par performance over the Old Course was stunning, finishing five clear of Nicklaus, who had hauled himself into contention early in R4; and Lema's star seemed to be in the ascendant. He was to finish prominently in a few more Majors, but before his true worth could be assessed, he was tragically killed in a private plane crash in 1966.

US PGA

COURSE:	Columbus CC
LOCATION:	Columbus, Ohio
DATE:	16-19 July
DISTANCE:	6851 yards
PAR:	71 (284)
WINNER:	$18000

Pos	Player	1st	2nd	3rd	4th	Total
1	**BOBBY NICHOLLS**	64	71	69	67	271
2 =	Jack Nicklaus	67	73	70	64	274
	Arnold Palmer	68	68	69	69	274
4	Mason Rudolph	73	66	68	69	276
5 =	Tom Nieporte	68	71	68	72	279
	Ken Venturi	72	65	73	69	279
7	Bo Wininger	69	68	73	70	280
8	Gay Brewer	72	71	71	67	281
9 =	Billy Casper	68	72	70	72	282
	Jon Gustin	69	76	71	66	282
	Ben Hogan	70	72	68	72	282
	Tony Lema	71	68	72	71	282
13 =	Ed Furgol	71	69	72	71	283
	Billy Maxwell	72	71	70	70	283
	Gary Player	70	71	71	71	283
	Mike Souchak	67	73	71	72	283
17 =	Walter Burkemo	70	71	72	71	284
	Jacky Cupit	72	71	72	69	284
19 =	Bob Charles	68	71	73	73	285
	Al Geiberger	73	72	72	68	285

In a Championship of records, 28 year-old Bobby Nicholls, partially paralysed only a few years earlier, won over Nicklaus and Palmer by three strokes. Record-equalling 64s came from Nicholls and Nicklaus; and the new low total of 271 for the PGA, was also, by three strokes, the record for any Major Championship. A consistent player for the next decade or so, Nicholls never won another Major, and his form left him after he was struck, along with Lee Trevino and Jerry Heard, by lightning during the Western Open in 1975.

THE MASTERS

COURSE:	Augusta National GC
LOCATION:	Augusta, Georgia
DATE:	8-11 April
DISTANCE:	6925 yards
PAR:	72 (288)
WINNER:	$20000

Pos	Player	1st	2nd	3rd	4th	Total
1	**JACK NICKLAUS**	67	71	64	69	271
2 =	Arnold Palmer	70	68	72	70	280
	Gary Player	69	72	72	73	280
4	Mason Rudolph	70	75	66	72	283
5	Dan Sikes	67	72	71	75	285
6 =	Gene Littler	71	74	67	74	286
	Ramon Sota	71	73	70	72	286
8 =	Frank Beard	68	77	72	70	287
	Tommy Bolt	69	78	69	71	287
10	George Knudson	72	73	69	74	288
11 =	Tommy Aaron	67	74	71	77	289
	Bruce Crampton	72	72	74	71	289
	Paul Harney	74	74	71	70	289
	Doug Sanders	69	72	74	74	289
15 =	George Bayer	69	74	75	72	290
	Bruce Devlin	71	76	73	70	290
	Wes Ellis, Jr	69	76	72	73	290
	Tommy Jacobs	71	74	72	73	290
	Kel Nagle	75	70	74	71	290
	Byron Nelson	70	74	72	74	290

Jack Nicklaus dismantled Ben Hogan's Masters low, and equalled Lloyd Mangrum's 1940 course record 64, when he shot 271, 17 under par, to win. The under-par figures and the margin of victory – nine strokes – were also records, and the low total matched Bobby Nicholls' outstanding effort in the previous year's PGA, to become the best-equal for any Major to that date.

US OPEN

COURSE:	Bellerive CC
LOCATION:	St Louis, Missouri
DATE:	17-21 June
DISTANCE:	7191 yards
PAR:	70 (280)
WINNER:	$26000

Pos	Player	1st	2nd	3rd	4th	Total
1	**GARY PLAYER***	70	70	71	71	282
2	Kel Nagle	68	73	72	69	282
3	Frank Beard	74	69	70	71	284
4 =	Julius Boros	72	75	70	70	287
	Al Geiberger	70	76	70	71	287
6 =	Bruce Devlin	72	73	72	71	288
	Ray Floyd	72	72	76	68	288
8 =	Tony Lema	72	74	73	70	289
	Gene Littler	73	71	73	72	289
	Dudley Wysong	72	75	70	72	289
11 =	Deane Beman (a)	69	73	76	72	290
	Mason Rudolph	69	72	73	76	290
	Doug Sanders	77	73	69	71	290
14	Billy Maxwell	76	73	71	71	291
15	Steve Oppermann	72	77	73	70	292
16	Gay Brewer	72	74	71	76	293
17 =	Billy Casper	73	73	76	72	294
	Charles Huckaby	73	74	73	74	294
	George Knudson	80	69	73	72	294
	Bob Verwey	73	74	75	72	294

* Gary Player (71) beat Kel Nagle (74) in the 18-Hole Play-off

South Africa's Gary Player became the first overseas winner of the US Open since Ted Ray in 1920; beating 1960 British Open Champion, Kel Nagle, after a play-off. In doing so he joined Gene Sarazen and Ben Hogan as only one of three golfers to win all four Majors – the Grand Slam. Player achieved this feat in six years, compared with seven for Hogan (who, of course only entered the British Open once) and 13 for Sarazen.

COURSE: Royal Birkdale GC	COURSE: Laurel Valley GC
LOCATION: Southport, Lancashire, England	LOCATION: Ligonier, Pennsylvania
DATE: 7-9 July	DATE: 12-15 August
DISTANCE: 7037 yards	DISTANCE: 7090 yards
PAR: 73 (292)	PAR: 71 (284)
WINNER: £1750	WINNER: $25000

Pos	Player	1st	2nd	3rd	4th	Total
1	**PETER THOMSON**	74	68	72	71	285
2 =	Brian Huggett	73	68	76	70	287
	Christy O'Connor, Sr	69	73	74	71	287
4	Roberto de Vicenzo	74	69	73	72	288
5 =	Bernard Hunt	74	74	70	71	289
	Tony Lema	68	72	75	74	289
	Kel Nagle	74	70	73	72	289
8 =	Bruce Devlin	71	69	75	75	290
	Sebastian Miguel	72	73	72	73	290
10 =	Max Faulkner	74	72	74	73	293
	John Panton	74	74	75	70	293
12 =	Hugh Boyle	73	69	76	76	294
	Neil Coles	73	74	77	70	294
	Jack Nicklaus	73	71	77	73	294
	Lionel Platts	72	72	73	77	294
16	Arnold Palmer	70	71	75	79	295
17 =	Eric Brown	72	70	77	77	296
	Tommy Horton	75	73	76	72	296
	Cobie Legrange	76	73	75	72	296
	Guy Wolstenholme	72	75	77	72	296

Pos	Player	1st	2nd	3rd	4th	Total
1	**DAVE MARR**	70	69	70	71	280
2 =	Billy Casper	70	70	71	71	282
	Jack Nicklaus	69	70	72	71	282
4	Bo Wininger	73	72	72	66	283
5	Gardner Dickinson	67	74	69	74	284
6 =	Bruce Devlin	68	75	72	70	285
	Sam Snead	68	75	70	72	285
8 =	Tommy Aaron	66	71	72	78	287
	Jack Burke, Jr	75	71	72	69	287
	Jacky Cupit	72	76	70	69	287
	Rod Funseth	75	72	69	71	287
	Bob McCallister	76	68	70	73	287
13 =	Wes Ellis, Jr	73	76	70	69	288
	RH Sykes	71	71	71	75	288
15 =	Ben Hogan	72	75	72	70	289
	Mike Souchak	70	72	77	70	289
17 =	Julius Boros	75	72	73	70	290
	Ray Floyd	68	73	72	77	290
19	Al Geiberger	74	71	71	75	291
20 =	Bruce Crampton	77	74	70	71	292
	Jack Fleck	76	71	72	73	292
	Doug Ford	73	70	77	72	292
	Gordon Jones	72	76	71	73	292
	George Knudson	75	69	73	75	292
	Kel Nagle	74	75	71	72	292
	Mason Rudolph	67	76	75	74	292
	Doug Sanders	71	73	74	74	292

Returning to the scene of his very first Open victory in 1954, Peter Thomson picked up his fifth win, and thereby joined Braid and Taylor on this mark, just one behind Harry Vardon's all-time record. It will always be argued that Thomson's four wins during the fifties were somewhat devalued because the competition was not of the very best; an arguement strengthened by Thomson's modest success in US Majors. However, no-one can demean his fifth, and final, win, with a strong American contingent trailing in his wake. Birkdale had, at last, like its inclusion on the Open roster, received its long-overdue Royal Charter.

Dave Marr won his only Major when he firstly cast off Tommy Aaron's challenge (whose 40 going out in R4 put him out of contention); then held firm to weather assaults from Nicklaus and Casper. 53 year-old ex-Champions, Sam Snead and Ben Hogan, came home sixth and 15th, respectively, while contemporary giants of the game, Palmer and Player, could only tie 33rd.

1966

COURSE:	Augusta National GC								
LOCATION:	Augusta, Georgia								
DATE:	7-11 April								
DISTANCE:	6925 yards								
PAR:	72 (288)								
WINNER:	$20000								

COURSE:	Olympic GC					
LOCATION:	San Francisco, California					
DATE:	16-20 June					
DISTANCE:	6719 yards					
PAR:	70 (280)					
WINNER:	$26500					

Pos	Player	1st	2nd	3rd	4th	Total
1	**JACK NICKLAUS***	68	76	72	72	288
2 =	Gay Brewer	74	72	72	70	288
	Tommy Jacobs	75	71	70	72	288
4 =	Arnold Palmer	74	70	74	72	290
	Doug Sanders	74	70	75	71	290
6 =	Don January	71	73	73	75	292
	George Knudson	73	76	72	71	292
8 =	Ray Floyd	72	73	74	74	293
	Paul Harney	75	68	76	74	293
10 =	Billy Casper	71	75	76	72	294
	Jay Hebert	72	74	73	75	294
	Bob Rosburg	73	71	76	74	294
13 =	Tommy Aaron	74	73	77	71	295
	Peter Butler	72	71	79	73	295
	Ben Hogan	74	71	73	77	295
16	Ken Venturi	75	74	73	74	296
17 =	Tommy Bolt	75	72	78	72	297
	Bruce Crampton	74	75	71	77	297
	Terry Dill	75	72	74	76	297
	Doug Ford	75	73	73	76	297
	Phil Rodgers	76	73	75	73	297

Pos	Player	1st	2nd	3rd	4th	Total
1	**BILLY CASPER***	69	68	73	68	278
2	Arnold Palmer	71	66	70	71	278
3	Jack Nicklaus	71	71	69	74	285
4 =	Tony Lema	71	74	70	71	286
	Dave Marr	71	74	68	73	286
6	Phil Rodgers	70	70	73	74	287
7	Bobby Nicholls	74	72	71	72	289
8 =	Wes Ellis, Jr	71	75	74	70	290
	Johnny Miller (a)	70	72	74	74	290
	Mason Rudolph	74	72	71	73	290
	Doug Sanders	70	75	74	71	290
12	Ben Hogan	72	73	76	70	291
13 =	Rod Funseth	75	75	69	73	292
	Rives McBee	76	64	74	78	292
15 =	Bob Murphy (a)	73	72	75	73	293
	Gary Player	78	72	74	69	293
17 =	George Archer	74	72	76	72	294
	Frank Beard	76	74	69	75	294
	Julius Boros	74	69	77	74	294
	Don January	73	73	75	73	294
	Ken Venturi	73	77	71	73	294

*Jack Nicklaus (70) beat Tommy Jacobs (72) and Gay Brewer (78) in the 18-Hole Play-off

Nicklaus' third Masters win was the first ever back-to-back. His fifth Major title took him equal with Braid and Taylor, Byron Nelson and Peter Thomson; but it was not his easiest. In a Tournament where the lead changed hands 17 times, a play-off seemed inevitable. Finally, Nicklaus had more trouble seeing off Tommy Jacobs than Gay Brewer, who struggled to a 78.

* Billy Casper (69) beat Arnold Palmer (73) in the 18-Hole Play-off

Arnold Palmer's attempt to collect his second US Open and eighth Major folded on the back nine of the final round. Although he eventually succumbed to Billy Casper in a play-off, in the fourth round of regulation play Palmer dropped seven shots to the eventual winner, after blitzing the outward holes in 32. This was Casper's second title, following his win at Winged Foot in 1959. Unknown Rives McBee equalled the low score of 64 in R2.

BRITISH OPEN

COURSE: Honourable Company of
Edinburgh Golfers
LOCATION: Muirfield, East Lothian, Scotland
DATE: 6-9 July
DISTANCE: 6887 yards
PAR: n/k
WINNER: £2100

Pos	Player	1st	2nd	3rd	4th	Total
1	**JACK NICKLAUS**	70	67	75	70	282
2 =	Doug Sanders	71	70	72	70	283
	Dave Thomas	72	73	69	69	283
4 =	Bruce Devlin	73	69	74	70	286
	Kel Nagle	72	68	76	70	286
	Gary Player	72	74	71	69	286
	Phil Rodgers	74	66	70	76	286
8 =	Dave Marr	73	76	69	70	288
	Sebastian Miguel	74	72	70	72	288
	Arnold Palmer	73	72	69	74	288
	Peter Thomson	73	75	69	71	288
12	RH Sikes	73	72	73	72	290
13 =	Harold Henning	71	69	75	76	291
	Christy O'Connor, Sr	73	72	74	72	291
15	Julius Boros	73	71	76	72	292
16 =	Peter Butler	73	65	80	75	293
	Alex Caygill	72	71	73	77	293
	Jimmy Hitchcock	70	77	74	72	293
	Ronnie Shade (a)	71	70	75	77	293
20 =	Peter Alliss	74	72	75	73	294
	Roberto de Vicenzo	74	72	71	77	294
	Doug Sewell	76	69	74	75	294

Jack Nicklaus became the fourth (and last, to date) golfer to win a clean sweep of all the Major Championships. Nicklaus' record is the greatest of them all; and even laid claim to such at that particular point in time. The Bobby Jones Grand Slams included six Amateur titles, but no Masters or PGA (through no fault of his own); Nicklaus had two Amateur Championships (although not the British Amateur) as well as matching the professional deeds of Sarazen, Hogan and Player. It is, indeed, an unique achievement. Moreover, his professional Grand Slam was accumulated in easily the fastest time – just four years. The R&A decided to follow the example of the US Open and spread the Championship over four days. The Masters had been a four-day event since inception, and the PGA since opting for medal play.

US PGA

COURSE: Firestone CC
LOCATION: Akron, Ohio
DATE: 21-24 July
DISTANCE: 7180 yards
PAR: 70 (280)
WINNER: $25000

Pos	Player	1st	2nd	3rd	4th	Total
1	**AL GEIBERGER**	68	72	68	72	280
2	Dudley Wysong	74	72	66	72	284
3 =	Billy Casper	73	73	70	70	286
	Gene Littler	75	71	71	69	286
	Gary Player	73	70	70	73	286
6 =	Julius Boros	69	72	75	71	287
	Jacky Cupit	70	73	73	71	287
	Arnold Palmer	75	73	71	68	287
	Doug Sanders	69	74	73	71	287
	Sam Snead	68	71	75	73	287
11	Frank Beard	73	72	69	74	288
12 =	Dow Finsterwald	74	70	73	72	289
	Jay Hebert	75	73	70	71	289
	Don January	69	71	73	76	289
15 =	Paul Harney	74	73	71	72	290
	Bill Martindale	73	75	70	72	290
	Ken Venturi	74	75	69	72	290
18 =	Gardner Dickinson	74	72	73	72	291
	Ray Floyd	74	75	74	68	291
	Dave Marr	75	75	68	73	291
	Ernie Vossler	77	70	75	69	291

Al Geiberger was the only player to achieve par as the course defeated the likes of Casper and Player (two over); Boros, Palmer and Snead (three over); and Nicklaus (eight over). It was the only Major Championship for Geiberger, who is one of the few golfers who will be remembered for something other than a win in a Major Championship: his 59 in the 1977 Memphis Classic was the first sub-60 score in a US Tour event. He went out in 30, back in 29, and shot 11 birdies, one eagle and no bogeys.

THE MASTERS

COURSE:	Augusta National GC
LOCATION:	Augusta, Georgia
DATE:	6-9 April
DISTANCE:	6925 yards
PAR:	72 (288)
WINNER:	$20000

Pos	Player	1st	2nd	3rd	4th	Total
1	**GAY BREWER**	73	68	72	67	280
2	Bobby Nicholls	72	69	70	70	281
3	Bert Yancey	67	73	71	73	284
4	Arnold Palmer	73	73	70	69	285
5	Julius Boros	71	70	70	75	286
6 =	Paul Harney	73	71	74	69	287
	Gary Player	75	69	72	71	287
8 =	Tommy Aaron	75	68	74	71	288
	Lionel Hebert	77	71	67	73	288
10 =	Roberto de Vicenzo	73	72	74	71	290
	Bruce Devlin	74	70	75	71	290
	Ben Hogan	74	73	66	77	290
	Mason Rudolph	72	76	72	70	290
	Sam Snead	72	76	71	71	290
15	Jacky Cupit	73	76	67	75	291
16 =	George Archer	75	67	72	78	292
	Wes Ellis, Jr	79	71	74	68	292
	Tony Jacklin	71	70	74	77	292
	Dave Marr	73	74	70	75	292
	Doug Sanders	74	72	73	73	292

After disappointing in the three-way play-off the previous year, Gay Brewer won his only Major; one stroke clear of 1964 PGA Champion, Bobby Nicholls, at Augusta National. With Bert Yancey fading, Brewer and Nicholls fought tooth and nail over the last round, the winner getting in front for the first time at the 13th.

US OPEN

COURSE:	Baltusrol GC
LOCATION:	Springfield, New Jersey
DATE:	15-18 June
DISTANCE:	7015 yards
PAR:	70 (280)
WINNER:	$30000

Pos	Player	1st	2nd	3rd	4th	Total
1	**JACK NICKLAUS**	71	67	72	65	275
2	Arnold Palmer	69	68	73	69	279
3	Don January	69	72	70	70	281
4	Billy Casper	69	70	71	72	282
5	Lee Trevino	72	70	72	70	284
6 =	Deane Beman	69	71	71	73	284
	Gardner Dickinson	70	73	68	73	284
	Bob Goalby	72	71	70	71	284
9 =	Dave Marr	70	74	70	71	285
	Kel Nagle	70	72	72	71	285
	Art Wall	69	73	72	71	285
12 =	Al Balding	75	72	71	68	286
	Wes Ellis, Jr	74	69	70	73	286
	Gary Player	69	73	73	71	286
15	Tom Weiskopf	72	71	74	70	287
16 =	Dutch Harrison	70	76	72	70	288
	Jerry Pittman	72	72	75	69	288
18 =	Miller Barber	71	71	69	78	289
	Marty Fleckman (a)	67	73	69	80	289
	Paul Harney	71	75	72	71	289
	Dave Hill	76	69	69	75	289
	Bob Verwey	75	71	69	74	289

Arnold Palmer may have been the first person in US Open history to shoot below 280 on more than one occasion, but he could not stop Nicklaus' second Open win, nor his lowering of the record total; a record which had stood since 1948 when Ben Hogan took the Riviera Country Club apart. At 27, Nicklaus was now well into one of his purple patches; collecting his seventh Major, to tie with Vardon, Jones, Sarazen, Snead and Palmer.

COURSE:	Royal Liverpool GC				
LOCATION:	Hoylake, Cheshire, England				
DATE:	12-15 July				
DISTANCE:	6995 yards				
PAR:	70 (280)				
WINNER:	£2100				

COURSE:	Columbine CC				
LOCATION:	Denver, Colorado				
DATE:	20-24 July				
DISTANCE:	7436 yards				
PAR:	72 (288)				
WINNER:	$25000				

Pos	Player	1st	2nd	3rd	4th	Total
1	**ROBERTO DE VICENZO**	70	71	67	70	278
2	Jack Nicklaus	71	69	71	69	280
3 =	Clive Clark	70	73	69	72	284
	Gary Player	72	71	67	74	284
5	Tony Jacklin	73	69	73	70	285
6 =	Harold Henning	74	70	71	71	286
	Sebastian Miguel	72	74	68	72	286
8 =	Al Balding	74	71	69	73	287
	Hugh Boyle	74	74	71	68	287
	Bruce Devlin	70	70	72	75	287
	Tommy Horton	74	74	69	70	287
	Peter Thomson	71	74	70	72	287
13 =	Deane Beman	72	76	68	73	289
	M Hoyle	74	75	69	71	289
	Stanley Peach	71	75	73	70	289
	Lionel Platts	68	73	72	76	289
	Guy Wolstenholme	74	71	73	71	289
18 =	Barry Coxon	73	76	71	70	290
	Hedley Muscroft	72	73	72	73	290
	Doug Sanders	71	73	73	73	290

Pos	Player	1st	2nd	3rd	4th	Total
1	**DON JANUARY***	71	72	70	68	281
2	Don Massingale	70	75	70	66	281
3 =	Jack Nicklaus	67	75	69	71	282
	Dan Sikes	69	70	70	73	282
5 =	Julius Boros	69	76	70	68	283
	Al Geiberger	73	71	69	70	283
7 =	Frank Beard	71	74	70	70	285
	Don Bies	69	70	76	70	285
	Bob Goalby	70	74	68	73	285
	Gene Littler	73	72	71	69	285
11 =	Billy Farrell	75	72	69	70	286
	Dave Hill	66	73	74	73	286
	Ken Venturi	73	74	71	68	286
14 =	Sam Carmichael	75	71	69	72	287
	Lionel Hebert	75	71	70	71	287
	Bobby Nichols	75	75	67	70	287
	Arnold Palmer	70	71	72	74	287
	RH Sikes	72	71	71	73	287
19	Billy Casper	75	70	75	68	288
20 =	Tommy Aaron	70	65	76	78	289
	Bill Bisdorf	72	71	77	69	289
	Dick Crawford	76	73	73	67	289
	Ray Floyd	74	69	74	72	289
	Mike Souchak	70	73	70	76	289

Already 44, Argentinian Roberto de Vicenzo became Britain's Champion Golfer, after being runner-up as long ago as 1950. This, the best player to come out of South America, was to collect 12 different national titles in all, over a professional career spanning 40 years. He then progressed to the Seniors Tour, winning the US title twice, and the World's senior title in 1974. The Royal Liverpool Golf Club at Hoylake sadly played host to the Open for the tenth and last time.

* Don January (69) beat Don Massingale (71) in the 18-Hole Play-off

Columbine hosted a Major for the one and only time and holds the record as being the longest course for any Major to date. For Don January, who had perished in the 1961 play-off, the extra holes this time were not to hold any gremlins. His 69 was too good for Don Massengale's one-under-par effort.

THE MASTERS

COURSE:	Augusta National GC
LOCATION:	Augusta, Georgia
DATE:	11-14 April
DISTANCE:	6925 yards
PAR:	72 (288)
WINNER:	$20000

Pos	Player	1st	2nd	3rd	4th	Total
1	**BOB GOALBY**	70	70	71	66	277
2	Roberto de Vicenzo	69	73	70	66	278
3	Bert Yancey	71	71	72	65	279
4	Bruce Devlin	69	73	69	69	280
5 =	Frank Beard	75	65	71	70	281
	Jack Nicklaus	69	71	74	67	281
7 =	Tommy Aaron	68	72	72	69	282
	Ray Floyd	71	71	69	71	282
	Lionel Hebert	72	71	71	68	282
	Jerry Pittman	70	73	70	69	282
	Gary Player	72	67	71	72	282
12 =	Miller Barber	75	69	68	71	283
	Doug Sanders	76	69	70	68	283
14 =	Don January	71	68	72	73	284
	Mason Rudolph	73	73	72	66	284
16 =	Julius Boros	73	71	70	71	285
	Billy Casper	68	75	73	69	285
	Tom Weiskopf	74	71	69	71	285
19	Bob Charles	75	71	70	70	286
20 =	Dave Marr	74	71	71	71	287
	Kermit Zarley	70	73	74	70	287

Following his late-career win in the British Open in 1967, Roberto de Vicenzo tied with Bob Goalby; after birdying 17 and dropping a shot at the last. The Argentinian was annoyed about that bogey at 18, but completely distraught when he was penalised one stroke for signing an incorrect card. The three at 17 was entered as a four – a mistake that was to haunt de Vicenzo, and Tommy Aaron, who was marking his playing partner's card – for some time to come. Goalby, in rather unsatisfactory circumstances, was outright winner.

US OPEN

COURSE:	Oak Hill CC
LOCATION:	Rochester, New York
DATE:	13-16 June
DISTANCE:	6962 yards
PAR:	70 (280)
WINNER:	$30000

Pos	Player	1st	2nd	3rd	4th	Total
1	**LEE TREVINO**	69	68	69	69	275
2	Jack Nicklaus	72	70	70	67	279
3	Bert Yancey	67	68	70	76	281
4	Bobby Nichols	74	71	68	69	282
5 =	Don Bies	70	70	75	69	284
	Steve Spray	73	75	71	65	284
7 =	Bob Charles	73	69	72	71	285
	Jerry Pittman	73	67	74	71	285
9 =	Gay Brewer	71	71	75	69	286
	Billy Casper	75	68	71	72	286
	Bruce Devlin	71	69	75	71	286
	Al Geiberger	72	74	68	72	286
	Sam Snead	73	71	74	68	286
	Dave Stockton	72	73	69	72	286
15	Dan Sikes	71	71	73	72	287
16 =	George Archer	74	72	73	69	288
	Julius Boros	71	71	71	75	288
	Charles Coody	69	71	72	76	288
	Rod Funseth	74	72	69	73	288
	Dave Hill	74	68	74	72	288
	Gary Player	76	69	70	73	288

Equalling Jack Nicklaus' previous year low total, Lee Trevino became the first man in history to win any Major with all four rounds under par and sub-70. When he wasn't winning, Nicklaus was notching up a high percentage of second places. Bert Yancey set a new Open 54-hole low of 205; and Sam Snead, now 56, still made the Top 10. Entries for the Open passed 3000 for the first time.

	BRITISH OPEN	
COURSE:	Carnoustie GC	
LOCATION:	Carnoustie, Angus, Scotland	
DATE:	10-13 July	
DISTANCE:	7252 yards	
PAR:	72 (288)	
WINNER:	£3000	

Pos	Player	1st	2nd	3rd	4th	Total
1	**GARY PLAYER**	74	71	71	73	289
2 =	Bob Charles	72	72	71	76	291
	Jack Nicklaus	76	69	73	73	291
4	Billy Casper	72	68	74	78	292
5	Maurice Bembridge	71	75	73	74	293
6 =	Brian Barnes	70	74	80	71	295
	Gay Brewer	74	73	72	76	295
	Neil Coles	75	76	71	73	295
9	Al Balding	74	76	74	72	296
10 =	Roberto de Vicenzo	77	72	74	74	297
	Bruce Devlin	77	73	72	75	297
	Arnold Palmer	77	71	72	77	297
13 =	Peter Alliss	73	78	72	75	298
	Bobby Cole	75	76	72	75	298
	Tommy Horton	77	74	73	74	298
	Brian Huggett	76	71	75	76	298
	Kel Nagle	74	75	75	74	298
18 =	Eric Brown	76	76	74	73	299
	Tony Jacklin	72	72	75	80	299
	Paddy Skerritt	72	73	77	77	299

Gary Player won his fifth Major when he won the Open at Carnoustie; and over the longest course set for the Championship. He beat a strong field which boasted six other Majors winners in the Top 10 and ties. A 54-hole cut was introduced for the first time, reducing the number to 45 who went out on the last day.

	US PGA	
COURSE:	Pecan Valley CC	
LOCATION:	San Antonio, Texas	
DATE:	18-21 July	
DISTANCE:	7096 yards	
PAR:	70 (280)	
WINNER:	$25000	

Pos	Player	1st	2nd	3rd	4th	Total
1	**JULIUS BOROS**	71	71	70	69	281
2 =	Bob Charles	72	70	70	70	282
	Arnold Palmer	71	69	72	20	282
4 =	George Archer	71	69	74	69	283
	Marty Fleckman	66	72	72	73	283
6 =	Frank Beard	68	70	72	74	284
	Billy Casper	74	70	70	70	284
8 =	Miller Barber	70	70	72	73	285
	Frank Boynton	70	73	72	70	285
	Charles Coody	70	77	70	68	285
	Al Geiberger	70	73	71	71	285
	Bob Goalby	73	72	70	70	285
	Lou Graham	73	70	70	72	285
	Doug Sanders	72	67	73	73	285
	Dan Sikes	70	72	73	70	285
	Kermit Zarley	72	75	68	70	285
17 =	Dave Hill	72	74	69	71	286
	Mason Rudolph	69	75	70	72	286
	Dave Stockton	75	71	68	72	286
20 =	Gay Brewer	71	72	72	72	287
	Al Mengert	71	73	70	73	287
	Dick Rhyan	72	72	68	75	287

If Julius Boros failed by a few days to set the record for the oldest winner of the US Open in 1963; he certainly set one which is going to be difficult to beat when he won the PGA at Pecan Valley, at the age of 48. Before that, the oldest winner of any Major was 46 year-old Tom Morris, Sr; and the oldest within the century, Jerry Barber in 1961, also in the PGA, was positively juvenile at 45!

THE MASTERS

US OPEN

COURSE:	Augusta National GC
LOCATION:	Augusta, Georgia
DATE:	10-13 April
DISTANCE:	6925 yards
PAR:	72 (288)
WINNER:	$20000

COURSE:	Champions GC
LOCATION:	Houston, Texas
DATE:	12-15 June
DISTANCE:	6967 yards
PAR:	70 (280)
WINNER:	$30000

Pos	Player	1st	2nd	3rd	4th	Total
1	**GEORGE ARCHER**	67	73	69	72	281
2 =	Billy Casper	66	71	71	74	282
	George Knudson	70	73	69	70	282
	Tom Weiskopf	71	71	69	71	282
5 =	Charles Coody	74	68	69	72	283
	Don January	74	73	70	66	283
7	Miller Barber	71	71	68	74	284
8 =	Tommy Aaron	71	71	73	70	285
	Lionel Hebert	69	73	70	73	285
	Gene Littler	69	75	70	71	285
11	Mason Rudolph	69	73	74	70	286
12	Dan Sikes	69	71	73	74	287
13 =	Bruce Crampton	69	73	74	72	288
	Al Geiberger	71	71	74	72	288
	Harold Henning	73	72	71	72	288
	Takaaki Kono	71	75	68	74	288
	Bert Yancey	69	75	71	73	288
18	Dave Stockton	71	71	75	72	289
19 =	Frank Beard	72	74	70	74	290
	Deane Beman	74	73	74	69	290
	Bruce Devlin	67	70	76	77	290
	Dale Douglass	73	72	71	74	290
	Lee Trevino	72	74	75	69	290

Pos	Player	1st	2nd	3rd	4th	Total
1	**ORVILLE MOODY**	71	70	68	72	281
2 =	Deane Beman	68	69	73	72	282
	Al Geiberger	68	72	72	70	282
	Bob Rosburg	70	69	72	71	282
5	Bob Murphy	66	74	72	71	283
6 =	Miller Barber	67	71	68	78	284
	Bruce Crampton	73	72	68	71	284
	Arnold Palmer	70	73	69	72	284
9	Bunky Henry	70	72	68	75	285
10 =	George Archer	69	74	73	70	286
	Bruce Devlin	73	74	70	69	286
	Dave Marr	75	69	71	71	286
13 =	Julius Boros	71	73	70	73	287
	Charles Coody	72	68	72	75	287
	Dale Douglass	76	69	70	72	287
	Ray Floyd	79	68	68	72	287
	Dave Hill	73	74	70	70	287
	Howie Johnson	72	73	72	70	287
	Dean Refram	69	74	70	74	287
	Phil Rodgers	76	70	69	72	287
	Kermit Zarley	74	72	70	71	287

George Archer only came to prominence in Major Championships in the PGA of 1968, when he finished fourth, two behind Julius Boros. Billy Casper, who had made all the running, wilted, leaving Archer the Masters Champion when Tom Wieskopf and Canadian George Knudson couldn't mount a sufficient challenge over the final holes.

Failing to make the cut in his first attempt the previous year, former career soldier Orville Moody won his only Major in only his second year on the Tour. Miller Barber held a three-stroke lead over Moody after 54 holes, but blew up, allowing Moody to close out Beman, Geiberger and 1959 PGA Champion, Bob Rosburg, over the final 18.

COURSE: Royal Lytham and St Anne's GC	COURSE: NCR CC
LOCATION: St Annes, Lancashire, England	LOCATION: Dayton, Ohio
DATE: 9-12 July	DATE: 14-17 August
DISTANCE: 6848 yards	DISTANCE: 6915 yards
PAR: 71 (284)	PAR: 71 (284)
WINNER: £4250	WINNER: $35000

Pos	Player	1st	2nd	3rd	4th	Total
1	**TONY JACKLIN**	68	70	70	72	280
2	Bob Charles	66	69	75	72	282
3 =	Roberto de Vicenzo	72	73	66	72	283
	Peter Thomson	71	70	70	72	283
5	Christy O'Connor, Sr	71	65	74	74	284
6 =	Davis Love, Jr	70	73	71	71	285
	Jack Nicklaus	75	70	68	72	285
8	Peter Alliss	73	74	73	66	286
9	Kel Nagle	74	71	72	70	287
10	Miller Barber	69	75	75	69	288
11 =	Neil Coles	75	76	70	68	289
	Tommy Horton	71	76	70	72	289
	Cobie Legrange	79	70	71	69	289
	Guy Wolstenholme	70	71	76	72	289
15	Gay Brewer	76	71	68	75	290
16 =	Eric Brown	73	76	69	73	291
	Bruce Devlin	71	73	75	72	291
	Harold Henning	72	71	75	73	291
	Brian Huggett	72	72	69	78	291
	Orville Moody	71	70	74	76	291
	Peter Townsend	73	70	76	72	291
	Bert Yancey	72	71	71	77	291

Pos	Player	1st	2nd	3rd	4th	Total
1	**RAY FLOYD**	69	66	67	74	276
2	Gary Player	71	65	71	70	277
3	Bert Greene	71	68	68	71	278
4	Jimmy Wright	71	68	69	71	279
5 =	Miller Barber	73	75	64	68	280
	Larry Ziegler	69	71	70	70	280
7 =	Charles Coody	69	71	72	69	281
	Orville Moody	70	68	71	72	281
	Terry Wilcox	72	71	72	66	281
10	Frank Beard	70	75	68	69	282
11 =	Don Bies	74	64	71	74	283
	Bunky Henry	69	68	70	76	283
	Larry Mowry	69	71	69	74	283
	Jack Nicklaus	70	68	74	71	283
15 =	Bruce Crampton	70	70	72	72	284
	Dave Hill	74	75	67	68	284
	Don January	75	70	70	69	284
	Chi Chi Rodriguez	72	72	71	69	284
19 =	Howie Johnson	73	68	72	72	285
	Johnny Pott	69	75	71	70	285

Raymond Floyd won the first of his two PGA titles, and four Majors, in holding out Gary Player over the last round. Player was the subject of anti-apartheid demonstrations during the Championship; but displaying his famous iron will he pushed Floyd all the way, pulling back four shots over the last round, and just failing to tie. As in the PGA of 1959, it was claustrophobic at the top of the R1 leaderboard, with nine tying for the lead.

After a wait of 18 years, the old Claret Jug was lifted by a home player again. Englishman Tony Jacklin became a national hero when he finished four under par, and ahead of three former Champions, to win at Lytham. As if to mark the occasion, the R&A's winner's prize was increased in 1969 by over 40% – a realistic increase, perhaps, but still way off the American pace of increases over the recent past. It may be simplistic to say that Jacklin's emergence at the top of world golf, albeit for a short time, was a pivotal point in the game's history; in that the emphasis of total American dominance was to change. But his exploits did act as a catalyst in Britain, in that the interest in golf surged; and within the next 15 years, two multiple Majors winners, Faldo and Lyle, had emerged, as well as parity or better in the Ryder Cup.

THE MASTERS

COURSE:	Augusta National GC
LOCATION:	Augusta, Georgia
DATE:	9-13 April
DISTANCE:	6925 yards
PAR:	72 (288)
WINNER:	$25000

Pos	Player	1st	2nd	3rd	4th	Total
1	**BILLY CASPER***	72	68	68	71	279
2	Gene Littler	69	70	70	70	279
3	Gary Player	74	68	68	70	280
4	Bert Yancey	69	70	72	70	281
5 =	Tommy Aaron	68	74	69	72	283
	Dave Hill	73	70	70	70	283
	Dave Stockton	72	72	69	70	283
8	Jack Nicklaus	71	75	69	69	284
9	Frank Beard	71	76	68	70	285
10 =	Bob Lunn	70	70	75	72	287
	Chi Chi Rodriguez	70	76	73	68	287
12 =	Charles Coody	70	74	67	77	288
	Bert Greene	75	71	70	72	288
	Tony Jacklin	73	74	70	71	288
	Don January	76	73	69	70	288
	Takaaki Kono	75	68	71	74	288
17	Bob Charles	75	71	71	72	289
18 =	Howie Johnson	75	71	73	71	290
	Dick Lotz	74	72	72	72	290
	Orville Moody	73	72	71	74	290

*Billy Casper (69) beat Gene Littler (74) in the 18-Hole Play-off

Billy Casper compensated for his defeat the previous year when he took the Masters in a play-off from 1961 Open Champion Gene Littler. The final round was very tight with five players jockeying for the lead, before Casper and Littler prevailed. This was Casper's third Major, following two successes in the US Open.

US OPEN

COURSE:	Hazeltine National GC
LOCATION:	Minnepolis, Minnesota
DATE:	18-21 June
DISTANCE:	7151 yards
PAR:	72 (288)
WINNER:	$30000

Pos	Player	1st	2nd	3rd	4th	Total
1	**TONY JACKLIN**	71	70	70	70	281
2	Dave Hill	75	69	71	73	288
3 =	Bob Charles	76	71	75	67	289
	Bob Lunn	77	72	70	70	289
5	Ken Still	78	71	71	71	291
6	Miller Barber	75	75	72	70	292
7	Gay Brewer	75	71	71	76	293
8 =	Billy Casper	75	75	71	73	294
	Bruce Devlin	75	75	71	73	294
	Lee Trevino	77	73	74	70	294
	Larry Ziegler	75	73	73	73	294
12 =	Julius Boros	73	75	70	77	295
	Bobby Cole	78	75	71	71	295
	Joel Goldstrand	76	76	71	72	295
	Howie Johnson	75	72	75	73	295
	Gene Littler	77	72	71	75	295
	Bobby Mitchell	74	78	74	69	295
18 =	Al Balding	75	74	75	72	296
	Paul Harney	78	73	75	70	296
	Johnny Miller	79	73	73	71	296
	Randy Wolff	78	67	76	75	296

Reigning British Open Champion Jacklin achieved a rare double with a remarkable win at Hazeltine. His victory by seven shots was the biggest since Jim Barnes in 1921; he led wire-to-wire, increasing his lead round-by-round; he was the only player under par. Second-placed Dave Hill was so critical of Robert Trent Jones' alterations to the course, he was fined $150 by the USGA for his remarks.

BRITISH OPEN

COURSE:	Royal & Ancient GC				
LOCATION:	St Andrews, Fife, Scotland				
DATE:	8-11 July				
DISTANCE:	6951 yards				
PAR:	72 (288)				
WINNER:	£5250				

Pos	Player	1st	2nd	3rd	4th	Total
1	**JACK NICKLAUS***	68	69	73	73	283
2	Doug Sanders	68	71	71	73	283
3 =	Harold Henning	67	72	73	73	285
	Lee Trevino	68	68	72	77	285
5	Tony Jacklin	67	70	73	76	286
6 =	Neil Coles	65	74	72	76	287
	Peter Oosterhuis	73	69	69	76	287
8	Hugh Jackson	69	72	73	74	288
9 =	Tommy Horton	66	73	75	75	289
	John Panton	72	73	73	71	289
	Peter Thomson	68	74	73	74	289
12	Arnold Palmer	68	72	76	74	290
13 =	Maurice Bembridge	67	74	75	76	292
	Bob Charles	72	73	73	74	292
	JC Richardson	67	72	76	77	292
	Bert Yancey	71	71	73	77	292
17 =	Roberto Bernadini	75	69	74	75	293
	Billy Casper	71	74	73	75	293
	Clive Clark	69	70	77	77	293
	Roberto de Vicenzo	71	76	71	75	293
	Christy O'Connor, Sr	72	68	74	79	293

* Jack Nicklaus (72) beat Doug Sanders (73) in the 18-Hole Play-off

Doug Sanders never won a Major, but will always be remembered for his glorious failure at St Andrews. Once Trevino fell away, Sanders always seemed to have the edge over Nicklaus. However, needing a par four at the relatively-easy 18th, he missed a three-foot putt for outright victory. In the play-off, Sanders, one behind going to the last, birdied the same hole; only for Nicklaus to do likewise and pick up his second Open, and first Major in, what was for him, a barren three years.

US PGA

COURSE:	Southern Hills CC				
LOCATION:	Tulsa, Oklahoma				
DATE:	13-16 August				
DISTANCE:	6962 yards				
PAR:	70 (280)				
WINNER:	$40000				

Pos	Player	1st	2nd	3rd	4th	Total
1	**DAVE STOCKTON**	70	70	66	73	279
2 =	Bob Murphy	71	73	71	66	281
	Arnold Palmer	70	72	69	70	281
4 =	Larry Hinson	69	71	74	68	282
	Gene Littler	72	71	69	70	282
6 =	Bruce Crampton	73	75	68	67	283
	Jack Nicklaus	68	76	73	66	283
8 =	Ray Floyd	71	73	65	75	284
	Dick Lotz	72	70	75	67	284
10 =	Billy Maxwell	72	71	73	69	285
	Mason Rudolph	71	70	73	71	285
12 =	Don January	73	71	73	69	286
	Johnny Miller	68	77	70	71	286
	Gary Player	74	68	74	70	286
	Sam Snead	70	75	68	73	286
16 =	Al Geiberger	72	74	71	71	288
	Mike Hill	70	71	74	73	288
18 =	Billy Casper	72	70	74	73	289
	Bruce Devlin	75	70	71	73	289
	Al Mengert	76	72	70	71	289
	Dan Sikes	74	70	75	70	289

Arnold Palmer's third runner-up spot in the PGA was to be his last serious attempt to be the fifth player to win all four Majors. The PGA was forever to elude him. Dave Stockton's R3 66 took him clear of the field and although Arnie was gradually clawing his way back he couldn't make enough of an impact on the leader to exert pressure. The Grand Slam was not to be.

US PGA

COURSE:	National GC
LOCATION:	Palm Beach Gardens, Florida
DATE:	25-28 February
DISTANCE:	7096 yards
PAR:	72 (288)
WINNER:	$40000

Pos	Player	1st	2nd	3rd	4th	Total
1	**JACK NICKLAUS**	66	69	70	73	281
2	Billy Casper	71	73	71	68	283
3	Tommy Bolt	72	74	69	69	284
4 =	Miller Barber	72	68	75	70	285
	Gary Player	71	73	68	73	285
6 =	Gibby Gilbert	74	67	72	73	286
	Dave Hill	74	71	71	70	286
	Jim Jamieson	72	72	72	70	286
9 =	Jerry Heard	73	71	72	71	287
	Bob Lunn	72	70	73	72	287
	Fred Marti	72	71	74	70	287
	Bob Rosburg	74	72	70	71	287
13 =	Frank Beard	74	71	73	70	288
	Bob Charles	70	75	70	73	288
	Bruce Devlin	71	71	74	72	288
	Larry Hinson	71	73	73	71	288
	Lee Trevino	71	73	75	69	288
18 =	Herb Hooper	74	71	73	71	289
	Arnold Palmer	75	71	70	73	289
20 =	Johnny Miller	71	76	72	71	290
	Bob E Smith	73	70	75	72	290

Going completely against the grain of previous years, the 1971 PGA Championship was held in February, at the PGA of America's home course, making it the first not the last Major of the season. The time of year made no difference to Jack Nicklaus though. He won, coasting home with shots to spare. In winning, he performed a unique double Grand Slam. Nicklaus became – and still is – the only golfer to win all the Major Championships at least twice.

THE MASTERS

COURSE:	Augusta National GC
LOCATION:	Augusta, Georgia
DATE:	8-11 April
DISTANCE:	6925 yards
PAR:	72 (288)
WINNER:	$25000

Pos	Player	1st	2nd	3rd	4th	Total
1	**CHARLES COODY**	66	73	70	70	279
2 =	Johnny Miller	72	73	68	68	281
	Jack Nicklaus	70	71	68	72	281
4 =	Don January	69	69	73	72	283
	Gene Littler	72	69	73	69	283
6 =	Gary Player	72	72	71	69	284
	Ken Still	72	71	72	69	284
	Tom Weiskopf	71	69	72	72	284
9 =	Frank Beard	74	73	69	70	286
	Roberto de Vicenzo	76	69	72	69	286
	Dave Stockton	72	73	69	72	286
12	Bert Greene	73	73	71	70	287
13 =	Billy Casper	72	73	71	72	288
	Bruce Devlin	72	70	72	74	288
	Ray Floyd	69	75	73	71	288
	Hale Irwin	69	72	71	76	288
	Bob Murphy	69	70	76	73	288
18 =	Bruce Crampton	73	72	74	70	289
	Arnold Palmer	73	72	71	73	289
20 =	Dave Eichelberger	76	71	70	73	290
	Orville Moody	79	69	70	72	290

In 1969, dropped shots over the last three holes cost Charles Coody the Masters Tournament. This year, despite Johnny Miller's six-under-par charge to hole 16 in the final round, Coody held his game together to see off Miller, who eventually ran out of steam, and Jack Nicklaus.

COURSE:	Merion GC
LOCATION:	Ardmore, Pennsylvania
DATE:	17-21 June
DISTANCE:	6544 yards
PAR:	70 (280)
WINNER:	$30000

COURSE:	Royal Birkdale GC
LOCATION:	Southport, Lancashire, England
DATE:	7-9 July
DISTANCE:	7080 yards
PAR:	73 (292)
WINNER:	£5500

Pos	Player	1st	2nd	3rd	4th	Total
1	**LEE TREVINO***	70	72	69	69	280
2	Jack Nicklaus	69	72	68	71	280
3 =	Jim Colbert	69	69	73	71	282
	Bob Rosburg	71	72	70	69	282
5 =	George Archer	71	70	70	72	283
	Johnny Miller	70	73	70	70	283
	Jim Simons (a)	71	71	65	76	283
8	Ray Floyd	71	75	67	71	284
9 =	Gay Brewer	70	70	73	72	285
	Larry Hinson	71	71	70	73	285
	Bobby Nichols	69	72	69	75	285
	Bert Yancey	75	69	69	72	285
13 =	Bob Charles	72	75	69	70	286
	Bobby Cole	72	71	72	71	286
	Jerry Heard	73	71	73	69	286
	Jerry McGee	72	67	77	70	286
	Chi Chi Rodriguez	70	71	73	72	286
	Lanny Wadkins (a)	68	75	75	68	286
19 =	Homero Blancas	71	71	75	70	287
	Dave Eichelberger	72	72	70	73	287
	Bob Goalby	68	76	74	69	287
	Hale Irwin	72	73	72	70	287
	Ken Still	71	72	69	75	287

Pos	Player	1st	2nd	3rd	4th	Total
1	**LEE TREVINO**	69	70	69	70	278
2	Liang-Huan Lu	70	70	69	70	279
3	Tony Jacklin	69	70	70	71	280
4	Craig DeFoy	72	72	68	69	281
5 =	Charles Coody	74	71	70	68	283
	Jack Nicklaus	71	71	72	69	283
7 =	Billy Casper	70	72	75	67	284
	Gary Player	71	70	71	72	284
9 =	Doug Sanders	73	71	74	67	285
	Peter Thomson	70	73	73	69	285
11 =	Harry Bannerman	73	71	72	71	287
	Roberto de Vicenzo	71	70	72	74	287
	Kel Nagle	70	75	73	69	287
	Ramon Sota	72	72	70	73	287
	Dave Stockton	74	74	68	71	287
	Bert Yancey	75	70	71	71	287
17	Dale Hayes	71	72	70	75	288
18 =	Bob Charles	77	71	71	70	289
	Peter Oosterhuis	76	71	66	76	289
20 =	Bernard Hunt	74	73	73	70	290
	Howie Johnson	69	76	72	73	290

* Lee Trevino (68) beat Jack Nicklaus (71) in the 18-Hole Play-off

Lee Trevino's second US Open win came after a superb 68 saw off Jack Nicklaus in a play-off. Amateur Jim Simons held a two-stroke lead at the end of R3, thanks to a sparkling 65. Nicklaus collected his second consecutive Majors runner-up prize of the season, after lifting the Masters title; while 1971 winner, Tony Jacklin, missed the cut, as had five other defending champions over the previous eight years. Entries passed 4000 for the first time.

The year of 'Mr Lu' and the constantly-doffed pork-pie hat: the first of Lee Trevino's British Opens. Liang-Huan Lu, from Taiwan, charmed the Birkdale crowds – and TV audiences – as he so nearly became the first Asian golfer to win a Major. Trevino's R1 69 was to make all the difference as the pair matched each other's scores from there in. His second consecutive Major of the year meant he joined Jones (twice), Sarazen and Hogan as the only players to lift both Opens in the same year.

1972

	COURSE:	Augusta National GC
	LOCATION:	Augusta, Georgia
	DATE:	6-9 April
	DISTANCE:	6925 yards
	PAR:	72 (288)
	WINNER:	$25000

Pos	Player	1st	2nd	3rd	4th	Total
1	**JACK NICKLAUS**	68	71	73	74	286
2 =	Bruce Crampton	72	75	69	73	289
	Bobby Mitchell	73	72	71	73	289
	Tom Weiskopf	74	71	70	74	289
5 =	Homero Blancas	76	71	69	74	290
	Bruce Devlin	74	75	70	71	290
	Jerry Heard	73	71	72	74	290
	Jim Jamieson	72	70	71	77	290
	Jerry McGee	73	74	71	72	290
10 =	Gary Player	73	75	72	71	291
	Dave Stockton	76	70	74	71	291
12 =	George Archer	73	75	72	72	292
	Charles Coody	73	70	74	75	292
	Al Geiberger	76	70	74	72	292
	Steve Melnyk	72	72	74	74	292
	Bert Yancey	72	69	76	75	292
17 =	Billy Casper	75	71	74	74	294
	Bob Goalby	73	76	72	73	294
19 =	Ben Crenshaw (a)	73	74	74	74	295
	Takaaki Kono	76	72	73	74	295
	Lanny Wadkins	72	72	77	74	295

After a period of three seasons when he won nothing, Jack Nicklaus was winning Majors again – and continuing to break records. He won his fourth Masters, tying the record of Arnold Palmer, and tenth Major overall; one ahead of Ben Hogan, one behind Walter Hagen. Australian Bruce Crampton was to follow Jack home in this, and his next two, Major Championship wins. In fact all Crampton's four Majors second places were behind Nicklaus.

	COURSE:	Pebble Beach GL
	LOCATION:	Pebble Beach, California
	DATE:	17-21 June
	DISTANCE:	6812 yards
	PAR:	72 (288)
	WINNER:	$30000

Pos	Player	1st	2nd	3rd	4th	Total
1	**JACK NICKLAUS**	71	73	72	74	290
2	Bruce Crampton	74	70	73	76	293
3	Arnold Palmer	77	68	73	76	294
4 =	Homero Blancas	74	70	76	75	295
	Lee Trevino	74	72	71	78	295
6	Kermit Zarley	71	73	73	79	296
7	Johnny Miller	74	73	71	79	297
8	Tom Weiskopf	73	74	73	78	298
9 =	Chi Chi Rodriguez	71	75	78	75	299
	Cesar Sanudo	72	72	78	77	299
11 =	Billy Casper	74	73	79	74	300
	Don January	76	71	74	79	300
	Bobby Nichols	77	74	72	77	300
	Bert Yancey	75	79	70	76	300
15 =	Don Massengale	72	81	70	78	301
	Orville Moody	71	77	79	74	301
	Gary Player	72	76	75	78	301
	Jim Simons (a)	75	75	79	72	301
19 =	Lou Graham	75	73	75	79	302
	Tom Kite (a)	75	73	79	75	302

Spectacular Pebble Beach played host to a Major Championship for the first time – and it proved a tough test. Nicklaus' second Major win in a row was the fifth time the Masters-US Open double in the same year was recorded. Craig Wood, Ben Hogan (twice) and Arnold Palmer had previously accomplished it. It was Jack's third US Open title and it also put him level with Walter Hagen atop the all-time lists with 11 – Masters (4), US Open (3), British Open (2), PGA (2). Mason Rudoph shot the low score for R1&2, but scored 80 and 86 in between to finish in 40th place.

COURSE: Honourable Company of
Edinburgh Golfers
LOCATION: Muirfield, East Lothian, Scotland
DATE: 12-15 July
DISTANCE: 6892 yards
PAR: 71 (284)
WINNER: £5500

Pos	Player	1st	2nd	3rd	4th	Total
1	**LEE TREVINO**	71	70	66	71	278
2	Jack Nicklaus	70	72	71	66	279
3	Tony Jacklin	69	72	67	72	280
4	Doug Sanders	71	71	69	70	281
5	Brian Barnes	71	72	69	71	283
6	Gary Player	71	71	76	67	285
7 =	Guy Hunt	75	72	67	72	286
	Arnold Palmer	73	73	69	71	286
	David Vaughan	74	73	70	69	286
	Tom Weiskopf	73	74	70	69	286
11 =	Clive Clark	72	71	73	71	287
	Dave Marr	70	74	71	72	287
13 =	Roberto Bernadini	73	71	76	68	288
	Peter Townsend	70	72	76	70	288
15 =	Peter Butler	72	75	73	69	289
	Bob Charles	75	70	74	70	289
	Jan Dorrestein	74	71	72	72	289
	Johnny Miller	76	66	72	75	289
19 =	Harry Bannerman	77	73	73	67	290
	Frank Beard	70	76	74	70	290
	Maurice Bembridge	73	71	75	71	290
	Bert Yancey	73	72	72	73	290

COURSE: Oakland Hills CC
LOCATION: Birmingham, Michigan
DATE: 3-6 August
DISTANCE: 6815 yards
PAR: 72 (288)
WINNER: $45000

Pos	Player	1st	2nd	3rd	4th	Total
1	**GARY PLAYER**	71	71	67	72	281
2 =	Tommy Aaron	71	71	70	71	283
	Jim Jamieson	69	72	72	70	283
4 =	Billy Casper	73	70	67	74	284
	Ray Floyd	69	71	74	70	284
	Sam Snead	70	74	71	69	284
7 =	Gay Brewer	71	70	70	74	285
	Jerry Heard	69	70	72	74	285
	Phil Rodgers	71	72	68	74	285
	Doug Sanders	72	72	68	73	285
11 =	Hale Irwin	71	69	75	71	286
	Lee Trevino	73	71	71	71	286
13 =	Jack Nicklaus	72	75	68	72	287
	Dan Sikes	70	72	73	73	287
15	Charles Coody	71	73	70	74	288
16 =	Miller Barber	73	74	72	70	289
	Hubert Green	75	71	73	70	289
	Arnold Palmer	69	75	72	73	289
	Lanny Wadkins	74	68	72	75	289
20 =	Johnny Miller	70	76	70	74	290
	Bob Shaw	72	72	74	72	290
	JC Snead	72	72	71	75	290
	Larry Wise	74	71	67	78	290

Lee Trevino's back-to-back Open win was destined to be. In the third round, he scrambled five consecutive birdies over the final five holes with an array of chips-in and outlandish putting unlikely to be seen again...or so Tony Jacklin hoped. It was bad enough for the Englishman watching his immaculate 67 being overhauled by Trevino's antics in R3; but when, tied going into the 72nd hole, he was 15 feet away in three, and saw Trevino, through the back of the green in four, run it in, it destroyed Jacklin – some say as a golfing force forever. Jacklin three-putted and allowed a Nicklaus charge to deprive him even of second place, Jack just failing to emulate Hogan's 1953 three Majors in-a-row record.

Just when it was rumoured that Gary Player was losing his form; and like Arnold Palmer – another of the modern triumvirate, who along with Nicklaus were now known as the 'Big Three' – he would never win another Major, he picked up his second PGA title and sixth Major Championship victory. He was now ranked above Taylor, Braid, Nelson and Thomson in the all-time lists, but still one behind the next group of Vardon, Jones, Sarazen, Snead and the aforementioned Palmer.

1973

COURSE:	Augusta National GC
LOCATION:	Augusta, Georgia
DATE:	5-9 April
DISTANCE:	6925 yards
PAR:	72 (288)
WINNER:	$30000

COURSE:	Oakmont CC
LOCATION:	Oakmont, Pennsylvania
DATE:	14-17 June
DISTANCE:	6921 yards
PAR:	71 (284)
WINNER:	$35000

Pos	Player	1st	2nd	3rd	4th	Total
1	**TOMMY AARON**	68	73	74	68	283
2	JC Snead	70	71	73	70	284
3 =	Jim Jamieson	73	71	70	71	285
	Jack Nicklaus	69	77	73	66	285
	Peter Oosterhuis	73	70	68	74	285
6 =	Bob Goalby	73	70	71	74	288
	Johnny Miller	75	69	71	73	288
8 =	Bruce Devlin	73	72	72	72	289
	Jumbo Ozaki	69	74	73	73	289
10 =	Gay Brewer	75	66	74	76	291
	Gardner Dickinson	74	70	72	75	291
	Don January	75	71	75	70	291
	Chi Chi Rodriguez	72	70	73	76	291
14 =	Hubert Green	72	74	75	71	292
	Mason Rudolph	72	72	77	71	292
	Dave Stockton	72	74	71	75	292
17 =	Billy Casper	75	73	72	73	293
	Bob Dickson	70	71	76	76	293
	Lou Graham	77	73	72	71	293
	Babe Hiskey	74	73	72	74	293
	Gene Littler	77	72	71	73	293
	Kermit Zarley	74	71	77	71	293

Pos	Player	1st	2nd	3rd	4th	Total
1	**JOHNNY MILLER**	71	69	76	63	279
2	John Schlee	73	70	67	70	280
3	Tom Weiskopf	73	69	69	70	281
4 =	Jack Nicklaus	71	69	74	68	282
	Arnold Palmer	71	71	68	72	282
	Lee Trevino	70	72	70	70	282
7 =	Julius Boros	73	69	68	73	283
	Jerry Heard	74	70	66	73	283
	Lanny Wadkins	74	69	75	65	283
10	Jim Colbert	70	68	74	72	284
11	Bob Charles	71	69	72	74	286
12	Gary Player	67	70	77	73	287
13 =	Al Geiberger	73	72	71	72	288
	Ralph Johnston	71	73	76	68	288
	Larry Ziegler	73	74	69	72	288
16	Ray Floyd	70	73	75	71	289
17	Marvin Giles (a)	74	69	74	73	290
18 =	Gene Littler	71	74	70	76	291
	Rocky Thompson	73	71	71	76	291
20 =	Rod Funseth	75	74	70	74	293
	Hale Irwin	73	74	75	71	293
	Denny Lyons	72	74	75	72	293
	Bob Murphy	77	70	75	71	293
	Bobby Nichols	75	71	74	73	293

Local boy, Tommy Aaron, won his first and last Major ahead of JC Snead – Sam's nephew. Englishman, Peter Oosterhuis, held a three-shot lead going into the last day, but couldn't hold it together, as Aaron, Snead and Jamieson challenged. A string of eight consecutive birdies helped Jack Nicklaus race up the leaderboard to tie with the Briton and Jamieson.

Johnny Miller followed up his second place at Augusta with his first Majors win in the US Open at Oakmont. In doing so he beat the Open low round score of 64 jointly held by Lee Mackey, Tommy Jacobs and Rives McBee – his 63 being the lowest score in any Major to date.

	BRITISH OPEN					US PGA	
COURSE:	Troon GC				COURSE:	Canterbury GC	
LOCATION:	Troon, Ayrshire, Scotland				LOCATION:	Cleveland, Ohio	
DATE:	11-14 July				DATE:	9-12 August	
DISTANCE:	7064 yards				DISTANCE:	6852 yards	
PAR:	72 (288)				PAR:	71 (284)	
WINNER:	£5500				WINNER:	$45000	

Pos	Player	1st	2nd	3rd	4th	Total
1	**TOM WEISKOPF**	68	67	71	70	276
2 =	Neil Coles	71	72	70	66	279
	Johnny Miller	70	68	69	72	279
4	Jack Nicklaus	69	70	76	65	280
5	Bert Yancey	69	69	73	70	281
6	Peter Butler	71	72	74	69	286
7 =	Bob Charles	73	71	73	71	288
	Christy O'Connor, Sr	73	68	74	73	288
	Lanny Wadkins	71	73	70	74	288
10 =	Brian Barnes	76	67	70	76	289
	Gay Brewer	76	71	72	70	289
	Harold Henning	73	73	73	70	289
	Lee Trevino	75	73	73	68	289
14 =	Tony Jacklin	75	73	72	70	290
	Doug McClelland	76	71	69	74	290
	Arnold Palmer	72	76	70	72	290
	Gary Player	76	69	74	69	290
18 =	Hugh Baiocchi	75	74	69	74	292
	Hugh Boyle	75	75	69	73	292
	Bruce Crampton	71	76	73	72	292
	Bruce Devlin	72	78	71	71	292
	Bernard Gallacher	73	69	75	75	292
	DJ Good	75	74	73	70	292
	Dave Hill	75	74	74	69	292

Pos	Player	1st	2nd	3rd	4th	Total
1	**JACK NICKLAUS**	72	68	68	69	277
2	Bruce Crampton	71	73	67	70	281
3 =	Mason Rudolph	69	70	70	73	282
	JC Snead	71	74	68	69	282
	Lanny Wadkins	73	69	71	69	282
6 =	Don Iverson	67	72	70	74	283
	Dan Sikes	72	68	72	71	283
	Tom Weiskopf	70	71	71	71	283
9 =	Hale Irwin	76	72	68	68	284
	Sam Snead	71	71	71	71	284
	Kermit Zarley	76	71	68	69	284
12 =	Bobby Brue	70	72	73	70	285
	Jim Colbert	72	70	69	74	285
	Larry Hinson	73	70	71	71	285
	Denny Lyons	73	70	67	75	285
	Dave Stockton	72	69	75	69	285
	Tom Watson	75	70	71	69	285
18 =	Al Geiberger	67	76	74	69	286
	Gibby Gilbert	70	70	73	73	286
	Bob Goalby	75	70	71	70	286
	Jim Jamieson	71	73	71	71	286
	Johnny Miller	72	71	74	69	286
	Lee Trevino	76	70	73	67	286

Tom Weiskopf's good finish in the US Open was in a run of superb form on the US Tour. He had already tied for second in the Masters, and running up to Pebble Beach, his results sequence read: W, W, 2, W. He played one other Tour event between the Opens, and must have been disappointed to finish fifth. His win at Troon, therefore, was as expected as it was popular – for if the game of golf awarded marks for artistic impression, then Weiskopf would have won more than one Major. US Open Champion, Johnny Miller, added another runner-up prize to his Masters earlier in the year.

Jack Nicklaus made history when he won his 12th Major and became the greatest player of Major Championships the game had ever seen. In passing Walter Hagen's total, he also – to the statistician's delight – eclipsed the old version of Grand Slam titles, which include the US and British Amateur Championship, held by Bobby Jones for 43 years. Nicklaus' two US Amateur wins took his grand haul past Jones' tally of 13 titles.

1974

COURSE:	Augusta National GC
LOCATION:	Augusta, Georgia
DATE:	11-14 April
DISTANCE:	6925 yards
PAR:	72 (288)
WINNER:	$35000

COURSE:	Winged Foot GC
LOCATION:	Mamaroneck, New York
DATE:	13-16 June
DISTANCE:	6961 yards
PAR:	70 (280)
WINNER:	$35000

Pos	Player	1st	2nd	3rd	4th	Total
1	**GARY PLAYER**	71	71	66	70	278
2 =	Dave Stockton	71	66	70	73	280
	Tom Weiskopf	71	69	70	70	280
4 =	Jim Colbert	67	72	69	73	281
	Hale Irwin	68	70	72	71	281
	Jack Nicklaus	69	71	72	69	281
7 =	Bobby Nichols	73	68	68	73	282
	Phil Rodgers	72	69	68	73	282
9 =	Maurice Bembridge	73	74	72	64	283
	Hubert Green	68	70	74	71	283
11 =	Bruce Crampton	73	72	69	70	284
	Jerry Heard	70	70	73	71	284
	Dave Hill	71	72	70	71	284
	Arnold Palmer	76	71	70	67	284
15 =	Buddy Allin	73	73	70	69	285
	Miller Barber	75	67	72	71	285
	Ralph Johnston	72	71	70	72	285
	Johnny Miller	72	74	69	70	285
	Dan Sikes	69	71	74	71	285
20 =	Chi Chi Rodriguez	70	74	71	71	286
	Sam Snead	72	72	71	71	286

Pos	Player	1st	2nd	3rd	4th	Total
1	**HALE IRWIN**	73	70	71	73	287
2	Forrest Fezler	75	70	74	70	289
3 =	Lou Graham	71	75	74	70	290
	Bert Yancey	76	69	73	72	290
5 =	Jim Colbert	72	77	69	74	292
	Arnold Palmer	73	70	73	76	292
	Tom Watson	73	71	69	79	292
8 =	Tom Kite	74	70	77	72	293
	Gary Player	70	73	77	73	293
10 =	Buddy Allin	76	71	74	73	294
	Jack Nicklaus	75	74	76	69	294
12 =	Frank Beard	77	69	72	77	295
	John Mahaffey	74	73	75	73	295
	Larry Ziegler	78	68	78	71	295
15 =	Ray Floyd	72	71	78	75	296
	Mike Reasor	71	76	76	73	296
	Tom Weiskopf	76	73	72	75	296
18 =	Dale Douglass	77	72	72	76	297
	Al Geiberger	75	76	78	68	297
	David Graham	73	75	76	73	297

Gary Player's seventh Major win, but only his second Masters, and after a 13 year span. 1970 PGA Champion Dave Stockton had led for much of the Tournament, but was caught and passed by Player in an exciting back nine. A nine iron to within inches of the pin at 17 set up the birdie that was to clinch it for the South African. Maurice Bembridge, a rare English visitor, equalled the low score with a 64 to finish tied for ninth.

Hale Irwin won his first Major by playing solid golf over the tough West Course at Winged Foot. That he was seven over par is testament to the demands of the golf course. 23 year-old Tom Watson held the lead after 54 holes, but collapsed – coming home in 41, as the pack overwhelmed him.

	BRITISH OPEN	
COURSE:	Royal Lytham and St Anne's GC
LOCATION:	St Annes, Lancashire, England
DATE:	10-13 July
DISTANCE:	6822 yards
PAR:	71 (284)
WINNER:	£5500

	US PGA	
COURSE:	Tanglewood GC
LOCATION:	Clemmons, North Carolina
DATE:	8-11 August
DISTANCE:	6852 yards
PAR:	71 (284)
WINNER:	$45000

Pos	Player	1st	2nd	3rd	4th	Total
1	**GARY PLAYER**	69	68	75	70	282
2	Peter Oosterhuis	71	71	73	71	286
3	Jack Nicklaus	74	72	70	71	287
4	Hubert Green	71	74	72	71	288
5 =	Danny Edwards	70	73	76	73	292
	Liang-Huan Lu	72	72	75	73	292
7 =	Bobby Cole	70	72	76	75	293
	Don Swaelens	77	73	74	69	293
	Tom Weiskopf	72	72	74	75	293
10	Johnny Miller	72	75	73	74	294
11 =	John Garner	75	78	73	69	295
	David Graham	76	74	76	69	295
13 =	Neil Coles	72	75	75	74	296
	Al Geiberger	76	70	76	74	296
	John Morgan	69	75	76	76	296
	Alan Tapie	73	77	73	73	296
	Peter Townsend	79	76	72	69	296
18 =	Peter Dawson	74	74	73	76	297
	Tony Jacklin	74	77	71	75	297
	Gene Littler	77	76	70	74	297
	Dewitt Weaver	73	80	70	74	297

Pos	Player	1st	2nd	3rd	4th	Total
1	**LEE TREVINO**	73	66	68	69	276
2	Jack Nicklaus	69	69	70	69	277
3 =	Bobby Cole	69	68	71	71	279
	Hubert Green	68	68	73	70	279
	Dave Hill	74	69	67	69	279
	Sam Snead	69	71	71	68	279
7	Gary Player	73	64	73	70	280
8	Al Geiberger	70	70	75	66	281
9 =	Don Bies	73	71	68	70	282
	John Mahaffey	72	72	71	67	282
11 =	Tommy Aycock	73	68	73	70	284
	Frank Beard	73	67	69	75	284
	Lee Elder	74	69	72	69	284
	Ray Floyd	68	73	74	70	284
	Mike Hill	76	72	68	68	284
	Tom Watson	69	72	73	70	284
17 =	Gay Brewer	72	72	72	69	285
	Tom Jenkins	70	73	71	71	285
	John Schlee	68	67	75	75	285
	Dan Sikes	71	75	71	68	285
	Leonard Thompson	69	71	70	75	285

Gary Player won his third Open and eighth Major in all when he was the only one to beat par at Royal Lytham. He climbed to fourth place outright in the all-time list, behind Nicklaus, Hagen and Hogan. The British Open, thanks to its support from Player (Champion first in 1959) and the Americans led by Palmer and Nicklaus, was unrecognisable from a decade or so before. Only one Englishman finished in the cosmopolitan Top 10, which also featured two South Africans, five Americans, a Taiwanese and a Belgian.

Wet conditions throughout the Championship favoured the maverick shotmaking genius that was Lee Trevino. He won his first PGA, and fifth Major, after shooting an opening 73 which left him tied-43rd, five shots off the lead. Thereafter he played brilliant golf in the conditions to card 203 for the last 54 holes. Jack Nicklaus continued to collect as many runner-up prizes as wins. Sam Snead, at the age of 62, was having a remarkable Indian summer in the PGA, finishing fourth, ninth and third over the last three years. It was 32 years after his first of seven Major titles.

THE MASTERS

COURSE:	Augusta National GC
LOCATION:	Augusta, Georgia
DATE:	10-13 April
DISTANCE:	6925 yards
PAR:	72 (288)
WINNER:	$40000

COURSE:	Medinah CC
LOCATION:	Medinah, Illinois
DATE:	19-23 June
DISTANCE:	7032 yards
PAR:	71 (284)
WINNER:	$40000

Pos	Player	1st	2nd	3rd	4th	Total
1	**JACK NICKLAUS**	68	67	73	68	276
2 =	Johnny Miller	75	71	65	66	277
	Tom Weiskopf	69	72	66	70	277
4 =	Hale Irwin	73	74	71	64	282
	Bobby Nichols	67	74	72	69	282
6	Billy Casper	70	70	73	70	283
7	Dave Hill	75	71	70	68	284
8 =	Hubert Green	74	71	70	70	285
	Tom Watson	70	70	72	73	285
10 =	Tom Kite	72	74	71	69	286
	JC Snead	69	72	75	70	286
	Lee Trevino	71	70	74	71	286
13 =	Arnold Palmer	69	71	75	72	287
	Larry Ziegler	71	73	74	69	287
15 =	Bobby Cole	73	71	73	71	288
	Rod Curl	72	70	76	70	288
	Bruce Devlin	72	70	76	70	288
	Allen Miller	68	75	72	73	288
	Art Wall	72	74	72	70	288
20 =	Buddy Allin	73	69	73	74	289
	Ralph Johnston	74	73	69	73	289

Pos	Player	1st	2nd	3rd	4th	Total
1	**LOU GRAHAM***	74	72	68	73	287
2	John Mahaffey	73	71	72	71	287
3 =	Frank Beard	74	69	67	78	288
	Ben Crenshaw	70	68	76	74	288
	Hale Irwin	74	71	73	70	288
	Bob Murphy	74	73	72	69	288
7 =	Jack Nicklaus	72	70	75	72	289
	Peter Oosterhuis	69	73	72	75	289
9 =	Pat Fitzsimons	67	73	73	77	290
	Arnold Palmer	69	75	73	73	290
	Tom Watson	67	68	78	77	290
12 =	Ray Floyd	76	71	72	72	291
	Andy North	75	72	72	72	291
14 =	Joe Inman, Jr	72	72	71	77	292
	Rik Massengale	71	74	71	76	292
	Eddie Pearce	75	71	70	76	292
	Jim Wiechers	68	73	76	75	292
18 =	Terry Dill	72	69	77	75	293
	Hubert Green	74	73	68	78	293
	Gary Groh	73	74	73	73	293
	Jay Haas (a)	74	69	72	78	293
	Grier Jones	69	73	79	72	293
	Jerry Pate (a)	79	70	72	72	293

Nicklaus' fifth win was a record for the Masters, while Tom Weiskopf equalled Ben Hogan's four second places. The two fought out a real dogfight over the last nine holes, but when Weiskopf missed his birdie putt on 18, Jack was home and dry for Major No.13. Attempting to make up 11 shots on Nicklaus over the last 36 holes, Johnny Miller fired 131, but just failed to tie for the lead when he again missed a putt for birdie at the last.

* Lou Graham (71) beat John Mahaffey (73) in the 18-Hole Play-off

With three strokes covering the first 11 players home, a play-off was perhaps inevitable. Frank Beard led by three going into the final round from Tom Watson and Pat Fitzsimmons, but all played R4 poorly allowing John Mahaffey through to tie with Lou Graham, who took a one-over five at the last. Graham steadied himself for the play-off to win his only Major. Unusually, Jack Nicklaus dropped a shot at each of the last three holes, and fell back into the pack.

COURSE:	Carnoustie GC
LOCATION:	Carnoustie, Angus, Scotland
DATE:	9-12 July
DISTANCE:	7065 yards
PAR:	72 (288)
WINNER:	£7500

Pos	Player	1st	2nd	3rd	4th	Total
1	**TOM WATSON***	71	67	69	72	279
2	Jack Newton	69	71	75	74	279
3 =	Bobby Cole	72	66	66	76	280
	Johnny Miller	71	69	66	74	280
	Jack Nicklaus	69	71	68	72	280
6	Graham Marsh	72	67	71	71	281
7 =	Neil Coles	72	69	67	74	282
	Peter Oosterhuis	68	70	71	73	282
9	Hale Irwin	69	70	69	75	283
10 =	George Burns	71	73	69	71	284
	John Mahaffey	71	68	69	76	284
12 =	Bob Charles	74	73	70	69	286
	P Leonard	70	69	73	74	286
	Andries Oosthuizen	69	69	70	78	286
15	Tom Weiskopf	73	72	70	72	287
16 =	Maurice Bembridge	75	73	67	73	288
	Arnold Palmer	74	72	69	73	288
	Alan Tapie	70	72	67	79	288
19 =	Bernard Gallacher	72	67	72	78	289
	Lon Hinckle	76	72	69	72	289
	Tommy Horton	72	71	71	75	289
	Sam Torrance	72	74	71	72	289

* Tom Watson (71) beat Jack Newton (72) in the 18-Hole Play-off

After succumbing to final round pressures in the US Open the previous month, and blowing up at Winged Foot in 1974, there was something of a question mark over Tom Watson's credentials when it came to converting winning positions into wins in Major Championships. There was always going to be something different about seaside golf for Watson, however – especially in Scotland – as he became only the third American after Ben Hogan and Tony Lema to play the British Open (and its particular linksland game) 'blind', and win at the first attempt.

COURSE:	Firestone CC
LOCATION:	Akron, Ohio
DATE:	7-10 August
DISTANCE:	7180 yards
PAR:	70 (280)
WINNER:	$45000

Pos	Player	1st	2nd	3rd	4th	Total
1	**JACK NICKLAUS**	70	68	67	71	276
2	Bruce Crampton	71	63	75	69	278
3	Tom Weiskopf	70	71	70	68	279
4	Andy North	72	74	70	65	281
5 =	Billy Casper	69	72	72	70	283
	Hale Irwin	72	65	73	73	283
7 =	Dave Hill	71	71	74	68	284
	Gene Littler	76	71	66	71	284
9	Tom Watson	70	71	71	73	285
10 =	Buddy Allin	73	72	70	71	286
	Ben Crenshaw	73	72	71	70	286
	Ray Floyd	70	73	72	71	286
	David Graham	72	70	70	74	286
	Don January	72	70	71	73	286
	John Schlee	71	68	75	72	286
	Leonard Thompson	74	69	72	71	286
17 =	Dale Douglass	74	72	74	67	287
	Gibby Gilbert	73	70	77	67	287
	Mike Hill	72	71	70	74	287
	Steve Melnyk	71	72	74	70	287
	Gil Morgan	73	71	71	72	287

Jack Nicklaus, who else, became the first person to do the Masters-PGA double in the same year – twice. Sam Snead and Jack Burke Jr were the only other players to achieve the feat once. Playing steady golf based on an overnight four-shot lead, Nicklaus coasted to his 14th Major, ahead of Bruce Crampton – runner up to Jack for the fourth time in a Major Championship. Crampton had the consolation of setting a new low of 63, however – the best in the PGA – and matched Johnny Miller, in the 1973 US Open, to tie for the all-time low round score in a Major.

THE MASTERS

	COURSE:	Augusta National GC
	LOCATION:	Augusta, Georgia
	DATE:	8-11 April
	DISTANCE:	6925 yards
	PAR:	72 (288)
	WINNER:	$40000

Pos	Player	1st	2nd	3rd	4th	Total
1	**RAY FLOYD**	65	66	70	70	271
2	Ben Crenshaw	70	70	72	67	279
3 =	Jack Nicklaus	67	69	73	73	282
	Larry Ziegler	67	71	72	72	282
5 =	Charles Coody	72	69	70	74	285
	Hale Irwin	71	77	67	70	285
	Tom Kite	73	67	72	73	285
8	Billy Casper	71	76	71	69	287
9 =	Roger Maltbie	72	75	70	71	288
	Graham Marsh	73	68	75	72	288
	Tom Weiskopf	73	71	70	74	288
12 =	Jim Colbert	71	72	74	72	289
	Lou Graham	68	73	72	76	289
	Gene Littler	71	72	74	72	289
15 =	Al Geiberger	75	70	73	73	291
	Dave Hill	69	73	76	73	291
	Jerry McGee	71	73	72	75	291
	Curtis Strange (a)	71	76	73	71	291
19 =	Buddy Allin	69	76	72	75	292
	Bruce Devlin	77	69	72	74	292
	Hubert Green	71	66	78	77	292
	Dale Hayes	75	74	73	70	292

Ray Floyd's second Major came as a result of spectacular scoring at Augusta. In tying Jack Nicklaus' all-time low for the Masters (and any Major Championship) he set new 36- and 54-hole record scores, to win by eight – only one shot less than Jack's 1965 margin. At the end of R3 Floyd led Nicklaus by eight, but as the latter faded, and Ben Crenshaw charged, he held firm to maintain the same gap.

US OPEN

	COURSE:	Atlanta Athletic Club
	LOCATION:	Duluth, Altanta, Georgia
	DATE:	17-20 June
	DISTANCE:	7015 yards
	PAR:	70 (280)
	WINNER:	$42000

Pos	Player	1st	2nd	3rd	4th	Total
1	**JERRY PATE**	71	69	69	68	277
2 =	Al Geiberger	70	69	71	69	279
	Tom Weiskopf	73	70	68	68	279
4 =	Butch Baird	71	71	71	67	280
	John Mahaffey	70	68	69	73	280
6	Hubert Green	72	70	71	69	282
7	Tom Watson	74	72	68	70	284
8 =	Ben Crenshaw	72	68	72	73	285
	Lyn Lott	71	71	70	73	285
10	Johnny Miller	74	72	69	71	286
11 =	Rod Funseth	70	70	72	75	287
	Jack Nicklaus	74	70	75	68	287
13	Ray Floyd	70	75	71	72	288
14 =	Mark Hayes	74	74	70	71	289
	Don January	71	74	69	75	289
	Mike Morley	71	71	70	77	289
	Andy North	74	72	69	74	289
	JC Snead	73	69	71	76	289
19 =	Danny Edwards	73	75	70	72	290
	Randy Glover	72	74	76	68	290
21 =	Dave Eichelberger	73	70	74	74	291
	Larry Nelson	75	74	70	72	291

Spectators numbered more than 100,000 for the four days for the first time, to see Jerry Pate play golf of a consistently-high standard to win from 1966 PGA Champion, Al Geiberger, and the British Open Champion of 1973, Tom Weiskopf. After Nicklaus in 1962, Pate, at 22, was the youngest US Open winner since Bobby Jones in 1923.

COURSE:	Royal Birkdale GC
LOCATION:	Southport, Lancashire, England
DATE:	7-10 July
DISTANCE:	7001 yards
PAR:	72 (288)
WINNER:	£7500

COURSE:	Congressional CC
LOCATION:	Bethesda, Maryland
DATE:	12-16 August
DISTANCE:	7054 yards
PAR:	70 (280)
WINNER:	$45000

Pos	Player	1st	2nd	3rd	4th	Total
1	**JOHNNY MILLER**	72	68	73	66	279
2 =	Seve Ballesteros	69	69	73	74	285
	Jack Nicklaus	74	70	72	69	285
4	Ray Floyd	76	67	73	70	286
5 =	Hubert Green	72	70	78	68	288
	Tommy Horton	74	69	72	73	288
	Mark James	76	72	74	66	288
	Tom Kite	70	74	73	71	288
	Christy O'Connor, Jr	69	73	75	71	288
10 =	George Burns	75	69	75	70	289
	Peter Butler	74	72	73	70	289
	Vicente Fernandez	79	71	69	70	289
	Norio Suzuki	69	75	75	70	289
14	Brian Barnes	70	73	75	72	290
15 =	Eamonn Darcy	78	71	71	71	291
	John Fourie	71	74	75	71	291
17 =	Graham Marsh	71	73	72	76	292
	Jack Newton	70	74	76	72	292
	Tom Weiskopf	73	72	76	71	292
	Guy Wolstenholme	76	72	71	73	292

Pos	Player	1st	2nd	3rd	4th	Total
1	**DAVE STOCKTON**	70	72	69	70	281
2 =	Ray Floyd	72	68	71	71	282
	Don January	70	69	71	72	282
4 =	David Graham	70	71	70	72	283
	Jack Nicklaus	71	69	69	74	283
	Jerry Pate	69	73	72	69	283
	John Schlee	72	71	70	70	283
8 =	Charles Coody	68	72	67	77	284
	Ben Crenshaw	71	69	74	70	284
	Jerry McGee	68	72	72	72	284
	Gil Morgan	66	68	75	75	284
	Tom Weiskopf	65	74	73	72	284
13 =	Tom Kite	66	72	73	75	286
	Gary Player	70	69	72	75	286
15 =	Lee Elder	68	74	70	75	287
	Mark Hayes	69	72	73	73	287
	Mike Hill	72	70	73	72	287
	Mike Morley	69	72	72	74	287
	Arnold Palmer	71	76	68	72	287
	JC Snead	74	71	70	72	287
	Tom Watson	70	74	70	73	287

Johnny Miller became the 13th winner of both Opens, first achieved by Harry Vardon when he claimed the US Open in 1900. In doing so he pulled away from the exciting, erratic Spaniard – the 19 year-old Severiano Ballesteros – with a blistering last round 66. Over the final 36 holes Miller played sensible, percentage golf: he used his one iron off the tee no fewer than 21 times. His achievement, however, almost took a back seat to Ballesteros' antics. Flirting with the Birkdale dunes, his scrambling brilliance was shown to the world for the first time. This was no ordinary golfer.

Dave Stockton won the PGA for the second time. He repeated his 1970 success by holing an awkward ten-foot putt for par at the last, to avoid a play-off with the 1967 and 1969 Champions. Congressional was at its meanest – denying par to any competitor over the 72 holes.

THE MASTERS

COURSE:	Augusta National GC
LOCATION:	Augusta, Georgia
DATE:	7-10 April
DISTANCE:	6925 yards
PAR:	72 (288)
WINNER:	$40000

Pos	Player	1st	2nd	3rd	4th	Total
1	**TOM WATSON**	70	69	70	67	276
2	Jack Nicklaus	72	70	70	66	278
3 =	Tom Kite	70	73	70	67	280
	Rik Massengale	70	73	67	70	280
5	Hale Irwin	70	74	70	68	282
6 =	David Graham	75	67	73	69	284
	Lou Graham	75	71	69	69	284
8 =	Ben Crenshaw	71	69	69	76	285
	Ray Floyd	71	72	71	71	285
	Hubert Green	67	74	72	72	285
	Don January	69	76	69	71	285
	Gene Littler	71	72	73	69	285
	John Schlee	75	73	69	68	285
14 =	Billy Casper	72	72	73	69	286
	Jim Colbert	72	71	69	74	286
	Rod Funseth	72	67	74	73	286
	Jerry Pate	70	72	74	70	286
	Tom Weiskopf	73	71	71	71	286
19 =	George Archer	74	74	69	70	287
	Andy Bean	74	70	71	72	287
	Danny Edwards	72	74	68	73	287
	Lee Elder	76	68	72	71	287
	Gary Player	71	70	72	74	287

Reigning British Open Champion, Tom Watson, won his second Major in under a year, when he beat Jack Nicklaus. Nicklaus' sequence of scores in the Majors before this event and following his success in the 1973 PGA, were as follows: 4, 10, 3, 2, W, 7, 3, W, 3, 11, 2, 4 – recording an amazing consistency, and posing a threat at every Championship. Watson's 20 foot birdie putt at 17 sealed his victory.

US OPEN

COURSE:	Southern Hills CC
LOCATION:	Tulsa, Oklahoma
DATE:	16-19 June
DISTANCE:	6873 yards
PAR:	70 (280)
WINNER:	$45000

Pos	Player	1st	2nd	3rd	4th	Total
1	**HUBERT GREEN**	69	67	72	70	278
2	Lou Graham	72	71	68	68	279
3	Tom Weiskopf	71	71	68	71	281
4	Tom Purtzer	69	69	72	72	282
5 =	Jay Haas	72	68	71	72	283
	Gary Jacobsen	73	70	67	73	283
7 =	Terry Diehl	69	68	73	74	284
	Lyn Lott	73	72	71	67	284
	Tom Watson	74	72	71	67	284
10 =	Rod Funseth	69	70	72	74	285
	Al Geiberger	70	71	75	69	285
	Mike McCullough	73	73	69	70	285
	Jack Nicklaus	74	68	71	72	285
	Peter Oosterhuis	71	70	74	70	285
	Gary Player	72	67	71	75	285
16 =	Wally Armstrong	71	70	70	75	286
	Joe Inman, Jr	70	70	72	74	286
	Steve Melnyk	70	73	70	73	286
19 =	Bill Kratzert	73	69	75	70	287
	Bruce Lietzke	74	68	71	74	287
	Jerry McGee	76	69	76	66	287
	Arnold Palmer	70	72	73	72	287

Hubert Green hung on to a lead he'd had since the first day to squeeze out 1975 Champion, Lou Graham, whose record-equalling last 36 holes took him to within one of a tie. Birdie-par-bogey over the last three holes, Green just about handled the pressure to stay ahead of Graham, already waiting nervously in the clubhouse.

BRITISH OPEN

COURSE: Turnberry GC
LOCATION: Turnberry, Ayrshire, Scotland
DATE: 6-9 July
DISTANCE: 6875 yards
PAR: 70 (280)
WINNER: £10000

Pos	Player	1st	2nd	3rd	4th	Total
1	**TOM WATSON**	68	70	65	65	268
2	Jack Nicklaus	68	70	65	66	269
3	Hubert Green	72	66	74	67	279
4	Lee Trevino	68	70	72	70	280
5 =	George Burns	70	70	72	69	281
	Ben Crenshaw	71	69	66	75	281
7	Arnold Palmer	73	73	67	69	282
8	Ray Floyd	70	73	68	72	283
9 =	Mark Hayes	76	63	72	73	284
	Tommy Horton	70	74	65	75	284
	Johnny Miller	69	74	67	74	284
	John Schroeder	66	74	73	71	284
13 =	Howard Clark	72	68	72	74	286
	Peter Thomson	74	72	67	73	286
15 =	Seve Ballesteros	69	71	73	74	287
	Peter Butler	71	68	75	73	287
	Bobby Cole	72	71	71	73	287
	Guy Hunt	73	71	71	72	287
	Graham Marsh	73	69	71	74	287
	Jerry Pate	74	70	70	73	287
	Bob Shearer	72	69	72	74	287

The Open came to Turnberry for the first time. Some argue that this was the best ever Open. Tom Watson defended his title and became the fifth player to do the Masters-British Open double in the same year; following no lesser lights than Hogan, Palmer, Nicklaus (twice, of course) and Player. His 268, in a wonderfully stirring two-horse race with Nicklaus, beat the Championship record by eight shots and lowered Jack's, Bobby Nicholls' and Ray Floyd's record score for any Major. Watson also set a new low of 130 for 36 holes. Nicklaus, unused to seeing a rival withstand the kind of pressure he was putting on Watson, was in the end beaten by his young compatriot. Even so, so much of a private duel was this titanic struggle, Jack's second place was ten shots clear of US Open Champion, Hubert Green. Mark Hayes' 63 was a new Championship low and tied with Johnny Miller's and Bruce Crampton's record for any Major.

US PGA

COURSE: Pebble Beach GL
LOCATION: Pebble Beach, California
DATE: 11-14 August
DISTANCE: 6804 yards
PAR: 72 (288)
WINNER: $45000

Pos	Player	1st	2nd	3rd	4th	Total
1	**LANNY WADKINS***	69	71	72	70	282
2	Gene Littler	67	69	70	76	282
3	Jack Nicklaus	69	71	70	73	283
4	Charles Coody	70	71	70	73	284
5	Jerry Pate	73	70	69	73	285
6 =	Al Geiberger	71	70	73	72	286
	Lou Graham	71	73	71	71	286
	Don January	75	69	70	72	286
	Jerry McGee	68	70	77	71	286
	Tom Watson	68	73	71	74	286
11 =	Joe Inman, Jr	72	69	73	73	287
	Johnny Miller	70	74	73	70	287
13 =	Tom Kite	73	73	70	72	288
	Lee Trevino	71	73	71	73	288
15 =	George Cadle	69	73	70	77	289
	Bruce Lietzke	74	70	74	71	289
	Gil Morgan	74	68	70	77	289
	Leonard Thompson	72	73	69	75	289
19 =	George Archer	70	73	76	72	291
	George Burns	71	76	70	74	291
	Mark Hayes	68	75	74	74	291
	Arnold Palmer	72	73	73	73	291
	John Schroeder	73	76	68	74	291
	JC Snead	76	71	72	72	291

* Lanny Wadkins beat Gene Littler at the third extra hole in the Sudden Death Play-off

In the first ever sudden death play-off employed in any Major, Lanny Wadkins won his only Major when he beat 1961 US Open Champion, Gene Littler. The tie was somewhat presented to Wadkins, who, five shots adrift at the turn, saw Littler bogey five of the next six holes; and Jack Nicklaus, who was then level with Littler, dropped a shot at the 17th. Wadkins then drew level with Littler by shooting the only birdie of his round at the last.

1978

COURSE:	Augusta National GC
LOCATION:	Augusta, Georgia
DATE:	6-9 April
DISTANCE:	6925 yards
PAR:	72 (288)
WINNER:	$45000

COURSE:	Cherry Hills CC
LOCATION:	Denver, Colorado
DATE:	15-18 June
DISTANCE:	7083 yards
PAR:	71 (284)
WINNER:	$45000

Pos	Player	1st	2nd	3rd	4th	Total
1	**GARY PLAYER**	72	72	69	64	277
2 =	Rod Funseth	73	66	70	69	278
	Hubert Green	72	69	65	72	278
	Tom Watson	73	68	68	69	278
5 =	Wally Armstrong	72	70	70	68	280
	Billy Kratzert	70	74	67	69	280
7	Jack Nicklaus	72	73	69	67	281
8	Hale Irwin	73	67	71	71	282
9 =	David Graham	75	69	67	72	283
	Joe Inman, Jr	69	73	72	69	283
11 =	Don January	72	70	72	70	284
	Jerry McGee	71	73	71	69	284
	Tom Weiskopf	72	71	70	71	284
14 =	Peter Oosterhuis	74	70	70	71	285
	Lee Trevino	70	69	72	74	285
16 =	Ray Floyd	76	71	71	68	286
	Lindy Miller (a)	74	71	70	71	286
18 =	Seve Ballesteros	74	71	68	74	287
	Tom Kite	71	74	71	71	287
	Gil Morgan	73	73	70	71	287
	Jerry Pate	72	71	72	72	287
	Ed Sneed	74	70	70	73	287
	Lanny Wadkins	74	70	73	70	287

Pos	Player	1st	2nd	3rd	4th	Total
1	**ANDY NORTH**	70	70	71	74	285
2 =	JC Snead	70	72	72	72	286
	Dave Stockton	71	73	70	72	286
4 =	Hale Irwin	69	74	75	70	288
	Tom Weiskopf	77	73	70	68	288
6 =	Andy Bean	72	72	71	74	289
	Bill Kratzert	72	74	70	73	289
	Johnny Miller	78	69	68	74	289
	Jack Nicklaus	73	69	74	73	289
	Gary Player	71	71	70	77	289
	Tom Watson	74	75	70	70	289
12 =	Ray Floyd	75	70	76	70	291
	Joe Inman, Jr	72	72	74	73	291
	Mike McCullough	75	75	73	68	291
	Lee Trevino	72	71	75	73	291
16 =	Seve Ballesteros	75	69	71	77	292
	Artie McNickle	74	75	70	73	292
	Jerry Pate	73	72	74	73	292
	Bob Shearer	78	72	71	71	292
20 =	Wally Armstrong	73	73	74	73	293
	Phil Hancock	71	73	75	74	293
	Tom Kite	73	73	70	77	293
	Bruce Lietzke	72	73	72	76	293

Gary Player, aged 42, won his ninth and last Major Championship at the Masters, thus drawing level with Ben Hogan to tie third on the all-time list. His first Major was back in 1959 when he lifted the British Open title at Muirfield, and his span of wins matched the 20 years of JH Taylor (1894-1913). Seven birdies over the last ten holes turned back the clock and set up his third Masters win – an improbable result when Hubert Green was defending a seven-shot lead after R3, and went round the last 18 holes in par. Tommy Nakajima of Japan shot 13 at the 13th. Unlucky for some, perhaps: certainly for accident-prone Tommy. He missed the cut.

No-one beat par at Cherry Hills. Andy North went to four under par after seven holes on the last day, a lead of five, with the benefit of two birdies. Then the next few holes saw some eccentric scoring from him: bogey, bogey, bogey, birdie, birdie, bogey, double-bogey! Despite that he still maintained a (diminished) lead. At the 15th it was cut to just one stroke when Dave Stockton birdied, but Stockton's own bogey at the 18th meant North only needed the same to win. He duly did.

COURSE:	Royal & Ancient GC				
LOCATION:	St Andrews, Fife, Scotland				
DATE:	12-15 July				
DISTANCE:	6933 yards				
PAR:	72 (288)				
WINNER:	£12500				

Pos	Player	1st	2nd	3rd	4th	Total
1	**JACK NICKLAUS**	71	72	69	69	281
2 =	Ben Crenshaw	70	69	73	71	283
	Ray Floyd	69	75	71	68	283
	Tom Kite	72	69	72	70	283
	Simon Owen	70	75	67	71	283
6	Peter Oosterhuis	72	70	69	73	284
7 =	Isao Aoki	68	71	73	73	285
	Nick Faldo	71	72	70	72	285
	John Schroeder	74	69	70	72	285
	Bob Shearer	71	69	74	71	285
11 =	Michael Cahill	71	72	75	68	286
	Dale Hayes	74	70	71	71	286
	Orville Moody	73	69	74	70	286
14 =	Mark Hayes	70	75	75	67	287
	Jumbo Ozaki	72	69	75	71	287
	Tom Watson	73	68	70	76	287
17 =	Seve Ballesteros	69	70	76	73	288
	Bob Byman	72	69	74	73	288
	Guy Hunt	71	73	71	73	288
	Tommy Nakajima	70	71	76	71	288
	Tom Weiskopf	69	72	72	75	288

In a Championship of might-have-beens it was totally fitting that Jack Nicklaus should win what was to be his last Open Championship at the Home of Golf. It was his 15th Major and his first for three years; and it presented him with a record that may never be beaten (Mr Woods may disagree!). He now became the only player to win each of the Grand Slam titles three times or more; and still no-one else apart from Sarazen, Hogan and Player have achieved the feat even once. New Zealander, Simon Owen, building on his R3 67, took the lead when he chipped in at the 15th. At this point he was playing the best golf of the round, and an upset seemed likely. However, he dropped two shots over the last three holes to tie second. After his disaster in the Masters, Nakajima effectively put himself out of contention when he took nine at the 17th (Road Hole) in the third round.

COURSE:	Oakmont CC				
LOCATION:	Oakmont, Pennsylvania				
DATE:	3-6 August				
DISTANCE:	6989 yards				
PAR:	71 (284)				
WINNER:	$50000				

Pos	Player	1st	2nd	3rd	4th	Total
1	**JOHN MAHAFFEY***	75	67	68	66	276
2 =	Jerry Pate	72	70	66	68	276
	Tom Watson	67	69	67	73	276
4 =	Gil Morgan	76	71	66	67	280
	Tom Weiskopf	73	67	69	71	280
6	Craig Stadler	70	74	67	71	282
7 =	Andy Bean	72	72	70	70	284
	Graham Marsh	72	74	68	70	284
	Lee Trevino	69	73	70	74	284
10	Fuzzy Zoeller	75	69	73	68	285
11	Joe Inman, Jr	72	68	69	77	286
12 =	Hale Irwin	73	71	73	70	287
	Bill Kratzert	70	77	73	67	287
	Larry Nelson	76	71	70	70	287
	John Schroeder	76	69	70	72	287
16 =	Ben Crenshaw	69	71	75	73	288
	Phil Hancock	70	73	70	75	288
	Grier Jones	70	73	71	74	288
19 =	Wally Armstrong	71	73	75	70	289
	George Burns	79	68	70	72	289
	Bob Gilder	74	71	70	74	289
	Don January	73	72	75	69	289
	Bobby Nichols	75	67	73	74	289
	Dave Stockton	68	75	74	72	289
	Kermit Zarley	75	71	67	76	289

* John Mahaffey beat Jerry Pate and Tom Watson at the second extra hole in the Sudden Death Play-off

Trailing Tom Watson by seven strokes going into the last round, John Mahaffey shot a 66 to tie him and Jerry Pate. He then birdied the second extra hole to win the first three-way sudden-death playoff, and his only Majors title. This was the first strokeplay PGA hosted by Oakmont CC, but two Championships were held there in matchplay days – and five US Opens to that date. This made Oakmont the most used venue for Majors in the US after Augusta National.

THE MASTERS

COURSE:	Augusta National GC				
LOCATION:	Augusta, Georgia				
DATE:	12-15 April				
DISTANCE:	6925 yards				
PAR:	72 (288)				
WINNER:	$50000				

Pos	Player	1st	2nd	3rd	4th	Total
1	**FUZZY ZOELLER***	70	71	69	70	280
2 =	Ed Sneed	68	67	69	76	280
	Tom Watson	68	71	70	71	280
4	Jack Nicklaus	69	71	72	69	281
5	Tom Kite	71	72	68	72	283
6	Bruce Lietzke	67	75	68	74	284
7 =	Craig Stadler	69	66	74	76	285
	Leonard Thompson	68	70	73	74	285
	Lanny Wadkins	73	69	70	73	285
10 =	Hubert Green	74	69	72	71	286
	Gene Littler	74	71	69	72	286
12 =	Seve Ballesteros	72	68	73	74	287
	Miller Barber	75	64	72	76	287
	Jack Newton	70	72	69	76	287
	Andy North	72	72	74	69	287
	Lee Trevino	73	71	70	73	287
17 =	Lee Elder	73	70	74	71	288
	Ray Floyd	70	68	73	77	288
	Billy Kratzert	73	68	71	76	288
	Artie McNickle	71	72	74	71	288
	Gary Player	71	72	74	71	288

*Fuzzy Zoeller beat Ed Sneed and Tom Watson at the second extra hole of the Sudden Death Play-off

Frank Urban (Fuzzy) Zoeller wrote himself into the record books with his first Major triumph, by winning the first-ever sudden death play-off in the Masters. He also collected the first $50000 winner's prize at Augusta, although the 1978 PGA Championship claims that for the first Major. Ed Sneed saw fame and glory dissipate after squandering a five-stroke lead at the start of the day. After the 15th he was still three clear, but three bogeys necessitated a play-off. For Tom Watson, after the aforementioned 1978 PGA, it was his second successive three-way sudden death play-off; but he was to be no luckier at the Masters. Zoeller's birdie at the second extra hole saw to that.

US OPEN

COURSE:	Inverness GC				
LOCATION:	Toledo, Ohio				
DATE:	14-17 June				
DISTANCE:	6982 yards				
PAR:	71 (284)				
WINNER:	$50000				

Pos	Player	1st	2nd	3rd	4th	Total
1	**HALE IRWIN**	74	68	67	75	284
2 =	Jerry Pate	71	74	69	72	286
	Gary Player	73	73	72	68	286
4 =	Larry Nelson	71	68	76	73	288
	Bill Rogers	71	72	73	72	288
	Tom Weiskopf	71	74	67	76	288
7	David Graham	73	73	70	73	289
8	Tom Purtzer	70	69	75	76	290
9 =	Keith Fergus	70	77	72	72	291
	Jack Nicklaus	74	77	72	68	291
11 =	Ben Crenshaw	75	71	72	75	293
	Lee Elder	74	72	69	78	293
	Andy North	77	74	68	74	293
	Calvin Peete	72	75	71	75	293
	Ed Sneed	72	73	75	73	293
16 =	Bob Gilder	77	70	69	78	294
	Graham Marsh	77	71	72	74	294
	Jim Simons	74	74	78	68	294
19 =	Al Geiberger	74	74	69	78	295
	Lee Trevino	77	73	73	72	295
	Lanny Wadkins	73	74	71	77	295
	Bobby Walzel	74	72	71	78	295
	DA Weibring	74	76	71	74	295

Par over the tough 72 holes at Inverness was only achieved by Hale Irwin, giving him another US Open title to add to his victory of 1974. Leading Tom Weiskopf by three overnight, he had extended his advantage to five by the 16th. Then the wheels almost came off. At the 17th, bunkered and two-putting, he carded a double-bogey six, then found sand again at the last to limp home just two ahead.

BRITISH OPEN

Pos	Player	1st	2nd	3rd	4th	Total
1	**SEVE BALLESTEROS**	73	65	75	70	283
2 =	Ben Crenshaw	72	71	72	71	286
	Jack Nicklaus	72	69	73	72	286
4	Mark James	76	69	69	73	287
5	Rodger Davis	75	70	70	73	288
6	Hale Irwin	68	68	75	78	289
7 =	Isao Aoki	70	74	72	75	291
	Bob Byman	73	70	72	76	291
	Graham Marsh	74	68	75	74	291
10 =	Bob Charles	78	72	70	72	292
	Greg Norman	73	71	72	76	292
	Jumbo Ozaki	75	69	75	73	292
13 =	Wally Armstrong	74	74	73	72	293
	Terry Gale	71	74	75	73	293
	John O'Leary	73	73	74	73	293
	Simon Owen	75	76	74	68	293
17 =	Peter McEvoy (a)	71	74	72	77	294
	Lee Trevino	71	73	74	76	294
19 =	Ken Brown	72	71	75	77	295
	Nick Faldo	74	74	78	69	295
	Sandy Lyle	74	76	75	70	295
	Orville Moody	71	74	76	74	295
	Gary Player	77	74	69	75	295

US PGA — 1979

COURSE: Oakland Hills CC
LOCATION: Birmingham, Michigan
DATE: 2-5 August
DISTANCE: 7014 yards
PAR: 70 (280)
WINNER: $60000

Pos	Player	1st	2nd	3rd	4th	Total
1	**DAVID GRAHAM***	69	68	70	65	272
2	Ben Crenshaw	69	67	69	67	272
3	Rex Caldwell	67	70	66	71	274
4	Ron Streck	68	71	69	68	276
5 =	Gibby Gilbert	69	72	68	69	278
	Jerry Pate	69	69	69	71	278
7 =	Jay Haas	68	69	73	69	279
	Don January	69	70	71	69	279
	Howard Twitty	70	73	69	67	279
10 =	Lou Graham	69	74	68	69	280
	Gary Koch	71	71	71	67	280
12 =	Andy Bean	76	69	68	68	281
	Jerry McGee	73	69	71	68	281
	Jack Renner	71	74	66	70	281
	Tom Watson	66	72	69	74	281
16 =	Bob Gilder	73	71	68	70	282
	Hubert Green	69	70	72	71	282
	Bruce Lietzke	69	69	71	73	282
	Gene Littler	71	71	67	73	282
	Graham Marsh	69	70	71	72	282

COURSE: Royal Lytham and St Anne's GC, LOCATION: St Annes, Lancashire, England, DATE: 18-21 July, DISTANCE: 6822 yards, PAR: 71 (284), WINNER: £15000

*David Graham beat Ben Crenshaw at the third extra hole in the Sudden Death Play-off

Ballesteros' victory at Lytham will not be remembered for the first Open Championship to be won by a continental European since Arnaud Massy in 1907, but for the manner in which it was won. A new star in the ascendant, the flamboyant Spaniard was aggressive and headstrong; foolish and cavalier in his approach to the game: and he announced himself to the world, displaying all those characteristics in just 18 holes on Saturday, 21 July 1979. Bashing his way from rough to sand, to car park to green, with scant regard for the fairway – only replacing brute strength with sublime touch when he neared his destination – Seve broke the hearts of Crenshaw and Nicklaus. As much as past icons like Ouimet, Jones, Hogan, Palmer or Nicklaus, he was changing the face of golf once again: and European golf, and pan-European golfing unity, was stirring.

David Graham became the second Australian, after Jim Ferrier in 1947, to take the PGA Championship. With play-offs coming thick and fast in recent Majors, this PGA was no exception; but while Ben Crenshaw played beautifully for his R4 67, Graham's 65 should have been a 63 (he double-bogeyed the last), and no play-off would have been necessary. Graham then sank two very missable putts before birdying the third extra hole for victory. This was Crenshaw's fourth second place in a Major, and second in succession, and he was spoken of at the time as the best golfer around never to have won such a coveted title.

183

THE MASTERS

COURSE:	Augusta National GC
LOCATION:	Augusta, Georgia
DATE:	10-13 April
DISTANCE:	6925 yards
PAR:	72 (288)
WINNER:	$55000

Pos	Player	1st	2nd	3rd	4th	Total
1	**SEVE BALLESTEROS**	66	69	68	72	275
2 =	Gibby Gilbert	70	74	68	67	279
	Jack Newton	68	74	69	68	279
4	Hubert Green	68	74	71	67	280
5	David Graham	66	73	72	70	281
6 =	Ben Crenshaw	76	70	68	69	283
	Ed Fiori	71	70	69	73	283
	Tom Kite	69	71	74	69	283
	Larry Nelson	69	72	73	69	283
	Jerry Pate	72	68	76	67	283
	Gary Player	71	71	71	70	283
12 =	Andy Bean	74	72	68	70	284
	Tom Watson	73	69	71	71	284
14 =	Jim Colbert	72	70	70	73	285
	Jack Renner	72	70	72	71	285
	JC Snead	73	69	69	74	285
17 =	Ray Floyd	75	70	74	67	286
	Jay Haas	72	74	70	70	286
19 =	Billy Kratzert	73	69	72	73	287
	Gil Morgan	74	71	75	67	287
	Calvin Peete	73	71	76	67	287
	Jim Simons	70	70	72	75	287
	Fuzzy Zoeller	72	70	70	75	287

US OPEN

COURSE:	Baltusrol GC
LOCATION:	Springfield, New Jersey
DATE:	12-15 June
DISTANCE:	7076 yards
PAR:	70 (280)
WINNER:	$55000

Pos	Player	1st	2nd	3rd	4th	Total
1	**JACK NICKLAUS**	63	71	70	68	272
2	Isao Aoki	68	68	68	70	274
3 =	Keith Fergus	66	70	70	70	276
	Lon Hinkle	66	70	69	71	276
	Tom Watson	71	68	67	70	276
6 =	Mark Hayes	66	71	69	74	280
	Mike Reid	69	67	75	69	280
8 =	Hale Irwin	70	70	73	69	282
	Mike Morley	73	68	69	72	282
	Andy North	68	75	72	67	282
	Ed Sneed	72	70	70	70	282
12 =	Bruce Devlin	71	70	70	72	283
	Joe Hager	72	70	71	70	283
	Lee Trevino	68	72	69	74	283
	Bobby Wadkins	72	71	68	72	283
16 =	Joe Inman, Jr	74	69	69	72	284
	Pat McGowan	69	69	73	73	284
	Gil Morgan	73	70	70	71	284
	Bill Rogers	69	72	70	73	284
	Craig Stadler	73	67	69	75	284
	Curtis Strange	69	74	71	70	284

Seve Ballesteros led the Masters by ten strokes going into the back nine on the last day. Typically, the flawed genius made some unspeakable errors coming home, so that in the end his lead was cut to four. If he had parred in from there, the Masters low total was his for the taking. But that was not the Ballesteros way. As it was, Seve's second Major was his first in the US and, after leading wire-to-wire, he became, at 23, the youngest winner of the Masters to date.

1980 was to be Jack Nicklaus' last really big year in Major Championships. Tom Watson's year-round play on the US Tour had been superior to Jack's for the last three seasons, but now turning 40, the Golden Bear honed himself pre-season for one last assault on the Majors. After disappointing in the Masters, he won the Open for the fourth time and joined the ranks of Willie Anderson, Bobby Jones and Ben Hogan, setting a new low total in the process. This included a 63, which tied Johnny Miller (1973) and Tom Weiskopf (in R1) on the US Open record round score.

COURSE:	Honourable Company of Edinburgh Golfers
LOCATION:	Muirfield, East Lothian, Scotland
DATE:	17-20 July
DISTANCE:	6806 yards
PAR:	71 (284)
WINNER:	£25000

Pos	Player	1st	2nd	3rd	4th	Total
1	**TOM WATSON**	68	70	64	69	271
2	Lee Trevino	68	67	71	69	275
3	Ben Crenshaw	70	70	68	69	277
4 =	Carl Mason	72	69	70	69	280
	Jack Nicklaus	73	67	71	69	280
6 =	Andy Bean	71	69	70	72	282
	Ken Brown	70	68	68	76	282
	Hubert Green	77	69	64	72	282
	Craig Stadler	72	70	69	71	282
10 =	Gil Morgan	70	70	71	72	283
	Jack Newton	69	71	73	70	283
12 =	Isao Aoki	74	74	63	73	284
	Nick Faldo	69	74	71	70	284
	Sandy Lyle	70	71	70	73	284
	Larry Nelson	72	70	71	71	284
16 =	John Bland	73	70	73	73	285
	Jerry Pate	71	67	74	73	285
	Tom Weiskopf	72	72	71	70	285
19 =	Seve Ballesteros	72	68	72	74	286
	Bruce Lietzke	74	69	73	70	286
	Bill Rogers	76	73	68	69	286
	Norio Suzuki	74	68	72	72	286

Tom Watson collected his third Open on Scottish links (all different) ahead of a resurgent Lee Trevino, and the nearly-man of the moment, Ben Crenshaw. Eight Americans, an Englishman, a Scotsman and an Australian made up the Top 10 and tie. Watson's fourth Major rubber-stamped the contention that he was the best player in the world in 1980. Finally, after lagging so far behind for so much of the century, the Open was accorded almost parity in prize money with its American counterparts. Twenty years previously, that would have been unthinkable.

COURSE:	Oak Hill CC
LOCATION:	Rochester, New York
DATE:	7-10 August
DISTANCE:	6964 yards
PAR:	70 (280)
WINNER:	$60000

Pos	Player	1st	2nd	3rd	4th	Total
1	**JACK NICKLAUS**	70	69	66	69	274
2	Andy Bean	72	71	68	70	281
3 =	Lon Hinckle	70	69	69	75	283
	Gil Morgan	68	70	73	72	283
5 =	Curtis Strange	68	72	72	72	284
	Howard Twitty	68	74	71	71	284
7	Lee Trevino	74	71	69	69	285
8 =	Bill Rogers	71	71	72	72	286
	Bobby Walzel	68	76	71	71	286
10 =	Terry Diehl	72	72	68	76	288
	Peter Jacobsen	71	73	74	70	288
	Jerry Pate	72	73	70	73	288
	Tom Watson	75	74	72	67	288
	Tom Weiskopf	71	73	72	72	288
15 =	John Mahaffey	71	77	69	72	289
	Andy North	72	70	73	74	289
17 =	George Archer	70	73	75	72	290
	Ray Floyd	70	76	71	73	290
	Joe Inman, Jr	72	71	75	72	290
20 =	Rex Caldwell	73	70	73	75	291
	Rod Curl	74	71	75	71	291
	Tom Kite	73	70	76	72	291
	Bob Murphy	68	80	72	71	291
	Jack Newton	72	73	73	73	291
	Alan Tapie	74	75	69	73	291

Gene Sarazen in 1922 was the only man in history to win both American National Championships – the US Open and the US PGA – in the same season. 58 years later the feat was eventually emulated by Jack Nicklaus; thus adding another record, or share of a record, to his name. He stretched his lead in the all-time list with this 1980 double to 17 Majors, and tied Walter Hagen's redoubtable PGA record of five wins. As an aesthetically boring piece of forward planning by the PGA of America, by coincidence the host site was the third in a row to feature the King of the Forest (after Oakmont and Oakland Hills).

THE MASTERS

COURSE:	Augusta National GC
LOCATION:	Augusta, Georgia
DATE:	9-12 April
DISTANCE:	6925 yards
PAR:	72 (288)
WINNER:	$60000

Pos	Player	1st	2nd	3rd	4th	Total
1	**TOM WATSON**	71	68	70	71	280
2 =	Johnny Miller	69	72	73	68	282
	Jack Nicklaus	70	65	75	72	282
4	Greg Norman	69	70	72	72	283
5 =	Tom Kite	74	72	70	68	284
	Jerry Pate	71	72	71	70	284
7	David Graham	70	70	74	71	285
8 =	Ben Crenshaw	71	72	70	73	286
	Ray Floyd	75	71	71	69	286
	John Mahaffey	72	71	69	74	286
11 =	George Archer	74	70	72	71	287
	Hubert Green	70	70	74	73	287
	Peter Jacobsen	71	70	72	74	287
	Bruce Lietzke	72	67	73	75	287
15 =	Gay Brewer	75	68	71	74	288
	Bob Gilder	72	75	69	72	288
	Gary Player	73	73	71	71	288
	Jim Simons	70	75	71	72	288
19 =	Don Pooley	71	75	72	71	289
	Curtis Strange	69	79	70	71	289

Tom Watson's contemporary superiority over Jack Nicklaus continued into 1981, when he won the first Major of the year at Augusta. A R3 75 undid Jack, who held a four-shot lead after 36 holes, and he was joined in second place by Johnny Miller. This win was Watson's second Green Jacket and fifth Major overall.

US OPEN

COURSE:	Merion GC
LOCATION:	Ardmore, Pennsylvania
DATE:	18-21 June
DISTANCE:	6544 yards
PAR:	70 (280)
WINNER:	$55000

Pos	Player	1st	2nd	3rd	4th	Total
1	**DAVID GRAHAM**	68	68	70	67	273
2 =	George Burns	69	66	68	73	276
	Bill Rogers	70	68	69	69	276
4 =	John Cook	68	70	71	70	279
	John Schroeder	71	68	69	71	279
6 =	Frank Conner	71	72	69	68	280
	Lon Hinkle	69	71	70	70	280
	Jack Nicklaus	69	68	71	72	280
	Sammy Rachels	70	71	69	70	280
	Chi Chi Rodriguez	68	73	67	72	280
11 =	Isao Aoki	72	71	71	67	281
	Ben Crenshaw	70	75	64	72	281
	Jim Thorpe	66	73	70	72	281
14 =	Mark Hayes	71	70	72	69	282
	Calvin Peete	73	72	67	70	282
	Lanny Wadkins	71	68	72	71	282
17 =	Bruce Lietzke	70	71	71	71	283
	Jack Renner	68	71	72	72	283
	Curtis Strange	71	69	72	71	283
20 =	Tom Kite	73	74	67	70	284
	Larry Nelson	70	73	69	72	284
	Mike Reid	71	72	69	72	284

David Graham added the US Open to the PGA Championship he picked up in 1979. He became the first Australian to win the Open and the first overseas player since Tony Jacklin in 1970. He turned a three-stroke deficit going into the last day into a victory by the same margin, thanks to a superb 67, and turned the tables on George Burns who had led from R2.

BRITISH OPEN

COURSE:	Royal St George's GC	
LOCATION:	Sandwich, Kent, England	
DATE:	16-19 July	
DISTANCE:	6857 yards	
PAR:	70 (280)	
WINNER:	£25000	

Pos	Player	1st	2nd	3rd	4th	Total
1	**BILL ROGERS**	72	66	67	71	276
2	Bernhard Langer	73	67	70	70	280
3 =	Ray Floyd	74	70	69	70	283
	Mark James	72	70	68	73	283
5 =	Sam Torrance	72	69	73	70	284
	Bruce Lietzke	76	69	71	69	285
	Manuel Pinero	73	74	68	70	285
8 =	Howard Clark	72	76	70	68	286
	Ben Crenshaw	72	67	76	71	286
	Brian Jones	73	76	66	71	286
11 =	Isao Aoki	71	73	69	74	287
	Nick Faldo	77	68	69	73	287
	Lee Trevino	77	67	70	73	287
14 =	Brian Barnes	76	70	70	72	288
	Eamonn Darcy	79	69	70	70	288
	David Graham	71	71	74	72	288
	Nick Job	70	69	75	74	288
	Sandy Lyle	73	73	71	71	288
19 =	Gordon J Brand	78	65	74	72	289
	Graham Marsh	75	71	72	71	289
	Jerry Pate	73	73	69	74	289
	Peter Townsend	73	70	73	73	289

The Open returned to Sandwich after a break of 32 years. Bill Rogers, who had finished strongly to tie for second in the US Open the previous month, played the best golf of his life to win on a links course at his first attempt – as had Hogan, Lema and Watson before him. His strength lay in the middle rounds, enabling him to take a five-shot lead into the last 18, and comfortably hold off two young European hopefuls, Langer and James, and double-Majors winner Floyd; who was never to get closer than this in the Open.

US PGA

COURSE:	Atlanta Athletic Club	
LOCATION:	Duluth, Atlanta, Georgia	
DATE:	6-9 August	
DISTANCE:	7070 yards	
PAR:	70 (280)	
WINNER:	$60000	

Pos	Player	1st	2nd	3rd	4th	Total
1	**LARRY NELSON**	70	66	66	71	273
2	Fuzzy Zoeller	70	68	68	71	277
3	Dan Pohl	69	67	73	69	278
4 =	Isao Aoki	75	68	66	70	279
	Keith Fergus	71	71	69	68	279
	Bob Gilder	74	69	70	76	279
	Tom Kite	71	67	69	72	279
	Bruce Lietzke	70	70	71	68	279
	Jack Nicklaus	71	68	71	69	279
	Greg Norman	73	67	68	71	279
11 =	Vance Heafner	68	70	70	72	280
	Andy North	68	69	70	73	280
	Jerry Pate	71	68	70	71	280
	Tommy Valentine	73	70	71	66	280
15	JC Snead	70	71	70	70	281
16 =	David Edwards	71	69	70	72	282
	Hale Irwin	71	74	68	69	282
18	Bob Murphy	66	69	73	75	283
19 =	John Cook	72	69	70	73	284
	Ray Floyd	71	70	71	72	284
	Jay Haas	73	68	74	69	284
	Joe Inman, Jr	73	71	67	73	284
	Don January	70	72	70	72	284
	Gil Morgan	70	69	74	71	284
	Don Pooley	74	70	69	71	284
	Tom Purtzer	70	70	73	71	284

Vietnam veteran Larry Nelson won his first Major at the Atlanta Athletic Club – just a few minutes from his front door. He hung on to Bob Murphy's coat-tails as Murphy blazed away with a 66, 69 start; then pulled away from the field with a 66 of his own to take a lead of four over Fuzzy Zoeller. He maintained the differential over the final round to cruise home.

THE MASTERS

COURSE:	Augusta National GC
LOCATION:	Augusta, Georgia
DATE:	8-11 April
DISTANCE:	6925 yards
PAR:	72 (288)
WINNER:	$64000

Pos	Player	1st	2nd	3rd	4th	Total
1	**CRAIG STADLER***	75	69	67	73	284
2	Dan Pohl	75	75	67	67	284
3 =	Seve Ballesteros	73	73	68	71	285
	Jerry Pate	74	73	67	71	285
5 =	Tom Kite	76	69	73	69	287
	Tom Watson	77	69	70	71	287
7 =	Ray Floyd	74	72	69	74	289
	Larry Nelson	79	71	70	69	289
	Curtis Strange	74	70	73	72	289
10 =	Andy Bean	75	72	73	70	290
	Mark Hayes	74	73	73	70	290
	Tom Weiskopf	75	72	68	75	290
	Fuzzy Zoeller	72	76	70	72	290
14	Bob Gilder	79	71	66	75	291
15 =	Yakata Hagawa	75	74	71	72	292
	Jack Nicklaus	69	77	71	75	292
	Gary Player	74	73	71	74	292
	Jim Simons	77	74	69	72	292
19	David Graham	73	77	70	73	293
20 =	Peter Jacobsen	78	75	70	71	294
	Bruce Lietzke	76	75	69	74	294
	Jodie Mudd (a)	77	74	67	76	294
	Jack Renner	72	75	76	71	294

*Craig Stadler beat Dan Pohl in the Sudden Death Play-off

Craig Stadler answered the $64000 question when he defeated Dan Pohl in the sudden-death play-off. He was being asked it all through the second half of the Tournament as Pohl, who shot an anonymous 150 for the first 36, then tore up the course with two 67s. He made up six shots on the 'Walrus', but Stadler clung on for a tie, steadied himself, and prevailed in overtime to claim his only Major victory.

US OPEN

COURSE:	Pebble Beach GL
LOCATION:	Pebble Beach, California
DATE:	17-20 June
DISTANCE:	6815 yards
PAR:	72 (288)
WINNER:	$60000

Pos	Player	1st	2nd	3rd	4th	Total
1	**TOM WATSON**	72	72	68	70	282
2	Jack Nicklaus	74	70	71	69	284
3 =	Bobby Clampett	71	73	72	70	286
	Dan Pohl	72	74	70	70	286
	Bill Rogers	70	73	69	74	286
6 =	David Graham	73	72	69	73	287
	Jay Haas	75	74	70	68	287
	Gary Koch	78	73	69	67	287
	Lanny Wadkins	73	76	67	71	287
10 =	Bruce Devlin	70	69	75	74	288
	Calvin Peete	71	72	72	73	288
12 =	Chip Beck	76	75	69	69	289
	Danny Edwards	71	75	73	70	289
	Lyn Lott	72	71	75	71	289
15 =	Larry Rinker	74	67	75	74	290
	Scott Simpson	73	69	72	76	290
	JC Snead	73	75	71	71	290
	Fuzzy Zoeller	72	76	71	71	290
19 =	Ben Crenshaw	76	74	68	73	291
	Larry Nelson	74	72	74	71	291
	Hal Sutton	73	76	72	70	291

Watson's penchant for seaside golf, and delight in keeping Jack Nicklaus at bay, was doubly manifested at Pebble Beach. His first – and so far, only US Open – was won after another momentous struggle between the two great golfers; and was only settled at the 17th, when Tom memorably pitched in for a birdie. Now only the PGA Championship stopped him from becoming the fifth player to win all the Grand Slam titles. Another record was set for entries filed, taking the figure over 5000 for the first time.

COURSE: Royal Troon GC
LOCATION: Ayrshire, Scotland
DATE: 15-19 July
DISTANCE: 7067 yards
PAR: 72 (288)
WINNER: £32000

COURSE: Atlanta Athletic Club
LOCATION: Duluth, Atlanta, Georgia
DATE: 6-9 August
DISTANCE: 7070 yards
PAR: 70 (280)
WINNER: $65000

Pos	Player	1st	2nd	3rd	4th	Total
1	**TOM WATSON**	69	71	74	70	284
2 =	Peter Oosterhuis	74	67	74	70	285
	Nick Price	69	69	74	73	285
4 =	Nick Faldo	73	73	71	69	286
	Masahiro Kuramoto	71	73	71	71	286
	Tom Purtzer	76	66	75	69	286
	Des Smyth	70	69	74	73	286
8 =	Sandy Lyle	74	66	73	74	287
	Fuzzy Zoeller	73	71	73	70	287
10 =	Bobby Clampett	67	66	78	77	288
	Jack Nicklaus	77	70	72	69	288
12	Sam Torrance	73	72	73	71	289
13 =	Seve Ballesteros	71	75	73	71	290
	Bernhard Langer	70	69	78	73	290
15 =	Ben Crenshaw	74	75	72	70	291
	Ray Floyd	74	73	77	67	291
	Curtis Strange	72	73	76	70	291
	Denis Watson	75	69	73	74	291
19	Ken Brown	70	71	79	72	292
20 =	Isao Aoki	75	69	75	74	293
	Tohru Nakamura	77	68	77	71	293

Pos	Player	1st	2nd	3rd	4th	Total
1	**RAY FLOYD**	63	69	68	72	272
2	Lanny Wadkins	71	68	69	67	275
3 =	Fred Couples	67	71	72	66	276
	Calvin Peete	69	70	68	69	276
5 =	Jay Haas	71	66	68	72	277
	Greg Norman	66	69	70	72	277
	Jim Simons	68	67	73	69	277
8	Bob Gilder	66	68	72	72	278
9 =	Lon Hinkle	70	68	71	71	280
	Tom Kite	73	70	70	67	280
	Jerry Pate	72	69	70	69	280
	Tom Watson	72	69	71	68	280
13	Seve Ballesteros	71	68	69	73	281
14 =	Nick Faldo	67	70	73	72	282
	Curtis Strange	72	70	71	69	282
16 =	Jim Colbert	70	72	72	69	283
	Dan Halldorsan	69	71	72	71	283
	Bruce Lietzke	73	71	70	69	283
	Jack Nicklaus	74	70	72	67	283
	Tom Purtzer	73	69	73	68	283
	Craig Stadler	71	70	70	72	283

Troon GC received its Royal Charter in the Queen's Silver Jubilee year of 1977. That year Tom Watson won his second British Open 20 miles down the coast at Turnberry; and in 1982 collected his fourth – all at different Scottish courses. He joined the Morrises, Willie Park Sr, Walter Hagen and Bobby Locke on four wins; he also joined Bobby Jones (twice), Gene Sarazen, Ben Hogan and Lee Trevino as the only winners of both Opens in the same year. He was chased hard by Peter Oosterhuis, and Nick Price was left to contemplate on what might have been.

Raymond Floyd's third Major was also his second PGA, after a gap of 13 years; the longest wait for a second win in any single Major. Floyd's records were not to stop there: 63 equalled the all-time low in the PGA and any Major; 131 was a new 36-hole record for the PGA; his 200 was the low for any 54 holes in any Major; and Floyd became the only winner of the PGA wire-to-wire on more than one occasion. 52-year-old Gene Littler, the 1961 US Open Champion, shot the low score of R3.

THE MASTERS

COURSE:	Augusta National GC
LOCATION:	Augusta, Georgia
DATE:	7-11 April – Friday washed out
DISTANCE:	6925 yards
PAR:	72 (288)
WINNER:	$90000

Pos	Player	1st	2nd	3rd	4th	Total
1	**SEVE BALLESTEROS**	68	70	73	69	280
2 =	Ben Crenshaw	76	70	70	68	284
	Tom Kite	70	72	73	69	284
4 =	Ray Floyd	67	72	71	75	285
	Tom Watson	70	71	71	73	285
6 =	Hale Irwin	72	73	72	69	286
	Craig Stadler	69	72	69	76	286
8 =	Gil Morgan	67	70	76	74	287
	Dan Pohl	74	72	70	71	287
	Lanny Wadkins	73	70	73	71	287
11	Scott Simpson	70	73	72	73	288
12 =	George Archer	71	73	71	74	289
	Wayne Levi	72	70	74	73	289
	Johnny Miller	72	72	71	74	289
	J C Snead	68	74	74	73	289
16 =	Keith Fergus	70	69	74	77	290
	Tommy Nakajima	72	70	72	76	290
	Jack Renner	67	75	78	70	290
19	Isao Aoki	70	76	74	71	291
20 =	Nick Faldo	70	70	76	76	292
	Mark Hayes	71	73	76	72	292
	Peter Jacobsen	73	71	76	72	292
	Peter Oosterhuis	73	69	78	72	292
	Lee Trevino	71	72	72	77	292
	Tom Weiskopf	75	72	71	74	292
	Fuzzy Zoeller	70	74	76	72	292

Ballesteros' second Masters win, and his third Major triumph, was a typical mixture of brilliance and bravura. He shot a last round 69 to overhaul the crumbling 1982 Champion Craig Stadler, and the reigning PGA Champion, Ray Floyd. Eligible 'bridesmaids', Crenshaw and Kite, were still awaiting the bouquet to be thrown in their direction. Both shot sub-70 but had too much ground to make up on the irrepressible Spaniard.

US OPEN

COURSE:	Oakmont CC
LOCATION:	Oakmont, Pennsylvania
DATE:	16-20 June – play carried over to Monday due to rain
DISTANCE:	6972 yards
PAR:	71 (284)
WINNER:	$72000

Pos	Player	1st	2nd	3rd	4th	Total
1	**LARRY NELSON**	75	73	65	67	280
2	Tom Watson	72	70	70	69	281
3	Gil Morgan	73	72	70	68	283
4 =	Seve Ballesteros	69	74	69	74	286
	Calvin Peete	75	68	70	73	286
6	Hal Sutton	73	70	73	71	287
7	Lanny Wadkins	72	73	74	69	288
8 =	David Graham	74	75	73	69	291
	Ralph Landrum	75	73	69	74	291
10 =	Chip Beck	73	74	74	71	292
	Andy North	73	71	72	76	292
	Craig Stadler	76	74	73	69	292
13 =	Lennie Clements	74	71	75	73	293
	Ray Floyd	72	70	72	79	293
	Pat McGowan	75	71	75	72	293
	Mike Nicolette	76	69	73	75	293
	David Ogrin	75	69	75	74	293
	Scott Simpson	73	71	73	76	293
	Jim Thorpe	75	70	75	73	293
20 =	Tom Kite	75	76	70	73	294
	Griff Moody	76	72	73	73	294
	Gary Player	73	74	76	71	294
	DA Weibring	71	74	80	79	294

Larry Nelson's second Major followed his 1981 PGA triumph; but victory was far from his mind after the first 36 holes, when he was standing on 148, seven shots back, and tying for 25th place. He then broke the US Open record for 36 holes with a ten-under-par 132 – four strokes better than the previous low. Arnold Palmer equalled Gene Sarazen's record of 31 consecutive US Open appearances, and finished tied for 60th.

BRITISH OPEN

COURSE: Royal Birkdale GC
LOCATION: Southport, Lancashire, England
DATE: 14-17 July
DISTANCE: 6968 yards
PAR: 71 (284)
WINNER: £40000

Pos	Player	1st	2nd	3rd	4th	Total
1	**TOM WATSON**	67	68	70	70	275
2 =	Andy Bean	70	69	70	67	276
	Hale Irwin	69	68	72	67	276
4	Graham Marsh	69	70	74	64	277
5	Lee Trevino	69	66	73	70	278
6 =	Seve Ballesteros	71	71	69	68	279
	Harold Henning	71	69	70	69	279
8 =	Denis Durnian	73	66	74	67	280
	Nick Faldo	68	68	71	73	280
	Christy O'Connor, Jr	72	69	71	68	280
	Bill Rogers	67	71	73	69	280
12 =	Peter Jacobsen	72	69	70	70	281
	Craig Stadler	64	70	72	75	281
14 =	Ray Floyd	72	66	69	75	282
	David Graham	71	69	67	75	282
	Gary Koch	75	71	66	70	282
	Mike Sullivan	72	68	74	68	282
	Fuzzy Zoeller	71	71	67	73	282
19 =	Tienie Britz	71	74	69	69	283
	Bernard Gallacher	72	71	70	70	283
	Hubert Green	69	74	72	68	283
	Jay Haas	73	72	68	70	283
	Simon Hobday	70	73	70	70	283
	Greg Norman	75	71	70	67	283
	Brian Waites	70	70	73	70	283

Playing steady golf as only he could, Tom Watson capitalised on a good start and mistakes by Craig Stadler to take the lead after 54 holes. He was headed by Nick Faldo briefly in R4, but kept his game together better than the 26-year-old Englishman, who was urged on by an excited home crowd. Last round charges by Andy Bean and twice US Open Champion, Hale Irwin, were not quite enough to undermine Watson; nor was a new final round low for the Championship by Australian, Graham Marsh. Watson, proving he could win south of the border, joined the rarified level of five Open wins – joint-second all-time with Taylor, Braid and Thomson, and one behind Vardon. This was his eighth and last Major title, to date.

US PGA

COURSE: Riviera CC
LOCATION: Pacific Palisades, California
DATE: 4-7 August
DISTANCE: 6946 yards
PAR: 71 (284)
WINNER: $100000

Pos	Player	1st	2nd	3rd	4th	Total
1	**HAL SUTTON**	65	66	72	71	274
2	Jack Nicklaus	73	65	71	66	275
3	Peter Jacobsen	73	70	68	65	276
4	Pat McGowan	68	67	73	69	277
5	John Fought	67	69	71	71	278
6 =	Bruce Lietzke	67	71	70	71	279
	Fuzzy Zoeller	72	71	67	69	279
8	Dan Pohl	72	70	69	69	280
9 =	Ben Crenshaw	68	66	71	77	282
	Jay Haas	68	72	69	73	282
	Mike Reid	69	71	72	70	282
	Scott Simpson	66	73	70	73	282
	Doug Tewell	74	72	69	67	282
14 =	Keith Fergus	68	70	72	73	283
	David Graham	79	69	74	70	283
	Hale Irwin	72	70	73	68	283
	Roger Maltbie	71	71	71	70	283
	Jim Thorpe	68	72	74	69	283
	Lee Trevino	70	68	74	71	283
20 =	John Cook	74	71	68	71	284
	Danny Edwards	67	76	71	70	284
	Ray Floyd	69	75	71	69	284

The Riviera CC, scene of Hogan's and Demaret's dismantling of the US Open and all-Majors low total in 1948, was host to a Major Championship for the first time since. Although the 1948 figure was lowered, the impact on the golfing world this time around was not so great – unless of course your name was Hal Sutton. Nothing could have seemed better for Sutton, winning his first Major in the season following his 'Rookie of the Year' award; but he had to withstand heavy pressure from Nicklaus and Peter Jacobsen to win through. The winner's prize money broke through the six-figure dollar mark for the first time in any Major.

THE MASTERS

US OPEN

	COURSE:	Augusta National GC
	LOCATION:	Augusta, Georgia
	DATE:	12-15 April
	DISTANCE:	6925 yards
	PAR:	72 (288)
	WINNER:	$108000

	COURSE:	Winged Foot GC
	LOCATION:	Mamaroneck, New York
	DATE:	14-18 June
	DISTANCE:	6930 yards
	PAR:	70 (280)
	WINNER:	$94000

Pos	Player	1st	2nd	3rd	4th	Total
1	**BEN CRENSHAW**	67	72	70	68	277
2	Tom Watson	74	67	69	69	279
3 =	David Edwards	71	70	72	67	280
	Gil Morgan	73	71	69	67	280
5	Larry Nelson	76	69	66	70	281
6 =	Ronnie Black	71	74	69	68	282
	David Graham	69	70	70	73	282
	Tom Kite	70	68	69	75	282
	Mark Lye	69	66	73	74	282
10	Fred Couples	71	73	67	72	283
11 =	Rex Caldwell	71	71	69	73	284
	Wayne Levi	71	72	69	72	284
	Larry Mize	71	70	71	72	284
	Jack Renner	71	73	71	69	284
15 =	Nick Faldo	70	69	70	76	285
	Ray Floyd	70	73	70	72	285
	Calvin Peete	79	66	70	70	285
18 =	Andy Bean	71	70	72	73	286
	Danny Edwards	72	71	70	73	286
	Jack Nicklaus	73	73	70	70	286

Pos	Player	1st	2nd	3rd	4th	Total
1	**FUZZY ZOELLER***	71	66	69	70	276
2	Greg Norman	70	68	69	69	276
3	Curtis Strange	69	70	74	68	281
4 =	Johnny Miller	74	68	70	70	282
	Jim Thorpe	68	71	70	73	282
6	Hale Irwin	68	68	69	79	284
7 =	Peter Jacobsen	72	73	73	67	285
	Mark O'Meara	71	74	71	69	285
9 =	Fred Couples	69	71	74	72	286
	Lee Trevino	71	72	69	74	286
11 =	Andy Bean	70	71	75	71	287
	Jay Haas	73	73	70	71	287
	Tim Simpson	72	71	68	76	287
	Lanny Wadkins	72	71	72	72	287
	Tom Watson	72	72	74	69	287
16 =	Isao Aoki	72	70	72	74	288
	Lennie Clements	69	76	72	71	288
	Mark McCumber	71	73	71	73	288
	Tom Purtzer	73	72	72	71	288
	Hal Sutton	72	72	74	70	288

After ten Top 10 finishes, including three runners-up places, Ben Crenshaw cast off the mantle of 'best player never to have won a Major' and won the 1984 Masters by two from Tom Watson. In doing so he collected Augusta's first $100000+ winner's prize, and left Tom Kite to wonder when it was going to happen for him. Kite held the third round lead, but disintegrated over the last day to finish five shots behind the crowd's favourite, Ben.

* Fuzzy Zoeller (67) beat Greg Norman (75) in the 18-Hole Play-off

Greg Norman's first of several near misses over the next few years gave Fuzzy Zoeller, somewhat surprisingly, even to him, his second Major Championship. Zoeller led by three at the turn, but Norman scrambled on to level terms; courtesy of a birdie at 17, then a 15-yard putt to save par at the last. His relief and ambition were only temporary however, and when Fuzzy sank a putt of almost 25 yards at the second play-off hole, and Greg made a double-bogey, that was the beginning of the end for 'the Shark'.

COURSE:	Royal & Ancient GC
LOCATION:	St Andrews, Fife, Scotland
DATE:	19-22 July
DISTANCE:	6968 yards
PAR:	72 (288)
WINNER:	£50000

Pos	Player	1st	2nd	3rd	4th	Total
1	**SEVE BALLESTEROS**	69	68	70	69	276
2 =	Bernard Langer	71	68	68	71	278
	Tom Watson	71	68	66	73	278
4 =	Fred Couples	70	69	74	68	281
	Lanny Wadkins	70	69	73	69	281
6 =	Nick Faldo	69	68	76	69	282
	Greg Norman	67	74	74	67	282
8	Mark McCumber	74	67	72	70	283
9 =	Hugh Baiocchi	72	70	70	72	284
	Ian Baker-Finch	68	66	71	79	284
	Graham Marsh	70	74	73	67	284
	Ronan Rafferty	74	72	67	71	284
	Sam Torrance	74	74	66	70	284
14 =	Andy Bean	72	69	75	69	285
	Bill Bergin	75	73	66	71	285
	Ken Brown	74	71	72	68	285
	Hale Irwin	75	68	70	72	285
	Sandy Lyle	75	71	72	67	285
	Peter Senior	74	70	70	71	285
	Lee Trevino	70	67	75	73	285
	Fuzzy Zoeller	71	72	71	71	285

Seve Ballesteros won his second Open to double his haul of Major wins; thereby denying Tom Watson immortality and a share in Harry Vardon's record of six Open wins. Neck-and-neck coming to the 17th, Ballesteros (via the rough, of course) found the green in regulation for the first time that week, and the usually rock-steady Watson sent his approach over the green to within two feet of the wall abutting the road by which the 17th hole at St Andrews is named. A dropped shot here coincided with Seve's birdie at 18, and there was no way back for Tom.

COURSE:	Shoal Creek CC
LOCATION:	Birmingham, Alabama
DATE:	16-19 August
DISTANCE:	7145 yards
PAR:	72 (288)
WINNER:	$125000

Pos	Player	1st	2nd	3rd	4th	Total
1	**LEE TREVINO**	69	68	67	69	273
2 =	Gary Player	74	63	69	71	277
	Lanny Wadkins	68	69	68	72	277
4	Calvin Peete	71	70	69	68	278
5	Seve Ballesteros	70	69	70	70	279
6 =	Gary Hallberg	69	71	68	72	280
	Larry Mize	71	69	67	73	280
	Scott Simpson	69	69	72	70	280
	Hal Sutton	74	73	64	69	280
10 =	Russ Cochran	73	68	73	67	281
	Tommy Nakajima	72	68	67	74	281
	Victor Regalado	69	69	73	70	281
13	Ray Floyd	68	71	69	74	282
14 =	Hubert Green	70	74	66	73	283
	Mike Reid	68	72	72	71	283
16 =	Andy Bean	69	75	70	70	284
	Donnie Hammond	70	69	71	74	284
18 =	Peter Jacobsen	70	72	72	71	285
	Craig Stadler	71	73	73	68	285
20 =	Fred Couples	72	72	75	67	286
	Nick Faldo	69	73	74	70	286
	Keith Fergus	72	72	72	70	286
	John Mahaffey	72	72	72	70	286
	Corey Pavin	73	72	74	67	286

Lee Trevino, at 44, won his second PGA, ten years after his win at Tanglewood. In doing so he frustrated Gary Player, now 48, and prevented him from achieving his tenth Major win; even though the South African shot a PGA low of 63 in R2. Lanny Wadkins, Champion in 1977, fought hard against the veteran maestros, but first he, then Player, buckled under the power of Trevino's impressive play on the greens. The affable Texan walked away with the record prize for any Major; his sixth title (two Masters, two British Opens and two PGAs – like Sam Snead, Trevino too missed out in the US Open), and became eleventh overall on the all-time list.

THE MASTERS

COURSE:	Augusta National GC
LOCATION:	Augusta, Georgia
DATE:	11-14 April
DISTANCE:	6925 yards
PAR:	72 (288)
WINNER:	$126000

Pos	Player	1st	2nd	3rd	4th	Total
1	**BERNHARD LANGER**	72	74	68	68	282
2 =	Seve Ballesteros	72	71	71	70	284
	Ray Floyd	70	73	69	72	284
	Curtis Strange	80	65	68	71	284
5	Jay Haas	73	73	72	67	285
6 =	Gary Hallberg	68	73	75	70	286
	Bruce Lietzke	72	71	73	70	286
	Jack Nicklaus	71	74	72	69	286
	Craig Stadler	73	67	76	70	286
10 =	Fred Couples	75	73	69	70	287
	David Graham	74	71	71	71	287
	Lee Trevino	70	73	72	72	287
	Tom Watson	69	71	75	72	287
14 =	Bill Kratzert	73	77	69	69	288
	John Mahaffey	72	75	70	71	288
16 =	Isao Aoki	72	74	71	72	289
	Gary Koch	72	70	73	74	289
18 =	Wayne Levi	75	72	70	73	290
	Mark McCumber	73	73	79	65	290
	Sam Randolph (a)	70	75	72	73	290
	Tim Simpson	73	72	75	70	290
	Jim Thorpe	73	71	72	74	290
	Lanny Wadkins	72	73	72	73	290

After tying second with Tom Watson at St Andrews the previous year, Bernhard Langer became the first German, and only the third continental European (after Arnaud Massy and Ballesteros) to win a Major Championship. Seve jointly led the chasing group, but despite catching the overnight leaders Floyd and Strange, he had no answer to the German's final-round 68. In the wake of the Spaniard, the European challenge on the Majors, and the Masters, in particular, albeit piecemeal at this stage, had begun.

US OPEN

COURSE:	Oakland Hills CC
LOCATION:	Birmingham, Michigan
DATE:	13-16 June
DISTANCE:	6966 yards
PAR:	70 (280)
WINNER:	$103000

Pos	Player	1st	2nd	3rd	4th	Total
1	**ANDY NORTH**	70	65	70	74	279
2 =	Dave Barr	70	68	70	72	280
	Tze-Chung Chen	65	69	69	77	280
	Denis Watson	72	65	73	70	280
5 =	Seve Ballesteros	71	70	69	71	281
	Payne Stewart	70	70	71	70	281
	Lanny Wadkins	70	72	69	70	281
8	Johnny Miller	74	71	68	69	282
9 =	Rick Fehr	69	67	73	74	283
	Corey Pavin	72	68	73	70	283
	Jack Renner	72	69	72	70	283
	Fuzzy Zoeller	71	69	72	71	283
13	Tom Kite	69	70	71	74	284
14	Hale Irwin	73	72	70	70	285
15 =	Andy Bean	69	72	73	72	286
	Jay Haas	69	66	77	74	286
	Greg Norman	72	71	71	72	286
	Mark O'Meara	72	67	75	72	286
	Don Pooley	73	69	73	71	286
	Tony Sills	75	70	71	70	286
	Scott Simpson	73	73	68	72	286
	Joey Sindelar	72	72	69	73	286

Andy North repeated his 1978 win at Cherry Hills by just holding off Dave Barr of Canada, and Taiwan's T-C Chen. Chen was four strokes to the good, and looking like being Asia's breakthrough into the Majors when, going out on the last day, he lost all his advantage with a disastrous eight at the fifth. North went ahead, but after bogeying nine, ten and 11, slipped behind Barr. Nerves got to everybody in the run-in and all but North dropped shots up to 17. North then bogeyed the final hole; but had a two-stroke buffer at the tee, to just edge home.

BRITISH OPEN

COURSE:	Royal St George's GC
LOCATION:	Sandwich, Kent, England
DATE:	18-21 July
DISTANCE:	6857 yards
PAR:	70 (280)
WINNER:	£65000

Pos	Player	1st	2nd	3rd	4th	Total
1	**SANDY LYLE**	68	71	73	70	282
2	Payne Stewart	70	75	70	68	283
3 =	David Graham	68	71	70	75	284
	Bernhard Langer	72	69	68	75	284
	Christy O'Connor, Jr	64	76	72	72	284
	Mark O'Meara	70	72	70	72	284
	Jose Rivero	74	72	70	68	284
8 =	Anders Forsbrand	70	76	69	70	285
	Tom Kite	73	73	67	72	285
	DA Weibring	69	71	74	71	285
11 =	Jose-Maria Canizares	72	75	70	69	286
	Eamonn Darcy	76	68	74	68	286
	Peter Jacobsen	71	74	68	73	286
	Gary Koch	75	72	70	69	286
	Fuzzy Zoeller	69	76	70	71	286
16 =	Simon Bishop	71	75	72	69	287
	Greg Norman	71	72	71	73	287
	Sam Torrance	74	74	69	70	287
	Ian Woosnam	70	71	71	75	287
20 =	Ian Baker-Finch	71	73	74	70	288
	Jaime Gonzalez	72	72	73	71	288
	Mark James	71	78	66	73	288
	Graham Marsh	71	75	69	73	288
	Lee Trevino	73	76	68	71	288

Jock Hutchison and Tommy Armour excepted (who, in 1921 and 1931, were domiciled in the USA), George Duncan was the last Scotsman to win the Open Championship – in 1920. This was a desperate return for a nation which had given the world the ancient game. Then, as a consequence of the sport's resurgence in Britain and Europe – with Jacklin perhaps the catalyst, and Ballesteros very much its swash-buckling lead role – Sandy Lyle won his first Major amid patriotic scenes at St George's. With this result, Langer's win at the Masters, and the development of Faldo and the emergence of Woosnam, the Ryder Cup – now the British Isles and Europe against the Americans (since 1979) – was won for the first time since 1957.

US PGA

COURSE:	Cherry Hills CC
LOCATION:	Englewood, Colorado
DATE:	8-11 August
DISTANCE:	7145 yards
PAR:	72 (288)
WINNER:	$125000

Pos	Player	1st	2nd	3rd	4th	Total
1	**HUBERT GREEN**	67	69	70	72	278
2	Lee Trevino	66	68	75	71	280
3 =	Andy Bean	71	70	72	68	281
	Tze-Ming Chen	69	76	71	65	281
5	Nick Price	73	73	65	71	282
6 =	Fred Couples	70	65	76	72	283
	Buddy Gardner	73	73	70	67	283
	Corey Pavin	66	75	73	69	283
	Tom Watson	67	70	74	72	283
10 =	Peter Jacobsen	66	71	75	72	284
	Lanny Wadkins	70	69	73	72	284
12 =	Scott Hoch	70	73	73	69	285
	Tom Kite	69	75	71	70	285
	Dan Pohl	72	74	69	70	285
	Scott Simpson	72	68	72	73	285
	Payne Stewart	72	72	73	68	285
	Doug Tewell	64	72	77	72	285
18 =	Bob Gilder	73	70	74	69	286
	Wayne Levi	72	69	74	71	286
	Bruce Lietzke	70	74	72	70	286
	Calvin Peete	69	72	75	70	286
	Craig Stadler	72	73	74	67	286

Lee Trevino, leading at the halfway point, could not cosolidate to win back-to-back PGAs. His 75 in R3 let in 1977 US Open Champion, Hubert Green, for his second Major. After eight years of anonymous performances, Green, despite his early pedigree, was not expected to win another Major title; but obviously 'they' failed to tell Hubert that!

THE MASTERS

COURSE:	Augusta National GC
LOCATION:	Augusta, Georgia
DATE:	10-13 April
DISTANCE:	6925 yards
PAR:	72 (288)
WINNER:	$144000

Pos	Player	1st	2nd	3rd	4th	Total
1	**JACK NICKLAUS**	74	71	69	65	279
2 =	Tom Kite	70	74	68	68	280
	Greg Norman	70	72	68	70	280
4	Seve Ballesteros	71	68	72	70	281
5	Nick Price	79	69	63	71	282
6 =	Jay Haas	76	69	71	67	283
	Tom Watson	70	74	68	71	283
8 =	Tommy Nakajima	70	71	71	72	284
	Payne Stewart	75	71	69	69	284
	Bob Tway	70	73	71	70	284
11 =	Donnie Hammond	73	71	67	74	285
	Sandy Lyle	76	70	68	71	285
	Mark McCumber	76	67	71	71	285
	Corey Pavin	71	72	71	71	285
	Calvin Peete	75	71	69	70	285
16 =	Dave Barr	70	77	71	68	286
	Ben Crenshaw	71	71	74	70	286
	Gary Koch	69	74	71	72	286
	Bernhard Langer	74	68	69	75	286
	Larry Mize	75	74	72	65	286

I doubt if there was ever a more popular win in the Majors than the one achieved at Augusta by Jack Nicklaus in 1986. Now aged 46, and not having won a Major for six years, the odds on the Golden Bear picking up another title, to add to the seemingly insurmountable tally of 17, were very long indeed. Nearly-men old and new, Kite and Norman (who agonisingly bogeyed the last), were shattered by a vintage Nicklaus charge which took him to a final round 65; and title No.18. In doing so, he became the oldest winner of the Masters, and the third-oldest Major winner of all time (after Julius Boros and Tom Morris, Sr). Along the way he collected six Masters – a record; four US Opens – a tied record; three British Opens; and five PGAs – another tied record. Looking at the winner's prize money, did Tom and Greg consider Jack's appetite for Major titles gross?

US OPEN

COURSE:	Shinnecock Hills GC
LOCATION:	Southampton, New York
DATE:	12-15 June
DISTANCE:	6912 yards
PAR:	70 (280)
WINNER:	$115000

Pos	Player	1st	2nd	3rd	4th	Total
1	**RAY FLOYD**	75	68	70	66	279
2 =	Chip Beck	75	73	68	65	281
	Lanny Wadkins	74	70	72	65	281
4 =	Hal Sutton	75	70	66	71	282
	Lee Trevino	74	68	69	71	282
6 =	Ben Crenshaw	76	69	69	69	283
	Payne Stewart	76	68	69	70	283
8 =	Bernhard Langer	74	70	70	70	284
	Mark McCumber	74	71	68	71	284
	Jack Nicklaus	77	72	67	68	284
	Bob Tway	70	73	69	72	284
12 =	Greg Norman	71	68	71	75	285
	Denis Watson	72	70	71	72	285
14	Mark Calcavecchia	75	75	72	65	287
15 =	David Frost	72	72	77	67	288
	David Graham	76	71	69	72	288
	Gary Koch	73	73	71	71	288
	Jodie Mudd	73	75	69	71	288
	Joey Sindelar	81	66	70	71	288
	Craig Stadler	74	71	74	69	288
	Scott Verplank	75	72	67	74	288
	Bobby Wadkins	75	69	72	72	288
	Fuzzy Zoeller	75	74	71	68	288

90 years after hosting the second-ever Championship, the US Open returned to a very different Shinnecock Hills. Ray Floyd, 43, picked up his fourth Major title; but in this, his first US Open win, he beat Ted Ray's 66-year-old record for being the oldest winner by some five months (and like Nicklaus in the Masters a few weeks before, found himself in the Top 10 for the oldest Majors winners). He also joined a group of only 12 players to have won three different Majors – Tom Watson being the last to do so in 1982. High quality last rounds by Chip Beck and Lanny Wadkins weren't quite enough and, shooting a 66 of his own, Floyd came home two strokes ahead. 54-hole leader, Norman, fell away again.

	BRITISH OPEN		US PGA
COURSE:	Turnberry GC	COURSE:	Inverness Club
LOCATION:	Turnberry, Ayrshire, Scotland	LOCATION:	Toledo, Ohio
DATE:	17-20 July	DATE:	7-10 August
DISTANCE:	6957 yards	DISTANCE:	6982 yards
PAR:	70 (280)	PAR:	71 (284)
WINNER:	£70000	WINNER:	$140000

Pos	Player	1st	2nd	3rd	4th	Total
1	**GREG NORMAN**	74	63	74	69	280
2	Gordon J Brand	71	68	75	71	285
3 =	Bernhard Langer	72	70	76	68	286
	Ian Woosnam	70	74	70	72	286
5	Nick Faldo	71	70	76	70	287
6 =	Seve Ballesteros	76	75	73	64	288
	Gary Koch	73	72	72	71	288
8 =	Brian Marchbank	78	70	72	69	289
	Tommy Nakajima	74	67	71	77	289
	Fuzzy Zoeller	75	73	72	69	289
11 =	Jose-Maria Canizares	76	68	73	73	290
	David Graham	75	73	70	72	290
	Christy O'Connor, Jr	75	71	75	69	290
14 =	Andy Bean	74	73	73	71	291
	Curtis Strange	79	69	74	69	291
16 =	Ray Floyd	78	67	73	74	292
	Anders Forsbrand	71	73	77	71	292
	Jose-Maria Olazabal	78	69	72	73	292
19 =	Bob Charles	76	72	73	72	293
	Manuel Pinero	78	71	70	74	293

Pos	Player	1st	2nd	3rd	4th	Total
1	**BOB TWAY**	72	70	64	70	276
2	Greg Norman	65	68	69	76	278
3	Peter Jacobsen	68	70	70	71	279
4	DA Weibring	71	72	68	69	280
5 =	Bruce Lietzke	69	71	70	71	281
	Payne Stewart	70	67	72	72	281
7 =	David Graham	75	69	71	67	282
	Mike Hulbert	69	68	74	71	282
	Jim Thorpe	71	67	73	71	282
10	Doug Tewell	73	71	68	71	283
11 =	Ben Crenshaw	72	73	72	67	284
	Donnie Hammond	70	71	68	75	284
	Lonnie Nielsen	73	69	72	70	284
	Lee Trevino	71	74	69	70	284
	Lanny Wadkins	71	75	70	68	284
16 =	Chip Beck	71	73	71	70	285
	Jack Nicklaus	70	68	72	75	285
	Don Pooley	71	74	69	71	285
	Tony Sills	71	72	69	73	285
	Tom Watson	72	69	72	72	285

Greg Norman put away, at least for a while, former miseries – including the recent US Open final round failure – and silenced his critics to boot; when he won wonderfully over a Turnberry links whipped up by heavy winds. His belated first Major was a performance of power tempered by worldy-wise experience. Now 31, his five years on the European Tour (as much as his previous close calls) helped him tame the conditions and silence the field. He seemed to have broken his jinx and was destined to win more Major honours; but, as we are about to see, old habits were to return. Only two Americans from a strong contingent made the Top 10.

In only his second year on the US Tour, Bob Tway was to burst Greg Norman's Turnberry bubble, and allow all the old doubts about his losing Majors from winning positions to return. Norman, leading all the way, and by four going into the last round, was caught by Tway as he squandered shots down the back nine. Then, in the cruellest way of all, when brittle confidence is starting to crumble, Tway won the Championship by chipping in from a bunker for a birdie at 18. Uniquely, Norman held the lead at the start of the final round in every Major of 1986.

THE MASTERS

COURSE:	Augusta National GC				
LOCATION:	Augusta, Georgia				
DATE:	9-12 April				
DISTANCE:	6925 yards				
PAR:	72 (288)				
WINNER:	$162000				

Pos	Player	1st	2nd	3rd	4th	Total
1	**LARRY MIZE***	70	72	72	71	285
2 =	Seve Ballesteros	73	71	70	71	285
	Greg Norman	73	74	66	72	285
4 =	Ben Crenshaw	75	70	67	74	286
	Roger Maltbie	76	66	70	74	286
	Jodie Mudd	74	72	71	69	286
7 =	Jay Haas	72	72	72	73	289
	Bernhard Langer	71	72	70	76	289
	Jack Nicklaus	74	72	73	70	289
	Tom Watson	71	72	74	72	289
	DA Weibring	72	75	71	71	289
12 =	Chip Beck	75	72	70	73	290
	Tze-Chung Chen	74	69	71	76	290
	Mark McCumber	75	71	69	75	290
	Curtis Strange	71	70	73	76	290
	Lanny Wadkins	73	72	70	75	290
17 =	Paul Azinger	77	73	69	72	291
	Mark Calcavecchia	73	72	78	68	291
	Sandy Lyle	77	74	68	72	291
	Craig Stadler	74	74	72	71	291

*Larry Mize beat Seve Ballesteros and Greg Norman at the second extra hole in the Sudden Death Play-off

Greg Norman would have hoped that the memory of the previous August's PGA nightmare would have faded during the winter; and have disappeared altogether with the optimistic airs of spring. He certainly came to Augusta full of expectation, and a R3 66 took him to the wire to tie with twice-Champion Ballesteros, and hitherto modest performer, Larry Mize. Seve blew out on the first extra hole; and with Norman on the green, and Mize to the right of it, some 30 yards from the flag, Greg was in prime position. The nightmare recurred when Mize, in an action which, in a less-gentlemanly sport would surely have been classed as sadistic, chipped in; leaving Norman crushed once more.

US OPEN

COURSE:	Olympic GC				
LOCATION:	San Francisco, California				
DATE:	16-19 June				
DISTANCE:	6709 yards				
PAR:	70 (280)				
WINNER:	$150000				

Pos	Player	1st	2nd	3rd	4th	Total
1	**SCOTT SIMPSON**	71	68	70	68	277
2	Tom Watson	72	65	71	70	278
3	Seve Ballesteros	68	75	68	71	282
4 =	Ben Crenshaw	67	72	72	72	283
	Bernhard Langer	69	69	73	72	283
	Larry Mize	71	68	72	72	283
	Curtis Strange	71	72	69	71	283
	Bobby Wadkins	71	71	70	71	283
9 =	Lennie Clements	70	70	70	74	284
	Tommy Nakajima	68	70	74	72	284
	Mac O'Grady	71	69	72	72	284
	Dan Pohl	75	71	69	69	284
	Jim Thorpe	70	68	73	73	284
14 =	Isao Aoki	71	73	70	71	285
	Bob Eastwood	73	66	75	71	285
	Tim Simpson	76	66	70	73	285
17 =	Mark Calcavecchia	73	68	73	72	286
	David Frost	70	72	71	73	286
	Kenny Knox	72	71	69	74	286
	Jodie Mudd	72	75	71	68	286
	Jumbo Ozaki	71	69	72	74	286
	Nick Price	69	74	69	74	286
	Jim Woodward	71	74	72	69	286

Overnight leader Tom Watson was denied a second US Open title when Scott Simpson birdied 14, 15, and 16 on the final stretch to overtake him and win his first Major title. Watson was undergoing a long slump in form, but still managed to raise his game for the events that mattered, and just failed to tie Simpson when his 45-foot putt for birdie at the 18th ended up inches from the hole.

BRITISH OPEN

COURSE: Honourable Company of Edinburgh Golfers
LOCATION: Muirfield, East Lothian, Scotland
DATE: 16-19 July
DISTANCE: 6963 yards
PAR: 71 (284)
WINNER: £75000

Pos	Player	1st	2nd	3rd	4th	Total
1	**NICK FALDO**	68	69	71	71	279
2 =	Paul Azinger	68	68	71	73	280
	Rodger Davis	64	73	74	69	280
4 =	Ben Crenshaw	73	68	72	68	281
	Payne Stewart	71	66	72	72	281
6	David Frost	70	68	70	74	282
7	Tom Watson	69	69	71	74	283
8 =	Nick Price	68	71	72	73	284
	Craig Stadler	69	69	71	75	284
	Ian Woosnam	71	69	72	72	284
11 =	Mark Calcavecchia	69	70	72	74	285
	Graham Marsh	69	70	72	74	285
	Mark McNulty	71	69	75	70	285
	Jose-Maria Olazabal	70	73	70	72	285
	Jumbo Ozaki	69	72	71	73	285
	Hal Sutton	71	70	73	71	285
17 =	Ken Brown	69	73	70	74	286
	Eamonn Darcy	74	69	72	71	286
	Ray Floyd	72	68	70	76	286
	Wayne Grady	70	71	76	69	286
	Bernhard Langer	69	69	76	72	286
	Sandy Lyle	76	69	71	70	286
	Mark Roe	74	68	72	72	286
	Lee Trevino	67	74	73	72	286

Nick Faldo, for many years seen by many as the heir-apparent to Tony Jacklin, eventually came out of the shadow of the double Open winner, (and nearly three years of technical rehabilitation with guru David Leadbeater), to win his first Major. He had been playing the Open since 1976 when he was a teenager, and although consistently winning on the European Tour, he was not by his own demanding standards making the breakthrough in the Majors. Leadbeater effectively rebuilt Faldo's swing. He won in the Muirfield haar (sea mist), grinding down Paul Azinger with 18 straight pars in R4, eventually nudging ahead at the last when the American missed his 30-foot par putt.

US PGA

COURSE: PGA National GC
LOCATION: Palm Beach Gardens, Florida
DATE: 6-9 August
DISTANCE: 7002 yards
PAR: 72 (288)
WINNER: $150000

Pos	Player	1st	2nd	3rd	4th	Total
1	**LARRY NELSON***	70	72	73	72	287
2	Lanny Wadkins	70	70	74	73	287
3 =	Scott Hoch	74	74	71	69	288
	DA Weibring	73	72	67	76	288
5 =	Mark McCumber	74	69	69	77	289
	Don Pooley	73	71	73	72	289
7 =	Ben Crenshaw	72	70	74	74	290
	Bobby Wadkins	68	74	71	77	290
9	Curtis Strange	70	76	71	74	291
10 =	Seve Ballesteros	72	70	72	78	292
	David Frost	75	70	71	76	292
	Tom Kite	72	77	71	72	292
	Nick Price	76	71	70	75	292
14 =	Curt Byrum	74	75	68	76	293
	David Edwards	69	75	77	72	293
	Ray Floyd	70	70	73	80	293
	Dan Pohl	71	78	75	69	293
	Jeff Sluman	72	69	78	74	293
	Tom Watson	70	79	73	71	293
20	Peter Jacobsen	73	75	73	73	294

*Larry Nelson beat Lanny Wadkins at the first extra hole in the Sudden Death Play-off

Larry Nelson may not have been the most consistent performer in the Majors, but he is only one of 15 players to have won the PGA Championship more than once. When the Championship returned to the Florida home of the PGA, he tied with 1977 Champion, Lanny Wadkins, then added to his 1981 success when Wadkins bogeyed the first hole in sudden death.

THE MASTERS

COURSE:	Augusta National GC
LOCATION:	Augusta, Georgia
DATE:	7-10 April
DISTANCE:	6925 yards
PAR:	72 (288)
WINNER:	$183000

Pos	Player	1st	2nd	3rd	4th	Total
1	**SANDY LYLE**	71	67	72	71	281
2	Mark Calcavecchia	71	69	72	70	282
3	Craig Stadler	76	69	70	68	283
4	Ben Crenshaw	72	73	67	72	284
5 =	Fred Couples	75	68	71	71	285
	Greg Norman	77	73	71	64	285
	Don Pooley	71	72	72	70	285
8	David Frost	73	74	71	68	286
9 =	Bernhard Langer	71	72	71	73	287
	Tom Watson	72	71	73	71	287
11 =	Seve Ballesteros	73	72	70	73	288
	Ray Floyd	80	69	68	71	288
	Lanny Wadkins	74	75	69	70	288
14 =	Nick Price	75	76	72	66	289
	Doug Tewell	75	73	68	73	289
16 =	Mark McNulty	74	71	73	72	290
	Dan Pohl	78	70	69	73	290
	Fuzzy Zoeller	76	66	72	76	290
19 =	Tze-Chung Chen	76	73	72	70	291
	Hubert Green	74	70	75	72	291

Sandy Lyle became the first Briton to win the Masters, and the third European in the decade to date. His R2 67 gave him the platform, and he led again after 54 holes. However, Mark Calcavecchia then caught Lyle and they were level when Lyle teed off at the last. Going for birdie, the Scot caught a fairway trap some 140 yards from the flag. Then, in one of the most dramatic approaches seen at Augusta's 18th, Lyle's seven iron sailed out of the bunker, over the pin and span back to within ten feet of the hole. He birdied against Calcavecchia's par to take the Green Jacket.

US OPEN

COURSE:	The Country Club
LOCATION:	Brookline, Massachusetts
DATE:	16-20 June
DISTANCE:	7010 yards
PAR:	71 (284)
WINNER:	$180000

Pos	Player	1st	2nd	3rd	4th	Total
1	**CURTIS STRANGE***	70	67	69	72	278
2	Nick Faldo	72	67	68	71	278
3 =	Mark O'Meara	71	72	66	71	280
	Steve Pate	72	69	72	67	280
	DA Weibring	71	69	68	72	280
6 =	Paul Azinger	69	70	76	66	281
	Scott Simpson	69	66	72	74	281
8 =	Bob Gilder	68	69	70	75	282
	Fuzzy Zoeller	73	72	71	66	282
10 =	Fred Couples	72	67	71	73	283
	Payne Stewart	73	73	70	67	283
12 =	Andy Bean	71	71	72	70	284
	Ben Crenshaw	71	72	74	67	284
	Larry Mize	69	67	72	76	284
	Dan Pohl	74	72	69	69	284
	Lanny Wadkins	70	71	70	73	284
17 =	Ray Floyd	73	72	73	67	285
	Hale Irwin	71	71	72	71	285
	Mark McNulty	73	72	72	68	285
	Joey Sindelar	76	68	70	71	285

* Curtis Strange (71) beat Nick Faldo (75) in the 18-Hole Play-off

Sandy Lyle projected his Masters form into the Open to shoot 68 and share the lead, but dropped out of contention after that. Another Briton, Nick Faldo, was trying to emulate Tony Jacklin by winning the US Open while still Britain's Champion Golfer, and tied with Curtis Strange when Strange bogeyed the 17th. The play-off – the third in three visits to Brookline (including the momentous 1913 affair between Ouimet, Vardon and Ray) – saw Curtis play much the better golf, and held the lead from the 7th, Faldo bogeying three of the last four holes.

BRITISH OPEN

COURSE: Royal Lytham and St Anne's GC
LOCATION: St Annes, Lancashire, England
DATE: 14-18 July (Sat play washed out)
DISTANCE: 6857 yards
PAR: 71 (284)
WINNER: £80000

Pos	Player	1st	2nd	3rd	4th	Total
1	**SEVE BALLESTEROS**	67	71	70	65	273
2	Nick Price	70	67	69	69	275
3	Nick Faldo	71	69	68	71	279
4 =	Fred Couples	73	69	71	68	281
	Gary Koch	71	72	70	68	281
6	Peter Senior	70	73	70	69	282
7 =	Isao Aoki	72	71	73	67	283
	David Frost	71	75	69	68	283
	Sandy Lyle	73	69	67	74	283
	Payne Stewart	73	75	68	67	283
11 =	Brad Faxon	69	74	70	71	284
	David J Russell	71	74	69	70	284
13 =	Larry Nelson	73	71	68	73	285
	Eduardo Romero	72	71	69	73	285
	Curtis Strange	79	69	69	68	285
16 =	Andy Bean	71	70	71	74	286
	Ben Crenshaw	73	73	68	72	286
	Don Pooley	70	73	69	74	286
	Jose Rivero	75	69	70	72	286
20 =	Gordon Brand, Jr	72	76	68	71	287
	Bob Charles	71	74	69	73	287
	Rodger Davis	76	71	72	68	287
	Tom Kite	75	71	73	68	287
	Bob Tway	71	71	72	73	287

Seve Ballesteros' third Open victory and fifth Major title came where it all started for the Spaniard in 1979. At his lucky Lytham links, Ballesteros' stunning 65 broke the heart of defending Champion, Faldo, and only Zimbabwean, Nick Price, could mount a challenge. In the end he had to capitulate to Seve's masterful performance. Rain washed away Saturday's play, disappointing the 36000 crowd, and after 117 Opens over 128 years, there was play on a Monday.

US PGA

COURSE: Oak Tree GC
LOCATION: Edmond, Oklahoma
DATE: 11-15 August
DISTANCE: 7015 yards
PAR: 71 (284)
WINNER: $160000

Pos	Player	1st	2nd	3rd	4th	Total
1	**JEFF SLUMAN**	69	70	68	65	272
2	Paul Azinger	67	66	71	71	275
3	Tommy Nakajima	69	68	74	67	278
4 =	Tom Kite	72	69	71	67	279
	Nick Faldo	67	71	70	71	279
6 =	Bob Gilder	66	75	71	68	280
	Dave Rummells	73	64	68	75	280
8	Dan Pohl	69	71	70	71	281
9 =	Ray Floyd	68	68	74	72	282
	Steve Jones	69	68	72	73	282
	Kenny Knox	72	69	68	73	282
	Greg Norman	68	71	72	71	282
	Mark O'Meara	70	71	70	71	282
	Payne Stewart	70	69	70	73	282
15 =	John Mahaffey	71	71	70	71	283
	Craig Stadler	68	73	75	67	283
17 =	Mark Calcavecchia	73	69	70	72	284
	Ben Crenshaw	70	71	69	74	284
	David Graham	70	67	73	74	284
	Mark McNulty	73	70	67	74	284
	Jay Overton	68	66	76	74	284
	Corey Pavin	71	70	75	68	284
	Nick Price	74	70	67	73	284
	Richard Zokol	70	70	74	70	284

Just as Ballesteros had done at Royal Lytham the previous month, a charging 65 from Jeff Sluman gave him a Major Championship win – except this was Sluman's first. For Paul Azinger, it was sense of Muirfield *déjà vu*; but instead of being ground down by Nick Faldo, he was blasted away by Sluman. All-round scoring was lower than expected on a notoriously difficult course.

THE MASTERS

	COURSE:	Augusta National GC
	LOCATION:	Augusta, Georgia
	DATE:	6-9 April
	DISTANCE:	6925 yards
	PAR:	72 (288)
	WINNER:	$200000

Pos	Player	1st	2nd	3rd	4th	Total
1	**NICK FALDO***	68	73	77	65	283
2	Scott Hoch	69	74	71	69	283
3 =	Ben Crenshaw	71	72	70	71	284
	Greg Norman	74	75	68	67	284
5	Seve Ballesteros	71	72	73	69	285
6	Mike Reid	72	71	71	72	286
7	Jodie Mudd	73	76	72	76	287
8 =	Chip Beck	74	76	70	68	288
	Jose-Maria Olazabal	77	73	70	68	288
	Jeff Sluman	74	72	74	68	288
11 =	Fred Couples	72	76	74	67	289
	Ken Green	74	69	73	73	289
	Mark O'Meara	74	71	72	72	289
14 =	Paul Azinger	75	75	69	71	290
	Don Pooley	70	77	76	67	290
	Tom Watson	72	73	74	71	290
	Ian Woosnam	74	76	71	69	290
18 =	David Frost	76	72	73	70	291
	Tom Kite	72	72	72	75	291
	Jack Nicklaus	73	74	73	71	291
	Jumbo Ozaki	71	75	73	72	291
	Curtis Strange	74	71	74	72	291
	Lee Trevino	67	74	81	69	291

*Nick Faldo (5,3) beat Scott Hoch (5,4) in the Sudden Death Play-off

With Nick Faldo winning his second Major in successive years, he also perpetuated the mini stranglehold that Europeans had on the Masters. After Ballesteros (twice), Langer and Lyle, Faldo's win meant that half the decade's Masters titles went overseas – a somewhat different picture to the previous 46 years of the Tournament. Faldo had to put together something special over the last round after an incongruous 77 in R3, and his best-of-the-event 65 tied him with Scott Hoch; and set him up for the play-off win and the first prize of $200000 – a record for any Major.

US OPEN

	COURSE:	Oak Hill CC
	LOCATION:	Rochester, New York
	DATE:	15-18 June
	DISTANCE:	6902 yards
	PAR:	70 (280)
	WINNER:	$200000

Pos	Player	1st	2nd	3rd	4th	Total
1	**CURTIS STRANGE**	71	64	73	70	278
2 =	Chip Beck	71	69	71	68	279
	Mark McCumber	70	68	72	69	279
	Ian Woosnam	70	68	73	68	279
5 =	Brian Claar	71	72	68	69	280
6 =	Jumbo Ozaki	70	71	68	72	281
	Scott Simpson	67	70	69	75	281
8	Peter Jacobsen	71	70	71	70	282
9 =	Paul Azinger	71	72	70	70	283
	Hubert Green	69	72	74	68	283
	Tom Kite	67	69	69	78	283
	Jose-Maria Olazabal	69	72	70	72	283
13 =	Scott Hoch	70	72	70	72	284
	Mark Lye	71	69	72	72	284
	Larry Nelson	68	73	68	75	284
	Tom Pernice	67	75	68	74	284
	Payne Stewart	66	75	72	71	284
18 =	Jay Don Blake	66	71	72	76	285
	Nick Faldo	68	72	73	72	285
	David Frost	73	72	70	70	285

Curtis Strange became the first player since Ben Hogan in 1951 to win back-to-back US Opens, and the sixth in all. Along with Hogan, he joined Willie Anderson, John McDermott, Bobby Jones and Ralph Guldahl. His win over Chip Beck, Mark McCumber and Welshman, Ian Woosnam, was a little more comfortable than his play-off win over Faldo the previous year. He could afford to three-putt the 18th and still win. With odds against it happening of 332000 to 1, four players – Doug Weaver, Mark Wiebe, Jerry Pate and Nick Price – all achieved a hole-in-one on the 167-yard 6th, and all within a few hours during R2.

BRITISH OPEN

COURSE:	Royal Troon GC
LOCATION:	Troon, Ayrshire, Scotland
DATE:	20-23 July
DISTANCE:	7067 yards
PAR:	71 (284)
WINNER:	£80000

Pos	Player	1st	2nd	3rd	4th	Total
1	**MARK CALCAVECCHIA***	71	68	68	68	275
2 =	Wayne Grady	68	67	69	71	275
	Greg Norman	69	70	72	64	275
4	Tom Watson	69	68	68	72	277
5	Jodie Mudd	73	67	68	70	278
6 =	Fred Couples	68	71	68	72	279
	David Feherty	71	67	69	72	279
8 =	Paul Azinger	68	73	67	72	280
	Eduardo Romero	68	70	75	67	280
	Payne Stewart	72	65	69	74	280
11 =	Nick Faldo	71	71	70	69	281
	Mark McNulty	75	70	70	66	281
13 =	Roger Chapman	76	68	67	71	282
	Howard Clark	72	68	72	70	282
	Mark James	69	70	71	72	282
	Steve Pate	69	70	70	73	282
	Craig Stadler	73	69	69	71	282
	Philip Walton	69	74	69	70	282
19 =	Derrick Cooper	69	70	76	68	283
	Tom Kite	70	74	67	72	283
	Larry Mize	71	74	66	72	283
	Don Pooley	73	70	69	71	283

* Mark Calcavecchia (4-3-3-3) beat Wayne Grady (4-4-4-4) and Greg Norman (3-3-4-x) in the 4-Hole Play-off

Another play-off was needed to settle a Major when the 1988 Masters runner-up, Mark Calcavecchia, tied with Australians Wayne Grady and Greg Norman at Troon. This time, however, it was an experimental four-hole play-off, starting at the 15th; and should there still be a tie after the 18th had been played, a further rotation of the same holes would take place. Norman had fought his way into contention with a record-equalling regulation fourth-round score, only to miss out again when it really mattered. Grady lost touch early in the play-off, and after controlling events early on, Norman's game collapsed over holes 3 and 4, to let Calcavecchia back in.

US PGA

COURSE:	Kemper Lakes GC
LOCATION:	Hawthorn Woods, Illinois
DATE:	10-13 August
DISTANCE:	7217 yards
PAR:	72 (288)
WINNER:	$200000

Pos	Player	1st	2nd	3rd	4th	Total
1	**PAYNE STEWART**	74	66	69	67	276
2 =	Andy Bean	70	67	74	66	277
	Mike Reid	66	67	70	74	277
	Curtis Strange	70	68	70	69	277
5	Dave Rummells	68	69	69	72	278
6	Ian Woosnam	68	70	70	71	279
7 =	Scott Hoch	69	69	69	73	280
	Craig Stadler	71	64	72	73	280
9 =	Nick Faldo	70	73	69	69	281
	Ed Fiori	70	67	75	69	281
	Tom Watson	67	69	74	71	281
12 =	Seve Ballesteros	72	70	66	74	282
	Jim Gallagher Jr	73	69	68	72	282
	Greg Norman	74	71	67	70	282
	Mike Sullivan	76	66	67	73	282
	Mark Wiebe	71	70	69	72	282
17 =	Isao Aoki	72	71	65	75	283
	Ben Crenshaw	68	72	72	71	283
	Buddy Gardner	72	71	70	70	283
	Davis Love III	73	69	72	69	283
	Blaine McCallister	71	72	70	70	283
	Larry Mize	73	71	68	71	283
	Chris Perry	67	70	70	76	283

For the first time in the same year, the three American Majors paid out the same amount to the winner. Payne Stewart, along with Australia's Rodger Davis, the only two top golfers of the day who regularly wore traditional plus-twos (or-fours) or knickerbockers, collected his first Major title, after some strong performances over the recent past. At the 13th hole in R4, a win for him looked most unlikely, but a seven-shot swing between Stewart (four birdies) and Mike Reid (bogey at 16, double-bogey at 17) allowed Payne to squeeze by, and also pip Andy Bean – already home with a 66.

THE MASTERS

COURSE:	Augusta National GC
LOCATION:	Augusta, Georgia
DATE:	5-8 April
DISTANCE:	6925 yards
PAR:	72 (288)
WINNER:	$225000

Pos	Player	1st	2nd	3rd	4th	Total
1	**NICK FALDO***	71	72	66	69	278
2	Ray Floyd	70	68	68	72	278
3 =	John Huston	66	74	68	75	283
	Lanny Wadkins	72	73	70	68	283
5	Fred Couples	74	69	72	69	284
6	Jack Nicklaus	72	70	69	74	285
7 =	Seve Ballesteros	74	73	68	71	286
	Bill Britton	68	74	71	73	286
	Bernhard Langer	70	73	69	74	286
	Scott Simpson	74	71	68	73	286
	Curtis Strange	70	73	71	72	286
	Tom Watson	77	71	67	71	286
13	Jose-Maria Olazabal	72	73	68	74	287
14 =	Ben Crenshaw	72	74	73	69	288
	Scott Hoch	71	68	73	76	288
	Tom Kite	75	73	66	74	288
	Larry Mize	70	76	71	71	288
	Ronan Rafferty	72	74	69	73	288
	Craig Stadler	72	70	74	72	288
20 =	Mark Calcavecchia	74	73	73	69	289
	Steve Jones	77	69	72	71	289
	Fuzzy Zoeller	72	74	73	70	289

*Nick Faldo (4,4) beat Ray Floyd (4,5) in the Sudden Death Play-off

Nick Faldo joined company with Jack Nicklaus (1965-66) to be the only players to have won consecutive Masters Tournaments. This time Faldo needed to play off against 48 year-old Raymond Floyd, and became the only man in Majors history to have to play off to win back-to-back titles. It was his third Major title. Mike Donald's 64 led by two after the first day: he then shot an 82 to make the cut by one. He followed this by playing the final 54 holes in 19-over par – a Masters record since the halfway cut was introduced in 1957 – to come in 47th out of 49 finishers.

US OPEN

COURSE:	Medinah CC
LOCATION:	Medinah, Illinois
DATE:	14-18 June
DISTANCE:	7195 yards
PAR:	72 (288)
WINNER:	$220000

Pos	Player	1st	2nd	3rd	4th	Total
1	**HALE IRWIN***	69	70	74	67	280
2	Mike Donald	67	70	72	71	280
3 =	Billy Ray Brown	69	71	69	72	281
	Nick Faldo	72	72	68	69	281
5 =	Mark Brooks	68	70	72	73	283
	Greg Norman	72	73	69	69	283
	Tim Simpson	66	69	75	73	283
8 =	Scott Hoch	70	73	69	72	284
	Steve Jones	67	76	74	67	284
	Jose-Maria Olazabal	73	69	69	73	284
	Tom Sieckmann	70	74	68	72	284
	Craig Stadler	71	70	72	71	284
	Fuzzy Zoeller	73	70	68	73	284
14 =	Jim Benepe	72	70	73	70	285
	John Huston	68	72	73	72	285
	John Inman	72	71	70	72	285
	Larry Mize	72	70	69	74	285
	Larry Nelson	74	67	69	75	285
	Scott Simpson	66	73	73	73	285
	Jeff Sluman	66	70	74	75	285

*Hale Irwin (74) beat Mike Donald (74) at the first extra hole after the 18-Hole Play-off was tied

No concessions are given for age, as 45-year-old Hale Irwin will tesify. He was taken into a sudden death extension to the play-off – effectively made to play 91 holes – for the privilege of becoming the oldest winner of the US Open. It was his third win; only Anderson, Jones, Hogan and Nicklaus had achieved more. Irwin beat Mike Donald, who led him by four shots going into the last regulation 18 holes. Donald, whose adventures in the Masters had not fazed him, had won his private duel with Billy Ray Brown, only to find Irwin in the clubhouse on 280 as well. There was a new record for entries filed - 6198.

BRITISH OPEN

COURSE:	Royal & Ancient GC
LOCATION:	St Andrews, Fife, Scotland
DATE:	19-22 July
DISTANCE:	6933 yards
PAR:	72 (288)
WINNER:	£85000

Pos	Player	1st	2nd	3rd	4th	Total
1	**NICK FALDO**	67	65	67	71	270
2 =	Mark McNulty	74	68	68	65	275
	Payne Stewart	68	68	68	71	275
4 =	Jodie Mudd	72	66	72	66	276
	Ian Woosnam	68	69	70	69	276
6 =	Ian Baker-Finch	68	72	64	73	277
	Greg Norman	66	66	76	69	277
8 =	David Graham	72	71	70	66	279
	Donnie Hammond	70	71	68	70	279
	Steve Pate	70	68	72	69	279
	Corey Pavin	71	69	68	71	279
12 =	Paul Broadhurst	74	69	63	74	280
	Robert Gamez	70	72	67	71	280
	Tim Simpson	70	69	69	72	280
	Vijay Singh	70	69	72	69	280
16 =	Peter Jacobsen	68	70	70	73	281
	Steve Jones	72	67	72	70	281
	Sandy Lyle	72	70	67	72	281
	Frank Nobilo	72	67	68	74	281
	Jose-Maria Olazabal	71	67	71	72	281

Nick Faldo shot the lowest total for any Major since Tom Watson's all-time low of 268 (and Nicklaus' 269) at Turnberry in 1977. In some ways, Faldo's performance could be considered superior, in that his total was 18 under par, compared to Watson's 12 under; he finished five ahead of reigning PGA Champion Payne Stewart and Zimbabwean, Mark McNulty, themselves leading home a classy-looking Top 10. It was Faldo's second Open Championship, and fourth Major, in under four years. In that time, influenced, at least psychologically, by the Leadbeater technique, his Majors sequence read: W, 28, 30, 2, 3, 4, W, 18, 11, 9, W, 3, W – a consistency over a period of time only put together by the very best in golfing history.

US PGA

COURSE:	Shoal Creek CC
LOCATION:	Birmingham, Alabama
DATE:	9-12 August
DISTANCE:	7145 yards
PAR:	72 (288)
WINNER:	$225000

Pos	Player	1st	2nd	3rd	4th	Total
1	**WAYNE GRADY**	72	67	72	71	282
2	Fred Couples	69	71	73	72	285
3	Gil Morgan	77	72	65	72	286
4	Bill Britton	72	74	72	71	289
5 =	Chip Beck	71	70	78	71	290
	Billy Mayfair	70	71	75	74	290
	Loren Roberts	73	71	70	76	290
8 =	Mark McNulty	74	72	75	71	292
	Don Pooley	75	74	71	72	292
	Tim Simpson	71	73	75	73	292
	Payne Stewart	71	72	70	79	292
12 =	Hale Irwin	77	72	70	74	293
	Larry Mize	72	68	76	77	293
14 =	Billy Andrade	75	72	73	74	294
	Morris Hatalsky	73	78	71	72	294
	Jose Maria Olazabal	73	77	72	72	294
	Corey Pavin	73	75	72	74	294
	Fuzzy Zoeller	72	71	76	75	294
19 =	Bob Boyd	74	74	71	76	295
	Nick Faldo	71	75	80	69	295
	Blaine McCallister	75	73	74	73	295
	Greg Norman	77	69	76	73	295
	Mark O'Meara	69	76	79	71	295
	Tom Watson	74	71	77	73	295
	Mark Wiebe	74	73	75	73	295

After tying for the British Open in 1989, Wayne Grady no doubt benefitted from that experience as he played mistake-free par golf coming home behind Fred Couples. Fred, feeling the pressure, lost out through bogeys at 13, 14, 15 and 16. Grady was the third Australian, after Jim Ferrier and David Graham, to hold the PGA title, which, along with the US Open, was the most American-dominated Major Championship at the time.

THE MASTERS

COURSE:	Augusta National GC
LOCATION:	Augusta, Georgia
DATE:	11-14 April
DISTANCE:	6925 yards
PAR:	72 (288)
WINNER:	$243000

Pos	Player	1st	2nd	3rd	4th	Total
1	**IAN WOOSNAM**	72	66	67	72	277
2	Jose-Maria Olazabal	68	71	69	70	278
3 =	Ben Crenshaw	70	73	68	68	279
	Steve Pate	72	73	69	65	279
	Lanny Wadkins	67	71	70	71	279
	Tom Watson	68	68	70	73	279
7 =	Ian Baker-Finch	71	70	69	70	280
	Andrew Magee	70	72	68	70	280
	Jodie Mudd	70	70	71	69	280
10 =	Hale Irwin	70	70	75	66	281
	Tommy Nakajima	74	71	67	69	281
12 =	Mark Calcavecchia	70	68	77	67	282
	Nick Faldo	72	73	67	70	282
	Billy Mayfair	72	72	72	66	282
	Craig Stadler	70	72	71	69	282
	Fuzzy Zoeller	70	70	75	67	282
17 =	Ray Floyd	71	68	71	73	283
	Jim Gallagher, Jr	67	74	71	71	283
	Peter Jacobsen	73	70	68	72	283
	Mark McCumber	67	71	73	72	283
	Larry Mize	72	71	66	74	283

Woosnam's win at Augusta took him to the top of the world ranking. Over the past half a dozen years or so the Welshman had not set the Majors world alight, but had made his name as a winner of tournaments world-wide, with a game based on long driving (for his 5'4" frame) and silky iron play. If his putting was half as good again, maybe he would have been in contention in more Majors, both before and after this. Once in contention, he knew how to win. Not that that was so much in evidence that April at Augusta, coming to the 72nd hole. Woosnam, tied with the young Spaniard Olazabal and the old maestro Watson, missed the green with his approach; but he scrambled up to five feet and down for a par while the others dropped shots, to claim his one and only Major.

US OPEN

COURSE:	Hazeltine National GC
LOCATION:	Minneapolis, Minnesota
DATE:	13-17 June
DISTANCE:	7149 yards
PAR:	72 (288)
WINNER:	$235000

Pos	Player	1st	2nd	3rd	4th	Total
1	**PAYNE STEWART***	67	70	73	72	282
2	Scott Simpson	70	68	72	72	282
3 =	Fred Couples	70	70	75	70	285
	Larry Nelson	73	72	72	68	285
5	Fuzzy Zoeller	72	73	74	67	286
6	Scott Hoch	69	71	74	73	287
7	Nolan Henke	67	71	77	73	288
8 =	Ray Floyd	73	72	76	68	289
	Jose-Maria Olazabal	73	71	75	70	289
	Corey Pavin	71	67	79	72	289
11 =	Jim Gallagher, Jr	70	72	75	73	290
	Hale Irwin	71	75	70	74	290
	Davis Love III	70	76	73	71	290
	Craig Parry	70	73	73	74	290
	DA Weibring	76	71	75	68	290
16 =	Nick Faldo	72	74	73	72	291
	Sandy Lyle	72	70	74	75	291
	Tom Watson	73	71	77	70	291
19 =	Mark Brooks	73	73	73	73	292
	Billy Ray Brown	73	71	77	71	292
	John Cook	76	70	72	74	292
	Peter Persons	70	75	75	72	292
	Nick Price	74	69	71	78	292
	Tom Sieckmann	74	70	74	74	292
	Craig Stadler	71	69	77	75	292

* Payne Stewart (75) beat Scott Simpson (77) in the 18-Hole Play-off

Payne Stewart had been injured for much of the early season, and didn't compete in the Masters. However, fit again, he led home an all-American Top 10 to collect his second Major Championship; adding to the PGA title he won in 1989. Leading almost throughout, he surrendered the lead to 1987 Champion, Scott Simpson, between holes 10 and 15 in the last round. Simpson then bogeyed 16 and 18 to make it the third US Open play-off in four years. Both played nondescript golf, but Stewart was just the steadier to win.

BRITISH OPEN

COURSE: Royal Birkdale GC
LOCATION: Southport, Lancashire, England
DATE: 18-21 July
DISTANCE: 6940 yards
PAR: 70 (280)
WINNER: £90000

Pos	Player	1st	2nd	3rd	4th	Total
1	**IAN BAKER-FINCH**	71	71	64	66	272
2	Mike Harwood	68	70	69	67	274
3 =	Fred Couples	72	69	70	64	275
	Mark O'Meara	71	68	67	69	275
5 =	Eamonn Darcy	73	68	66	70	277
	Jodie Mudd	72	70	72	63	277
	Bob Tway	75	66	70	66	277
8	Craig Parry	71	70	69	68	278
9 =	Seve Ballesteros	66	73	69	71	279
	Bernhard Langer	71	71	70	67	279
	Greg Norman	74	68	71	66	279
12 =	Roger Chapman	74	66	71	69	280
	Rodger Davis	70	71	73	66	280
	Vijay Singh	71	69	69	71	280
	Magnus Sunesson	72	73	68	67	280
	David Williams	74	71	68	67	280
17 =	Chip Beck	67	78	70	66	281
	Paul Broadhurst	71	73	68	69	281
	Nick Faldo	68	75	70	68	281
	Barry Lane	68	72	71	70	281
	Mark Mouland	68	74	68	71	281
	Peter Senior	74	67	71	69	281
	Andrew Sherborne	73	70	68	70	281
	Lee Trevino	71	72	71	67	281
	Ian Woosnam	70	72	69	70	281

In 1984, then aged 23, Australian Ian Baker-Finch shot a fourth-round 79 over the Old Course at St Andrews to bow out of Open Championship contention. Baker-Finch was not the first person to blow up in the last round of a Major, and won't be the last, but the combination of surnames made him a headline writer's delight. It was with some satisfaction, then, when the most famous hyphen in golf became the first double-barrelled surname to win any Major. At Birkdale he shot a record-equalling R3 score, and birdied five of the first seven holes on the last day. Although chased hard by compatriot, Mike Harwood, this burst of scoring secured him the title. Englishman, Richard Boxhall, trailing the lead in R3 by just three, freakishly broke his leg while driving off the 3rd tee.

US PGA

COURSE: Crooked Stick GC
LOCATION: Carmel, Indiana
DATE: August
DISTANCE: 7295 yards
PAR: 72 (288)
WINNER: $230000

Pos	Player	1st	2nd	3rd	4th	Total
1	**JOHN DALY**	69	67	69	71	276
2	Bruce Lietzke	68	69	72	70	279
3	Jim Gallagher, Jr	70	72	72	67	281
4	Kenny Knox	67	71	70	74	282
5 =	Bob Gilder	73	70	67	73	283
	Steven Richardson	70	72	72	69	283
7 =	David Feherty	71	74	71	68	284
	Ray Floyd	69	74	72	69	284
	John Huston	70	72	70	72	284
	Steve Pate	70	75	70	69	284
	Craig Stadler	68	71	69	76	284
	Hal Sutton	74	67	72	71	284
13 =	Jay Don Blake	75	70	72	68	285
	Andrew Magee	69	73	68	75	285
	Payne Stewart	74	70	71	70	285
16 =	Nick Faldo	70	69	71	76	286
	Ken Green	68	73	71	74	286
	Wayne Levi	73	71	72	70	286
	Sandy Lyle	68	75	71	72	286
	Rocco Mediate	71	71	73	71	286
	Gil Morgan	70	71	74	71	286
	Howard Twitty	70	71	75	70	286

Every sport has its share of fairy stories – golf more than most. There have not been many more remarkable than when John Daly won the PGA in 1991. Virtually unknown, he didn't qualify high enough to merit an automatic entry for the Championship. In fact, he was only ninth on the reserve list –ninth alternate; and his chance only came when Nick Price scratched to be at the birth of his child, and several higher on the list declined the invitation to play. Daly hit the ball consistently longer, and usually straighter, than any player before in the history of the Majors. Without a practice round, he shot a 69 and, from R2 onwards, his ferocious hitting backed up by some magical pressure putting, he was not headed; finally victorious by three strokes.

THE MASTERS

COURSE:	Augusta National GC
LOCATION:	Augusta, Georgia
DATE:	9-12 April
DISTANCE:	6925 yards
PAR:	72 (288)
WINNER:	$270000

Pos	Player	1st	2nd	3rd	4th	Total
1	**FRED COUPLES**	69	67	69	70	275
2	Ray Floyd	69	68	69	71	277
3	Corey Pavin	72	71	68	67	278
4 =	Mark O'Meara	74	67	69	70	280
	Jeff Sluman	65	74	70	71	280
6 =	Ian Baker-Finch	70	69	68	74	281
	Nolan Henke	70	71	70	70	281
	Larry Mize	73	69	71	68	281
	Greg Norman	70	70	73	68	281
	Steve Pate	73	71	70	67	281
	Nick Price	70	71	67	73	281
	Ted Schultz	68	69	72	72	281
13 =	Nick Faldo	71	72	68	71	282
	Wayne Grady	68	75	71	68	282
	Bruce Lietzke	69	72	68	73	282
	Craig Parry	69	66	69	78	282
	Dillard Pruitt	75	68	70	69	282
	Scott Simpson	70	71	71	70	282
19 =	Billy Ray Brown	70	74	70	69	283
	John Daly	71	71	73	68	283
	Mike Hulbert	68	74	71	70	283
	Andrew Magee	73	70	70	70	283
	Ian Woosnam	69	66	73	75	283
	Fuzzy Zoeller	71	70	73	69	283

Ian Woosnam, tying with Craig Parry at halfway, looked to be on course to a successful defence of his title, but disappointingly fell away to finish eight shots adrift of Freddie Couples at the end. Parry still led after 54 holes, but the Australian of Woosnam-esque stature also capitulated, shooting a final round 78. Couples' first Major was extremely popular, and he played a consistent, and at times brilliant, set of four rounds to head Ray Floyd – six months short of his 50th birthday – by two.

US OPEN

COURSE:	Pebble Beach GL
LOCATION:	Pebble Beach, California
DATE:	18-21 June
DISTANCE:	6809 yards
PAR:	72 (288)
WINNER:	$275000

Pos	Player	1st	2nd	3rd	4th	Total
1	**TOM KITE**	71	72	70	72	285
2	Jeff Sluman	73	74	69	71	287
3	Colin Montgomerie	70	71	77	70	288
4 =	Nick Faldo	70	76	68	77	291
	Nick Price	71	72	77	71	291
6 =	Billy Andrade	72	74	72	74	292
	Jay Don Blake	70	74	75	73	292
	Bob Gilder	73	70	75	74	292
	Mike Hulbert	74	73	70	75	292
	Tom Lehman	69	74	72	77	292
	Joey Sindelar	74	72	68	78	292
	Ian Woosnam	72	72	69	79	292
13 =	Ian Baker-Finch	74	71	72	76	293
	John Cook	72	72	74	75	293
	Mark McCumber	70	76	73	74	293
	Gil Morgan	66	69	77	81	293
17 =	Fred Couples	72	70	78	74	294
	Andy Dillard	68	70	79	77	294
	Wayne Grady	74	76	81	73	294
	Andrew Magee	77	69	72	76	294
	Tray Tyner	74	72	78	70	294
	Willie Wood	70	75	75	74	294

Tom Kite probably held the tag of 'best player never..', etc, longer than most. He had appeared in the US Open as far back as 1970, and had three runner-up slots in Major Championships; he may have thought, at the age of 42, his career (in which he became the biggest money-earner in golf history at the time) was going to end without that elusive claim to immortality – a Major. It took a wild and windy Pebble Beach to elevate his status into Majors folklore: an Open that confirmed Jeff Sluman's credentials as a worthy Majors Champion (he won the 1988 PGA title); and the promise of Scotsman, Colin Montgomerie; while being 46 year-old Gil Morgan's last serious attempt to win.

COURSE:	Honourable Company of Edinburgh Golfers
LOCATION:	Muirfield, Angus, Scotland
DATE:	16-19 July
DISTANCE:	6970 yards
PAR:	71 (284)
WINNER:	£95000

COURSE:	Bellerive CC
LOCATION:	St Louis, Missouri
DATE:	13-16 August
DISTANCE:	7148 yards
PAR:	71 (284)
WINNER:	$280000

Pos	Player	1st	2nd	3rd	4th	Total
1	**NICK FALDO**	66	64	69	73	272
2	John Cook	66	67	70	70	273
3	Jose-Maria Olazabal	70	67	69	68	274
4	Steve Pate	64	70	69	73	276
5 =	Gordon Brand, Jr	65	68	72	74	279
	Ernie Els	66	69	70	74	279
	Donnie Hammond	70	65	70	74	279
	Robert Karlsson	70	68	70	71	279
	Malcolm Mackenzie	71	67	70	71	279
	Andrew Magee	67	72	70	70	279
	Ian Woosnam	65	73	70	71	279
12 =	Chip Beck	71	68	67	74	280
	Ray Floyd	64	71	73	72	280
	Sandy Lyle	68	70	70	72	280
	Mark O'Meara	71	68	72	69	280
	Larry Rinker	69	68	70	73	280
	Jamie Spence	71	68	70	71	280
18	Greg Norman	71	72	70	68	281
19 =	Ian Baker-Finch	71	71	72	68	282
	Hale Irwin	70	73	67	72	282
	Tom Kite	70	69	71	72	282

Pos	Player	1st	2nd	3rd	4th	Total
1	**NICK PRICE**	70	70	68	70	278
2 =	John Cook	71	72	67	71	281
	Nick Faldo	68	70	76	67	281
	Jim Gallagher, Jr	72	66	72	71	281
	Gene Sauers	67	69	70	75	281
6	Jeff Maggert	71	72	65	74	282
7 =	Russ Cochran	69	69	76	69	283
	Dan Forsman	70	73	70	70	283
9 =	Brian Claar	68	73	73	70	284
	Anders Forsbrand	73	71	70	70	284
	Duffy Waldorf	74	73	68	69	284
12 =	Billy Andrade	72	71	70	72	285
	Corey Pavin	71	73	70	71	285
	Jeff Sluman	73	71	72	69	285
15 =	Mark Brooks	71	72	68	75	286
	Brad Faxon	72	69	75	70	286
	Greg Norman	71	74	71	70	286
18 =	Steve Elkington	74	70	71	72	287
	Rick Fehr	74	73	71	69	287
	John Huston	73	75	71	68	287

Nick Faldo won his third Open to match the feat of Jones, Cotton, Player, Nicklaus and Ballesteros during the twentieth century. He's still tied-11th on the all-time list of Open winners however, only halving Vardon's haul of titles. At the same venue in 1987, Paul Azinger was the American worn down by Faldo's attritional style. This time, after wasting a four-shot lead overnight, he stood on the 15th tee two behind another American, John Cook, with the tide going the way of his rival. Faldo's reserves of grit are famously deep, however, and the outstanding winner of Majors in recent years proved why, when he birdied 15 and 17, forcing Cook to crack on 18, and win by one.

John Cook was to be unlucky again at Bellerive, but this time he could take some comfort knowing that Nick Price was also a two-time second placer (British Opens in 1982 and 1988) before landing his first Major. Zimbabwean Price, with an English father and Welsh mother, spent much of his early career on the European circuit before settling in the US where he was now establishing himself as one of the world's best players. Faldo's charge to become the first European to win the PGA did not fluster the calm African who, after the leader throughout, Gene Sauers, blew up, held on for a comfortable win.

THE MASTERS

COURSE:	Augusta National GC				
LOCATION:	Augusta, Georgia				
DATE:	8-11 April				
DISTANCE:	6925 yards				
PAR:	72 (288)				
WINNER:	$306000				

Pos	Player	1st	2nd	3rd	4th	Total
1	**BERNHARD LANGER**	68	70	69	70	277
2	Chip Beck	72	67	72	70	281
3 =	John Daly	70	71	73	69	283
	Steve Elkington	71	70	71	71	283
	Tom Lehman	67	75	73	68	283
	Lanny Wadkins	69	72	71	71	283
7 =	Dan Forsman	69	69	73	73	284
	Jose-Maria Olazabal	70	72	74	68	284
9 =	Brad Faxon	74	70	72	69	285
	Payne Stewart	74	70	72	69	285
11 =	Seve Ballesteros	74	70	71	71	286
	Ray Floyd	68	71	74	73	286
	Anders Forsbrand	71	74	75	66	286
	Corey Pavin	67	75	73	71	286
	Scott Simpson	72	71	71	72	286
	Fuzzy Zoeller	75	67	71	73	286
17 =	Mark Calcavecchia	71	70	74	72	287
	Jeff Sluman	71	72	71	73	287
	Howard Twitty	70	71	73	73	287
	Ian Woosnam	71	74	73	69	287

Eight years after winning his first Masters, Bernhard Langer proved he was still a force in world golf with a repeat victory at Augusta. It was also ten years after Seve Ballesteros' second win, which paved the way for Lyle, Faldo (twice) and Woosnam, along with Langer, to dominate the event for Europe. Jose-Maria Olazabal apart, the German was the only European to finish in this year's Top 10: a signal, perhaps, along with form from the other Majors later in the year, that the US were to retain the Ryder Cup this year. Winner's prize money topped $300000 for the first time.

US OPEN

COURSE:	Baltusrol GC				
LOCATION:	Springfield, New Jersey				
DATE:	17-20 June				
DISTANCE:	7152 yards				
PAR:	70 (280)				
WINNER:	$290000				

Pos	Player	1st	2nd	3rd	4th	Total
1	**LEE JANZEN**	67	67	69	69	272
2	Payne Stewart	70	66	68	70	274
3 =	Paul Azinger	71	68	69	69	277
	Craig Parry	66	74	69	68	277
5 =	Scott Hoch	66	72	72	68	278
	Tom Watson	70	66	73	69	278
7 =	Ernie Els	71	73	68	67	279
	Ray Floyd	68	73	70	68	279
	Fred Funk	70	72	67	70	279
	Nolan Henke	72	71	67	69	279
11 =	John Adams	70	70	69	71	280
	David Edwards	70	72	66	72	280
	Nick Price	71	66	70	73	280
	Loren Roberts	70	70	71	69	280
	Jeff Sluman	71	71	69	69	280
16 =	Fred Couples	68	71	71	71	281
	Barry Lane	74	68	70	69	281
	Mike Standly	70	69	70	72	281
19 =	Ian Baker-Finch	70	70	70	72	282
	Dan Forsman	73	71	70	68	282
	Tom Lehman	71	70	71	70	282
	Blaine McCallister	68	73	73	68	282
	Steve Pate	70	71	71	70	282
	Corey Pavin	68	69	75	70	282

Failing to make the cut in three former attempts, it was deemed a little early in his career for 28 year-old Lee Janzen to win a Major. However, leading from R2, he headed a strong field thereafter, and held on to be a worthy winner from 1991 Champion Payne Stewart. Joey Sindelar tied for the first round lead with a 66. He then shot a 79 to miss the cut. John Daly, the 1991 PGA Champion and prodigious hitter *extraordinaire,* playing the 630 yard 17th – the longest hole in Majors history – drove, then one-ironed the green in two.

BRITISH OPEN

COURSE:	Royal St George's GC
LOCATION:	Sandwich, Kent, England
DATE:	15-18 July
DISTANCE:	6860 yards
PAR:	70 (280)
WINNER:	£100000

Pos	Player	1st	2nd	3rd	4th	Total
1	**GREG NORMAN**	66	68	69	64	267
2	Nick Faldo	69	63	70	67	269
3	Bernhard Langer	67	66	70	67	270
4 =	Corey Pavin	68	66	68	70	272
	Peter Senior	66	69	70	67	272
6 =	Ernie Els	68	69	69	68	274
	Paul Lawrie	72	68	69	65	274
	Nick Price	68	70	67	69	274
9 =	Fred Couples	68	66	72	69	275
	Wayne Grady	74	68	64	69	275
	Scott Simpson	68	70	71	66	275
12	Payne Stewart	71	72	70	63	276
13	Barry Lane	70	68	71	68	277
14 =	Mark Calcavecchia	66	73	71	68	278
	John Daly	71	66	70	71	278
	Tom Kite	72	70	68	68	278
	Mark McNulty	67	71	71	69	278
	Gil Morgan	70	68	70	70	278
	Jose Rivero	68	73	67	70	278
	Fuzzy Zoeller	66	70	71	71	278

Greg Norman set the lowest score in Majors history when his 64 in the last round gave him a two-shot lead over reigning Champion, Nick Faldo. Norman's 13-under-par 267 was one lower than Tom Watson's at Turnberry in 1977, where Norman won his only other title. In repeating his win he scotched further accusations of his fragility in Major Championships, but he was not to get rid of them completely. Ernie Els shot four sub-70 rounds, but only finished sixth – the lowest position for such an achievement in a Major Championship. Nick Faldo and Payne Stewart each tied with the all-time low of 63. The winning prize money reached six figures in pounds Sterling for the first time.

US PGA

COURSE:	Inverness Club
LOCATION:	Toledo, Ohio
DATE:	12-15 August
DISTANCE:	7024 yards
PAR:	71 (284)
WINNER:	$300000

Pos	Player	1st	2nd	3rd	4th	Total
1	**PAUL AZINGER***	69	66	69	68	272
2	Greg Norman	68	68	67	69	272
3	Nick Faldo	68	68	69	68	273
4	Vijay Singh	68	63	73	70	274
5	Tom Watson	69	65	70	72	276
6 =	John Cook	72	66	68	71	277
	Bob Estes	69	66	69	73	277
	Dudley Hart	66	68	71	72	277
	Nolan Henke	72	70	67	68	277
	Scott Hoch	74	68	68	67	277
	Hale Irwin	68	69	67	73	277
	Phil Mickelson	67	71	69	70	277
	Scott Simpson	64	70	71	72	277
14 =	Steve Elkington	67	66	74	71	278
	Brad Faxon	70	70	65	73	278
	Bruce Fleisher	69	74	67	68	278
	Gary Hallberg	70	69	68	71	278
	Lanny Wadkins	65	68	71	74	278
	Richard Zokol	66	71	71	70	278
20 =	Jay Haas	69	68	70	72	279
	Eduardo Romero	67	67	74	71	279

*Paul Azinger beat Greg Norman at the second extra hole in the Sudden Death Play-off

Paul Azinger, twice a runner-up in Majors (British Open 1987 and the PGA itself a year later), and close finisher in this year's US Open, eventually collected an overdue Major Championship. Greg Norman's propensity to fail in Majors showdowns continued, as he succumbed once again to events at Inverness. Here, in 1986, it was Bob Tway's greenside bunker blow: this time it was down to Greg himself. He rimmed the hole from four feet to bogey the second extra hole in the play-off. Vijay Singh, from Fiji, and easily the greatest golfer to come from the South Seas, shot a record-equalling 63 in R2.

1994

COURSE:	Augusta National GC
LOCATION:	Augusta, Georgia
DATE:	7-10 April
DISTANCE:	6925 yards
PAR:	72 (288)
WINNER:	$306000

COURSE:	Oakmont CC
LOCATION:	Oakmont, Pennsylvania
DATE:	16-20 June
DISTANCE:	6946 yards
PAR:	71 (284)
WINNER:	$320000

Pos	Player	1st	2nd	3rd	4th	Total
1	**JOSE-MARIA OLAZABAL**	74	67	69	69	279
2	Tom Lehman	70	70	69	72	281
3	Larry Mize	68	71	72	71	282
4	Tom Kite	69	72	71	71	283
5 =	Jay Haas	72	72	72	69	285
	Jim McGovern	72	70	71	72	285
	Loren Roberts	75	68	72	70	285
8 =	Ernie Els	74	67	74	71	286
	Corey Pavin	71	72	73	70	286
10 =	Ian Baker-Finch	71	71	71	74	287
	Ray Floyd	71	74	71	72	287
	John Huston	72	72	74	69	287
13	Tom Watson	70	71	73	74	288
14	Dan Forsman	74	66	76	73	289
15 =	Chip Beck	71	71	75	74	291
	Brad Faxon	71	73	73	74	291
	Mark O'Meara	75	70	76	70	291
18 =	Seve Ballesteros	70	76	75	71	292
	Ben Crenshaw	74	73	73	72	292
	David Edwards	73	72	73	74	292
	Bill Glasson	72	73	75	72	292
	Hale Irwin	73	68	79	72	292
	Greg Norman	70	70	75	77	292
	Lanny Wadkins	73	74	73	72	292

Pos	Player	1st	2nd	3rd	4th	Total
1	**ERNIE ELS***	69	71	66	73	279
2 =	Colin Montgomerie	71	65	73	70	279
	Loren Roberts	76	69	74	70	279
4	Curtis Strange	70	70	70	70	280
5	John Cook	73	65	73	71	282
6 =	Tom Watson	68	73	68	74	283
	Clark Dennis	71	71	70	71	283
	Greg Norman	71	71	69	72	283
9 =	Jeff Maggert	71	68	75	70	284
	Frank Nobilo	69	71	68	76	284
	Jeff Sluman	72	69	72	71	284
	Duffy Waldorf	74	68	73	69	284
13 =	David Edwards	73	65	75	72	285
	Scott Hoch	72	72	70	71	285
	Jim McGovern	73	69	74	69	285
16 =	Fred Couples	72	71	69	74	286
	Steve Lowery	71	71	68	76	286
18 =	Seve Ballesteros	72	72	70	73	287
	Hale Irwin	69	69	71	78	287
	Scott Verplank	70	72	75	70	287

* Ernie Els (74) beat Colin Montgomerie (78) and tied with Loren Roberts (74) in the 18-Hole Play-off, before winning at the second extra hole

The rich promise of Jose-Maria Olazabal matured at Augusta, as Seve's prodigy and countryman won a Major for the first time. Six off the lead after R1 (held by 1987 Masters Champion, Larry Mize, in his best Majors performance since that year), Olazabal powered his way up the leaderboard; going around the final 54 holes in 11 under par, to overtake third-round leader, Tom Lehman. This win made it nine wins for Europeans since Ballesteros himself in 1980, and the third for Spain.

There was a three-way play-off in the Open for the first time since Brookline in 1963. Arnold Palmer, along with Jacky Cupit, missed out to Julius Boros that year: now Arnold, aged 64, started the US Open for the last time. Ernie Els, 40 years his junior, became the first South African since Gary Player to win the Championship, and only the third after Bobby Locke and Player to win any Major Championship. After 18 holes, Colin Montgomerie was eliminated, leaving Els to fight it out, sudden death, with Loren Roberts. It took two holes before Roberts' bogey let in Ernie. The R1 leaderboard had a nostalgic feel to it: Tom Watson led Jack Nicklaus by one.

COURSE:	Turnberry GC	
LOCATION:	Turnberry, Ayrshire, Scotland	
DATE:	14-17 July	
DISTANCE:	6957 yards	
PAR:	70 (280)	
WINNER:	£110000	

COURSE:	Southern Hills CC	
LOCATION:	Tulsa, Oklahoma	
DATE:	11-14 August	
DISTANCE:	6824 yards	
PAR:	70 (280)	
WINNER:	$310000	

Pos	Player	1st	2nd	3rd	4th	Total
1	**NICK PRICE**	69	66	67	66	268
2	Jesper Parnevik	68	66	68	67	269
3	Fuzzy Zoeller	71	66	64	70	271
4 =	David Feherty	68	69	66	70	273
	Anders Forsbrand	72	71	66	64	273
	Mark James	72	67	66	68	273
7	Brad Faxon	69	65	67	73	274
8 =	Nick Faldo	75	66	70	64	275
	Tom Kite	71	69	66	69	275
	Colin Montgomerie	72	69	65	69	275
11 =	Mark Calcavecchia	71	70	67	68	276
	Russell Claydon	72	71	68	65	276
	Jonathan Lomas	66	70	72	68	276
	Mark McNulty	71	70	68	67	276
	Larry Mize	73	69	64	70	276
	Frank Nobilo	69	67	72	68	276
	Greg Norman	71	67	69	69	276
	Ronan Rafferty	71	66	65	74	276
	Tom Watson	68	65	69	74	276
20 =	Mark Brooks	74	64	71	68	277
	Peter Senior	68	71	67	71	277
	Vijay Singh	70	68	69	70	277
	Greg Turner	65	71	70	71	277

Pos	Player	1st	2nd	3rd	4th	Total
1	**NICK PRICE**	67	65	70	67	269
2	Corey Pavin	70	67	69	69	275
3	Phil Mickelson	68	71	67	70	276
4 =	John Cook	71	67	69	70	277
	Nick Faldo	73	67	71	66	277
	Greg Norman	71	69	67	70	277
7 =	Steve Elkington	73	70	66	69	278
	Jose-Maria Olazabal	72	66	70	70	278
9 =	Ben Crenshaw	70	67	70	72	279
	Tom Kite	72	68	69	70	279
	Loren Roberts	69	72	67	71	279
	Tom Watson	69	72	67	71	279
	Ian Woosnam	68	72	73	66	279
14	Jay Haas	71	66	68	75	280
15 =	Glen Day	70	69	70	72	281
	Mark McNulty	72	68	70	71	281
	Larry Mize	72	72	67	70	281
	Kirk Triplett	71	69	71	70	281
19 =	Bill Glasson	71	73	68	70	282
	Mark McCumber	73	70	71	68	282
	Craig Parry	70	69	70	73	282
	Craig Stadler	70	70	74	68	282
	Curtis Strange	73	71	68	70	282
	Fuzzy Zoeller	69	71	72	70	282

Nick Price was to end 1994 atop the (Sony) World Ranking: only Langer (in the first week of the Ranking), Ballesteros, Faldo, Woosnam and Couples, at times kept that spot from the dominant Greg Norman since the computerised tables were first produced in 1986. Greg was to regain the No.1 position for the eighth time again in 1995. Price's second Major occurred in a display of blistering scoring over the Turnberry Links. His battle-royal throughout R4 with Jesper Parnevik, culminated with the Swede, going to the last two ahead, dropping a shot at the last; while Price was holing a 17-yard putt for eagle at the 17th.

Nick Price's 11-under par 269 was a new low for the PGA Championship and formed part of a remarkable 23-under par back-to-back Majors double for the Zimbabwean. He became the first golfer since Faldo in 1990 to win more than one Major in the same season; and only the second person to achieve the British Open-PGA double in the same year since Walter Hagen's achievement 70 years before. His win by six strokes over an outstanding field emphasised Price's superiority in 1994.

THE MASTERS

COURSE:	Augusta National GC
LOCATION:	Augusta, Georgia
DATE:	6-9 April
DISTANCE:	6925 yards
PAR:	72 (288)
WINNER:	$396000

Pos	Player	1st	2nd	3rd	4th	Total
1	**BEN CRENSHAW**	70	67	69	68	274
2	Davis Love III	69	69	71	66	275
3 =	Jay Haas	71	64	72	70	277
	Greg Norman	73	68	68	68	277
5 =	Steve Elkington	73	67	67	72	279
	David Frost	66	71	71	71	279
7 =	Scott Hoch	69	67	71	73	280
	Phil Mickelson	66	71	70	73	280
9	Curtis Strange	72	71	65	73	281
10 =	Fred Couples	71	69	67	75	282
	Brian Henninger	70	68	68	76	282
12 =	Lee Janzen	69	69	74	71	283
	Kenny Perry	73	70	71	69	283
14 =	Hale Irwin	69	72	71	72	284
	Jose-Maria Olazabal	66	74	72	72	284
	Tom Watson	73	70	69	72	284
17 =	Paul Azinger	70	72	73	70	285
	Brad Faxon	76	69	69	71	285
	Ray Floyd	71	70	70	74	285
	John Huston	70	66	72	77	285
	Colin Montgomerie	71	69	76	69	285
	Corey Pavin	67	71	72	75	285
	Ian Woosnam	69	72	71	73	285

Ben Crenshaw's second Masters, and second Major, was an emotional occasion. 'Gentle' Ben had been one of the game's most popular players for over two decades; and when he won his second Green Jacket, 11 years after the first, and just a few days after the death of his friend and mentor, Harvey Penick, no one complained. Davis Love III, whose grandfather and father had featured in various Majors over the years, was beginning to assume the mantle that Crenshaw once had – and Kite had discarded in 1992.

US OPEN

COURSE:	Shinnecock Hills GC
LOCATION:	Southampton, New York
DATE:	15-18 June
DISTANCE:	6912 yards
PAR:	70 (280)
WINNER:	$350000

Pos	Player	1st	2nd	3rd	4th	Total
1	**COREY PAVIN**	72	69	71	68	280
2	Greg Norman	68	67	74	73	282
3	Tom Lehman	70	72	67	74	283
4 =	Bill Glasson	69	70	76	69	284
	Jay Haas	70	73	72	69	284
	Neal Lancaster	70	72	77	65	284
	Davis Love III	72	68	73	71	284
	Jeff Maggert	69	72	77	66	284
	Phil Mickelson	68	70	72	74	284
10 =	Frank Nobilo	72	72	70	71	285
	Vijay Singh	70	71	72	72	285
	Bob Tway	69	69	72	75	285
13 =	Brad Bryant	71	75	70	70	286
	Lee Janzen	70	72	72	72	286
	Mark McCumber	70	71	77	68	286
	Nick Price	66	73	73	74	286
	Mark Roe	71	69	74	72	286
	Jeff Sluman	72	69	74	71	286
	Steve Stricker	71	70	71	74	286
	Duffy Waldorf	72	70	75	69	286

Davis Love was inheriting the label 'the best player never to have won a Major', championship by championship; and this was reinforced when the US Open celebrated its centennial at Shinnecock. Corey Pavin had also been linked with the tag, but his first win eliminated him from the maiden stakes to leave Love, with another creditable performance, looking over his shoulder for new competition in Mickelson and Montgomerie. Greg Norman finished second for the seventh time in a Major.

BRITISH OPEN

COURSE: Royal & Ancient GC
LOCATION: St Andrews, Fife, Scotland
DATE: 20-23 July
DISTANCE: 6933 yards
PAR: 72 (288)
WINNER: £125000

Pos	Player	1st	2nd	3rd	4th	Total
1	**JOHN DALY***	67	71	73	71	282
2	Costantino Rocca	69	70	70	73	282
3 =	Steven Bottomley	70	72	72	69	283
	Mark Brooks	70	69	73	71	283
	Michael Campbell	71	71	65	76	283
6 =	Steve Elkington	72	69	69	74	284
	Vijay Singh	68	72	73	71	284
8 =	Bob Estes	72	70	71	72	285
	Mark James	72	75	68	70	285
	Corey Pavin	69	70	72	74	285
11 =	Ernie Els	71	68	72	75	286
	Brett Ogle	73	69	71	73	286
	Payne Stewart	72	68	75	71	286
	Sam Torrance	71	70	71	74	286
15 =	Robert Allenby	71	74	71	71	287
	Ben Crenshaw	67	72	76	72	287
	Brad Faxon	71	67	75	74	287
	Per-Ulrik Johansson	69	78	68	72	287
	Greg Norman	71	74	72	70	287
20 =	Andrew Coltart	70	74	71	73	288
	David Duval	71	75	70	72	288
	Barry Lane	72	73	68	75	288
	Peter Mitchell	73	74	71	70	288

* John Daly beat Constantino Rocca in the 4-hole play-off

John Daly, flirting with alcoholics' rehabilitation centres since his 1991 PGA triumph, held his nerve to outplay an emotionally-drained Costantino Rocca in the four-hole play-off. After completing R4, Daly was in the clubhouse watching the Italian approach Tom Morris' green. He needed to chip and putt for two to tie. With not much green to work with, Rocca fluffed his shot. Daly, with TV cameras watching his every gesture, kept calm, but must have thought the Claret Jug was his. His expression hardly changed when Costantino sensationally holed his next shot; but the Italian collapsed in a mixture of relief and exhaustion. Despite seeing the Jug dashed away from his lips at the last, it was Daly, in overtime, who stayed calmer to win his second Major.

US PGA

COURSE: Riviera CC
LOCATION: Pacific Palisades, California
DATE: 10-13 August
DISTANCE: 6956 yards
PAR: 71 (284)
WINNER: $360000

Pos	Player	1st	2nd	3rd	4th	Total
1	**STEVE ELKINGTON***	68	67	68	64	267
2	Colin Montgomerie	68	67	67	65	267
3 =	Ernie Els	66	65	66	72	269
	Jeff Maggert	66	69	65	69	269
5	Brad Faxon	70	67	71	63	271
6 =	Bob Estes	69	68	68	68	273
	Mark O'Meara	64	67	69	73	273
8 =	Jay Haas	69	71	64	70	274
	Justin Leonard	68	66	70	70	274
	Steve Lowery	69	68	68	69	274
	Jeff Sluman	69	67	68	70	274
	Craig Stadler	71	66	66	71	274
13 =	Jim Furyk	68	70	69	68	275
	Miguel Jimenez	69	69	67	70	275
	Payne Stewart	69	70	69	67	275
	Kirk Triplett	71	69	68	67	275
17 =	Michael Campbell	71	65	71	69	276
	Constantino Rocca	70	69	68	69	276
	Curtis Strange	72	68	68	68	276
20 =	Greg Norman	66	69	70	72	277
	Jesper Parnevik	69	69	70	69	277
	Duffy Waldorf	69	69	67	72	277

*Steve Elkington beat Colin Montgomerie at the first extra hole in the Sudden Death Play-off

Quiz question: Which golfer ties the record low score in Major Championships, but has never won any? Answer: Colin Montgomerie. His 267 took him level with Steve Elkington, whose 25-foot birdie putt sealed the play-off. If the Europeans had taken a shine to the Masters, then the PGA was starting to become the preserve of golfers from the Southern Hemisphere. Between 1916 and 1962 only Australia's Jim Ferrier and South Africa's Gary Player had taken the trophy ahead of native or naturalised Americans. Following Player's second win in 1972, David Graham, Wayne Grady, Price (twice), Ernie Els and now Elkington had won the Championship – the last five in six years.

THE MASTERS

COURSE:	Augusta National GC
LOCATION:	Augusta, Georgia
DATE:	11-14 April
DISTANCE:	6925 yards
PAR:	72 (288)
WINNER:	$435000

Pos	Player	1st	2nd	3rd	4th	Total
1	**NICK FALDO**	69	67	73	67	276
2	Greg Norman	63	69	71	78	281
3	Phil Mickelson	65	73	72	72	282
4	Frank Nobilo	71	71	72	69	283
5 =	Scott Hoch	67	73	73	71	284
	Duffy Waldorf	72	71	69	72	284
7 =	Davis Love III	72	71	74	68	285
	Jeff Maggert	71	73	72	69	285
	Corey Pavin	75	66	73	71	285
10 =	David Frost	70	68	74	74	286
	Scott McCarron	70	70	72	74	286
12 =	Ernie Els	71	71	72	73	287
	Lee Janzen	68	71	75	73	287
	Bob Tway	67	72	76	72	287
15 =	Mark Calcavecchia	71	73	71	73	288
	Fred Couples	78	68	71	71	288
17	John Huston	71	71	71	76	289
18 =	Paul Azinger	70	74	76	70	290
	David Duval	73	72	69	76	290
	Tom Lehman	75	70	72	73	290
	Mark O'Meara	72	71	75	72	290
	Nick Price	71	75	70	74	290

Perhaps this was the most astounding final round in Majors history. World No.1, Greg Norman, twice winner of the British Open, became a Majors runner-up for the eighth, and perhaps most-damaging, time when he surrendered a six-shot overnight lead to Nick Faldo; and to then capitulate completely, finally losing by five (an 11-stroke swing). His eight runners-up places put him tied with Sam Snead in third place of all time. But Sam won seven Majors as well, and proportionately the best players have a similar number of winning and second place positions. Above Snead and Norman are Nicklaus with 18 and 18; followed by Palmer (nine and seven). Against Faldo, Norman's capitulation included a seven-shot swing in as many holes, and ten over the last 12. Faldo, to his credit, remains one of the best head-to-head scrappers in the history of the Majors.

US OPEN

COURSE:	Oakland Hills CC
LOCATION:	Birmingham, Michigan
DATE:	13-16 June
DISTANCE:	6996 yards
PAR:	70 (280)
WINNER:	$405000

Pos	Player	1st	2nd	3rd	4th	Total
1	**STEVE JONES**	74	66	69	69	278
2 =	Tom Lehman	71	72	65	71	279
	Davis Love III	71	69	70	69	279
4	John Morse	68	74	68	70	280
5 =	Ernie Els	72	67	72	70	281
	Jim Furyk	72	69	70	70	281
7 =	Ken Green	73	67	72	70	282
	Scott Hoch	73	71	71	67	282
	Vijay Singh	71	72	70	69	282
10 =	Lee Janzen	68	75	71	69	283
	Colin Montgomerie	70	72	69	72	283
	Greg Norman	73	66	74	70	283
13 =	Dan Forsman	72	71	70	71	284
	Frank Nobilo	69	71	70	74	284
	Tom Watson	70	71	71	72	284
16 =	David Berganio	69	72	72	72	285
	Mark Brooks	76	68	69	72	285
	Stewart Cink	69	73	70	73	285
	John Cook	70	71	71	73	285
	Nick Faldo	72	71	72	70	285
	Mark O'Meara	72	73	68	72	285
	Sam Torrance	71	69	71	74	285

Steve Jones had to pre-qualify for the Open – being the first winner to do so since 1976, when Jerry Pate had to endure the same ordeal. Jones had faded from the golf scene a few years previously due to an awful motorcycle accident, but it was he who had the right stuff as holes were running out. Jones, Davis Love and Tom Lehman were battling for supremacy. Love should have been in the clubhouse with a 67, but missing a putt on the 18th reminiscent of that required to win the British Open in 1970 by Doug Sanders; and after bogeying 17, he could only sit and wait. Driving off the 18th tee, Lehman found a fairway bunker to nullify any hope he had of making the green in regulation. Jones steadied and drove truly down the middle to set up the par that was to win it.

COURSE: Royal Lytham and St Anne's GC	COURSE: Valhalla GC
LOCATION: St Annes, Lancashire, England	LOCATION: Louisville, Kentucky
DATE: 18-21 July	DATE: 8-11 August
DISTANCE: 6892 yards	DISTANCE: 7144 yards
PAR: 71 (284)	PAR: 72 (288)
WINNER: £200000	WINNER: $430000

Pos	Player	1st	2nd	3rd	4th	Total
1	**TOM LEHMAN**	67	67	64	73	271
2 =	Ernie Els	68	67	71	67	273
	Mark McCumber	67	69	71	66	273
4	Nick Faldo	68	68	68	70	274
5 =	Mark Brooks	67	70	68	71	276
	Jeff Maggert	69	70	72	65	276
7 =	Fred Couples	67	70	69	71	277
	Peter Hedblom	70	65	75	67	277
	Greg Norman	71	68	71	67	277
	Greg Turner	72	69	68	68	277
11 =	Alexander Cejka	73	67	71	67	278
	Darren Clarke	70	68	69	71	278
	Vijay Singh	69	67	69	73	278
14 =	David Duval	76	67	66	70	279
	Paul McGinley	69	65	74	71	279
	Mark McNulty	69	71	70	69	279
	Shigeki Maruyama	68	70	69	72	279
18 =	Padraig Harrington	68	68	73	71	280
	Rocco Mediate	69	70	69	72	280
	Loren Roberts	67	69	72	72	280
	Michael Welch	71	68	73	68	280

Pos	Player	1st	2nd	3rd	4th	Total
1	**MARK BROOKS***	68	70	69	70	277
2	Kenny Perry	66	72	71	68	277
3 =	Steve Elkington	67	74	67	70	278
	Tommy Tolles	69	71	71	67	278
5 =	Justin Leonard	71	66	72	70	279
	Jesper Parnevik	73	67	69	70	279
	Vijay Singh	69	69	69	72	279
8 =	Lee Janzen	68	71	71	70	280
	Per-Ulrik Johansson	73	72	66	69	280
	Phil Mickelson	67	67	74	72	280
	Larry Mize	71	70	69	70	280
	Frank Nobilo	69	72	71	68	280
	Nick Price	68	71	69	72	280
14 =	Mike Brisky	71	69	69	72	281
	Tom Lehman	71	71	69	70	281
	Joey Sindelar	73	72	69	67	281
17 =	Russ Cochran	68	72	65	77	282
	David Edwards	69	71	72	70	282
	Brad Faxon	72	68	73	69	282
	Jim Furyk	70	70	73	69	282
	Greg Norman	68	72	69	73	282
	Tom Watson	69	71	73	69	282
	DA Weibring	71	73	71	67	282

With the first prize doubling within four years, the 125th Open, although mostly dominated by the top Americans, was still not supported by as many as the R&A would have liked. Demands imposed upon them by the ever more competitive PGA Tour forced many to stay at home; especially those not exempt and who would have to have invested extra time in qualifying. This would change in a few years, with the inclusion of the Open as an official PGA Tour event. Nick Faldo kept home hopes alive with three successive 68s, but was too far away from Tom Lehman's 54-hole record score of 198 to make an impression. 1994 US Open Champion, Ernie Els, and 45-year-old Mark McCumber, kept up the pressure, and Mark Brooks was in the hunt as he was last year; but Lehman's cushion was too comfortable. His two-over par 73 still gave him a two-stroke advantage at the end. After several good finishes in recent years, his first Major was well-deserved.

*Mark Brooks beat Kenny Perry in the Sudden Death Play-off at the first extra hole

Carrying on his good form from Royal Lytham, Mark Brooks from Texas was involved in the finish once again. This time his immediate competition came from Kenny Perry, who was two strokes clear of the field going to the last hole. R3 leader Russ Cochrane had blown up and challenges from Vijay Singh and Steve Elkington were dissipating. With Perry's lead then reduced to one after a wayward drive, Brooks birdied the last to force extra holes. He repeated the dose at the same hole in the play-off. The two-shot swing at the end of regulation play was a stern lesson to Perry who was actively playing to the crowd going to the 18th tee.

1997

THE MASTERS

COURSE:	Augusta National GC
LOCATION:	Augusta, Georgia
DATE:	10-13 April
DISTANCE:	6925 yards
PAR:	72 (288)
WINNER:	$486000

Pos	Player	1st	2nd	3rd	4th	Total
1	**TIGER WOODS**	70	66	65	69	270
2	Tom Kite	77	69	66	70	282
3	Tommy Tolles	72	72	72	67	283
4	Tom Watson	75	68	69	72	284
5 =	Costantino Rocca	71	69	70	75	285
	Paul Stankowski	68	74	79	74	285
7 =	Fred Couples	72	69	73	72	286
	Bernhard Langer	72	72	74	68	286
	Justin Leonard	76	69	71	70	286
	Davis Love III	72	71	72	71	286
	Jeff Sluman	74	67	72	73	286
12 =	Steve Elkington	76	72	72	67	287
	Per-Ulrik Johannson	72	73	73	69	287
	Tom Lehman	73	76	69	69	287
	Jose-Maria Olazabal	71	70	74	72	287
	Willie Wood	72	76	71	68	287
17 =	Mark Calcavecchia	74	73	72	69	288
	Ernie Els	73	70	71	74	288
	Fred Funk	74	73	69	72	288
	Vijay Singh	75	74	69	70	288

Records galore fell to the new *enfant terrible* of golf. Eldrick 'Tiger' Woods, after many years of hype and a sparkling amateur record, had arrived. At 21 he became the youngest winner of the Masters, and in so doing, changed the public perception of this middle-class, middle-brow, middle-aged, white man's sport so dramatically it may be now be irrevocable. Tiger so destroyed the Augusta course (a record low for the Masters) and the field (a record winning margin for the Masters), and created so many records on the way (first rookie to win a Major since Jerry Pate in 1976; shot the last 54 holes in 200; the first black golfer to win a Major, etc.) he almost disguised the most amazing facet of his emergence. Here was a role model for all youth, black and white alike. His maturity off course was commented upon as much as his golfing genius – and left all in awe and wonder at what this new comet was about to inflict on the world of golf over the next couple of decades.

US OPEN

COURSE:	Congressional GC
LOCATION:	Bethesda, Maryland
DATE:	12-15 June
DISTANCE:	7213 yards
PAR:	70 (280)
WINNER:	$465000

Pos	Player	1st	2nd	3rd	4th	Total
1	**ERNIE ELS**	71	67	69	69	276
2	Colin Montgomerie	65	76	67	69	277
3	Tom Lehman	67	70	68	73	278
4	Jeff Maggert	73	66	68	74	281
5 =	Olin Browne	71	71	69	71	282
	Jim Furyk	74	68	69	71	282
	Jay Haas	73	69	68	72	282
	Tommy Tolles	74	67	69	72	282
	Bob Tway	71	71	70	70	282
10 =	Scott Hoch	71	68	72	72	283
	Scott McCarron	73	71	69	70	283
	David Ogrin	70	69	71	73	283
13 =	Billy Andrade	75	67	69	73	284
	Stewart Cink	71	67	74	72	284
	Loren Roberts	72	69	72	71	284
16 =	Bradley Hughes	75	70	71	69	285
	Davis Love III	75	70	69	71	285
	Jose-Maria Olazabal	71	71	72	71	285
19 =	Nick Price	71	74	71	70	286
	Paul Stankowski	75	70	68	73	286
	Hal Sutton	66	73	73	74	286
	Lee Westwood	71	71	73	71	286
	Tiger Woods	74	67	73	72	286

The Woods bandwagon could not get up the expected head of steam, and despite a R2 67 which put him briefly in contention, Tiger rarely threatened in what was to become a three-horse race amongst those consistent performers, Lehman, Montgomerie and Els. Once again, though, Montgomerie was to be found wanting at the very end, as Lehman faded and the Scotsman was tying with Els, coming into the 17th. True, the juxtaposition of the 18th green where Lehman and Maggert were putting out created a diversion, but Monty's temperament failed him as he delayed, and perhaps dithered, over a fatal five-footer. Els was made of sterner stuff and the South African collected his second US Open at the age of 27.

BRITISH OPEN

COURSE:	Royal Troon GC
LOCATION:	Troon, Ayrshire, Scotland
DATE:	17-20 July
DISTANCE:	7079 yards
PAR:	71 (284)
WINNER:	£250000

Pos	Player	1st	2nd	3rd	4th	Total
1	**JUSTIN LEONARD**	69	66	72	65	272
2 =	Darren Clarke	67	66	71	71	275
	Jesper Parnevik	70	66	66	73	275
4	Jim Furyk	67	72	70	70	279
5 =	Stephen Ames	74	69	66	71	280
	Padraig Harrington	75	69	69	67	280
7 =	Fred Couples	69	68	70	74	281
	Peter O'Malley	73	70	70	68	281
	Eduardo Romero	74	68	67	72	281
10 =	Robert Allenby	76	68	66	72	282
	Mark Calacavecchia	74	67	72	69	282
	Ernie Els	75	69	69	69	282
	Retief Goosen	75	69	70	68	282
	Tom Kite	72	67	74	69	282
	Davis Love III	70	71	74	67	282
	Shigeki Maruyama	74	69	70	69	282
	Frank Nobilo	74	72	68	68	282
	Tom Watson	71	70	70	71	282
	Lee Westwood	73	70	67	72	282
20 =	Stuart Appleby	72	72	68	71	283
	Brad Faxon	77	67	72	67	283
	Mark James	76	67	70	70	283
	Jose-Maria Olazabal	75	68	73	67	283

After Woods and Els, Justin Leonard become the third twentysomething in a row to a win a Major. He shot a brilliant last round to destroy Parnevik, who had been in a similar position three years earlier at Turnberry, that time succumbing to Nick Price. With all the early attention in R4 on the scrap between Ulsterman Clarke and the quirky Swede, Leonard proceeded to compile the lowest score of the day up ahead; he was almost unnoticed until he birdied 17, and set a meaningful target for those behind. Playing in-and-out golf, Parnevik still had the Championship in his grasp when he approached the 13th. Four bogeys home, including 16, 17 and 18, sealed his fate and put a question mark over his big-time nerve. Leonard continued the good form of the Americans in recent years, making it three in a row.

US PGA

COURSE:	Winged Foot GC
LOCATION:	Mamaroneck, New York
DATE:	14-17 August
DISTANCE:	6987 yards
PAR:	70 (280)
WINNER:	$470000

Pos	Player	1st	2nd	3rd	4th	Total
1	**DAVIS LOVE III**	66	71	66	66	269
2	Justin Leonard	68	70	65	71	274
3	Jeff Maggert	69	69	73	65	276
4	Lee Janzen	69	67	74	69	279
5	Tom Kite	68	71	71	70	280
6 =	Phil Blackmar	70	68	74	69	281
	Jim Furyk	69	72	72	68	281
	Scott Hoch	71	72	68	70	281
9	Tom Byrum	69	73	70	70	282
10 =	Tom Lehman	69	72	72	70	283
	Scott McCarron	74	71	67	71	283
	Joey Sindelar	72	71	71	69	283
13 =	David Duval	70	70	71	73	284
	Tim Herron	72	73	68	71	284
	Colin Montgomerie	74	71	67	72	284
	Greg Norman	68	71	74	71	284
	Mark O'Meara	69	73	75	67	284
	Nick Price	72	70	72	70	284
	Vijay Singh	73	66	76	69	284
	Tommy Tolles	75	70	73	66	284
	Kirk Triplett	73	70	71	70	284
	Bob Tway	68	75	72	69	284

An emotional Davis Love finally made the Majors breakthrough he had been seeking for so long, by first seeing off in-form Leonard and then pulling away from the field to win in the end by some margin; and with some panache (he birdied the last). The win was much more than just quenching an overlong thirst: it was the manifestation of a family dream after his father, Davis Love Jr, had contested several Majors without success (he was sixth in the 1969 British Open). The win was even more poignant as his father was killed in an air crash in 1988. Love's win continued the uncanny sequence of a new champion every year since the advent of strokeplay. The last back-to-back winner of the Wanamaker Trophy was Denny Shute, way back in 1937.

THE MASTERS

COURSE:	Augusta National GC	
LOCATION:	Augusta, Georgia	
DATE:	9-12 April	
DISTANCE:	6925 yards	
PAR:	72 (288)	
WINNER:	$576000	

Pos	Player	1st	2nd	3rd	4th	Total
1	**MARK O'MEARA**	74	70	68	67	279
2 =	Fred Couples	69	70	71	70	280
	David Duval	71	68	74	67	280
4	Jim Furyl	76	70	67	68	281
5	Paul Azinger	71	72	69	70	283
6 =	Jack Nicklaus	73	72	70	68	285
	David Toms	75	72	72	64	285
8 =	Darren Clarke	76	73	67	69	286
	Justin Leonard	74	73	69	69	286
	Colin Montgomerie	71	75	69	70	286
	Tiger Woods	71	72	72	70	285
12 =	Jay Haas	72	71	71	72	286
	Per-Ulrik Johannson	74	75	67	70	286
	Phil Mickelson	74	69	69	74	286
	Jose-Maria Olazabal	70	73	71	72	286
16 =	Mark Calcavecchia	74	74	69	70	287
	Ernie Els	75	70	70	72	287
	Scott Hoch	70	71	73	73	287
	Scott McCarron	73	71	72	71	287
	Ian Woosnam	74	71	72	70	287

In a memorable Masters for golden oldies, Mark O'Meara, at 41, won his first Major at the 57th time of asking. He birdied the final two holes – something which hadn't been achieved since Palmer's landmark win in 1960 – to overcome the stuttering (and in both cases, increasingly profligate in Major championship run-ins) Duval and Couples at the death. Nicklaus rolled back the years, before breaking his run of 154 consecutive Majors after the upcoming US Open with a hip operation, by becoming the oldest Top 10 finisher in the Masters. His venerable partner in crime, Gary Player, at 62, became the oldest to beat the cut at Augusta; whilst Gay Brewer shot the oldest par-or-better round, aged 66.

US OPEN

COURSE:	Olympic Club	
LOCATION:	San Francisco, California	
DATE:	18-21 June	
DISTANCE:	6979 yards	
PAR:	70 (280)	
WINNER:	$535000	

Pos	Player	1st	2nd	3rd	4th	Total
1	**LEE JANZEN**	73	66	73	68	280
2	Payne Stewar	66	71	70	74	281
3	Bob Tway	68	70	73	73	284
4	Nick Price	73	68	71	73	285
5 =	Tom Lehman	68	75	68	75	286
	Steve Stricker	73	71	69	73	286
7 =	David Duval	75	68	75	69	287
	Jeff Maggert	69	69	75	74	287
	Lee Westwood	72	74	70	71	287
10 =	Stuart Appleby	73	74	70	71	288
	Stewart Cink	73	68	73	74	288
	Phil Mickelson	71	73	74	70	288
	Jeff Sluman	72	74	74	68	288
14 =	Paul Azinger	75	72	77	65	289
	Jim Furyk	74	73	68	74	289
	Matt Kuchar (a)	70	69	76	74	289
	Jesper Parnevik	69	74	76	74	289
18 =	Frank Lickliter	73	71	72	74	290
	Colin Montgomerie	70	74	77	69	290
	Jose-Maria Olazabal	68	77	72	74	290
	Loren Roberts	71	76	71	72	290
	Tiger Woods	74	72	71	73	290

Two major pieces of good fortune on the Olympic Club's testing course, at the 5th and the 11th, on the last day, helped Lee Janzen turn around a five-shot disadvantage to overcome a faltering Payne Stewart, and win his second US Open. Janzen, in all fairness, had played the most solid golf of all the leading protagonists over the last 18; repeating his triumph over the luckless Stewart in 1993. Stewart, ahead of the field by four starting the day, had enough in hand to win over the rest of the pack, and indeed finished three clear of Tway in third place. But Janzen's second-best-of-the-day 68 was enough to make him a multiple Major champion, and elevate him from the mediocre list of one-win wonders which had started to typify the Majors.

BRITISH OPEN

COURSE: Royal Birkdale GC
LOCATION: Southport, Lancashire, England
DATE: 16-19 July
DISTANCE: 7018 yards
PAR: 70 (280)
WINNER: £300000

Pos	Player	1st	2nd	3rd	4th	Total
1	**MARK O'MEARA***	72	68	72	68	280
2	Brain Watts	68	69	73	70	280
3	Tiger Woods	65	73	77	66	281
4 =	Jim Furyk	70	70	72	70	282
	Jesper Parnevik	68	72	72	70	282
	Justin Rose (a)	72	66	75	69	282
	Raymond Russell	68	73	75	66	282
8	Davis Love III	67	73	77	68	283
9 =	Thomas Bjorn	68	71	76	71	286
	Costantino Rocca	72	74	70	70	286
11 =	David Duval	70	71	75	71	287
	Brad Faxon	67	74	74	72	287
	John Husto	65	77	73	72	287
14	Gordon Brand, Jr	71	70	76	71	288
15 =	Peter Baker	69	72	77	71	289
	Jose-Maria Olazabal	73	72	75	69	289
	Des Smyth	74	69	75	71	289
	Greg Turner	68	75	75	71	289
19 =	Robert Allenby	67	76	78	69	290
	Mark James	71	74	74	71	290
	Sandy Lyle	70	73	75	72	290
	Vijay Singh	67	74	78	71	290
	Curtis Strange	73	73	74	70	290

*Mark O'Meara beat Brian Watts in the 4-Hole Play-off

In a magical last day, which capped the best Major since the Faldo-Norman Masters of 1996, Mark O'Meara's sheer 1998 impetus saw him squeak home for his second Major of the year, after a play-off with US exile Brian Watts. The severity of the weather on the Saturday sorted out the field, much like the mayhem caused at a fence in a steeplechase race; leaving just a handful of serious contenders left to fight for the spoils. A new British sporting hero appeared to be born in a mercurial performance from the teenage amateur Justin Rose; he finished at the 72nd hole with an outrageous chip-in, and in fourth place. The birth was to prove somewhat premature, however, as almost every cut in tournaments he played over the next 12 months was missed.

US PGA

COURSE: Sahalee CC
LOCATION: Redmond, Washington State
DATE: 13-16 August
DISTANCE: 6906 yards
PAR: 70 (280)
WINNER: $540000

Pos	Player	1st	2nd	3rd	4th	Total
1	**VIJAY SINGH**	70	66	67	68	271
2	Steve Stricker	69	68	66	70	273
3	Steve Elkington	69	69	69	67	274
4 =	Frank Lickliter	68	71	69	68	276
	Mark O'Meara	69	70	69	68	276
	Nick Price	70	73	68	65	276
7 =	Davis Love III	70	68	69	70	277
	Billy Mayfair	73	67	67	70	277
9	John Cook	71	68	70	69	278
10 =	Skip Kendall	72	68	68	71	279
	Kenny Perry	69	72	70	68	279
	Tiger Woods	66	72	70	71	279
13 =	Robert Allenby	72	68	69	71	280
	Paul Azinger	68	73	70	69	280
	Fred Couples	74	71	67	68	280
	Brad Faxon	70	68	74	68	280
	Steve Flesch	75	69	67	69	280
	Bill Glasson	68	74	69	69	280
	John Huston	70	71	68	71	280
	Bob Tway	69	76	67	68	280

Popular Fijian, Vijay Sigh, deservedly collected his first Major at the typically tight Salahee course. Overcoming many a turmoil during his globe-trotting career, his solid game seems ideally suited to the strictures of the PGA Championship; proved here when pulling away from the promising Stricker over the last round. Once again the winner came from the Southern Hemisphere, and once again there was an almost non-existent challenge from a disappointing group of Europeans. O'Meara tinkered with the immortality that sharing Ben Hogan's 1953 three-Majors record would surely bring, picking up three shots over the final day's first five holes; but staggered back into the pack, to finish five adrift of the winner, no doubt contemplating on what a wonderful game golf is.

THE MASTERS

COURSE:	Augusta National GC
LOCATION:	Augusta, Georgia
DATE:	8-11 April
DISTANCE:	6985 yards
PAR:	72 (288)
WINNER:	$720000

Pos	Player	1st	2nd	3rd	4th	Total
1	**JOSE-MARIA OLAZABAL**	70	66	73	71	280
2	Davis Love III	69	72	71	73	282
3	Greg Norman	71	68	71	73	283
4 =	Bob Estes	71	72	69	72	284
	Steve Pate	71	75	65	73	284
6 =	David Duval	71	74	70	70	285
	Carlos Franco	72	72	68	73	285
	Phil Mickelson	74	69	71	71	285
	Nick Price	69	72	72	72	285
	Lee Westwood	75	71	68	71	285
11 =	Steve Elkington	72	70	71	74	287
	Bernhard Langer	76	66	72	73	287
	Colin Montgomerie	70	72	71	74	287
14 =	Jim Furyk	72	73	70	73	288
	Lee Janzen	70	69	73	76	288
	Brandt Jobe	72	71	74	71	288
	Ian Woosnam	71	74	71	72	288
18 =	Brandel Chamblee	69	73	75	72	289
	Bill Glasson	72	70	73	74	289
	Justin Leonard	70	72	73	74	289
	Scott McCarron	69	68	76	76	289
	Tiger Woods	72	72	70	75	289

In a Masters tournament that resembled a windswept British Open, two Augusta favourites reprised the good old days when Olazabal and Norman dominated the fourth round. And a third, and the man to whom the appeal of the Masters owes so much, Gene Sarazen, was, sadly for all concerned, to tee off ceremonially for the last time, aged 97. That the two latter-day heroes should even be playing at the top level again was remarkable, as Norman missed most of 1998, and all the Majors, having his shoulder rebuilt; and of course Olazabal's gloomy prognosis during 1995 and 1996 that he may never walk again is well-known. Olazabal returned to golf in 1997 and played solidly, if not spectacularly: the Masters win hopefully means a return to a hugely successful career. Greg just seemed genuinely happy to be in contention again.

US OPEN

COURSE:	Pinehurst Resort & CC
LOCATION:	Pinehurst, North Carolina
DATE:	17-20 June
DISTANCE:	7175 yards
PAR:	70 (280)
WINNER:	$625000

Pos	Player	1st	2nd	3rd	4th	Total
1	**PAYNE STEWART**	68	69	72	70	279
2	Phil Mickelson	67	70	73	70	280
3 =	Vijay Singh	69	70	73	69	281
	Tiger Woods	68	71	72	70	281
5	Steve Stricker	70	73	69	73	285
6	Tim Herron	69	72	70	75	286
7 =	David Duval	67	70	75	75	287
	Jeff Maggert	71	69	74	73	287
	Hal Sutton	69	70	76	72	287
10 =	Darren Clarke	73	70	74	71	288
	Billy Mayfair	67	72	74	75	288
12 =	Paul Azinger	72	72	75	70	289
	Paul Goydos	67	74	74	74	289
	Davis Love III	70	73	74	72	289
15 =	Justin Leonard	69	75	73	73	290
	Colin Montgomerie	72	72	74	72	290
17 =	Jim Furyk	69	73	77	72	291
	Jay Haas	74	72	73	72	291
	Dudley Hart	73	73	76	69	291
	John Huston	71	69	75	76	291
	Jesper Parnevik	71	71	76	73	291
	Scott Verplank	72	73	72	74	291

Pinehurst, arguably the spiritual home of US golf, finally played host to American golf's premier event. 42-year-old Payne Stewart added a second US Open title and third Major (with his PGA win in 1989) when he fought back into contention over the last few holes at Pinehurst No.2 course. Five months later he was to be forever taken from the world of golf in a tragic, bizarre flying accident. Two long saving putts from Stewart on 16 and 18 sandwiched a meticulously set-up birdie on the 17th; clawing back shots on leaders Phil Mickelson and Tiger Woods, and eventually finishing ahead of them at one under par. Payne had wiped out the memories of 1993 and 1998 and the spectre of Lee Janzen. Mickelson was consigned to the next Major still as a Majors nearly-man and John Daly, after an opening round 68, finished 77, 81 and 83, cursed the USGA and threatened to boycott Pebble Beach in 2000.

COURSE:	Carnoustie GC
LOCATION:	Carnoustie, Angus, Scotland
DATE:	15-18 July
DISTANCE:	7361 yards
PAR:	71 (284)
WINNER:	£350000

COURSE:	Medinah CC
LOCATION:	Medinah, Illinois
DATE:	12-15 August
DISTANCE:	7398 yards
PAR:	72 (288)
WINNER:	$650000

Pos	Player	1st	2nd	3rd	4th	Total
1	PAUL LAWRIE*	73	74	76	67	290
2 =	Justin Leonard	73	74	71	72	290
	Jean Van de Velde	75	68	70	77	290
4 =	Angel Cabrera	75	69	77	70	291
	Craig Parry	76	75	67	73	291
6	Greg Norman	76	70	75	72	293
7 =	David Frost	80	69	71	74	294
	Davis Love III	74	74	77	69	294
	Tiger Woods	74	72	74	74	294
10 =	Scott Dunlap	72	77	76	70	295
	Jim Furyk	78	71	76	70	295
	Retief Goosen	76	75	73	71	295
	Jesper Parnevik	74	71	78	72	295
	Hal Sutton	73	78	72	72	295
15 =	Colin Montgomerie	74	76	72	74	296
	Scott Verplank	80	74	73	69	296
	Tsuyoshi Yoneyama	77	74	73	72	296
18 =	Andrew Coltart	74	74	72	77	297
	Bernhard Langer	72	77	73	75	297
	Frank Nobilo	76	76	70	75	297
	Costantino Rocca	81	69	74	73	297
	Patrik Sjoland	74	72	77	74	297
	Lee Westwood	76	75	74	72	297

Pos	Player	1st	2nd	3rd	4th	Total
1	TIGER WOODS	70	67	68	72	277
2	Sergio Garcia	66	73	68	71	278
3 =	Stewart Cink	69	70	68	73	280
	Jay Haas	68	67	75	70	280
5	Nick Price	70	71	69	71	281
6 =	Bob Estes	71	70	72	69	282
	Colin Montgomerie	72	70	70	70	282
8 =	Jim Furyk	71	70	69	74	284
	Steve Pate	72	70	73	69	284
10 =	David Duval	70	71	72	72	285
	Miguel Jimenez	70	70	73	72	285
	Jesper Parnevik	72	70	73	70	285
	Corey Pavin	69	74	71	71	285
	Chris Perry	70	73	71	71	285
	Mike Weir	68	68	69	80	285
16 =	Mark Brooks	70	73	70	74	287
	Gabriel Hjertstedt	72	70	73	72	287
	Brandt Jobe	69	74	69	75	287
	Greg Turner	73	69	70	75	287
	Lee Westwood	70	68	74	75	287

*Paul Lawrie (5 4 3 3) beat Justin Leonard (5 4 4 5) and Jean Van de Velde (6 4 3 5) in the 4-Hole Play-off

Few sporting events can match the 1999 Open for the heroic, suspenseful, heart-wrenching, and sporting scenes witnessed at Carnoustie on the Sunday evening. Paul Lawrie won the Open after beating Justin Leonard and Jean Van de Velde in the four-hole play-off – these are the facts. But they don't tell the story, though, of the punishing rough; of Rodney Pampling's R1 lead and cut demise - unique in Majors history; of Sergio Garcia's tearful finish; of Lawrie being the first qualifier to win, and a Scotsman on his own soil since James Braid in 1910. Nor do they tell the tale of Van de Velde's farce at the 72nd hole and his self-destruction in the Barry Burn. Who says this is only a game?

Since winning the Masters in 1997, despite being the only golfer to have made the Top 30 in every one of the ten intervening Majors, Tiger Woods has disappointed by his own high standards. It was only a matter of time, however, before he would win again. He did so at Medinah No.3, but in a fashion which suggests he may not have it all his own way in future. Enter then Sergio Garcia. He stunned everyone in leading the field at Medinah, and was just two behind the Tiger after a R3 68. Mike Weir's challenge evaporated (he became the only player in the history of the Majors to have carded, over four rounds, scores in the sixties and eighties, but none in the seventies!), but Garcia kept the pressure on with the best moment of the Championship. Stuck 170 yards from the pin on the 16th, the ball trapped amongst some tree roots, he blasted the ball to within 40 feet, chasing and leaping after his ball like some demented animal. Woods dropped a shot but just about held out for his second Major. But what of El Niño?

Most Wins in Major Championships

1	**JACK NICKLAUS**	18
2	Walter Hagen	11
3 =	Ben Hogan	9
	Gary Player	9
5	Tom Watson	8
6 =	Bobby Jones	7
	Arnold Palmer	7
	Gene Sarazen	7
	Sam Snead	7
	Harry Vardon	7
11 =	Nick Faldo	6
	Lee Trevino	6
13 =	Seve Ballesteros	5
	James Braid	5
	Byron Nelson	5
	JH Taylor	5
	Peter Thomson	5
18 =	Willie Anderson Jr	4
	Jim Barnes	4
	Ray Floyd	4
	Bobby Locke	4
	Tom Morris Jr	4
	Tom Morris Sr	4
	Willie Park Sr	4
25 =	Jamie Anderson	3
	Tommy Armour	3
	Julius Boros	3
	Billy Casper	3
	Henry Cotton	3
	Jimmy Demaret	3
	Bob Ferguson	3
	Ralph Guldahl	3
	Hale Irwin	3
	Cary Middlecoff	3
	Larry Nelson	3
	Nick Price	3
	Denny Shute	3
	Payne Stewart	3

Most Wins in Individual Majors

British Open

1	**HARRY VARDON**	6
2 =	James Braid	5
	JH Taylor	5
	Peter Thomson	5
	Tom Watson	5
6 =	Walter Hagen	4
	Tom Morris Jr	4
	Tom Morris Sr	4
	Willie Park Sr	4
11 =	Jamie Anderson	3
	Seve Ballesteros	3
	Henry Cotton	3
	Nick Faldo	3
	Bob Ferguson	3
	Bobby Jones	3
	Jack Nicklaus	3
	Gary Player	3

US Open

1 =	**WILLIE ANDERSON**	4
	BEN HOGAN	4
	BOBBY JONES	4
	JACK NICKLAUS	4
5	Hale Irwin	3
6 =	Julius Boros	2
	Billy Casper	2
	Ernie Els	2
	Ralph Guldahl	2
	Walter Hagen	2
	Lee Janzen	2
	John McDermott	2
	Cary Middlecoff	2
	Andy North	2
	Gene Sarazen	2
	Alex Smith	2
	Payne Stewart	2
	Curtis Strange	2
	Lee Trevino	2

US PGA

1 =	**WALTER HAGEN**	5
	(All Matchplay – MP)	
	JACK NICKLAUS	5
	(All Strokeplay – SP)	
3 =	Gene Sarazen (All MP)	3
	Sam Snead (All MP)	3
5 =	Jim Barnes (All MP)	2
	Leo Diegel (All MP)	2
	Ray Floyd (All SP)	2
	Ben Hogan (All MP)	2
	Byron Nelson (All MP)	2
	Larry Nelson (All SP)	2
	Gary Player (All SP)	2
	Nick Price (All SP)	2
	Paul Runyan (All MP)	2
	Denny Shute (All MP)	2
	Dave Stockton (All SP)	2
	Lee Trevino (All SP)	2

The Masters

1	**JACK NICKLAUS**	6
2	Arnold Palmer	4
3 =	Jimmy Demaret	3
	Nick Faldo	3
	Gary Player	3
	Sam Snead	3
7 =	Seve Ballesteros	2
	Ben Crenshaw	2
	Ben Hogan	2
	Bernhard Langer	2
	Byron Nelson	2
	Jose-Maria Olazabal	2
	Horton Smith	2
	Tom Watson	2

Multiple Wins in the Same Year

JACK NICKLAUS (5)	MAS, PGA (1963)
	MAS, BOP (1966)
	MAS, USO (1972)
	MAS, PGA (1975)
	USO, PGA (1980)
Ben Hogan (3)	MAS, USO, BOP (1953)
(The only occasion when three Majors were won)	
	USO, PGA (1948)
	MAS, USO (1951)
Bobby Jones (2)	USO, BOP (1926)
	USO, BOP (1930)
Arnold Palmer (2)	MAS, USO (1960)
	MAS, BOP (1962)
Gene Sarazen (2)	USO, PGA (1922)
	USO, BOP (1932)
Tom Watson (2)	MAS, BOP (1977)
	USO, BOP (1982)
Jack Burke, Jr (1)	MAS, PGA (1956)
Nick Faldo (1)	MAS, BOP (1990)
Walter Hagen (1)	BOP, PGA (1924)
Mark O'Meara (1)	MAS, BOP (1998)
Gary Player (1)	MAS, BOP (1974)
Nick Price (1)	BOP, PGA (1994)
Sam Snead (1)	MAS, PGA (1949)
Craig Wood (1)	MAS, USO (1941)

Youngest Winners

TOM MORRIS, Jr (BOP, 1868)	17 yrs 5 months 8 days
Tom Morris, Jr (BOP, 1869)	18 yrs 5 months 1 day
Tom Morris, Jr (BOP, 1870)	19 yrs 5 months
John McDermott (USO, 1911)	19 yrs 10 mnths 12 days
Francis Ouimet (USO, 1913)	20 yrs 4 months 11 days
Gene Sarazen (USO, 1922)	20 yrs 4 months 16 days
Gene Sarazen (PGA, 1922)	20 yrs 5 months 20 days
Tom Creavy (PGA, 1931)	20 yrs 7 months 17 days
John McDermott (USO, 1912)	20 yrs 11 mnths 21 days
Willie Auchterlonie (BOP, 1893)	21 yrs 24 days
Tiger Woods (MAS, 1997)	21 yrs 3 months 15 days

Oldest Winners

JULIUS BOROS (PGA, 1968)	48 yrs 4 months 18 days
Tom Morris, Sr (BOP, 1867)	46 yrs 3 months 9 days
Jack Nicklaus (MAS, 1986)	46 yrs 2 months 23 days
Jerry Barber (PGA, 1961)	45 yrs 3 months 6 days
Hale Irwin (USO, 1990)	45 yrs 15 days
Lee Trevino (PGA, 1984)	44 yrs 8 months 18 days
Roberto de Vicenzo (BOP, 1967)	44 yrs 3 months 3 days
Ray Floyd (USO, 1986)	43 yrs 9 months 11 days
Ted Ray (USO, 1920)	43 yrs 4 months 16 days
Julius Boros (USO, 1963)	43 yrs 3 months 20 days
Ben Crenshaw (MAS, 1995)	43 yrs 2 months 29 days

Largest Winning Margins

13	Tom Morris Sr	BOP, 1862
12	Tom Morris Jr	BOP, 1870
	Tiger Woods	MAS, 1997
11	Willie Smith	USO, 1899
9	Jim Barnes	USO, 1921
	Jack Nicklaus	MAS, 1965
8	James Braid	BOP, 1908
	Ray Floyd	MAS, 1976
	JH Taylor	BOP, 1900
	JH Taylor	BOP, 1913
7	Fred Herd	USO, 1898
	Tony Jacklin	USO, 1970
	Cary Middlecoff	MAS, 1955
	Jack Nicklaus	PGA, 1980

Longest Gaps between Wins

11 years	Julius Boros (USO 1952 to USO 1963)
	Henry Cotton (BOP 1937 to BOP 1948)
	Ben Crenshaw (MAS 1984 to MAS 1995)
	Hale Irwin (USO 1979 to USO 1990)

Coincidentally these time spans bridge the same Major Championship. The longest span between victories in two different Majors is nine years for Gene Sarazen (PGA 1923 to BOP 1932). The longest gap between two wins in the same Major (although he achieved success elsewhere between-times) was 13 years for Ray Floyd (PGA 1969 to PGA 1982).

Most Runners-up (against no of wins)

1	**JACK NICKLAUS**	19 (18)
	(BOP7; USO 4; PGA 4; MAS 4)	
2	Arnold Palmer	10 (6)
	(BOP 1; USO 4; PGA 3; MAS 2)	
3 =	Greg Norman	8 (2)
	(BOP 1; USO 2; PGA 2; MAS 3)	
	Sam Snead	8 (6)
	(USO 4; PGA 2; MAS 2)	
4 =	JH Taylor	7 (5)
	(BOP6; USO 1)	
	Tom Watson	7 (8)
	(BOP 1; USO 2; PGA 1; MAS 3)	
6 =	Ben Hogan	6 (9)
	(USO 2; MAS 4)	
	Byron Nelson	6 (5)
	(USO 1; PGA 3; MAS 2)	
	Gary Player	6 (9)
	(USO 2; PGA 2; MAS 2)	
	Harry Vardon	6 (7)
	(BOP 4; USO 2)	
10 =	Ben Crenshaw	5 (2)
	(BOP 2; PGA 1; MAS 2)	
	Ray Floyd	5 (4)
	(BOP 1; PGA 1; MAS 3)	
	Tom Weiskopf	5 (1)
	(USO 1; MAS 4)	
	Craig Wood	5 (2)
	(BOP 1; USOP 1; PGA 1; MAS 2)	

It is also worth noting that the following players have recorded the most runner-up positions without ever winning a Major title:

Harry Cooper	4
(USO 2; MAS 2)	
Bruce Crampton*	4
(USO 1; PGA 2; MAS 1)	
Doug Sanders	4
(BOP 2; USO 1; PGA 1)	
Macdonald Smith	4
(BOP 2; USO 2)	
Andy Bean	3
(BOP 1; PGA 2)	
Chip Beck	3
(USO 2; MAS 1)	
Johnny Bulla	3
(BOP 2; MAS 1)	
Andrew Kirkaldy	3
(BOP 3)	
Tom McNamara	3
(USOP 3)	
Colin Montgomerie	3
(USOP 2; PGA 1)	
Ed Oliver	3
(USOP 1; PGA 1; MAS 1)	
Dai Rees	3
(BOP 3)	
Frank Stranahan	3
(BOP 2; MAS 1)	
Davie Strath	3
(BOP 3)	

On every occasion he was runner-up, Bruce Crampton was beaten by Jack Nicklaus!

Most Top 5 Finishes

1	**JACK NICKLAUS**	56
2 =	Arnold Palmer	26
	Sam Snead	26
4 =	Gene Sarazen	24
	Tom Watson	24
6 =	Walter Hagen	22
	Ben Hogan	22
8	Gary Player	19
9 =	Nick Faldo	18
	Byron Nelson	18
	Greg Norman	18
	JH Taylor	18
	Harry Vardon	18

The players with most top 5 finishes who have never recorded a win are:

Harry Cooper	11
Macdonald Smith	10
Bobby Cruickshank	8
Andrew Kirkaldy	8
Doug Sanders	8

The players with most top 5 finishes who have never recorded a win or a second place are:

Jay Haas	8
Ed Dudley	6
Bruce Devlin	6

Most Top 10 Finishes

1	**JACK NICKLAUS**	73
2	Sam Snead	46
3	Tom Watson	44
4	Gary Player	40
5	Ben Hogan	39
6	Arnold Palmer	38
7	Gene Sarazen	35
8 =	Ray Floyd	28
	Walter Hagen	28
	Byron Nelson	28

The players with most top 10 finishes who have never recorded a win are:

Ed Dudley	19
Bruce Devlin	16
Macdonald Smith	15

Most Top 20 Finishes

1	**JACK NICKLAUS**	84
2	Sam Snead	65
3	Tom Watson	61
4	Ray Floyd	60
5	Gary Player	56
6	Arnold Palmer	54
7	Gene Sarazen	52
8	Ben Hogan	45
8 =	Billy Casper	44
10	Lee Trevino	43

The players with most top 20 finishes who have never recorded a win are:

Ed Dudley	31
Bruce Devlin	25
Doug Sanders	24

Lowest Scores

Totals

267	**STEVE ELKINGTON**	Riviera CC, PGA 1995
	COLIN MONTGOMERIE*	Riviera CC, PGA 1995
	GREG NORMAN	Royal St George's, BOP 1993
268	Nick Price	Turnberry, BOP 1994
	Tom Watson	Turnberry, BOP 1977
269	Ernie Els*	Riviera CC, PGA 1995
	Nick Faldo*	Royal St George's, BOP 1993
	Davis Love III	Winged Foot, PGA 199
	Jeff Maggert*	Riviera CC, PGA 1995
	Jack Nicklaus*	Turnberry, BOP 1977
	Jesper Parnevik*	Turnberry, BOP 1994
	Nick Price	Southern Hills, PGA 1994
270	Nick Faldo	St Andrews, BOP 1990
	Bernhard Langer*	Royal St George's, BOP 1993
	Tiger Woods	Augusta National, MAS 1997
271	Brad Faxon*	Riviera CC, PGA 1995
	Ray Floyd	Augusta National, MAS 1976
	Tom Lehman	Royal Lytham, BOP 1996
	Bobby Nichols	Columbus CC, PGA 1964
	Jack Nicklaus	Augusta National, MAS 1965
	Tom Watson	Muirfield, BOP 1980
	Fuzzy Zoeller*	Turnberry, BOP 1994
272	Paul Azinger	Inverness, PGA 1993
	Ian Baker-Finch	Royal Birkdale, BOP 1991
	Ben Crenshaw*	Oakland Hills, PGA 1979
	Nick Faldo	Muirfield, BOP 1992
	Ray Floyd	Southern Hills, PGA 1982
	David Graham	Oakland Hills, PGA 1979
	Lee Janzen	Baltusrol, USO 1993
	Jack Nicklaus	Baltusrol, USO 1980
	Greg Norman*	Inverness, PGA 1993
	Corey Pavin*	Royal St George's, BOP 1993
	Peter Senior*	Royal St George's, BOP 1993
	Jeff Sluman	Oak Tree GC, PGA 1988

not winning totals

18 Holes

63	**MICHAEL BRADLEY**	Riviera CC, PGA 1995
	RAY FLOYD	Southern Hills, PGA 1982
	JACK NICKLAUS	Baltusrol, USO 1980
	GREG NORMAN	Augusta National, MAS 1996
	TOM WEISKOPF	Baltusrol, USO 1980
64	Rodger Davis	Muirfield, BOP 1987
	Mike Donald	Augusta National, MAS 1990
	Ray Floyd	Muirfield, BOP 1992
	Jim Gallagher, Jr	Riviera CC, PGA 1995
	Lee Mackey, Jr	Merion, USO 1950
	Lloyd Mangrum	Augusta National, MAS 1940
	Bobby Nichols	Columbus CC, PGA 1964
	Christy O'Connor, Jr	Royal St George's, BOP 1985
	Mark O'Meara	Riviera CC, PGA 1995
	Steve Pate	Muirfield, BOP 1982
	Scott Simpson	Inverness, PGA 1993
	Craig Stadler	Royal Birkdale, BOP 1983
	Doug Tewell	Cherry Hills, PGA 1985
	David Toms	Augusta National, MAS 1998

36 Holes

130	**NICK FALDO** (66,64)	Muirfield, BOP 1992
131	Ernie Els (66,65)	Riviera CC, PGA 1995
	Ray Floyd (65,66)	Augusta National, MAS 1976
	Mark O'Meara (64,67)	Riviera CC, PGA 1995
	Vijay Singh (68,63)	Inverness, PGA 1993
	Hal Sutton (65,66)	Riviera CC, PGA 1983
132	Nick Faldo (67,65)	St Andrews, BOP 1990
	Nick Faldo (69,63)	Royal St George's, BOP 1993
	Ray Floyd (63,69)	Southern Hills, PGA 1982
	Nick Price (67,65)	Southern Hills, PGA 1994

54 Holes

197	**ERNIE ELS** (66,65,66)	Riviera CC, PGA 1995	
198	Tom Lehman (67,67,64)	Royal Lytham, BOP 1996	
199	Nick Faldo (67,65,67)	St Andrews, BOP 1990	
200	Ray Floyd (63,69,68)	Southern Hills, PGA 1982	
	Jeff Maggert (66,69,65)	Riviera CC, PGA 1995	
	Mark O'Meara (64,67,69)	Riviera CC, PGA 1995	
201	Ray Floyd (65,66,70)	Augusta National, MAS 1976	
	Tiger Woods (70, 66,65)	Augusta National, MAS 1997	

MAJORS HALL OF FAME

Each year in the author's *The Golf Majors – Records and Yearbook* points are allocated to players for wins, second places, Top 5 etc. down to Top 30 finishes in the Majors. At the end of 1999, this is what the Top 20 list of all-time looked like, with the number of points amassed (1998 positions in brackets):

1	(1)	**JACK NICKLAUS**	697
2	(2)	Gary Player	383
3	(3)	Sam Snead	374
4	(4)	Tom Watson	362
5	(5)	Arnold Palmer	341
6	(6)	Walter Hagen	339
7	(7)	Ben Hogan	329
8	(8)	Gene Sarazen	320
9	(9)	Ray Floyd	256
10	(10)	Lee Trevino	241
11	(11)	Nick Faldo	236
12	(12)	Harry Vardon	232
13	(13)	Byron Nelson	231
14	(14)	Seve Ballesteros	207
15	(15)	JH Taylor	206
16 =	(16)	Billy Casper	203
	(18)	Greg Norman	203
18	(17)	Ben Crenshaw	197
19	(19)	Bobby Jones	189
20	(20)	Julius Boros	185

Some other movers:

28(37) Payne Stewart; 29(33) Nick Price; 40(43) Fred Couples; 67(92) Jose-Maria Olazabal; 75(76) Ernie Els; 81(90) Jay Haas; 89(92) Ian Woosnam; 95(-) Davis Love III

THE DEVELOPMENT OF THE RYDER CUP

The Ryder Cup has been through a very strange first 73 years. It almost expired at least twice, and even the very first official meeting nearly didn't happen. The one-sidedness of the competition, after a fairly even start to the matches, required the advent of World War II, paradoxically, to assist in the Cup's long-term continuity. By 1939, for example, the US had begun their first period of total dominance, and one can only imagine that with the likes of Nelson, Snead and Hogan in their early-1940s pomp, backed up by Demaret, Guldahl, the Mangrums and others, the interest in still a fairly young, and increasingly meaningless, fixture could have been snuffed out totally. By the end of the twentieth century, the Ryder Cup was not quite the competition the purists had in mind during the duelling days of the early twenties, when Brits could still cross the Atlantic to settle – or tour, even at advanced age – and plunder the US Open. But by 1927 it is hard to imagine that the Americans, at least, could see much of a future in such a series in a sport where Old World dominance had visibly and dramatically waned in the few years since the Armistice, swept away with the advent of the new US 'super' golfer, both professional and amateur. One can only surmise that when the first official matches started – after a few years of verbal argy-bargy – the Americans, stung by a one-off mauling in an *ad hoc* competiton in 1926, wanted quick revenge, and an opportunity for a few years to place on record its superiority over the British. For the Ryder Cup to be still around, and to have attained such an exalted status as a gobal event, not just in golf, but in sport in general, is really quite amazing, therefore. That it has survived, is down to the application of a number of 'fixes' along the way; some quick, some desperate, and one, at least, inspired. But how did it all start?

The origin of the idea to stage international matches between the best American professionals and those of Great Britain is a subject of debate among golf historians. 1909 US Open Champion and English exile, George Sargent, was PGA President during the early 1920s, and gave the credit for the idea to the wonderfully-monickered Sylvanus P Jermain, President of the Inverness Club in Toledo, Ohio, for first presenting the concept in 1921. However, Bob Harlow, founder of *Golf World* and former manager of Walter Hagen (yes, even then there were managers and agents about), claimed in 1951 that the

matches were first proposed in 1920 by James Harnett, who worked for *Golf Illustrated*. Harnett got the support he needed from a PGA of America AGM in December 1920, which advanced Harnett some funds to get things off the ground. The corollary of this was a series of informal matches played in 1921 in Gleneagles, Scotland, which the Americans tied in with other British events to make the trip worthwhile. Harnett, most likely with Hagen's assistance, selected the American team. The British soundly defeated the US Team, 9-3. In the same year, the professionals' amateur cousins had already got their proto-Walker Cup going, and in their unofficial match at Hoylake the score was exactly reversed. Interest in international golf was obviously there.

It was not until 1926, though, mainly because post-War Britain was not amenable to transatlantic jollies for the playing of golf, that another unofficial match for the professionals occurred. The R&A had decreed regional qualifying rounds before the Open Championship, forcing overseas US hopefuls to make their journeys earlier. With extra time on their hands, the American contingent agreed to form a team for an unofficial match against the British professionals at Wentworth. This time, the Americans were humiliated, 13$\frac{1}{2}$ to 1$\frac{1}{2}$. Abe Mitchell beat the reigning British Open Champion, Jim Barnes, 8&7, in the singles, and then partnered George Duncan in the Foursomes to hammer Hagen and Barnes, 9&8. Considering the considerable shift in the balance of power of the previous few years, this was a thumping the Americans could hardly have expected, and were certainly not going to leave unsanswered, if they could help it. It is conceivable, though, that if another five years were to elapse before the next unofficial scrap, even this considerable US dudgeon may have evaporated; their total dominance of the next few years' golfing itineraries, especially in Major championships, making such a competition irrelevant. However, events to formalise the fixture happened very quickly indeed: among the appreciative gallery was English seed merchant and entrepreneur, Samuel Ryder.

Ryder was a mail-order seed sales tycoon from St Albans, where he had also held the position of Mayor. In his youth he was a bit of a cricketer, but had never lifted a golf club in anger. Then, as is so often the case, he becamed consumed by the magic of the royal and ancient game only when taking it up for medical reasons after he was 50 years of age. Never one to endow his enthusiasms with half-measures, he engaged his own personal golf tutor. He hired, at the princely retainer of £1000 a year, arguably the best British player of the immediate post-Triumvirate years: the above-mentioned Mitchell, no less! You might say he had the bug.

Mitchell was the reason he came to Wentworth, and Ryder, now into his seventies, was struck particularly by the Americans' dignity in defeat and largesse towards their British opponents. Of course, deep-down, the visitors were feeling someway towards the other end of the emotional pendulum, but these were still the days when Corinthian values in sport were at least superficially displayed. Golf, the sport, and the way of life, had done yet another remarkable selling job on Mr Ryder that day.

After the matches Ryder met up with his tutor, who was in conversation with fellow Brit, Archie Duncan, American player Emmett French, and the still hugely-influential Walter Hagen. When Ryder muttered excitedly about doing something like this again, Duncan put it to him to provide a trophy which should be competed for at regular intervals. Ryder, fired with boyish enthusiasm, agreed at once, and commissioned Mappin & Webb to produce the £250 gold chalice that bears his name, with Abe Mitchell as the model for the golfer perched on top. (1927 was prone to such golden imagery: a secretary at Hollywood's Academy of Motion Pictures Arts and Sciences, so the legend goes, thought that their inaugural awards statuette reminded her of her Uncle Oscar!).

Unfortunately for Mitchell, he was to miss out on the first 'Ryder' Cup, which was held at the Worcester Country Club in New England, laid low with appendicitis, and Herbert Jolly stepped in. Samuel Ryder had to step in last minute, too, as the funds needed to send the British team to the States fell short by £500. He continued to support the home matches in person until his death in 1936, and his daughter Joan was still attending them almost a half a century later. The original deed demanded that only home-born and home-based players could represent either side; so either side was immediately shorn of people like Jim Barnes, Jock Hutchison and Tommy Armour, Brits already making their homes and careers in the US. The 1921 and 1926 formats were still adhered too: matchplay singles, and foursomes – pairs who play alternate shots with the same ball – which had a proving ground in the Walker Cup as well. Changes to the format throughout time were to be

expected, but for the first 32 years, remained as per 1927. (Details of the changes follow later within this section.) In 1927, the British were captained by one of golf's legends – Ted Ray – who had won the US Open in 1920, ahead of an ageing Harry Vardon, and others. Now Ray was 50 himself, the same age as Vardon was when they contested that event seven years earlier at the Inverness Club, in front of none other than Sylvanus P Jermain. Was this, maybe, the occasion which sparked off Mr J's putative brainwave for the 'Ryder' Cup? The American team was led by the first superstar of golf, and founding PGA of America stalwart, Walter Hagen. With such high-profile leaders, all looked promising that June when the teams met at the Worcester Club.

History tells us little more than the bald statistics: the Americans, so superior around, and on, the greens, and always able to talk a better game, demolished an overawed British team, 9½ - 2½; many of whom had only left Britain before to fight a war. Not an auspicious start for what was hoped was going to be a series of titanic struggles. Nevertheless, it was Britain who pulled off a surprising win at Moortown two years later, and the first four series of matches, through to 1933, were won by the home side. Without really thinking about it too much, the captain was initially one of the selected players, but in the 1933 matches, the British chose one of the Triumvirate, JH Taylor, to lead the team, leaving all the players to concentrate on playing only. Indeed, the Great Triumvirate had taken a good deal of interest in the matches from the outset, and the 1927 pioneers were picked to play by a committee made up of Taylor, Braid and Vardon.

The selection of the teams on both sides down the years has varied in concept enormously, but rather than clog up a nice story with the nitty-gritty here, there is a brief chronology on team selection procedure for both sides, courtesy of the PGA of America, at the end of this section.

In 1935, the US won easily once more on home soil, with Hagen in position as playing captain for the fifth and final time. Then, as non-playing captain in 1937, he broke the home-team's winning routine when his team of stars, established and emerging, convincingly triumphed at Southport and Ainsdale. There may have been no 'Haig', but there was still the mercurial Sarazen, and debuts for Byron Nelson and Sam Snead. With Ben Hogan waiting in the wings, and several others to boot, the first lucky break in the Cup's survival came when the 1939 fixture was postponed, pending some unpleasantries in Europe that needed attending to. It's not very often that anyone or anything can owe a debt of gratitude to World War Two; but with the British golfers now starting to lose heavily, both home and away, and with such a depth of talent beginning, like some kind of capillary action, to reach the surface in the States, it is difficult to envisage the competition continuing for too much longer. Whereas in Britain, there would be perhaps one outstanding product per generation (in the thirties it was Henry Cotton), the Americans could match that calibre of player at least ten times, and exceed it once or twice too.

With the outbreak of the War and the suspension of the Ryder Cup, both countries had more or less picked their sides for the 1939 event scheduled to be held at Florida's Ponte Vedra Country Club on 18-19 November. The eight out of ten players named for the British team that never was, were:

(Playing) Captain: Henry Cotton; Jimmy Adams, Dick Burton, Sam King, Alf Padgham, Dai Rees, Charles and Reg Whitcombe.

The US selected:

Captain: Walter Hagen; Vic Ghezzi, Ralph Guldahl, Jimmy Hines, Harold (Jug) McSpaden, Dick Metz, Byron Nelson, Henry Picard, Paul Runyan, Horton Smith, Sam Snead.

Indeed the Americans continued to pick 'Ryder Cup' teams that participated in internal challenge matches throughout the War to raise funds for the US Red Cross and other war-related efforts. Their wartime teams and fixtures were:

1940 Captain: Walter Hagen; Vic Ghezzi, Ralph Guldahl, Jimmy Hines, Dick Metz, Byron Nelson, Henry Picard, Horton Smith, Sam Snead. (Defeated Gene Sarazen's Challengers, 7-5; 16-17 July at Oakland Hills Country Club, Bloomfield Hills, Michigan.)

1941 Captain: Walter Hagen; Vie Ghezzi, Ralph Guldahl, Jimmy Hines, Harold (Jug) McSpaden, Dick Met:, Byron Nelson, Henry Picard, Paul Runyan, Horton Smith, Sam Snead. (Lost to Bobby Jones' Challengers 8½- 6½; 23-24 August at Detroit Golf Club.)

1942 Captain: Craig Wood; Jimmy Demaret, Ed Dudley Vie Ghezzi, Ben Hogan, Lloyd Mangrum, Harold (Jug) McSpaden, Byron Nelson,Gene Sarazen, Horton Smith. (Defeated Walter Hagen's Challengers;10-5,18-19 July at Oakland Hills Country Club.)

1943 Captain: Craig Wood; Jimmy Demaret, Vie Ghezzi, Lloyd Mangrum, Harold (Jug) McSpaden, Byron Nelson, Gene Sarazen, Al Watrous. (Defeated Walter Hagen's Challengers, 8½ to 3½; 7-8 August, at Plum Hollow Country Club, Detroit.)

The US, then, had already built a huge advantage in having player superiority in depth. Many of their players also missed the war and the PGA Tour, as it was, continued almost unbroken. Their British counterparts were not so lucky with the war being on their doorsteps. Few were able to maintain regular play, and many answered the call to arms. On being demobbed, the austere atmosphere pervading the whole of Europe deprived golf of money and, thus, potential professional players. There was not the spirit or the wherewithal to raise interest in the Ryder Cup when a resumption was mooted in 1947. As is often the case – Samuel Ryder being a case most obvious – some form of philanthropic gesture which supersedes the atmosphere of apathy (and the question of whether it was worth reviving a competition between class players and mere artisans) picks up destiny and runs away with it. The picker-upper here was an Oregon fruit grower called Robert A Hudson. It says something for the influence he had that even with an 11-1 embarrassment, the British were persuaded not to throw in the towel, and did much better at Ganton two years later.

Hudson supported other British visits to the States for a few years thereafter, when some woeful performances from them only suggested that they may have been taking the Michael; or in this case, the Robert. Indeed if it wasn't for gritty home showings at Ganton, and then again at Wentworth in 1953, maybe the Americans would be thinking twice about the whole thing once more. Then, in 1957, came the injection that the Ryder Cup needed: the first British win since 1933. Diminutive scrapper, Dai Rees, led an emotional sporting nation almost to tears, as TV stuck its first real pervasive lens into the matches in Britain for the first time. Galleries at the British-hosted Ryder Cups had always been large and enthusiastic: now through technology, the British sports fan at large became a golf fan for the first time. It had happened to other sports earlier in the decade: soccer, of course, with the Matthews Final of 1953; Roger Bannister's first-ever four-minute mile; and, the year before, the Devon Loch Grand National. Sport was a natural for TV. National sports like soccer, rugby and cricket would obviously benefit from such broad coverage: but, for the first time, a sport not high in the national consciousness, golf, was given its time in the limelight. Consequently, the Ryder Cup became, in Britain at least, now something to look forward to every two years, not some section of the sporting summaries on the inside of a newspaper's back page.

One swallow, etc: the Lindrick experience was powerful, it had to be. Given the maulings that the British experienced over the next decade, they needed every bit of morale stored up since 1957 just to keep going. As Hogan and Snead bowed out, there was no respite, as the amazing Arnold Palmer, both as player and motivator, took over. Paradoxically, Palmer, who injected fresh interest from US golfers in the Open Championship and the heritage of British Golf, was now doing his darndest (that's Palmer-parlance) to send the Ryder Cup into some ignominious demise. As if to say, we are going to exact every last ounce of revenge for Lindrick, the US came to Birkdake in 1969, with Jack Nicklaus making a belated bow, thinking, we are going to squeeze you to death. The British performance in 1969, spearheaded by the new Cotton, Tony Jacklin, gave the Americans a severe shock. The drama as the last singles pair approached the eighteenth green all square with the match likewise, gave everyone, on colour televison for the first time, and peeking through fingers on the fringes of the green, severe palpitations. The sportmanship of the Jack Nicklaus gesture, when ignoring the Emperor's down-turned thumb and sparing Jacklin that putt at the death, was an unique occasion in sport. Despite Nicklaus never receiving a Christmas card from captain Sam Snead ever again, everyone acknowledged that the Ryder Cup, tied for the first time in history, was now an occasion – one that Sam Ryder had striven for, but never really saw.

So, once more, the inevitable seemed postponed for a while longer, and the fixture lived for a few more years on the inertia of events at Birkdale. Officially, in 1973, the British team became Great Britain and Ireland, even though Christy O'Connor Sr had been playing under the Union flag since 1957. For many years the ruling with regard to residency and the circuit on which a golfer played had been relaxed, but the move was seen as a diplomatic one which was favoured by the US. The Americans had reverted to type since 1969, and by 1977 had easily won all four matches that decade, to date. The 1977 series had

reached a new low, with player power demanding a less-hectic schedule. The resulting pedestrian continuity of play bored the usually supportive British golf fans stiff; and as a result, the matches were played in an atmosphere akin to that found in a Trappist monastery. To add to it, the US won, very comfortably, their eighteenth out of 22 Ryder Cups played, and were on the point of taking their ball home.

Then, for the second time in eight years, Jack Nicklaus was very much responsible for saving the ailing non-entity. Since 1933, a win at Lindrick and a tie at Brikdale was all that Great Britain (and Ireland) could boast. Surely after another debacle in 1977, perhaps fittingly after a full 50 years, it was time to put the moribund excuse for a sporting contest to final rest. Nicklaus, though, gentleman, sportsman and one for whom the history of golf held so much, suggested that a transplant was the only way to save the dying man. Once initial opposition from the most deep-rooted chauvinists within the British PGA was swept away, the operation took place. A couple of token Spaniards were included in a new 'Europe' team selected to take on the US in 1979: inauspicious, perhaps, but either this was the first chapter of the sequel, or the last chapter of the Ryder Cup for ever. Two series of matches; the emergence of Seve Ballesteros as the most exciting player in the world; and the return of Tony Jacklin, were all that were needed for the publisher to sign a new contract. After the US' narrow win in 1983, the Ryder Cup, as we know it today – a passionate, thunderously exciting sporting pageant of inordinate quality – was played at the Belfry for the first time; a timely tribute to the Ryder family, as daughter Joan witnessed the matches for the last time, and called them 'the most exciting ever'.

She didn't come close! Sam Torrance, the lake, the carnival afterwards – immediate recollections of a momentous day in sporting history. Jacklin's creed was being absorbed; his coaxing, his enthusiam, his energy, were all rubbing off. Faldo, Langer, Lyle and Woosnam, were now world stars in their own right, and could stack up against anything the Americans could muster. Oh, and Ballesteros. What inspirations these were to be: not just in 1985, but for the first win on US soil at, so ironically, Nicklaus' own Muirfield Village, with Jack as US captain; and again in the heart-stopping tie (and Cup retention) in 1989. Lyle may have gone by the end of the decade, but

another Spaniard, Olazabal, was to come in and form, with
Seve, the best-ever partnership in Ryder Cup history.
Personnel had improved, but the greatest legacy of Jacklin
was to instil into the lesser mortals the belief they could
overcome these US icons.

Honours, from then on, as the end of the twentieth
century came to a close, were fairly even. With this new-
found competitiveness, arose, unfortunately, some
unpleasantness, particularly among the crowds supporting
both sides. A US hardening to the indignity of regular
defeat for the first time led to an escalation of crowd
'partisanship', to use a polite euphemism, and to a distinct
xenophobic undertone in some of the press on both sides.
The 'War on the Shore', the intense drama of the Kiawah
Island matches in 1991, was the start. Thoughout the
nineties, there was an unwanted growth in heckling, cat-
calling and jeering amongst the galleries; then, after two
successive European wins in 1995 and 1997, including
the first ever matches to be held in continental Europe,
came the 'Battle of Brookline'. Justin Leonard's marvellous
45-foot putt on Francis Ouimet's seventeenth green to win
the Cup back for America, set in motion a series of events,
which, for the first time in over seventy years, witnessed
uncontrolled jubilation among the players. The local daily,
the *Boston Globe*, referring to the 'battle', announced that
'golf had got a black eye'. Once players forget the etiquette
which holds the game of golf together, and their opponents
are disadvantaged because of it, the sport spirals into the
depths that some others have already gone, never to
resurface the same. It is to be hoped in 2001 at the Belfry
and, perhaps more importantly, at Oakland Hills two years
later, the spirit of old will return to complement the
competition of recent times. Together, these characteristics
will make the future of the Ryder Cup an unsurpassable
spectacle for golf fans on both sides of the Atlantic. I am,
you may have gathered, an incurable romantic!

COURSE:	Worcester CC
LOCATION:	Worcester, Massachusetts
DATE:	3-4 June
US CAPTAIN:	Walter Hagen (playing)
GB CAPTAIN:	Ted Ray (playing)
RESULT:	US – 9½ GB 2½

Despite the elation among professional golfers and the cognoscenti over the unofficial win the previous year, the public mood in the Britain for the Ryder Cup was disappointing in the approach to the first formal competition in 1927. The team, selected by the Great Triumvirate, no less, had the dickens of a job raising funds for the trip to America. Once blood had been finally squeezed from the stone (the stone being none other than Samuel Ryder, himself, who stumped up the final £500 needed), and they were just about to get under way, team captain Abe Mitchell was struck by appendicitis. The team couldn't delay, so off they sailed from Southampton on the *Aquitania,* getting word to Herbert Jolly, at home in Jersey, to pack his bags and follow on. The main core of the party arrived in New York four days ahead of Jolly, who had subsequently boarded the *Majestic* in something of a daze. Following the format already employed by the Walker Cup of four foursomes and eight singles, play got under way at the Worcester Country Club, and soon it became apparent that the Americans wanted to put the spat of 1926 firmly behind them. The British team were in surprisingly good spirits, considering their preparation, but that was soon to change. Immediately, it seemed, the pattern of events for the next 50 years or so (with one or two exceptions on the way) was set. The US ran out 3-1 winners on the first day, having comfortably claimed the first three matches; thereby creating the supreme confidence which led to a near whitewash in the second day singles. Only Charles Whitcombe survived the debacle unbowed, with a win and a half; and the British must have been wondering what they had begun to let themselves in for every two years. Ted Ray, at 50, was the oldest British competitor ever, and only Ray Floyd was to be older on either side, in 1993.

US TEAM	GB TEAM
Leo Diegel (1)	Aubrey Boomer (1)
Al Espinosa (1)	Archie Compston (1)
Johnny Farrell (1)	George Duncan (1)
Johnny Golden (1)	George Gadd (1)
Walter Hagen (1)	Arthur Havers (1)
Bill Mehlhorn (1)	Herbert Jolly (1)
Gene Sarazen (1)	Ted Ray (1)
Joe Turnesa (1)	Fred Robson (1)
Al Watrous (1)	Charles Whitcombe (1)

(Figures in brackets denote the number of Ryder Cup appearances)

Foursomes (Day 1)

Hagen & Golden (2&1) beat Ray & Robson	1-0
Farrell & Turnesa (8&6) beat Compston & Duncan	2-0
Sarazen & Watrous (3&2) beat Havers & Jolly	3-0
Diegel & Mehlhorn lost to Boomer & Whitcombe (7&5)	3-1
Day 1 totals	**3-1**

Singles (Day 2)

Mehlhorn (1 up) beat Compston	1-0
Farrell (5&4) beat Boomer	2-0
Golden (8&7) beat Jolly	3-0
Diegel (7& 5) beat Ray	4-0
Sarazen halved with Whitcombe	4½-½
Hagen (2&1) beat Havers	5½-½
Watrous (3&2) beat Robson	6½-½
Turnesa lost to Duncan (1 up)	6½-1½
Day 2 totals	**6½-1½**
MATCH TOTALS	*9½-2½*

1929

COURSE:	Moortown GC
LOCATION:	Leeds, England
DATE:	26-27 May
GB CAPTAIN:	George Duncan (playing)
US CAPTAIN:	Walter Hagen (playing)
RESULT:	GB 7 – US 5

As it happened, the next few years were to see the GB team more or less hold their own against some very strong-looking American sides. the 1929 matches at the Moortown club threw up an altogether more exciting series than the one-sided affair of two years earlier. Large crowds, often partisan, turned out over the two days to see the home team make a much better fist of the foursomes this time, thus giving themselves a chance on the second day.

Charles Whitcombe became a national hero with his hammering of 1928 US Open Champion, Johnny Farrell. He not only levelled the match score, but became the only undefeated British and Irish golfer after two Ryder Cup series (Johnny Golden would be the sole American, surprisingly, and he was omitted from the singles, only playing in three matches to Whitcombe's four). In a clash of the captains, Hagen was sensationally thumped, losing with eight holes remaining: Sarazen was also unceremoniously dumped by Compston, while Aubrey Boomer pulled off a surprise win over Joe Turnesa. However, it was the 22 year-old Henry Cotton, chipping in to even things up at halfway with Al Watrous, who finally nailed the Americans down. While Charlie Whitcombe's brother Ernie was holding Espinosa at bay, Cotton displayed a maturity beyond his years to see off Watrous, and pull off a famous victory for the home side.

Foursomes (Day 1)

Compston & C Whitcombe halved with Farrell & Turnesa	½-½
Boomer & Duncan lost to Diegel & Espinosa (7&5)	½-1½
Mitchell & Robson (2&1) beat Dudley & Sarazen	1½-1½
Cotton & E Whitcombe lost to Golden & Hagen (2 up)	1½-2½
Day 1 totals	**1½-2½**

Singles (Day 2)

C Whitcombe (8&6) beat Farrell	1 - 0
Duncan (10&8) beat Hagen	2 - 0
Mitchell lost to Diegel (9&8)	2 - 1
Compston (6&4) beat Sarazen	3 - 1
Boomer (4&3) beat Turnesa	4 - 1
Robson lost to Smith (4&2)	4 - 2
Cotton (4&3) beat Watrous	5 - 2
E Whitcombe halved with Espinosa	5½-2½
Day 2 totals	**5½-2½**
MATCH TOTALS	**7-5**

GB TEAM	US TEAM
Percy Alliss (1)	Leo Diegel (2)
Aubrey Boomer (2)	Ed Dudley (1)
Stewart Burns (1)	Al Espinosa (2)
Archie Compston (2)	Johnny Farrell (2)
Henry Cotton (1)	Johnny Golden (2)
George Duncan (2)	Walter Hagen (2)
Abe Mitchell (1)	Gene Sarazen (2)
Fred Robson (1)	Horton Smith (2)
Charles Whitcombe (2)	Joe Turnesa (2)
Ernest Whitcombe (1)	Al Watrous (2)

COURSE:	Scioto CC
LOCATION:	Columbus, Ohio
DATE:	26-27 June
US CAPTAIN:	Walter Hagen
GB CAPTAIN:	Charles Whitcombe (playing)
RESULT:	US 9 – GB 3

Politics, red tape and general silliness rather spoiled the 1931 series at the Scioto Club as a meaningful competition. The original Trust Deed concerning the Ryder Cup matches specifically disbarred players who were not natives of their country, or even resident. This means that GB could not even consider for selection players of the calibre of Aubrey Boomer, because of his association with clubs in Belgium (the Royal Golf Club) and France (Paris, St Cloud); or Percy Alliss, initially included in the team, who was the professional at the Wannsee Club, Berlin. The US had a similar predicament, in that naturalised Americans – Jim Barnes and Jock Hutchison in the inaugural event particularly, while they were still in their pomp; and more latterly, Tommy Armour – were also disqualified. Britain's PGA then exacerbated the position by throwing in a petty rule of their own: that all players must sail out to the States and back as one party. Henry Cotton, as the new shining light in the British game, should have been encouraged to spend more time on the US circuit, but instead of receiving the PGA's blessing to stay and play tournaments he had committed to after the Cup matches, they withdrew his invitation.

Whereas the US may have found suitable replacements falling out of locker rooms all over the country, the sparse resources of the visitors were exposed from the outset. The Americans cruised to a 2-0 foursomes lead with many holes to spare, and only Mitchell and Robson saved the away side's blushes on the first day. The even more exposed nature of the singles cruelly really found them out on Day 2, with the US, led by Burke's and Sarazen's easy opening wins, sweeping aside the opposition with some disdain.

US TEAM	GB TEAM
Billy Burke (1)	Percy Alliss (1)*
Wiffy Cox (1)	Archie Compston (3)
Leo Diegel (3)	Bill Davies (1)
Al Espinosa (3)	George Duncan (3)
Johnny Farrell (3)	Syd Easterbrook (1)
Walter Hagen (3)	Arthur Havers (2)
Gene Sarazen (3)	Bert Hodson (1)
Denny Shute (1)	Abe Mitchell (2)
Horton Smith (2)	Fred Robson (3)
Craig Wood (1)	Charles Whitcombe (3)
	Ernest Whitcombe (2)

* Not allowed to compete

Foursomes (Day 1)

Farrell & Sarazen (8&7) beat		
Compston & Davies		1 - 0
Hagen & Shute (10&9) beat		
Duncan & Havers		2 - 0
Diegel & Espinosa lost to		
Mitchell & Robson (3&1)		2 - 1
Burke & Cox (3&2) beat		
Easterbrook & E Whitcombe		3 - 1
Day 1 totals		**3 - 1**

Singles (Day 2)

Burke (7&6) beat Compston	1 - 0
Sarazen (7&6) beat Robson	2 - 0
Farrell lost to Davies (4&3)	2 - 1
Cox (3&1) beat Mitchell	3 - 1
Hagen (4&3) beat C Whitcombe	4 - 1
Shute (8&6) beat Hodson	5 - 1
Espinosa (2&1) beat E Whitcombe	6 - 1
Craig Wood lost to Havers (4&3)	6 - 2
Day 2 totals	**6 - 2**
MATCH TOTALS	*9-3*

COURSE:	Southport & Ainsdale GC
LOCATION:	Southport, Lancashire, England
DATE:	26-27 June
GB CAPTAIN:	JH Taylor (non-playing)
US CAPTAIN:	Walter Hagen (playing)
RESULT:	GB 6½ – US 5½

John H Taylor ran a tough outfit in the 1933 matches; with physical training, no less, and *Chariots of Fire* excursions along Southport beach. The Americans for once were a little wet behind the ears, in that not many had played links golf before, and only four had previously visited Britain. The home side had to make do without Cotton again (now resident in Belgium), but looked a match for the visitors. The crowds once again were huge for the day, even bigger than at Moortown, and they roared on the home side, as for once the Americans could not steal a march in the foursomes.

The second day was the greatest day of drama so far in the fledgling Ryder Cup – fitting, perhaps, that is was the last day's play witnessed by Samuel Ryder before he died. His vision could be appreciated, at least in microcosm, for what he was trying to achieve: it would take the event longer than he could ever have imagined to reach its optimum set-up, but at least he, and some 15000 others that day, got a feel of how great a sporting event could be on one of its very best occasions.

Nip-and-tuck, the protagonists went at it all day, with heroics performed everywhere. After some early reverses, Alliss and Havers seemed to have turned things the hosts' way, but the last two matches were close, with holes running out. Whitcombe then succumbed to Horton Smith; and a tantalising, charging putt from Shute at the last, against a quaking Easterbrook, nearly won it for the Americans. Unfortunately it slipped four feet or more past the hole: Shute failed to sink it coming back and the series stood even again, with all the matches so far home wins.

GB TEAM / US TEAM

GB TEAM	US TEAM
Percy Alliss (2)	Billy Burke (2)
Allan Dailey (1)	Leo Diegel (4)
Bill Davies (2)	Ed Dudley (2)
Syd Easterbrook (2)	Olin Dutra (1)
Arthur Havers (3)	Walter Hagen (4)
Arthur Lacey (1)	Paul Runyan (1)
Abe Mitchell (3)	Gene Sarazen (4)
Alf Padgham (1)	Denny Shute (2)
Alf Perry (1)	Horton Smith (3)
Charles Whitcombe (4)	Craig Wood (2)

Foursomes (Day 1)

Alliss & Whitcombe halved with	
Hagen & Sarazen	½-½
Havers & Mitchell (3&2) beat	
Dutra & Shute	1½-½
Davies & Easterbrook (1 up) beat	
Runyan & Wood	2½-½
Padgham & Perry lost to	
Burke & Dudley (1 up)	2½-1½
Day 1 totals	**2½-1½**

Singles (Day 2)

Padgham lost to Sarazen (6&4) beat	0 - 1	
Mitchell (9&8) beat Dutra	1 - 1	
Lacey lost to Hagen (2&1)	1 - 2	
Davies lost to Wood (4&3)	1 - 3	
Alliss (2&1) beat Runyan	2 - 3	
Havers (4&3) beat Diegel	3 - 3	
Easterbrook (1 up) beat Shute	4 - 3	
Whitcombe lost to Smith (2&1)	4 - 4	
Day 2 totals	**4 - 4**	
MATCH TOTALS	6½ - 5½	

COURSE:	Ridgewood CC
LOCATION:	Ridgewood, New Jersey
DATE:	28-29 September
US CAPTAIN:	Walter Hagen (playing)
GB CAPTAIN:	Charles Whitcombe (playing)
RESULT:	US 9 – GB 3

There was a certain sense of *déja vu* in that the captains and the score were identical to 1931 at Scioto. Sadly it was becoming a little predictable: close-fought matches so far in Britain; but quite embarrassing maulings in the sticky heat of an American summer for the visitors. The American team was now bristling with talent: Sarazen, Smith, Dutra, Runyan and Parks, were all Major Championship winners since the last event; and Johnny Revolta would go on to collect the US PGA title later that autumn. The away team boasted the first three in the Open Championship that year (Perry, Padgham and Charles Whitcombe) but only Henry Picard out of the American team even competed; and the 1934 Champion, Henry Cotton, was still exiled. After the first three matches in the foursomes were non-events, it needed Ernie and Charlie, two of the three Whitcombe boys on show, to save the Old World blushes on Day 1.

The first four singles went the way of the US the following day; and the match was already won before there was really any contest. Percy Alliss' solitary singles win, after it was all too late, summed up the British misery. US captain, Walter Hagen, knew he had enough in hand to take the day off (at least from playing). It was all so easy. This was to be his last ever appearance as a Ryder Cup player, having been a prime mover in setting up the competition. Just as one would imagine, he left a pretty impressive Cup record for anyone to follow: 7(Won) - 1 (Lost) - 1 (Halved).

US TEAM	GB TEAM
Olin Dutra (2)	Percy Alliss (3)
Walter Hagen (5)	Dick Burton (1)
Ky Laffoon (1)	Jack Busson (1)
Sam Parks, Jr (1)	Bill Cox (1)
Henry Picard (1)	Edward Jarman (1)
Johnny Revolta (1)	Alf Padgham (2)
Paul Runyan (2)	Alf Perry (2)
Gene Sarazen (5)	Charles Whitcombe (5)
Horton Smith (4)	Ernest Whitcombe (3)
Craig Wood (3)	Reg Whitcombe (1)

Foursomes (Day 1)

Hagen & Sarazen (7&6) beat Busson & Perry	1 - 0
Picard & Revolta (6&5) beat Alliss & Padgham	2 - 0
Runyan & Smith (9&8) Cox & Jarman	3 - 0
Dutra & Laffoon lost to C & E Whitcombe (1 up)	3 - 1
Day 1 totals	**3 - 1**

Singles (Day 2)

Sarazen (3&2) beat Busson	1 - 0
Runyan (5&3) beat Burton	2 - 0
Revolta (2&1) beat R Whitcombe	3 - 0
Dutra (4&2) beat Padgham	4 - 0
Craig Wood lost to Alliss (1 up)	4 - 1
Smith halved with Cox	4½-1½
Picard (3&2) beat E Whitcombe	5½-1½
Parks halved with Perry	6 - 2
Day 2 totals	**6 - 2**
MATCH TOTALS	*9 - 3*

COURSE:	Southport & Ainsdale GC
LOCATION:	Southport, Lancashire, England
DATE:	29-30 June
GB CAPTAIN:	Charles Whitcombe (playing)
US CAPTAIN:	Walter Hagen (non-playing)
RESULT:	GB 4 – US 8

The US team became the first to win away from home, and the Southport & Ainsdale Club became the first venue to be used on more than one occasion. This was some formidable outfit that Walter Hagen, now as a non-playing captain, had brought back to Lancashire four years on. Every player was, or was soon to be, a Major Championship winner, and they were up against a fairly ageing side. For GB, the Americans would only fear the past exploits of Percy Alliss, perhaps, now that Charlie Whitcombe seemed to be happy to sit out the singles contests, whilst the return of Cotton after eight years was of some concern to them. Newcomers Sam King and young Dai Rees were the only unknown quantities that could, perhaps, cause them an upset.

This was to prove partly right, but the visitors were soon into their stride in the foursomes, coming back strongly after a promising home start fizzled out, to lead by just one intriguing point after the first day. Rees proved to be the unknown problem, as he and Cotton brought the scores equal at 4-4 during the singles. Hopes were starting to build that the others still out would just get back on terms in later matches. However, an outstanding Sam Snead debut singles win over Dick Burton led the Americans home without dropping a further point. The next match in the series, set for the Ponte Vedra Club in Florida for November 1939, was tragically superseded by another form of war, altogether less agreeable. The Ryder Cup therefore faced a ten-year enforced sabbatical, before its eventual resumption in the autumn of 1947.

GB TEAM	US TEAM
Percy Alliss (4)	Ed Dudley (3)
Dick Burton (2)	Ralph Guldahl (1)
Henry Cotton (2)	Tony Manero (1)
Bill Cox (2)	Byron Nelson (1)
Sam King (1)	Henry Picard (2)
Arthur Lacey (1)	Johnny Revolta (2)
Alf Padgham (3)	Gene Sarazen (6)
Alf Perry (3)	Denny Shute (3)
Dai Rees (1)	Horton Smith (4)
Charles Whitcombe (6)	Sam Snead (1)

Foursomes (Day 1)

Cotton & Padgham lost to	
Dudley & Nelson (4&2)	0 - 2
Cox & Lacey lost to	
Guldahl & Manero (2&1)	0 - 2
Rees & Whitcombe halved with	
Sarazen & Shute	½-2½
Alliss & Burton (2&1)	
Picard & Revolta	1½-2½
Day 1 totals	**1½-2½**

Singles (Day 2)

Padgham lost to Guldahl (8&7)	0 - 1
King halved with Shute	½-1½
Rees (3&1) beat Nelson	1½-1½
Cotton (5&3) beat Manero	2½-1½
Alliss lost to Sarazen (1 up)	2½-2½
Burton lost to Snead (5&4)	2½-3½
Perry lost to Dudley (2&1)	2½-4½
Lacey lost to Picard (2&1)	2½-5½
Day 2 totals	**2½-5½**
MATCH TOTALS	*4 - 8*

COURSE:	Portland GC
LOCATION:	Portland, Oregon
DATE:	1-2 November
US CAPTAIN:	Ben Hogan (playing)
GB CAPTAIN:	Henry Cotton (playing)
RESULT:	US 11 – GB 1

Just as Samuel Ryder took the bull by the horns to set up the competition after seeing its potential back in 1926, so the Ryder Cup needed another catalyst to give it its momentum after the break for the hostilities. Post-war austerity in Europe made a return to competition in 1947 remote; and the event itself could easily have foundered at this point. Then riding out of the Pacific North West on his white charger came one Robert Hudson. He not only offered the services of the Portland Club to host the matches, he paid for the British team's passages and provided food hampers for the players to take back! This may look very patronising today, but at the time, the average British pro was scraping a living in a profession which itself seemed almost illicit in the context of everyday events. Moreover, Hudson continued this largesse towards British teams in the Ryder Cup series well after rationing had finished.

It would be easy to make excuses for the near-whitewash. The US Tour had kept going throughout the War, although several of the US team had seen active service. Unofficial 'Ryder Cup' teams had been selected each year during the enforced break, and put into competition against other US 'star' teams. The visitors' journey on the *Queen Mary*, plus a four-day train hike to the West Coast, meant they would be travelling for the best part of a month, both ways, for two days of competitive golf. All points are valid. However, this was a mean US team, led by one of the greatest winners of them all, Ben Hogan. Gone may be the greats, Hagen and Sarazen, and other slightly lesser mortals; but Hogan, along with Snead and Nelson, would be in most people's Top 10 Greats of all time; and Demaret, Mangrum and the others, were all as tough as they come. That only one match out of 12 reached the final hole over two days' play, just emphasises how easy the US win was. Just imagine how Herman Keiser must have felt, though.

US TEAM	GB TEAM
Herman Barron (1)	Jimmy Adams (1)
Jimmy Demaret (1)	Henry Cotton (3)
Dutch Harrison (1)	Fred Daly (1)
Ben Hogan (1)	Max Faulkner (1)
Herman Keiser (1)	Eric Green (1)
Lloyd Mangrum (1)	Reg Horne (1)
Byron Nelson (2)	Sam King (2)
Ed Oliver (1)	Arthur Lees (1)
Sam Snead (2)	Dai Rees (2)
Lew Worsham (1)	Charlie Ward (1)

Foursomes (Day 1)

Oliver & Worsham (10&9) beat	
Cotton & Lees	1 - 0
Mangrum & Snead (6&5) beat	
Daly & Ward	2 - 0
Demaret & Hogan (2 up) beat	
Adams & Faulkner	3 - 0
Barron & Nelson (2&1) beat	
King & Rees	4 - 0
Day 1 totals	**4 - 0**

Singles (Day 2)

Harrison (5&4) beat Daly	1 - 0
Worsham (3&2) beat Adams	2 - 0
Mangrum (6&5) beat Faulkner	3 - 0
Oliver (4&3) beat Ward	4 - 0
Nelson (2&1) beat Lees	5 - 0
Demaret (3&2) beat Rees	6 - 0
Herman Keiser lost to King (4&3)	6 - 1
Day 2 totals	**6 - 1**
MATCH TOTALS	*11 - 1*

COURSE:	Ganton GC
LOCATION:	Scarborough, Yorkshire, England
DATE:	16-17 September
GB CAPTAIN:	Charles Whitcombe (non-playing)
US CAPTAIN:	Ben Hogan (non-playing)
RESULT:	GB 5 – US 7

Henry Cotton had 'queried' the legality of Ben Hogan's golf balls in Portland in 1947. He couldn't believe the amount of backspin the great man was getting from the ball. All seemed in order, however, and with the Americans taking the moral high ground, they proceeded to give the British team a good stuffing – in the name of fair play, of course. Was Hogan just getting his own back in 1949 when he 'queried' the grooves on some British clubs? Whatever, Bernard Darwin, the golf-writers' guru, then a member of the R&A Rules Committee, agreed with Ben, and poor old Ganton pro, Jock Ballantine, spent the entire night before the foursomes filing away the offending grooves.

If Cotton's wheeze had backfired and Hogan's trumping of his card gave the US the white hats and GB the black ones, the home team came at the Americans in the foursomes in a perfidious ambush. Completely unexpected, going against the script, almost not being British, the hosts murdered their guests on that first day; only Demaret and Heafner surviving the carnage. What sweet revenge for 1947 it seemed. By the middle of the second afternoon, though, the mugging was over. Adams and Rees had kept the home side two points ahead after half the singles, but victory was even then doubtful with the remaining four matches moving heavily America's way. So it was to prove. The bulldog's teeth had been drawn, and the eagle soared away with the spoils yet again.

GB TEAM

Jimmy Adams (2)
Laurie Ayton (1)
Ken Bousfield (1)
Dick Burton (3)
Fred Daly (2)
Max Faulkner (2)
Sam King (3)
Arthur Lees (2)
Dai Rees (3)
Charlie Ward (2)

US TEAM

Skip Alexander (1)
Jimmy Demaret (2)
Bob Hamilton (1)
Chick Harbert (1)
Dutch Harrison (2)
Clayton Heafner (1)
Lloyd Mangrum (2)
Johnny Palmer (1)
Sam Snead (3)

Foursomes (Day 1)

Adams & Faulkner (2&1) beat Harrison & Palmer	1 - 0	
Bousfield & Daly (4&2) beat Alexander & Hamilton	2 - 0	
King & Ward lost to Demaret and Heafner (4&3)	2 - 1	
Burton & Lees (1 up) Mangrum & Snead	3 - 1	
Day 1 totals	**3 - 1**	

Singles (Day 2)

Faulkner lost to Harrison (8&7)	0 - 1
Adams (2&1) beat Palmer	1 - 1
Ward lost to Snead (6&5)	1 - 2
Rees (6&4) beat Hamilton	2 - 2
Burton lost to Heafner (3&2)	2 - 3
King lost to Harbert (4&3)	2 - 4
Lees lost to Demaret (7&6)	2 - 5
Daly lost to Mangrum (4&3)	2 - 6
Day 2 totals	**2 - 6**
MATCH TOTALS	**5 - 7**

COURSE:	Pinehurst CC
LOCATION:	Pinehurst, North Carolina
DATE:	2-4 November
US CAPTAIN:	Sam Snead (playing)
GB CAPTAIN:	Arthur Lacey (non-playing)
RESULT:	US 9 – GB 2½

What a shame such glorious surroundings as Pinehurst No.2 should play host to so poor a competition. Of course, that was the not the fault of the hosts, who really didn't have to play inspired golf to thrash what was a sorry British team. Lees and Ward did even the scores early on in the foursomes, but really, the writing was on the wall once Heafner and Burke took reigning Open Champion Faulkner, and perennial scrapper, Rees, apart in the first foursomes match. Thereafter only a 100% record from Lees saved the visitors from total ignominy.

Another, even more remarkable 100% score was to occur during the matches. Jimmy Demaret bowed out of Ryder Cup competition, with a perfect score: three Ryder Cups, a 6-0-0 sequence, and a record which has yet to be equalled for the number of matches played. Demaret, on being commended by Dai Rees for the ten out of 11 sand saves he made which surely earned him his result over the Welshman, generously gave the sand wedge to his opponent.

US TEAM	GB TEAM
Skip Alexander (2)	Jimmy Adams (3)
Jack Burke, Jr (1)	Ken Bousfield (2)
Jimmy Demaret (3)	Fred Daly (3)
Dutch Harrison (3)	Max Faulkner (3)
Clayton Heafner (1)	Jack Hargreaves (1)
Ben Hogan (2)	Arthur Lees (3)
Lloyd Mangrum (3)	John Panton (1)
Ed Oliver (2)	Dai Rees (4)
Henry Ransom (1)	Charlie Ward (3)
Sam Snead (4)	Harry Weetman (1)

Foursomes (Day 1)

Burke & Heafner (5&3) beat Faulkner & Rees	1 - 0
Oliver & Ransom lost to Lees & Ward (2&1)	1 - 1
Mangrum & Snead (5&4) beat Adams & Panton	2 - 1
Demaret & Hogan (5&4) beat Bousfield & Daly	3 - 1
Day 1 totals	**3 - 1**

Singles (Day 2)

Burke (4&3) beat Adams	1 - 0
Demaret (2 up) beat Rees	2 - 0
Heafner halved with Daly	2½-½
Mangrum (6&5) beat Weetman	3½-½
Oliver lost to Lees (2&1)	3½-1½
Hogan (3&2) beat Ward	4½-1½
Alexander (8&7) beat Panton	5½-1½
Snead (4&3) beat Faulkner	6½-1½
Day 2 totals	**6½-1½**
MATCH TOTALS	*9½ - 2½*

COURSE:	Wentworth GC
LOCATION:	Virginia Water, Surrey, England
DATE:	2-3 October
GB CAPTAIN:	Henry Cotton (non-playing)
US CAPTAIN:	Lloyd Mangrum (playing)
RESULT:	GB 5½ – US 6½

Classy Wentworth's famous West Course played host to the 1953 series of matches, which the Americans came to without the all-conquering Ben Hogan. Earlier that year he collected the three Major Championships he had entered for, but had already made it a policy to forego the week-long physical purgatory that was the US PGA Championship, since his much-reported 1949 road accident. Although he took part in 1951, he now felt that he could not do justice to the 36-hole matchplay marathon which was prevalent in Ryder Cup matches at the time. He was to be missed, as a spirited display by Britain, let down only by Cotton's naive foursomes strategy, only narrowly failed to win the Cup for the first time in 20 years.

Leaving out experienced campaigners Faulkner and Rees, Cotton gave all the new boys a chance; but it backfired, and it was only Bradshaw, paired with fellow-Irishman Daly, who won through on the first day. Eric Brown and Bernard Hunt, in their respective debut matches, with their partners, each received a fearful hammering: Burke and Kroll, for example, combined to shoot a wonderful, and uncatchable, 66-equivalent over the morning 18. Rees couldn't get the better of Jack Burke when he was eventually let loose in the first singles match; but whole-hearted, successive wins for Daly (9&7 over Kroll), Brown and Weetman (over Mangrum and Snead, respectively), suddenly put the home side back in the frame. Faulkner went down to Middlecoff, but in the last three matches there was all to play for. Bradshaw heroically gained his second point on his first appearance; and the penultimate match would go on to tie. Meanwhile, ahead at the seventeenth, young Peter Alliss, son of Percy, drove out of bounds to drop two shots in two holes and go one down to Joe Turnesa. Joe, after Jim, the second of the brothers to represent the US in the Ryder Cup, halved the hole with a six, after both players displayed a fit of nerves on the greens; and the Cup was retained for another two years.

GB TEAM	US TEAM
Jimmy Adams (4)	Jack Burke, Jr (1)
Peter Alliss (1)	Walter Burkemo (1)
Harry Bradshaw (1)	Dave Douglas (1)
Eric Brown (1)	Fred Haas, Jr (1)
Fred Daly (4)	Ted Kroll (1)
Max Faulkner (4)	Lloyd Mangrum (4)
Bernard Hunt (1)	Cary Middlecoff (1)
John Panton (2)	Ed Oliver (3)
Dai Rees (5)	Sam Snead (5)
Harry Weetman (2)	Joe Turnesa (1)

Foursomes (Day 1)

Alliss & Weetman lost to	
Douglas & Oliver (2&1)	0 - 1
Brown & Panton lost to	
Mangrum & Snead (8&7)	0 - 2
Adams & Hunt lost to	
Burke & Kroll (7&5)	0 - 3
Bradshaw & Daly (1 up) beat	
Burkemo & Middlecoff	1 - 3
Day 1 totals	**1 - 3**

Singles (Day 2)

Rees lost to Burke (2&1)	0 - 1
Daly (9&7) beat Kroll	1 - 1
Brown (2 up) beat Mangrum	2 - 1
Weetman (1 up) beat Snead	3 - 1
Faulkner lost to Middlecoff (3&1)	3 - 2
Alliss lost to Turnesa (1 up)	3 - 3
Hunt halved with Douglas	3½-3½
Bradshaw (3&2) beat Haas	4½-3½
Day 2 totals	**4½-3½**
MATCH TOTALS	*5½ - 6½*

COURSE:	Thunderbird G & CC
LOCATION:	Palm Springs, California
DATE:	5-6 November
US CAPTAIN:	Chick Harbert (playing)
GB CAPTAIN:	Dai Rees (playing)
RESULT:	US 8 – GB 4

At this time in the US, the heritage of foregone conclusions tagged the Ryder Cup as a meaningless competition, and it now held little value for the public at large, if ever it really did. With TV getting involved with the Tour, tournament golf was one thing, but Americans believed the only international sport outside the Olympic Games was the World Series. The Ryder Cup was deemed a tin-pot affair, and, just like the British Open, was it worth bothering about? There were some within the sport who wanted to do away with this backwater competition and focus on the money-spinning Tour only. Thankfully, at least, the US professional golfer still saw it as his privilege to represent his country in the only way open to him: but time for the Ryder Cup, as it was, was running out.

The GB team was selected on Order of Merit positions for the first time; the first seven on the list gaining automatic selection and then choosing their three 'wild-card' team-mates themselves. Perhaps, because of this, they collected more points on US soil than ever before – but were still comprehensively beaten. As usual, the team gave themselves a mountain to climb, allowing the traditional US head start in the foursomes. The singles were a little more even, although the Americans, at one point 5-1 ahead in the match, were never really troubled in the singles they subsequently won; and the home team never looked in danger at any time over the two days.

US TEAM	GB TEAM
Jerry Barber (1)	Ken Bousfield (2)
Tommy Bolt (1)	Harry Bradshaw (2)
Jack Burke, Jr (2)	Eric Brown (2)
Doug Ford (1)	Johnny Fallon (1)
Marty Furgol (1)	John Jacobs (1)
Chick Harbert (2)	Arthur Lees (4)
Chandler Harper (1)	Christy O'Connor, Sr (1)
Ted Kroll (2)	Dai Rees (6)
Cary Middlecoff (2)	Syd Scott (1)
Sam Snead (6)	Harry Weetman (3)

Foursomes (Day 1)

Barber & Harper lost to Fallon & Jacobs (1 up)	0 - 1
Ford & Kroll (5&4) beat Brown & Scott	1 - 1
Bolt & Burke (1 up) beat Lees & Weetman	2 - 1
Middlecoff & Snead (3&2) beat Bradshaw & Rees	3 - 1
Day 1 totals	**3 - 1**

Singles (Day 2)

Bolt (4&2) beat O'Connor	1 - 0
Harbert (3&2) beat Scott	2 - 0
Middlecoff lost to Jacobs (1 up)	2 - 1
Snead (3&1) beat Rees	3 - 1
Furgol lost to Lees (3&2)	3 - 2
Barber lost to Brown (3&2)	3 - 3
Burke (3&2) beat Bradshaw	4 - 3
Ford (4&3) beat Weetman	5 - 3
Day 2 totals	**5 - 3**
MATCH TOTALS	*8 - 4*

1957

COURSE:	Lindrick GC
LOCATION:	Sheffield, Yorkshire, England
DATE:	4-5 October
GB CAPTAIN:	Dai Rees (playing)
US CAPTAIN:	Jack Burke, Jr (playing)
RESULT:	GB 7½ – US 4½

Of course interest in the Ryder Cup will always pick up if, suddenly, it becomes competitive again. By winning an historic victory at Lindrick, the chosen golf course of benefactor, Sir Stuart Goodwin, Dai Rees' British team bought the Ryder Cup a good few years. After the first four competitions were shared, the Americans had won seven off the reel. This time, however, for the first time, the US team didn't have an outstanding star name. Only Snead was still playing with something like his old gusto, but by 1957 he was already 45, and, although he still had another Ryder Cup in him, he was not the force he was. Arnold Palmer was waiting in the wings, but in 1957, the Americans, away from home, were caught in something of a vulnerable vacuum; and lost the Ryder Cup for the first time since 1933.

After the first day, however, the spectators might have thought that this was business as usual, with the US team taking a two-point lead. The home side's singles selection for the following day was interesting, depending on which version of the story you take. Apparently Max Faulkner wished to be left out, his game was not good enough in his view. Initially, it was also thought that his first round partner, Harry Weetman, volunteered to step down, too. The story goes, however, that Weetman was not at all happy.

Whatever, the outcome proved to be beyond the wildest dreams of the home team and its ecstatic (unsporting? – Tommy Bolt thought so!) supporters. Big early leads were built up by Brown, rookie Peter Mills, Bousfield, Rees and Hunt. Amazingly they were retained, sometimes improved upon, and the winning scores, the Hawkins/Alliss match apart, were met with huge gasps of disbelief around the course and, via radio and medieval TV outside broadcast, across the nation – and even in America. Dai Rees, making a record seventh appearance, became a household name after 20 years of Ryder Cup heartache; and golf, suddenly, became close to a mainstream sport with British fans for the first time.

GB TEAM	US TEAM
Peter Alliss (2)	Tommy Bolt (2)
Ken Bousfield (3)	Jack Burke, Jr (3)
Harry Bradshaw (3)	Dow Finsterwald (1)
Eric Brown (2)	Doug Ford (1)
Max Faulkner (5)	Ed Furgol (1)
Bernard Hunt (2)	Fred Hawkins (1)
Peter Mills (1)	Lionel Hebert (1)
Christy O'Connor, Sr (2)	Ted Kroll (3)
Dai Rees (7)	Dick Mayer (1)
Syd Scott (1)	Cary Middlecoff (2)
Harry Weetman (3)	Art Wall (1)

Foursomes (Day 1)

Alliss & Hunt lost to Finsterwald & Ford (2&1)	0 - 1
Bousfield & Rees (3&2) beat Hawkins & Wall	1 - 1
Faulkner & Weetman lost to Burke & Kroll (4&3)	1 - 2
Brown & O'Connor lost to Bolt & Mayer (7&5)	1 - 3
Day 1 totals	**1 - 3**

Singles (Day 2)

Brown (4&3) beat Bolt	1 - 0
Mills (5&3) beat Burke	2 - 0
Alliss lost to Hawkins (2&1)	2 - 1
Bousfield (4&3) beat Hebert	3 - 1
Rees (7&6) beat Furgol	4 - 1
Hunt (6&5) beat Ford	5 - 1
O'Connor (7&6) beat Finsterwald	6 - 1
Bradshaw halved with Mayer	6½-1½
Day 2 totals	**6½-1½**
MATCH TOTALS	*7½ - 4½*

COURSE:	Eldorado CC
LOCATION:	Palm Desert, California
DATE:	6-7 November
US CAPTAIN:	Sam Snead (playing)
GB CAPTAIN:	Dai Rees (playing)
RESULT:	US 8½ – GB 3½

A return to the States in 1959 was a return to reality for the British side. The US recalled Sam Snead as a player, for one last time, as it turned out, and made him captain, while Jay Hebert's appearance made him and brother Lionel (from 1957) the third pair of brothers after the Turnesas and the Furgols, to represent the US in the competition. There was nearly no competition in which to participate, however. A similar pressure loss to that which occurred in 1999 in a plane carrying Payne Stewart, was also the reason why the plane carrying the British, on an internal US flight to the host site, plunged 4000 feet, before it was thankfully in this instance corrected. On returning to Los Angeles airport, the stiff upper lip was quivering slightly, so the last leg of the journey was taken by bus. The team arrived late, uncomfortable, unprepared: really no different from previous visits.

After the standard give-away start, the visitors kept the score differential down to one point after the first day; one of the better away performances. It might have been even better if Weetman, in the last match with shots in hand, hadn't followed Snead into the water, then saw the veteran snatch a half with a ten-foot putt. In the singles the away team could have won the final three matches, but by then a procession of heavyweight American wins had made them academic. As it was, Rees was edged out and Alliss could only manage a half, anyway. After 32 years, this was to be the last Ryder Cup with a 36-hole format; and the last time the GB team crossed the Atlantic by cruise ship.

US TEAM	GB TEAM
Julius Boros (1)	Peter Alliss (3)
Jack Burke, Jr (4)	Ken Bousfield (4)
Dow Finsterwald (2)	Eric Brown (3)
Doug Ford (2)	Norman Drew (1)
Jay Hebert (2)	Bernard Hunt (3)
Cary Middlecoff (3)	Peter Mills (2)
Bob Rosburg (1)	Christy O'Connor, Sr (3)
Sam Snead (7)	Dai Rees (8)
Mike Souchak (1)	Dave Thomas (1)
Harry Weetman (4)	Art Wall (2)

Foursomes (Day 1)

Rosburg & Souchak (5&4) beat Brown & Hunt	1 - 0
Boros & Finsterwald (2 up) beat Bousfield & Rees	2 - 0
Ford & Wall lost to Alliss & O'Connor (3&2)	2 - 1
Middlecoff & Snead halved with Thomas & Weetman	2½-1½
Day 1 totals	**2½-1½**

Singles (Day 2)

Ford halved with Drew	½ - ½
Souchak (3&2) beat Bousfield	1½-½
Rosburg (6&5) beat Weetman	2½-½
Snead (6&5) beat Thomas	3½-½
Wall (7&6) beat O'Connor	4½-½
Finsterwald (1 up) beat Rees	5½-½
Hebert halved with Alliss	6 - 1
Brown (4&3) beat Middlecoff	6 - 2
Day 2 totals	**6 - 2**
MATCH TOTALS	**8½ - 3½**

COURSE:	Royal Lytham and St Annes GC
LOCATION:	St Annes, Lancashire, England
DATE:	13-14 October
GB CAPTAIN:	Dai Rees (playing)
US CAPTAIN:	Jerry Barber (playing)
RESULT:	GB 9½ – US 14½

For once the R&A and Britain's PGA saw eye to eye, and the 1961 series of matches was hosted by an Open Championship links at last, and the first links of any sort since the early days at Southport & Ainsdale. With this psychological move (none of the US team had any professional links experience except Palmer, who was, of course, the Open Champion); a new format which, in theory, should give the British a better chance of picking up points; and the knowledge that the Americans were beaten in the British Isles the last time around, home hopes were high. When will they ever learn, as the song goes. The format, moved by the PGA in Britain, made the matches of 18-hole duration, but doubled their number, and thereby doubled the points on offer. The PGA of America went along with the changes, and also proposed that a four-ball event be included from 1963. Sam Snead qualified for the team but was then disqualified over a bizarre ruling about a non-PGA-sanctioned tournament. His appeal was only heard after the Ryder Cup event, and he never appeared as a player again. His final record after eight series of matches (of which only one was lost) – 10-2-1!

Whatever the changes, whatever the omens, the result remained much the same as usual, with the US stretching away by three on the first morning, and were four clear going into their stronger suit, the singles. Palmer was quickly into Ryder Cup stride (being a former US Amateur champion, he was comfortable with matchplay), winning three and halving one of his four matches. The Americans pulled away like some purring limo leaving a Reliant Robin in its wake – quietly and effortlessly – to seal a win by five points. As usual, however, Dai Rees, for the ninth and last time, proved a thorn in the side of the visitors. As if to bow out with a cameo of his 24-year unbroken (apart from the War years), uphill battle against the Yankee slickers, the pugnacious Welshman put Jay Hebert and Doug Ford to the sword. He also came out honours even over the foursomes in which he was involved, before exiting the

Ryder Cup stage. He would still be involved, later, but like his old adversary, Snead, never again as a player. His final statistics after nine series: 7-9-1 – in the context of an 8-1 record of team defeats, pretty impressive.

GB TEAM	US TEAM
Peter Alliss (4)	Jerry Barber (2)
Ken Bousfield (5)	Billy Casper (1)
Neil Coles (1)	Bill Collins (1)
Tom Haliburton (1)	Dow Finsterwald (3)
Bernard Hunt (4)	Doug Ford (3)
Ralph Moffitt (1)	Jay Hebert (2)
Christy O'Connor, Sr (4)	Gene Littler (1)
John Panton (3)	Arnold Palmer (1)
Dai Rees (9)	Mike Souchak (1)
Harry Weetman (5)	Art Wall (3)

Morning Foursomes (Day 1)

Alliss & O'Connor beat
Ford & Littler   1 - 0
Hunt & Panton lost to
Hebert & Wall (4&3)   1 - 1
Bousfield & Rees lost to
Casper & Palmer (2&1)   1 - 2
Coles & Haliburton lost to
Collins & Souchak (1 up)   1 - 3

Afternoon Foursomes (Day 1)

Alliss & O'Connor lost to
Hebert & Wall (1 up)   1 - 4
Hunt & Panton lost to
Casper & Palmer (5&4)   1 - 5
Bousfield & Rees (4&2) beat
Collins & Souchak   2 - 5
Coles & Haliburton lost to
Barber & Finsterwald (1 up)   2 - 6

Day 1 totals   **2 - 6**

Morning Singles (Day 2)

Weetman lost to Ford (1 up)   0 - 1
Moffitt lost to Souchak (5&4)   0 - 2
Alliss halved with Palmer   ½-2½
Bousfield lost to Casper (5&3)   ½-3½
Rees (2&1) beat Hebert   1½-3½
Coles halved with Littler   2 - 4
Hunt (5&4) beat Barber   3 - 4
O'Connor lost to Finsterwald (2&1)   3 - 5

Afternoon Singles (Day 2)

Weetman lost to Wall (1up)   3 - 6
Alliss (3&2) beat Collins   4 - 6
Hunt lost to Souchak (2&1)   4 - 7
Haliburton lost to Palmer (2&1)   4 - 8
Rees (4&3) beat Ford   5 - 8
Bousfield (1 up) beat Barber   6 - 8
Coles (1 up) beat Finsterwald   7 - 8
O'Connor halved with Littler   7½-8½

Day 2 totals   **7½-8½**

MATCH TOTALS   *9½ - 14½*

COURSE:	East Lake CC
LOCATION:	Atlanta, Georgia
DATE:	11-13 October
US CAPTAIN:	Arnold Palmer (playing)
GB CAPTAIN:	Johnny Fallon (non-playing)
RESULT:	US 23 – GB 9

With the advent of fourball (better ball), an extra day was needed: an extra day for the US team to accumulate even more points and claim even bigger victories. With 32 points now up for grabs, the 1963 score more resembled that of a rugby match – or, perhaps more aptly, an American Football game. Just two years after his debut, the irrepressible Palmer was given the captaincy. The US team were still sceptical about the value of a non-playing captain. The British and Irish had appointed Johnny Fallon, a well-respected, but rather low-key figure, with a couple of Open runners-up spots to boast about, but no tournament victories and experience of only one (100% success – from one foursome!) Ryder Cup.

Palmer was just an aura, a beacon for his players to follow. He led, typically, from the front, inspiring by deed more than by word; and despite getting the wind taken out of his sails in the very first foursome, and losing to Peter Alliss in the first singles, he played in all six phases, generally lifting American spirits along the way, and professionally putting the visitors to the sword as clinically as possible. He was to be the last playing captain, to date. Maintaining almost perfect arithmetic progression throughout the three days, the US racked up the highest points score and margin of victory in the series to date. There was worse to come.

US TEAM	GB TEAM
Julius Boros (2)	Peter Alliss (5)
Billy Casper (2)	Neil Coles (2)
Dow Finsterwald (4)	Tom Haliburton (2)
Bob Goalby (1)	Brian Huggett (1)
Gene Littler (2)	Bernard Hunt (5)
Tony Lema (1)	Geoff Hunt (1)
Billy Maxwell (1)	Christy O'Connor, Sr (5)
Arnold Palmer (2)	Dave Thomas (2)
Johnny Pott (1)	Harry Weetman (6)
Dave Ragan (1)	George Will (1)

Morning Foursomes (Day 1)

Palmer & Pott lost to Huggett & Will (3&2)	1 - 0
Casper & Ragan (1 up) beat	
Alliss & O'Connor	1 - 1
Boros & Lema halved with Coles & B Hunt	1½-1½
Finsterwald & Littler halved with	
Thomas & Weetman	2 - 2

Afternoon Foursomes (Day 1)

Goalby & Maxwell (4&3) beat	
Thomas & Weetman	3 - 2
Casper & Palmer (5&4) beat	
Huggett & Will	4 - 2
Finsterwald & Littler (2&1) beat	
Coles & G Hunt	5 - 2
Boros & Lema (1 up) beat	
Haliburton & B Hunt	6 - 1
Day 1 totals	**6 - 2**

Morning Fourballs (Day 2)

Finsterwald & Palmer (5&4) beat	
Huggett & Thomas	1 - 0
Boros & Littler halved with Alliss & B Hunt	1½-½
Casper & Maxwell (2&1) beat	
Weetman & Will	2½-½
Goalby & Ragan lost to	
Coles & O'Connor (1 up)	2½-1½

Afternoon Fourballs (Day 2)

Finsterwald & Palmer (3&2) beat	
Coles & O'Connor	3½-1½
Lema & Pott (1 up) beat Alliss & B Hunt	4½-1½
Casper & Maxwell (2&1) beat	
Haliburton & G Hunt	5½-1½
Goalby & Ragan halved with	
Huggett & Thomas	6 - 2
Day 2 totals	**6 – 2**
RUNNING MATCH TOTALS	*12 - 4*

Morning Singles (Day 3)

Lema (5&3) beat G Hunt	1 - 0
Pott lost to Huggett (3&1)	1 - 1
Palmer lost to Alliss (1 up)	1 - 2
Casper halved with Coles	1½-2½
Goalby (3&2) beat Thomas	2½-2½
Littler (1up) beat O'Connor	3½-2½
Boros lost to Weetman (1 up)	3½-3½
Finsterwald lost to hunt (2 up)	3½-4½

Afternoon Singles (Day 3)

Palmer (3&2) beat Will	4½-4½
Ragan (2&1) beat Coles	5½-4½
Lema halved with Alliss	6 - 5
Littler (6&5) beat Haliburton	7 - 5
Boros (2&1) beat Weetman	8 - 5
Maxwell (2&1) beat O'Connor	9 - 5
Finsterwald (4&3) beat Thomas	10- 5
Goalby (2&1) beat Hunt	11- 5
Day 3 Totals	**11 – 5**
MATCH TOTALS	*23 - 9*

253

COURSE:	Royal Birkdale GC
LOCATION:	Southport, Lancashire, England
DATE:	7-9 October
GB CAPTAIN:	Harry Weetman (non-playing)
US CAPTAIN:	Byron Nelson (non-playing)
RESULT:	GB 12½ – US 19½

Class told once again as the Ryder Cup returned to the Southport area for the first time since the thirties. Because of a PGA of America ruling that a player must be a member for five years before he could become eligible for Ryder Cup selection, Palmer didn't make the team until 1961, yet because of his exploits, he was already the best golfer in the world. For the same reason, despite winning four Major Championships by 1965, and seven by 1967, Jack Nicklaus was sidelined until 1969! Can't imagine Tiger Woods being left out for the same reason today. Even without Jack, this was still some American team, bristling with Majors, themselves, and as purposeful as ever. Captained, to boot, by the legendary Nelson, who had not been directly involved since 1947, what could Britain offer in return? Weetman moved on from six playing experiences, obviously still driven on by being part of the 1957 win, to become non-playing captain. Bernard Hunt, Alliss and O'Connor still relished the memory of Lindrick, but there were no Majors winners in the team, nor had there been since Faulkner's swansong, also at Lindrick. This was the biggest problem, this chasm in class between the respective teams over the years. One would expect the US' fifth-choice ten at any time still to be too good for the British. It is difficult for the observer to understand why the US continued with the processional victories. It wasn't box-office in the States; the triumphs had to be hollow. There was no financial reward, as now (although after 1999 we may see a change there). The only reason for continuing must have been the Americans' deeply-felt patriotism; and the Ryder Cup gave sportsmen one of the only meaningful vehicles available to them to represent their country in a team event.

The results: the usual gritty performance from the home team; hanging on to the US shirt-tails after Day 2 but increasingly and inexorably being ground into the dust thereafter. Yet Alliss collected five points out of six.

GB TEAM	US TEAM
Peter Alliss (6)	Julius Boros (3)
Peter Butler (1)	Billy Casper (3)
Neil Coles (3)	Tommy Jacobs (1)
Jimmy Hitchcock (1)	Don January (1)
Bernard Hunt (6)	Tony Lema (2)
Jimmy Martin (1)	Gene Littler (3)
Christy O'Connor, Sr (6)	Dave Marr (1)
Lionel Platts (1)	Arnold Palmer (3)
Dave Thomas (3)	Johnny Pott (2)
George Will (2)	Ken Venturi (1)

Morning Foursomes (Day 1)

Butler & Platts lost to Boros & Lema (1 up)	0 - 1
Thomas & Will (6&5) beat Marr & Palmer	1 - 1
Coles & Hunt lost to		
Casper & Littler (2&1)	1 - 2
Alliss & O'Connor (5&4) beat		
January & Venturi	2 - 2

Afternoon Foursomes (Day 1)

Thomas & Will lost to		
Marr & Palmer (6&5)	2 - 3
Alliss & O'Connor (2&1) beat		
Casper & Littler	3 - 3
Hitchcock & Martin lost to		
Boros & Lema (5&4)	3 - 4
Coles & Hunt (3&2) beat		
January & Venturi	4 - 4
Day 1 totals	**4 - 4**

Morning Fourballs (Day 2)

Thomas & Will lost to		
Jacobs & January (1up)	0 - 1
Butler & Platts halved with Casper & Littler	½-1½
Alliss & O'Connor lost to		
Marr & Palmer (6&4)	½-2½
Coles & Hunt (1 up) beat Boros & Lema	1½-2½

Afternoon Fourballs (Day 2)

Alliss & O'Connor (2 up)		
Marr & Palmer	2½-2½
Thomas & Will lost to		
Jacobs & January (1 up)	2½-3½
Butler & Platts halved with Casper & Littler	3 - 4
Coles & Hunt lost to Lema & Venturi (1 up)	3 - 5
Day 2 totals	**3 - 5**
RUNNING MATCH TOTALS	*7 - 9*

Morning Singles (Day 3)

Hitchcock lost to Palmer (3&2)	0 - 1
Platts lost to Boros (4&2)	0 - 2
Butler lost to Lema (1 up)	0 - 3
Coles lost to Marr (2 up)	0 - 4
Hunt (2 up) beat Littler	1 - 4
Thomas lost to Jacobs (2&1)	1 - 5
Alliss (1 up) beat Casper	2 - 5
Will halved with January	2½-5½

Afternoon Singles (Day 3)

O'Connor lost to Lema (6&4)	2½-6½
Hitchcock lost to Boros (2&1)	2½-7½
Butler lost to Palmer (2 up)	2½-8½
Alliss (3&1) beat Venturi	3½-8½
Coles (3&2) beat Casper	4½-8½
Will lost to Littler (2&1)	4½-9½
Hunt lost to Marr (1 up)	4½-10½
Platts (1 up) beat Jacobs	5½-10½
Day 3 totals	**5½ - 10**
MATCH TOTALS	*12½ - 19½*

COURSE:	Champions GC
LOCATION:	Houston, Texas
DATE:	20-22 October
US CAPTAIN:	Ben Hogan (non-playing)
GB CAPTAIN:	Dai Rees (non-playing)
RESULT:	US 23½ – GB 8½

The lowest ebb for the Ryder Cup? It had come close to extinction before, and had been rescued from the brink by philanthropists and the odd, but timely injection of on-course drama here and there. The new philanthropist was television, and the second-rate nature of the opposition was not at all appealing to the US networks. There would be no white knight riding to the rescue there. Even the players queried the usefulness of the seemingly antiquated arrangement, and after events at the Champions Golf Club, things had come to a pretty pass. Another Lindrick was urgently required to make the Americans smart and want revenge for a few more years again. The interest in the UK for the home matches was still healthy, if met with some forboding; but an idea to play all the matches in Britain would have led to apathy from US players. They really are home birds, and believe the US is the centre of the world – and they are probably right.

By the end of Day 2, when the British could only gain a half from the whole day, the Americans needed just three points out of 16 to retain the Ryder Cup. Who would buy entrance tickets for Day 3 in advance? Predictably they got there after the opening three matches. Rookie, Gardner Dickinson, and Arnold Palmer, who else, each came out of the 'competition' with 100% records from five matches played; their points contribution was almost as much as the British and Irish team's put together. This summed up the position perfectly, and something desperate was needed from Britain if the 1969 series was not to be the last.

US TEAM	GB TEAM
Julius Boros (4)	Peter Alliss (7)
Gay Brewer (1)	Hugh Boyle (1)
Billy Casper (4)	Neil Coles (4)
Gardner Dickinson (1)	Malcolm Gregson (1)
Al Geiberger (1)	Brian Huggett (2)
Gene Littler (4)	Bernard Hunt (7)
Bobby Nichols (1)	Tony Jacklin (1)
Arnold Palmer (4)	Christy O'Connor, Sr (7)
Johnny Pott (3)	Dave Thomas (4)
Doug Sanders (1)	George Will (3)

Morning Foursomes (Day 1)

Boros & Casper halved with Huggett & Will	½ - ½
Dickinson & Palmer (2&1) beat	
Alliss & O'Connor	1½-½
Brewer & Sanders lost to	
Jacklin & Thomas (4&3)	1½-1½
Nichols & Pott (6&5) beat Coles & Hunt	2½-1½

Afternoon Foursomes (Day 1)

Boros & Casper (1 up) beat Huggett & Will	3½-1½
Dickinson & Palmer (5&4) beat	
Boyle & Gregson	4½-1½
Geiberger & Littler lost to	
Jacklin & Thomas (3&2)	4½-2½
Nichols & Pott (2&1)	
Alliss & O'Connor	5½-2½
Day 1 totals	**5½-2½**

Morning Fourballs (Day 2)

Brewer & Casper (3&2) beat	
Alliss & O'Connor	1 - 0
Nichols & Pott (1 up) beat Coles & Hunt	2 - 0
Geiberger & Littler (1 up) beat	
Jacklin & Thomas	3 - 0
Dickinson & Sanders (3&2) beat	
Huggett & Will	4 - 0

Afternoon Fourballs (Day 2)

Brewer & Casper (5&3)	
Coles & Hunt	5 - 0
Dickinson & Sanders (3&2) beat	
Alliss & Gregson	6 - 0
Boros & Palmer (1 up) beat Boyle & Will	7 - 0
Geiberger & Littler halved with	
Jacklin & Thomas	7 - ½
Day 2 totals	**7 - ½**
RUNNING MATCH TOTALS	*13 - 3*

Morning Singles (Day 3)

Brewer (4&3) beat Boyle	1 - 0
Casper (2&1) beat Alliss	2 - 0
Palmer (3&2) beat Jacklin	3 - 0
Boros lost to Huggett (1 up)	3 - 1
Sanders lost to Coles (2&1)	3 - 2
Geiberger (4&2) beat Gregson	4 - 2
Littler halved with Thomas	4½-2½
Nichols halved with Hunt	5 - 3

Afternoon Singles (Day 3)

Palmer (5&3) beat Huggett	6 - 3
Brewer lost to Alliss (2&1)	6 - 4
Dickinson (3&2) beat Jacklin	7 - 4
Nichols (3&2) beat O'Connor	8 - 4
Pott (3&1) beat Will	9 - 4
Geiberger (2&1) beat Gregson	10- 4
Boros halved with Hunt	10½-4½
Sanders lost to Coles (2&1)	10½-5½
Day 3 totals	**10½-5½**
MATCH TOTALS	*23½ - 8½*

COURSE:	Royal Birkdale GC
LOCATION:	Southport, Lancashire, England
DATE:	18-20 October
GB CAPTAIN:	Eric Brown (non-playing)
US CAPTAIN:	Sam Snead (non-playing)
RESULT:	GB 16 – US 16

The glory of sport at its greatest – both in its deeds and in those who participate – is not among the very highest echelons of human nobility, perhaps; to be compared, say, with the valour of war, or even man's reaching the moon. However, on Saturday, 18 October 1969, just a few months after Neil Armstrong's historic 'One small step...', one giant step in the advancement of the sporting ethos was made on the very last green of the very last match of the latest series of Ryder Cup matches, by a man who was making his very first appearance in the competition. In a gesture which effectively conceded the last chance for a US victory, Jack Nicklaus will be forever remembered and respected by those who love sport for sport's sake; even if he hadn't gone on to become the greatest golfer the world has ever seen. Perhaps it is fitting that the two go together: the mightiest and the most honourable. So much that is distasteful in sport is done under that euphemism 'competitiveness'.

By conceding a nasty three-foot putt to Tony Jacklin after he and the young English hero had been going at it hammer-and-tongs for eighteen holes, and with increasingly-hysterical and partisan galleries adding to the fervour of the occasion, Nicklaus had acknowledged the place of the honourable draw in sport. Once all has been given by both sides, and there is nothing to choose between the protagonists, there is only one fair result. It meant the difference between another GB defeat in the series and the first ever tie. It was a decision taken which would have massive consequences.

Initially Sam Snead, back as non-playing captain, was furious with Nicklaus, and probably is to this day; Sam coming from the archetypal American 'gotta have an edge' school of sportsmanship. Jack's gesture, coupled with the result and overall spectacle of that nail-biting last day, put golf on the front pages for a while, and gave it a much higher, permanent, profile on the back pages. Jacklin's presence at the climax was also good for golf's perception at the time. He was between his British and US Open

victories, and the sportsman in Britain at the time who was carrying his nation's aspirations for the future. Nicklaus made sure that Tony's reputation didn't get a chance to be dented. It was also another reason why new golfing talent, inspired by the events going on in golf, would soon start to come forward. And, finally, it guaranteed the future of the Ryder Cup for some time yet. Not only did events on the last green stiffen US sinews for a future fight, but the ebb and flow of a classic sporting contest over three days suggested what a magnificent spectacle the Ryder Cup, at its best, could be. Another crisis had been averted.

In the excitement it is easy to forget that Nicklaus' belated curtain-raiser was a quiet affair, with his results 1-2-1 from four matches; while Jacklin scored four wins and two halves, and was very much the champion of the home forces. Apart, obviously, from the first series in 1927, the US team fielded more rookies (10 out of the 12 now allowed, the company of Nicklaus, Floyd and Trevino, notwithstanding) than ever before. Was there a moral there too?

GB TEAM	US TEAM
Peter Alliss (8)	Tommy Aaron (1)
Brian Barnes (1)	Miller Barber (1)
Maurice Bembridge (1)	Frank Beard (1)
Peter Butler (2)	Billy Casper (5)
Alex Caygill (1)	Dale Douglass (1)
Neil Coles (5)	Ray Floyd (1)
Bernard Gallacher (1)	Dave Hill (1)
Brian Huggett (3)	Gene Littler (5)
Bernard Hunt (8)	Jack Nicklaus (1)
Tony Jacklin (2)	Dan Sikes (1)
Christy O'Connor, Sr (8)	Ken Still (1)
Peter Townsend (1)	Lee Trevino (1)

Morning Foursomes (Day 1)

Coles & Huggett (3&2) beat Barber & Floyd	1 - 0
Bembridge & Gallacher (2&1) beat Still & Trevino	2 - 0
Jacklin & Townsend (3&1) beat Aaron & Hill	3 - 0
Alliss & O'Connor halved with Beard & Casper	3½-½

Afternoon Foursomes (Day 1)

Coles & Huggett lost to Aaron & Hill (1 up)	3½-1½
Bembridge & Gallacher lost to Littler & Trevino (1 up)	3½-2½
Jacklin & Townsend (1 up) beat Beard & Casper	4½-2½
Butler & Hunt lost to Nicklaus & Sikes (1 up)	4½-3½
Day 1 totals	**4½-3½**

Morning Fourballs (Day 2)

O'Connor & Townsend (1 up) beat Douglass & Hill	1 - 0
Caygill & Huggett halved with Barber & Miller	1½-½
Alliss & Barnes lost to Littler & Trevino (1 up)	1½-1½
Coles & Jacklin (1 up) beat Nicklaus & Sikes	2½-1½

Afternoon Fourballs (Day 2)

Butler & Townsend lost to Beard & Casper (2 up)	2½-2½
Gallacher & Huggett lost to Hill & Still (2&1)	2½-3½
Bembridge & Hunt halved with Aaron & Floyd	3 - 4
Coles & Jacklin halved with Barber & Trevino	3½-4½
Day 2 totals	**3½-4½**
RUNNING MATCH TOTALS	*8 - 8*

Morning Singles (Day 3)

Alliss lost to Trevino (2&1)	0 - 1
Townsend lost to Hill (5&4)	0 - 2
Coles (1 up) beat Aaron	1 - 2
Barnes lost to Casper (1 up)	1 - 3
O'Connor (5&4) beat Beard	2 - 3
Bembridge (1 up) beat Still	3 - 3
Butler (1 up) beat Floyd	4 - 3
Jacklin (4&3) beat Nicklaus	5 - 3

Afternoon Singles (Day 3)

Barnes lost to Hill (4&2)	5 - 4
Gallacher (4&3) beat Trevino	6 - 4
Bembridge lost to Barber (7&6)	6 - 5
Butler (3&2) beat Douglass	7 - 5
Coles lost to Sikes (1 up)	7 - 6
O'Connor lost to Littler (2&1)	7 - 7
Huggett halved with Casper	7½-7½
Jacklin halved with Nicklaus	8 - 8
Day 3 totals	**8 - 8**
MATCH TOTALS	*16 - 16*

COURSE:	Old Warson CC
LOCATION:	St Louis, Missouri
DATE:	16-18 September
US CAPTAIN:	Jay Hebert (non-playing)
GB CAPTAIN:	Eric Brown (non-playing)
RESULT:	US 18½ – GB 13½

There was a knock-on effect of sorts in 1971, following on from events at Birkdale two years earlier, in that the British team pushed the Americans quite hard for much of the way, with a cracking start and a valiant, if vain, flourish at the end. They unfortunately lost their way somewhat in the middle. This was encouraging when previous matches hosted by the US were invariably runaway victories for the Americans. From a purist's viewpoint, the highlight of the series must have been the pairing of Nicklaus and Palmer in the afternoon fourballs. The Snead family was further represented with JC, Sam's nephew making his first appearance for the US.

Peter Oosterhuis, in his debut series, had the temerity to defeat both Gene Littler and Arnold Palmer in singles matches, while Brian Barnes also recorded two singles wins. The overall strength of the American professional ranks, however, still won through, and points were picked up at crucial times. For example, from being behind after the first day, they routed the British in the fourballs, making Day 2 theirs, and entering the singles with a healthy four-point lead. The British rallied to collect their best ever points haul on US soil, but realised that to compete with the Americans in their own back yard, they needed to have at least half a dozen players of a similar calibre to the Americans, not just the odd Cotton, or Jacklin, or Oosterhuis, to add to the usual qualities of tenacity and effort.

US TEAM	GB TEAM
Miller Barber (2)	Harry Bannerman (1)
Frank Beard (2)	Brian Barnes (2)
Billy Casper (6)	Maurice Bembridge (2)
Charles Coody (1)	Peter Butler (3)
Gardner Dickinson (2)	Neil Coles (6)
Gene Littler (6)	Bernard Gallacher (2)
Jack Nicklaus (2)	John Garner (1)
Arnold Palmer (5)	Brian Huggett (4)
Mason Rudolph (1)	Tony Jacklin (3)
JC Snead (1)	Christy O'Connor, Sr (9)
Dave Stockton (1)	Peter Oosterhuis (1)
Lee Trevino (2)	Peter Townsend (2)

Morning Foursomes (Day 1)

Barber & Casper lost to	
Coles & O'Connor (2&1)	0 - 1
Dickinson & Palmer (2 up) beat	
Oosterhuis & Townsend	1 - 1
Nicklaus & Stockton lost to	
Huggett & Jacklin (3&2)	1 - 2
Beard & Coody lost to	
Bembridge & Butler (1 up)	1 - 3

Afternoon Foursomes (Day 1)

Barber & Casper lost to	
Bannerman & Gallacher (2&1)	1 - 4
Dickinson & Palmer (1 up) beat	
Oosterhuis & Townsend	2 - 4
Rudolph & Trevino halved with	
Huggett & Jacklin	2½-4½
Nicklaus & Snead (5&3) beat	
Bembridge & Butler	3½-4½
Day 1 totals	**3½-4½**

Morning Fourballs (Day 2)

Rudolph & Trevino (2&1) beat	
Barnes & O'Connor	1 - 0
Beard & Snead (2&1) beat	
Coles & Garner	2 - 0
Dickinson & Palmer (5&4) beat	
Gallacher & Oosterhuis	3 - 0
Littler & Nicklaus (2&1) beat	
Bannerman & Townsend	4 - 0

Afternoon Fourballs (Day 2)

Casper & Trevino lost to	
Gallacher & Oosterhuis (1 up)	4 - 1
Littler & Snead (2&1) beat	
Huggett & Jacklin	5 - 1
Nicklaus & Palmer (1 up) beat	
Bannerman & Townsend	6 - 1
Beard & Coody halved with	
Coles & O'Connor	6½-1½
Day 2 totals	**6½-1½**
RUNNING MATCH TOTALS	***10 - 6***

Morning Singles (Day 3)

Trevino (1 up) beat Jacklin	1 - 0
Stockton halved with Gallacher	1½-½
Rudolph lost to Barnes (1 up)	1½-1½
Littler lost to Oosterhuis (4&3)	1½-2½
Nicklaus (3&2) beat Townsend	2½-2½
Dickinson (5&4) beat O'Connor	3½-2½
Palmer halved with Bannerman	4 - 3
Beard halved with Coles	4½-3½

Afternoon Singles (Day 3)

Trevino (7&6) beat Huggett	5½-3½
Snead (1 up) beat Jacklin	6½-3½
Barber lost Barnes (2&1)	6½-4½
Stockton (1 up) beat Townsend	7½-4½
Coody lost to Gallacher (2&1)	7½-5½
Nicklaus (5&3) beat Coles	8½-5½
Palmer lost to Oosterhuis (3&2)	8½-6½
Dickinson lost to Bannerman (2&1)	8½-7½
DAY 3 totals	**8½-7½**
MATCH TOTALS	***18½ - 13½***

261

COURSE:	Muirfield GC
LOCATION:	Muirfield, East Lothian, Scotland
DATE:	20-22 September
GB CAPTAIN:	Bernard Hunt (GB & I-non-playing)
US CAPTAIN:	Jack Burke, Jr (non-playing)
RESULT:	GB and Ireland 13 – US 19

If the GB team were officially called Great Britain and Ireland from 1973, no-one told Christy O'Connor. This son of Galway had been playing for 'Britain' since the fairy-tale at Lindrick back in 1957, and a little incongruously he was to bow out after this, his record tenth appearance, aged 48. He went one better than Dai Rees, his captain on that day of fading memory; and was two ahead of Peter Alliss, who would commentate on the 1973 event for BBC television, and the 1973 captain, Bernard Hunt. A Ryder Cup for the Celtic fringe, perhaps, in that, O'Connor's record apart, the British host site was, for the first time, held outside of England, and the team comprised two Scots, two Irish, one Welsh: the English, however, were still in the majority. If the 'British' team's fringe was Celtic, then the Americans was certainly Latino, with Trevino joined by fellow Hispanics Blancas and Rodriguez.

The format was tinkered with again, in that the foursome and fourball sections were now interwoven to provide a morning and afternoon contrast, rather than one between Day 1 and Day 2. Muirfield was a fitting setting for the Ryder Cup, and all seemed to be going really well for the home side. After leading by three after the first day, Bernard Gallacher, in the thick of the early wins, fell ill with food poisoning. Even so, by midway in the competition the British and Irish led 7½-4½. Once again, however, the US showed that they could not only rally strongly when in adversity, but they had the ability and mental strength to turn defence into attack and completely rewrite the scenario. By the end of the second day they had wiped out the homeside's lead, and when they strung the first three singles together the following morning they had won 7½ points off the reel, put themselves three points ahead, and were home and dry. Their traditional strength in the singles matches would see them through. So it proved.

GB TEAM	US TEAM
Brian Barnes (3)	Tommy Aaron (2)
Maurice Bembridge (3)	Homero Blancas (1)
Peter Butler (4)	Gay Brewer (2)
Clive Clark (1)	Billy Casper (7)
Neil Coles (7)	Lou Graham (1)
Bernard Gallacher (3)	Dave Hill (2)
John Garner (2)	Jack Nicklaus (3)
Brian Huggett (5)	Arnold Palmer (6)
Tony Jacklin (4)	Chi Chi Rodriguez (1)
Christy O'Connor, Sr (10)	JC Snead (2)
Peter Oosterhuis (2)	Lee Trevino (3)
Eddie Polland (1)	Tom Wesikopf (1)

Morning Foursomes (Day 1)

Barnes & Gallacher (1 up) beat	
Casper & Trevino	1 - 0
Coles & O'Connor (3&2) beat	
Snead & Weiskopf	2 - 0
Jacklin & Oosterhuis halved with	
Graham & Rodriguez	2½-½
Bembridge & Polland lost to	
Nicklaus & Palmer (6&5)	2½-1½

Afternoon Fourballs

Barnes & Gallacher (5&4) beat	
Aaron & Brewer	3½-1½
Bembridge & Huggett (3&1) beat	
Nicklaus & Palmer	4½-1½
Jacklin & Oosterhuis (3&1) beat	
Casper & Weiskopf	5½-1½
Coles & O'Connor lost to	
Blancas & Trevino (2&1)	5½-2½
Day 1 totals	**5½-2½**

Morning Foursomes (Day 2)

Barnes & Butler lost to	
Nicklaus & Weiskopf (1 up)	0 - 1
Jacklin & Oosterhuis (2 up) beat	
Hill & Palmer	1 - 1
Bembridge & Huggett (5&4) beat	
Graham & Rodriguez	2 - 1
Coles & O'Connor lost to	
Casper & Trevino (2&1)	2 - 2

Afternoon Fourballs (Day 2)

Barnes & Butler lost to	
Palmer & Snead (2 up)	2 - 3
Jacklin & Oosterhuis lost to	
Brewer & Casper (3&2)	2 - 4
Clark & Polland lost to	
Nicklaus & Weiskopf (3&2)	2 - 5
Bembridge & Huggett halved with	
Blancas & Trevino	2½-5½
Day 2 totals	**2½-5½**
RUNNING MATCH TOTALS	*8 - 8*

Morning Singles (Day 3)

Barnes lost to Casper (2&1)	0 - 1
Gallacher lost to Weiskopf (3&1)	0 - 2
Butler lost to Blancas (5&4)	0 - 3
Jacklin (3&1) beat Aaron	1 - 3
Coles halved with Brewer	1½-3½
O'Connor lost to Snead (1 up)	1½-4½
Bembridge halved with Nicklaus	2 - 5
Oosterhuis halved with Trevino	2½-5½

Afternoon Singles (Day 3)

Huggett (4&2) beat Blancas	3½-5½
Barnes lost to Snead (3&1)	3½-6½
Gallacher lost to Brewer (6&5)	3½-7½
Jacklin lost to Casper (2&1)	3½-8½
Coles lost to Trevino (6&5)	3½-9½
O'Connor halved with Weiskopf	4 - 10
Bembridge lost to Nicklaus (2 up)	4 - 11
Oosterhuis (4&2) beat Palmer	5 - 11
Day 3 totals	**5 - 11**
MATCH TOTALS	*13 - 19*

COURSE:	Laurel Valley GC
LOCATION:	Ligonier, Pennsylvania
DATE:	19-21 September
US CAPTAIN:	Arnold Palmer (non-playing)
GB CAPTAIN:	Bernard Hunt (GB & I-non-playing)
RESULT:	US 21 – GB & Ireland 11

The foursomes and fourballs arrangements for the second day were turned around, but otherwise the 1975 format remained the same. Christy O'Connor's name appeared on the roster for the eleventh time, but, this time, it was the nephew O'Connor filling the shoes of his uncle. Also, another Hunt, this time Guy, became the third of that ilk to represent the Europeans in the Ryder Cup, although no blood relation to the two brothers Bernard and Geoff. Despite Hunt being in the team, once again when confronting the Americans on their own turf, unfortunately the team was not in the hunt. There had almost always appeared in the Ryder Cup to date, a part of the three days over which the US held complete sway. On occasions when the GB (and Ireland) team seemed to be playing well and giving their adversaries as good as they were getting, a mist seemed to fall over proceedings, and like some film dream sequence, a grotesque fantasy scene was played out. By the time we get back to real-time action, the Americans, inexplicably, have won a handful of points without return, and the series is effectively over. This happened at the beginning of the matches very often, rendering the competition null and void sometimes by the end of the first morning. This was just the case at Laurel Valley.

The only other real point of note was Brian Barnes' double singles defeat of Jack Nicklaus. Although the match result was not affected by the first of these results, Jack's pride was. He had had his best year of six of the best: since winning the Open Championship at St Andrews in 1970, he had missed a Top 10 spot in the Major Championships only once; winning seven times, runner up four times and third three times, in 22 consecutive events. To say that the world's best-ever golfer was in form would have been some understatement. Imagine the great man's dander, therefore, at this Scotsman's nerve. Jack manoeuvred a rematch for the afternoon singles, told Barnes on the tee, mortals shouldn't meddle in the affairs of gods, or something akin, and got himself away with two birdies. Barnes has always been renowned for his phlegmatic approach, however, and he steadily reeled in the Golden Bear before the final hole was reached. Nicklaus' manner in a second deflating defeat was characteristically noble. Billy Casper set an American appearances record of eight.

US TEAM	GB TEAM
Billy Casper (8)	Brian Barnes (4)
Ray Floyd (2)	Maurice Bembridge (4)
Al Geiberger (2)	Eamonn Darcy (1)
Lou Graham (2)	Bernard Gallacher (4)
Hale Irwin (1)	Tommy Horton (1)
Gene Littler (7)	Brian Huggett (6)
Johnny Miller (1)	Guy Hunt (1)
Bob Murphy (1)	Tony Jacklin (5)
Jack Nicklaus (4)	Christy O'Connor, Jr (1)
JC Snead (3)	John O'Leary (1)
Lee Trevino (4)	Peter Oosterhuis (3)
Tom Wesikopf (2)	Norman Wood (1)

Morning Foursomes (Day 1)

Nicklaus & Weiskopf (5&4) beat	
Barnes & Gallacher	1 - 0
Irwin & Littler (4&3) beat	
Bembridge & Wood	2 - 0
Geiberger & Miller (3&1) beat	
Jacklin & Oosterhuis	3 - 0
Snead & Trevino (2&1) beat	
Horton & O'Leary	4 - 0

Afternoon Fourballs (Day 1)

Casper & Floyd lost to	
Jacklin & Oosterhuis (2&1)	4 - 1
Graham & Weiskopf (3&2) beat	
Darcy & O'Connor	5 - 1
Murphy & Nicklaus halved with	
Barnes & Gallacher	6½-1½
Irwin & Trevino (2&1) beat	
Horton & O'Leary	6½-1½
Day 1 totals	**6½-1½**

Morning Fourballs (Day 2)

Casper & Miller halved with	
Jacklin & Oosterhuis	½ - ½
Nicklaus & Snead (4&2) beat	
Horton & Wood	1½-½
Graham & Littler (5&3) beat	
Barnes & Gallacher	2½-½
Floyd & Geiberger halved with	
Darcy & Hunt	3 - 1

Afternoon Foursomes (Day 2)

Murphy & Trevino lost to	
Huggett & Jacklin (3&2)	3 - 2
Miller & Weiskopf (5&3) beat	
O'Connor & O'Leary	4 - 2
Casper & Irwin (3&2) beat	
Bembridge & Oosterhuis	5 - 2
Geiberger & Graham (3&2) beat	
Darcy & Hunt	6 - 2
Day 2 totals	**6 - 2**
RUNNING MATCH TOTALS	**_12 - 3½_**

Morning Singles (Day 3)

Murphy (2&1) beat Jacklin	1 - 0
Miller lost to Oosterhuis (2 up)	1 - 1
Trevino halved with Gallacher	1½-1½
Irwin halved with Horton	2 - 2
Littler (4&2) beat Huggett	3 - 2
Casper (3&2) beat Darcy	4 - 2
Weiskopf (5&3) beat Hunt	5 - 2
Nicklaus lost to Barnes (4&2)	5 - 3

Afternoon Singles (Day 3)

Floyd (1 up) beat Jacklin	6 - 3
Snead lost to Oosterhuis (3&2)	6 - 4
Geiberger halved with Gallacher	6½-4½
Graham lost to Horton (2&1)	6½-5½
Irwin (2&1) beat O'Leary	7½-5½
Murphy (2&1) beat Bembridge	8½-5½
Trevino lost to Wood (2&1)	8½-6½
Nicklaus lost to Barnes (2&1)	8½-7½
Day 3 totals	**8½-7½**
MATCH TOTALS	**_21 - 11_**

COURSE:	Royal Lytham & St Annes GC
LOCATION:	St Annes, Lancashire, England
DATE:	15-17 September
GB CAPTAIN:	Brian Huggett (GB & I-non-playing)
US CAPTAIN:	Dow Finsterwald (non-playing)
RESULT:	GB and Ireland 7½ – US 12½

The 1977 Ryder Cup series was something of a debacle. Not only was there yet another American victory, aided and abetted by a familiar GB & Ireland collapse – courtesy of some big second-day defeats – the event had become characterless, as well as meaningless. The players, via the British PGA, had complained that the three days' golf was too intensive, and that competition would be brighter, sharper, if the number of matches were reduced. The format was trimmed down, therefore, but had the effect of killing any spectacle capable of engendering crowd excitement. Each match over the first two days teed off at 45 minute intervals, thereby losing any continuity (galleries were sometimes split as much as three holes away from each other) and creating precious little atmosphere. If Britain and Ireland had ever done well in the Ryder Cup, it was at home and with a strongly supportive crowd. By the sixteenth hole of the second singles match, the US just required a half to retain the Cup; yet another third-day non-event. It seemed that this might be the end. Sad, if that was to be the case, for Britain and Ireland, who were fielding the youngest player to date to appear for either side in the Ryder Cup: Nick Faldo, just 20, completed a 100% winning performance over his three matches, and looked like the kind of player the home team had been crying out for since Jacklin first hit the scene.

However, amidst the gloom and despair for the future, Jack Nicklaus, hob-nobbing with the British PGA's Lord Derby, lent his weight to an idea that had been fermenting for a little while: he proposed that the British and Irish embrace other world players to keep the Ryder Cup meaningful for the American golfer. Although as tactful as ever, Jack was making a very serious point: make a match of it or we won't bother to turn up again. The idea gained ground, although the British PGA threw out the idea of taking on board Australians, Japanese, South Africans, and the like. They, after much gnashing of teeth, approved the inclusion of European players, however, as the

practicability of selection, based on the fledgling European Tour, was not considered a problem. In 1979, the Ryder Cup was to come of age, although it wasn't to know it at the time. After over half a century when the real essence of the Ryder Cup was only fleetingly glimpsed, it now had its chance to grow into one of the great events in world sport. And, incongruously, it was to be contested by teams representing the (fairly) homogenous United States of America, and a disparate, amorphous juxtaposition of peoples, who had spent millennia divided by language and culture; and, off and on, even massacring one another when the mood was felt.

GB& I TEAM	US TEAM
Brian Barnes (5)	Ray Floyd (3)
Ken Brown (1)	Lou Graham (3)
Howard Clark (1)	Hubert Green (1)
Neil Coles (8)	Dave Hill (3)
Eamonn Darcy (1)	Hale Irwin (2)
Peter Dawson (1)	Don January (2)
Nick Faldo (1)	Jerry McGee (1)
Bernard Gallacher (5)	Jack Nicklaus (5)
Tommy Horton (2)	Ed Sneed (1)
Tony Jacklin (6)	Dave Stockton (2)
Mark James (1)	Lanny Wadkins
Peter Oosterhuis (4)	Tom Watson (1)

Foursomes (Day 1)

Gallacher & Barnes lost to	
Irwin & Wadkins (3&1)	0 - 1
Coles & Dawson lost to	
McGee & Stockton (1 up)	0 - 2
Faldo & Oosterhuis (2&1) beat	
Floyd & Graham	1 - 2
Darcy & Jacklin halved with	
January & Sneed	1½-2½
Horton & James lost to	
Nicklaus & Watson (5&4)	1½-3½
Day 1 totals	**1½-3½**

Fourballs (Day 2)

Barnes & Horton lost to	
Green & Watson (5&4)	0 - 1
Coles & Dawson lost to	
Sneed & Wadkins (5&3)	0 - 2
Faldo & Oosterhuis (3&1) beat	
Floyd & Nicklaus	1 - 2
Darcy & Jacklin lost to	
Hill & Stockton (5&3)	1 - 3
Brown & James lost to	
Graham & Irwin (1 up)	1 - 4
Day 2 totals	**1- 4**
RUNNING MATCH TOTALS	*2½ - 7½*

Singles (Day 3)

Clark lost to Wadkins (4&3)	0 - 1
Coles lost to Graham (5&3)	0 - 2
Dawson (5&4) beat January	1 - 2
Barnes (1 up) beat Irwin	2 - 2
Horton lost to Hill (5&4)	2 - 3
Gallacher (1 up) beat Nicklaus	3 - 3
Darcy lost to Green (1 up)	3 - 4
James lost to Floyd (2&1)	3 - 5
Faldo (1 up) beat Watson	4 - 5
Oosterhuis (2 up) beat McGee	5 - 5
Day 3 totals	**5 - 5**
MATCH TOTALS	*7½ - 12½*

COURSE:	The Greenbrier
LOCATION:	White Sulphur Springs, West Virginia
DATE:	14-16 September
US CAPTAIN:	Billy Casper (non-playing)
EUROPE CAPTAIN:	John Jacobs (non-playing)
RESULT:	US 17 — Europe 11

Ironically, Jack Nicklaus did not qualify for the expanded 1979 Ryder Cup for which he had so persuasively lobbied. A rare blip in the master's form before the days of US 'Wild Card' selections as we now know them, accounted for that. The Europeans did use the captain's discretion, however, for the first time, to select two players outside of normal qualifying. John Jacobs chose Peter Oosterhuis and Des Smyth. The factoring of European players into the Ryder Cup equation was obviously going to take some time to take effect. As far as 1979 was concerned, it was much the same as before: in the States, the home team, including a black player in Lee Elder for the first time, were still unbeatable, with rookie Larry Nelson the star performer. He maintained a 100% win record over five matches, and accounted for the historic Spanish debutant, Severiano Ballesteros, in four of them. Ballesteros was the first continental European to be selected along with countryman Antonio Garrido; and rather than the Spaniards being integrated within the team, the European strategy was to pair them, believing that intra- rather than inter-national spirit was probably stronger. It was to no avail, however, as they were to collect only one point from the four paired and two singles matches in which they competed.

The format was altered for the fourth series running, after only three changes in the entire history of the competition before that. The lunacy of 1977 was put right, and apart from a little tinkering, the format we know today, with all twelve players selected competing in singles matches on Day 3, put in place. Mark James was a beneficiary of another convention begun in 1979. Each captain selected a player who would sit out the singles in the event of an opponent having to cry off for any reason, and the names were put in envelopes. James was unfit, and the unlucky American was Gil Morgan. James, too, along with old chum Ken Brown, got himself into hot water for being what they were; silly young men not conforming to the rules of old buffers, and were fined on their return. I wonder what these upstanding patriarchs of the 1999

Ryder Cup establishment think about that now? As often before, the Americans won the match by putting together a purple patch to which the Europeans had no answer. After a good second day Bernard Gallacher's first win of the singles drew the sides level, and an exciting last day was in prospect, any chance the visitors had in causing an upset was immediately blown away, with the US sweeping through the next five matches.

US TEAM	EUROPE TEAM
Andy Bean (1)	Seve Ballesteros (1)
Lee Elder (1)	Brian Barnes (6)
Hubert Green (2)	Ken Brown (2)
Mark Hayes (1)	Nick Faldo (2)
Hale Irwin (3)	Bernard Gallacher (6)
Tom Kite (1)	Antonio Garrido (1)
John Mahaffey (1)	Tony Jacklin (7)
Gil Morgan (1)	Mark James (2)
Larry Nelson (1)	Michael King (1)
Lee Trevino (5)	Sandy Lyle (1)
Lanny Wadkins (2)	Peter Oosterhuis (5)*
Fuzzy Zoeller (1)	Des Smyth (1)*

* Indicates captain's 'wild card' selections

Morning Fourballs (Day 1)

Nelson & Wadkins (2&1) beat	
Ballesteros & Garrido	1 - 0
Trevino & Zoeller (3&2) beat	
Brown & James	2 - 0
Bean & Elder (2&1) beat	
Faldo & Oosterhuis	3 - 0
Irwin & Mahaffey lost to	
Barnes & Gallacher (2&1)	3 - 1

Afternoon Foursomes (Day 1)

Irwin & Kite (7&6) beat	
Brown & Smyth	4 - 1
Green & Zoeller lost to	
Ballesteros & Garrido (3&2)	4 - 2
Morgan & Trevino halved with	
Jacklin & Lyle	4½-2½
Nelson & Wadkins (4&3) beat	
Barnes & Gallacher	5½-2½
Day 1 totals	**5½-2½**

Morning Foursomes (Day 2)

Elder & Mahaffey lost to	
Jacklin & Lyle (5&4)	0 - 1
Bean & Kite lost to	
Faldo & Oosterhuis (6&5)	0 - 2
Hayes & Zoeller lost to	
Barnes & Gallacher (3&2)	0 - 3
Nelson & Wadkins (3&2) beat	
Ballesteros & Garrido	1 - 3

Afternoon Fourballs (Day 2)

Nelson & Wadkins (5&4) beat	
Ballesteros & Garrido	2 - 3
Irwin & Kite (1 up) beat	
Jacklin & Lyle	3 - 3
Trevino & Zoeller lost to	
Barnes & Gallacher (3&2)	3 - 4
Elder & Hayes lost to	
Faldo & Oosterhuis (1 up)	3 - 5
Day 2 totals	**3 - 5**
RUNNING MATCH TOTALS	*8½ - 7½*

Singles (Day 3)

Wadkins lost to Gallacher (3&2)	0 - 1
Nelson (3&2) beat Ballesteros	1 - 1
Kite (1 up) beat Jacklin	2 - 1
Hayes (1 up) beat Garrido	3 - 1
Bean (4&3) beat King	4 - 1
Mahaffey (1 up) beat Barnes	5 - 1
Elder lost to Faldo (3&2)	5 - 2
Irwin (5&3) beat Smyth	6 - 2
Green (2 up) beat Oosterhuis	7 - 2
Zoeller lost to Brown (1 up)	7 - 3
Trevino (2&1) beat Lyle	8 - 3
Morgan halved (match not played) with James	8½-3½
DAY 3 totals	**8½-3½**
MATCH TOTALS	*17 - 11*

COURSE:	Walton Heath GC
LOCATION:	Walton Heath, Surrey, England
DATE:	18-20 September
EUROPE CAPTAIN:	John Jacobs (non-playing)
US CAPTAIN:	Dave Marr (non-playing)
RESULT:	Europe 9½ – US 18½

I suppose it is fair to give a new relationship time to bed down. After events at The Greenbrier in 1979, the Europeans could just about get away with suggesting that their new multi-national blend was still maturing, and accounted for the home thrashing in 1981. Excuses like that would not be acceptable for very much longer, however. The Americans wanted a competition, not an end-of-season junket and a chance to collect even more blazers, sweaters and other goodies. Excuses apart, Walton Heath was not what the visitors really wanted. When they, themselves, took the Ryder Cup so seriously – why else pair Watson and Nicklaus throughout – imagine what they must have thought about Europe expelling their best player, just because he didn't play regularly on the European Tour. Ballesteros was still learning his trade in world golf. By 1981 he had already picked up the Open Championship and the Masters, but the competition on the still-young European Tour was too thin for such a wonderful talent to achieve his full promise. The US PGA Tour was where he needed to cut his teeth; but in doing so he incurred the short-sighted wrath of the hierarchy this side of the Atlantic, and several of the top European players as well. Ballesteros was never a shrinking violet, and his obstinacy was a factor in his not being considered as a 'wild card' pick; but in hindsight he was right to take his stance. Since Ballesteros, other players have been penalised by the people who determine how Ryder Cup teams are selected; just because they have the aspiration to succeed week-in, week-out against the best golfers in the world – not just on alternate years. And until there is some form of World Tour with regional feeder tours based on the current ones, more players will be sacrificed for the 'good' of their domestic set up.

Walton Heath was a last-minute venue, as the British PGA's own baby at the Belfry was overdue. Once again the foursomes and fourballs did a jig, but everything else remained the same. Europe began so promisingly; a point clear after the first day. Then came the steamroller effect on

Day 2. As if hypnotised as a unit to go out and thrash the opposition without mercy, the US collected all but one of the eight points on offer: only Floyd and Irwin, probably too mentally tough to be hypnotised, slipped up. The singles were won by a ratio of two to one, but the three and a half points needed to retain the trophy were obtained in the first four matches (this included Larry Nelson's ninth match win on the trot). The Europeans were shell-shocked. The team was quite young still, and it was hoped that they would not become totally demoralised by such a mauling. The Americans may have been disappointed at how the opposition rolled over: they may just care to scrutinise their own team that year, though. It was one of the better ones!

EUROPE TEAM	US TEAM
Jose-Maria Canizares (1)	Ben Crenshaw (1)
Howard Clark (2)	Ray Floyd (4)
Eamonn Darcy (3)	Hale Irwin (4)
Nick Faldo (3)	Tom Kite (2)
Bernard Gallacher (7)	Bruce Lietzke (1)
Mark James (3)*	Johnny Miller (2)
Bernhard Langer (1)	Larry Nelson (2)
Sandy Lyle (1)	Jack Nicklaus (6)
Peter Oosterhuis (6)*	Jerry Pate (1)
Manuel Pinero (1)	Bill Rogers (1)
Des Smyth (2)	Lee Trevino (6)
Sam Torrance (1)	Tom Watson (2)

* Indicates captain's 'wild card' selections

Morning Foursomes (Day 1)

Langer & Pinero lost to Nelson & Trevino (1 up)	0 - 1
James & Lyle (2&1) beat Lietzke & Rogers	1 - 1
Gallacher & Smyth (3&2) beat Floyd & Irwin	2 - 1
Faldo & Oosterhuis lost to Nicklaus & Watson (4&3)	2 - 2

Afternoon Fourballs (Day 1)

Clark & Torrance halved with Kite & Miller	2½-2½
James & Lyle (3&2) beat Crenshaw & Pate	3½-2½
Canizares & Smyth (6&5) beat Lietzke & Rogers	4½-2½
Darcy & Gallacher lost to Floyd & Irwin (2&1)	4½-3½
Day 1 totals	**4½-3½**

Morning Fourballs (Day 2)

Faldo & Torrance lost to Pate & Trevino (7&5)	0 - 1
James & Lyle lost to Kite & Nelson (1 up)	0 - 2
Langer & Pinero (2&1) beat Floyd & Irwin	1 - 2
Canizares & Smyth lost to Nicklaus & Watson (3&2)	1 - 3

Afternoon Foursomes (Day 2)

Oosterhuis & Torrance lost to Pate & Trevino (2&1)	1 - 4
Langer & Pinero lost to Nicklaus & Watson (3&2)	1 - 5
James & Lyle lost to Floyd & Rogers (3&2)	1 - 6
Gallacher & Smyth lost to Kite & Nelson (3&2)	1 - 7
Day 2 totals	**1 - 7**
RUNNING MATCH TOTALS	*5½ - 10½*

Singles (Day 3)

Torrance lost to Trevino (5&3)	0 - 1
Lyle lost to Kite (3&2)	0 - 2
Gallacher halved with Rogers	½-2½
James lost to Nelson (2 up)	½-3½
Smyth lost to Crenshaw (6&4)	½-4½
Langer halved with Lietzke	1 - 5
Pinero (4&2) beat Pate	2 - 5
Canizares lost to Irwin (1 up)	2 - 6
Faldo (2&1) beat Miller	3 - 6
Clark (4&3) beat Watson	4 - 6
Oosterhuis lost to Floyd (1 up)	4 - 7
Darcy lost to Nicklaus (5&3)	4 - 8
Day 3 totals	**4 - 8**
MATCH TOTALS	*9½ - 18½*

COURSE:	PGA National GC
LOCATION:	Palm Beach Gardens, Florida
DATE:	14-16 October
US CAPTAIN:	Jack Nicklaus (non-playing)
EUROPE:	Tony Jacklin (non-playing)
RESULT:	US 14½ – Europe 13½

Jack Nicklaus had wanted it competitive. I'm sure in retrospect he thoroughly enjoyed the 1983 Ryder Cup, even though, involved in a non-playing capacity for the first time, he went through torment, particularly in the nail-biting climax on the final day. It was so apt that both captains should lead their respective teams to such a thrilling Ryder Cup denouement; their dramatic half on the very last hole at Birkdale in 1969 tied the match, a climactic end to the last great series of matches before this magnificent golfing showcase. But was this another false dawn? After the very early competitions, we had seen magnificent British performances rarely, really only twice: the inexplicable win at Lindrick in 1957; and the aforementioned 1969 classic. Hopes were high then that a new era was blowing in, only on both occasions for such aspirations to be crushed under the weight of numbers of quality players the States could bring on from a seemingly bottomless mine of talent. In 1983, however, the continental European facet of the Ryder Cup was very different from 1969, or even from ten years earlier. Now, the European Tour was burgeoning, providing opportunities the European golfer, outside of the British Isles, had hitherto been unable to obtain, at least not to such an extent. More and more events in more and more European locations attracted the latent hidden depths of European talent: talent, which although it could not yet be matched against the stock of US golfing prowess, certainly began to provide what was still a British and Irish-spined Ryder Cup team with an in-depth reserve for the first time, and of better quality than at any time before.

The paired competitions swung hither and thither over the first two days, without the US making its expected, almost traditional, clean break. When Ballesteros, cajoled back into the fray by Jacklin, in an inspired teaming with rookie Paul Way, saw off World No. 1 Tom Watson and Bob Gilder at the seventeenth, the Europeans had closed the second day level on points. This had never before happened on US soil, making the American public for the first time sit up and take an interest in what was going on.

On the third day the first singles match was struck by the genius of Ballesteros, and really set up the Europeans for the forthcoming battles. Having typically squandered a winning lead against Fuzzy Zoeller (at one point after the turn he was three up), the Spaniard then looked done for as he drove into a fairway bunker some 250 yards from the pin on the par-five eighteenth. With scant regard for his poor position up against the lip of the trap, Seve took out a three wood and blasted the ball to the fringe of the green in one of the great shots of golf. He got up and down for a hallmark scrambled half. Buoyed up by this piece of Iberian magic, the Europeans then went ahead by two, courtesy of wins by Faldo and Langer, only to be overhauled by a mini charge from the Americans towards the middle of the day. Then Way sunk Curtis Strange; but Stadler did for Woosnam. With other matches tying, the one point US advantage could still be made up at any time though. Ken Brown, in the penultimate match out, saw off Ray Floyd at the sixteenth, leaving two evenly-balanced scraps, which looked as if they could go either way. At the eighteenth Canizares was one up on Wadkins: Watson was one up at the seventeenth against Gallacher. Great sporting occasions usually have at least one defining moment. After three days' play, this Ryder Cup had several. However, it is the crucial timing of some brilliant play, or stroke of luck, which turns a result around. Ballesteros' wonderful shot at the last in the first of the singles really set up the day, and provided a rallying call for the Europeans: now Lanny Wadkins was to take away that day-long aspiration of a first win on American soil, with a 60-yard chip so precise, it was conceded by Canizares for an unlikely half. Watson duly did what Watson does and the home team squeaked home by one point. Nicklaus' dream had come true: he had led his team to victory in an epic encounter, the kind of battle which was to be commonplace in years to come. The Ryder Cup had grown up.

US TEAM	EUROPE TEAM
Ben Crenshaw (2)	Seve Ballesteros (2)
Ray Floyd (5)	Gordon J Brand (Sr) (1)
Bob Gilder (1)	Ken Brown (3)
Jay Haas	Jose-Maria Canizares (2)
Tom K...	Nick Faldo (4)
Gil M...	Bernard Gallacher (8)
	Bernhard Langer (2)
	Sandy Lyle (2)
	Sam Torrance (1)
	Brian Waites (1)
	Paul Way (1)
	Ian Woosnam (1)

Morning Foursomes (Day 1)

Crenshaw & Watson (5&4) beat Gallacher & Lyle	1 - 0
Stadler & Wadkins lost to Faldo & Langer (4&2)	1 - 1
Kite & Peete (2&1) beat Ballesteros & Way	2 - 1
Floyd & Gilder lost to Canizares & Torrance	2 - 2

Afternoon Fourballs (Day 1)

Morgan & Zoeller lost to Brown & Waites (2&1)	2 - 3
Haas & Watson (2&1) beat Faldo & Langer	3 - 3
Floyd & Strange lost to Ballesteros & Way (1 up)	3 - 4
Crenshaw & Peete halved with ...osnam	3½-4½
	3½-4½

Morning Fourballs (Day 2)

Stadler & Wadkins (1 up) beat Brown & Waites	1 - 0
Crenshaw & Peete lost to Faldo & Langer (4&2)	1 - 1
Haas & Morgan halved with Ballesteros & Way	1½-1½
Gilder & Watson (5&4) beat Torrance & Woosnam	2½-1½

Afternoon Foursomes (Day 2)

Floyd & Kite lost to Faldo & Langer (3&2)	2½-2½
Haas & Strange (3&2) beat Brown & Waites	3½-2½
Morgan & Wadkins (7&5) beat Canizares & Torrance	4½-2½
Gilder & Watson lost to Ballesteros & Way (2&1)	4½-3½
Day 2 totals	**4½ - 3½**
RUNNING MATCH TOTALS	***8 - 8***

Singles (Day 3)

Zoeller halved with Ballesteros	½ - ½
Haas lost to Faldo (2&1)	½-1½
Morgan lost to Langer (2 up)	½-2½
Gilder (2 up) beat Brand	1½-2½
Crenshaw (3&1) beat Lyle	2½-2½
Peete (1 up) beat Waites	3½-2½
Strange lost to Way (2&1)	3½-3½
Kite halved with Torrance	4 - 4
Stadler (3&2) beat Woosnam	5 - 4
Wadkins halved with Canizares	5½-4½
Floyd lost to Brown (4&3)	5½-5½
Watson (2&1) beat Gallacher	6½-5½
Day 3 totals	**6½-5½**
MATCH TOTALS	***14½ - 13½***

273

COURSE:	The Belfry
LOCATION:	Sutton Coldfield, West Midlands, England
DATE:	13-15 September
EUROPE CAPTAIN:	Tony Jacklin (non-playing)
US CAPTAIN:	Lee Trevino (non-playing)
RESULT:	Europe 16½ – US 11½

The Europeans felt they should have at least tied the last series, held at the home of the US PGA in Florida. The defeat at the death, after so much had gone right for once, was devastating. It was because of the bitterness of losing when it should have been a better result in 1983, not just because another Ryder Cup had been lost, as in the past – and a new belief in European golf – that when 1985 came around at the Belfry, the air was one of some confidence in the home camp. The Masters and Open Championship of 1985 now belonged to Europeans (Langer and Lyle, respectively), and the aura of Ballesteros still counted strongly. Add in some world-class performances from Woosnam; and with Faldo, already a Cup veteran, although not at his best (coming to the end of a long period of technical re-building), for the first time ever, the Americans were matched for star names.

Old habits die hard, however, and the Americans were allowed to get away with their customary head start. Going into the afternoon fourballs, three rather easy US wins had put them two points ahead. These were immediately clawed back, however, and the Europeans could have won all four matches. As it was, after the first day, there was just one point in favour of the Americans. The transition took place on Day 2, when, so often in the past, the US had sown the seeds of ultimate victory. Defeats for the first two US fourballs, whose pairings included that year's other Majors winners, Andy North and Hubert Green, put European noses in front for the first time. For once, when in such a position, the home team managed to stay there. Strong performances from the continental Europeans, especially the Spanish quartet in the opening two foursomes of the afternoon, repaid the faith of those in 1977 who could see only good coming of a pan-European team, and sent them to bed two ahead.

The traditional American strength in the singles meant that on paper the match was still well-balanced. There was a different mentality to the European team now, though, than to any that had opposed the US down the years. Even up to and including the events of 1969, any 'British' success or near success was (so it was perceived) achieved through Corinthian endeavour: the plucky underdog overcoming the strutting mastiff, that sort of thing. Tony Jacklin's leadership, Ballesteros' medieval-grandee-of-Cantabria ambience, and a number of hard-bitten winners, had changed all that. OK, there was now a hard streak running through the team, but it was not cynical. Golf doesn't produce the cynical behaviour, thankfully, witnessed in other headline sports. Not even the 'shocking' affairs of 1999 at Brookline could ever be termed cynical, or premeditated. Jacklin had melded strong characters with a sense of team discipline and spirit, and for the first time, following on from the beliefs of 1983, the Europeans were a thoroughly professional outfit.

They outfought and outplayed the Americans where the Americans believed they were best. Instead of producing a singles charge that would have turned the match around by the middle of the day, the US was constantly on the back foot. By the time Clark pipped O'Meara, only Stadler (with a repeat of his 1983 win over Woosnam) and Kite (halving with Ballesteros) had salvaged US pride, and the Europeans had notched up a series-winning six and a half points. In fact, the matches had been won, memorably, in the game before Clark and O'Meara, when Sam Torrance took the glory. Against US Open Champion, Andy North, Torrance had turned around a three-hole deficit, and when North found water at the last, Sam needed a par to win the whole shebang. Famously hitting the green to enormous cheers, the popular Scot didn't need his two putts: his sweet twenty-footer arced tantalisingly into the hole. Arms aloft, surrounded by team-mates going barmy, and a home crowd going barmier, he broke down and cried. I am sure that many, many golf nuts, inured to the traditional lack of success of the Europeans in the Ryder Cup, did exactly the same.

EUROPE TEAM	US TEAM
Seve Ballesteros (3)	Ray Floyd (6)
Ken Brown (3)*	Hubert Green (3)
Jose-Maria Canizares (3)	Peter Jacobsen (1)
Howard Clark (3)	Tom Kite (3)
Nick Faldo (5)*	Andy North (1)
Bernhard Langer (3)	Calvin Peete (2)
Sandy Lyle (3)	Mark O'Meara (1)
Manuel Pinero (2)	Craig Stadler (2)
Jose Rivero (1)*	Hal Sutton (1)
Sam Torrance (2)	Curtis Strange (2)
Paul Way (2)	Lanny Wadkins (4)
Ian Woosnam (2)	Fuzzy Zoeller (3)

* Indicates captain's 'wild card' selections

Morning Foursomes (Day 1)

Ballesteros & Pinero (2&1) beat
O'Meara & Strange — 1 - 0
Faldo & Langer lost to
Kite & Peete (3&2) — 1 - 1
Brown & Lyle lost to
Floyd & Wadkins (4&3) — 1 - 2
Clark & Torrance lost to
Stadler & Sutton (3&2) — 1 - 3

Afternoon Fourballs (Day 1)

Way & Woosnam (1 up) beat
Green & Zoeller — 2 - 3
Ballesteros & Pinero (2&1) beat
Jacobsen & North — 3 - 3
Canizares & Langer halved with
Stadler & Sutton — 3½-3½
Clark & Torrance lost to
Floyd & Wadkins — 3½-4½

Day 1 totals — **3½-4½**

Morning Fourballs (Day 2)

Clark & Torrance (2&1) beat
Kite & North — 1 - 0
Way & Woosnam (4&3) beat
Green & Zoeller — 2 - 0
Ballesteros & Pinero lost to
O'Meara & Wadkins (3&2) — 2 - 1
Langer & Lyle halved with
Stadler & Strange — 2½-1½

Afternoon Foursomes (Day 2)

Canizares & Rivero (7&5) beat
Kite & Peete — 3½-1½
Ballesteros & Pinero (5&4) beat
Stadler & Sutton — 4½-1½
Way & Woosnam lost to
Jacobsen & Strange (4&2) — 4½-2½
Brown & Langer (3&2) beat
Floyd & Wadkins — 5½-2½

Day 2 totals — **5½—2½**

RUNNING MATCH TOTALS — ***9 - 7***

Singles (Day 3)

Pinero (3&1) beat Wadkins	1 - 0
Woosnam lost to Stadler (2&1)	1 - 1
Way (2 up) beat Floyd	2 - 1
Ballesteros halved with Kite	2½-1½
Lyle (3&2) beat Jacobsen	3½-1½
Langer (5&4) beat Sutton	4½-1½
Torrance (1 up) beat North	5½-1½
Clark (1 up) beat O'Meara	6½-1½
Rivero lost to Peete (1 up)	6½-2½
Faldo lost to Green (3&1)	6½-3½
Canizares (2 up) beat Zoeller	7½-3½
Brown lost to Strange (4&2)	7½-4½

Day 3 totals — **7½-4½**

MATCH TOTALS — ***16½ - 11½***

COURSE:	Muirfield Village GC
LOCATION:	Dublin, Ohio
DATE:	25-27 September
US CAPTAIN:	Jack Nicklaus (non-playing)
EUROPE CAPTAIN:	Tony Jacklin (non-playing)
RESULT:	US 13 – Europe 15

If the American public was stirred from its Ryder Cup slumber with what it witnessed in 1983, it was rubbing its eyes with some disbelief after 1985. For the first time in its 60-year history, then, the 1987 event was getting the kind of media hype in the States normally reserved for baseball. The Americans regarded themselves as the underdogs – who'd have thought it possible? The European bandwagon, however, had been on a roll since 1983; Jacklin's positive leadership combining a skilful and dedicated bunch into a team to be feared. Previously, US 'teams' would stroll through Ryder Cup matches because individually there were at least eight of their team with superior skills to their opposite numbers. They never needed to 'gel'; they never really needed to like each other. But the new, greater depth of player-quality the opposition had, allied with a curious cross-continental camaraderie never before (or since) seen in any other form of endeavour in Europe made Jacklin's men stand apart from what convention had witnessed to date. So it was with some trepidation that America welcomed the 1987 European Ryder Cup team to Muirfield Village.

Jack Nicklaus had been having something of an Indian summer since the last series. At 46, in 1986, he had become the oldest player to win the Masters; and his golf was still good enough to have posed a threat in this Ryder Cup if he had been playing. If the series of 1983 was fitting in rejoining the former battles of Jack and Tony Jacklin, and in vindicating Nicklaus' intervention to broaden the base of 'British' teams; then there was some sense of irony in the 1987 series being played at the Nicklaus architectural *magnum opus*. Even its very name, reverently acknowledging the great Scottish links and its connection with the Golden Bear's first Open win, could now be construed as another 'pro' for the Europeans, or a 'con' for the home side. Jack's ideal from 1977 may now have seemed to the great man to be not such a good idea. After the three days, I am sure it came to mind. Jacklin, on the other hand, was now taking the war to the European Tour as well as the American team. So magisterial was his

position in the European Ryder Cup set-up at this point, he demanded, and got, several issues agreed, and concessions made, for his players, from an *ad hoc* meeting called between the Opening Ceremony and the first matches. What it did, importantly, was to clear those players' minds of nagging concerns, leaving them free to concentrate fully on the matter in hand.

The 1987 Ryder Cup settled on its present format of matches, and the Europeans, led by some of their big guns, for once were not left at the starting post: the first outings for those soon-to-be legendary pairings, Faldo and Woosnam, and Ballesteros and Olazabal, ensured the morning points were shared. Then, the impossible happened. After over a half a century of US victories, often set up by a golden period during the competition when the opposition was not allowed a look in, they themselves received their first-ever whitewash in a complete session. Four straight wins without return in the afternoon fourballs opened up an unprecedented European lead. But could it last? The second day, with the Americans stung into a dangerous mood, was one of heroic battles, with players on both sides mentioned in dispatches. When hurt in the past, the US had shown a swift, usually match-winning, riposte. The sheer hate of losing is an enormous strength within the American psyche; its power is such that it can seem to move mountains. This outpouring of vengeful vitriol, however, was met with higher and greater mountains than in the past; the Alps and the Pyrenees, not just the Grampians and Snowdonia. The battles went to and fro, and as the European usurpers won one skirmish, the defenders redoubled and fought back. Looking out of it, the Americans, through the Stewart/Bean and Sutton/Mize teams, fought back to reduce the overall lead to its overnight proportions and still leaving them hope in their strong suit, the singles, to come. But the steel in this European side was exemplified by a stubborn win in the last match by Lyle and Langer, and that hope was, it seemed, effectively snuffed out.

Hit us once, and we'll come back at you. Hit us again and watch out. That is what you might find America saying at time of war. If not exactly war, the 1987 Ryder Cup was starting to take on the same kind of offence to the national feel-good factor, and public outcry and some Nicklaus morale-lifting tried, one last time, to reverse the position on the third day. It almost worked. Never take the Americans lightly: never believe they are beaten. Tearing into the superior-feeling European upper order like Test Match fast bowlers against England in cricket, they won five of the first seven matches, and halved another. They had clawed back to within half a point of what should have been an unassailable European lead. It took one of the visitors' lesser lights to stem the tide of vengeance. Eamonn Darcy, while Woosnam, Faldo, Olazabal, Lyle, and the like were being put to the sword, toughed it out against Ben Crenshaw in an amazing match to earn a vital point. Crenshaw, two down at one point, broke his putter in disgust, and thereafter fought his way back using the edge of his wedge or his one iron on the greens. But Darcy's brave putt at the 18th finished it, and it was left to the swashbuckling buccaneer, Ballesteros, to steer the damaged, drifting ship into port, with his match-winning point against Curtis Strange.

US TEAM	EUROPE TEAM
Andy Bean (2)	Seve Ballesteros (4)
Mark Calcavecchia (1)	Gordon Brand, Jr (1)
Ben Crenshaw (3)	Ken Brown (4)*
Tom Kite (4)	Howard Clark (4)
Larry Mize (1)	Eamonn Darcy (4)
Larry Nelson (3)	Nick Faldo (6)
Dan Pohl (1)	Bernhard Langer (4)
Scott Simpson (1)	Sandy Lyle (4)*
Payne Stewart (1)	Jose-Maria Olazabal (1)*
Curtis Strange (3)	Jose Rivero (2)
Hal Sutton (2)	Sam Torrance (3)
Lanny Wadkins (5)	Ian Woosnam (3)

* Indicates captain's 'wild card' selections

Morning Foursomes (Day 1)

Strange & Kite (4&2) beat Clark & Torrance	1 - 0
Pohl & Sutton (2&1) beat Brown & Langer	2 - 0
Mize & Wadkins lost to Faldo & Woosnam (2 up)	2 - 1
Nelson & Stewart lost to Ballesteros & Olazabal (1 up)	2 - 2

Afternoon Fourballs

Crenshaw & Simpson lost to Brand & Rivero (3&2)	2 - 3
Bean & Calcavecchia lost to Langer & Lyle (1 up)	2 - 4
Pohl & Sutton lost to Faldo & Woosnam (2&1)	2 - 5
Kite & Strange lost to Ballesteros & Olazabal (2&1)	2 - 6
Day 1 totals	**2 - 6**

Morning Foursomes (Day 2)

Kite & Strange (3&1) beat Brand & Rivero	1 - 0
Mize & Sutton halved with Faldo & Woosnam	1½-½
Nelson & Wadkins lost to Langer & Lyle (2&1)	1½-1½
Crenshaw & Stewart lost to Ballesteros & Olazabal (1 up)	1½-2½

Afternoon Fourballs (Day 2)

Kite & Strange lost to Faldo & Woosnam (5&4)	1½-3½
Bean & Stewart (3&2) beat Brand & Darcy	2½-3½
Mize & Sutton (2&1) beat Ballesteros & Olazabal	3½-3½
Nelson & Wadkins lost to Langer & Lyle (1 up)	3½-4½
Day 2 totals	**3½-4½**
RUNNING MATCH TOTALS	**5½ - 10½**

Singles (Day 3)

Bean (1 up) beat Woosnam	1 - 0
Pohl lost to Clark (1 up)	1 - 1
Mize halved with Torrance	1½-1½
Calcavecchia (1 up) beat Faldo	2½-1½
Stewart (2 up) beat Olazabal	3½-1½
Simpson (2&1) beat Rivero	4½-1½
Kite (3&2) beat Lyle	5½-1½
Crenshaw lost to Darcy (1 up)	5½-2½
Nelson halved with Langer	6 - 3
Strange lost to Ballesteros (2&1)	6 - 4
Wadkins (3&2) beat Brown	7 - 4
Sutton halved with Brand	7½-4½
Day 3 totals	**7½-4½**
MATCH TOTALS	**13 - 15**

COURSE:	The Belfry
LOCATION:	Sutton Coldfield, West Midlands, England
DATE:	22-24 September
EUROPE CAPTAIN:	Tony Jacklin (non-playing)
US CAPTAIN:	Ray Floyd (non-playing)
RESULT:	Europe 14 – US 14

Tony Jacklin signed off as captain after four successive Ryder Cups, at the Belfry. When he took over, the Europeans were individuals or cliques with no logical reason for bonding, no nationalistic cause to espouse – really just a synthesis of the best talent available to try to keep the US interested in the Ryder Cup. At the end of the 28th series of matches he had left the Americans with a devil of a complex. They could still see they had the best players in depth, but how could they get the better of this international potpourri whose whole was greater than its individual parts. Jacklin had masterminded not just the winning of a Ryder Cup twice in succession (including the first time on US soil), a feat never done before by European teams, but left the Belfry in 1989 with the Cup still in European hands. His record of 2-1-1 over four matches compares with the 3-1-20 complete record of previous teams against the Americans – and 1-1-16 between 1935 and 1981. Jacklin will always be remembered for his playing prowess, especially the holding of both Opens when he won the US title at Hazeldine in 1970. His greatest legacy to golf, though, is undoubtedly his transformation, almost single-handedly, of a doomed anachronism into one of the greatest spectacles in the world of sport.

No one can blame him for exiting the scene after the second Battle of the Belfry. The pressure, both on and off the course, had become exceptionally wearing on the captains. The intensified competition placed more and more demands on them, and in the case of Jacklin, the expectancy next time around was greater than the superhuman effort just made. The US dander was up. Never before had they been treated so in a sport considered now so much their own. The hype leading up to the 1989 event piled pressure on the new American captain, Raymond Floyd. He attempted to stir up pride in his men and intensify morale before the event, but this badly misfired. Taking a leaf out of Ben Hogan's 1967 book when he announced at the Opening Ceremony that the

American team were the 'twelve best golfers in the world', Ray had miscalculated: not only weren't they (the 'Sony' ranking of the time stated that the first three on the list were non-American, and only six of the remaining twelve were), but this was not 1967. In those balmy days when the only stiffness in the competition to US superiority in the Ryder Cup was perceived on the upper lip, Hogan had a point, and the British attitude had been brow-beaten into a state of defeatism. It was considered part of the increasing gamesmanship surrounding the event, now that the competition was fairly even. Floyd's comment, not surprisingly, went down like a lead balloon, and had the opposite effect to what it was intended on the European troops.

Nevertheless the Americans didn't need patronising words. Their self-motivation to regain that which was perceived to be their own was enough, and they came in for lunch with an encouraging 3 - 1 advantage. In 1987, the defining period which led to the European victory was the second session on Day 1, when they whitewashed the Americans for the first time. Now again, the US pairings inexplicably crumbled in the afternoon fourballs, as the inspiring Spaniards and the grittily-talented partnership of Faldo and Woosnam topped and tailed another clean sweep of matches. A four-point swing set up Europe for the second day with a two-point lead. Again mirroring 1987, Day 2 was an exciting, close-fought affair in match results, although many individual matches were won and lost well before the 18th hole. Two wins from Beck and Azinger equalled those now expected from Ballesteros and Olazabal, and honours were even for the day.

Thus on the final day of singles, Europe still maintained a two-point cushion, and needed to win five points out of the twelve on offer to retain the Cup, five-and-a-half to win outright. But the US team went out to eradicate such premature thoughts as quickly as possible. Tom Kite first inflicted a record 18-hole win over hapless Howard Clark, and the lead was wiped out when Beck eased to dormie-three, after winning the 17th, over Langer. In the fourth single, James put Europe ahead again briefly, only for the champion, Seve, to go down to Azinger at the last. Four years earlier Andy North infamously found the lake at the 18th on the Belfry in the pivotal singles match against Sam Torrance. The destiny of the Ryder Cup was to take a huge turn there again, as the hazard came into play. Even going into the 18th, both Stewart and Calcavecchia, in successive matches, found the water and Europe now just required two points to win from the remaining six matches. These were all fairly even, and could go either way, although Canizares was inching to victory over Ken Green, and Woosnam, as backstop, seemed to be having the better of things with Strange. All-square going into the last, the next match to finish was Couples and O'Connor. Left yards behind Freddie's imposing drive, the Irishman needed a long iron to even make the green. His now-famous impeccably-hit two iron, after some divine intervention from Jacklin, closed to four feet. Couples' previously-considered academic nine iron was now no longer a formality. With the crowd getting into a fair old lather and becoming ever-more claustrophobic to the players, the American could only push his approach to the right of the green and that was that, apart from another crying Celt (remember Torrance in 87?). Canizares quietly accomplished his task, and with four matches left, the Cup was safe.

Whether the American gall was raised by the ignominy of all this, or the Europeans still playing suddenly found all the pent-up emotion drained by the news, the last four matches happened to go America's way. I believe there is more to the former conjecture, especially in the way Curtis Strange strung together four birdies over the last four holes to see off Woosnam, leaving the Welshman still looking for his first Ryder Cup singles win. The matches thus ended in the most exciting tie, matching the only other occasion in 1969 when Nicklaus picked up Jacklin's ball on Birkdale links. The all-important singles points had been won for Europe by the so-called journeymen of the team, not the stars. Such was the legacy of Tony Jacklin.

EUROPE TEAM	US TEAM
Seve Ballesteros (5)	Paul Azinger (1)
Gordon Brand, Jr (2)	Chip Beck (1)
Jose-Maria Canizares (4)	Mark Calcavecchia (2)
Howard Clark (5)*	Fred Couples (1)
Nick Faldo (7)	Ken Green (1)
Mark James (4)	Tom Kite (5)
Bernhard Langer (5)*	Mark McCumber (1)
Christy O'Connor, Jr (2)*	Mark O'Meara (2)
Jose-Maria Olazabal (2)	Payne Stewart (2)
Ronan Rafferty (1)	Curtis Strange (4)
Sam Torrance (4)	Lanny Wadkins (6)*
Ian Woosnam (4)	Tom Watson (4)*

* Indicates captain's 'wild card' selections

Morning Foursomes (Day 1)

Faldo & Woosnam halved with	
Kite & Strange	½ - ½
Clark & James lost to	
Stewart & Wadkins (1 up)	½-1½
Langer & Rafferty lost to	
Calcavecchia & Green (2&1)	½-2½
Ballesteros & Olazabal halved with	
Beck & Watson	1 - 3

Afternoon Fourballs (Day 1)

Ballesteros & Olazabal (6&5) beat	
O'Meara & Watson	2 - 3
Clark & James (3&2) beat	
Couples & Wadkins	3 - 3
Brand & Torrance (1 up) beat	
Azinger & Strange	4 - 3
Faldo & Woosnam (2 up) beat	
Calcavecchia & McCumber	5 - 3
Day 1 totals	**5 - 3**

Morning Foursomes (Day 2)

Brand & Torrance lost to	
Azinger & Beck (4&3)	0 - 1
Faldo & Woosnam (3&2) beat	
Stewart & Wadkins	1 - 1
O'Connor & Rafferty lost to	
Calcavecchia & Green (3&2)	1 - 2
Ballesteros & Olazabal (1 up) beat	
Kite & Strange	2 - 2

Afternoon Fourballs (Day 2)

Faldo & Woosnam lost to	
Azinger & Beck (2&1)	2 - 3
Canizares & Langer lost to	
Kite & McCumber (2&1)	2 - 4
Ballesteros & Olazabal (4&2) beat	
Calcavecchia & Green	3 - 4
Clark & James (1 up) beat	
Stewart & Strange	4 - 4
Day 2 totals	**4 - 4**
RUNNING MATCH TOTALS	*9 - 7*

Singles (Day 3)

Clark lost to Kite (8&7)	0 - 1
Langer lost to Beck (3&1)	0 - 2
Ballesteros lost to Azinger (1 up)	0 - 3
James (3&2) beat O'Meara	1 - 3
Olazabal (1 up) beat Stewart	2 - 3
Rafferty (1 up) beat Calcavecchia	3 - 3
O'Connor (1 up) beat Couples	4 - 3
Canizares (1 up) beat Green	5 - 3
Torrance lost to Watson (3&1)	5 - 4
Brand lost to McCumber (1up)	5 - 5
Faldo lost to Wadkins (1 up)	5 - 6
Woosnam lost to Strange (2 up)	5 - 7
Day 3 totals	**5 - 7**
MATCH TOTALS	*14 - 14*

COURSE:	Ocean Course
LOCATION:	Kiawah Island, South Carolina
DATE:	26 -29 September
US CAPTAIN:	Dave Stockton (non-playing)
EUROPE CAPTAIN:	Bernard Gallacher (non-playing)
RESULT:	US 14½ – Europe 13½

After the era of Jacklin, his more down-to-earth aide-de-camp of the previous three encounters, Bernard Gallacher, should have made for a seamless transition. The popular Scot was not of the same stature as the statesmanlike Jacklin, and his homespun low-key methodology was worlds away from the high-profile leadership perhaps required in the modern Ryder Cup. Take his opposite number, for example, Dave Stockton. A no-nonsense professional, twice a Major Champion, he was raising the temperature of the upcoming event by almost inciting the media into anti-European hysteria. By the time Kiawah Island's time had arrived, the most partisan of crowds for any of the series of matches was baying for an American win. Crowds, from the earliest days, especially large in Britain, had always cheered on their favourites, and sometimes there was an excited cheer from a few when something hadn't gone right for the opposition. What we began to see at Kiawah Island, though, was the start of a very disturbing trend: perhaps a natural corollary of these matches being so competitive since 1983. The American fans, so unused to seeing Americans getting beaten at anything, and whipped up by a bellicose golfing press, now had in their midst the heckler and the jeerer, the bad sportsman prepared to win at all costs. There may have only been a few, and the instances rare, but since 1991, there has been a development of bad feeling between visiting players and home galleries, something that graduated to player-player bad feeling in 1999. Of course this does not go back to the stance of Stockton in 1991 alone, but he was the first captain on either side to seek an edge which was on the fringe of sportsmanship.

As a series, the 1991 Ryder Cup was as magnificent as any in latter years. After the first two days, the teams were classically locked at 8 - 8. The mornings were dominated by the home team, but the Europeans came back strongly after lunch, taking the honours for the day. For America, Fred Couples and Ray Floyd, happier to be back in harness as a player, were in the thick of things; whilst, for Europe, if the Faldo/Woosnam bubble had burst, the Ballesteros and Olazabal partnership was still doing more than its bit.

Day 3 then, and a day of spectacular singles jousting. No explanation was given, but Steve Pate who had been injured in a road accident on his way to South Carolina, missed the first day's play. He played seemingly without any ill-effects in the second set of fourballs on Day 2, yet was withdrawn following the publication of the pairing sheets for the singles. Whether Dave Stockton would have allowed Pate to play anyone other than a pumped-up Ballesteros, we may never know. Gallacher was fuming, Seve was drawn to play Wayne Levi, and David Gilford the unlucky name in the envelope. When play got under way, the earlier matches, broadly speaking, seemed to be going the way of Europe, and those starting later favouring the Americans. So with half the results in, a European lead of two looked secure, but the US were finishing strongly. Colin Montgomerie, one who was to become susceptible to gallery barracking over the coming years, stamped his arrival in the Ryder Cup, winning the last four holes for a memorable half with Mark Calcavecchia. It was becoming increasingly obvious though that Beck, Couples and Wadkins would win their matches against Woosnam, Torrance and James, respectively, leaving only an unlikely Paul Broadhurst point over O'Meara to count. So it panned out, and all the interest swung to the very last match; surely one of the greatest of all Ryder Cup climaxes. Playing against wily old Hale Irwin and a sometimes over-exuberant crowd, Bernhard Langer had drawn level going into the last hole, having been two adrift with four to play. He needed to win, however, if the Europeans were to share the spoils and retain the trophy. Irwin, who had won his third US Open the previous year, even with all his experience, had never known pressure like this. He miscued his approach to the green and the ball clattered into the gallery, seemingly lost. Then, almost as if an afterthought, it popped back out again, and an Irwin life had been saved. Eventually on the green he went to pieces over a putt that left him anything but stone dead, but it was the German who still had to go for the win, and that meant holing a mean five and a half footer. Barely able to keep itself in control, the crowd willed Langer's putt past the edge of the cup. America had won back the Ryder Cup for the first time since 1985, by a coat of paint. Langer was distraught, but the fans went wild, as they say.

US TEAM	EUROPE TEAM
Paul Azinger (2)	Seve Ballesteros (5)
Chip Beck (2)*	Paul Broadhurst (1)
Mark Calcavecchia (3)	Nick Faldo (8)*
Fred Couples (2)	David Feherty (1)
Ray Floyd (7)*	David Gilford (1)
Hale Irwin (5)	Mark James (5)*
Wayne Levi (1)	Bernhard Langer (6)
Mark O'Meara (3)	Colin Montgomerie (1)
Steve Pate (1)	Jose-Maria Olazabal (3)
Corey Pavin (1)	Steven Richardson (1)
Payne Stewart (3)	Sam Torrance (5)
Lanny Wadkins (7)*	Ian Woosnam (5)

* Indicates captain's 'wild card' selections

Morning Foursomes (Day 1)

Azinger & Beck lost to	
Ballesteros & Olazabal (2&1)	0 - 1
Irwin & Wadkins (4&2) beat	
Gilford & Montgomerie	1 - 1
Couples & Floyd (2&1) beat	
James & Langer	2 - 1
Calcavecchia & Stewart (1 up) beat	
Faldo & Woosnam	3 - 1

Afternoon Fourballs (Day 1)

Calcavecchia & Pavin lost to	
James & Richardson (5&4)	3 - 2
O'Meara & Wadkins halved with	
Feherty & Torrance	3½-2½
Couples & Floyd (5&3) beat	
Faldo & Woosnam	4½-2½
Azinger & Beck lost to	
Ballesteros & Olazabal (2&1)	4½-3½
Day 1 totals	**4½-3½**

Morning Foursomes (Day 2)

Azinger & O'Meara (7&6) beat	
Faldo & Gilford	1 - 0
Irwin & Wadkins (4&2) beat	
Feherty & Torrance	2 - 0
Calcavecchia & Stewart (1 up) beat	
James & Richardson	3 - 0
Couples & Floyd lost to	
Ballesteros & Olazabal (3&2)	3 - 1

Afternoon Fourballs (Day 2)

Azinger & Irwin lost to	
Broadhurst & Woosnam (2&1)	3 - 2
Pate & Pavin lost to	
Langer & Montgomerie (2&1)	3 - 3
Levi & Wadkins lost to	
James & Richardson (3&1)	3 - 4
Couples & Stewart halved with	
Ballesteros & Olazabal	3½-4½
Day 2 totals	**3½-4½**
RUNNING MATCH TOTALS	**8 - 8**

Singles (Day 3)

Stewart lost to Feherty (2&1)	0 - 1
Floyd lost to Faldo (2 up)	0 - 2
Calcavecchia halved with Montgomerie	½-2½
Pavin (2&1) beat Richardson	1½-2½
Levi lost to Ballesteros (3&2)	1½-3½
Azinger (2 up) beat Olazabal	2½-3½
Beck (3&1) beat Woosnam	3½-3½
O'Meara lost to Broadhurst (3&1)	3½-4½
Couples (3&2) beat Torrance	4½-4½
Wadkins (3&2) beat James	5½-4½
Irwin halved with Langer	6 - 5
Pate halved (match not played) with Gilford	6½-5½
Day 3 totals	**6½-5½**
MATCH TOTALS	***14½ - 13½***

1993

COURSE:	The Belfry
LOCATION:	Sutton Coldfield, West Midlands, England
DATE:	24-26 September
EUROPE CAPTAIN:	Bernard Gallacher (non-playing)
US CAPTAIN:	Tom Watson (non-playing)
RESULT:	Europe 13 – US 15

Tom Watson used all his mid-West charm to ensure the antics of 1991 didn't undermine what had become a wonderful international sporting competition. He made a gentlemen's pact with Bernard Gallacher, a man after his own heart, to keep the rivalry within bounds and to let the respective play of the two sides do the talking. In doing so, the atmosphere surrounding the 1993 series at the Belfry was much more ambient, and the three days as good as they ever were. Ray Floyd created a record for being the oldest-ever player, from either side, to play in the Ryder Cup. He was a jaunty 51. He shared another, with Lanny Wadkins: they both equalled Billy Casper's American record of eight appearances.

The home side shaded the first day with Wadkins and Pavin starring for the visitors: Woosnam in his two matches with different partners was also 100%, and Faldo with Montgomerie were unbeaten. The second day was looking promising with the Europeans taking the less-fancied foursomes, the above-mentioned British stalwarts again to the fore, and a healthy lead of three at lunch. There then occurred a bizarre series of events, the blame for the outcome of which one has to lay at the door of Gallacher. In fairness, neither Bernard Langer nor Seve Ballesteros were the established players they were in 1993, when Tony Jacklin got their support for the cause in the mid-eighties. Greats in the making, yes, yet still young and malleable in the right hands. It makes one ponder, however, whether Jacklin would have succumbed to player-power as Gallacher did that day at the Belfry. With the Americans rocking, Langer and Ballesteros persuaded Gallacher to rest them from the fourballs, usually so profitable for the Europeans, arguing that they wanted to be at their best for the following day's singles. Instead of going for the jugular, and putting the Cup effectively out of the Americans' grasp by winning the fourballs 3-1, say, Gallacher drafted in rookies Rocca and Haeggman; and the weakened home pairings lost the session by the same

margin. Therefore, the Europeans who would have anticipated a lead going unto the singles of four or five points, undoubtedly let the US team off the hook; leaving them not just relieved, but amused and highly motivated by events which left them only one behind.

When the third day arrived, Sam Torrance cried off injured, and Watson chose to leave out veteran Lanny Wadkins. Chip Beck, three behind Barry Lane on the 14th tee, came through to make it three wins out of three in his Ryder cup singles record to bring the teams level. But for the immediate period thereafter, it looked as if Bernard Gallacher's decision of the previous day might not matter anyway. Montgomerie, Baker and Haeggman all won, against tough opposition, and Woosnam, for a change, forced a half with Freddie Couples. Two and a half points were needed for victory from the six remaining singles, and with Olazabal, Faldo, plus the refreshed Ballesteros and Langer still out, who would have bet against them? The Americans began to play inspired golf, however, and as news spread that they were winning holes in the later matches, so the momentum built up. Before too long we were witnessing a familiar US charge of old, something the Europeans may have thought could never happen to them again. Payne Stewart swept away Mark James; then a European banker coming into the 17th, Costantino Rocca, blew up, conceding the last two holes and the match to Davis Love. Thereafter the stars were toppled ignominiously, with only Faldo, halving in the final match with Paul Azinger, doing his reputation little harm, but then only when it was all done and dusted. After a period of European dominance which had lasted only six years, two successive Ryder Cup wins, albeit exciting, nail-biting affairs, had placed the Americans firmly back in the driving seat and at the pinnacle of world golf once more. Had the European challenge been seen off for another several decades, or could they continue to provide meaningful opposition for the US in the future? They just had two years to find out.

EUROPE TEAM	US TEAM
Peter Baker (1)	Paul Azinger (3)
Seve Ballesteros (6)*	Chip Beck (3)
Nick Faldo (9)	John Cook (1)
Joakim Haeggman (1)*	Fred Couples (3)
Mark James (6)	Ray Floyd (8)*
Barry Lane (1)	Jim Gallagher, Jr (1)
Bernhard Langer (7)	Lee Janzen (1)
Colin Montgomerie (2)	Tom Kite (7)
Jose-Maria Olazabal (4)*	Davis Love III (1)
Costantino Rocca (1)	Corey Pavin (2)
Sam Torrance (6)	Payne Stewart (4)
Ian Woosnam (6)	Lanny Wadkins (8)*

* Indicates captain's 'wild card' selections

Morning Foursomes (Day 1)

James & Torrance lost to Pavin & Wadkins (4&3)	0 - 1
Langer & Woosnam (7&5) beat Couples & Stewart	1 - 1
Ballesteros & Olazabal lost to Kite & Love (2&1)	1 - 2
Faldo & Montgomerie (4&3) beat Couples & Floyd	2 - 2

Afternoon Fourballs (Day 1)

Baker & Woosnam (1 up) beat Gallagher & Janzen	3 - 2
Lane & Langer lost to Pavin & Wadkins (4 & 2)	3 - 3
Faldo & Montgomerie halved with Azinger & Couples	3½-3½
Ballesteros & Olazabal (2&1) beat Kite & Love	4½-3½
Day 1 totals	**4½-3½**

Morning Foursomes (Day 2)

Faldo & Montgomerie (3&2) beat Pavin & Wadkins	1 - 0
Langer & Woosnam (2&1) beat Azinger & Couples	2 - 0
Baker & Lane lost to Floyd & Stewart (3&2)	2 - 1
Ballesteros & Olazabal (2&1) beat Kite & Love	3 - 1

Afternoon Fourballs (Day 2)

Faldo & Montgomerie lost to Beck & Cook (2 up)	3 - 2
James & Rocca lost to Gallagher & Pavin (5&4)	3 - 3
Baker & Woosnam (6&5) beat Azinger & Couples	4 - 3
Haeggman & Olazabal lost to Floyd & Stewart	4 - 4
Day 2 totals	**4 - 4**
RUNNING MATCH TOTALS	**8½ - 7½**

Singles (Day 3)

Lane lost to Beck (1 up)	0 - 1
Montgomerie (1 up) beat Janzen	1 - 1
Baker (2 up) beat Pavin	2 - 1
Woosnam halved with Couples	2½-1½
Haeggman (1 up) beat Cook	3½-1½
James lost to Stewart (3&2)	3½-2½
Rocca lost to Love (1 up)	3½-3½
Ballesteros lost to Gallagher (3&2)	3½-4½
Olazabal lost to Floyd (2up)	3½-5½
Langer lost to Kite (5&3)	3½-6½
Faldo halved with Azinger	4 - 7
Torrance halved (match not played) with Wadkins	4½-7½
Day 3 totals	**4½-7½**
MATCH TOTALS	**13 - 15**

COURSE:	Oak Hill CC
LOCATION:	Rochester, New York
DATE:	22 -24 September
US CAPTAIN:	Lanny Wadkins (non-playing)
EUROPE CAPTAIN:	Bernard Gallacher (non-playing)
RESULT:	US 13½ – Europe 14½

Bernard Gallacher had been involved with the Ryder Cup man and boy. Making his Cup debut in 1969 as a 21 year-old, he played in an unbroken sequence until 1983, Tony Jacklin's first year as captain. Although not officially appointed, he was to be Jacklin's No. 2 for the next three series, and it seemed almost inevitable he would climb into the great man's shoes when he called it a day. Gallacher was all too aware that in an official capacity, either as player on eight occasions, or as captain in now his third consecutive Ryder Cup, he had never been on the winning side. Certain to bow out after 1995, this was his last chance therefore for glory. To help bolster a familiar mix of top players and promising rookies, Gallacher kept faith with two proven scrappers from the good old days, when he chose Faldo and Woosnam (included when Olazabal cried off unfit), now both starting to decline, as his 'wild cards'. Ballesteros, who had seen a temporary return to some form, and Langer, as ever, were still around like a pair of knowing sixth-formers. Against this, the US captain, Lanny Wadkins, chose Fred Couples, still in the World Top 10 according to the Official Ranking, but incongruously not in the US Top 10 over the period that points were being counted for selection; and another old chum, Curtis Strange. With Ben Crenshaw qualifying after his emotional second Masters win earlier in the season, and the doggedly consistent Tour pro Peter Jacobsen, and a resurgent Jay Haas, also making the team on merit, fortysomethings were well-represented in the home side. After several series when the US seemed happier with foursomes pairs, and the Europeans with the freer fourballs format, the trend was bucked at the Belfry two years earlier. It continued to be bucked at Oak Hill. Following an even first morning, the Americans inflicted some heavy defeats on the visitors after lunch, taking the fourballs 3 - 1, and moving into the second day with this two-point advantage. Thereupon, the visitors got much the better of the morning foursomes, bringing the scores level, only for the first afternoon to be repeated. Over the two days, the Americans

had won six of the eight fourballs, while Europe had triumphed in five of the eight foursomes. Who'd be a betting man? Phil Mickelson impressed as he moved toward a 100% three-match record on his debut; and Corey Pavin sent the fans a-hollerin' and a-whoopin' when he pitched in on the eighteenth to steal the last fourball. For Europe, Costantino Rocca, blamed by many for throwing away the Europeans' last chance in 1995, featured in three pairs wins out of four. The upshot of all this was that the US were heading into their favourite singles format, already holding a healthy two-point lead, leaving themselves just five points out of the twelve on offer on the Sunday to keep the Cup for the third series in a row.

The signs on the third morning were not initially good for Europe, with Seve being blown away in the first match by Tom Lehman, and the score in favour of the US now 10-7, with only four points needed for overall victory. Thereafter, it almost all went wrong for the home side. A superb win for Mark James over Jeff Maggert started the ball rolling, then Clark pipped Jacobsen. Woosnam, against his 1993 opponent, Couples, had never won a singles in six previous outings. But Woosie wobbled to a half, and the Europeans breathed a sigh of relief. They had pulled back on the US, now only one behind, and had consolidated. Davis Love briefly renewed American optimism, and a two-point gap, when he beat Rocca convincingly. But then, aided by some fairly inept performances, the wheels came off the home wagon in spectacular fashion, with Faxon, Crenshaw, Strange, then Roberts losing out in turn to Gilford, Montgomerie, Faldo (one down with two to play) and Torrance. A two-point lead had been transformed into a two-point deficit over just four matches. Although the tide was in Europe's favour, there was much oar-work to be done yet. A gutsy display by Corey Pavin overcame the awkward Langer, and with Mickelson looking as if he was going to shade the last match against Johansson, unknown Philip Walton of

Ireland was suddenly shoved into centre stage, the destiny of the Ryder Cup squarely on his shoulders. He was coasting it, three up and only three holes left against Jay Haas. At least a half was guaranteed then, but if Johansson lost, the series would be tied and America would hold on to the trophy. Then on the 16th, Haas holed his bunker shot, and made everyone very nervous indeed. Walton was definitely cracking when he bogeyed 17; and he and Haas headed for the eighteenth and their doom. Mickelson was seeing off the Swede behind them, so everything was down to these two. For all his experience (he was fifth in the US Open as far back as 1975, and a seven-time winner on the US Tour) it was Haas who was to crumble more than the young Irishman. While Walton made the green in a shaky three, Haas' third sailed left into some trees. His approach span back to the edge, the par putt slipping by. Walton needed, and took, the two putts in hand to secure victory. He entered the folklore of golf, and Bernard Gallacher withdrew with honour.

US TEAM	EUROPE TEAM
Fred Couples (4)*	Seve Ballesteros (7)
Ben Crenshaw (4)	Howard Clark (6)
Brad Faxon (1)	Nick Faldo (10)*
Jay Haas (2)	David Gilford (2)
Peter Jacobsen (2)	Mark James (7)
Tom Lehman (1)	Per-Ulrik Johansson (1)
Davis Love III (1)	Bernhard Langer (8)
Jeff Maggert (1)	Colin Montgomerie (3)
Phil Mickelson (1)	Costantino Rocca (2)
Corey Pavin (3)	Sam Torrance (7)
Loren Roberts (1)	Philip Walton (1)
Curtis Strange (5)*	Ian Woosnam (7)*

* Indicates captain's 'wild card' selections

Morning Foursomes (Day 1)

Lehman & Pavin (1 up) beat	
Faldo & Montgomerie	1 - 0
Couples & Haas lost to	
Rocca & Torrance	1 - 1
Love & Maggert (4&3) beat	
Clark & James	2 - 1
Crenshaw & Strange lost to	
Johansson & Langer	2 - 2

Afternoon Fourballs (Day 1)

Faxon & Jacobsen lost to	
Ballesteros & Gilford	2 - 3
Maggert & Roberts (6&5) beat	
Rocca & Torrance	3 - 3
Couples & Love (3&2) beat	
Faldo & Montgomerie	4 - 3
Mickelson & Pavin (6&4) beat	
Johansson & Langer	5 - 3
Day 1 totals	**5 - 3**

Morning Foursomes (Day 2)

Haas & Strange lost to	
Faldo & Montgomerie (4&2)	0 - 1
Love & Maggert lost to	
Rocca & Torrance (6&5)	0 - 2
Jacobsen & Roberts (1 up) beat	
Walton & Woosnam	1 - 2
Lehman & Pavin lost to	
Gilford & Langer (4&3)	1 - 3

Afternoon Fourballs (Day 2)

Couples & Faxon (4&2) beat	
Faldo & Montgomerie	2 - 3
Crenshaw & Love lost to	
Walton & Woosnam (3&2)	2 - 4
Haas & Mickelson (3&2) beat	
Ballesteros & Gilford	3 - 4
Pavin & Roberts (1 up) beat	
Faldo & Langer	4 - 4
Day 2 totals	**4 - 4**
RUNNING MATCH TOTALS	**9 - 7**

Singles (Day 3)

Lehman (4&3) beat Ballesteros	1 - 0
Jacobsen lost to Clark (1 up)	1 - 1
Maggert lost to James (4&3)	1 - 2
Couples halved with Woosnam	1½-2½
Love (3&2) beat Rocca	2½-2½
Faxon lost to Gilford (1 up)	2½-3½
Crenshaw lost to Montgomerie (3&1)	2½-4½
Strange lost to Faldo (1 up)	2½-5½
Roberts lost to Torrance (2&1)	2½-6½
Pavin (3&2) beat Langer	3½-6½
Haas lost to Walton (1 up)	3½-7½
Mickelson (2&1) beat Johansson	4½-7½
Day 3 totals	**4½-7½**
MATCH TOTALS	*13½ - 14½*

COURSE:	Valderrama GC
LOCATION:	Sotogrande, Spain
DATE:	26-28 September
EUROPE CAPTAIN:	Seve Ballesteros (non-playing)
US CAPTAIN:	Tom Kite (non-playing)
RESULT:	Europe 14½ – US 13½

Despite the gradual spread of cosmopolitan personnel involved in the Ryder Cup up to 1995, the British PGA had only allowed the British, British and Irish, or the European hosting of the Ryder Cup outside of England once – Muirfield in 1973. So the Scots had the privilege just once: nothing for the Welsh or Irish – the small nations which had been an integral part of Ryder Cup history through the characters, and some great players, they had produced. In a European context, Spain could therefore consider itself quite lucky that it was honoured so soon. Once the venue was settled at Valderrama, Seve needn't have lobbied for the job of captain: it was his for the taking. No-one else was in the frame. Right to the end he was optimistic about making the team as a player, and perhaps becoming the first European playing captain since Dai Rees in 1961; the first for any side since Palmer's effervescent leadership in 1963. As it turned out, his omnipresence would not have left him enough time. If walkie-talkies had been around since fairly early on, it was under the captaincy of Tony Jacklin that they became really effective. Jacklin would relay and receive information to and from those matches he couldn't physically get to. With Ballesteros, that wasn't good enough. He felt he had to career about all the sites of the battlefield, visiting his troops in person, his mere presence inspiring his charges to greater things. It was a case of have buggy, will travel; his charger was a motorised golf cart, surging over hill and down dale like some rally-cross enthusiast, Miguel Angel Jimenez, his petrified No. 2 hanging on for grim death.

Against this larger-than-life whirlwind, the US had pitched Tom Kite, as polarised a character to that of Seve's as one could get. A really professional, dedicated player, he went about his captain's role with the same quiet efficiency, determined not to be completely over-powered by the Ballesteros *tour de force*. He selected Couples and Lee Janzen to supplement his team: Seve, his erstwhile

partner-in-crime, Olazabal, happily fit again, and US-based Jesper Parnevik. Faldo created a new record, on either side, of eleven appearances, and the world waited with baited breath to see what the new phenomenon, 21 year-old Tiger Woods, could add to the lore and tradition of 70 years. The foursomes and fourballs timetables were tampered with again, but the overall framework remained the same; and it all started, as it often does, quietly enough, the early sparring producing no outright leader by lunchtime, and only one point in favour of the Europeans by nightfall, on the first day. Woods, playing with mentor O'Meara, took his first Ryder Cup blood.

Seve stirred up his men for Day 2 and the Europeans took three and a half points from the morning session, the captain highly visible and getting every last ounce of performance from both his men and his buggy. The recent tendency for the teams to abandon their hitherto favourite pair-formats came to an abrupt halt, at least from the European viewpoint. After doing well in the foursomes, the Europeans got much their own way in the preferred fourballs on the second day. The morning damage took the home side clear by an unprecedented five points by the end of the day. Day 3 saw the Americans wake up to a gloomy prospect. The Costa del Sol's legendary sunshine had turned its back on the event, so the three days were littered with frequent heavy downpours issuing from permanently-leaden clouds. Add to this the visitors needing to collect nine of the twelve available points left to win back the Cup, and you wouldn't have been surprised to hear that the Americans had decided to declare and stay in bed.

Tom Kite was a miserly golfer, though, and his attitude as captain was no different. If these European grandees and hidalgos wanted this Ryder Cup, they would have to fight for every last half-point, until the last bitter resistance was finally overcome, and that would be a long time coming. He told his men that obtaining the required points could be achieved, and that US teams in the past had achieved near whitewashes of the opposition in the singles. What he omitted to say was that no team had ever chased such a last-day target and succeeded. He couldn't have wished for a better start. Fred Couples, playing inspirational golf, swatted a disgruntled, and in his own view, underplayed, Ian Woosnam, by a record-equalling score. The overnight score and his wretched performance left the Welshman with no argument. The points were shared over the next five matches, the biggest story being Woods' lesson from Rocca. So far, so good for the Europeans: six matches to go and one point to retain the Ryder Cup, one-and-a-half to win the series. Urging his men to one final effort, and with the pride of securing at least a tie, at stake, Kite got a spirited fightback from his remaining players. Finally, Bernhard Langer produced the point that mattered, but the Americans were to win four of the five matches left. In the last match out, Colin Montgomerie, whose steady, unfussy play over the three days had provided an interesting contrast to Ballesteros' intrusive style of management, coolly shepherded his match against Scott Hoch to the conclusion required for the team. Colin was not so amused, however, when, with Hoch unable to do anything to change the overall result, Seve told him to concede a 20-footer to the American, leaving the final matched halved, and an unwelcome dent in Monty's Ryder Cup figures. In the end, the European victory was done the hard way, but the US had left themselves an insurmountable mountain to climb. Since 1985, the Europeans had accumulated a 4-2-1 record.

EUROPE TEAM	US TEAM
Thomas Bjorn (1)	Fred Couples (5)*
Darren Clarke (1)	Brad Faxon (2)
Nick Faldo (11)	Jim Furyk (1)
Ignacio Garrido (1)	Scott Hoch (1)
Per-Ulrik Johansson (2)	Lee Janzen (2)*
Bernhard Langer (9)	Tom Lehman (2)
Colin Montgomerie (4)	Justin Leonard (1)
Jose-Maria Olazabal (5)*	Davis Love III (2)
Jesper Parnevik (1)*	Jeff Maggert (2)
Costantino Rocca (3)	Phil Mickelson (2)
Lee Westwood (1)	Mark O'Meara (4)
Ian Woosnam (8)	Tiger Woods (1)

* Indicates captain's 'wild card' selections

Morning Fourballs (Day 1)

Olazabal & Rocca (1 up) beat	
Love & Mickelson	1 - 0
Faldo & Westwood lost to	
Couples & Faxon (1 up)	1 - 1
Johansson & Parnevik (1 up) beat	
Furyk & Lehman	2 - 1
Langer & Montgomerie lost to	
O'Meara & Woods (3&2)	2 - 2

Afternoon Foursomes (Day 1)

Olazabal & Rocca lost to	
Hoch & Janzen (1 up)	2 - 3
Langer & Montgomerie (5&3) beat	
O'Meara & Woods	3 - 3
Faldo & Westwood (3&2) beat	
Leonard & Maggert	4 - 3
Garrido & Parnevik halved with	
Lehman & Mickelson	4½-3½

Day 1 totals	**4½-3½**

Morning Fourballs (Day 2)

Clarke & Montgomerie (1 up) beat	
Couples & Love	1 - 0
Bjorn & Woosnam (2&1) beat	
Faxon & Leonard	2 - 0
Faldo & Westwood (2&1) beat	
O'Meara & Woods	3 - 0
Garrido & Olazabal halved with	
Lehman & Mickelson	3½-½

Afternoon Foursomes (Day 2)

Langer & Montgomerie (1 up) beat	
Furyk & Janzen	4½-½
Faldo & Westwood lost to	
Hoch & Maggert (2&1)	4½-1½
Garrido & Garrido halved with	
Leonard & Woods	5 - 2
Olazabal & Rocca (5&4 beat)	
Couples & Love	6 - 2

Day 2 totals	**6 - 2**
RUNNING MATCH TOTALS	***10½ - 5½***

Singles (Day 3)

Woosnam lost to Couples (8&7)	0 - 1
Johansson (3&2) beat Love	1 - 1
Parnevik lost to O'Meara (5&4)	1 - 2
Clarke lost to Mickelson (2&1)	1 - 3
Rocca (4&2) beat Woods	2 - 3
Bjorn halved with Leonard	2½-3½
Garrido lost to Lehman (7&6)	2½-4½
Langer (2&1) beat Faxon	3½-4½
Westwood lost to Maggert (3&2)	3½-5½
Olazabal lost to Janzen (1 up)	3½-6½
Faldo lost to Furyk (3&2)	3½-7½
Montgomerie halved with Hoch	4 - 8

Day 3 totals   **4 - 8**

MATCH TOTALS   *14½ - 13½*

COURSE:	The Country Club
LOCATION:	Brookline, Boston, Massachusetts
DATE:	24 -26 September
US CAPTAIN:	Ben Crenshaw (non-playing)
EUROPE CAPTAIN:	Mark James (non-playing)
RESULT:	US 14½ – Europe 13½

And so to the last Ryder Cup of the century; and if it didn't serve to line the coffers of the respective PGAs so well, it may have been the last competition ever. Ever since the mid-eighties when a newly found composite having been created, was then, for the first time, threatening US hegemony in world golf, the attitude of the Americans gradually changed with every niggling chip the Europeans were taking out of their veneer of superiority. The air of the Europeans was changing too. No longer the cap-touching subservience of previous 'thank you for the humiliation, sir'-types, which had characterised the down-trodden, grey, I-know-my-place British professional for so many decades. Now from the blousiness of Ballesteros to the meanness of Montgomerie, no more ground was being conceded to the Americans. The US team's general beneficence in the massacres before 1983 was hardening, through, first of all, disbelief in what was happening, then through sheer frustration in not being able to do too much about it. Momentum in European golf had led to an unheard-of expectancy in the Ryder Cup: and Americans were now starting to play 'hardball'. This was clear after the Europeans' 1985-89 reign as holders, when Dave Stockton choreographed the 'War on the Shore' at Kiawah Island. It worked along one dimension only, in that the Ryder Cup was regained. The shrewd appointment of Tom Watson as the next US captain then did much to calm things down, if only to brush some of the nastiness under the carpet. Subsequent European wins at Oak Hill and Valderrama were typified by jingoistic celebrations of a type which smacked now openly of triumphalism: far from the rosy-hued vista of Ian Woosnam dangling over the Belfry Clubhouse in 1985, spraying a stunned crowd with champagne in naive, disbelieving celebration after Jacklin's first win. The crowds throughout the nineties had become more than partisan: now, more than at any time they were a part of the home side's weaponry, and thuggish misdemeanours, like the growth of heckling, were tut-

tutted at rather than openly rebuked. Something had to give, and it was so sad that in concluding a wonderful series of matches over the best part of two decades with one of the greatest collapses/fight-backs (depending on your stance) ever seen in sporting competition, the overriding memory will not be of the golf.

Coming into the meeting at the Country Club, all was not right. Peeved that the PGA of America was to earn a multi-million dollar profit from the 1999 event, some of the selected US team wanted to be rewarded too. They were led openly by David Duval (who, never having played in a Ryder Cup, had likened it to a corporate junket) and Tiger Woods, the world's top two players, and, more surprisingly, Mark O'Meara, who had been something of a traditionalist, and a vet of three previous Ryder Cups. Of course, they weren't really saying we want to be paid, *per se*: what concerned them was how the PGA were going to use this grotesque pile of money. Unfortunately that's the way it was construed though, and some unseemly bickering occurred within the American team. Payne Stewart, for one, was sickened by the suggestion of being paid to represent his country, while captain, Ben Crenshaw, as reverential towards golfing traditions as anyone, must have wondered whether his team was being infected by Philistines. So not united, this States' team, then, when they arrived at Brookline. It seemed that this lack of togetherness was going to prove the US downfall. In the vanguard of an irresistible European charge on Day 1 was Spain's new *El Cid*, Sergio Garcia, except that because he was only 19 and the youngest player on either side of the Atlantic to play in the Ryder Cup, he was already known as *El Niño*, 'The Kid'. It alluded also to the destructive climatic phenomenon which had been battering away at America's Pacific coastline for some months earlier – a metaphor for American ruin. Going into Saturday, the US were 2 - 6 down (3½ of the points coming from the irresistible combination of the exuberant young Spaniard and the eccentric Swede, Parnevik) and rocking. Their disarray contrasted sharply to Mark James' buoyant, confident troops. It took a super-human effort from Crenshaw to get the US juggernaut underway, and although twice taking the lead within the morning session of matches, each time they were hauled back by the Europeans. The wins had sparked some life into the home team though, and they hung on to the Europeans in the afternoon fixtures, leaving the overnight score differential the same, at four.

The Europe side had led at Valderrama after two days by five, and just held on, as the Americans, although always in vain, pulled them almost back to parity. Both sides were aware then of what was possible: I doubt, deep down, though, no matter what Ben Crenshaw said beforehand, that either side believed the visitors would lose. James gambled slightly, in making the upper order more lightweight than those last going out: numbers 3, 4 and 5 in the order, all rookies, and hadn't yet played in a match. Crenshaw had thought differently and sent out a strong opening group of stars, and by the middle of the day the Americans, after the first six matches, were unbelievably two points ahead. They had not just won the matches either, they had pulverised the opposition. The crowd by now had been whipped into a frenzy by the prospect of a most unlikely, yet glorious, in the context of sporting history, home victory. Montgomerie, ever a target, and sadly over time, one who now expected it, was cruelly barracked; so much that his father left the course after seven holes. It is difficult to criticise players when the abuse they receive is constant and demeaning, but Monty has now made himself a target for these louts by his gestures of distaste and some over-emphasis when withdrawing from his ball. That said, he was the main rallying point for the Europeans still out: as long as his match was still relevant at the end, it seemed that Europe might yet escape. A plucky win by Padraig Harrington against Mark O'Meara stemmed the juggernaut, now threatening to run out of control, but Steve Pate's win over Jimenez left the Americans needing just a half for victory. Next up, Olazabal and Leonard were on the 17th, now neck and neck, while Montgomerie was holding Stewart at bay, and the final two matches had already closed out for one point apiece. The Olazabal/Leonard match was the key, therefore; a half would be enough to take the Cup. Leonard's revival to this point was a microcosm of the changes in US fortunes over the three days. Four down

coming into the 12th, he, surely, had little chance against the rejuvenated Masters Champion. Mistakes by the Spaniard on 12 and 13 let the American, himself 1997 Open Champion, back in, just as a tactical error by James partially accounted for the US storming back earlier in the day. With his mood changing to positive, and Olazabal becoming more and more pressurised, 14 and 15 were won. But champion golfers have other attributes, not just talent, and Ollie steeled himself for the *denouement*, one which would have a shattering effect on one side, and a feeling like nothing on earth for the other. After ending all-square at 16, Olazabal was in pole position on the green on 17: Justin's approach gave him an impossible 45-foot putt for birdie; Jose-Maria was inside that with a good chance for birdie from 20 feet. The crowd was wetting itself by now, and many were chanting 'USA, USA', but nothing really untoward. In fact, a caucus of visiting supporters were doing their best to match it with a spirited 'Jose, Jose'. Silence fell over Leonard's putt, and as he struck it the world went into suspended animation, like one of those cinematic tricks: this though was life imitating art. After an interminable journey the ball plopped in, Justin whooped with unbridled joy, and pandemonium broke out.

What happened next is generally interpreted somewhat differently by each side. That it did happen has led to one of the sorriest episodes in the history of such a gracious game. All now know that the US fans and members of the media, and, more importantly, the team members who were anxiously fringing the green, erupted in spontaneous celebration, and spilled on to it. To be fair to Justin Leonard, he had made some attempt to get off the putting surface in his excitement, but was overwhelmed by his team mates. All players must subconsciously have had the line of Olazabal's yet-to-be-taken putt in their minds, as they steered away from it. Unfortunately some hangers-on didn't. This, all sides agree in retrospect, should never have happened. The conventions of the Royal and Ancient game are immensely strong still, and courtesy should have been given to the other player to play out. All who were there and have spoken since have publicly acknowledged it. When things eventually settled down, Olazabal missed his putt, and the Ryder Cup had been lost. To his credit and professional pride, he birdied the dormied 18th.

The aftermath of events at the 17th hole are now well-documented, but it is important to look back after a few months to see whether there has been any lasting harm done to the Ryder Cup, or golf itself. Initially Ben Crenshaw could sing nothing but praise, quite rightly, for his team's remarkable come-back: his immediate recollections of the 17th hole, were, understandably to do with the magical putt which had won back the Ryder Cup. He even tried to infer some kind of fatalism, by recalling that is was on the 17th hole in the play-off of the 1913 US Open Championship, that Harry Vardon double-bogeyed, leaving Francis Ouimet to open up nearly a century of US golfing dominance over its Old World teachers. 'Mystical' he called the coincidence. He profusely apologised for the action of his players when the mystical putt was sunk, though, and would do so for days to come, as did many of those, like Tom Lehman, who were involved. The Europeans responded immediately with natural unsportsman-like references to the event, but there it should have ended. Public outbursts from experienced players like Sam Torrance, who called the Americans' impromptu actions 'disgusting'; and Mark James' attempt to diffuse matters sounding only to be 'holier than thou', only added fuel to the fire. Some local press were sympathetic to the Europeans, but as the mumblings went on, they hardened and instead of supporting maligned sportsmen, they now berated 'whining foreigners'. In addition to the 17th-hole debacle, which over time tempers have eased, there became, from the European side, claims which may do long-term damage to the Ryder Cup's future. We have already seen that Montgomerie was a target for some in the galleries, which was borne out by his playing partner in the singles, Payne Stewart, who, characteristically, was disheartened by what he had heard coming from his fellow-Americans. There was a claim that Mark James' wife was spat upon: and a counter-claim from US pro Billy Andrade who was at Brookline, that she was a 'nut-case'. Unsavoury claims often are met with even more unsavoury counter claims, and the American press had a field day for a while thereafter airing, in the genteel confines of such a game, some monstrosities apparently perpetrated by the crowds at Valderrama. Both Crenshaw and James unequivocally announced that they would not be seeking the captaincy again: Ben for what the whole two-year sabbatical had taken out of him; the Englishman even considering refusing to play again in a series held in the US, should he qualify.

There is no winner in this situation, and the *cliché* says that the only loser is golf. In this instance, this could very well be the case. The Ryder Cup will carry on: David Duval was right in that respect – it is too much of a commercial snowball to be dropped by the US PGA or the European Tour. The wounds of 1999 might heal by the 2001 Belfry meeting, but with a pair of potential

combustibles like Curtis Strange and Sam Torrance as captains, who can say. What we witnessed at the Country Club, though, was the erosion of golfing values. There had been coming, through a hardening of competition over the last two decades, a developing undertow of unpleasantness from spectators, and not just those at US home matches. This disturbing trend must be stopped in its tracks, or golf will go the way of other so-called gentlemanly sports in the latter part of the twentieth century, like rugby union, cricket and tennis. Here fans are whipped up into open hatred of the opposition at times, using usually the excuse of race, nationality or creed: the sport, or the event, has then outgrown itself. It is now up to golfers to try to reverse such incitement, for the good of the game, and their own futures.

US TEAM	EUROPE TEAM
David Duval (1)	Darren Clarke (2)
Jim Furyk (2)	Andrew Coltart (1)*
Tom Lehman (3)*	Sergio Garcia (1)
Justin Leonard (2)	Padraig Harrington (1)
Davis Love III (3)	Miguel Jimenez (1)
Jeff Maggert (3)	Paul Lawrie (1)
Phil Mickelson (3)	Colin Montgomerie (5)
Mark O'Meara (5)	Jose-Maria Olazabal (6)
Steve Pate (2)*	Jesper Parnevik (2)*
Payne Stewart (5)	Jarmo Sandelin (1)
Hal Sutton (3)	Jean Van de Velde (1)
Tiger Woods (2)	Lee Westwood (2)

* Indicates captain's 'wild card' selections

Morning Foursomes (Day 1)

Duval & Mickelson lost to	
Lawrie & Montgomerie (3&2)	0 - 1
Lehman & Woods lost to	
Garcia & Parnevik (2&1)	0 - 2
Love & Stewart halved with	
Harrington & Jimenez	½ -2½
Maggert & Sutton (3&2) beat	
Clarke & Westwood	1½-2½

Afternoon Fourballs (Day 1)

Leonard & Love halved with	
Lawrie & Montgomerie	2 - 3
Furyk & Mickelson lost to	
Garcia & Parnevik (1 up)	2 - 4
Maggert & Sutton lost to	
Jimenez & Olazabal (2&1)	2 - 5
Duval & Woods lost to	
Clarke & Westwood (1 up)	2 - 6
Day 1 totals	**2 - 6**

Morning Foursomes (Day 2)

Maggert & Sutton (1 up) beat	
Lawrie & Montgomerie	1 - 0
Furyk & O'Meara lost to	
Clarke & Westwood (3&2)	1 - 1
Pate & Woods (1 up) beat	
Harrington & Jimenez	2 - 1
Leonard & Stewart lost to	
Garcia & Parnevik (3&2)	2 - 2

Afternoon Fourballs (Day 2)

Lehman & Mickelson (2&1) beat	
Clarke & Westwood	3 - 2
Duval & Love halved with	
Garcia & Parnevik	3½-2½
Leonard & Sutton halved with	
Jimenez & Olazabal	4 - 3
Pate & Woods lost to	
Lawrie & Montgomerie (2&1)	4 - 4
Day 2 totals	**4 - 4**
RUNNING MATCH TOTALS	***6 - 10***

Singles (Day 3)

Lehman (3&2) beat Westwood	1 - 0
Sutton (4&2) beat Clarke	2 - 0
Michelin (4&3) beat Sandelin	3 - 0
Love (6&5) beat Van de Velde	4 - 0
Woods (3&2) beat Coltart	5 - 0
Duval (5&4) beat Parnevik	6 - 0
O'Meara lost to Harrington (1 up)	6 - 1
Pate (2&1) beat Jimenez	7 - 1
Leonard halved with Olazabal	7½-1½
Stewart lost to Montgomerie (1 up)	7½-2½
Furyk (4&3) beat Garcia	8½-2½
Maggert lost to Lawrie (4&3)	8½-3½
Day 3 totals	**8½-3½**
MATCH TOTALS	***14½ - 13½***

RYDER CUP FORMAT CHANGES

1927-59 From the beginning of the series through to 1959, the Ryder Cup competition was comprised of four foursome (alternate shot) matches on one day and eight singles matches on the other day, each of 36 holes.

1961 The format was changed in 1961, to provide four 18-hole foursome matches the morning of the first day, four more foursomes that afternoon; eight 18-hole singles the morning of the second day and eight more singles that afternoon. With one point at stake in each match, the total number of points was doubled to 24.

1963-75 In 1963, four-ball (better-ball) matches were added for the first time, boosting the total number of points available to 32. After 1973, the foursomes and fourballs were swapped around.

1977 The format was altered again in 1977, this time with five foursomes on opening day, five four-ball matches on the second day, and 10 singles matches on the final day. This reduced the total points to 20.

1979 In 1979, when the Great Britain/Ireland team was expanded to include players from European countries; the format was revised to provide for four fourball and four foursome matches the first day, the same playing format for the second day and 12 singles matches scheduled for the third day. Total points were 28. This format continued, with minor adjustments to the timings of the foursomes and fourballs sessions – latterly at the joint agreement of both captains – through to the 1999 Matches.

TEAM SELECTION AND/OR QUALIFICATION

US Team

1927-29 Only American-born players were eligible to compete, and eight players were chosen based 'on performance' over the previous three years, by a PGA Selection Committee.

1931 Five players were selected during the PGA Annual Meeting. Three others were chosen from 14 players invited to compete in a 72-hole competition at Scioto Country Club a week before the Ryder Cup.

1933 Team selected by vote of PGA Executive Committee and PGA section presidents.

1935 Selection based on playing records of previous two years. Automatic qualifiers: Walter Hagen, team captain; Paul Runyan, 1934 PGA Champion; Olin Dutra, 1934 US Open Champion; Sam Parks, 1935 US Open Champion; and six players based on scoring average: Ky Laffoon, Henry Picard, Johnny Revolta, Gene Sarazen, Horton Smith and Craig Wood.

1937-39 Six players were chosen on basis of performance during past two years. Four more players added after performance in the US. Open.

1947-51 Points system used for the first time. Current US Open and PGA Champions were automatic choices. The remainder of the team was selected by a PGA Executive Committee largely based on a points list. Points were awarded to Top 10 finishers in all events except the PGA Championship, where only the first eight earned points. Points accrued from 1 January 1946 to 1 September 1947. The winners of the PGA Championship and US Open received 100 points; the Masters champion, 95; the Western Open champion, 80; and winners of all other PGA-sanctioned events received 70 points.

1953 The PGA Executive Committee added 1952 PGA Champion Jim Turnesa to the automatic qualifier list, along with 1953

PGA Champion Walter Burkemo. The remainder of the team was from the points list.

1955 As per 1947

1957 Team members must have played in both the 1956 and 57 PGA Championships. The 1957 PGA Champion was an automatic choice.

1959-61 Points standings from to years to September of current year. Point values assigned were the same as in 1947.

1963-67 Selection based on two-year point standings up to the current year PGA Championship.

1969-75 Team increased by two players to 12, and selection based primarily on points accrued from previous year PGA Championship to the current year PGA Championship. Must have competed in two PGA Championships unless excused for reasons justified by the PGA Executive Committee.

1977 Points earned from July 1976 to July 1977. Bonus points awarded for winning the 1976 PGA Championship and World Series of Golf. Automatic berths to winners of 1977 PGA Championship and World Series of Golf.

1979 Selections based on the top 12 players from the points list.

1981-83 Selections based on the top 11 players from the points list and the current year PGA Champion.

1985 Selections based on points from 1 January 1985, to 1985 PGA Championship. Bonus points awarded for PGA Championship, US Open and Tournament Players Championship. The current US Open and PGA Champions were automatic choices.

1987 Selections based on points from 1 January 1986, to 1987 PGA Championship. Bonus points awarded for 1986 and 1987 PGA Championships. The current US Open and PGA Champions were automatic choices.

1989 For the first time, the captain was given two nominations of his own, provided the PGA Champion already qualified; otherwise one choice. Bonus points were awarded for PGA Championship, US Open, British Open and the Masters. The 1989 PGA Champion was an automatic choice. Captain Raymond Floyd picked Lanny Wadkins and Tom Watson.

1991 The PGA Champion was no longer given an automatic berth. The captain's two nominations continued.

1993-99 The points system was changed to allow added 'weight (double points)' to the current year and added importance to the four Majors (triple points in previous year; quadruple points in current year. Two captain's wild-card' choices continued.

British, Great Britain-Ireland and European Teams

1927 The initial selection committee was comprised of Harry Vardon, James Braid and JH Taylor

1929 Five-man selection committee.

1931 Three trial matches were held at Royal Lytham, Frilford Heath and Fulwell. The team was then chosen by a committee drawn from British PGA regions.

1933-39 Chosen by selection committee.

1947 Selection committee drew up a list of 14 candidates. The PGA Matchplay champion earned an automatic berth.

1949 Selection committee agreed to use 'List of Merit' in compiling a list of 16 candidates.

1951 Selection committee picked eight players, and the newly-organized Order of Merit (Money List) acted as a guide. The final two berths were determined at the conclusion of the PGA Matchplay Championship.

1953 Selection committee drawn from PGA regions was replaced by a tournament committee. A list of 17 candidates was drawn from those who played a sequence of trial matches at Wentworth.

1955 The first seven places from the Order of Merit following the Open Championship. The remaining three places were determined by a PGA tournament sub-committee in consultation with players already chosen.

1957 For the first time, the team was chosen by a points system. Points were awarded to Top 20 finishers in all strokeplay events, including the the Open. Further points were awarded to Top 10 finishers in the Dunlop Masters and the final 16 players in the PGA Matchplay Championship.

1959 The top seven players in the Order of Merit earned automatic berths. The remaining three spots were filled by PGA Matchplay champion and Dunlop Masters champion or – if already qualified, by ballot among team members and the PGA sub-committee.

1961 The Open and PGA Matchplay champion were added to eight players selected from the Order of Merit. Eligibility was based on players competing in seven of the nine PGA events.

1963 The points system was reintroduced. Points were awarded to top 40 players. The Open and PGA Matchplay champions earned automatic berths. No points were awarded for limited-field events such as the Dunlop Masters.

1965-67 The points system was extended over two seasons, beginning with the previous year's Open to the 1965 Esso tournament. The Open Champion earned an automatic berth, and the remaining places were determined by the points system.

1969 The team was expanded to 12 players, but the selection process remained the same as in 1965, with the Open champion earning an automatic berth, and the remaining places determined by the points system.

1971 Six players were automatic selections from the Order of Merit, and the remaining six chosen by selection committee.

1973 The points system ran from August 1972 to August 1973. Thirty points were awarded to winners of major PGA tournaments. Additional points were awarded in increments of 24, 23, 22, down

to one point for 25th place. Eight players were selected automatically, and four by invitation.

1975-77 The leading eight players from the Order of Merit were chosen. The remaining four were by invitation from a three-member selection committee chaired by the captain.

1979-81 The Top 10 players from the Money List earned berths, and two were selected by invitation. 1979 was the first time in Ryder Cup history that players from Continental Europe were included.

1983 The entire 12-player team was chosen on the basis of finish in the Order of Merit.

1985-93 The top nine players from the Order of Merit list were automatic selections. The three other team members were chosen at the discretion of the captain.

1995 For the first time, European players' performances in US-based Majors are used to determine the makeup of the European Ryder Cup Team. Player earnings in the US Major championships were converted from dollars to pounds to make up the points list. The currency exchange rate is determined on the first day of each championship. Captain's selections are reduced to two players, and 10 automatic qualifiers through the Order of Merit standings complete the team.

1997 The Top 10 automatic qualifiers from the Ryder Cup Point Standings the same, with the Captain having two selections. Should the captain qualify on points he may nominate to stand down and select another player of his own choice.

1999 The Top 10 automatic qualifiers from the Ryder Cup Point Standings the same. Captain's selections from the PGA European Tour's membership. Official money gained in the three US Majors included along with the inaugural World Golf Championship Matchplay event contested in February 1999. A player must compete in four PGA European Tour ranking tournaments to be eligible.

United States 24 Wins: Britain/GB and Ireland/Europe 7 Wins: 2 Ties

1927	Worcester CC, Worcester, Massachusetts	US	9½	Britain	2½
1929	Moortown GC, Leeds, Yorkshire, England	**Britain**	7	US	5
1931	Scioto CC, Columbus, Ohio	US	9	Britain	3
1933	Southport & Ainsdale GC, Southport, Lanca, Eng	**Britain**	6½	US	5½
1935	Ridgewood CC, Ridgewood, New Jersey	US	9	Britain	3
1937	Southport & Ainsdale GC, Southport, Lancs, Eng	US	8	Britain	4
1939-1945	*No Matches Played — World War II*				
1947	Portland GC, Portland, Oregon	US	11	Britain	I
1949	Ganton GC, Scarborough, Yorkshire, England	US	7	Britain	5
1951	Pinehurst CC, Pinehurst, North Carolina	US	9½	Britain	2½
1953	Wentworth GC, Wentworth, Surrey, England	US	6½	Britain	5½
1955	Thunderbird CC, Palm Springs, California	US	8	Britain	4
1957	Lindrick GC, Sheffield, Yorkshire, England	**Britain**	7½	US	4½
1959	El Dorado CC, Palm Desert, California	US	8½	Britain	3½
1961	Royal Lytham & St. Annes, St. Annes, Lancs, Eng	US	14½	Britain	9½
1963	East Lake CC, Atlanta, Georgia	US	23	Britain	9
1965	Royal Birkdale GC, Southport, Lancashire, Eng	US	19½	Britain	12½
1967	Champions GC, Houston, Texas	US	23½	Britain	8½
1969	Royal Birkdale GC, Southport, Lancashire, Eng	**Tied (US)**	16	Britain	16
1971	Old Warson CC, St. Louis, Missouri	US	18½	Britain	13½
1973	Muirfield GC, East Lothian, Scotland	US	19	GB&I	13
1975	Laurel Valley GC, Ligonier, Pennsylvania	US	21	GB&I	11
1977	Royal Lytham & St. Annes, St. Annes, Lancs, Eng	US	12½	GB&I	7½
1979	The Greenbrier, White Sulphur Springs, W Virginia	US	17	Europe	11
1981	Walton Health GC, Walton Heath, Surrey, England	US	18½	Europe	9½
1983	PGA National GC, Palm Beach Gardens, Florida	US	14½	Europe	13½
1985	The Belfry, Sutton Coldfield, West Midlands, Eng	**Europe**	16½	US	11½
1987	Muirfield Village GC, Dublin, Ohio	**Europe**	15	US	13
1989	The Belfry, Sutton Coldfield, West Midlands, Eng	**Tied (Europe)**	14	US	14
1991	The Ocean Course, Kiawah Island, South Carolina	US	14½	Europe	13½
1993	The Belfry, Sutton Coldfield, West Midlands, Eng	US	14	Europe	13
1995	Oak Hill CC, Rochester, New York	**Europe**	14½	US	13½
1997	Vaderrama GC, Sotogrande, Spain	**Europe**	14½	US	13½
1999	The Country Club, Brookline, Massachusetts	US	14½	Europe	13½

MOST APPEARANCES

Players

NICK FALDO (GB&I/Eur)	11	(1977-97)
Christy O'Connor, Sr (GB/GB&I)	10	(1957-73)
Bernhard Langer (Eur)	9	(1981-97)
Dai Rees (GB)	9	(1937-61)
Peter Alliss (GB)	8	(1953-69)
Seve Ballesteros (Eur)	8	(1979-95)
Billy Casper (US)	8	(1961-75)
Neil Coles (GB/GB&I)	8	(1961-77)
Ray Floyd (US)	8	(1969-93)
Bernard Gallacher (GB/GB&I/Eur)	8	(1969-83)
Bernard Hunt (GB)	8	(1953-69)
Sam Torrance (Eur)	8	(1981-95)
Lanny Wadkins (US)	8	(1977-93)
Ian Woosnam (Eur)	8	(1983-97)
Tony Jacklin (GB/GB&I/Eur)	7	(1967-79)
Mark James (GB&I/Eur)	7	(1977-95)
Tom Kite (US)	7	(1979-93)
Gene Littler (US)	7	(1961-75)
Sam Snead (US)	7	(1937-59)
Harry Weetman (GB)	7	(1951-63)
Brian Barnes (GB/GB&I/Eur)	6	(1969-79)
Ken Bousfield (GB)	6	(1949-61)
Howard Clark (GB&I/Eur)	6	(1977-95)
Brian Huggett (GB/GB&I)	6	(1963-75)
Jack Nicklaus (US)	6	(1969-81)
Jose-Maria Olazabal (Eur)	6	(1987-99)
Peter Oosterhuis (GB/GB&I/Eur)	6	(1971-81)
Arnold Palmer (US)	6	(1961-73)
Gene Sarazen (US)	6	(1927-37)
Lee Trevino (US)	6	(1969-81)
Charles Whitcombe (GB)	6	(1927-37)

Captains

WALTER HAGEN (US)	5	(4 playing)
DAI REES (GB)	5	(4 playing)
Tony Jacklin (Eur)	4	
Charles Whitcombe (GB)	4	(3 playing)
Bernard Gallacher (Eur)	3	
Sam Snead (US)	3	(2 playing)
Eric Brown (GB)	2	
Henry Cotton (GB)	2	(1 playing)
Ben Hogan (US)	2	(1 playing)
John Jacobs (Eur)	2	
Bernard Hunt (GB&I)	2	
Jack Nicklaus (US)	2	
Arnold Palmer (US)	2	(1 playing)

Most Matches (against Appearances)

NICK FALDO	46	(11)
Neil Coles	40	(8)
Bernhard Langer	38	(9)
Seve Ballesteros	37	(8)
Billy Casper	37	(8)
Christy O'Connor, Sr	36	(10)
Tony Jacklin	35	(7)
Lanny Wadkins	34	(8)
Arnold Palmer	32	(6)
Ray Floyd	31	(8)
Bernard Gallacher	31	(8)
Ian Woosnam	31	(8)
Peter Alliss	30	(8)
Lee Trevino	30	(6)
Bernard Hunt	28	(8)
Tom Kite	28	(7)
Jack Nicklaus	28	(6)
Jose-Maria Olazabal	28	(6)
Peter Oosterhuis	28	(6)
Sam Torrance	28	(8)
Gene Littler	27	(7)
Brian Barnes	25	(6)
Brian Huggett	24	(6)
Mark James	24	(7)
Colin Montgomerie	23	(5)
Fred Couples	20	(5)
Hale Irwin	20	(5)

Most Points Won (against Matches)

NICK FALDO	25	(46)
Billy Casper	23½	(37)
Arnold Palmer	23	(32)
Seve Ballesteros	22½	(37)
Lanny Wadkins	21½	(34)
Bernhard Langer	20½	(38)
Lee Trevino	20	(30)
Jack Nicklaus	18½	(28)
Gene Littler	18	(27)
Jose-Maria Olazabal	17½	(28)
Tom Kite	17	(28)
Ian Woosnam	16½	(31)
Neil Coles	15½	(40)
Bernhard Gallacher	15½	(31)
Peter Oosterhuis	15½	(28)
Hale Irwin	14	(20)
Colin Montgomerie	14	(23)
Ray Floyd	13½	(31)
Christy O'Connor, Sr	13	(36)
Peter Alliss	12½	(30)
Julius Boros	11	(16)
Brian Huggett	11	(24)
Brian Barnes	10½	(25)
Sam Snead	10½	(13)
Tom Watson	10½	(15)
Sam Torrance	10	(28)

Most Wins (against Matches)

NICK FALDO	23	(46)
Arnold Palmer	22	(32)
Seve Ballesteros	20	(37)
Billy Casper	20	(37)
Lanny Wadkins	20	(34)
Bernhard Langer	18	(38)
Jack Nicklaus	17	(28)
Lee Trevino	17	(30)
Tom Kite	15	(28)
Jose-Maria Olazabal	15	(28)
Gene Littler	14	(27)
Peter Oosterhuis	14	(28)
Ian Woosnam	14	(31)
Bernard Gallacher	13	(31)
Hale Irwin	13	(20)
Tony Jacklin	13	(35)
Neil Coles	12	(40)
Ray Floyd	12	(31)
Colin Montgomerie	12	(23)
Christy O'Connor, Sr	11	(36)
Peter Alliss	10	(30)
Brian Barnes	10	(25)
Sam Snead	10	(13)
Tom Watson	10	(15)

Most Singles Wins (aganst Singles Matches)

BILLY CASPER	6	(10)
NICK FALDO	6	(11)
PETER OOSTERHUIS	6	(9)
ARNOLD PALMER	6	(11)
SAM SNEAD	6	(7)
Peter Alliss	5	(12)
Brian Barnes	5	(10)
Neil Coles	5	(15)
Tom Kite	5	(7)
Gene Littler	5	(10)
Dai Rees	5	(9)
Eric Brown	4	(4)
Ray Floyd	4	(8)
Bernard Gallacher	4	(11)
Bernard Hunt	4	(10)
Jack Nicklaus	4	(10)
Gene Sarazen	4	(6)
Lanny Wadkins	4	(10)

Most Foursomes Wins (against Foursomes Matches)

SEVE BALLESTEROS	10	(14)
NICK FALDO	10	(18)
BERNHARD LANGER	10	(16)
Arnold Palmer	9	(12)
Lanny Wadkins	9	(15)
Billy Casper	8	(15)
Tony Jacklin	8	(13)
Jack Nicklaus	8	(9)
Tom Kite	7	(13)
Jose-Maria Olazabal	7	(10)
Hale Irwin	6	(7)
Colin Montgomerie	6	(9)
Christy O'Connor, Sr	6	(13)

Most Fourballs Wins (against Fourballs Matches)

IAN WOOSNAM	10	(14)
Seve Ballesteros	8	(15)
Nick Faldo	7	(17)
Jose-Maria Olazabal	7	(12)
Arnold Palmer	7	(9)
Lanny Wadkins	7	(11)
Billy Casper	6	(12)
Lee Trevino	6	(10)
Mark James	5	(9)
Bernhard Langer	5	(13)
Gene Littler	5	(9)
Peter Oosterhuis	5	(9)

Youngest Players	Years	Months	Days
SERGIO GARCIA (1999)	19	8	15
Nick Faldo (1977)	20	1	28
Paul Way (1983)	20	7	3
Bernard Gallacher (1969)	20	7	9
Horton Smith (1929)	21	0	4
Tiger Woods (1997)	21	8	27

Oldest Players	Years	Months	Days
RAY FLOYD (1993)	51	0	20
Ted Ray (1927)	50	2	5
Christy O'Connor, Sr (1973)	48	8	30
Don January (1977)	47	9	26
Julius Boros (1967)	47	7	17

RYDER CUP RECORDS

Best Performances (% of Points to Matches)

(minimum of 3 Ryder Cup Appearances/Matches)

	A/M	W - L - H	Pts	%
JIMMY DEMARET	3/6	6 - 0 - 0	6	100
Jack Burke, Jr	5/8	7 - 1 - 0	7	87.5
Horton Smith	5/4	3 - 0 - 1	3½	87.5
Walter Hagen	5/9	7 - 1 - 1	7½	83.3
JC Snead	3/11	9 - 2 - 0	9	81.8
Sam Snead	7/13	10 - 2 - 1	10½	80.8
Lloyd Mangrum	4/8	6 - 2 - 0	6	75
Ed Dudley	3/4	3 - 1 - 0	3	75
Ted Kroll	3/4	3 - 1 - 0	3	75
Dow Finsterwald	4/13	9 - 3 - 1	9½	73.1
Larry Nelson	3/13	9 - 3 - 1	9½	73.1
Chip Beck	3/9	6 - 2 - 1	6½	72.2
Arnold Palmer	6/32	22 - 8 - 2	23	71.9
Johnny Pott	3/7	5 - 2 - 0	5	71.4
Gene Sarazen	6/12	7 - 2 - 3	8½	70.8
Hale Irwin	5/20	13 - 5 -2	14	70
Tom Watson	4/15	10 - 4 - 1	10½	70
Julius Boros	5/16	9 - 3 - 4	11	68.8
Lee Trevino	6/30	17 - 7 - 6	20	66.7
Gene Littler	7/27	14 - 5 - 8	18	66.7
Dave Hill	3/9	6 - 3 - 0	6	66.7
Art Wall	3/6	4 - 2 - 0	4	66.7
Dutch Harrison	3/3	2 - 1 - 0	2	66.7
Jack Nicklaus	6/28	17 - 8 - 3	18½	66.1
Billy Casper	8/37	20 - 10 - 7	23½	63.5
Lanny Wadkins	8/34	20 - 11 - 3	21½	63.2
Jose-Maria Olazabal	6/28	15 - 8 - 5	17½	62.5
Corey Pavin	3/13	8 - 5 - 0	8	61.5
Lou Graham	3/9	5 - 3 - 1	5½	61.1
Colin Montgomerie	5/23	12 - 7 - 4	14	60.9
Seve Ballesteros	8/37	20 - 12- 5	22½	60.8
Tom Kite	7/28	15 - 9 - 4	17	60.7
Ed Oliver	3/5	3 - 2 - 0	3	60
Percy Alliss	5/6	3 - 2 - 1	3½	58.3
Johnny Farrell	3/6	3 - 2 - 1	3½	58.3
Hubert Green	3/7	4 - 3 - 0	4	57.1
Charles Whitcombe	6/9	3 - 2 - 4	5	55.6
Peter Oosterhuis	6/28	14 - 11-3	15½	55.4
Jose-Maria Canizares	4/11	5 - 4 - 2	6	54.5
Costantino Rocca	3/11	6 - 5 - 0	6	54.5
Nick Faldo	11/46	23 - 19 - 4	25	54.3
Bernhard Langer	9/38	18 - 15 - 5	20½	53.9
Ian Woosnam	8/31	14 - 12 - 5	16½	53.2
Bernard Gallacher	8/31	13 - 13 - 5	15½	50
Howard Clark	6/15	7 - 7 - 1	7½	50
Ken Bousfield	6/10	5 - 5 - 0	5	50
Doug Ford	4/9	4 - 4 - 1	4½	50
Eric Brown	4/8	4 - 4 - 0	4	50
Arthur Havers	3/6	3 - 3 - 0	3	50
Denny Shute	3/6	2 - 2 - 2	3	50
Harry Bradshaw	3/5	2 - 2 - 1	2½	50

In 1916, with the ritzy Walter Hagen very much to the fore, the PGA of America was founded – partly along the lines of the British example of 1903, to protect the club golfer. It had an extra dimension over its British cousin, however, in that through players with the drive of Hagen, joining publicists and businessmen outside the game, the top-flight US professional was being honed into a very marketable 'product'. One such guru was Bob Harlow – he who reputedly came up with the idea for the 'Ryder' Cup. He also happened to be Hagen's manager, and it was Harlow who planted the first seeds of a regular, well-orderd tour. The US Open, the fledgling PGA Championship, the Western Open and others, were all held annually, and when early season 'warm weather' events got under way in the 1920s with the likes of the Texas and Los Angeles Opens and the North and South at Pinehurst, the basis for the tour was there. Harlow, however, formalised the itinerary and got on board equipment and clothing manufacturers to subsidise the prize money stumped up by local businesses. By 1934, the first Money List was published, headed by Paul Runyan with the grand sum of $6767. The PGA parent body were concerned that the primary ethos of protecting the club professional would go out of the window, as the Tour now began to exude a 'them-and-us' atmosphere: that fear was to pervade the PGA for another thirty-odd years before coming to a head.

There was very little they could do, however, to stop the steam-roller effect. The Tour pros were as much *bona fide* members as the journeymen and, they had to admit it secretly, their very success, bringing with it increasingly higher profiles, was the driving force behind the movement's rapid advance in the 1930s. With Hagen and Sarazen to the fore, the only doubt was that momentum may be held up by the war clouds developing over Europe. As it turned out, apart from 1943 when the Tour almost ground to a halt, the war years proved to be no more than a contemplative easing of the pace, and by 1945 three more giants of the game had emerged to accelerate things once more. In fact, in 1945, Byron Nelson won an astonishing 19 events, famously collecting 11 of them in a row, and he, Sam Snead, and the human story of Ben Hogan, upped the public perception to an all-time high. The number of events and the total prize money continued to increase. Then in 1953, TV came with a bang, and there was to be no looking back. Television and golf went together extremely well, perhaps surprisingly when the

American sports fan likes a bit of pace and action as a norm. It was undoubtedly helped early on by an amazing long-range pitch-in by Lew Worsham to win a match already, it seemed, won by Chandler Harper. The drama of golf had announced itself to the viewing millions, and the sport joined those of the first rank.

Now accessible to the armchair enthusiast, TV revolutionised the numbers: the numbers watching the sport (galleries consquently were getting much bigger); the numbers financially; and, most importantly, the numbers taking up the game. During the fifties and sixties the quantity, and therefore the in-depth quality, of professional players multiplied. The standard of the less-gifted Tour pro was now much higher than in earlier years, and failure to make the cut and get into the prize money may be by just one or two strokes. There was greater demand for more of the prize money to be released therefore, and the PGA, who had done very nicely thank you out of its cut from the Tour, were urged to give up some of theirs. The break-away factor that had been grumbling along as the 'them-and-us' element for many years, was now bringing things to a head. In an historic secession in 1968, the American Professional Golfers was formed; or, as it was neatly termed by the spurned PGA, acting like some smothering mother who won't let her grown-up son leave home, as their Tour Players' Division. In 1968, then, the Tour had a name, and a commissioner – Joseph Dey – and was 'official' for the first time.

It was Dey's successor, former US and British Amateur Champion, and four times a winner as a pro, Deane Beman, who really turned the already hugely lucrative Tour into a machine for making money. His vision, aided by an astute business mind, presaged an enormous increase in Tour activities, and by the time he retired in 1994, he had increased its assets from $730000 to $200 million! He was also instrumental in setting up both the Seniors Tour (1980) and the Ben Hogan Tour in 1986 (the Nike Tour, 1993-99; the BUY.COM Tour from 2000). The man who replaced Beman, Tim Finchem, has set his store on 'internationalising' the Tour. Whereas Beman operated a form of protectionism, in that overseas players had virtually to commit to the Tour at the expense of their domestic tours, or just come to the US for the Majors, Finchem has introduced a happier system, allowing the non-Americans access to invitations for up to six events in addition to the Majors. He was also quick to support an alternative to the vision of Greg Norman to create a sort of global golfing 'premier league', when he backed the 1999 launch of the World Golf Championship events, allowing, effectively, the best players further opportunities to play in the States. Whether he, and others, will be able to stop such a World Tour eventually, only the future will tell. Already with a handful and more prestigious events taking place for the elite, other tournaments have to be set up for the mere mortals. Will the US Tour have to find more, perhaps?

EVENTS/WINNERS

All events listed in alphabetical order, and cross referred to current/most recent tournament names

AIR CANADA CHAMPIONSHIP

Greater Vancouver Open

1996	Guy Boros
1997	Mark Calcavecchia
1998	David Duval

Air Canada Championship

1999	Mike Weir

Most Wins
No multiple winners

American Express Westchester Classic
See Buick Classic

American Motors' Inverrary Classic
See Honda Classic

American Optical Classic
See CVS Charity Classic

Andy Williams-San Diego Open Invitational
See Buick Invitational

Andersen Consulting World Championship of Golf
See World Golf Championships section

Anheuser-Busch Golf Classic
See Michelob Championship at Kingsmill

Arizona Open
See Phoenix Open Invitational

AT&T PEBBLE BEACH NATIONAL PRO-AM

Bing Crosby Professional-Amateur

1937	Sam Snead
1938	Sam Snead
1939	Dutch Harrison
1940	Ed Oliver
1941	Sam Snead
1942	John Dawson
1943-46	*No Tournaments – World War Two*
1947	George Fazio, Ed Furgol – tied
1948	Lloyd Mangrum
1949	Ben Hogan
1950	Jack Burke, Jr, Dave Douglas, Smiley Quick, Sam Snead – tied

1951	Byron Nelson
1952	Jimmy Demaret

Bing Crosby Professional-Amateur Invitational

1953	Lloyd Mangrum
1954	Dutch Harrison
1955	Cary Middlecoff

Bing Crosby National Professional-Amateur Golf Championship

1956	Cary Middlecoff
1957	Jay Hebert
1958	Billy Casper
1959	Gene Littler, Art Wall – tied

Bing Crosby National

1960	Ken Venturi
1961	Bob Rosburg
1962	Doug Ford
1963	Billy Casper

Bing Crosby National Professional-Amateur

1964	Tony Lema
1965	Bruce Crampton
1966	Don Massengale
1967	Jack Nicklaus
1968	Johnny Pott
1969	George Archer
1970	Bert Yancey
1971	Tom Shaw
1972	Jack Nicklaus
1973	Jack Nicklaus
1974	Johnny Miller
1975	Gene Littler
1976	Ben Crenshaw
1977	Tom Watson
1978	Tom Watson
1979	Lon Hinkle
1980	George Burns
1981	John Cook
1982	Jim Simons
1983	Tom Kite
1984	Hale Irwin
1985	Mark O'Meara

AT&T Pebble Beach National Pro-Am

1986	Fuzzy Zoeller
1987	Johnny Miller
1988	Steve Jones
1989	Mark O'Meara
1990	Mark O'Meara

1991	Paul Azinger
1992	Mark O'Meara
1993	Brett Ogle
1994	Johnny Miller
1995	Peter Jacobsen
1996	No Tournament – Bad weather cancellation
1997	Mark O'Meara
1998	Phil Mickelson
1999	Payne Stewart

Most Wins

5	Mark O'Meara
4	Sam Snead (including one tie)

Atlanta Classic
See BellSouth Classic

AVCO Golf Classic
See CVS Charity Classic

Bank of Boston Classic
See CVS Charity Classic

Bay Hill Citrus Classic; Bay Hill Classic
See Bay Hill Invitational

BAY HILL INVITATIONAL

Florida Citrus Open Invitational

1966	Lionel Hebert
1967	Julius Boros
1968	Dan Sikes
1969	Ken Still
1970	Bob Lunn
1971	Arnold Palmer
1972	Jerry Heard
1973	Buddy Allin
1974	Jerry Heard
1975	Lee Trevino
1976	Hale Irwin
1977	Gary Koch
1978	Mac McLendon

Bay Hill Citrus Classic

1979	Bob Byman

Bay Hill Classic

1980	Dave Eichelberger
1981	Andy Bean
1982	Tom Kite

1983	Mike Nicolette
1984	Gary Koch

Hertz Bay Hill Classic

1985	Fuzzy Zoeller
1986	Dan Forsman
1987	Payne Stewart
1988	Paul Azinger

Nestle Invitational

1989	Tom Kite
1990	Robert Gamez
1991	Andrew Magee
1992	Fred Couples
1993	Ben Crenshaw
1994	Loren Roberts
1995	Loren Roberts

Bay Hill Invitational

1996	Paul Goydos
1997	Phil Mickelson
1998	Ernie Els
1999	Tim Herron

Most Wins

2	Jerry Heard, Tom Kite, Gary Koch, Loren Roberts

BC OPEN

(*Unofficial tour events)

Broome County Open

*1971	Butch Harmon

BC Open

*1972	Bob Payne
1973	Hubert Green
1974	Richie Karl
1975	Don Iverson
1976	Bob Wynn
1977	Gil Morgan
1978	Tom Kite
1979	Howard Twitty
1980	Don Pooley
1981	Jay Haas
1982	Calvin Peete
1983	Pat Lindsey
1984	Wayne Levi
1985	Joey Sindelar
1986	Rick Fehr
1987	Joey Sindelar

1988	Bill Glasson
1989	Mike Hulbert
1990	Nolan Henke
1991	Fred Couples
1992	John Daly
1993	Blaine McCallister
1994	Mike Sullivan
1995	Hal Sutton
1996	Fred Funk
1997	Gabriel Hjertstedt
1998	Chris Perry
1999	Brad Faxon

Most Wins

2	Joey Sindelar

Beatrice Western Open

See Motorola Western Open

BELL CANADIAN OPEN

Canadian Open

1904	JH Oke
1905	George Gumming
1906	Charles Murray
1907	Percy Barrett
1908	Albert Murray
1909	Karl Keffer
1910	Dan Kenney
1911	Charles Murray
1912	George Sargent
1913	Albert Murray
1914	Karl Keffer
1915-18	*No Tournaments – World War One*
1919	Douglas Edgar
1920	Douglas Edgar
1921	WH Trovinger
1922	Al Watrous
1923	Clarence Hackney
1924	Leo Diegel
1925	Leo Diegel
1926	Macdonald Smith
1927	Tommy Armour
1928	Leo Diegel
1929	Leo Diegel
1930	Tommy Armour
1931	Walter Hagen

1932	Harry Cooper
1933	Joe Kirkwood, Sr
1934	Tommy Armour
1935	Gene Kunes
1936	Lawson Little
1937	Harry Cooper
1938	Sam Snead
1939	Harold McSpaden
1940	Sam Snead
1941	Sam Snead
1942	Craig Wood
1943-44	*No Tournaments – World War Two*
1945	Byron Nelson
1946	George Fazio
1947	Bobby Locke
1948	Chuck Congdon
1949	Dutch Harrison
1950	Jim Ferrier
1951	Jim Ferrier
1952	Johnny Palmer
1953	Dave Douglas
1954	Pat Fletcher
1955	Arnold Palmer
1956	Doug Sanders (a)
1957	George Bayer
1958	Wes Ellis, Jr
1959	Doug Ford
1960	Art Wall
1961	Jacky Cupit
1962	Ted Kroll
1963	Doug Ford
1964	Kel Nagle
1965	Gene Littler
1966	Don Massengale
1967	Billy Casper
1968	Bob Charles
1969	Tommy Aaron
1970	Kermit Zarley
1971	Lee Trevino
1972	Gay Brewer
1973	Tom Weiskopf
1974	Bobby Nichols
1975	Tom Weiskopf
1976	Jerry Pate
1977	Lee Trevino
1978	Bruce Lietzke

1979	Lee Trevino
1980	Bob Gilder
1981	Peter Oosterhuis
1982	Bruce Lietzke
1983	John Cook
1984	Greg Norman
1985	Curtis Strange
1986	Bob Murphy
1987	Curtis Strange
1988	Ken Green
1989	Steve Jones
1990	Wayne Levi
1991	Nick Price
1992	Greg Norman
1993	David Frost

Bell Canadian Open

1994	Nick Price
1995	Mark O'Meara
1996	Dudley Hart
1997	Steve Jones
1998	Billy Andrade
1999	Hal Sutton

Most Wins

4	Leo Diegel
3	Tommy Armour, Sam Snead, Lee Trevino

BellSouth Atlanta Golf Classic
See BellSouth Classic

BELLSOUTH CLASSIC
Atlanta Classic

1967	Bob Charles
1968	Bob Lunn
1969	Bert Yancey
1970	Tommy Aaron
1971	Gardner Dickinson
1972	Bob Lunn
1973	Jack Nicklaus
1974	No Tournament
1975	Hale Irwin
1976	No Tournament
1977	Hale Irwin
1978	Jerry Heard
1979	Andy Bean

1980	Larry Nelson
1981	Tom Watson

Georgia-Pacific Atlanta Golf Classic

1982	Keith Fergus
1983	Calvin Peete
1984	Tom Kite
1935	Wayne Levi
1986	Bob Tway
1987	Dave Barr
1988	Larry Nelson

BellSouth Atlanta Golf Classic

1989	Scott Simpson
1990	Wayne Levi
1991	Corey Pavin

BellSouth Classic

1992	Tom Kite
1993	Nolan Henke
1994	John Daly
1995	Mark Calcavecchia
1996	Paul Stankowski
1997	Scott McCarron
1998	Tiger Woods
1999	David Duval

Most Wins

2	Hale Irwin, Tom Kite, Wayne Levi, Bob Lunn, Larry Nelson

Big I Houston Open
See Shell Houston Open

Bing Crosby National; Bing Crosby National Professional-Amateur; Bing Crosby National Professional-Amateur Golf Championship; Bing Crosby Professional-Amateur; Bing Crosby Professional-Amateur Invitational
See AT&T Pebble Beach National Pro-Am

BOB HOPE CHRYSLER CLASSIC

Palm Springs Desert Classic

1960	Arnold Palmer
1961	Billy Maxwell
1962	Arnold Palmer
1963	Jack Nicklaus
1964	Tommy Jacobs

Bob Hope Desert Classic

1965	Billy Casper
1966	Doug Sanders
1967	Tom Nieporte
1968	Arnold Palmer
1969	Billy Casper
1970	Bruce Devlin
1971	Arnold Palmer
1972	Bob Rosburg
1973	Arnold Palmer
1974	Hubert Green
1975	Johnny Miller
1976	Johnny Miller
1977	Rik Massengale
1978	Bill Rogers
1979	John Mahaffey
1980	Craig Stadler
1981	Bruce Lietzke
1982	Ed Fiori
1983	Keith Fergus

Bob Hope Classic

1984	John Mahaffey
1985	Lanny Wadkins

Bob Hope Chrysler Classic

1986	Donnie Hammond
1987	Corey Pavin
1988	Jay Haas
1989	Steve Jones
1990	Peter Jacobsen
1991	Corey Pavin
1992	John Cook
1993	Tom Kite
1994	Scott Hoch
1995	Kenny Perry
1996	Mark Brooks
1997	John Cook
1998	Fred Couples
1999	David Duval

Most Wins

5	Arnold Palmer
2	Billy Casper, John Mahaffey, Johnny Miller, Corey Pavin

Bob Hope Classic; Bob Hope Desert Classic
See Bob Hope Chrysler Classic

Broome County Open
See BC Open

BUICK CHALLENGE

Green Island Open Invitational

1970	Mason Rudolph

Southern Open Invitational

1971	Johnny Miller
1972	DeWitt Weaver
1973	Gary Player
1974	Forrest Fezler
1975	Hubert Green
1976	Mac McLendon
1977	Jerry Pate
1978	Jerry Pate
1979	Ed Fiori
1980	Mike Sullivan
1981	JC Snead
1982	Bobby Clampett
1983	Ronnie Black
1984	Hubert Green
1985	Tim Simpson
1986	Fred Wadsworth
1987	Ken Brown
1998	David Frost
1999	Ted Schulz

Buick Southern Open

1990	Kenny Knox
1991	David Peoples
1992	Gary Hallberg
1993	John Inman
1994	Steve Elkington

Buick Challenge

1995	Fred Funk
1996	Michael Bradley
1997	Davis Love III
1998	Steve Elkington
1999	David Toms

Most Wins

2	Steve Elkington, Jerry Pate

BUICK CLASSIC

Westchester Classic

1967	Jack Nicklaus
1968	Julius Boros

1969	Frank Beard
1970	Bruce Crampton
1971	Arnold Palmer
1972	Jack Nicklaus
1973	Bobby Nichols
1974	Johnny Miller
1975	Gene Littler

American Express Westchester Classic

1976	David Graham
1977	Andy North
1978	Lee Elder

Manufacturers Hanover Westchester Classic

1979	Jack Renner
1980	Curtis Strange
1981	Ray Floyd
1982	Bob Gilder
1983	Seve Ballesteros
1984	Scott Simpson
1985	Roger Maltbie
1986	Bob Tway
1987	JC Snead
1988	Seve Ballesteros
1989	Wayne Grady

Buick Classic

1990	Hale Irwin
1991	Billy Andrade
1992	David Frost
1993	Vijay Singh
1994	Lee Janzen
1995	Viiay Singh
1996	Ernie Els
1997	Ernie Els
1998	JP Hayes
1999	Duffy Waldorf

Most Wins

2	Seve Ballesteros, Ernie Els, Jack Nicklaus, Vijay Singh

Buick Goodwrench Open
See Buick Open

BUICK INVITATIONAL

San Diego Open

1952	Ted Kroll
1953	Tommy Bolt
1954	Gene Littler

Convair-San Diego Open

1955	Tommy Bolt
1956	Bob Rosburg

San Diego Open Invitationa

1957	Arnold Palmer
1958	No Tournament
1959	Marty Furgol
1960	Mike Souchak
1961	Arnold Palmer
1962	Tommy Jacobs
1963	Gary Player
1964	Art Wall
1965	Wes Ellis, Jr
1966	Billy Casper
1967	Bob Goalby

Andy Williams-San Diego Open Invitational

1968	Tom Weiskopf
1969	Jack Nicklaus
1970	Pete Brown
1971	George Archer
1972	Paul Harney
1973	Bob Dickson
1974	Bobby Nichols
1975	JC Snead
1976	JC Snead
1977	Tom Watson
1978	Jay Haas
1979	Fuzzy Zoeller
1980	Tom Watson

Wickes-Andy Williams San Diego Open

1981	Bruce Lietzke
1982	Johnny Miller

Isuzu/Andy Williams San Diego Open

1983	Gary Hallberg
1984	Gary Koch
1985	Woody Blackburn

Shearson Lehman Brothers Andy Williams Open

1986	Bob Tway
1987	George Burns

Shearson Lehman Hutton Andy Williams Open

1988	Steve Pate

Shearson Lehman Hutton Open

1989	Greg Twiggs
1990	Dan Forsman

Shearson Lehman Brothers Open

1991	Jay Don Blake

Buick Invitational of California

1992	Steve Pate
1993	Phil Mickelson
1994	Craig Stadler
1995	Peter Jacobsen

Buick Invitational

1996	Davis Love III
1997	Mark O'Meara
1998	Scott Simpson
1999	Tiger Woods

Most Wins

2	Tommy Bolt, Arnold Palmer, Steve Pate, JC Snead, Tom Watson

Buick Invitational of California

See Buick Invitational

BUICK OPEN

(Tournaments marked* not official tour events)

Buick Open Invitational

1958	Billy Casper
1959	Art Wall
1960	Mike Souchak
1961	Jack Burke, Jr
1962	Bill Collins
1963	Julius Boros
1964	Tony Lema
1965	Tony Lema
1966	Phil Rodgers
1967	Julius Boros
1968	Tom Weiskopf
1969	Dave Hill
1970-71	No Tournaments

Vern Parsell Buick Open

1972*	Gary Groh

Lake Michigan Classic

1973*	Wilf Homenuik

Flint Elkes Open

1974*	Bryan Abbott
1975*	Spike Kelley
1976*	Ed Sabo
1977*	Bobby Cole
1978*	Jack Newton

Buick Goodwrench Open

1979	John Fought
1980	Peter Jacobsen

1981	Hale Irwin

Buick Open

1982	Lanny Wadkins
1983	Wayne Levi
1984	Denis Watson
1985	Ken Green
1986	Ben Crenshaw
1987	Robert Wrenn
1988	Scott Verplank
1989	Leonard Thompson
1990	Chip Beck
1991	Brad Faxon
1992	Dan Forsman
1993	Larry Mize
1994	Fred Couples
1995	Woody Austin
1996	Justin Leonard
1997	Vijay Singh
1998	Billy Mayfair
1999	Tom Pernice

Most Wins

2	Tony Lema

Buick Open Invitational
See Buick Open

Buick Southern Open
See Buick Challenge

Byron Nelson Golf Classic
See GTE Byron Nelson Golf Classic

Canadian Open
See Bell Canadian Open

CANON GREATER HARTFORD OPEN

Insurance City Open

1952	Ted Kroll
1953	Bob Toski
1954	Tommy Bolt
1955	Sam Snead
1956	Arnold Palmer
1957	Gardner Dickinson
1958	Jack Burke, Jr
1959	Gene Littler
1960	Arnold Palmer

1961	Billy Maxwell
1962	Bob Goalby
1963	Billy Casper
1964	Ken Venturi
1965	Billy Casper
1966	Art Wall

Greater Hartford Open Invitational

1967	Charles Sifford
1968	Billy Casper
1969	Bob Lunn
1970	Bob Murphy
1971	George Archer
1972	Lee Trevino

Sammy Davis, Jr Greater Hartford Open

1973	Billy Casper
1974	Dave Stockton
1975	Don Bies
1976	Rik Massengale
1977	Bill Kratzert
1978	Rod Funseth
1979	Jerry McGee
1980	Howard Twitty
1981	Hubert Green
1982	Tim Norris
1983	Curtis Strange
1984	Peter Jacobsen

Canon Sammy Davis, Jr Greater Hartford Open

1985	Phil Blackmar
1986	Mac O'Grady
1987	Paul Azinger
1988	Mark Brooks
1989	Paul Azinger

Canon Greater Hartford Open

1990	Wayne Levi
1991	Billy Ray Brown
1992	Lanny Wadkins
1993	Nick Price
1994	David Frost
1995	Greg Norman
1996	DA Weibring
1997	Stewart Cink
1998	Olin Browne
1999	Brent Geiberger

Most Wins

4	Billy Casper
2	Paul Azinger, Arnold Palmer

Canon Sammy Davis, Jr Greater Hartford Open
See Canon Greater Hartford Open

Carling World Open
See CVS Charity Classic

Centel Western Open
See Motorola Western Open

Colonial National Invitation Tournament
See Mastercard Colonial

COMPAQ CLASSIC OF NEW ORLEANS

Greater New Orleans Open Invitational

1938	Harry Cooper
1939	Henry Picard
1940	Jimmy Demaret
1941	Henry Picard
1942	Lloyd Mangrum
1943	*No Tournament – World War Two*
1944	Sam Byrd
1945	Byron Nelson
1946	Byron Nelson
1947	No Tournament
1949-57	No Tournaments
1958	Billy Casper
1959	Bill Collins
1960	Dow Finsterwald
1961	Doug Sanders
1962	Bo Wininger
1963	Bo Wininger
1964	Mason Rudolph
1965	Dick Mayer
1966	Frank Beard
1967	George Knudson
1968	George Archer
1969	Larry Hinson
1970	Miller Barber
1971	Frank Beard
1972	Gary Player
1973	Jack Nicklaus
1974	Lee Trevino

First NBC New Orleans Open

1975	Billy Casper
1976	Larry Ziegler
1977	Jim Simons
1978	Lon Hinkle
1979	Hubert Green

Greater New Orleans Open

1980	Tom Watson

USF&G New Orleans Open

1981	Tom Watson

USF&G Classic

1982	Scott Hoch
1983	Bill Rogers
1984	Bob Eastwood
1985	Seve Ballesteros
1986	Calvin Peete
1987	Ben Crenshaw
1988	Chip Beck
1989	Tim Simpson
1990	David Frost
1991	Ian Woosnam

Freeport-McMoran Classic

1992	Chip Beck
1993	Mike Standly
1994	Ben Crenshaw
1995	Davis Love III

Freeport-McDermott Classic

1996	Scott McCarron
1997	Brad Faxon
1998	Lee Westwood

Compaq Classic of New Orleans

1999	Carlos Franco

Most Wins

2	Chip Beck, Billy Casper, Ben Crenshaw, Byron Nelson, Henry Picard, Tom Watson, Bo Wininger

Convair-San Diego Open
See Buick Invitational

CVS CHARITY CLASSIC

*(Tournaments marked with * held at Pleasant Valley CC, but not related to CVC Charity Classic history)*

*Carling World Open**

1965	Tony Lema
1966-67	No Tournaments

Kemper Open (see also entry for Kemper Open)*

1968	Arnold Palmer

AVCO Golf Classic

1969	Tom Shaw
1970	Billy Casper

Massachusetts Classic

1971	Dave Stockton

USI Classic

1972	Bruce Devlin
1973	Lanny Wadkins

Pleasant Valley Classic

1974	Victor Regalado
1975	Roger Maltbie
1976	Buddy Allin
1977	Ray Floyd

American Optical Classic

1978	John Mahaffey
1979	Lou Graham

Pleasant Valley Jimmy Fund Classic

1980	Wayne Levi
1981	Jack Renner

Bank of Boston Classic

1982	Bob Gilder
1983	Mark Lye
1984	George Archer
1985	George Burns
1986	Gene Sauers
1987	Sam Randolph
1988	Mark Calcavecchia
1989	Blaine McCallister
1990	Morris Hatalsky

New England Classic

1991	Bruce Fleisher
1992	Brad Faxon
1993	Paul Azinger
1994	Kenny Perry

Ideon Classic at Pleasant Valley

1995	Fred Funk

CVS Charity Classic

1996	John Cook
1997	Loren Roberts
1998	Steve Pate
1999	No Tournament

Most Wins

No multiple winners

Dallas Centennial; Open Dallas
See GTE Byron Nelson Golf Classic

Danny Thomas Memphis Classic
See FedEx St Jude Classic

Dean Martin Tuscon Open
See Touchstone Energy Tuscon Open

Deposit Guaranty Golf Classic
See Southern Farm Bureau Classic

Doral CC Open Invitational;Doral-Eastern Open Invitational
See Doral-Ryder Open

DORAL-RYDER OPEN

Doral CC Open Invitational

1962	Billy Casper
1963	Dan Sikes
1964	Billy Casper
1965	Doug Sanders
1966	Phil Rodgers
1967	Doug Sanders
1968	Gardner Dickinson
1969	Tom Shaw

Doral-Eastern Open Invitational

1970	Mike Hill
1971	JC Snead
1972	Jack Nicklaus
1973	Lee Trevino
1974	Buddy Allin
1975	Jack Nicklaus
1976	Hubert Green
1977	Andy Bean
1978	Tom Weiskopf
1979	Mark McCumber
1980	Ray Floyd
1981	Ray Floyd
1982	Andy Bean
1983	Gary Koch
1984	Tom Kite
1985	Mark McCumber
1986	Andy Bean

Doral-Ryder Open

1987	Lanny Wadkins
1988	Ben Crenshaw

1989	Bill Glasson
1990	Greg Norman
1991	Rocco Mediate
1992	Ray Floyd
1993	Greg Norman
1994	John Huston
1995	Nick Faldo
1996	Greg Norman
1997	Steve Elkington
1998	Michael Bradley
1999	Steve Elkington

Most Wins

3	Ray Floyd, Greg Norman

Ed McMahon-Jaycees Quad City Open
See John Deere Classic

Federal Express St Jude Classic
See FedEx St Jude Classic

FEDEX ST JUDE CLASSIC

Memphis Invitational Open

1958	Billy Maxwell
1959	Don Whitt
1960	Tommy Bolt
1961	Cary Middlecoff
1962	Lionel Hebert
1963	Tony Lema
1964	Mike Souchak
1965	Jack Nicklaus
1966	Bert Yancey
1967	Dave Hill
1968	Bob Lunn
1969	Dave Hill

Danny Thomas Memphis Classic

1970	Dave Hill
1971	Lee Trevino
1972	Lee Trevino
1973	Dave Hill
1974	Gary Player
1975	Gene Littler
1976	Gibby Gilbert
1977	Al Geiberger
1978	Andy Bean
1979	Gil Morgan

1980	Lee Trevino
1981	Jerry Pate
1982	Ray Floyd
1983	Larry Mize
1984	Bob Eastwood

Jude Memphis Classic

1985	Hal Sutton

Federal Express St Jude Classic

1986	Mike Hulbert
1987	Curtis Strange
1988	Jodie Mudd
1989	John Mahaffey
1990	Tom Kite
1991	Fred Couples
1992	Jay Haas
1993	Nick Price
1994	Dicky Pride
1995	Jim Gallagher, Jr

FedEx St Jude Classic

1996	John Cook
1997	Greg Norman
1998	Nick Price
1999	Ted Tryba

Most Wins

4	Dave Hill
3	Lee Trevino

First NBC New Orleans Open
See Compaq Classic of New Orleans

Flint Elkes Open
See Buick Open

Florida Citrus Open Invitational
See Bay Hill International

Freeport-McDermott Classic; Freeport-McMoran Classic
See Compaq Classic of New Orleans

Georgia-Pacific Atlanta Golf Classic
See BellSouth Classic

Glen Campbell Los Angeles Open
See Nissan Open

GREATER GREENSBORO CHRYSLER CLASSIC

Greater Greensboro Open

1938	Sam Snead
1939	Ralph Guldahl
1940	Ben Hogan
1941	Byron Nelson
1942	Sam Byrd
1943-44	*No Tournament – World War Two*
1945	Byron Nelson
1946	Sam Snead
1947	Vic Ghezzi
1948	Lloyd Mangrum
1949	Sam Snead
1950	Sam Snead
1951	Art Doering
1952	Dave Douglas
1953	Earl Stewart
1954	Doug Ford
1955	Sam Snead
1956	Sam Snead
1957	Stan Leonard
1958	Bob Goalby
1959	Dow Finsterwald
1960	Sam Snead
1961	Mike Souchak
1962	Billy Casper
1963	Doug Sanders
1964	Julius Boros
1965	Sam Snead
1966	Doug Sanders
1967	George Archer
1968	Billy Casper
1969	Gene Littler
1970	Gary Player
1971	Buddy Allin
1972	George Archer
1973	Chi Chi Rodriguez
1974	Bob Charles
1975	Tom Weiskopf
1976	Al Geiberger
1977	Danny Edwards
1978	Seve Ballesteros
1979	Ray Floyd
1980	Craig Stadler
1981	Larry Nelson
1982	Danny Edwards
1983	Lanny Wadkins
1984	Andy Bean
1985	Joey Sindelar
1986	Sandy Lyle
1987	Scott Simpson

KMart Greater Greensboro Open

1988	Sandy Lyle
1989	Ken Green
1990	Steve Elkington
1991	Mark Brooks
1992	Davis Love III
1993	Rocco Mediate
1994	Mike Springer
1995	Jim Gallagher, Jr

Greater Greensboro Chrysler Classic

1996	Mark O'Meara
1997	Frank Nobilo
1998	Trevor Dodds
1999	Jesper Parnevik

Most Wins

8	Sam Snead
2	George Archer, Billy Casper, Danny Edwards, Sandy Lyle, Byron Nelson, Doug Sanders

Greater Greensboro Open
See Greater Greensboro Chrysler Classic

Greater Hartford Open Invitational
See Canon Greater Hartford Open

GREATER MILWAUKEE OPEN

1968	Dave Stockton
1969	Ken Still
1970	Deane Beman
1971	Dave Eichelberger
1972	Jim Colbert
1973	Dave Stockton
1974	Ed Sneed
1975	Art Wall
1976	Dave Hill
1977	Dave Eichelberger
1978	Lee Elder
1979	Calvin Peete
1980	Bill Kratzert
1981	Jay Haas

1982	Calvin Peete
1983	Morris Hatalsky
1984	Mark O'Meara
1985	Jim Thorpe
1986	Corey Pavin
1987	Gary Hallberg
1988	Ken Green
1989	Greg Norman
1990	Jim Gallagher, Jr
1991	Mark Brooks
1992	Richard Zokol
1993	Billy Mayfair
1994	Mike Springer
1995	Scott Hoch
1996	Loren Roberts
1997	Scott Hoch
1998	Jeff Sluman
1999	Carlos Franco

Most Wins

2	Dave Eichelberger, Scott Hoch, Calvin Peete, Dave Stockton

Greater New Orleans Open; Greater New Orleans Open Invitational
See Compaq Classic of New Orleans

Greater Vancouver Open
See Air Canada Championship

Green Island Open Invitational
See Buick Challenge

GTE BYRON NELSON GOLF CLASSIC

Texas Victory Open

1944	Byron Nelson

Dallas Open

1945	Sam Snead
1946	Ben Hogan
1947-55	No Tournament

Dallas Centennial Open

1956i	Don January

Texas Invitational Open

1956ii	Peter Thomson

Dallas Open

1957	Sam Snead
1958	Sam Snead

1959	Julius Boros
1960	Johnny Pott
1961	Earl Stewart
1962	Billy Maxwell
1963	No Tournament
1964	Charles Coody
1965	No Tournament
1966	Roberto de Vicenzo
1967	Bert Yancey

Byron Nelson Golf Classic

1968	Miller Barber
1969	Bruce Devlin
1970	Jack Nicklaus
1971	Jack Nicklaus
1972	Chi Chi Rodriguez
1973	Lanny Wadkins
1974	Buddy Allin
1975	Tom Watson
1976	Mark Hayes
1977	Ray Floyd
1978	Tom Watson
1979	Tom Watson
1980	Tom Watson
1981	Bruce Lietzke
1982	Bob Gilder
1983	Ben Crenshaw
1984	Craig Stadler
1985	Bob Eastwood
1986	Andy Bean
1987	Fred Couples

GTE Byron Nelson Golf Classic

1988	Bruce Lietzke
1989	Jodie Mudd
1990	Payne Stewart
1991	Nick Price
1992	Billy Ray Brown
1993	Scott Simpson
1994	Neal Lancaster
1995	Ernie Els
1996	Phil Mickelson
1997	Tiger Woods
1998	John Cook
1999	Loren Roberts

Most Wins

4	Tom Watson
3	Sam Snead

Hardee's Golf Classic
See John Deere Classic

Hawaiian Open
See Sony Open in Hawaii

H-E-B Texas Open
See Westin Texas Open

Heritage Classic
See MCI Classic – The Heritage of Golf

Hertz Bay Hill Classic
See Bay Hill Invitational

Home of the Sun Invitational
See Touchstone Energy Tuscon Open

HONDA CLASSIC

Jackie Gleason's Inverrary Classic
1972	Tom Weiskopf

Jackie Gleason's Inverrary National Airlines Classic
1973	Lee Trevino

Jackie Gleason's Inverrary Classic
1974	Leonard Thompson
1975	Bob Murphy
1976	No Tournament (1976 TPC hosted by Inverrary G&CC)
1977	Jack Nicklaus
1978	Jack Nicklaus
1979	Larry Nelson
1980	Johnny Miller

American Motors' Inverrary Classic
1981	Tom Kite

Honda Inverrary Classic
1982	Hale Irwin
1983	Johnny Miller

Honda Classic
1984	Bruce Lietzke
1985	Curtis Strange
1986	Kenny Knox
1987	Mark Calcavecchia
1988	Joey Sindelar
1989	Blaine McCallister
1990	John Huston
1991	Steve Pate
1992	Corey Pavin
1993	Fred Couples
1994	Nick Price
1995	Mark O'Meara
1996	Tim Herron
1997	Stuart Appleby
1998	Mark Calcavecchia
1999	Vijay Singh

Most Wins
2	Mark Calcavecchia, Jack Nicklaus

Honda Inverrary Classic
See Honda Classic Houston Champions International;

Houston Classic; Houston Coca Cola Open; Houston Open
See Shell Houston Open

Ideon Classic at Pleasant Valley
See CVS Charity Classic

Independent Insurance Agent Open
See Shell Houston Open

Infiniti Tournament of Champions
See Mercedes Championships

Insurance City Open
See Canon Greater Hartford Open

(The) International
See Sprint International

Isuzu/Andy Williams San Diego Open
See Buick Invitational

Jackie Gleason's Inverrary Classic; Jackie Gleason's Inverrary National Airlines Classic
See Honda Classic

Joe Garagiola Tuscon Open
See Touchstone Energy Tuscon Open

JOHN DEERE CLASSIC

Quad Cities Open
1972	Deane Beman
1973	Sam Adams
1974	Dave Stockton

Ed McMahon-Jaycees Quad City Open
1975	Roger Maltbie
1976	John Lister

1977	Mike Morley
1978	Victor Regalado
1979	DA Weibring

Quad Cities Open

1980	Scott Hoch
1981	Dave Barr

Miller High-Life Quad Cities Open

1982	Payne Stewart
1983	Danny Edwards
1984	Scott Hoch

Lite Quad Cities Open

1985	Dan Forsman

Hardee's Golf Classic

1986	Mark Wiebe
1987	Kenny Knox
1988	Blaine McCallister
1989	Curt Byrum
1990	Joey Sindelar
1991	DA Weibring
1992	David Frost
1993	David Frost
1994	Mark McCumber

Quad City Classic

1995	DA Weibring
1996	Ed Fiori
1997	David Toms
1998	Steve Jones

John Deere Classic

1999	JL Lewis

Most Wins

3	DA Weibring
2	David Frost, Scott Hoch

Jude Memphis Classic
See FedEx St Jude Classic

Kaiser International Open Invitational
See Michelob Championship at Kingsmill

KEMPER OPEN

1968	Arnold Palmer
1969	Dale Douglas
1970	Dick Lotz
1971	Tom Weiskopf
1972	Doug Sanders
1973	Tom Weiskopf

1974	Bob Menne
1975	Ray Floyd
1976	Joe Inman, Jr
1977	Tom Weiskopf
1978	Andy Bean
1979	Jerry McGee
1980	John Mahaffey
1981	Craig Stadler
1982	Craig Stadler
1983	Fred Couples
1984	Greg Norman
1985	Bill Glasson
1986	Greg Norman
1987	Tom Kite
1988	Morris Hatalsky
1989	Tom Byrum
1990	Gil Morgan
1991	Billy Andrade
1992	Bill Glasson
1993	Grant Waite
1994	Mark Brooks
1995	Lee Janzen
1996	Steve Stricker
1997	Justin Leonard
1998	Stuart Appleby
1999	Rich Beem

Most Wins

3	Tom Weiskopf
2	Bill Glasson, Greg Norman, Craig Stadler

KMart Greater Greensboro Open
See Greater Greensboro Chrysler Classic

LaCantera Texas Open
See Westin Texas Open

Lake Michigan Classic
See Buick Open

LAS VEGAS INVITATIONAL

Panasonic Las Vegas Pro-Celebrity Classic

1983	Fuzzy Zoeller

Panasonic Las Vegas Invitational

1984	Denis Watson
1985	Curtis Strange
1986	Greg Norman

1987	Paul Azinger
1988	Gary Koch

Las Vegas Invitational

1989	Scott Hoch
1990	Bob Tway
1991	Andrew Magee
1992	John Cook
1993	Davis Love III
1994	Bruce Lietzke
1995	Jim Furyk
1996	Tiger Woods
1997	Bill Glasson
1998	Jim Furyk
1999	Jim Furyk

Most Wins

3	Jim Furyk

Lite Quad Cities Open
See John Deere Open

Los Angeles Open; Los Angeles Open presented by Nissan
See Nissan Open

Magnolia State Classic
See Southern Farm Bureau Classic

Manufacturers Hanover Westchester Classic
See Buick Classic

Massachusetts Classic
See CVS Charity Classic Mastercard Colonial

COLONIAL NATIONAL INVITATION TOURNAMENT

1946	Ben Hogan
1947	Ben Hogan
1948	Clayton Heafner
1949	No Tournament
1950	Sam Snead
1951	Cary Middlecoff
1952	Ben Hogan
1953	Ben Hogan
1954	Johnny Palmer
1955	Chandler Harper
1956	Mike Souchak
1957	Roberto de Vicenzo
1958	Tommy Bolt
1959	Ben Hogan

1960	Julius Boros
1961	Doug Sanders
1962	Arnold Palmer
1963	Julius Boros
1964	Billy Casper
1965	Bruce Crampton
1966	Bruce Devlin
1967	Dave Stockton
1968	Billy Casper
1969	Gardner Dickinson
1970	Homero Blancas
1971	Gene Littler
1972	Jerry Heard
1973	Tom Weiskopf
1974	Rod Curl
1975	No Tournament
1976	Lee Trevino
1977	Ben Crenshaw
1973	Lee Trevino
1979	Al Geiberger
1930	Bruce Lietzke
1931	Fuzzy Zoeller
1982	Jack Nicklaus
1983	Jim Colbert
1984	Peter Jacobsen
1985	Corey Pavin
1986	Dan Pohl
1987	Keith Clearwater
1988	Lanny Wadkins
1989	Ian Baker-Finch

Southwestern Bell Colonial

1980	Ben Crenshaw
1991	Tom Purtzer
1992	Bruce Lietzke
1993	Fulton Allem
1994	Nick Price

Mastercard Colonial

1995	Tom Lehman
1996	Corey Pavin
1997	David Frost
1998	Tom Watson
1999	Olin Browne

Most Wins

5	Ben Hogan
2	Julius Boros, Ben Crenshaw, Bruce Lietzke, Corey Pavin, Lee Trevino

MCI CLASSIC –THE HERITAGE OF GOLF

Heritage Classic

1969	Arnold Palmer
1970	Bob Goalby

Sea Pines Heritage Classic

1971	Hale Irwin
1972	Johnny Miller
1973	Hale Irwin
1974	Johnny Miller
1975	Jack Nicklaus
1976	Hubert Green
1977	Graham Marsh
1978	Hubert Green
1979	Tom Watson
1980	Doug Tewell
1981	Bill Rogers
1982	Tom Watson
1983	Fuzzy Zoeller
1984	Nick Faldo
1985	Bernhard Langer
1986	Fuzzy Zoeller

MCI Heritage Classic

1987	Davis Love III
1988	Greg Norman
1989	Payne Stewart
1990	Payne Stewart
1991	Davis Love III
1992	Davis Love III
1993	David Edwards
1994	Hale Irwin

MCI Classic – The Heritage of Golf

1995	Bob Tway
1996	Loren Roberts
1997	Nick Price
1998	Davis Love III
1999	Glen Day

Most Wins

4	Davis Love III
3	Hale Irwin

MCI Heritage Classic

See MCI Classic – The Heritage of Golf

MEMORIAL TOURNAMENT

1976	Roger Maltbie
1977	Jack Nicklaus
1978	Jim Simons
1979	Tom Watson
1980	David Graham
1981	Keith Fergus
1982	Ray Floyd
1983	Hale Irwin
1984	Jack Nicklaus
1985	Hale Irwin
1986	Hal Sutton
1987	Don Pooley
1988	Curtis Strange
1989	Bob Tway
1990	Greg Norman
1991	Kenny Perry
1992	David Edwards
1993	Paul Azinger
1994	Tom Lehman
1995	Greg Norman
1996	Tom Watson
1997	Vijay Singh
1998	Fred Couples
1999	Tiger Woods

Most Wins

2	Hale Irwin, Jack Nicklaus, Greg Norman, Tom Watson

Memphis Invitational Open

See FedEx St Jude Classic

MERCEDES CHAMPIONSHIPS

Mercedes Tournament of Champions

1953	Al Besselink
1954	Art Wall
1955	Gene Littler
1956	Gene Littler
1957	Gene Littler
1958	Stan Leonard
1959	Mike Souchak
1960	Jerry Barber
1961	Sam Snead
1962	Arnold Palmer
1963	Jack Nicklaus
1964	Jack Nicklaus
1965	Arnold Palmer
1966	Arnold Palmer

1967	Frank Beard
1968	Don January
1969	Gary Player
1970	Frank Beard
1971	Jack Nicklaus
1972	Bobby Mitchell
1973	Jack Nicklaus

Mony Tournament of Champions

1974	Johnny Miller
1975	Al Geiberger
1978	Don January
1977	Jack Nicklaus
1978	Gary Player
1979	Tom Watson
1981	Lee Trevino
1980	Tom Watson
1982	Lanny Wadkins
1983	Lanny Wadkins
1984	Tom Watson
1985	Tom Kite
1986	Calvin Peete
1987	Mac O'Grady
1988	Steve Pate
1989	Steve Jones

Infiniti Tournament of Champions

1990	Paul Azinger
1991	Tom Kite
1992	Steve Elkington
1993	Davis Love III

Mercedes Championships

1994	Phil Mickelson
1995	Steve Elkington
1996	Mark O'Meara
1997	Tiger Woods
1998	Phil Mickelson
1999	David Duval

Most Wins

5	Jack Nicklaus
3	Gene Littler, Arnold Palmer, Tom Watson

Mercedes Tournament of Champions
See Mercedes Championships

MICHELOB CHAMPIONSHIP AT KINGSMILL

Kaiser International Open Invitational

1968	Kermit Zarley
1969i	Miller Barber
1969ii	Jack Nicklaus
1970	Ken Still
1971	Billy Casper
1972	George Knudson
1973	Ed Sneed
1974	Johnny Miller
1975	Johnny Miller
1970	JC Snead

Anheuser-Busch Golf Classic

1977	Miller Barber
1978	Tom Watson
1979	John Fought
1980	Ben Crenshaw
1981	John Mahaffey
1982	Calvin Peete
1983	Calvin Peete
1984	Ronnie Black
1985	Mark Wiebe
1986	Fuzzy Zoeller
1987	Mark McCumber
1988	Tom Sieckmann
1989	Mike Donald
1990	Lanny Wadkins
1991	Mike Hulbert
1992	David Peoples
1993	Jim Gallagher, Jr
1994	Mark McCumber
1995	Ted Tryba

Michelob Championship at Kingsmill

1996	Scott Hoch
1997	David Duval
1998	David Duval
1999	Notah Begay III

Most Wins

2	Miller Barber, David Duval, Mark McCumber, Johnny Miller, Calvin Peete

Michelob Houston Open
See Shell Houston Open

Miller High-Life Quad Cities Open
See John Deere Classic

Mony Tournament of Champions
See Mercedes Championships

MOTOROLA WESTERN OPEN

Western Open

1899	Willie Smith
1900	No Tournament
1901	Laurie Auchterlonie
1902	Willie Anderson, Jr
1903	Alex Smith
1904	Willie Anderson, Jr
1905	Arthur Smith
1906	Alex Smith
1907	Robert Simpson
1908	Willie Anderson, Jr
1909	Willie Anderson, Jr
1910	Charles Evans, Jr (a)
1911	Robert Simpson
1912	Macdonald Smith
1913	John McDermott
1914	Jim Barnes
1915	Tom McNamara
1916	Walter Hagen
1917	Jim Barnes
1918	*No Tournament – World War One*
1919	Jim Barnes
1920	Jock Hutchison
1921	Walter Hagen
1922	Mike Brady
1923	Jock Hutchison
1924	Bill Mehlhorn
1925	Macdonald Smith
1926	Walter Hagen
1927	Walter Hagen
1928	Abe Espinosa
1929	Tommy Armour
1930	Gene Sarazen
1931	Ed Dudley
1932	Walter Hagen
1933	Macdonald Smith
1934	Harry Cooper
1935	Johnny Revolta
1936	Ralph Guldahl
1937	Ralph Guldahl
1938	Ralph Guldahl
1939	Byron Nelson
1940	Jimmy Demaret
1941	Ed Oliver
1942	Herman Barron
1943-45	*No Tournaments –World War Two*
1946	Ben Hogan
1947	Johnny Palmer
1948	Ben Hogan
1949	Sam Snead
1950	Sam Snead
1951	Marty Furgol
1952	Lloyd Mangrum
1953	Dutch Harrison
1954	Lloyd Mangrum
1955	Gary Middlecoff
1956	Mike Fetchick
1957	Doug Ford
1958	Doug Sanders
1959	Mike Souchak
1960	Stan Leonard
1961	Arnold Palmer
1962	Jacky Cupit
1963	Arnold Palmer
1964	Chi Chi Rodriguez
1965	Billy Casper
1966	Billy Casper
1967	Jack Nicklaus
1968	Jack Nicklaus
1969	Billy Casper
1970	Hugh Royer
1971	Bruce Crampton
1972	Jim Jamieson
1973	Billy Casper
1974	Tom Watson
1975	Hale Irwin
1976	Al Geiberger
1977	Tom Watson
1978	Andy Bean
1979	Larry Nelson
1980	Scott Simpson
1981	Ed Fiori
1982	Tom Weiskopf

1983	Mark McCumber
1984	Tom Watson
1985	Scott Verplank
1986	Tom Kite

Beatrice Western Open

1987	DA Weibring
1988	Jim Benepe
1989	Mark McCumber

Centel Western Open

1990	Wayne Levi
1991	Russ Cochran
1992	Ben Crenshaw

Sprint Western Open

1993	Nick Price

Motorola Western Open

1994	Nick Price
1995	Billy Mayfair
1996	Steve Stricker
1997	Tiger Woods
1998	Joe Durant
1999	Tiger Woods

Most Wins

5	Walter Hagen
4	Willie Anderson, Jr, Billy Casper

Nabisco Championships of Golf; Nabisco Golf Championships of Golf; Nabisco Championships
See (The) Tour Championship

NATIONAL CAR RENTAL GOLF CLASSIC AT WALT DISNEY WORLD RESORT

Walt Disney World Invitational Open

1971	Jack Nicklaus
1972	Jack Nicklaus
1973	Jack Nicklaus

Walt Disney World National Team Championship

1974	Hubert Green/Mac McLendon
1975	Jim Colbert/Dean Refram
1976	Woody Blackburn/Bill Kratzert
1977	Gibby Gilbert/Grier Jones
1978	Wayne Levi/Bob Mann
1979	George Burns/Ben Crenshaw
1980	Danny & David Edwards
1981	Vance Heafner/Mike Holland

Walt Disney World Golf Classic

1982	Hal Sutton
1983	Payne Stewart
1984	Larry Nelson

Walt Disney World/Oldsmobile Golf Classic

1985	Lanny Wadkins
1986	Ray Floyd
1987	Larry Nelson
1988	Bob Lohr
1989	Tim Simpson
1990	Tim Simpson
1991	Mark O'Meara
1992	John Huston
1993	Jeff Maggert
1994	Rick Fehr
1995	Brad Bryant
1996	Tiger Woods
1997	David Duval

NATIONAL CAR RENTAL GOLF CLASSIC AT WALT DISNEY WORLD RESORT

1998	John Huston
1999	Tiger Woods

Most Wins

3	Jack Nicklaus
2	John Huston, Larry Nelson, Tim Simpson, Tiger Woods

NBC Tuscon Open
See Touchstone Energy Tuscon Open

NEC WORLD SERIES OF GOLF

(*Unofficial tour events – four-man, 36-hole exhibition strokeplay matches)

*1962	Jack Nicklaus
*1963	Jack Nicklaus
*1964	Tony Lema
*1965	Gary Player
*1966	Gene Littler
*1967	Jack Nicklaus
*1968	Gary Player
*1969	Orville Moody
*1970	Jack Nicklaus
*1971	Charles Goody
*1972	Gary Player
*1973	Tom Weiskopf
*1974	Lee Trevino

*1975	Tom Watson
1976	Jack Nicklaus
1977	Lanny Wadkins
1978	Gil Morgan
1979	Lon Hinkle
1980	Tom Watson
1981	Bill Rogers
1982	Craig Stadler
1983	Nick Price
1984	Denis Watson
1985	Roger Maltbie
1986	Dan Pohl
1987	Curtis Strange
1988	Mike Reid
1989	David Frost
1990	Jose-Maria Olazabal
1991	Tom Purtzer
1992	Craig Stadler
1993	Fulton Allem
1994	Jose-Maria Olazabal
1995	Greg Norman
1996	Phil Mickelson
1997	Greg Norman
1998	David Duval
1999	No Tournament

(see World Golf Championship – WGC – Section)

Most Wins
(including unofficial events)

5	Jack Nicklaus
3	Gary Player

(excluding unofficial events)

2	Jose-Maria Olazabal, Greg Norman

Nestle Invitational
See Bay Hill Invitational

New England Classic
See CVS Charity Classic

Nissan Los Angeles Open
See Nissan Open

NISSAN OPEN

Los Angeles Open

1926	Harry Cooper
1927	Bobby Cruickshank

1928	Macdonald Smith
1929	Macdonald Smith
1930	Denny Shute
1931	Ed Dudley
1932	Macdonald Smith
1933	Craig Wood
1934	Macdonald Smith
1935	Vic Ghezzi
1936	Jimmy Hines
1937	Harry Cooper
1938	Jimmy Thomson
1939	Jimmy Demaret
1940	Lawson Little
1941	Johnny Bulla
1942	Ben Hogan
1943	*No Tournaments – World War Two*
1944	Harold McSpaden
1945	Sam Snead
1946	Byron Nelson
1947	Ben Hogan
1948	Ben Hogan
1949	Lloyd Mangrum
1950	Sam Snead
1951	Lloyd Mangrum
1952	Tommy Bolt
1953	Lloyd Mangrum
1954	Fred Wampler
1955	Gene Littler
1956	Lloyd Mangrum
1957	Doug Ford
1958	Frank Stranahan
1959	Ken Venturi
1960	Dow Finsterwald
1961	Bob Goalby
1962	Phil Rodgers
1963	Arnold Palmer
1964	Paul Harney
1965	Paul Harney
1966	Arnold Palmer
1967	Arnold Palmer
1968	Billy Casper
1969	Charles Sifford
1970	Billy Casper

Glen Campbell Los Angeles Open

1971	Bob Lunn
1972	George Archer

1973	Rod Funseth
1974	Dave Stockton
1975	Pat Fitzsimons
1976	Hale Irwin
1977	Tom Purtzer
1978	Gil Morgan
1979	Lanny Wadkins
1980	Tom Watson
1981	Johnny Miller
1982	Tom Watson
1983	Gil Morgan

Los Angeles Open

1984	David Edwards
1985	Lanny Wadkins
1986	Doug Tewell

Los Angeles Open presented by Nissan

| 1987 | Tze-Chung Chen |
| 1988 | Chip Beck |

Nissan Los Angeles Open

1989	Mark Calcavecchia
1990	Fred Couples
1991	Ted Schulz
1992	Fred Couples
1993	Tom Kite
1994	Corey Pavin

Nissan Open

1995	Corey Pavin
1996	Craig Stadler
1997	Nick Faldo
1998	Billy Mayfair
1999	Ernie Els

Most Wins

| 4 | Lloyd Mangrum, Macdonald Smith |
| 3 | Ben Hogan, Arnold Palmer |

Nortel Open

See Touchstone Energy Tuscon Open

Northern Telecom Open; Northern Telecom Tuscon Open

See Touchstone Energy Tuscon Open

Palm Springs Desert Classic

See Bob Hope Chrysler Classic

Panasonic Las Vegas Invitational; Panasonic Las Vegas Pro-Celebrity Classic

See Las Vegas Invitational

PHOENIX OPEN INVITATIONAL

Arizona Open

1932	Ralph Guldahl
1933	Harry Cooper
1934	No Tournament

Phoenix Open Invitational

1935	Ky Laffoon
1936-38	No Tournaments
1939	Byron Nelson
1940	Ed Oliver
1941-43	*No Tournaments – World War Two*
1944	Harold McSpaden
1945	Byron Nelson
1946	Ben Hogan
1947	Ben Hogan
1948	Bobby Locke
1949	Jimmy Demaret
1950	Jimmy Demaret
1951	Lew Worsham
1952	Lloyd Mangrum
1953	Lloyd Mangrum
1954	Ed Furgol
1955	Gene Littler
1956	Gary Middlecoff
1957	Billy Casper
1958	Ken Venturi
1959	Gene Littler
1960	Jack Fleck
1981	Arnold Palmer
1962	Arnold Palmer
1963	Arnold Palmer
1964	Jack Nicklaus
1965	Rod Funseth
1988	Dudley Wysong
1967	Julius Boros
1968	George Knudson
1969	Gene Littler
1970	Dale Douglas
1971	Miller Barber
1972	Homero Blancas

1973	Bruce Crampton
1974	Johnny Miller
1975	Johnny Miller
1976	Bob Gilder
1977	Jerry Pate
1978	Miller Barber
1979	Ben Grenshaw
1980	Jeff Mitchell
1981	David Graham
1982	Lanny Wadkins
1983	Bob Gilder
1984	Tom Purtzer
1985	Calvin Peete
1986	Hal Sutton
1987	Paul Azinger
1988	Sandy Lyle
1989	Mark Calcavecchia
1990	Tommy Armour III
1991	Nolan Henke
1992	Mark Calcavecchia
1993	Lee Janzen
1994	Bill Glasson
1995	Vijay Singh
1996	Phil Mickelson
1997	Steve Jones
1998	Jesper Parnevik
1999	Rocco Mediate

Most Wins
3	Gene Littler, Arnold Palmer

(THE) PLAYERS CHAMPIONSHIP

Tournament Players Championship
1974	Jack Nicklaus
1975	Al Geiberger
1976	Jack Nicklaus
1977	Mark Hayes
1978	Jack Nicklaus
1979	Lanny Wadkins
1980	Lee Trevino
1981	Ray Floyd
1982	Jerry Pate
1983	Hal Sutton
1984	Fred Couples
1985	Calvin Peete

1986	John Mahaffey
1987	Sandy Lyle

The Players Championship
1988	Mark McCumber
1989	Tom Kite
1990	Jodie Mudd
1991	Steve Elkington
1992	Davis Love III
1993	Nick Price
1994	Greg Norman
1995	Lee Janzen
1996	Fred Couples
1997	Steve Elkington
1998	Justin Leonard
1999	David Duval

Most Wins
3	Jack Nicklaus
2	Fred Couples, Steve Elkington

Pleasant Valley Classic; Pleasant Valley Jimmy Fund Classic
See CVS Charity Classic

Quad Cities Open; Quad City Classic
See John Deere Classic

RENO-TAHOE OPEN
1999	Notah Begay III

Sammy Davis, Jr Greater Hartford Open
See Canon Greater Hartford Open

San Antonio Texas Open
See Westin Texas Open

San Diego Open; San Diego Open Invitational
See Buick Invitational

Sea Pines Heritage Classic
See MCI Classic – The Heritage of Golf

Seiko-Tuscon Match Play Championship; Seiko-Tuscon Open
See Touchstone Energy Tuscon Open

SHELL HOUSTON OPEN

Tournament of Champions
1946	Byron Nelson
1947	Bobby Locke
1948	No Tournament
1949	Johnny Palmer

Houston Open
1950	Cary Middlecoff
1951	Marty Furgol
1952	Jack Burke, Jr
1953	Cary Middlecoff
1954	Dave Douglas
1955	Mike Souchak
1956	Ted Kroll
1957	Arnold Palmer
1958	Ed Oliver

Houston Classic
1959	Jack Burke, Jr
1960	Bill Collins
1961	Jay Hebert
1962	Bobby Nichols
1963	Bob Charles
1964	Mike Souchak
1965	Bobby Nichols

Houston Champions International
1966	Arnold Palmer
1967	Frank Beard
1968	Roberto de Vicenzo
1969	No Tournament
1970	Gibby Gilbert
1971	Hubert Green
1972	Bruce Devlin

Houston Open
1973	Bruce Crampton
1974	Dave Hill
1975	Bruce Crampton
1976	Lee Elder
1977	Gene Littler
1978	Gary Player
1979	Wayne Levi

Michelob Houston Open
1980	Curtis Strange
1981	Ron Streck
1982	Ed Sneed

Houston Coca-Cola Open
1983	David Graham
1984	Corey Pavin

Houston Open
1985	Ray Floyd
1986	Curtis Strange

Big I Houston Open
1987	Jay Haas

Independent Insurance Agent Open
1988	Curtis Strange
1989	Mike Sullivan
1990	Tony Sills
1991	Fulton Allem

Shell Huston Open
1992	Fred Funk
1993	Jim McGovern
1994	Mike Heinen
1995	Payne Stewart
1996	Mark Brooks
1997	Phil Blackmar
1998	David Duval
1999	Stuart Appleby

Most Wins
3	Curtis Strange
2	Jack Burke, Jr, Bruce Crampton, Cary Middlecoff, Bobby Nichols, Arnold Palmer, Mike Souchak

Shearson Lehman Brothers Andy Williams Open; Shearson Lehman Brothers Open; Shearson Lehman Hutton Andy Williams Open; Shearson Lehman Hutton Open

See Buick Invitational

SONY OPEN IN HAWAII

Hawaiian Open
1965	Gay Brewer
1966	Ted Makalena
1967	Dudley Wysong
1968	Lee Trevino
1969	Bruce Crampton
1970	No Tournament
1971	Tom Shaw
1972	Grier Jones
1973	John Schlee
1974	Jack Nicklaus

1975	Gary Groh
1976	Ben Crenshaw
1977	Bruce Lietzke
1978	Hubert Green
1979	Hubert Green
1980	Andy Bean
1981	Hale Irwin
1982	Wayne Levi
1983	Isao Aoki
1984	Jack Renner
1985	Mark OMeara
1986	Corey Pavin
1987	Corey Pavin
1988	Lanny Wadkins
1989	Gene Sauers
1990	David Ishii

United Hawaiian Open

1991	Lanny Wadkins

United Airlines Hawaiian Open

1992	John Cook
1993	Howard Twitty
1994	Brett Ogle
1995	John Morse
1996	Jim Furyk
1997	Paul Stankowski
1998	John Huston

Sony Open in Hawaii

1999	Jeff Sluman

Most Wins

2	Hubert Green, Corey Pavin, Lanny Wadkins

SOUTHERN FARM BUREAU CLASSIC

(Upgraded to an official tour event in 1994)

Magnolia State Classic

1968	Mac McLendon
1969	Larry Mowry
1970	Chris Blocker
1971	Roy Pace
1972	Mike Morley
1973	Dwight Nevil
1974	Dwight Nevil
1975	Bob Wynn
1976	Dennis Meyer
1977	Mike McCullough

1978	Craig Stadler
1979	Bobby Walzel
1980	Roger Maltbie
1981	Tom Jones
1982	Payne Stewart
1983	Russ Cochran
1984	Lance Ten Broeck
1985	Jim Gallagher, Jr

Deposit Guaranty Golf Classic

1986	Dan Halldorson
1987	David Ogrin
1988	Frank Conner
1989	Jim Boros
1990	Gene Sauers
1991	Larry Silveira
1992	Richard Zokol
1993	Greg Kraft
1994	Brian Henninger
1995	Ed Dougherty
1996	Willie Wood
1997	Billy Ray Brown
1998	Fred Funk

Southern Farm Bureau Classic

1999	Brian Henninger

Most Wins

2	Brian Henninger, Dwight Nevil

Southern Open Invitational
See Buick Challenge

Southwestern Bell Colonial
See Mastercard Colonial

SPRINT INTERNATIONAL

(Modified Stableford System)

The International

1986	Ken Green
1987	John Cook
1988	Joey Sindelar
1989	Greg Norman
1990	Davis Love III
1991	Jose-Maria Olazabal
1992	Brad Faxon

Sprint International

1993	Phil Mickelson
1994	Steve Lowery

1995	Lee Janzen
1996	Clarence Rose
1997	Phil Mickleson
1998	Vijay Singh
1999	David Toms

Most Wins

2	Phil Mickelson

Sprint Western Open
See Motorola Western Open

SUBARU SARAZEN WORLD OPEN CHAMPIONSHIP
US PGA Tour official event until 1998

1994	Ernie Els
1995	Frank Nobilo
1996	Frank Nobilo
1997	Mark Calcavecchia
1998	Dudley Hart
1999	

See PGA European Tour section

Most Wins

2	Frank Nobilo

Texas Invitational Open; Texas Victory Open
See GTE Byron Nelson Golf Classic

Texas Open; Texas Open Presented by Nabisco
See Westin Texas Open

TOUCHSTONE ENERGY TUSCON OPEN

Tuscon Open

1945	Ray Mangrum
1946	Jimmy Demaret
1947	Jimmy Demaret
1948	Skip Alexander
1949	Lloyd Mangrum
1950	Chandler Harper
1951	Lloyd Mangrum
1952	Henry Williams
1953	Tommy Bolt
1954	No Tournament
1955	Tommy Bolt
1956	Ted Kroll
1957	Dow Finsterwald
1958	Lionel Hebert
1959	Gene Littler

1960	Don January

Home of the Sun Invitational

1961	Dave Hill

Tuscon Open

1962	Phil Rodgers
1963	Don January
1964	Jacky Cupit
1965	Bob Charles
1966	Joe Campbell
1967	Arnold Palmer
1968	George Knudson
1969	Lee Trevino
1970	Lee Trevino
1971	JC Snead
1972	Miller Barber

Dean Martin Tuscon Open

1973	Bruce Crampton
1974	Johnny Miller
1975	Johnny Miller

NBC Tuscon Open

1976	Johnny Miller

Joe Garagiola Tuscon Open

1977	Bruce Lietzke
1978	Tom Watson
1979	Bruce Lietzke
1980	Jim Colbert
1981	Johnny Miller
1982	Craig Stadler
1983	Gil Morgan

Seiko-Tuscon Match Play Championship

1984	Tom Watson
1985	Jim Thorpe
1986	Jim Thorpe

Seiko-Tuscon Open

1987	Mike Reid

Northern Telecom Tuscon Open

1988	David Frost
1989	No Tournament
1990	Robert Gamez

Northern Telecom Open

1991	Phil Mickelson
1992	Lee Janzen
1993	Larry Mize
1994	Andrew Magee
1995	Phil Mickelson

Nortel Open
| 1996 | Phil Mickelson |

Tuscon Chrysler Classic
| 1997 | Jeff Sluman |
| 1998 | David Duval |

Touchstone Energy Tuscon Open
| 1999 | Gabriel Hjertstedt |

Most Wins
| 4 | Johnny Miller |
| 3 | Phil Mickelson |

(THE) TOUR CHAMPIONSHIP

Top 30 on PGA money-list compete.
(*Played at Oak Hills CC instead of Texas Open)

Nabisco Championships of Golf
| 1987* | Tom Watson |

Nabisco Golf Championships
| 1988 | Curtis Strange |
| 1989 | Tom Kite |

Nabisco Championships
| 1990 | Jodie Mudd |

The Tour Championship
1991	Craig Stadler
1992	Paul Azinger
1993	Jim Gallagher, Jr
1994	Mark McCumber
1995	Billy Mayfair
1996	Tom Lehman
1997	David Duval
1998	Hal Sutton
1999	Tiger Woods

Most Wins

No multiple winners

Tournament of Champions
See Shell Houston Open

Tournament Players Championship
See (The) Players Championship

Tuscon Chrysler Classic; Tuscon Open
See Touchstone Energy Tuscon Open

United Airlines Hawaiian Open; United Hawaiian Open
See Sony Open in Hawaii

USF&G Classic; USF&G New Orleans Open
See Compaq Classic of New Orleans

USI Classic
See CVS Charity Classic

Vantage Championship
See Westin Texas Open

Vern Parsell Buick Open
See Buick Open

Walt Disney World Golf Classic; Walt Disney World Invitational Open; Walt Disney World National Team Championship; Walt Disney World/Oldsmobile Classic
See National Car Rental Golf Classic at Walt Disney World Resort

Westchester Classic
See Buick Classic

Western Open
See Motorola Western Open

WESTIN TEXAS OPEN

(* Nabisco Championship of Golf in 1987 became the current-day Tour Championship)

Texas Open
1922	Bob MacDonald
1923	Walter Hagen
1924	Joe Kirkwood, Sr
1925	Joe Turnesa
1926	Macdonald Smith
1927	Bobby Cruickshank
1928	Bill Mehlhorn
1929	Bill Mehlhorn
1930	Denny Shute
1931	Abe Espinosa
1932	Clarence Clark
1933	No Tournament
1934	Wiffy Cox
1935-38	No Touranaments
1939	Dutch Harrison
1940	Byron Nelson
1941	Lawson Little
1942	Chick Harbert
1943	*No Tournament – World War Two*

1944	Johnny Revolta
1945	Sam Byrd
1946	Ben Hogan
1947	Ed Oliver
1948	Sam Snead
1949	Dave Douglas
1950	Sam Snead
1951	Dutch Harrison
1952	Jack Burke, Jr
1953	Tony Holguin
1954	Chandler Harper
1955	Mike Souchak
1956	Gene Littler
1957	Jay Hebert
1958	Bill Johnston
1959	Wes Ellis, Jr
1960	Arnold Palmer
1961	Arnold Palmer
1962	Arnold Palmer
1963	Phil Rodgers
1964	Bruce Crampton
1965	Frank Beard
1966	Harold Henning
1967	Chi Chi Rodriguez
1968	No Tournament
1969	Deane Beman

San Antonio Texas Open

1970	Ron Cerrudo
1971	No Tournament
1972	Mike Hill
1973	Ben Crenshaw
1974	Terry Diehl
1975	Don January
1976	Butch Baird
1977	Hale Irwin
1978	Ron Streck
1979	Lou Graham
1980	Lee Trevino

Texas Open

1981	Bill Rogers
1982	Jay Haas
1983	Jim Colbert
1984	Calvin Peete
1985	John Mahaffey

Vantage Championship

| 1986 | Ben Crenshaw |

| 1987 | No Tournament – see *The Tour Championship* |

Texas Open Presented by Nabisco

| 1988 | Corey Pavin |
| 1989 | Donnie Hammond |

H-E-B Texas Open

1990	Mark O'Meara
1991	Blaine McCalister
1992	Nick Price
1993	Jay Haas

Texas Open

| 1994 | Bob Estes |

LaCantera Texas Open

1995	Duffy Waldorf
1996	David Ogrin
1997	Tim Herron

Westin Texas Open

| 1998 | Hal Sutton |
| 1999 | Duffy Waldorf |

Most Wins

| 3 | Arnold Palmer |
| 2 | Ben Crenshaw, Jay Haas, Dutch Harrison, Bill Mehlhorn, Sam Snead, Duffy Waldorf |

Wickes-Andy Williams San Diego Open

See Buick Invitational

LEADING MONEY WINNERS

US unless stated $

Year	Winner	$
1934	Paul Runyan	6767
1935	Johnny Revolta	9543
1936	Horton Smith	7682
1937	Harry Cooper	14138
1938	Sam Snead	19534
1939	Henry Picard	10303
1940	Ben Hogan	10655
1941	Ben Hogan	18358
1942	Ben Hogan	13143
1943	*No Listings – World War Two*	
1944	Byron Nelson	*37967
1945	Byron Nelson	*63335
1946	Ben Hogan	42556
1947	Jimmy Demaret	27936
1948	Ben Hogan	32112
1949	Sam Snead	31593
1950	Sam Snead	35758
1951	Lloyd Mangrum	26088
1952	Julius Boros	37032
1953	Lew Worsham	34002
1954	Bob Toski	65819
1955	Julius Boros	63121
1956	Ted Kroll	72835
1957	Dick Mayer	65835
1958	Arnold Palmer	42607
1959	Art Wall	53167
1960	Arnold Palmer	75262
1961	Gary Player (RSA)	64540
1962	Arnold Palmer	81448
1963	Arnold Palmer	129230
1964	Jack Nicklaus	113284
1965	Jack Nicklaus	140752
1966	Billy Casper	121944
1967	Jack Nicklaus	188998
1968	Billy Casper	205168
1969	Frank Beard	184707
1970	Lee Trevino	157037
1971	Jack Nicklaus	244490
1972	Jack Nicklaus	320542
1973	Jack Nicklaus	308362
1974	Johnny Miller	353021
1975	Jack Nicklaus	298149
1976	Jack Nicklaus	266438
1977	Tom Watson	310653
1978	Tom Watson	362428
1979	Tom Watson	462636
1980	Tom Watson	530808
1981	Tom Kite	375698
1982	Craig Stadler	446462
1983	Hal Sutton	426668
1984	Tom Watson	476260
1985	Curtis Strange	542321
1986	Greg Norman (Aus)	653296
1987	Curtis Strange	925941
1988	Curtis Strange	1147644
1989	Tom Kite	1395278
1990	Greg Norman (Aus)	1165477
1991	Corey Pavin	979430
1992	Fred Couples	1344188
1993	Nick Price (Zim)	1478557
1994	Nick Price (Zim)	1499927
1995	Greg Norman (Aus)	1654959
1996	Tom Lehman	1780159
1997	Tiger Woods	2066833
1998	David Duval	2591031
1999	Tiger Woods	6616585

* Paid in War Bonds

MOST LEADING MONEY WINS

8	Jack Nicklaus
5 =	Ben Hogan
	Tom Watson
4	Arnold Palmer
3 =	Greg Norman
	Sam Snead
	Curtis Strange
2 =	Julius Boros
	Billy Casper
	Tom Kite
	Byron Nelson
	Nick Price
	Tiger Woods

LEADERS IN CAREER EARNINGS

		$
1	Greg Norman	12507322
2	Davis Love III	12487462
3	Payne Stewart	11737008

4	Nick Price	11386236
5	Tiger Woods	*11315129
6	Fred Couples	11305068
7	Mark O'Meara	11162269
8	Tom Kite	10533102
9	Scott Hoch	10308995
10	David Duval	10047947

By February 2000 this figure had increased to $12821129!

MOST TOUR WINS

81	Sam Snead
70	Jack Nicklaus
63	Ben Hogan
60	Arnold Palmer
52	Byron Nelson
51	Billy Casper
40 =	Walter Hagen
	Cary Middlecoff
38	Gene Sarazen
36	Lloyd Mangrum

Selected others

34	Tom Watson
27	Lee Trevino
21	Gary Player
19	Tom Kite
18	Greg Norman
16 =	Mark O'Meara
	Nick Price
15	Tiger Woods

MOST TOUR WINS IN A SEASON

18	Byron Nelson (1945)
	(including 11 in a row)
13	Ben Hogan (1946)
11	Sam Snead (1950)
10	Ben Hogan (1948)
9	Paul Runyan (1933)
8 =	Harry Cooper (1937)
	Johnny Miller (1974)
	Byron Nelson (1944)
	Arnold Palmer (1960)
	Henry Picard (1939)
	Gene Sarazen (1930)
	Horton Smith (1929)

Sam Snead (1938)
Tiger Woods (1999)

LOWEST SCORING

18 Holes

59	Chip Beck, *Las Vaegas invitational, 1991*
	Al Geiberger, *Memphis Classic, 1977*
	David Duval, *Bob Hope Chrysler Classic, 1999*
	All 13 under par
60	Tommy Bolt, *Insurance City Open, 1954*
	Al Brosch, *Texas Open, 1951*
	David Frost*, *Northern Telecom Tuscon Open, 1990*
	Ted Kroll, *Texas Open, 1954*
	Davis Love III*, *United Airlines Hawaiian Open, '94*
	Steve Lowery*, *Buick Challenge, 1997*
	Bill Nary, *El Paso Open, 1952*
	Sam Snead, *Dallas Open, 1957*
	Mike Souchak, *Texas Open, 1955*
	Grant Waite, *Phoenix Open, 1996*
	* All 12 under par

72 holes

257	Mike Souchak, *Texas Open, 1955*
	27 under par
258	John Cook*, *FedEx St Jude Classic, 1996*
	Donnie Hammond, *Texas Open, 1989*
	Steve Jones*, *Pheonix Open, 1997*
	* Both 26 under par
259	David Frost, *Hardee's Golf Classic, 1993*
	Chandler Harper*, *Texas Open, 1954*
	Byron Nelson, *Seattle Open, 1945*
	Tim Norris*, *Sammy Davis, Jr Greater Hartford Open, 1982*
	Corey Pavin, *Texas Open, 1988*
	* Both 25 under par

The lowest under par round on Tour (28 under) was by John Huston, United Airlines Hawaiian Open, 1998, when shooting 260

For once the PGA was behind Europe when it came to developing the golfers of the future for role of Tour professional. It wasn't until 1990, under the auspicies of Deane Beman, that the Ben Hogan Tour was launched, renamed after its first sponsor, Nike, in 1993. It has proved to be a rich well of talent nevertheless, and has provided invaluable experience, acting as it does as a bridge for the budding young pro to move from the college circuit to the full tour. If proof were needed, Nike Tour alumni to the end of 1999 provided the following impressive array of PGA Tour winners, totalling 79, 76 of them 'official events', after John Daly set the ball rolling in 1991 in somewhat spectacular fashion, by winning a Major! In 1999, of the 47 official/recognised events, the Nike tour had produced 21 winners. Take away the Tiger's eight wins, that means over 50% of the rest were won by golfers having cut their teeth on the junior tour. From 2000 the supporting tour will be known as the BUY.COM Tour.

PGA TOUR VICTORIES BY NIKE TOUR GRADUATES

Majors wins in brackets

11	David Duval
7	Ernie Els (2)
5	Jim Furyk
4 =	John Daly (2)
	Tom Lehman (1)
3 =	Stuart Appleby
	Tim Herron
	Mike Springer *(inc 1 unofficial)*
	Paul Stankowski *(inc 1 unofficial)*
	David Toms
2 =	Notah Begay III
	Olin Browne
	Brian Henninger
	Gabriel Hjertstedt
	Jeff Maggert
	Ted Tryba
1 =	Woody Austin
	Guy Boros
	Brandel Chamblee
	Stewart Cink
	Glen Day
	Trevor Dodds
	Joe Durant
	Brent Geiberger
	Paul Goydos
	JP Hayes
	Mike Heinen
	Greg Kraft (unofficial)
	JL Lewis
	Steve Lowery
	Jim McGovern
	John Morse
	Tom Pernice, Jr
	Chris Perry
	Clarence Rose
	Mike Standly
	Willie Wood

What other sport could effectively pension you off in your mid-forties, when you are struggling to maintain the standards of erstwhile glory days, only to resurrect you at 50, and pay you more than you have ever earned before? Sounds loopy, doesn't it, but ask Hale Irwin, who in 1998 won nearly $3m dollars – about a quarter of a million more than David Duval, who finished atop the regular PGA Tour Money List. Irwin earned nearly $6 million in a twenty-five year career that took in 20 Tour victories and three US Opens: in the five years since he turned 50, has grossed almost $10 million more!

Beginning in 1980 proper, although the prestigious PGA Seniors Championship had been providing a little extra pocket-money for the successful over-fifties since 1937, the biggest gravy train in world sport cannot even claim to be representative of top-class sport. What began though as an understandable attempt to add a few years bonus to those who wanted competitive golf still, albeit once in a while, snowballed into a hugely successful industry. The sponsors' chequebooks have always been open, with the number of events and the purse expanding sometimes geometrically over the past 20 years or so. As a by-product, the leisurely camaraderie of the early eighties has developed into a very serious professional series of contests, where the rewards are staggeringly high, and the pressure is as great on the players as it was when in their so-called prime.

The driving force behind the Tour was a PGA Senior Advisory Council, chaired by Dan Sikes, and comprising Sam Snead (then 68), Julius Boros, Don January, Bob Goalby and Gardner Dickinson; but their star weapon was, as if by destiny to be golf's greatest talisman, Arnold Palmer once more. Happy coincidence that Palmer's fiftieth birthday fell in 1979? Let's say it was superb timing. Arnie's form went from bad to worse during the 1970s, but the Army, maybe on furlough now and then, were still there to see their hero take on his new challenge. On cue he won his first-ever Senior event; and, naturally, it was the biggest around – the PGA Seniors. Already the Tour was tinged with magic. The genteel applause of the curious early galleries soon evaporated. The crowds became more voluble, and even the odd golf fan's version of a brainless soccer chant, the obnoxious 'You're the man', or a primordial ancestor of it, was reportedly heard. In the case of Palmer, that 'epithet' was always most convincing.

Palmer apart, what was it that would make the seniors Tour such a monster affair two decades on? Surely, after a while, once the novelty and nostalgia for the old timers wore off, the Tour would struggle to attract the kind of money needed to carry on. It has, however, two secret ingredients that the regular tour could never have. It has a constant stream of recognised 'new' talent every year, when the giants of the recent past hit fifty. It also has a quality that no one could have envisaged: it has managed to make winners of one-time also-rans. Taking the former point, look at the impact of Nicklaus, Player and Trevino after Arnold Palmer's initial impetus. Carry it on, through Raymond Floyd and Hale Irwin to Larry Nelson and Tom Kite; and with Tom Watson waiting in the wings, and Crenshaw and others just behind, the Tour has a streaming hall of fame for ever. Included in that list is the 1985 leading money-winner, Peter Thomson, who finally banished the myth that he couldn't play in America. The second advantage is more difficult to understand; a sort of serendipity, really. Journeymen golfers such as Gil Morgan, Jim Colbert and Bruce Fleisher; amateurs like the exceptional Jay Sigel and Allen Doyle; European golfers who previously were fishes out of water in America, like Brian Barnes and Jose-Maria Canizares – all started to win, and win as regularly as the greats of yore. What a delight to witness a win for Christy O'Connor, Jr in the State Farm Senior Classic in 1999 – Uncle Christy would have been most impressed, I'm sure.

So there can only be balmy days ahead for the Senior Golfer, at least in the States. The European picture, as always, is a little more austere, but with qualifying schools, burgeoning crowds and only the seemingly dissatisfied sponsors being those on the waiting list, who'd be a fortysomething player in America?

US SENIOR OPEN

1980	Roberto de Vicenzo	Winged Foot GC	285
1981	Arnold Palmer	Oakland Hills CC	289
1982	Miller Barber	Portland GC	282
1983	Billy Casper	Hazeltine National GC	288
1984	Miller Barber	Oak Hill CC	286
1985	Miller Barber	Edgewood Tahoe GC	285
1986	Dale Douglass	Scioto CC	279
1987	Gary Player	Brooklawn CC	270
1988	Gary Player	Medinah CC	288
1989	Orville Moody	Laurel Valley CC	279
1990	Lee Trevino	Ridgewood CC	275
1991	Jack Nicklaus	Oakland Hills CC	282
1992	Larry Laoretti	Saucon Valley CC	275
1993	Jack Nicklaus	Cherry Hills CC	278
1994	Simon Hobday	Pinehurst CC	274
1995	Tom Wesikopf	Congressional CC	275
1996	Dave Stockton	Canterbury GC	277
1997	Graham Marsh	Olympia Fields CC	280
1998	Hale Irwin	Riviera CC	285
1999	Dave Eichelberger	Des Moines G & CC	281

Most Wins

3	Miller Barber
2	Jack Nicklaus, Gary Player

PGA SENIORS CHAMPIONSHIP

PGA National GC, Palm Beach Gardens unless stated. 36- or 54-hole until 1957, then 72-hole event

1937	Jock Hutchison	Augusta National	223
1938	Fred McLeod	Augusta National	154
1939		No Championship	
1940	Otto Hackbarth	North Shore CC & Bobby Jones GC	146
1941	Jack Burke, Sr	Sarasota Bay CC & Bobby Jones GC	142
1942	Eddie Williams	Ft Myers G & CC	138
1943-44	*No Championship – World War Two*		
1945	Eddie Williams	PGA National GC, Dunedin	148
1946	Eddie Williams	PGA National GC, Dunedin	146
1947	Jock Hutchison	PGA National GC, Dunedin	145
1948	Charles McKenna	PGA National GC, Dunedin	141
1949	Marshall Crichton	PGA National GC, Dunedin	145
1950	Al Watrous	PGA National GC, Dunedin	142
1951	Al Watrous	PGA National GC, Dunedin	142
1952	Ernest Newnham	PGA National GC, Dunedin	146
1953	Harry Schwab	PGA National GC, Dunedin	142
1954	Gene Sarazen	PGA National GC, Dunedin	214
1955	Mortie Dutra	PGA National GC, Dunedin	213
1956	Pete Burke	PGA National GC, Dunedin	215
1957	Al Watrous	PGA National GC, Dunedin	210
1958	Gene Sarazen	PGA National GC, Dunedin	288
1959	Willie Goggin	PGA National GC, Dunedin	284
1960	Dick Metz	PGA National GC, Dunedin	284
1961	Paul Runyan	PGA National GC, Dunedin	278
1962	Paul Runyan	PGA National GC, Dunedin	278
1963	Herman Barron	Port St Lucie CC	272
1964	Sam Snead		279
1965	Sam Snead	Ft Lauderdale CC	278
1966	Fred Haas		286
1967	Sam Snead		279
1968	Chandler Harper		279
1969	Tommy Bolt		278
1970	Sam Snead		290
1971	Julius Boros		285
1972	Sam Snead		286
1973	Sam Snead		268
1974	Roberto de Vicenzo	Port St Lucie CC	174
1975	Charles Sifford	Walt Disney World	280
1976	Pete Cooper	Walt Disney World	283
1977	Julius Boros	Walt Disney World	283
1978	Joe Jimenez	Walt Disney World	286
1979i	Jack Fleck	Walt Disney World	289
1979ii	Don January	Turnberry Isle CC	270

1980	Arnold Palmer	Turnberry Isle CC	289
1981	Miller Barber	Turnberry Isle CC	281
1982	Don January		288
1983		*No Championship*	
1984i	Arnold Palmer		282

General Foods PGA Seniors Championship

1984ii	Peter Thomson		286
1985		*No Championship*	
1986	Gary Player		281
1987	Chi Chi Rodriguez		282
1988	Gary Player		284
1989	Larry Mowry		281

PGA Seniors Championship

1990	Gary Player	281
1991	Jack Nicklauas	271
1992	Lee Trevino	278
1993	Tom Wargo	275
1994	Lee Trevino	279
1995	Ray Floyd	277
1996	Hale Irwin	280
1997	Hale Irwin	274
1998	Hale Irwin	275
1999	Allen Doyle	274

LEADING SENIOR TOUR MONEY WINNERS

US unless stated		*$*
1980	Don January	44100
1981	Miller Barber	83136
1982	Miller Barber	106890
1983	Don January	237571
1984	Don January	328597
1985	Peter Thomson (Aus)	386724
1986	Bruce Crampton (Aus)	454299
1987	Chi Chi Rodriguez	509145
1988	Bob Charles (NZ)	533929
1989	Bob Charles (NZ)	725887
1990	Lee Trevino	1190518
1991	Mike Hill	1065657
1992	Lee Trevino	1027002
1993	Dave Stockton	1175944
1994	Dave Stockton	1402519
1995	Jim Colbert	1444386
1996	Jim Colbert	1627890
1997	Hale Irwin	2343364
1998	Hale Irwin	2861945
1999	Bruce Fleisher	2515705

Most Wins

| 3 | Don January |
| 2 | Miller Barber, Bob Charles, Jim Colbert, Hale Irwin, Dave Stockton, Lee Trevino |

Charles Blair Macdonald, an imposing businessman and pretty handy amateur golfer (after all he did receive some coaching from Old Tom Morris when a student at St Andrews University, and reputedly played a few rounds with Tom, Jr), came back from Scotland imbued with the spirit of the game. In 1893 he is credited with building the first 18-hole golf course in the US, at the Chicago Club's Wheaton location; in 1894 he called together the handful of clubs with any prestige and influence to arrange the formation of the USGA; and later in life did much to marry the egos of that organisation and the R&A to provide a remarkably consistent degree of unanimity world-wide on the rules of the game. In 1895, however, he had his crowning moment. He won the inaugural US Amateur Championship at Newport, RI, an event he was pivotal in creating. Because of its matchplay format, the event was started before the first ever US Open at the same venue, and finished after Horace Rawlins entered golfing folklore. The amateurs had all the privileges of course, and their event was the most prestigious of the two. It was another 20 years and more before the US professional got its act together, and by that time the position of the amateur in US golf was secure.

The early years of the US Amateur were dominated by the similarly named and often confused Walter Travis and Jerome Travers. They couldn't have been more different, however. Travis was a nuggety Australian, late to the game, and one who saw no horizons: he won the British Amateur at Sandwich after collecting the first two of three US titles. Travers was 20 years his junior, a product, as often, of a well-to-do New York dynasty, and won four national titles before Bobby Jones came on to the scene to equal, and then better, that record. This was now something of a Golden Age for the US amateur, reinforcing the position they had set up over the professional golfers. US Amateur Champions were regularly winning the US Open, as Jerome Travers had done in 1915 and Chick Evans following year. Francis Ouimet even won the Open before the Amateur, when, in one of golf history's great turning points, he struck a blow for all American golfers in snatching the 1913 US Open on the 17th hole of a play-off at Brookline (a location and occasion that 86 years on an emotional Ben Crenshaw was to recall), from the 'unbeatable' Brits, Vardon and Ray. In 1916 a Walter Hagen-led movement gave the pros their own championship, and for a decade or so, the hegemony in

US golf swung to and fro between the amateurs and the professionals. By right, the amateur should have been swept away, as the amazing feats of Hagen, supported by ex-Brits Hutchison and Barnes, and Gene Sarazen and Leo Diegel, took the lion's share of the limelight. The amateurs during the 1920s, apart from some fitful enterprise from Ouimet and Evans, and the newcomers Sweetser and Guilford, really only had one weapon. For a decade that one weapon was enough.

Robert Tyre Jones, Jr crept onto the scene, really, when he lost in the US Amateur final of 1919, at just 17 years of age. Studying the law, he took several more years to find his feet, and it wasn't until 1923 when things started to happen. Then did it happen! From 1923 until his retirement in 1930, he collected the US Amateur five times and the US Open four times. He crossed the Atlantic regularly and won the Open Championship on three occasions. Then in 1930 he collected the last remaining leg of the 'Grand Slam' of the time, the British Amateur, over the Old Course at St Andrews. Most golfers around would have thought that most acceptable. Indeed, only his great rival Hagen, and Jim Barnes, had, since 1914, put together the 'hat-trick' of both the Open Championships and the PGA Championship, so in his own spheres of golf, Bob Jones had won four 'Majors'. Jones, however, was not content. In this, his last year of serious competition, in addition to this last piece of the jigsaw, he added all the other bits as well for good measure. No one since, even the greats Hogan and Nicklaus, with their propensity for Majors, could do the real Grand Slam – all in one year.

After Jones, the professional game began to exert more and more influence. Jones' legacy, however, still gave US amateur golf a reasonably high profile. With his 'Masters' Tournament from 1934, he ensured a representative number of amateur players would be featured. John Goodman, in 1933, became the last amateur to win any of the Majors as we know them, but amateur golf was now seen to be a means of getting the right kind of background to break into the increasingly lucrative professional game. Double-double Amateur champion, Lawson Little, turned pro and won the US Open in 1940, and others followed. It was in the 50s, though, that this trend really took off, with Gene Littler, Arnold Palmer, Deane Beman and, of course, Jack Nicklaus, all adding the US Amateur to their CVs before turning pro. A steady stream of future Major champions has continued right through to this day. Craig Stadler, Jerry Pate, Mark O'Meara, Hal Sutton and Justin Leonard were all US Amateur Champions, and if there wasn't enough kudos in winning the world's most prestigious amateur title, then along came Tiger Woods to give it his endorsement. Grooming a future star and knowing just when to let him loose on the golf world at large is a difficult branch of science to pin down. Woods, however, obviously had to do it in threes. Three Junior Championships; three US Amateurs – OK, you can go! And the Tiger achieved what even the great Bob Jones couldn't. He won his three titles consecutively. Moreover, he did it in some style, and with each final going to the wire, he left, like Jones, a healthy endowment for the future of the US Amateur Championships.

WINNERS AND BEATEN FINALISTS

US unless stated

Matchplay over 36 holes until 1964 and from 1973 to date; otherwise strokeplay

1895	Charles Macdonald beat Charles Sands, 12&11
1896	HJ Whigham beat JG Thorp, 8&7
1897	HJ Whigham beat W Rossiter Betts, 8&6
1898	Findlay Douglas beat Walter Smith, 5&3
1899	HM Harriman beat Findlay Douglas, 3&2
1900	Walter Travis (Aus) beat Findlay Douglas, 2 up
1901	Walter Travis (Aus) beat Walter Egan, 5&4
1902	Louis James beat Eben Byers, 4&2
1903	Walter Travis (Aus) beat Eben Byers, 5&4
1904	H Chandler Egan beat Fred Herreshoff, 8&6
1905	H Chandler Egan beat DE Sawyer, 6&5
1906	Eben Byers beat George Lyon, 2 up
1907	Jerome Travers beat Archibald Graham, 6&5
1908	Jerome Travers beat Max Behr, 8&7
1909	Robert Gardner beat H Chandler Egan, 4&3
1910	Willian Fownes, Jr beat Warren Wood, 4&3
1911	Harold Hilton (Eng) beat Fred Herreshoff, after 37
1912	Jerome Travers beat Charles Evans, Jr, 7&6
1913	Jerome Travers beat John Anderson, 5&4
1914	Francis Ouimet beat Jerome Travers, 6&5
1915	Robert Gardner beat John Anderson, 5&4
1916	Charles Evans, Jr beat Robert Gardner, 4&3

1917-18 No Championships – World War One

1919	S Davidson Herron beat Bobby Jones, 5&4
1920	Charles Evans, Jr beat Francis Ouimet, 7&6
1921	Jesse Guilford beat Robert Gardner, 7&6
1922	Jess Sweetser beat Charles Evans, Jr, 3&2
1923	Max Marston beat Jess Sweetser, after 38
1924	Bobby Jones beat George Von Elm, 9&8
1925	Bobby Jones beat Watts Gunn, 8&7
1926	George Von Elm beat Bobby Jones, 2&1
1927	Bobby Jones beat Charles Evans, Jr, 8&7
1928	Bobby Jones beat Phil Perkins (Eng), 10&9
1929	Harrison Johnston beat Dr OF Willing, 4&3
1930	Bobby Jones beat Euegen V Homens, 8&7
1931	Francis Ouimet beat Jack Westland, 6&5
1932	C Ross Somerville beat Johnny Goodman, 2&1
1933	George Dunlap, Jr beat Max Marston, 6&5
1934	Lawson Little beat David Goldman, 8&7
1935	Lawson Little beat Walter Emery, 4&2
1936	John Fischer beat Jack McLean, after 37
1937	Johnny Goodman beat Raymond Billows, 2 up
1938	Willie Turnesa beat Patrick Abbott, 8&7
1939	Bud Ward beat Raymond Billows,7&5
1940	Dick Chapman beat WB McCullough, Jr, 11&9
1941	Bud Ward beat Patrick Abbott, 4&2

1942-45 No Championships – World War Two

1946	Ted Bishop beat Smiley Quick, after 37
1947	Skee Riegel beat John Dawson, 2&1
1948	Willie Turnesa beat Raymond Billows, 2&1
1949	Charles R Coe beat Rufus King, 11&10
1950	Sam Urzetta beat Frank Stranahan, after 39
1951	Billy Maxwell beat Joe Gagliardi, 4&3
1952	Jack Westland beat Al Mengert, 3&2
1953	Gene Littler beat Dale Morey, 1up
1954	Arnold Palmer beat Bob Sweeney, Jr, 1up
1955	E Harvie Ward, Jr beat Bill Hyndman, 9&8
1956	E Harvie Ward, Jr beat Charles Kocsis, 5&4
1957	Hillman Robbins, Jr beat Frank Taylor, 5&4
1958	Charles R Coe beat Tommy Aaron, 5&4
1959	Jack Nicklaus beat Charles R Coe, 1up
1960	Deane Beman beat Robert Gardner, 6&4
1961	Jack Nicklaus beat Dudley Wysong, 8&6
1962	Labron Harris, Jr beat Downing Gray, 1up
1963	Deane Beman beat Richard Sikes, 2&1
1964	Bill Campbell beat Edgar Tutwiler, 1 up

1965	Bob Murphy 291
1966	Gary Cowan 285
1967	Bob Dickson 285
1968	Brice Fleisher 284
1969	Steve Melnyk 286
1970	Lanny Wadkins 279
1971	Gary Cowan 280
1972	Marvin Giles III 285
1973	Craig Stadler beat David Strawn, 6&5
1974	Jerry Pate beat John Grace, 2&1
1975	Fred Ridley beat Keith Fergus, 2 up
1976	Bill Sander beat C Parker Moore, Jr 8&6
1977	John Fought beat Doug Fischesser, 9&8
1978	John Cook beat Scott Hoch, 5&4
1979	Mark O'Meara beat John Cook,8&7
1980	Hal Sutton beat Bob Lewis, 9&8
1981	Nat Crosbie beat Brian Lindley, after 37
1982	Jay Sigel beat David Tolley, 8&7
1983	Jay Sigel beat Chris Perry, 8&7
1984	Scott Verplank beat Sam Randolph, 4&3
1985	Sam Randolph beat beat Peter Persons, 1up
1986	Stewart Alexander beat Chris Kite, 5&3
1987	Billy Mayfair beat Eric Rebmann, 4&3
1988	Eric Meeks beat Danny Yates, 7&6
1989	Chris Patton beat Danny Green, 3&1
1990	Phil Mickelson beat Manny Zerman, 5&4
1991	Mitch Voges beat Manny Zerman, 7&6
1992	Justin Leonard beat Tom Scherrer, 8&7
1993	John Harris beat Danny Ellis, 5&3
1994	Tiger Woods beat Trip Kuehne, 2 up
1995	Tiger Woods beat Buddy Marucci, 2 up
1996	Tiger Woods beat Steve Scott, after 38
1997	Matt Kuchar beat Joel Kribel, 2&1
1998	Hank Kuehne beat Tom McKnight, 2&1
1999	David Gossett beat Sun Toon Kim (Kor), 9&8

Mildred Didrickson is not a name to conjure with: unless of, course, you nick-name her after a baseball legend because of her ability to hit anything that moved – or not; and marry her off to a wrestler called Zaharias. Not a Hollywood plot, but perhaps should be, for a biopic of Babe Zaharias would reveal an incredible talent for almost anything she did. For the annals of golf, we have to be grateful she chose sport. Golf fans had to wait until after the 1932 Los Angeles Olympics, however, for the golden girl to collect gold medals in the 80 Metres Hurdles and the Javelin. The film plot would have taken a dramatic twist here too as, then still Didrickson, she broke the world high jump record, only to be disqualified and placed second. She also qualified for two further events, but as the Olympic rules are for a maximum of three, she wasn't allowed to compete in them.

Taking up golf, she, by the end of the War, had been a professional touring the world, had been reinstated as an amateur, and won the US Women's Amateur title in 1946. She was, by far, the biggest name in the women's side of the sport, 13 consecutive victories emphatically bearing that out. The females were disorganised, however, and had little corporate support to help them. In 1944 the Women's PGA was founded to try to kick-start the professional game. In 1948 Wilson, the sports goods manufacturer did get behind it, the Women's PGA changed its name to the LPGA (seen as less brassy?) and in a tentative start, the first Tour chugged off in 1950 with just nine events. Zaharias, now pushing forty, was still seen as the standard bearer, and her esteem was such that sponsorship started to to trickle in. Babe, typically, left the Tour a few years later giving it the best send-off it could possibly get by being Money Leader for the first two years, thereby ensuring the headlines and a greater volume of sponsors in years to come.

By the end of the first decade, another superstar, Mickey Wright, had come along, and she was vying with oh-so consistent Kathy Whitworth for tour supremacy. Sport needs these rivalries to stimulate interest and further corporate whip-rounds. By 1972, the Tour had increased to 30 events and has never looked back. Outstanding golfers combined with modern fashions to improve the look of the game for golf fans and others previously not enamoured. Nancy Lopez and Jan Stephenson were to the fore, providing a further platform for growth and prosperity for the next generation – but the Americans had a shock when

it came from an unexpected direction. For so long the dominant nation in women's professional golf, it seemed, for a while, with players of the calibre of Betsy King, Beth Daniel and Pat Bradley, that reign would continue. Then in 1987, Ayako Okamoto became the first winner of the Money List from overseas. In 1992, US hegemony began to crumble when the Europeans won an historic Solheim Cup. Laura Davies topped the list in 1994, and there has not been an American top dog since. The Tour, however, has not suffered any sponsor backlash, the game now being so international, petty home-biased jealousies do not come in to it.

US WOMEN'S OPEN

Matchplay for 1946, then strokeplay
US unless stated

1946	Patty Berg beat Betty Jameson, 5&4		Spokane CC
1947	Betty Jameson	300	Starmount Forest CC
1948	Babe Zaharias	300	Atlantic City CC
1949	Lousie Suggs	291	Prince George's CC
1950	Babe Zaharias	291	Rolling Hills CC
1951	Betsy Rawls	294	Druid Hills GC
1952	Louise Suggs	284	Bala GC
1953	Betsy Rawls	302	CC of Rochester
1954	Babe Zaharias	291	Salem CC
1955	Fay Crocker	299	Wichita CC
1956	Kathy Cornelius	302	Northland CC
1957	Betsy Rawls	299	Winged Foot GC
1958	Mickey Wright	290	Forest Lake CC
1959	Mickey Wright	287	Churchill Valley CC
1960	Betsy Rawls	292	Worcester CC
1961	Mickey Wright	293	Baltusrol GC
1962	Marie Lindstrom	301	Dunes G&CC
1963	Mary Mills	289	Kenwood CC
1964	Mickey Wright	290	San Diego CC
1965	Carol Mann	290	Atlantic City CC
1966	Sandra Spuzich	297	Hazeltine National CC
1967	Cath'ne Lacoste (Fra) (a)	294	Hot Springs G&Tennis C
1968	Susie Maxwell	289	Moselem Spring GC
1969	Donna Caponi	294	Scenic Hills CC
1970	Donna Caponi	287	Muskogee CC
1971	JoAnne Carner	288	Kahkwa Club
1972	Susie (Maxwell) Berning	299	Winged Foot GC
1973	Susie Berning	290	CC of Rochester
1974	Sandra Haynie	295	La Grange CC
1975	Sandra Palmer	295	Atlantic City CC

1976	JoAnne Carner	292	Rolling Green GC
1977	Hollis Stacy	292	Hazeltine National GC
1978	Hollis Stacy	289	CC of Indianapolis
1979	Jerilyn Britz	284	Brooklawn CC
1980	Amy Alcott	280	Richland CC
1981	Pat Bradley	279	La Grange CC
1982	Janet Alex	283	Del Paso CC
1983	Jan Stephenson (Aus)	290	Cedar Ridge CC
1984	Hollis Stacy	290	Salem CC
1985	Kathy Baker	280	Baltusrol GC
1986	Jane Geddes	287	NCR CC
1987	Laura Davies (Eng)	285	Plainfield CC
1988	Liselotte Neumann (Swe)	277	Baltimore CC
1989	Betsy King	278	Indianwood G & CC
1990	Betsy King	284	Atlanta Athletic C
1991	Meg Mallon	283	Colonial CC
1992	Patty Sheehan	280	Oakmont CC
1993	Lauri Merten	280	Crooked Stick
1994	Patty Sheehan	277	Indianwood G & CC
1995	Annika Sorenstam (Swe)	278	Broadmoor
1996	Annika Sorenstam (Swe)	272	Pine Needles Lodge & CC
1997	Alison Nicholas (Eng)	274	Pumpkin Ridge GC
1998	Se Ri Pak (Kor)	290	Blackwolf Run GC
1999	Juli Inkster	272	Old Waverly GC

Most Wins

4	Betsy Rawls, Mickey Wright
3	Susie (Maxwell) Berning, Hollis Stacy, Babe Zaharias

LEADING LPGA TOUR MONEY WINNERS

US unless stated

		$
1950	Babe Zaharias	14800
1951	Babe Zaharias	15087
1952	Betsy Rawls	14505
1953	Louise Suggs	19816
1954	Patty Berg	16011
1955	Patty Berg	16492
1956	Marlene Hagge	20235
1957	Patty Berg	16272
1958	Beverly Hanson	12639
1959	Betsy Rawls	26774
1960	Louise Suggs	16892
1961	Mickey Wright	22236
1962	Mickey Wright	21641
1963	Mickey Wright	31269

1964	Mickey Wright	29800
1965	Kathy Whitworth	28658
1966	Kathy Whitworth	33517
1967	Kathy Whitworth	32937
1968	Kathy Whitworth	48379
1969	Carol Mann	49152
1970	Kathy Whitworth	30235
1971	Kathy Whitworth	41181
1972	Kathy Whitworth	85063
1973	Kathy Whitworth	82864
1974	JoAnne Carner	87094
1975	Sandra Palmer	76374
1976	Judy Rankin	150734
1977	Judy Rankin	122890
1978	Nancy Lopez	189814
1979	Nancy Lopez	197489
1980	Beth Daniel	231000
1981	Beth Daniel	206998
1982	JoAnne Carner	310400
1983	JoAnne Carner	291404
1984	Betsy King	266771
1985	Nancy Lopez	418772
1986	Pat Bradley	492021
1987	Ayako Okamato (Jap)	466034
1988	Sherri Turner	350851
1989	Betsy King	654132
1990	Beth Daniel	863578
1991	Pat Bradley	763118
1992	Dottie Pepper	693335
1993	Betsy King	595992
1994	Laura Davies (Eng)	687201
1995	Annika Sorenstam (Swe)	666533
1996	Karrie Webb (Aus)	1002000
1997	Annika Sorenstam (Swe)	1236789
1998	Annika Sorenstam (Swe)	1092748
1999	Karrie Webb (Aus)	1591959

Most Wins

8	Kathy Whitworth
4	Mickey Wright

GOLF IN BRITAIN AND EUROPE

If the US Tour has been somewhat isolationist, then the European Tour has been geographically all-embracing in recent years, thanks to co-sanctioned events with other Tours. In 1971, when pros on this side of the Atlantic saw what was happening in the States it didn't take them long to set up their own Tour, and with a similar structure. Successful professional and top teacher, John Jacobs, was a popular choice as the British PGA's inaugural Tournament Director-General, and his brief was to co-ordinate the disparate and historically individualistic golf map of Europe. The continent was graced with any number of traditional national championships, and in Britain, apart from the Open, Jacobs had the core of several revered long-standing events like the Dunlop Masters, the Penfold, and, of course, the *News of the World* Matchplay, to build upon. It was all Jacobs could do though, in the early years, to maximise the existing structure. Then in 1975, a young Scots banking high-flier called Ken Schofield was brought in to expand the tournaments and prize money available, and he couldn't have started at a more opportune time.

In 1976, a certain young Spaniard set the world alight when he nearly won the Open Championship. Golf in Europe had not received the impetus it had had early in the decade in Britain, with the feats of Tony Jacklin 'spawning' a new crop of hopefuls with a difference, perhaps. Certainly Peter Oosterhuis, after dominating the domestic Order of Merit, was doing quite well on the US Tour, and Mark James, Howard Clark and Sam Torrance looked promising. But it was in young Nick Faldo to whom a nation looked for the next Jacklin, and in a year or two to a Scottish Shropshire lad, who seemed to be making quicker headway than another talented member of his county's boys team, this time though a Welshman. Britain's immediate future looked relatively rosy, but it wasn't until Ballesteros' rude intervention that the rest of the continent looked up. By 1979, the Europeans, after some nifty intervening by Jack Nicklaus, no less, were incorporated into the British and Irish Ryder Cup team, and over the next two years a quietly spoken German was starting to win events, when, hitherto, Germans were not supposed to do so. In his first decade in charge, therefore, Schofield's search for sponsors and attempts to attain for the Tour the highest popular recognition were made all the more easy when Ballesteros, Faldo, Langer, Lyle and Woosnam, and a new Spanish hope in Olazabal, became world stars. They were not only winning events regularly in Europe and elsewhere, they were frightening the Americans to death in Major Championships and the Ryder Cup. With the arrival of the 'Sony' Official World Ranking in 1986, there were regularly more European Tour players in the Top 10 than American. Schofield opened his office door and waited for the money to run in. Much came from Volvo, whose unbroken support since 1988 has been worth over £100 million to the Tour, and whose name for several years was associated with the Tour.

It was one of the key factors of this success that nearly upset the Tour applecart. The Ryder Cup was now huge, with the Europeans winning in 1985 and 1987. A bitter wrangle ensued between Schofield and the PGA about his organisation's rights to a share of the enormous profits the PGA were making from the matches. After much mud-slinging, worthy of any big fight promo, the Chairman of the PGA John Lindsey was ousted and a deal was struck to share the lucre 50-50. Henceforward, somewhat disappointingly, it would be money which would decide the home venues for the Ryder Cup – thus Valderrama (1997) and the K Club (2005). The Tour's image was unsurprisingly tarnished by this openly greedy behaviour, and Schofield, acting on behalf of a presumably consenting membership, was not doing anything really different to Duval, O'Meara and others' open-palming before 1999 and Brookline. This had an affect on how potential sponsors were now viewing a once seemingly unsullied sport, and as the 1990s were entered, the relative recession made money harder to get. Since mid-decade, however, Schofield's efforts have been far more seemly. Beginning the season with events in Australia, South Africa and Asia – and South America in 2000 – players have the best conditions outside of the US Tour. A trimmed-down 'European' schedule is efficiently planned during the summer months, and the US Majors are now part of the official itinerary, with domestic tournaments arranged as alternatives . A Seniors and Satellite (renamed Challenge) Tour have been started; the former a little low-key, the latter a little low on prize money. The Challenge Tour, along with the Qualifing School, is, however, the way to the stars – ask Thomas Bjorn, Costantino Rocca and others. As this book goes to press, Ken Schofield was seriously considering the association of all the Tours outside of the US, based on the ATP schedules in tennis. If such a thing happened, how would the US PGA Tour react? What would the future be for golf in Europe; and would the European Tour automatically rule over the rest of the world outside of the States? Interesting times.

EVENTS/WINNERS

All events featured on the tour since its inception in 1971; listed in their latest incarnations and cross-referred to previous or associated events

AGF Biarritz Open
See AGF Open

AGF OPEN

(France)

AGF Biarritz Open

| 1988 | David Llewellyn |

AGF Open

| 1989 | Mark James |
| 1990 | Brett Ogle |

No Tournaments since

Most Wins

| | No multiple winners |

AGFA-GEVAERT

(England)

Gevacolor Film

| 1963 | Bernard Hunt |
| 1964 | Angel Miguel |

Agfa-Gevaert

1965	Jimmy Hitchcock
1966	Angel Miguel
1967	Peter Alliss

Agfacolor Film

1968	Clive Clark
1969	Brian Barnes
1970	Bernard Hunt

Agfa-Gevaert

| 1971 | Peter Oosterhuis |

No Tournaments since

Most Wins

| 3 | Bernard Hunt, Angel Miguel |

Agfacolor Film

See Agfa-Gevaert

Air France Cannes Open

See Cannes Open

Alamo English Open

See Compass Group English Open

ALFRED DUNHILL OPEN

36-hole Tournament until 1927

Belgian Open

1910	Arnaud Massy
1911	Charles Mayo
1912	George Duncan
1913	Tom Ball
1914	Tom Ball
1915-19	*No Tournaments – World War One*
1920	Rowland Jones
1921	E Laffite
1922	Aubrey Boomer
1923	PH Boomer
1924	Walter Hagen
1925	E Laffite
1926	Aubrey Boomer
1927	Marcel Dallemagne
1928	Albert Tingey, Jr
1929	Sid Brews
1930	Henry Cotton
1931	Arthur Lacey
1932	Arthur Lacey
1933	Auguste Boyer
1934	Henry Cotton
1935	Bill Branch
1936	Auguste Boyer
1937	Marcel Dallemagne
1938	Henry Cotton
1939	Flory van Donck
1940-45	*No Tournaments – World War Two*
1946	Flory van Donck
1947	Flory van Donck
1948	WS Forrester
1949	Jimmy Adams
1950	Roberto de Vicenzo
1951	A Pelissier
1952	Antonio Cerda
1953	Flory van Donck
1954	Dai Rees
1955	Dave Thomas
1956	Flory van Donck
1957	Bernard Hunt

1958	Ken Bousfield
1959-77	*No Tournaments*
1978	Noel Ratcliffe
1979	Gavin Levenson
1980-86	*No Tournaments*

Volvo Belgian Open

1987	Eamonn Darcy
1988	Jose-Maria Olazabal
1989	Gordon J Brand (Sr)

Peugeot-Trends Belgian Open

1990	Ove Sellberg

Renault Belgian Open

1991	Per-Ulrik Johansson

PIAGET Belgian Open

1992	Miguel Jimenez

Alfred Dunhill Open

1993	Darren Clarke
1994	Nick Faldo

No Tournaments since – See Belgacom Open

Most Wins

5	Flory van Donck
3	Henry Cotton

ALFRED DUNHILL SOUTH AFRICAN PGA CHAMPIONSHIP

Lexington South African PGA Championship

1995	Ernie Els

Alfred Dunhill South African PGA Championship

1996	Sven Struver
1997	Nick Price
1998	Tony Johnstone
1999	Ernie Els

Most Wins

2	Ernie Els

ALGARVE PORTUGUESE OPEN

1984-85 replaced the TCP; 1989 incorporated the TCP (see Deutsche Bank/SAP – TPC of Europe) Portuguese Open

1953	Eric Brown
1954	Angel Miguel
1955	Flory van Donck
1956	Angel Miguel

1957	No Tournamnent
1958	Peter Alliss
1959	Sebastian Miguel
1960	Ken Bousfield
1961	Ken Bousfield
1962	Alfonso Angelini
1963	Ramon Sota
1964	Angel Miguel
1965	*No Tournament*
1966	Alfonso Angelini
1967	Angel Gallardo
1968	Max Faulkner
1969	Ramon Sota
1970	Ramon Sota
1971	Lionel Platts
1972	German Garrido
1973	J Benito
1974	Brian Huggett
1975	H Underwood
1976	Salvador Balbuena
1977	M Ramos
1978	Howard Clark
1979	Brian Barnes
1980-81	*No Tournaments*
1982	Sam Torrance
1983	Sam Torrance

Quinta do Lago Portuguese Open

1984	Tony Johnstone
1985	Warren Humphreys
1986	Mark McNulty

Portuguese (Algarve) Open

1987	Robert Lee
1988	Mike Harwood
1989	Colin Montgomerie
1990	Mike McLean
1991	Steven Richardson
1992	Ronan Rafferty
1993	David Gilford
1994	Phillip Price
1995	Adam Hunter
1996	Wayne Riley
1997	Michael Jonzon
1998	Peter Mitchell

Algarve Portuguese Open
1999	Van Phillips

Most Wins
3	Angel Miguel, Ramon Sota
2	Alfonso Angelini, Ken Bousfield, Sam Torrance

Amex Open de Mediterrania
See Turespana Open de Mediterrania

ANDERSEN CONSULTING WORLD CHAMPIONSHIP OF GOLF
(US)
Official event on European Tour only
1995	Barry Lane
1996	Greg Norman
1997	Colin Montgomerie
1998	Colin Montgomerie
1999	See World Golf Championships section

Most Wins
2	Colin Montgomerie

Austrian Open
See Hohe Brucke Austrian Open

Avis Jersey Open
See DHL Jersey Open

Barcelona Open
See Torras Hostench Barcelona Open

BELGACOM OPEN
(Belgium)
1999	Robert Karlsson

Belgian Open
See Alfred Dunhill Open

Bells Scottish Open
See Scottish Open

Benson & Hedges Festiva
See Benson & Hedges International Open

BENSON & HEDGES INTERNATIONAL OPEN
(England)

Benson & Hedges Festival
1971	Tony Jacklin
1972	Jack Newton
1973	Vince Baker
1974	Phillipe Toussaint
1975	Vicente Fernandez

Benson & Hedges International Open
1976	Graham Marsh
1977	Antonio Garrido
1978	Lee Trevino
1979	Maurice Bembridge
1980	Graham Marsh
1981	Tom Weiskopf
1982	Greg Norman
1983	John Bland
1984	Sam Torrance
1985	Sandy Lyle
1986	Mark James
1987	Noel Ratcliffe
1988	Peter Baker
1989	Gordon Brand, Jr
1990	Jose-Maria Olazabal
1991	Bernhard Langer
1992	Peter Senior
1993	Paul Broadhurst
1994	Seve Ballesteros
1995	Peter O'Malley
1996	Stephen Ames
1997	Bernhard Langer
1998	Darren Clarke
1999	Colin Montgomerie

Most Wins
2	Bernhard Langer, Graham Marsh

BENSON & HEDGES MALAYSIAN OPEN
1999	Gerry Norquist

Benson & Hedges Open de Espana
See Peugeot Open de Espana

Benson & Hedges PGA Matchplay Tournament
See Sun Alliance PGA Matchplay Tournament

Billy Butlin Jersey Open
See DHL Jersey Open

BMW INTERNATIONAL OPEN
(Germany)

1989	David Feherty
1990	Paul Azinger
1991	Sandy Lyle
1992	Paul Azinger
1993	Peter Fowler
1994	Mark McNulty
1995	Frank Nobilo
1996	Marc Farry
1997	Robert Karlsson
1998	Russell Claydon
1999	Colin Montgomerie

Most wins
2	Paul Azinger

BNP Jersey Open Open
See DHL Jersey Open

Bob Hope British Classic
See European Pro-Celebrity Tournament

Braun German Open
See German Open

British Airways/Avis Jersey Open
See DHL Jersey Open

British Masters
See Victor Chandler British Masters

CALLERS OF NEWCASTLE OPEN
(England)

1977	John Fourie

No Tournaments since

CANNES OPEN

Compagnie de Chauffe Cannes Open
1984	David Frost
1985	Robert Lee

Suze Cannes Open
1986	John Bland
1987	Seve Ballesteros

Credit Lyonnaise Cannes Open
1988	Mark McMulty

1989	Paul Broadhurst
1990	Mark McNulty
1991	David Feherty
1992	Anders Forsbrand

Air France Cannes Open
1993	Rodger Davis
1994	Ian Woosnam
1995	Andre Bossert
1996	Raymond Russell

Europe 1 Cannes Open
1997	Stuart Cage

Cannes Open
1998	Thomas Levet

No Tournaments since

Most Wins
2	Mark McNulty

CANON EUROPEAN MASTERS (INCORPORATING SWISS OPEN)

36-hole Tournament until 1938

Swiss Open
1923	Alex Ross
1924	PH Boomer
1925	Alex Ross
1926	Alex Ross
1927-28	*No Tournaments*
1929	A Wilson
1930	Auguste Boyer
1931	Marcel Dallemagne
1932-33	*No Tournaments*
1934	Auguste Boyer
1935	Auguste Boyer
1936	Francis Francis (a)
1937	Marcel Dallemagne
1938	Jean Saubaber
1939	F Cavalo
1940-47	*No Tournaments – World War Two*
1948	Ugo Grappasonni
1949	Marcel Dallemagne
1950	Aldo Casera
1951	Eric Brown
1952	Ugo Grappasonni
1953	Flory van Donck

1954	Bobby Locke
1955	Flory van Donck
1956	Dai Rees
1957	Alfonso Angelini
1958	Ken Bousfield
1959	Dai Rees
1960	Harold Henning
1961	Kel Nagle
1962	Bob Charles
1963	Dai Rees
1964	Harold Henning
1965	Harold Henning
1966	Alfonso Angelini
1967	Randall Vines
1968	Roberto Bernardini
1969	Roberto Bernardini
1970	Graham Marsh
1971	Peter Townsend
1972	Graham Marsh
1973	Hugh Baiocchi
1974	Bob Charles
1975	Dale Hayes
1976	Manuel Pinero
1977	Seve Ballesteros
1978	Seve Ballesteros
1979	Hugh Baiocchi
1980	Nick Price
1981	Mauel Pinero

Ebel Swiss Open

1982	Ian Woosnam

Ebel European Masters

1983	Nick Faldo
1984	Jerry Anderson
1985	Craig Stadler
1986	Jose-Maria Olazabal
1987	Anders Forsbrand
1988	C Moody
1989	Seve Ballesteros
1990	Ronan Rafferty

Canon European Masters

1991	Jeff Hawkes
1992	Jamie Spence
1993	Barry Lane
1994	Eduardo Romero
1995	Mathias Gronberg
1996	Colin Montgomerie
1997	Costantino Rocca
1998	Sven Struver
1999	Lee Westwood

Most Wins

3	Seve Ballesteros, Auguste Boyer, Marcel Dallemagne, Harold Henning, Dai Rees, Alex Ross
2	Alfonso Angelini, Roberto Bernardini, Hugh Baiocchi, Bob Charles, Ugo Grappasonni, Graham Marsh, Manuel Pinero, Flory van Donck

CAR CARE PLAN INTERNATIONAL
(England)

1982	Brian Waites
1983	Nick Faldo
1984	Nick Faldo
1985	David J Russell
1986	Mark Mouland

No Tournaments since

Most Wins

2	Nick Faldo

Carrolls Sweet Afton
See Carrolls International

CARROLLS INTERNATIONAL
(Ireland)

Carrolls Sweet Afton

1963	Bernard Hunt
1964	Christy O'Connor, Sr
1965	Neil Coles

Carrolls International

1966	Christy O'Connor, Sr
1967	Christy O'Connor, Sr
1968	Jimmy Martin
1969	Ronnie Shade
1970	Brian Huggett
1971	Neil Coles
1972	Christy O'Connor, Sr
1973	P McGuirk
1974	Bernard Gallacher

No Tournaments since

Most Wins

4	Christy O'Connor, Sr
2	Neil Coles

Carrolls Irish Open
See Murphys Irish Open

Cepsa Madrid Open
See Madrid Open

CHEMAPOL TROPHY CZECH OPEN

1994	Per-Ulrik Johansson
1995	Peter Teravainen
1996	Jonathan Lomas
1997	Bernhard Langer

No Tournaments since

Most Wins
No multiple winners

CLASSIC INTERNATIONAL

(England)

1970	Hedley Muscroft
1971	Peter Butler

No Tournaments since

Most Wins
No multiple winners

COLD SHIELD GREATER MANCHESTER OPEN

Greater Manchester Open

1976	John O'Leary
1977	Eamonn Darcy
1978	Brian Barnes
1979	Mark McNulty

Cold Shield Greater Manchester Open

1980	Des Smyth
1981	Bernard Gallacher

No Tournaments since

Most Wins
No multiple winners

Colgate PGA Championship
See Volvo PGA Championship

Collingtree British Masters
See Victor Chandler British Masters

Compagnie de Chauffe Cannes Open
See Cannes Open

COMPAQ EUROPEAN GRAND PRIX

(England)

Slaley Hall Northumberland Challenge

1996	Retief Goosen

Compaq European Grand Prix

1997	Colin Montgomerie
1998	*No Tournament*
1999	David Park

Most Wins
No multiple winners

COMPASS GROUP ENGLISH OPEN

Lada English Open

1979	Seve Ballesteros

Mazda English Open

1980	Manuel Pinero

State Express English Open

1981	Rodger Davis
1982	Greg Norman
1983	Hugh Baiocchi
1984-87	*No Tournaments*

English Open

1988	Howard Clark

NM English Open

1989	Mark James
1990	Mark James
1991	David Gilford

Murphy's English Open

1992	Vicente Fernandez
1993	Ian Woosnam
1994	Colin Montgomerie
1995	Philip Walton

Alamo English Open

1996	Robert Allenby
1997	Per-Ulrik Johansson

National Car Rental English Open

1998	Lee Westwood

Compass Group English Open

1999	Darren Clarke

Most Wins

2	Mark James

Conte of Florence Italian Open
See Fiat & Fila Italian Open

CORAL CLASSIC
(Wales)

Welsh Golf Classic
1979	Mark James

Coral Classic
1980	Sandy Lyle
1981	Des Smith
1982	Gordon Brand, Jr

No Tournaments since

Most Wins

No multiple winners

Credit Lyonnaise Cannes Open
See Cannes Open

(THE) DAKS GOLF TOURNAMENT
(England)

1950	Norman Sutton
1951	John Panton
1952	Fred Daly
1953	Dai Rees
1954	Peter Alliss
1955	JS Pritchett
1956	Trevor Wilkes
1957	Bobby Locke
1958	Harold Henning, Peter Thomson – *tied*
1959	Christy O'Connor, Sr
1960	Peter Thomson
1961	Bernard Hunt
1962	Bob Charles, Dai Rees – *tied*
1963	Peter Alliss, Neil Coles – *tied*
1964	Neil Coles
1965	Peter Thomson
1966	Hugh Boyle
1967	Malcolm Gregson
1968	Malcolm Gregson
1969	Brian Huggett
1970	Neil Coles
1971	Neil Coles, Brian Huggett – *tied*
	No Tournaments since

Most Wins
4	Neil Coles (inc 2 ties)
3	Peter Thomson (inc 1 tie)

DEUTSCHE BANK - SAP OPEN TPC OF EUROPE
(Various countries – now Germany)

Tournament Players Championship (TPC)
1977	Neil Coles
1978	Brian Waites

SOS Talisman TPC
1979	Michael King

Haig Whisky TPC
1980	Bernard Gallacher
1981	Brian Barnes
1982	Nick Faldo

St Mellion Timeshare TPC
1983	Bernhard Langer
1984	Jaime Gonzalez
1985	*No Tournament*
1986	See Lawrence Batley International
1987-88	*No Tournaments*
1989-90	*See Portuguese Algarve Open*
1991-94	*No Tournaments*

Deutsche Bank - SAP Open TPC of Europe
1995	Bernhard Langer
1996	Frank Nobilo
1997	Ross McFarlane
1998	Lee Westwood
1999	Lee Westwood

Most Wins
2	Bernhard Langer, Lee Westwood

DHL JERSEY OPEN

British Airways/Avis Jersey Open
1978	Brian Huggett
1979	Sandy Lyle

Avis Jersey Open
1980	Jose-Maria Canizares

Billy But/in Jersey Open
1981	Tony Jacklin

Jersey Open
1982	Bernard Gallacher
1983	J Hall
1984	Bernard Gallacher
1985	Howard Clark
1986	John Morgan
1987	Ian Woosnam

BNP Jersey Open
| 1988 | Des Smyth |

Jersey European Airways Open
1989	Christy O'Connor, Jr
1990	*No Tournament*
1991	Sam Torrance
1992	Daniel Silva
1993	Ian Palmer
1994	Paul Curry

DHL Jersey Open
| 1995 | Andrew Oldcorn |

No Tournaments since

Most Wins
| 2 | Bernard Gallacher |

DIMENSION DATA PRO-AM
(S Africa)
| 1996 | Mark McNulty |
| 1997 | Nick Price |

No Tournaments since

Most Wins
No multiple winners

Dixcel Tissues European Open
See Smurfit European Open

DOUBLE DIAMOND STROKE PLAY
(Scotland)
1974	Maurice Bembridge
1975	Peter Dawson
1976	Simon Owen

No Tournaments since

Most Wins
No multiple winners

Dubai Classic
See Dubai Desert Classic

DUBAI DESERT CLASSIC
Karl Litten Desert Classic
| 1989 | Mark James |

Emirates Airline Desert Classic
| 1990 | Eamonn Darcy |

| 1991 | *No Tournament* |

Dubai Classic
1992	Seve Ballesteros
1993	Wayne Westner
1994	Ernie Els
1995	Fred Couples
1996	Colin Montgomerie

Dubai Desert Classic
1997	Richard Green
1998	Jose-Maria Olazabal
1999	David Howell

Most Wins
No multiple winners

Dunhill British Masters
See Victor Chandler British Masters

Dunlop Masters
See Victor Chandler British Masters

Dutch Open
See TNT Dutch Open

Ebel European Masters
See Canon European Masters

Ebel Swiss Open
See Canon European Masters

EL BOSQUE OPEN
(Spain)
| 1990 | Vijay Singh |

No Tournaments since

EL PARAISO OPEN
(Spain)
| 1974 | Peter Oosterhuis |

No Tournaments since

Emirates Airline Desert Classic
See Dubai Desert Classic

English Open
See Compass Group English Open

EPSON GRAND PRIX OF EUROPE
(Wales)
Matchplay until 1989, then Strokeplay
| 1986 | Ove Sellberg |
| 1987 | Mats Lanner |

1988	Berhard Langer
1989	Seve Ballesteros
1990	Ian Woosnam
1991	Jose-Maria Olazabal

No Tournaments since

Most Wins

No multiple winners

EQUITY & LAW CHALLENGE
(England)

1987	Barry Lane
1988	Ronan Rafferty
1989	Brett Ogle
1990	Brian Marchbank
1991	Brian Marchbank
1992	Anders Forsbrand

No Tournaments since

Most Wins

2	Brian Marchbank

ESTORIL OPEN
(Portugal)

1999	Jeff Remesy

Europe 1 Cannes Open
See Cannes Open

(THE) EUROPEAN NEWSPAPER MONTE CARLO OPEN

Monte Carlo Open

1984	Ian Mosey

Johnnie Walker Monte Carlo Open

1985	Sam Torrance
1986	Seve Ballesteros
1987	Peter Senior

Torras Monte Carlo Open

1988	Jose Rivero
1989	Mark McNulty
1990	Ian Woosnam
1991	Ian Woosnam

The European Newspaper Monte Carlo Open

1992	Ian Woosnam

No Tournaments since

Most Wins

3	Ian Woosnam

European Open
See Smurfit European Open

EUROPEAN PRO-CELEBRITY TOURNAMENT
(England)

Bob Hope British Classic

1980	Jose-Maria Canizares
1981	Bernhard Langer
1982	Gordon Brand, Jr
1983	Jose-Maria Canizares
1984	*No Tournament*

Four Stars Pro-Celebrity

1985	Ken Brown

London Standard Four Stars Pro-Celebrity

1986	Antonio Garrido
1987	Mark McNulty

Wang Four Stars Pro-Celebrity

1988	Rodger Davis
1989	Craig Parry
1990	Rodger Davis

European Pro-Celebrity

1991	Paul Broadhurst

No Tournaments since

Most Wins

2	Jose-Maria Canizares, Rodger Davis

FIAT & FILA ITALIAN OPEN

Italian Open

1925	F Pasquali
1926	Auguste Boyer
1927	Percy Alliss
1928	Auguste Boyer
1929	R Golias
1930	Auguste Boyer
1931	Auguste Boyer
1932	Aubrey Boomer
1933	*No Tournament*
1934	N Nutley
1935	Percy Alliss
1936	Henry Cotton
1937	Marcel Dallemagne
1938	Flory van Donck
1939-46	*No Tournaments – World War Two*
1947	Flory van Donck
1948	A Casera

1949	H Hassenain
1950	Ugo Grappasonni
1951	Jimmy Adams
1952	Eric Brown
1953	Flory van Donck
1954	Ugo Grappasonni
1955	Flory van Donck
1956	Antonio Cerda
1957	Harold Henning
1958	Peter Alliss
1959	Peter Thomson
1960	Brian Wilkes
1961-70	*No Tournaments*
1971	Ramon Sota
1972	Norman Wood
1973	Tony Jacklin
1974	Peter Oosterhuis
1975	Billy Casper
1976	Baldovino Dassu
1977	Angel Gallardo
1978	Dale Hayes
1979	Brian Barnes
1980	M Mannelli
1981	Jose-Maria Canizares
1982	Mark James
1983	Bernhard Langer
1984	Sandy Lyle
1985	Manuel Pinero
1986	David Feherty

Lancia Italian Open

1987	Sam Torrance
1988	Greg Norman
1989	Ronan Rafferty

Lancia-Martini Italian Open

1990	Richard Boxall
1991	Craig Parry
1992	Sandy Lyle
1993	Greg Turner

Tissetanta Italian Open

1994	Eduardo Romero
1995	Sam Torrance

Conte of Florence Italian Open

1996	Jim Payne
1997	Bernhard Langer

Fiat & Fila Italian Open

1998	Patrik Sjoland
1999	Dean Robertson

Most Wins

4	Auguste Boyer, Flory van Donck
2	Percy Alliss, Ugo Grappasonni, Bernhard Langer, Sandy Lyle, Sam Torrance

FNB PLAYERS CHAMPIONSHIP

(S Africa)

1996	Wayne Westner

No Tournaments since

Four Stars Pro-Celebrity

See European Pro-Celebrity Tournament

French Open

See Novotel Perrier Open de France

Fujitsu Open de Mediterrania

See Turespana Open de Mediterrania

GALLAHER ULSTER

(N Ireland)

1965	Bernard Hunt
1966	Christy O'Connor, Sr
1967	Bernard Hunt
1968	Christy O'Connor, Sr
1969	Christy O'Connor, Sr
1970	John Lister
1971	Tommy Horton

No Tournaments since

Most Wins

3	Christy O'Connor, Sr
2	Bernard Hunt

General Accident European Open

See Smurfit European Open

German Masters   See Linde German Masters

GERMAN OPEN

1911	Harry Vardon
1912	JH Taylor
1913-25	*No Tournaments – World War One and aftermath*
1926	Percy Alliss
1927	Percy Alliss
1928	Percy Alliss

1929	Percy Alliss
1930	Auguste Boyer
1931	R Golias
1932	Auguste Boyer
1933	Percy Alliss
1934	Alf Padgham
1935	Auguste Boyer
1936	Auguste Boyer
1937	Henry Cotton
1938	Henry Cotton
1939	Henry Cotton
1940-50	No Tournaments – World War Two and aftermath
1951	Antonio Cerda
1952	Antonio Cerda
1953	Flory van Donck
1954	Bobby Locke
1955	Ken Bousfield
1956	Flory van Donck
1957	Harry Weetman
1958	Fidel de Luca
1959	Ken Bousfield
1960	Peter Thomson
1961	Bernard Hunt
1962	Booby Verwey
1963	Brian Huggett
1964	Roberto de Vicenzo
1965	Harold Henning
1966	Bob Stanton
1967	Don Swaelens
1968	B Franklin
1969	Jean Garaialde
1970	Jean Garaialde
1971	Neil Coles
1972	Graham Marsh
1973	Tito Abreu
1974	Simon Owen
1975	Maurice Bembridge
1976	Simon Hobday
1977	Tiene Britz

Braun German Open

1978	Seve Ballesteros
1979	Tony Jacklin
1980	Mark McNulty

German Open

1981	Bernhard Langer

Lufthansa German Open

1982	Bernhard Langer
1983	Corey Pavin
1984	Wayne Grady
1985	Bernhard Langer
1986	Bernhard Langer
1987	Mark McNulty
1988	Seve Ballesteros

German Open

1989	Craig Parry

Volvo German Open

1990	Mark McNulty
1991	Mark McNulty
1992	Vijay Singh
1993	Bernhard Langer
1994	Colin Montgomerie
1995	Colin Montgomerie
1996	Ian Woosnam

German Open

1997	Ignacio Garrido
1998	Stephen Allan
1999	Jarmo Sandelin

Most Wins

5	Percy Alliss, Bernhard Langer
4	Auguste Boyer, Mark McNulty

Gevacolor Film
See Agfa-Gevaert

GIRONA OPEN

(Spain)

1991	Steven Richardson

No Tournaments since

Glasgow Golf Classic
See Glasgow Open

GLASGOW OPEN

Glasgow Golf Classic

1983	Bernhard Langer

Glasgow Open

1984	Ken Brown
1985	Howard Clark

No Tournaments since

Most Wins

No multiple winners

Greater Manchester Open
See Cold Shield Greater Manchester Open

Haig Whisky TPC
See Deutsche Bank – SAP Open TPC of Europe

HEINEKEN CLASSIC
(Australia)

1996	Ian Woosnam
1997	Miguel Martin
1998	Thomas Bjorn
1999	Jarrod Moseley

Most Wins

No multiple winners

Heineken Dutch Open
See TNT Dutch Open

Heineken Open de Catalonia
See Open de Catalonia

HOHE BRUCKE AUSTRIAN OPEN

Austrian Open

1990	Bernhard Langer

Mitsubishi and Denzel Austrian Open

1991	Mark Davis

Mitsubishi Austrian Open

1992	Peter Mitchell
1993	Ronan Rafferty

Hohe Brucke Austrian Open

1994	Mark Davis
1995	Alex Cejka
1996	Paul McGinley

No Tournaments since

Most Wins

2	Mark Davis

HONDA OPEN
(Germany)

1992	Bernhard Langer
1993	Sam Torrance
1994	Robert Allenby

No Tournaments since

Most Wins

No multiple winners

Iberia Madrid Open
See Madrid Open

Irish Open
See Murphy's Irish Open

Italian Open
See Fiat & Fila Italian Open

Jersey European Airways Open
See DHL Jersey Open

Jersey Open
See DHL Jersey Open

JOHN PLAYER CLASSIC
(England & Scotland)

1970	Christy O'Connor, Sr
1971	*No Tournament*
1972	Bob Charles
1973	Charles Coody

No Tournaments since

Most Wins

No muliple winners

JOHN PLAYER TROPHY
(England)
36 holes, 1970

1970	Clive Clark
1971	*No Tournament*
1972	Ross Whitehead

No Tournaments since

Most Wins

No multiple winners

JOHNNIE WALKER CLASSIC
(Far East/Australia)

1992	Ian Palmer
1993	Nick Faldo
1994	Greg Norman
1995	Fred Couples
1996	Ian Woosnam
1997	Ernie Els
1998	Tiger Woods
1999	Michael Campbell

Most Wins

No multiple winners

Johnnie Walker Monte Carlo Open
See (The) European Newspaper Monte Carlo Open

Karl Litten Desert Classic
See Dubai Desert Classic

KERRYGOLD INTERNATIONAL CLASSIC
(Ireland)

1975	George Burns
1976	Tony Jacklin
1977	Liam Higgins

No Tournaments since

Most Wins

No multiple winners

KLM Dutch Open
See TNT Dutch Open

KRONENBOURG OPEN
(Italy)

1993	Sam Torrance

No Tournaments since

Lada English Open
See Compass Group English Open

LANCIA D'ORO OPEN
(Italy)

1972	Jose-Maria Canizares

No Tournaments since

Lancia Italian Open
See Fiat & Fila Italian Open

Lancia-Martini Italian Open
See Fiat & Fila Italian Open

Lancome Trophy
See Trophee Lancome

LAWRENCE BATLEY INTERNATIONAL
(England)
1986 event incorporated the TPC (see Deutsche Bank/SAP - TPC of Europe)

1981	Sandy Lyle
1982	Sandy Lyle
1983	Nick Faldo
1984	Jose Rivero
1985	Graham Marsh
1986	Ian Woosnam
1987	Mark O'Meara

No Tournaments since

Most Wins

2	Sandy Lyle

Lexington South African PGA Championship
See Alfred Dunhill South African PGA Championship

LINDE GERMAN MASTERS

German Masters

1987	Sandy Lyle
1988	Jose-Maria Olazabal
1989	Bernhard Langer

Mercedes German Masters

1990	Sam Torrance
1991	Bernhard Langer
1992	Barry Lane
1993	Steven Richardson
1994	Seve Ballesteros
1995	Anders Forsbrand

Linde German Masters

1996	Darren Clarke
1997	Bernhard Langer
1998	Colin Montgomerie
1999	Sergio Garcia

Most Wins

3	Bernhard Langer

Loch Lomond World Invitational
See Standard Life Loch Lomond

London Standard Four Stars Pro-Celebrity
See European Pro-Celebrity Tournament

Long John Whisky PGA Matchplay Tournament
See Sun Alliance PGA Matchplay Tournament

Lufthansa German Open
See German Open Madeira Island Open

1993	Mark James
1994	Mats Lanner
1995	Santiago Luna
1996	Jarmo Sandelin
1997	Peter Mitchell
1998	Mats Lanner
1999	Pedro Linhart

Most Wins
2	Mats Lanner

MADRID OPEN

Madrid Open
1968	German Garrido
1969	Ramon Sota
1970	M Cabrera
1971	Valentin Barrios
1972	Jimmy Kinsella
1973	German Garrido
1974	Manuel Pinero
1975	Bob Shearer
1976	Tito Abreu
1977	Antonio Garrido
1978	Howard Clark
1979	Simon Hobday
1980	Seve Ballesteros
1981	Manuel Pinero
1982	Seve Ballesteros

Cepsa Madrid Open
1983	Sandy Lyle
1984	Howard Clark
1985	Manuel Pinero
1986	Howard Clark
1987	Ian Woosnam
1988	Derrick Cooper
1989	Seve Ballesteros
1990	Bernhard Langer

Madrid Open
1991	Andrew Sherborne

Iberia Madrid Open
1992	David Feherty

Madrid Open
1993	Des Smyth

No Tournaments since

Most Wins
3	Seve Ballesteros, Manuel Pinero
2	Howard Clark, German Garrido

Mallorca Open de Baleares
See Turespana Open de Baleares

MARTINI INTERNATIONAL

(Great Britain)
1961	Bernard Hunt
1962	Peter Thomson
1963	Neil Coles, Christy O'Connor, Sr – *tied*
1964	Christy O'Connor
1965	Peter Butler
1966	Peter Alliss, Bill Large – *tied*
1967	Malcolm Gregson, Brian Huggett – *tied*
1968	Brian Huggett
1969	Alex Caygill, G Henning – *tied*
1970	Doug Sewell, Peter Thomson
1971	Bernard Gallacher
1972	Brian Barnes
1973	Maurice Bembridge
1974	Stewart Ginn
1975	Christy O'Connor, Jr, Ian Stanley – *tied*
1976	Sam Torrance
1977	Greg Norman
1978	Seve Ballesteros
1979	Greg Norman
1980	Seve Ballesteros
1981	Greg Norman
1982	Bernard Gallacher
1983	Nick Faldo

No Tournaments since

Most Wins
3	Greg Norman
2	Seve Ballesteros, Bernard Gallacher, Brian Huggett (inc 1 tie), Christy O'Connor, Sr (inc 1 tie), Peter Thomson (inc 1 tie)

Mazda English Open
See Compass Group English Open

Mediterranean Open
See Turespana Open de Mediterrania

MERCEDES BENZ - VODACOM SOUTH AFRICAN OPEN

1997	Vijay Singh
1998	Ernie Els
1999	David Frost

Most Wins

No multiple winners

Mercedes German Masters
See Linde German Masters

MERSEYSIDE INTERNATIONAL

1980	Ian Mosey

No Tournaments since

Mitsubishi and Denzel Austrian Open
See Hohe Brucke Austrian Open

Mitsubishi Austrian Open
See Hohe Brucke Austrian Open

Monte Carlo Open
See (The) European Newspaper Monte Carlo Open

MORROCAN OPEN

1987	Howard Clark
1988-91	*No Tournaments*
1992	David Gilford
1993	David Gilford
1994	Anders Forsbrand
1995	Mark James
1996	Peter Hedblom
1997	Clinton Whitelaw
1998	Stephen Leaney
1999	Miguel Martin

Most Wins

2	David Gilford

MOTOROLA CLASSIC

(England)

Incorporated PGA Southern Open 1988

1988	D Williams
1989	David Llewellyn
1990	Paul Broadhurst

No Tournaments since

Most Wins

No multiple winners

MURPHY'S CUP

(England & Wales)

Stableford format. Unofficial event 1989 and 1990

1989	Hugh Baiocchi
1990	Tony Johnstone
1991	Tony Johnstone

No Tournaments since

Most Wins

2	Tony Johnstone

Murphy's English Open
See Compass Group English Open

MURPHY'S IRISH OPEN

Irish Open

1927	George Duncan
1928	Ernest (R) Whitcombe
1929	Abe Mitchell
1930	Charles Whitcombe
1931	Ernest Kenyon
1932	Alf Padgham
1933	Ernest Kenyon
1934	Syd Easterbrook
1935	Ernest (R) Whitcombe
1936	Reg Whitcombe
1937	Bert Gadd
1938	Bobby Locke
1939	Arthur Lees
1940-45	*No Tournaments – World War Two*
1946	Fred Daly
1947	Harry Bradshaw
1948	Dai Rees

1949	Harry Bradshaw
1950	Ossie Pickworth
1951-52	*No Tournaments*
1953	Eric Brown
1954-74	*No Tournaments*

Carrolls Irish Open

1975	Christy O'Connor, Jr
1976	Ben Crenshaw
1977	Hubert Green
1978	Ken Brown
1979	Mark James
1980	Mark James
1981	Sam Torrance
1982	John O'Leary
1983	Seve Ballesteros
1984	Bernhard Langer
1985	Seve Ballesteros
1986	Seve Ballesteros
1987	Bernhard Langer
1988	Ian Woosnam
1989	Ian Woosnam
1990	Jose-Maria Olazabal
1991	Nick Faldo
1992	Nick Faldo
1993	Nick Faldo

Murphy's Irish Open

1994	Bernhard Langer
1995	Sam Torrance
1996	Colin Montgomerie
1997	Colin Montgomerie
1998	David Carter
1999	Sergio Garcia

Most Wins

3	Seve Ballesteros, Nick Faldo, Bernhard Langer
2	Harry Bradshaw, Mark James, Ernest Kenyon, Colin Montgomerie, Sam Torrance, Ernest (R) Whitcombe, Ian Woosnam

National Car Rental English Open
See Compass Group English Open

NEWCASTLE BROWN '900' OPEN
(England)

1980	Des Smyth

No Tournaments since

News of the World PGA Matchplay Tournament
See Sun Alliance PGA Matchplay Tournament

NM English Open
See Compass Group English Open

NOVOTEL PERRIER OPEN DE FRANCE

Open de France

1906	Arnaud Massy
1907	Arnaud Massy
1908	JH Taylor
1909	JH Taylor
1910	James Braid
1911	Arnaud Massy
1912	Jean Gassiat
1913	George Duncan
1914	J Douglas Edgar
1915-19	*No Tournaments – World War One*
1920	Walter Hagen
1921	Aubrey Boomer
1922	Aubrey Boomer
1923	James Ockenden
1924	Cyril Tolley (a)
1925	Arnaud Massy
1926	Aubrey Boomer
1927	George Duncan
1928	Cyril Tolley (a)
1929	Aubrey Boomer
1930	Ernest (R) Whitcombe
1931	Aubrey Boomer
1932	Arthur Lacey
1933	Bert Gadd
1934	Sid Brews
1935	Sid Brews
1936	Marcel Dallemagne
1937	Marcel Dallemagne
1938	Marcel Dallemagne
1939	Martin Pose
1940-45	*No Tournaments – World War Two*
1946	Henry Cotton
1947	Henry Cotton

1948	F Cavalo
1949	Ugo Grappasonni
1950	Roberto de Vicenzo
1951	H Hassenein
1952	Bobby Locke
1953	Bobby Locke
1954	Flory van Donck
1955	Byron Nelson
1956	Angel Miguel
1957	Flory van Donck
1959	Flory van Donck
1959	Dave Thomas
1960	Roberto de Vicenzo
1961	Kel Nagle
1962	A Murray
1963	Bruce Devlin
1964	Roberto de Vicenzo
1965	Ramon Sota
1966	Denis Hutchinson
1967	Bernard Hunt
1968	Peter Butler
1969	Jean Garaialde
1970	David Graham
1971	Lu Liang Huan
1972	Barry Jaeckel
1973	Peter Oosterhuis
1974	Peter Oosterhuis
1975	Brian Barnes
1976	Vincent Tshabalala
1977	Seve Ballesteros
1978	Dale Hayes
1979	Bernard Gallacher

Paco Rabanne Open de France

1980	Greg Norman
1981	Sandy Lyle
1982	Seve Ballesteros
1983	Nick Faldo

Peugeot Open de France

1984	Bernhard Langer
1985	Seve Ballesteros
1986	Seve Ballesteros
1987	Jose Rivero
1988	Nick Faldo
1989	Nick Faldo
1990	Philip Walton
1991	Eduardo Romero

1992	Miguel Martin
1993	Costantino Rocca
1994	Mark Roe
1995	Paul Broadhurst
1996	Robert Allenby
1997	Retief Goosen
1998	Sam Torrance

Novotel Perrier Open de France

| 1999 | Retief Goosen |

Most Wins

| 5 | Aubrey Boomer |
| 4 | Seve Ballesteros, Arnaud Massy |

OKI PRO-AM

(Spain)

| 1996 | Tom Kite |
| 1997 | Paul McGinley |

No Tournaments since

Most Wins

No multiple winners

One 2 One British Masters

See Victor Chandler British Masters

OPEN DE CATALONIA

Open de Catalonia

1989	Mark Roe
1990	No Tournament
1991	Jose-Maria Olazabal
1992	Jose Rivero

Heineken Open de Catalonia

| 1993 | Sam Torrance |
| 1994 | Jose Coceres |

Turespana Open de Catalonia

| 1995 | Philip Walton |

Open de Catalonia

| 1996 | Paul Lawrie |

No Tournaments since

Most Wins

No multiple winners

OPEN DE EXTRADEMURA
(Spain)

1994	Paul Eales

No Tournaments since

Open de Espana
See Peugeot Open de Espana

Open de France
See Novotel Perrier Open de France

Open de Lyon
See V33 Open de Lyon

Open de Mediterrania
See Turespana Open de Mediterrania

OPEN NOVOTEL PERRIER
(France)

Strokeplay Foursomes

1996	Steven Bottomley & Jonathan Lomas
1997	Anders Forsbrand & Michael Jonzon
1998	Olle Karlsson & Jarmo Sandelin

No Tournaments since

Most Wins

No multiple winners

Paco Rabanne Open de France
See Novotel Perrier Open de France

Panasonic European Open
See Smurfit European Open

PARMECO GOLF CLASSIC
(England)

1971	Eddie Polland

No Tournaments since

Penfold-Bournemouth
See Penfold Tournament

Penfold PGA Championship
See Volvo PGA Championship

Penfold-Swallow
See Penfold Tournament

PENFOLD TOURNAMENT
(Great Britain)

Matchplay 1949, 1950. Mixed event 1950

Penfold

1932	Percy Alliss
1933	John Burton
1934	Reg Whitcombe
1935	Percy Alliss
1936	Jimmy Adams
1939	Henry Cotton
1940-45	*No Tournaments – World War Two*
1946	Norman Sutton
1947	Dai Rees, Norman von Nida, Reg Whitcombe – tied
1948	Fred Daly
1949	John Burton & Max Faulkner
1950	N. Sutton & a certain Mrs Gee
1951	Arthur Lees
1952	Eric Brown
1953	Arthur Lees
1954	Henry Cotton
1955	Christy O'Connor

Penfold-Swallow

1956	Eric Lester

Swallow-Penfold

1957	Harry Weetman

Penfold-Swallow

1958	Harry Weetman

Swallow-Penfold

1959	Peter Butler

Penfold-Swallow

1960	Harry Weetman

Swallow-Penfold

1961	Ken Bousfield

Penfold-Swallow

1962	Harry Weetman

Swallow-Penfold

1963	Bernard Hunt

Penfold-Swallow

1964	Peter Alliss

Swallow-Penfold

1965	Angel Miguel

Penfold-Swallow

1966	Dave Thomas

Swallow-Penfold
1967	J Cockin

Penfold-Swallow
1968	Peter Butler

Swallow-Penfold
1969	Alex Caygill

Penfold-Swallow
1970	Bernard Hunt

Penfold-Bournemouth
1971	Neil Coles
1972	Peter Oosterhuis
1973	Eddie Polland

Penfold
1974	Tommy Horton

No Tournaments since

Most Wins
4	Harry Weetman
2	Percy Alliss, John Burton (inc 1 Matchplay pairing), Peter Butler, Henry Cotton, Bernard Hunt, Arthur Lees, Norman Sutton (inc 1 Matchplay pairing), Reg Whitcombe

PEUGEOT OPEN DE ESPANA

Open de Espana
1912	Arnaud Massy
1913-15	*No Tournaments*
1916	Angel de la Torre
1917	Angel de la Torre
1918	*No Tournament*
1919	Angel de la Torre
1920	*No Tournament*
1921	E Laffite
1922	*No Tournament*
1923	Angel de la Torre
1924	*No Tournament*
1925	Angel de la Torre
1926	J Bernardino
1927	Arnaud Massy
1928	Arnaud Massy
1929	E Laffite
1930	J Bernardino
1931	*No Tournament*
1932	G Gonzalez

1933	G Gonzalez
1934	J Bernardino
1935	Angel de la Torre
1936-40	*No Tournaments – Spanish Civil War*
1941	M Provencio
1942	G Gonzalez
1943	M Provencio
1944	N Sargardia
1945	C Celles
1946	M Morcillo
1947	Mario Gonzalez (a)
1948	M Morcillo
1949	M Morcillo
1950	Antonio Cerda
1951	M Provencio
1952	Max Faulkner
1953	Max Faulkner
1954	Sebastian Miguel
1955	Henri de Lamaze (a)
1956	Peter Alliss
1957	Max Faulkner
1958	Peter Alliss
1959	Peter Thomson
1960	Sebastian Miguel
1961	Angel Miguel
1962	*No Tournament*
1963	Ramon Sota
1964	Angel Miguel
1965	*No Tournament*
1966	Roberto de Vicenzo
1967	Sebastian Miguel
1968	Bob Shaw
1969	Jean Garaialde
1970	Angel Gallardo
1971	Dale Hayes
1972	Antonio Garrido
1973	Neil Coles
1974	Jerry Heard
1975	Arnold Palmer
1976	Eddie Polland
1977	Bernard Gallacher
1978	Brian Barnes
1979	Dale Hayes

Benson & Hedges Open de Espana
1980	Eddie Polland
1981	Seve Ballesteros

1982	Sam Torrance
1983	Eamonn Darcy
1984	Bernhard Langer
1985	Seve Baltesteros

Peugeot Open de Espana

1986	Howard Clark
1987	Nick Faldo
1988	Mark James
1989	Bernhard Langer
1990	Rodger Davis
1991	Eduardo Romero
1992	Andrew Sherborne
1993	Joakim Haeggman
1994	Colin Montgomerie
1995	Seve Ballesteros
1996	Padraig Harrington
1997	Mark James
1998	Thomas Bjorn
1999	Jarmo Sandelin

Most Wins

6	Angel de la Torre
3	J Bernardino, Max Faulkner, G Gonzalez, Arnaud Massy, Sebastian Miguel, M Morcillo, M Provencio

Peugeot Open de France

See Novotel Perrier Open de France

Peugeot-Trends Belgian Open

See Alfred Dunhill Open

PGA Championship

See Volvo PGA Championship

PGA Matchplay Tournament

See Sun Alliance PGA Matchplay Tournament

PIAGET Belgian Open

See Alfred Dunhill Open

Piccadilly

See Piccadilly Medal

PICCADILLY MEDAL

(England)

72-hole Strokeplay, except: Matchplay Four-ball, 1968; Matchplay decided on strokes, 1969-75

Piccadilly (Strokeplay)

1962	Peter Thomson
1963	No Tournament
1964	Jimmy Martin
1965	Peter Butler
1966	Bernard Hunt
1967	Peter Butler

Piccadilly (Four-ball)

1968	R Emery & Hugh Jackson

Piccadilly Medal

1969	Peter Alliss
1970	John Lister
1971	Peter Oosterhuis
1972	Tommy Horton
1973	Peter Oosterhuis
1974	Maurice Bembridge
1975	Bob Shearer
1976	Sam Torrance

No Tournaments since

Most Wins

2	Peter Butler, Peter Oosterhuis

PLM OPEN

(Sweden)

1986	Peter Senior
1987	Howard Clark
1988	Frank Nobilo
1989	Mike Harwood
1990	Ronan Rafferty

No Tournaments since

Most Wins

No multiple winners

Portuguese Algarve Open

See Algarve Portuguese Open

PRINGLE OF SCOTLAND

(Scotland & England)

Seniors event only, 1969-74

1964	Harold Henning
1965	Cobie Legrange
1966	Neil Coles
1967	Tony Jacklin
1968	*No Tournament*
1969	John Panton
1970	Max Faulker
1971	Kel Nagle
1972	Ken Bousfield
1973	Kel Nagle
1974	Eric Lester

No Tournaments since

Most Wins

2	Kel Nagle

QATAR MASTERS

1998	Andrew Coltart
1999	Paul Lawrie

Most Wins

No multiple winners

Quinta do Lago Portuguese Open
See Portuguese Algarve Open

Renault Belgian Open
See Alfred Dunhill Open

Renault Open de Baleares
See Turespana Open de Baleares

ROMA MASTERS

1992	Jose-Maria Canizares
1993	Jean Van de Velde

No Tournaments since

Most Wins

No multiple winners

ST Mellion Time Share TPC
See Deutsche Bank – SAP Open TPC of Europe

SANYO OPEN

(Spain)

1982	Neil Coles
1983	Des Smyth
1984	Sam Torrance
1985	Seve Ballesteros
1986	Jose-Maria Olazabal

No Tournaments since

Most Wins

No multiple winners

SARAZEN WORLD OPEN

(US until 1998, then Spain)
Official US PGA Tour event until 1998

Subaru Sarazen World Open

1994	Ernie Els
1995	Frank Nobilo
1996	Frank Nobilo
1997	Mark Calcavecchia
1998	Dudley Hart

Sarazen World Open

1999	Thomas Bjorn

Most Wins

2	Frank Nobilo

SCANDINAVIAN ENTERPRISE OPEN

1973	Bob Charles
1974	Tony Jacklin
1975	George Burns
1976	Hugh Baiocchi
1977	Bob Byman
1978	Seve Ballesteros
1979	Sandy Lyle
1980	Greg Norman
1981	Seve Ballesteros
1982	Bob Byman
1983	Sam Torrance
1984	Ian Woosnam
1985	Ian Baker-Finch
1986	Greg Turner
1987	Gordon Brand, Jr
1988	Seve Ballesteros

1989	Ronan Rafferty
1990	Craig Stadler

No Tournaments since

Most Wins

3	Seve Ballesteros
2	Bob Byman

Scandinavian Masters
See Volvo Scandinavian Masters

SCOTTISH OPEN

1972-73	*See Sunbeam Electric*
1974-85	*No Tournaments*

Bells Scottish Open

1986	David Feherty
1987	Ian Woosnam
1988	Barry Lane
1989	M Allen
1990	Ian Woosnam
1991	Craig Parry
1992	Peter O'Malley
1993	Jesper Parnevik
1994	Carl Mason

Scottish Open

1995	Wayne Riley
1996	Ian Woosnam

No Tournaments since

Most Wins

3	Ian Woosnam

SCOTTISH PGA CHAMPIONSHIP

Originally played in 1907

1999	Warren Bennett

Silk Cut Masters
See Victor Chandler British Masters

Slaley Hall Northumberland Challenge
See Compaq European Grand Prix

SMURFIT EUROPEAN OPEN
(GB and Ireland)

European Open

1978	Bobby Wadkins

1979	Sandy Lyle
1980	Tom Kite

Dixcel Tissues European Open

1981	Graham Marsh

European Open

1982	Manuel Pinero

Panasonic European Open

1983	Isao Aoki
1984	Gordon Brand, Jr
1985	Bernhard Langer
1986	Greg Norman
1987	Paul Way
1988	Ian Woosnam
1989	Andrew Murray
1990	Peter Senior

General Accident European Open

1991	Mike Harwood
1992	Nick Faldo
1993	Gordon Brand Jr
1994	David Gilford

Smurfit European Open

1995	Bernhard Langer
1996	Per-Ulrik Johansson
1997	Per-Ulrik Johansson
1998	Mathias Gronberg
1999	Lee Westwood

Most Wins

2	Gordon Brand, Jr, Per-Ulrik Johansson, Bernhard Langer

SOS Talisman TPC
See Deutsche Bank – SAP Open TPC of Europe

Spanish Open
See Peugeot Open de Espana

STANDARD LIFE LOCH LOMOND
(Scotland)

Loch Lomond World Invitational

1996	Thomas Bjorn
1997	Tom Lehman

Standard Life Loch Lomond

1998	Lee Westwood
1999	Colin Montgomerie

Most wins

No multiple winners

State Express English Open
See Compass Group English Open

Subaru Sarazen World Open
See Sarazen World Open

SUMRIE-BOURNEMOUTH
(England & Scotland)
72-hole Strokeplay, 1968, thereafter Better-ball

Sumrie Clothes

1968	Brian Huggett
1969	Maurice Bembridge & Angel Gallardo
1970	Neil Coles & Bernard Hunt
1971	*No Tournament*
1972	Malcolm Gregson & Brian Huggett
1973	Neil Coles & Bernard Hunt

Sumrie-Bournemouth

1974	Peter Butler & Clive Clark
1975	Jack Newton & John O'Leary
1976	Eamonn Darcy & Christy O'Connor, Jr
1977	*No Tournament*
1978	Eamonn Darcy & Christy O'Connor, Jr

No Tournaments since

Most Wins

2	Neil Coles, Eamonn Darcy, Brian Huggett (inc 1 individual), Bernard Hunt, Christy O'Connor, Jr

Sumrie Clothes
See Sumrie-Bournemouth

Sun Alliance PGA Championship
See Volvo PGA Championship

SUN ALLIANCE PGA MATCHPLAY TOURNAMENT
(Great Britain & N Ireland)
News of the World PGA Matchplay Tournament

1903	James Braid
1904	JH Taylor
1905	James Braid
1906	Sandy Herd
1907	James Braid
1908	JH Taylor

1909	Tom Ball
1910	James Sherlock
1911	James Braid
1912	Harry Vardon
1913	George Duncan
1914-18	*No Tournaments – World War One*
1919	Abe Mitchell
1920	Abe Mitchell
1921	B Seymour
1922	George Gadd
1923	Reg Wilson
1924	Ernest (R) Whitcombe
1925	Archie Compston
1926	Sandy Herd
1927	Archie Compston
1928	Charles Whitcombe
1929	Abe Mitchell
1930	Charles Whitcombe
1931	Alf Padgham
1932	Henry Cotton
1933	Percy Alliss
1934	Jack Busson
1935	Alf Padgham
1936	Dai Rees
1937	Peter Alliss
1938	Dai Rees
1940	Henry Cotton
1941-44	*No Tournaments – World War Two*
1945	Reg Horne
1946	Henry Cotton
1947	Fred Daly
1948	Fred Daly
1949	Dai Rees
1950	Dai Rees
1951	Harry Weetman
1952	Fred Daly
1953	Max Faulkner
1954	Peter Thomson
1955	Ken Bousfield
1956	John Panton
1957	Christy O'Connor, Sr
1958	Harry Weetman
1959	David Snell
1960	Eric Brown
1961	Peter Thomson
1962	Eric Brown

1963	Dave Thomas
1964	Neil Coles
1965	Neil Coles
1966	Peter Thomson
1967	Peter Thomson
1968	Brian Huggett
1969	Maurice Bembridge

Long John Whisky PGA Matchplay Tournament

1970	Tommy Horton
1971	No Tournament
1972	John Garner

Benson & Hedges PGA Matchplay Tournament

1973	Neil Coles
1974	Jack Newton
1975	Eddie Polland

Sun Alliance PGA Matchplay Tournament

1976	Brian Barnes
1977	Hugh Baiocchi
1978	Mark James
1979	Des Smyth

No Tournaments since

Most Wins

4	James Braid, Dai Rees, Peter Thomson
3	Neil Coles, Henry Cotton, Fred Daly, Abe Mitchell

Sun Microsystems Dutch Open
See TNT Dutch Open

SUNBEAM ELECTRIC
(England & Scotland)
Incorporated the Scottish Open, 1972-73

1971	Peter Oosterhuis
1972	Neil Coles
1973	Graham Marsh

No Tournaments since

Most Wins

No multiple winners

Suze Cannes Open
See Cannes Open

Swallow-Penfold
See Penfold Tournament

Swiss Open
See Canon European Masters

Tenerife Open
See Turespana Open de Canarias

Tisettanta Italian Open
See Fiat & Fila Italian Open

TIMEX OPEN
(France)

1983	Manuel Ballesteros
1984	Michael Clayton

No Tournaments since

Most Wins

No multiple winners

TNT DUTCH OPEN
36 hole tournament until 1934

Dutch Open

1919	D Oosterveer
1920	H Burrows
1921	H Burrows
1922	George Pannell
1923	Aubrey Boomer
1924	Aubrey Boomer
1925	Aubrey Boomer
1926	Aubrey Boomer
1927	PH Boomer
1929	JJ Taylor
1930	J Oosterveer
1931	F Dyer
1932	Auguste Boyer
1933	Marcel Dallemagne
1934	Sid Brews
1935	Sid Brews
1936	Flory van Donck
1937	Flory van Donck
1938	Alf Padgham
1939	Bobby Locke
1940-45	No Tournaments – World War Two
1946	Flory van Donck
1947	G Ruhl
1948	CS Denny
1949	Jimmy Adams

1950	Roberto de Vicenzo
1951	Flory van Donck
1952	CS Denny
1953	Flory van Donck
1954	Ugo Grappasonni
1955	Alfonso Angelini
1956	Antonio Cerda
1957	John Jacobs
1958	Dave Thomas
1959	Sewsunker Sewgolum
1960	Sewsunker Sewgolum
1961	Brian Wilkes
1962	Brian Huggett
1963	R Waltman
1964	Sewsunker Sewgolum
1965	Angel Miguel
1966	Ramon Sota
1967	Peter Townsend
1968	J Cockin
1969	Guy Wolstenholme
1970	Vicente Fernandez
1971	Ramon Sota
1972	Jack Newton
1973	Doug McClelland
1974	Brian Barnes
1975	Hugh Baiocchi
1976	Seve Ballesteros
1977	Bob Byman
1978	Bob Byman
1979	Graham Marsh
1980	Seve Ballesteros

KLM Dutch Open

1981	Harold Henning
1982	Paul Way
1983	Ken Brown
1984	Bernhard Langer
1985	Graham Marsh
1986	Seve Ballesteros
1987	Gordon Brand, Jr
1988	Mark Mouland
1989	Jose-Maria Olazabal
1990	Stephen McAllister

Heineken Dutch Open

1991	Payne Stewart
1992	Bernhard Langer
1993	Colin Montgomerie
1994	Miguel Jimenez
1995	Scott Hoch

Sun Microsystems Dutch Open

1996	Mark McNulty
1997	Sven Struver

TNT Dutch Open

1998	Stephen Leaney
1999	Lee Westwood

Most Wins

5	Flory van Donck
3	Seve Ballesteros, Aubrey Boomer, Sewsunker Sewgolum

TORRAS HOSTENCH BARCELONA OPEN

1988	S Whelan

No Tournaments since – See Open Catalonia

Torras Monte Carlo Open

See (The) European Newspaper Monte Carlo Open

Tournament Players Championship

See Deutsche Bank – SAP Open TPC of Europe

TROPHEE LANCOME

(France)
Official Order of Merit event from 1982

1970	Tony Jacklin
1971	Arnold Palmer
1972	Tommy Aaron
1973	Johnny Miller
1974	Billy Casper
1975	Gary Player
1976	Seve Ballesteros
1977	Graham Marsh
1978	Lee Trevino
1979	Johnny Miller
1980	Lee Trevino
1981	David Graham
1982	David Graham
1983	Seve Ballesteros
1984	Sandy Lyle
1985	Nick Price
1986	Seve Ballesteros, Bernhard Langer – *tied* (after play-off)
1987	Ian Woosnam
1998	Seve Ballesteros

1989	Eduardo Romero
1990	Jose-Maria Olazabal
1991	Frank Nobilo
1992	Mark Roe
1993	Ian Woosnam
1994	Vijay Singh
1995	Colin Montgomerie
1996	Jesper Parnevik
1997	Mark O'Meara
1998	Miguel Jimenez
1999	Pierre Fulke

Most Wins

4	Seve Ballesteros (inc 1 tie)
2	Johnny Miller, Lee Trevino, Ian Woosnam

TUNISIAN OPEN

1982	Antonio Garrido
1983	Mark James
1984	Sam Torrance
1985	Stephen Bennett

No Tournaments since

Most Wins

No multiple winners

TURNOI PERRIER DE PARIS

Better-ball

1994	Peter Baker & David J Russell
1995	Seve Ballesteros & Jose-Maria Olazabal

No Tournaments since

Most Wins

No multiple winners

Turespana Iberia Open de Baleares
See Turespana Open de Baleares

Turespana Masters; Turespana Masters Open de Andalucia; Turespana Masters Open Communitat Valenciana Paradores de Turismo
See Turespana Masters Open de Baleares

TURESPANA MASTERS OPEN DE BALEARES

Turespana Masters Open de Andalucia

1992	Vijay Singh
1993	Andrew Oldcorn
1994	Carl Mason
1995	Alex Cejka
1996	Diego Borrego

Turespana Masters Open Communitat Valenciana Paradores de Turismo

1997	Jose-Maria Olazabal

Turespana Masters Open de Canarias

1998	Miguel Jimenez

Turespana Masters Open de Baleares

1999	Miguel Jimenez

Most Wins

2	Miguel Jimenez

Turespana Masters Open de Canarias
See Turespana Masters Open de Baleares

Turespana Iberia Open de Canarias
See Turespana Open de Canarias

TURESPANA OPEN DE BALEARES

Mallorca Open de Baleares

1988	Seve Ballesteros

Renault Open de Baleares

1989	Ove Sellberg
1990	Seve Ballesteros

Mallorca Open de Baleares

1991	Gavin Levenson

Turespana Open de Baleares

1992	Seve Ballesteros

Turespana Iberia Open de Baleares

1993	Jim Payne

Turespana Open de Baleares

1994	Barry Lane
1995	Greg Turner

No Tournaments since

Most Wins

3	Seve Ballesteros

TURESPANA OPEN DE CANARIAS

Tenerife Open
1989	Jose-Maria Olazabal
1990	Vicente Fernandez
1991	No Tournament

Turespana Open de Tenerife
1992	Jose-Maria Olazabal

Turespana Iberia Open de Canarias
1993	Mark James

Turespana Open de Tenerife
1994	David Gilford

Turespana Open de Canarias
1995	Jarmo Sandelin

No Tournaments since

Most Wins
2	Jose-Maria Olazabal

Turespana Open de Catalonia
See Open de Catalonia

TURESPANA OPEN DE MEDITERRANIA
(Spain)

Amex Mediterranean Open
1990	Ian Woosnam

Fujitsu Mediterranean Open
1991	Ian Woosnam

Open de Mediterrania
1992	Jose-Maria Olazabal

Turespana Open de Mediterrania
1993	Frank Nobilo
1994	Jose-Maria Olazabal
1995	Robert Karlsson

No Tournaments since

Most Wins
2	Jose-Maria Olazabal, Ian Woosnam

Turespana Open de Tenerife
See Turespana Open de Canarias

UNIROYAL INTERNATIONAL
(England)
1976	Tommy Hortom
1977	Seve Ballesteros

No Tournaments since

Most Wins

No multiple winners

V33 OPEN DE LYON
1992	David J Russell
1993	Costantino Rocca
1994	Stephen Ames

No Tournaments since

Most Wins

No multiple winners

VICTOR CHANDLER BRITISH MASTERS

Dunlop Masters
1946	Jimmy Adams, Bobby Locke – *tied*
1947	Arthur Lees
1948	Norman von Nida
1949	Charlie Ward
1950	Dai Rees
1951	Max Faulkner
1952	Harry Weetman
1953	Harry Bradshaw
1954	Bobby Locke
1955	Harry Bradshaw
1956	Christy O'Connor, Sr
1957	Eric Brown
1958	Harry Weetman
1959	Christy O'Connor, Sr
1960	Jimmy Hitchcock
1961	Peter Thomson
1962	Dai Rees
1963	Bernard Hunt
1964	Cobie Legrange
1965	Bernard Hunt

1966	Neil Coles
1967	Tony Jacklin
1968	Peter Thomson
1969	Cobie Legrange
1970	Brian Huggett
1971	Maurice Bembridge
1972	Bob Charles
1973	Tony Jacklin
1974	Bernard Gallacher
1975	Bernard Gallacher
1976	Baldovino Dassu
1977	Guy Hunt
1978	Tommy Horton
1979	Graham Marsh
1980	Bernhard Langer
1981	Greg Norman
1982	Greg Norman

Silk Cut Masters

1983	Ian Woosnam
1984	No Tournament

Dunhill British Masters

1985	Lee Trevino
1986	Seve Ballesteros
1987	Mark McNulty
1988	Sandy Lyle
1989	Nick Faldo
1990	Mark James
1991	Seve Ballesteros
1992	Christy O'Connor, Jr
1993	Peter Baker
1994	Ian Woosnam

Collingtree British Masters

1995	Sam Torrance

One 2 One British Masters

1996	Robert Allenby
1997	Greg Turner
1998	Colin Montgomerie

Victor Chandler British Masters

1999	Bob May

Most Wins

2	Seve Ballesteros, Harry Bradshaw, Bernard Gallacher, Bernard Hunt, Tony Jacklin, Cobie Legrange, Greg Norman, Christy O'Connor, Sr, Peter Thomson, Harry Weetman, Ian Woosnam

Viyella PGA Championship
See Volvo PGA Championship

VINHO VERDE ATLANTIC OPEN
(Portugal)

1990	Stephen McAllister

No Tournaments since

Volvo Belgian Open
See Alfred Dunhill Open

Volvo German Open
See German Open

VOLVO MASTERS
(Spain)

1988	Nick Faldo
1989	Ronan Rafferty
1990	Mike Harwood
1991	Rodger Davis
1992	Sandy Lyle
1993	Colin Montgomerie
1994	Bernhard Langer
1995	Alex Cjeka
1996	Mark McNulty
1997	Lee Westwood
1998	Darren Clarke
1999	Miguel Jimenez

Most Wins

No multiple winners

Volvo Open
See Volvo Open di Firenze

VOLVO OPEN DI FIRENZE
(Spain 1989, then Italy)

Volvo Open

1989	Vijay Singh

Volvo Open di Firenze

1990	Eduardo Romero
1991	Anders Forsbrand
1992	Anders Forsbrand

No Tournaments since

Most Wins

2	Anders Forsbrand

VOLVO PGA CHAMPIONSHIP

(England/Wales)

Closed to GB and Irish pros until 1966. In 1967 and 1968 there were 'open' and 'closed' tournaments.

PGA Championship

1955	Ken Bousfield
1956	Charlie Ward
1957	Peter Alliss
1958	Harry Bradshaw
1959	Dai Rees
1960	AF Strickley
1961	Brian Bamford
1962	Peter Alliss
1963	Peter Butler
1964	Tony Grubb
1965	Peter Alliss
1966	Guy Wolstenholme

Schweppes PGA Championship

1967c	Brian Huggett
1967o	Malcolm Gregson
1968c	Peter Townsend
1968o	David Talbot

PGA Championship

1969	Bernard Gallacher
1970-71	*No Tournaments*

Viyella PGA Championship

1972	Tony Jacklin
1973	Peter Oosterhuis
1974	Maurice Bembridge

Penfo/d PGA Championship

1975	Arnold Palmer
1976	Neil Coles
1977	Manuel Pinero

Colgate PGA Championship

1978	Nick Faldo
1979	Vicente Fernandez

Sun Alliance PGA Championship

1980	Nick Faldo
1981	Nick Faldo
1982	Tony Jacklin
1983	Seve Ballesteros

Whyte & Mackay PGA Championship

1984	Howard Clark
1985	Paul Way
1986	Rodger Davis
1987	Berhard Langer

Volvo PGA Championship

1988	Ian Woosnam
1989	Nick Faldo
1990	Mike Harwood
1991	Seve Ballesteros
1992	Tony Johnstone
1993	Bernhard Langer
1994	Jose-Maria Olazabal
1995	Bernhard Langer
1996	Costantino Rocca
1997	Ian Woosnam
1998	Colin Montgomerie
1999	Colin Montgomerie

Most Wins

4	Nick Faldo
3	Peter Alliss, Bernhard Langer

VOLVO SCANDINAVIAN MASTERS

(Sweden)

Scandinavian Masters

1991	Colin Montgomerie
1992	Nick Faldo
1993	Peter Baker
1994	Vijay Singh
1995	Jesper Parnevik

Volvo Scandinavian Masters

1996	Lee Westwood
1997	Joakim Haeggman
1998	Jesper Parnevik
1999	Colin Montgomerie

Most Wins

2	Colin Montgomerie, Jesper Parnevik

Wang Four Stars Pro-Celebrity

See European Pro-Celebrity Tournament

WD & HO WILLS

(England & N Ireland)

1968	Peter Butler
1969	Bernard Gallacher
1970	Tony Jacklin
1971	Bernard Hunt
1972	Peter Thomson
1973	Charles Coody
1974	Neil Coles

No Tournaments since

Most Wins

No multiple winners

Welsh Golf Classic

See Coral Classic

WEST OF IRELAND CLASSIC

Also counted as a challenge Tour event

1999 Costantino Rocca

Whyte & McKay PGA Championship   See Volvo PGA Championship

THE HARRY VARDON TROPHY

(Not to be confused with the Vardon Trophy, presented since 1937 to the player with the lowest stroke average on the [US] PGA Tour).

Awarded since 1937 by the PGA to the leading player in the (Volvo) Order of Merit

1937	Charles Whitcombe (Eng)
1938	Henry Cotton (Eng)
1939	Reg Whitcombe (Eng)
1940-45	*Not awarded – World War Two*
1946	Bobby Locke (RSA)
1947	Norman von Nida (Aus)
1948	Charlie Ward (Eng)
1949	Charlie Ward (Eng)
1950	Bobby Locke (RSA)
1951	John Panton (Eng)
1952	Harry Weetman (Eng)
1953	Flory van Donck (Bel)
1954	Bobby Locke (RSA)
1955	Dai Rees (Wal)
1956	Harry Weetman (Eng)
1957	Eric Brown (Sco)
1958	Bernard Hunt (Eng)
1959	Dai Rees (Wal)
1960	Bernard Hunt (Eng)
1961	Christy O'Connor, Sr (Ire)
1962	Christy O'Connor, Sr (Ire)
1963	Neil Coles (Eng)
1964	Peter Alliss (Eng)
1965	Bernard Hunt (Eng)
1966	Peter Alliss (Eng)
1967	Malcolm Gregson (Eng)
1968	Brian Huggett (Wal)
1969	Bernard Gallacher (Sco)
1970	Neil Coles (Eng)
1971	Peter Oosterhuis (Eng)
1972	Peter Oosterhuis (Eng)
1973	Peter Oosterhuis (Eng)
1974	Peter Oosterhuis (Eng)
1975	Dale Hayes (RSA)
1976	Seve Ballesteros (Sp)
1977	Seve Ballesteros (Sp)
1978	Seve Ballesteros (Sp)
1979	Sandy Lyle (Sco)
1980	Sandy Lyle (Sco)
1981	Bernhard Langer (Ger)
1982	Greg Norman (Aus)
1983	Nick Faldo (Eng)
1984	Bernhard Langer (Ger)
1985	Sandy Lyle (Sco)
1986	Seve Ballesteros (Sp)
1987	Ian Woosnam (Wal)
1988	Seve Ballesteros (Sp)
1989	Ronan Rafferty (NI)
1990	Ian Woosnam (Wal)
1991	Seve Ballesteros (Sp)
1992	Nick Faldo (Eng)
1993	Colin Montgomerie (Sco)
1994	Colin Montgomerie (Sco)
1995	Colin Montgomerie (Sco)
1996	Colin Montgomerie (Sco)
1997	Colin Montgomerie (Sco)
1998	Colin Montgomerie (Sco)
1999	Colin Montgomerie (Sco)

Most Order of Merit Wins

7	Colin Montgomerie
6	Seve Ballesteros
4	Peter Oosterhuis
3	Sandy Lyle
2 =	Peter Alliss
	Neil Coles
	Nick Faldo
	Bernard Hunt
	Bernhard Langer
	Bobby Locke
	Christy O'Connor, Sr
	Dai Rees
	Charlie Ward
	Harry Weetman
	Ian Woosnam

VOLVO ORDER OF MERIT, TOP 10, 1995-99 (WITH OFFICIAL PRIZEMONEY)

1995		£
1	Colin Montgomerie (Sco)	835051
2	Sam Torrance (Sco)	755706
3	Bernhard Langer (Ger)	655854
4	Costantino Rocca (Ita)	516320
5	Michael Campbell (NZ)	400977
6	Alex Cjeka (Ger)	308114
7	Mark James (Eng)	297377

8	Barry Lane (Eng)	284406
9	Anders Forsbrand (Swe)	281726
10	Peter O'Malley (Aus)	260726

1996

1	Colin Montgomerie (Sco)	875146
2	Ian Woosnam (Wal)	650423
3	Robert Allenby (Aus)	532143
4	Costantino Rocca (Ita)	482585
5	Mark McNulty (Zim)	463847
6	Lee Westwood (Eng)	428693
7	Andrew Coltart (Sco)	345936
8	Darren Clarke (NI)	329795
9	Paul Broadhurst (Eng)	300364
10	Thomas Bjorn (Den)	292478

1997

1	Colin Montgomerie (Sco)	798947
2	Bernhard Langer (Ger)	692398
3	Lee Westwood (Eng)	588718
4	Darren Clarke (NI)	537409
5	Ian Woosnam (Wal)	503562
6	Ignacio Garrido (Sp)	411479
7	Retief Goosen (RSA)	394597
8	Padraig Harrington (Ire)	388982
9	Jose-Maria Olazabal (Sp)	385648
10	Robert Karlsson (Swe)	364542

1998

1	Colin Montgomerie (Sco)	993077
2	Darren Clarke (NI)	902867
3	Lee Westwood (Eng)	814386
4	Miguel Jimenez (Sp)	518819
5	Patrik Sjoland (Swe)	500136
6	Thomas Bjorn (Den)	470798
7	Jose-Maria Olazabal (Sp)	449132
8	Ernie Els (RSA)	433884
9	Andrew Coltart (Sco)	388816
10	Mathias Gronberg (Swe)	358779

1999

1	Colin Montgomerie (Sco)	1302057
2	Lee Westwood (Eng)	943432
3	Sergio Garcia (Sp)	941209
4	Miguel Jimenez (Sp)	820206
5	Retief Goosen (RSA)	757131
6	Paul Lawrie (Sco)	643894
7	Padraig Harrington (Ire)	610830
8	Darren Clarke (NI)	522350

9	Jarmo Sandelin (Swe)	449379
10	Angel Cabrera (Arg)	444894

MOST WINS IN A SEASON

7 = Flory van Donck (1953)
(included five national Opens)
Norman von Nida (1947)
6 = Seve Ballesteros (1986)
Nick Faldo (1992)
(includes 'approved' events:
Toyota World Matchplay and
Johnnie Walker World Championship)
Colin Montgomerie (1999)
(includes 'approved' event:
Cisco World Matchplay)
5 = Seve Ballesteros (1988)
Nick Faldo (1983)
Bernard Hunt (1963)
Bobby Locke (1854)
Norman von Nida (1948)
Ian Woosnam (1987)
(includes 'approved' event:
Suntory World Matchplay)
Ian Woosnam (1990)
(includes 'approved' event:
Suntory World Matchplay)

LOWEST SCORING

18 Holes

60 Darren Clarke, *(The) European Newspaper Monte Carlo Open, 1992*
  Paul Curry, *Bells Scottish Open, 1992*
  Baldovino Dassu, *Swiss Open, 1971*
  Bernhard Langer*, *Linde German Masters, 1997*
  David Llewellyn, *AGF Biarritz Open, 1988*
  Johan Rystrom, *(The) European Newspaper Monte Carlo Open, 1992*
  Jamie Spence*, *Canon European Masters, 1992*
  Ian Woosnam, *Torras Monte Carlo Open, 1990*
  *Both 12 under par

72 holes

258 David Llewellyn, *AGF Biarritz Open, 1988*
  Ian Woosnam, *Torras Monte Carlo Open, 1990*
259 Mark McNulty*, *German Open, 1987*
260 Mike Clayton, *Timex Open, 1984*
  Colin Montgomerie, *Canon European Masters, 1996*

Peter Senior, *Johnnie Walker Monte Carlo Open, 1987*
Ian Woosnam, *Panasonic European Open, 1988*
261 Jerry Anderson, *Ebel European Masters - Swiss Open, 1984*

25 under par

The Satellite tour was introduced in 1986 and the first formal Order of Merit compiled three years later. In 1990 it was renamed the Challenge Tour. Initially, the Top 5 in the Order of Merit qualified automatically for the PGA European Tour. This was increased to the Top 10 in 1991, and Top 15 from 1996. Moreover, the number of players who don't have to pre-qualify for the Qualifying School has been increased over the years, so by 1999, those who finished between places 16 and 45 won automatic places at the School. It is a feature of the Challenge Tour to break new ground by taking quality golf tournaments to places so far not visited by the main Tour. In 1996, events were staged in Russia and Poland; the following year, Turkey and Slovenia. As in the case of its US elder cousin, players have made it to the top of the game through the Challenge Tour, as the following tables bear out; but, on the downside, nearly half of those who have qualified have susbsequently lost their cards. Others, because of a lofty Challenge Tour ranking, have made the most of the few main Tour invitations that come their way. David Park, in 1999, was a classic case in point. He finished 29th on the Challenge Tour in 1998 and gained an invite to the Moroccan Open. He nearly beat Greg Norman's 1977 record when the Australian won on only his second time out; but agonisingly succumbed to Miguel Angel Martin only at the sixth play-off hole. His endeavours brought him a further invitation the following week, where he duly pocketed the winner's cheque at the Compaq European Grand Prix, and tied Greg's 22-year old record.

AUTOMATIC QUALIFIERS ANNUALLY TO THE PGA EUROPEAN TOUR

1989

1	Neal Briggs (Eng)
2	Peter Smith (Sco)
3	Costantino Rocca (Ita)
4	Silvio Grappasonni (Ita)
5	Roger Sabarros (Fra)

1990

1	Giuseppe Cali (Ita)
2	Eoghan O'Connell (Ire)
3	David James (Eng)
4	Mikail Hoegberg (Swe)
5	Quentin Dabson (Fra)

1991

1	David R Jones (Eng)
2	Jonathan Sewell (Eng)
3	Roger Winchester (Eng)
4	John McHenry (Ire)
5	Jeremy Robinson (Eng)
6	Eric Giraud (Fra)
7	Chris Platts (Eng)
8	Silvio Grappasonni (Ita)
9	Heinz Peter Thul (Ger)
10	Jorge Berendt (Arg)

1992

1	Paul Affleck (Wal)
2	Michel Besanceney (Fra)
3	Paul Eales (Eng)
4	Nick Godin (Eng)
5	Craig Cassells (Eng)
6	Pierre Fulke (Swe)
7	Mikael Krantz (Swe)
8	Anders Gilner (Swe)
9	Jeremy Robinson (Eng)
10	Roy Mackenzie (Chi)

1993

1	Klas Eriksson (Swe)
2	Jean Louis Guepy (Fra)
3	Jonathan Lomas (Eng)
4	Gordon Manson (Sco)
5	Frederic Regard (Fra)
6	Frederik Larsson (Swe)
7	Olle Nordberg (Swe)
8	Charles Raulerson (US)
9	Niclas Fasth (Swe)
10	Ignacio Garrido (Sp)

1994

1	Raymond Burns (NI)
2	Jon Robson (Eng)
3	Michael Campbell (NZ)
4	Michael Archer (Eng)
5	Neal Briggs (Eng)
6	John Bickerton (Eng)
7	Mats Hallberg (Swe)
8	Stuart Cage (Eng)
9	Jarmo Sandelin (Swe)
10	Daniel Westermark (Swe)

1995

CHALLENGE TOUR

1	Thomas Bjorn (Den)
2	Tim Planchin (Fra)
3	Diego Borrego (Sp)
4	Eric Giraud (Fra)
5	Simon Hurley (Eng)
6	Per Nyman (Swe)
7	Emanuele Bolognesi (Ita)
8	Francisco Valera (Sp)
9	Ricky Willison (Eng)
10	Stephen Field (Eng)

1996

1	Ian Garbutt (Eng)
2	Dennis Edlund (Swe)
3	Robert Lee (Eng)
4	Andrew Sandywell (Eng)
5	Massimo Florioli (Ita)
6	Van Phillips (Eng)
7	Frederik Jacobson (Swe)
8	Joakim Rask (Swe)
9	Ignacio Feliu (Sp)
10	Adam Mednick (Swe)
11	John Mellor (Eng)
12	Carl Watts (Eng)
13	Stephen Scahill (Aus)
14	Marten Olander (Swe)
15	Kalle Vainola (Swe)

1997

1	Michele Reale (Ita)
2	Kalle Brink (Swe)
3	Greg Chalmers (Aus)
4	Raphael Jacquelin (Fra)
5	Anssi Kankkolen (Fin)
6	Nicolas Joakimides (Fra)
7	David Lynn (Eng)
8	Steen Tinning (Den)
9	Knut Storgaard (Den)
10	Craig Hainline (US)
11	Stephen Leaney (Aus)
12	Heinz Peter Thul (Ger)
13	Nicolas van Hootegem (Bel)
14	Soren Kjeldsen (Den)
15	Bradley Dredge (Wal)

1998

1	Warren Bennett (Eng)
2	Per Nyman (Swe)
3	Massimo Scarpa (Ita)
4	Roger Winchester (Eng)
5	Ricardo Gonzalez (Arg)
6	John Bickerton (Eng)
7	John Mellor (Eng)
8	Fredrik Lindgren (Swe)
9	John Senden (Aus)
10	Soren Hansen (Den)
11	Max Anglert (Swe)
12	Jorge Berendt (Arg)
13	Christopher Hanell (Swe)
14	Stephen Gallacher (Sco)
15	Daren Lee (Eng)

1999

1	Carl Suneson (Sp)
2	Iain Pyman (Eng)
3	Markus Brier (Aus)
4	Gustavo Rojas (Arg)
5	Stephen Scahill (Aus)
6	Hennie Otto (RSA)
7	Maarten Lafeber (Hol)
8	Bradley Dredge (Wal)
9	Benoit Teilleria (Fra)
10	Lucas Parsons (Aus)
11	Didier de Vooght (Bel)
12	Knud Storgaard (Den)
13	Philip Golding (Eng)
14	Johan Skold (Swe)
15	Greig Hutcheon (Sco)

MOST WINS ON SATELLITE/CHALLENGE TOUR

7	Warren Bennett
5 =	Adam Mednick
	Per Nyman
	Jeremy Robinson
4 =	Kevin Carissimi (US)
	Dennis Edlund
	Niclas Fasth
	Nick Godin
	Simon Hurley
	Mikail Krantz
	Mats Lanner (Swe)

Mark Litton (Wal)
Frederik Larsson
Erol Simsek (Ger)
Carl Suneson
3 = Thomas Bjorn
Michael Campbell
Jose Cantero (Arg)
Alex Cjeka (Ger)
Andrew Collison
Klas Eriksson
Ignacio Feliu
Anders Gilner
Philip Golding
Mats Hallberg
Peter Hedblom (Swe)
Anssi Kankkonen
Jonathan Lomas
John McHenry
Magnus Persson (Swe)
Joakim Rask
Heinz Peter Thul

As always in the wake of US innovation, it took a while for a Seniors tour to get under way in the UK. The senior members of the PGA had had their own closed championship since 1957, but it was another thirty years before a long-awaited Seniors Open came to fruition, and the first 'Tour' event arrived as late as 1990. It took another two years for the first Order of Merit compilation to be made. Since then, without attracting enormous galleries or prize money on an American scale, the tour has only just ticked over, waiting, no doubt, for the arrival within the next five years of James, Clark, Torrance and perhaps Ballesteros. Within the decade, Langer, Lyle, Faldo and Woosnam will all be eligible, but will the European Tour for Seniors have what it takes to attract the greats? In order to push on, some of these names one feels will have to get involved. The real star of the Tour to date has been Tommy Horton, who has turned the tables on many regarded as his betters in the prime of their lives, and walked off with the Order of Merit, the John Jacobs Trophy, five times in the eight years of its existence, including the last four years in a row. It has to be fair though to say that Tommy's competition has not always been out of the top drawer. A scan down the lists below may induce a heckle from the gallery, 'Same old faces'!

THE JOHN JACOBS TROPHY (ORDER OF MERIT)

1992
		£
1	John Fourie (RSA)	47856
2	Tommy Horton (Eng)	
3	Neil Coles (Eng)	
4	Peter Butler (Eng)	
5	Brian Huggett (Wal)	
6	David Butler (Eng)	
7	Tony Grubb (Eng)	
8	Bobby Verwey (RSA)	
9	Michael Murphy (Ire)	
10	Christy O'Connor, Sr (Ire)	

1993
1	Tommy Horton	56935
2	Brian Huggett	
3	Bobby Verwey	
4	Brian Waites (Eng)	
5	John Fourie	
6	Tony Grubb	
7	Peter Butler	
8	David Butler	
9	Neil Coles	
10	Michael Murphy	

1994
1	John Morgan (Eng)	57209
2	Brian Huggett	
3	Tommy Horton	
4	Malcolm Gregson (Eng)	
5	Antonio Garrido (Sp)	
6	Liam Higgins (Ire)	
7	Renato Compagnoli (Ita)	
8	Brian Waites	
9	Neil Coles	
10	Doug Dalziel (US)	

1995
1	Brian Barnes (Sco)	63620
2	John Morgan	
3	Brian Huggett	
4	Tommy Horton	
5	Neil Coles	
6	Antonio Garrido	
7	Malcolm Gregson	
8	Alberto Croce (Ita)	

1996
1	Tommy Horton	133195
2	John Morgan	
3	Malcolm Gregson	
4	Noel Ratcliffe (Aus)	
5	David Oakley (US)	
6	Antonio Garrido	
7	Maurice Bembridge (Eng)	
8	Bobby Verwey	
9	Brian Huggett	
10	Neil Coles	

1997
1	Tommy Horton	158427
2	Noel Ratcliffe	
3	Antonio Garrido	
4	Brian Waites	
5	Jim Rhodes (Eng)	
6	Malcolm Gregson	
7	Jose-Maria Canizares (Sp)	
8	David Creamer (Eng)	
9	Maurice Bembridge	
10	Ian Richardson (Eng)	

1998

1	Tommy Horton	127656
2	Brian Huggett	
3	Eddie Polland (NI)	
4	David Jones (NI)	
5	Noel Ratcliffe	
6	Jim Rhodes	
7	Bobby Verwey	
8	Neil Coles	
9	Denis O'Sullivan (Ire)	
10	Brian Waites	

1999

1	Tommy Horton	138943
2	Eddie Polland	
3	Jerry Bruner (US)	
4	Neil Coles	
5	Alan Tapie (US)	
6	Antonio Garrido	
7	Bill Brask (US)	
8	Ross Metherell (Aus)	
9	David Jones (NI)	
10	David Oakley	

MOST WINS ON TOUR (SINCE 1989)

22	Tommy Horton
9	Brian Huggett
7	Neil Coles
6 =	John Morgan
	Brian Waites
5	Bobby Verwey
4	Gary Player
3 =	Malcolm Gregson
	Liam Higgins

MOST PRESTIGIOUS EVENTS

Senior British Open

1987	Neil Coles	Turnberry	279
1988	Gary Player	Turnberry	272
1989	Bob Charles	Turnberry	269
1990	Gary Player	Turnberry	280
1991	Bobby Verwey	R Lytham & St Annes	285
1992	John Fourie	R Lytham & St Annes	282
1993	Bob Charles	R Lytham & St Annes	291
1994	Tom Wargo	Royal Portrush	281
1995	Brian Barnes	Royal Portrush	277
1996	Brian Barnes	Royal Portrush	278
1997	Gary Player	Royal Portrush	283
1998	Brian Huggett	Royal Portrush	283
1999	Christy O'Connor, Jr	Royal Portrush	282

Most Wins

3	Gary Player
2	Brian Barnes, Bob Charles, Brian Huggett

The Belfry PGA Seniors Championship
54 holes until 1967, in 1987 and between 1993-95; otherwise 72 holes

Teachers PGA Seniors Classic

1957	John Burton
1958	Norman Sutton
1959	Arthur Lees
1960	Reg Horne
1961	Sam King
1962	Sam King
1963	G Evans
1964	Syd Scott
1965	Charlie Ward
1966	Dai Rees
1967	John Panton
1968	Max Faulkner

Pringle PGA Seniors Championship

1969	John Panton
1970	Max Faulkner
1971	Kel Nagle
1972	Ken Bousfield
1973	Kel Nagle
1974	Eric Lester

Ben Sayers & Allied Hotels PGA Seniors Championship

1975	Kel Nagle
1976	Christy O'Connor, Sr

Cambridgeshie Hotel Hotels PGA Seniors Championship

1977	Christy O'Connor, Sr
1978	Paddy Skerritt
1979	Christy O'Connor, Sr
1980	Paddy Skerritt

Forte Hotels PGA Seniors Championship

1981	Christy O'Connor, Sr
1982	Christy O'Connor, Sr
1983	Christy O'Connor, Sr

1984	E Jones
1985	Neil Coles
1986	Neil Coles
1987	Neil Coles
1988	Peter Thomson
1989	Neil Coles
1990	Brian Waites
1991	Brian Waites
1992	Tommy Horton
1993	Brian Huggett
1994	John Morgan
1995	John Morgan

The Belfry Hotels PGA Seniors Championship

1996	Terry Gale
1997	Walter Hall
1998	Tommy Horton
1999	Ross Metherell

Most Wins

6	Christy O'Connor, Sr
4	Neil Coles

ENERGIS WENTWORTH SENIOR MASTERS

Shell Wentworth Senior Masters

1997	Gary Player

Schroder Wentworth Senior Masters

1998	Brian Huggett

Energis Wentworth Senior Masters

1999	Neil Coles

Most wins

No multiple winners

It is a sign of the times that the British Amateur Championship is not now regarded as one of the world's premier golfing events. Until World War Two, and, arguably for a time after, it was revered alongside the Open Championship, and integral to any aspiring American amateur who aimed for those erstwhile Grand Slam factors, the cutely-named 'Little Slam', of the US and British titles. Already by that time, however, the British amateur was not the force he was, in both quality and quantity. After the belatedly acknowledged inaugural Championship at Hoylake in 1885, players of the calibre of John Ball, Harold Hilton, Horace Hutchinson, Johnny Laidlay and the tragic Freddie Tait (killed in the Boer War), were a real scourge of the pros in the Open Championship; but their heyday was to end, as many other things did, with the Great War. The American influence was starting to take place as early as 1904, when the naturalised Australian Walter Travis won with the secret weapon, the middle-shafted Schenectady putter, banned by the R&A in 1910 and only allowed again after World War Two. But it was the advent of the Walker Cup and Bobby Jones in the 1920s which heralded the total eclipse of the British amateur, and gradually the Amateur Championship.

After the Jones victory in 1930, a series of outstanding US amateurs picked up the title more often on sporadic visits straddling the War than the home players did trying year-in, year-out. Lawson Little achieved the Little Slam uniquely in consecutive years: Charlie Yates, still involved in the Masters administration until quite recently, won at Troon in 1938; the fourth Turnesa brother, Willie, at Carnoustie; and twice Open runner-up Frank Stranahan at St George's and St Andrews. For Britain during this period, Cyril Tolley had notched up two wins, and Phil Perkins looked a world-beater and went to the States where his pro career was curtailed by injury. Otherwise, there was little to offer in the way of a sustained British defence. Even the well-respected Roger Wethered only won once. During the fifties, Irishman Joe Carr bravely collected the title twice, but you could usually tell when the Walker Cup was played at home as the draw for the Amateur championship's latter stages was punctuated with parentheses carrying 'USA'. Then in 1961, a Corinthian of the stature of those of yore emerged. Michael Bonallack was easily the best British amateur of the post-War era, and arguably the best in the entire twentieth century. By 1971, he had won five times, and probably should have won more. Immersed in the administration of the game, Bonallack went on to become, rather incongruously – and certainly uniquely – Chairman of the British PGA in 1976 and Secretary of the R&A between 1983 and 1998, the year in which he was knighted. Had he played more frequently, there was every chance of his emulating the immortal Jones in collecting the Open Championship on one of his beloved links courses: he was certainly good enough. Bonallack apart, there was no further icon upon which to build regular hopes. Peter McEvoy was easily the most enduring.

When the Walker Cup was not scheduled alongside the Amateur Championship on the calendar after 1981, the Americans stopped coming in quantity, and the quality of competition was eroded somewhat. The Jay Sigel-Scott Hoch final of 1979 at Hillside was the last real transatlantic blast. But the emergence of some quality home pros in the making, and the gradual influence of European amateurs was in evidence thereafter, and that has no doubt helped to retain the status of the competition in a world perspective. Philip Parkin oozed class when he won in 1983, but injury and other things nipped a promising future in the bud: the 1984 final could have been a World Matchplay Final a decade and a half on. The winner of the title still has super rewards. He gains automatic entry to the Open and, somewhat nostalgically, to the Masters, thanks to the Bob Jones connection. Sometimes, though, the expectancy to go on a build a great career, now almost always as a pro, is too high. Look at Gordon Sherry. The 1995 winner went on to do well in the Scottish Open and the Open, was part of the successful Walker Cup win at Porthcawl, but on turning pro after a disastrous Masters in 1996, he has really gone nowhere. Sometimes, just sometimes, though, it is the final amateur accolade before moving on to something even bigger. Ask Sergio Garcia.

WINNERS AND BEATEN FINALISTS

(GB & Ireland, unless stated)

Matchplay over 36 holes

1885	Allan Macfie beat Horace Hutchinson, 7&6
1886	Horace Hutchinson beat Henry Lamb, 7&6
1887	Horace Hutchinson beat John Ball, Jr, 1 hole
1988	John Ball, Jr beat Johnny Laidlay, 5&4
1889	Johnny Laidlay beat Leslie Balfour-Melville, 2&1
1990	John Ball, Jr beat Johnny Laidlay, 4&3
1891	Johnny Laidlay beat Harold Hilton, after 37
1892	John Ball, Jr beat Harold Hilton, 3&1
1893	PC Anderson beat J Laidlay, 2 holes
1894	John Ball, Jr beat S Mure Fergusson, 1 hole
1895	Leslie Balfour-Melville beat John Ball, Jr after 37
1896	Freddie Tait beat Harold Hilton, 8&7
1897	Jack Allan beat James Robb, 4&2
1898	Freddie Tait beat S Mure Fergusson, 7&5
1999	John Ball, Jr beat Freddie Tait, after 37
1900	Harold Hilton beat James Robb, 8&7
1901	Harold Hilton beat James Low, 1 hole
1902	Charles Hutchings beat SH Fry, 1 hole
1903	Robert Maxwell beat Horace Hutchison, 7&5
1904	Walter Travis (Aus/US) beat Edward (BH) Blackwell, 4&3
1905	A Barry beat Hon Osmund Scott, 3&2
1906	James Robb beat C Lingen, 4&3
1907	J Ball, Jr beat C Palmer 6&4
1908	Bertie Lassen beat HE Taylor, 7&6
1909	Robert Maxwell beat Capt CK Hutchison 1 hole
1910	John Ball, Jr beat C Aylmer, 10&9
1911	Harold Hilton beat Bertie Lassen, 4&3
1912	John Ball, Jr beat Abe Mitchell, after 38
1913	Harold Hilton beat Robert Harris, 6&5
1914	JLC Jenkins beat Charles Hezlet, 3&2

1915-19 No Championships – World War One

1920	Cyril Tolley beat Bob Gardner (US), after 37
1921	Willie Hunter, Jr (Sco/US) beat Allan Graham, 12&11
1922	Sir Ernest Holderness beat J Caven, 1 hole
1923	Roger Wethered beat Robert Harris, 7&8
1924	Sir Ernest Holderness beat Eustace Storey, 3&2
1925	Robert Harris beat K Fradgley, 3&2
1920	Jess Sweetser (US) beat A Simpson, 6&5
1927	Dr William Tweddell beat D Landale,7&6
1928	Phil Perkins beat Roger Wethered, 6&4

1929	Cyril Tolley beat J Smith, 4&3
1930	Bobby Jones (US) beat Roger Wethered, 7&6
1931	E Smith beat John de Forest, 1 hole
1932	John de Forest beat E Fiddian, 3&1
1933	Hon Michael Scott beat Dale Bourn, 4&3
1934	Lawson Little (US) beat J Wallace, 14&13
1935	Lawson Little (US) beat Dr William Tweddell, 1 hole
1936	Hector Thomson beat Jim Ferrier (Aus), 2 holes
1937	Bob Sweeny, Jr (US) beat Lionel Munn, 3&2
1938	Charlie Yates (US) beat Cecil Ewing, 3&2
1939	Alex Kyle beat Tony Duncan, 2&1

1940-45 No Championships – World War Two

1946	Jimmy Bruen beat Bob Sweeny Jr, 4&3
1947	Willie Turnesa (US) beat Dick Chapman (US), 3&2
1948	Frank Stranahan (US) beat Charlie Stowe, 5&4
1949	Max McCready beat Willie Turnesa (US), 2&1
1950	Frank Stranahan (US) beat Dick Chapman (US), 8&6
1951	R Chapman (US) beat Charles R Coe (US), 5&4
1952	E Harvie Ward, Jr (US) beat Frank Stranahan (US), 6&5
1953	Joe Carr beat E Harvie Ward (USA), 2 holes
1954	Doug Bachli (Aus) beat Bill Campbell (US) 2&1
1955	Joe Conrad (US) beat Alan Slater, 3&2
1956	John Beharrell beat Leslie Taylor, 5&4
1957	Reid Jack beat Harold Ridgley (US), 2&1
1958	Joe Carr beat Alan Thirlwell, 3&2
1959	Deane Beman (US) beat Bill Hyndman (US), 3&2
1960	Joe Carr beat Bob Cochran (US), 8&7
1961	Michael Bonallack beat Jimmy Walker, 6&4
1962	Richard Davies (US) beat John Povall, 1 hole
1963	Micahel Lunt beat John Blackwell, 2&1
1964	Gordon Clark beat Michael Lunt, after 39
1965	Micahel Bonallack beat Clive Clark, 2&1
1966	Bobby Cole (RSA) beat Ronnie Shade, 3&2
1967	Bob Dickson (US) beat Ron Cerrudo (US), 2&1
1968	Michael Bonallack beat Joe Carr, 7&6
1969	Michael Bonallack beat Bill Hyndman (US), 3&2
1970	Michael Bonallack beat Bill Hyndman (US), 8&7
1971	Steve Melnyk (US) beat Jim Simons (US), 3&2
1972	Trevor Homer beat Alan Thirlwell, 4&3
1973	Dicj Siderowf (US) beat Peter Moody, 5&3
1974	Trevor Homer beat Jim Gabrielsen (US), 2 holes
1975	Marvin Giles III (US) beat Mark James, 8&7
1976	Bob Siderowf (US) beat John Davies, after 37
1977	Peter McEvoy beat H Campbell, 5&4
1978	Peter McEvoy beat P McKeller, 4&3

1979	Jay Sigel (US) beat Scott Hoch (US) 3&2
1980	Duncan Evans beat D Suddards (RSA) 4&3
1981	P Ploujoux (Fra) beat J Hirsch (US), 4&2
1982	M Thompson beat A Stubbs, 4&3
1983	Philip Parkin beat Jim Holtgrieve (US) 5&4
1984	Jose-Maria Olazabal (Sp) beat Colin Montgomerie, 5&4
1985	G McGimpsey beat C Homewood, 8&7
1986	D Curry beat G Birtwell, 11&9
1987	P Mayo beat Peter McEvoy 3&1
1988	C Hardin (Swe) beat B Fouchee (RSA), 1 hole
1989	Stephen Dodd beat C Cassells, 5&3
1990	Rolf Muntz (Hol) beat A Macara, 7&6
1991	Gary Wolstenholme beat Bob May (US), 8&6
1992	S Dundas beat Bradley Dredge, 7&6
1993	Iain Pyman beat P Page after 37
1994	L James beat Gordon Sherry 2&1
1995	Gordon Sherry beat M Reynard 7&6
1996	W Bladon beat R Bearnes, 1 hole
1997	Craig Watson beat Trevor Immelman (RSA), 3&2
1998	Sergio Garcia (Sp) beat Craig Williams 7&6
1999	Graeme Storm beat Aran Wainwright, 7&6

* 18-hole Final

Most wins

8	John Ball, Jr
5	Michael Bonallack

British and European lady golfers were, unsurprisingly, not as well-organised as their US conterparts, and really until quite recently the only golf being played was amateur. The early days were dominated by Lady Margaret Scott, the Hezlet sisters and the likes of all-round sportswoman, Olympic archery silver-medallist and multiple Wimbledon Champion, Lottie Dod. The French, too, were taking an interest and Thione de la Chaume, who would soon marry into the famous sporting and sportswear Lacoste family, won the Ladies Open Amateur Championship in 1927. The memory of Joyce Wethered, she of the melifluous swing and prodigious yardage; the sad eclipse in mid-career of Pam Barton; and the endeavours of Bunty Smith in the 50s, are tinged rosy. But, to be honest, there was never much more than the parochial tweeness of the county set, or the odd European unseated aristo, lorded over as it was by the privileged.

Whether there would have been a European Tour yet without direct overseas involvement is dubious. Any ladies talented or headstrong enough to want to turn pro and make a go of it had to go through qualifying for the LPGA Tour in America, a punishing, expensive and often ignominious ordeal. Few were, and fewer did. Vivien Saunders was definitely an exception to the rule, as she was to prove many times afterwards. Indeed, the Ladies Golf Union actively discouraged professionalism, to the degree that when Saunders enquired how she went about it, she was told that by merely musing about the subject she already was deemed to be professional! By the 70s though, several US tour regulars felt ready to do some missionary work, and in addition to their US Tour ties, took in Europe for a part of the year. Already so different from those players of a generation earlier, some of these girls were like models or film stars. Indeed a few went in front of TV screens to endorse this and that. Jan Stephenson, a lissome Aussie who joined the US tour in 1974, was the most glamorous of all: golfwear suddenly became a fashion statement – females the world over took an interest, and males wondered what on earth was happening to the Royal and Ancient game. Coupled with their good looks, these girls could play a bit too, and galleries in the UK started to pick up. In the van from a playing point of view was the exceptional and bankable Nancy Lopez. Coming to Britain in 1978 and 1979 she created a stir by taking the the Colgate European Open in successive years. Suddenly sponsors were interested in

golf and Carlsberg went as far as supporting a dozen events in 1979. Other corporate help took the number of events to over thirty, and from a membership of virtually nil, the Women's Professional Golfers Association, a contradiction in terms a few years before, had almost 50 paid-up subscribers. A corollary of this was the organisation in the same year of the associated Women Professional Golfers' European Tour (WPGET), and with it the first real year of the Tour as we know it today.

Just like many things in life, golf being no exception, a fledgling venture needs a bit of luck. Francis Ouimet set golfing America and the US Open aflame; Gene Sarazen's amazing 220-yard fairway wood in 1935 turned the Augusta National Invitational, Bob Jones' semi-social off-season event, into 'The Masters'. Even established events or scenarios need that vital injection that sometimes only some bravado from, or presence of, an individual can provide. I have no doubt that if you were to ask many in golf what saved the Open Championship from oblivion, it would not be 'what', but 'who' – Arnold Palmer. Would the Ryder Cup be the mega-event it is today – would there still be a Ryder Cup – without Jack Nicklaus' intervention in 1977? Similarly the toddling Ladies' European Tour, come the age of four or five, began to look in need of some nourishment. Then along came manna from heaven, or, at least, Laura from Coventry. A natural ball-player and overt tomboy, Laura Davies took the British golf scene by storm, raising its lowly profile, and attracting the very income it so needed for survival. After the 1985 Curtis Cup she turned professional and immediately won the Order of Merit. In 1986 she won the British Open at Birkdale, and startled the Americans with her massive hitting, to finish eleventh at her first attempt in the US Open. She returned to win it the following year. British and European womens' golf seemed to take off from there. The sensational Solheim Cup victory in 1992 over the Americans at Dalmahoy was the next landmark, and the onset of such talent as Annika Sorenstam, Liselotte Neumann, Trish Johnson, Alison Nicholas and others should have guaranteed the Tour in Europe continued success. Ironically, however, it is because of these very players cherry-picking their events to play the much more lucrative US Tour, that the Tour, renamed the European Ladies PGA Tour in 1998, cannot rest on its laurels.

EUROPEAN LADIES PGA TOUR

WEETABIX WOMEN'S BRITISH OPEN

Women's British Open
1976	Jenny Lee Smith (Eng)(a)	Fulford	299

Pretty Polly Women's British Open
1977	Vivien Saunders (Eng)	Lindrick	306
1978	Janet Melville (Eng)(a)	Foxhills	310
1979	Alison Sheard (RSA)	Southport & Ain	301
1980	Debbie Massey (US)	Wentworth	294
1981	Debbie Massey (US)	Ganton	295
1982	Marta Figueras-Dotti (Sp) (a)	Royal Birkdale	296
1983		No Championship	

Hitachi Women's British Open
| 1984 | Ayako Okamoto (Jap) | Woburn | 289 |

Women's British Open
| 1985 | Betsy King (US) | Moor Park | 300 |
| 1986 | Laura Davies (Eng) | Royal Birkdale | 283 |

Weetabix Women's British Open
1987	Alison Nicholas (Eng)	St Mellion	296
1988	Corinne Dibnah (Aus)	Lindrick	295
1989	Jane Geddes (US)	Ferndown	274
1990	Helen Alfredsson (Swe)	Woburn	288
1991	Penny Grice-Whittaker (Eng)	Woburn	284
1992	Patty Sheehan (US)	Woburn	207*
1993	Karen Lunn (Aus)	Woburn	275
1994	Liselotte Neumann (Swe)	Woburn	280
1995	Karrie Webb (Aus)	Woburn	278
1996	Emilee Klein (US)	Woburn	277
1997	Karrie Webb (Aus)	Sunningdale	269
1998	Sherri Steinhauser (US)	R Lytham	292
1999	Sherri Steinhauser (US)	Woburn	283

*54 holes

Most Wins
2 Debbie Massey, Sherri Steinhauser, Karrie Webb

EUROPEAN LADIES PGA TOUR ORDER OF MERIT

1979	Catherine Panton
1980	Muriel Thomson
1981	Jenny Lee Smith
1982	Jenny Lee Smith
1983	Muriel Thomson
1984	Dale Reid
1985	Laura Davies
1986	Laura Davies
1987	Dale Reid
1988	Marie-Laure Taya
1989	Marie-Laure Taya de Lorenzi
1990	Trish Johnson
1991	Corinne Dibnah
1992	Laura Davies
1993	Karen Lunn
1994	Liselotte Neumann
1995	Annika Sorenstam
1996	Laura Davies
1997	Alison Nicholas
1998	Helen Alfredsson
1999	Laura Davies

Most Wins
| 5 | Laura Davies |
| 2 | Jenny Lee Smith, Dale Reid, Marie-Laure Taya (de Lorenzi), Muriel Thomson |

Following Greg Norman's attempt at a breakaway World Tour for golf's elite, Messrs Finchem and Schofield, along with the the heads of the other three majors tours, to wit, the International Federation of International Tours, came up with a compromise which may or may not work. In the inaugural season of 1999, three events, each worth a cool $1 million to the winner, were adapted or introduced, for those players at the top of the rankings or had qualified, or were qualifying, for the Ryder and Presidents Cups, repectively. This, of course, produced two very similar fields. Apart from the Andersen Consulting Matchplay, the events were relatively successful in turnout, popularity and quality. Problems may lie ahead however in just those areas that a Norman tour would have hit – clashes with domestic events and some event locations themselves. Already the 2001 Andersen Consulting, to be held at Royal Melbourne over the first weekend of the New Year, is not at all popular with those northern hemisphere pros for whom traditionally this is still a family time. The Americans are just disgruntled with having to traipse to Australia: mind you, some would only play in the British Open if was held in Florida.

After no one in the World's Top 20 survived the vagaries of matchplay into the final two days, the Sunday at La Costa, with respect to Jeff Maggert, Andrew Magee, John Huston and Steve Pate, was a disappointingly low-key affair. Maggert's reSolve was the strongest and he held out for his first win. Thereafter things went very much to form as Tiger Woods entered a purple patch not witnessed since Hogan's heyday of 1948. Between the WGC NEC Invitational at the end of August to February 2000, the Tiger won all seven events he entered, which included the third part of the WGC trilogy at Valderrama.

WGC EVENTS 1999

ANDERSON CONSULTING MATCHPLAY CHAMPIONSHIP

VENUE:	La Costa Resort & Spa
LOCATION:	Carlsbad, California
DATE:	24-28 February
QUALIFYING:	64 Top-ranked players in the World
ROUNDS/HOLES:	R1,2,3,QF, 18holes; SF,F, 36 holes
WINNER'S PURSE:	$1000000
FINAL:	JEFF MAGGERT
	beat
	ANDREW MAGEE, after 37
3rd/4th PLAY-OFF	John Huston
	beat
	Steve Pate, 5&4

Round by Round Details

(Figures in brackets the then Official World Ranking position)

ROUND 1

Tiger Woods (1) beat Nick Faldo (64), 4&3; Bob Tway (33) beat Tom Watson (32), 6&4; Craig Parry (49) beat Jesper Parnevik (16), 1 up; Stewart Cink (48) beat Payne Stewart (17), 3&2; Vijay Singh (8) beat Rocco Mediate (57), 5&3; Bernhard Langer (25) beat Brad Faxon (40), 4&2; Nick Price (9) beat Frankie Minoza (56); 4&3; JEFF MAGGERT (24), beat Fred Funk (41), 2 up; Lee Janzen (21) beat Glen Day (44), 3&2; Phil Mickelson (12) beat Joe Ozaki (53), 3&2; Greg Norman (28) beat John Cook (37), 3&2; Eduardo Romero (60) beat Lee Westwood (5), 3&2; Scott Hoch (20) beat Ian Woosnam (45), 3&2; Fred Couples (13) beat Dudley Hart (52), 2 up; Brandt Jobe (36) beat Jeff Sluman (29), 3&2; Steve Pate (61) beat Davis Love III (4), 1 up; Michael Bradley (62) beat Mark O'Meara (3), 4&2; Jose-Maria Olazabal (30) beat Billy Mayfair (35), 5&3; Steve Jones (51) beat Steve Elkington (14), 2&1; Scott Verplank (46) beat Tom Lehman (19), 3&1; Craig Stadler (59) beat Colin Montgomerie (6), 5&3; John Huston (27) beat Bob Estes (38), 3&2; Patrik Sjoland (54) beat Jim Furyk (11), 5&3; Carlos Franco (43) beat Mark Calcavecchia (22), 2&1; Shigeki Maruyama (42) beat Steve Stricker (23), 3&2; Justin Leonard (10) beat Miguel Jimenez (55), 4&3; Loren Roberts (39) beat Hal Sutton (26), 5&4; Paul Azinger (58) beat Ernie Els (7), 1 up;

Thomas Bjorn (47) beat Brian Watts (18), 1 up; ANDREW MAGEE (50) beat Darren Clarke (15), 1 up; Bill Glasson (34) beat Stuart Appleby (31); 2&1; David Duval (2) beat Stephen Leaney (63), 2&1

ROUND 2 (Last 32)
Woods beat Tway, 1 up
Cink beat Parry, 3&2
Langer beat Singh, 2&1
MAGGERT beat Price, 1 up
Mickelson beat Janzen, 2&1
Romero beat Norman, after 21
Couples beat Hoch, 1 up
Pate beat jobe, 1 up
Olazabal beat Bradley, 2&1
Jones beat Verplank, 5&4
Huston beat Sadler, 3&2
Sjoland beat Franco, 1 up
Maruyama beat Leonard, 4&2
Roberts beat Azinger, 2&1
MAGEE beat Bjorn, 1 up
Glasson beat Duval, 2&1

ROUND THREE (Last 16)
Woods beat Cink, 2&1
MAGGERT beat Langer, 1 up
Romero beat Mickelson, 2&1
Pate by Couples, 1 up
Olazabal beat Jones, 1 up
Huston beat Sjoland, 1 up
Maruyama beat Roberts, 2&1
MAGEE beat Glasson, 2&1

QUARTER FINAL (Last 8)
MAGGERT beat Woods, 2&1
Pate beat Romero, 3&2
Huston beat Olazabal, 2&1
MAGEE beat Maruyama, 1 up

SEMI FINAL (Last 4)
MAGGERT beat Pate, 1 up
MAGEE beat Huston, 3&1

NEC INVITATIONAL

	VENUE:	Firestone CC				
	LOCATION:	Akron, Ohio				
	DATE:	26-29 August				
	YARDAGE:	7139				
	PAR:	70 (280)				
	WINNER'S PURSE:	$1000000				
1	TIGER WOODS	66	71	62	71	270
2	Phil Mickelson	69	67	70	65	271
3 =	Craig Parry	71	66	69	69	275
	Nick Price	67	69	68	71	275
5	Ernie Els	71	69	67	69	276
6	Shigeki Maruyama	72	67	70	68	277
7 =	Carlos Franco	68	67	70	73	278
	Sergio Garcia	67	70	69	72	278
	Jeff Maggert	71	67	69	71	278
10 =	Jim Furyk	67	72	69	71	279
	Davis Love III	68	69	70	72	279
12 =	Mark Calcavecchia	68	69	73	70	280
	Padraig Harrington	72	67	70	71	280
	Steve Pate	69	71	68	72	280
15 =	Fred Couples	71	70	63	77	281
	Tom Lehman	67	72	67	75	281
	Vijay Singh	71	67	72	71	281
	Payne Stewart	70	67	69	75	281
	Hal Sutton	69	67	72	73	281
20	Justin Leonard	73	68	69	72	282

AMERICAN EXPRESS CHAMPIONSHIP

	VENUE:	Valderrama GC				
	LOCATION:	Sotogrande, Spain				
	DATE:	4-7 November				
	YARDAGE:	6830				
	PAR:	71 (284)				
	WINNER'S PURSE:	$1000000				
1	TIGER WOODS*	71	69	70	68	278
2	Miguel Jimenez	72	68	69	69	278
3	Dudley Hart	75	68	70	70	283
4 =	Stewart Cink	75	65	71	73	284
	Nick Price	69	71	70	74	284
	Lee Westwood	73	67	71	73	284
7 =	Fred Funk	71	68	74	72	285
	Sergio Garcia	74	69	69	73	285
	Scott Hoch	69	70	72	74	285
	Chris Perry	70	67	72	76	285

11 =	Bob Estes	69	72	72	73	286
	Jim Furyk	68	73	71	74	286
	Justin Leonard	71	67	72	76	286
	Jose-Maria Olazabal	73	69	69	75	286
	David Toms	72	68	71	75	286
16 =	Tim Herron	71	66	75	75	287
	Davis Love III	74	70	73	70	287
	Vijay Singh	67	71	75	74	287
19	Hal Sutton	75	66	69	78	288
20 =	Bob May	77	69	74	69	289
	Colin Montgomerie	70	72	72	75	289
	Craig Parry	72	73	71	73	289
	Dennis Paulson	76	71	68	74	289
	Jarmo Sandelin	70	74	75	70	289

Tiger Woods beat Miguel Jiminez at the 1st extra hole of
the sudden-death Play-off

CISCO WORLD MATCHPLAY CHAMPIONSHIP

*Mark McCormack-inspired invitational at Wentworth;
originally 8 players; now 16*

Piccadilly World Matchplay

1964	Arnold Palmer beat Neil Coles, 2&1
1965	Gary Player beat Peter Thomson, 3&2
1966	Gary Player beat Jack Nicklaus, 6&4
1967	Arnold Palmer beat Peter Thomson, 1 up
1968	Gary Player beat Bob Charles, 1 up
1969	Bob Charles beat Gene Littler, after 37
1970	Jack Nicklaus beat Lee Trevino, 2&1
1971	Gary Player beat Jack Nicklaus, 5&4
1972	Tom Weiskopf beat Lee Trevino, 4&3
1973	Gary Player beat Graham Marsh, after 40
1974	Hale Irwin beat Gary Player, 3&1
1975	Hale Irwin beat Al Geiberger, 4&2
1976	David Graham beat Hale Irwin, after 38

Colgate World Matchplay

1977	Graham Marsh beat Ray Floyd, 5&3
1978	Isao Aoki beat Simon Owen, 3&2

Suntory World Matchplay

1979	Bill Rogers beat Isao Aoki, 1 up
1980	Greg Norman beat Sandy Lyle, 1 up
1981	Seve Ballesteros beat Ben Crenshaw, 1 up
1982	Seve Ballesteros beat Sandy Lyle, after 37
1983	Greg Norman beat Nick Faldo, 3&2
1984	Seve Ballesteros beat Bernhard Langer, 2&1
1985	Seve Ballesteros beat Bernhard Langer, 6&5
1986	Greg Norman beat Sandy Lyle, 2&1
1987	Ian Woosnam beat Sandy Lyle, 1 up
1988	Sandy Lyle beat Nick Faldo, 2&1
1989	Nick Faldo beat Ian Woosnam, 1 up
1990	Ian Woosnam beat Mark McNulty, 4&2

Toyota World Matchplay

1991	Seve Ballesteros beat Nick Price, 3&2
1992	Nick Faldo beat Jeff Sluman, 8&7
1993	Corey Pavin beat Nick Faldo, 1 up
1994	Ernie Els beat Colin Montgomerie, 4&2
1995	Ernie Els beat Steve Elkington, 3&1
1996	Ernie Els beat Vijay Singh, 3&2
1997	Vijay Singh beat Ernie Els, 1 up

Cisco World Matchplay

1998	Mark O'Meara beat Tiger Woods, 1 up
1999	Colin Montgomerie beat Mark O'Meara, 3&2

Most Wins

5	Seve Ballesteros, Gary Player
3	Ernie Els, Greg Norman

There are several Heath Robinson concoctions about, and in the main they do not work. Anything so convoluted goes against the natural grain. For decades the Ryder Cup was an anachronistic nod to the historical roots of the game, due, sooner rather than later, to fail completely and quietly go away. Pure desperation, surely, that Europeans were invited into the 'competition' in 1979, to buy the ailing embarrassment just a few more years. In two decades, however, it has become one of golf's glittering prizes, and on a world scale for team events, perhaps only behind the soccer World Cup in importance and esteem. The main reason is an uncommon bond amongst the Europeans, which historically, racially, linguistically, they shouldn't have. The only true European Union, perhaps.

Never ones to miss an opportunity, the PGA of America saw dollar signs while others in the game just wondered at this chemistry. On the premise that so many of the world's great players were ineligible for the Ryder Cup, they launched the Presidents Cup to be played between the US and anybody else in the world who didn't fit into any neat compartment; and to be played in those lonely, fallow, alternate years when the Ryder Cup wasn't being contested. Fair enough, it gave Greg Norman and Nick Price and others a belated opportunity to play on a world stage previously denied them; but it is noticeable that this chance was not around when the Ryder Cup was not profitable. Even the name seems like a strained attempt to give the tournament some credibility and that certain *je ne sais quoi.* Gerald Ford presided over the first matches, and George Bush in 1996. However, when the 'others', the international Team, hosted the 1998 event in Australia, they could only come up with a prime minister, John Howard, to perform the role.

Predictably, the US ran away with the first event, but that special ingredient — is it really America-bashing, perhaps? — that you get when you throw together a disparate bunch of Antipodeans, a few Asiatics and the odd Latino, started to kick in again and the visitors came close in the 1996 matches. Just as had happened in Europe, the team without the apparent common denominator gelled much better than the US, and after the 1998 matches, they were sent home soundly beaten.

MATCH RESULTS

1994

	VENUE:	Robert Trent Jones GC
	LOCATION:	Lake Manassas, Virginia
DATE:		16-18 September
	CAPTAINS:	US – Hale Irwin (playing)
		International - David Graham (non-playing)
	RESULT:	US 20, INTERNATIONAL 8

Day 1 Four-balls and Foursomes

US 7½	International 2½

Day 2 Four-balls and Foursomes

US 4½ (12)	International 5½ (8)

Day 3 Singles

US 8 (20)	International 4 (12)

TEAMS (Scores W-L-H)

US	International
Fred Couples (3-0-0)	Robert Allenby (Aus, 1-4-0)
Jim Gallagher, Jr (3-1-1)	Fulton Allem (RSA, 1-3-1)
Jay Haas (3-2-0)	Steve Elkington (Aus, 2-2-1)
Scott Hoch (2-1-1)	David Frost (RSA, 1-2-1)
John Huston (1-3-0)	Bradley Hughes (Aus, 1-3-0)
Hale Irwin (2-1-0)	Mark McNulty (Zim, 1-2-1)
Tom Lehman (2-2-1)	Frank Nobilo (NZ, 1-3-1)
Davis Love III (4-0-1)	Craig Parry (Aus, 2-3-0)
Jeff Maggert (2-2-0)	Nick Price (Zim, 0-2-2)
Phil Mickelson (2-1-2)	Peter Senior (Aus, 2-1-0)
Corey Pavin (2-2-1)	Vijay Singh (Fij, 3-1-1)
Loren Roberts (2-1-1)	Tsukasa Watanabe (Jap, 1-2-0)

1996

VENUE:	Robert Trent Jones GC
LOCATION:	Lake Manassas, Virginia
DATE:	13-15 September
CAPTAINS:	US - Arnold Palmer (non-playing)
	International - Peter Thomson
	(non- playing)
RESULT:	US 16½, INTERNATIONAL 8½

Day 1 Fourballs and Foursomes
US 7½   International 2½

Day Fourballs and Foursomes
US 3 (10½)   International 7 (9½)

Day 3 Singles
US 6 (16½)   International 6 (15½)

TEAMS (Scores W-L-H)

US	International
Mark Brooks (0-3-0)	Robert Allenby (1-4-0)
Fred Couples (3-1-0)	Steve Elkington (3-2-0)
David Duval (4-0-0)	Ernie Els (RSA, 3-1-1)
Scott Hoch (3-1-0)	David Frost (2-1-0)
Tom Lehman (1-4-0)	Mark McNulty (2-2-1)
Justin Leonard (1-3-0)	Frank Nobilo (2-3-0)
Davis Love III (4-0-1)	Greg Norman (Aus, 3-2-0)
Phil Mickelson (1-2-1)	Jumbo Ozaki (Jap, 1-2-0)
Mark O'Meara (5-0-0)	Craig Parry (1-2-0)
Corey Pavin (1-3-1)	Nick Price (2-3-0)
Kenny Perry (2-2-0)	Peter Senior (1-2-0)
Steve Stricker (2-3-0)	Vijay Singh (2-3-0)

1998

VENUE:	Royal Melbourne GC
LOCATION:	Melbourne, Australia
DATE:	11-13 December
CAPTAINS:	US – Jack Nicklaus (non-playing)
	International - Peter Thomson
	(non-playing)
RESULT:	INTERNATIONAL 20½, US 11½

Day 1 Foursomes and Fourballs
International 7   US 3

Day 2 Foursomes and Fourballs
International 7½ (14½)   US 2½ (5½)

Day 3 Singles
US 6 (20½)   International 6 (11½)

TEAMS (Scores W-L-H)

International	US
Stuart Appleby (Aus, 2-1-1)	Mark Calcavecchia (1-1-2)
Steve Elkington (3-0-2)	Fred Couples (2-2-1)
Ernie Els (3-1-1)	David Duval (0-4-1)
Carlos Franco (Par, 0-2-1)	Jim Furyk (1-3-0)
Shigeki Maruyama (Jap, 5-0-0)	Scott Hoch (2-2-0)
Frank Nobilo (2-2-0)	John Huston (0-4-0)
Greg Norman (3-1-1)	Lee Janzen (1-1-2)
Joe Ozaki (Jap, 2-1-0)	Justin Leonard (0-3-1)
Craig Parry (3-1-0)	Davis Love III (1-3-1)
Nick Price (2-1-2)	Phil Mickelson (0-2-2)
Vijay Singh (3-1-1)	Mark O'Meara (2-2-0)
Greg Turner (NZ, 2-1-1)	Tiger Woods (2-3-0)

SeriesPosition

US	2
International Team	1

Best Performances
(% of Points to Matches – min 5 points)
A/M = Appearances/Matches

	A/M	W	L	H	Pts	%
SHIGEKI MARUYAMA	1/5	5	0	0	5	100
Mark O'Meara	2/9	7	2	0	7	77.8
Fred Couples	3/12	8	3	1	8½	70.8
Ernie Els	2/10	6	2	2	7	70
Greg Norman	2/10	6	3	1	6½	65
Steve Elkington	3/15	8	4	3	9½	63.3
Scott Hoch	3/12	7	4	1	7½	62.5
Davis Love III	3/15	8	5	2	9	60
Vijay Singh	3/15	8	5	2	9	60
Craig Parry	3/12	6	6	0	6	50

Originally the Dunhill Nations Cup. Mark McCormack-inspired 16 international team invitational; played at St Andrews, matches head-to-head medal strokeplay, lowest scorer winning. Knock-out until 1991, then mini-leagues, 4x4.

1985	AUSTRALIA	3-0	US
	David Graham		Ray Floyd
	Graham Marsh		Mark O'Meara
	Greg Norman		Curtis Strange

1986	AUSTRALIA	3-0	JAPAN
	Rodger Davis		Tommy Nakajima
	David Graham		Jet Ozaki
	Greg Norman		Joe Ozaki

1987	ENGLAND	2-1	SCOTLAND
	Gordon (J) Brand, Sr		Gordon Brand, Jr
	Howard Clark		Sandy Lyle
	Nick Faldo		Sam Torrance

1988	IRELAND	2-1	AUSTRALIA
	Eamonn Darcy		Rodger Davis
	Ronan Rafferty		David Graham
	Des Smyth		Greg Norman

1989	US	3½-2½*	JAPAN
	Mark Calcavecchia		Hajime Meshiai
	Tom Kite		Joe Ozaki
	Curtis Strange		Koichi Suzuki

1990	IRELAND	3½-2½*	ENGLAND
	David Feherty		Richard Boxhall
	Ronan Rafferty		Howard Clark
	Philip Walton		Mark James

1991	SWEDEN	2-1	S AFRICA
	Anders Forsbrand		John Bland
	Per-Ulrik Johansson		David Frost
	Mats Lanner		Gary Player

1992	ENGLAND	2½-½	SCOTLAND
	David Gilford		Gordon Brand, Jr
	Steven Richardson		Sandy Lyle
	Jamie Spence		Colin Montgomerie

1993	US	2-1	ENGLAND
	Fred Couples		Peter Baker
	John Daly		Nick Faldo
	Payne Stewart		Mark James

1994	CANADA	2-1	US
	Dave Barr		Fred Couples
	Rick Gibson		Tom Kite
	Ray Stewart		Curtis Strange

1995	SCOTLAND	2-1	ZIMBABWE
	Andrew Coltart		Tony Johnstone
	Colin Montgomerie		Mark McNulty
	Sanm Torrance		Nick Price

1996	US	2-1	NEW ZEALAND
	Phil Mickelson		Frank Nobilo
	Mark O'Meara		Greg Turner
	Steve Stricker		Grant Waite

1997	S AFRICA	3-0	SWEDEN
	Ernie Els		Joakim Haeggman
	David Frost		Per-Ulrik Johansson
	Retief Goosen		Jesper Parnevik

1998	S AFRICA	3-0	SPAIN
	Ernie Els		Santiago Luna
	David Frost		Miguel Jimenez
	Retief Goosen		Jose-Maria Olazabal

1999	SPAIN	2-1	AUSTRALIA
	Sergio Garcia		Stephen Leaney
	Miguel Jimenez		Peter O'Malley
	Jose-Maris Olazabal		Craig Parry

* All players played two matches in the Final

Most Wins		
2		Australia, England, Ireland, South Africa, US

The Alfred Dunhill Cup may never have got a look in if the World Cup, originally the Canada Cup, during the near half-century of its existence, had been as consistent in reality as it always has been in its ideals. It was devised by a Canadian-based industrialist-cum-philanthropist (golf history seems littered with them; but without them whither golf today?) who in 1953 felt that the time was right to introduce a truly universal team competition. It has been, and still is, the only genuine world 'open' in golf, and less-developed golfing nations send their teams in Olympian fashion just to compete; and have even hosted the event from time to time. Contrary to this missionary and all-embracing zeal, some of the more powerful nations, depending on the calendar slot, or just how the weight of the event was perceived at the time, would scour the membership sending out 'Would anyone like to play?' messages; whereas at other times, ageing ambassadors were called upon (the US twosome which lifted the Cup in 1961 had a combined age of 100!); or, incongruously, walking legends were conscripted.

Much of the above, of course, is aimed at the US, who could probably field one of a dozen duos which on paper would be good enough to win the Cup; but it was because of their seriousness during the nineties that the event has become realtively revered once more. For four consecutive years the pairing of Couples and Love won for the States, and that lifted the stock of the event very considerably. There has been talk about its eventual revamping (currently two players whose 72-hole strokeplay aggregate score is counted; with a parallel individual competiton, the International Trophy), and incorporation within the World Golf Championships.

WORLD CUP RESULTS

Canada Cup

Team	Individual	Venue

1953
ARGENTINA, 287* Antonio Cerda (140) Beaconsfield,
Antonio Cerda   Montreal, Canada
Roberto de Vicenzo

1954
AUSTRALIA, 556 Stan Leonard (Can, 275) Laval-sur-Lac,
Kel Nagle   Montreal, Canada
Peter Thomson

1955
US, 560   Ed Furgol (279)   Columbia,
Ed Furgol   Washington, USA
Chick Harbert

1956
US, 567   Ben Hogan (277)   Wentworth,
Ben Hogan   Surrey, England
Sam Snead

1957
JAPAN, 557   Torakichi Nakamura (274)Kasumigaseki,
Torakichi Nakamura   Tokyo, Japan
Koichi Ono

1958
IRELAND, 579   Angel Miguel (Sp, 286) Club de Golf,
Harry Bradshaw   Mexico City, Mexico
Christy O'Connor, Sr
1959
AUSTRALIA, 563   Stan Leonard (Can, 275)   Royal
Kel Nagle   Melbourne,
Peter Thomson   Melbourne, Australia

1960
US, 565   Flory van Donck (Bel, 279)   Portmarnock,
Arnold Palmer   Dublin, Ireland

1961
US, 560   Sam Snead (272)   Dorado Beach,
\Jimmy Demaret   Puerto Rico
Sam Snead

1962
US, 557   R de Vicenzo (Arg, 276) Jockey Club,
Arnold Palmer   Buenos Aires, Argentina
Sam Snead

1963
US, 482***   Jack Nicklaus (237***)   St Nom-la-
Jack Nicklaus   Breteche,
Arnold Palmer   Paris, France

1964
US, 554   Jack Nicklaus (276)   Kasnapali,
Jack Nicklaus   Hawaii, USA
Arnold Palmer

1965
SOUTH AFRICA, 554 Gary Player (281) Club de Campo,
Harold Henning   Madrid, Spain
Gary Player

1966
US, 548   George Knudson (Can, 272) Yomiuri,
Jack Nicklaus   Tokyo, Japan
Arnold Palmer

World Cup of Golf

1967
US, 557   Arnold Palmer (276)   Club de Golf,
Jack Nicklaus   Mexico City, Mexico
Arnold Palmer

1968
CANADA, 569   Al Balding (274)   Olgiata,
Al Balding   Rome, Italy
George Knudson

1969
US, 552   Lee Trevino (275)   Singapore Island,
Orville Moody   Singapore
Lee Trevino

1970
AUSTRALIA, 544   R de Vicenzo (Arg, 269) Jockey Club,
Bruce Devlin   Buenos Aires, Argentina
David Graham

1971
US, 555   Jack Nicklaus (271)   Palm Beach,
Jack Nicklaus   Florida, USA
Lee Trevino

1972
TAIWAN, 438**   Hsieh Min Nan (217)Royal Melbourne,
Hsieh Min Nan   Melbourne, Australia
Lu Liang-Huan

1973
US, 558   Johnny Miller (277)Neuva Andalucia'
Johnny Miller   Spain
Jack Nicklaus

1974
SOUTH AFRICA, 554   Bobby Cole (271)   Caracas,
Bobby Cole   Venezuela
Dale Hayes

1975
US, 554   Johnny Miller (275)   Navatanee,
Lou Graham   Bangkok, Thailand
Johnny Miller

1976
SPAIN, 574   Ernesto Acosta (Mex, 282)   Palm
Seve Ballesteros   Springs,
Manuel Pinero   California, USA

1977
SPAIN, 591   Gary Player (RSA, 289)   Wack Wack,
Seve Ballesteros   Manila, Philippines
Antonio Garrido

1978
US, 564   John Mahaffey (281)   Princeville,
John Mahaffey   Hawaii, USA
Andy North

1979
US, 575   Hale Irwin (285)   Glyfada,
Hale Irwin   Greece
John Mahaffey

1980
CANADA, 572   Sandy Lyle (Sco, 282)   El Rimcon,
Dan Halldorson   Bogota, Colombia
Jim Nelford

1981
No Event

1982
SPAIN, 563   Manuel Pinero (281) Pierre Marques,
Jose-Maria Canizares   Acapulco, Mexico
Manuel Pinero

1983
US, 565   Dave Barr (Can, 276)   Pondok Indah,
Rex Caldwell   Indonesia
John Cook

1984
SPAIN, 414**   J-M Canizares (205**)   Ogliata,
Jose-Maria Canizares   Rome, Italy
Jose Rivero

1985
CANADA, 559   Howard Clark (Eng, 272)   La Quinta,
Dave Barr   California, USA
Dan Halldorson

1986
No Event

1987

WALES, 574   Ian Woosnam (274)   Kapalua,
David Llewellyn   Hawaii, USA
Ian Woosnam

1988

US, 560   Ben Crenshaw (275)Royal Melbourne,
Ben Crenshaw   Melbourne, Australia
Mark McCumber

World Cup of Golf by Philip Morris

1989

AUSTRALIA, 278* Peter Fowler (137*)   Las Brisas,
Peter Fowler   Spain
Wayne Grady

World Cup of Golf by Kraft General Foods

1990

GERMANY, 556   Payne Stewart (US, 271)   Grand
Bernhard Langer   Cypress,
Torsten Giedeon   Florida, USA

World Cup of Golf by Philip Morris

1991

SWEDEN, 563   Ian Woosnam (Wal, 273)   La Querce,
Anders Forsbrand   Rome, Italy
Per-Ulrik Johansson

1992

US, 548   Brett Ogle (Aus, 270)   La Moraleja,
Fred Couples   Spain
Davis Love III

World Cup of Golf by Heineken

1993

US, 556   Bernhard Langer (Ger, 272)Lake Nona,
Fred Couples   Florida, USA
Davis Love III

1994

US, 536   Fred Couples (265)   Dorado Beach,
Fred Couples   Puerto Rico
Davis Love III

1995

US, 543   Davis Love III (267)   Mission Hills,
           Fred Couples   Shenzheng, China
           Davis Love III

1996

SOUTH AFRICA, 547   Ernie Els (272)   Erinvale,
Ernie Els   South Africa
Wayne Westner

World Cup of Golf

1997

IRELAND, 545   C Montgomerie (Sco, 266)   Kiawah
Padraig Harrington   Island,
                                  South Carolina, USA

1998

ENGLAND, 568   Scott Verplank (US, 279)Gulf Habour,
David Carter   New Zealand
Nick Faldo

1999

US, 545   Tiger Woods (263)   Mines Resort,
Mark O'Meara   Kuala Lumpur, Malaysia
Tiger Woods
* 36 Holes   ** 54 Holes   *** 63 Holes

Most Team Wins

22	US
4	Australia, Spain

Most Wins as a Pairing

4	Fred Couples/Davis Love III, Jack Nicklaus/Arnold Palmer
2	Kel Nagle/Peter Thomson, Arnold Palmer/Sam Snead

Most Wins by an Individual

6	Jack Nicklaus, Arnold Palmer
4	Fred Couples, Davis Love III, Sam Snead

Most International Trophy Wins

3	Jack Nicklaus
2	Roberto de Vicenzo, Stan Leonard, Johnny Miller, Gary Player, Ian Woosnam

Record Low Team Score

536	US (1996)
543	US (1995)

Record Low Individual Score

263	Tiger Woods (US, 1999)
265	Fred Couples (US, 1994)

Back in the days when amateur golfers were regarded as superior to the professionals on course as well as off it (well, at the end of World War One, the US Open had been claimed since 1913 by Francis Ouimet, Jerome Travers and Chick Evans), the USGA felt it was opportune to initiate some grand international gala of amateur golf. Golf had formed part of the Olympics in 1900 and 1904, when the eccentric Canadian George Lyon beat twice-US Amateur Champion, Chandler Egan, 3&2 in the final. (Lyon picked up a club for the first time at 38, after being, among other things, Canadian Pole Vault champion, and having a personal best as a batsman in cricket of 238 not out. He finished runner up in the 1906 US Amateur to little Eben Byers when he was 44, and when he collected the Gold Medal at the St Louis Games, he made his approach to the podium by walking on his hands! Where *have* all the characters gone?). It all fell apart in London in 1908, though, when the British players pulled out over a dispute, and golf has not been represented in anger at the Olympics since. Then in 1920, USGA President, George Herbert Walker, offered a trophy for all those nations who wanted to compete for it in the United States; but nobody bothered. Then after an impromptu 'international' match set up by a group of Americans, including the aforementioned Evans and Ouimet (before the British Amateur at Hoylake), gave people the taste for such a competition, the R&A, in an unprecedented rush of blood, threw down the gauntlet and proposed to send a team to the US in 1922 to challenge for Mr Walker's cup. It could have been *Boy's Own* stuff when GB captain Robert Harris took sick and, rather than selecting a replacement from their own ranks, they appointed *The Times* correspondent Bernard Darwin. Darwin was such a force within the British game as an observer; so that, and playing off scratch, made him the obvious choice. He promptly put down his pen and beat US Captain Bill Fownes in his singles match. Alas, the story didn't have a happy ending – and not for the last time: Darwin's new-found colleagues couldn't match their skipper's feat and the team went down 8-4. The format for all the other team matchplay events, both amateur and professional, emanated from that first series in New York.

From the very beginning, at least until fairly recent times, the anachronism of amateur sport in a modern context cannot have been better embodied than in the Walker Cup (except, perhaps, the Curtis Cup). It sounds like a Mony Python sketch – who in their right minds

would want to come back to be massacred every two years? – 'I've come back to be massacred please.' 'Certainly sir, that will be half a crown.' But that's what used to happen. The sheer volume of excellent amateurs from the early days, through the great Bobby Jones to post-war giants like Nicklaus and Woods, made the Walker Cup one of the most one-sided regular events in all sport. All done in the Corinthian ethic of the playing of the game. The sheer patience of the Americans is awe-inspiring, if positively head-scratching, but in the end, and this is where the world is completely daft, it has been rewarding for us all. The last decade or so has at last thrown up some decent competition and really excellent sporting occasions – remember Tiger and Co lashed by the Bristol Channel and an inspired home team at Porthcawl? But after such a history, surely the massacres will continue once more, and probably sooner rather than later.

WALKER CUP MATCH RESULTS

(Including some of the more interesting participants in selected years)

1922

US 8, GB&I 4 NGL of America
(US – Jesse Guilford, Francis Ouimet, Chick Evans, Jess Sweetser, Bobby Jones; GB – Bernard Darwin (by default!), Roger Wethered, Cyril Tolley)

1923

GB&I 5½, US 6½ St Andrews

1924

US 9, GB&I 3 Garden City
(GB – Hon Michael Scott, Charles Hezlet)

1926

GB&I 5½, US 6½ St Andrews
(US – George Von Elm)

1928

US 11, GB&I 1 Chicago
(GB – Dr William Tweddell, Phil Perkins)

1930

GB&I 2, US 10 Royal St George's

1932

US 9½,   GB&I 2½   Brookline

1934

GB 2½,   US 9½ St Andrews

(US – Johnny Goodman, Lawson Little)

1936

US 10½,   GB 1½   Pine Valley

(US – Charlie Yates)

1938

GB&I 7½,   US 4½   St Andrews

(GB – Jimmy Bruen; US – Bud Ward, Chuck
Kocsis, Fred Haas)

1940-46

No Matches – World War Two

1947

GB&I 4,   US 8   St Andrews

(GB – Joe Carr, Gerald Micklem, Laddie Lucas; US
– Skee Riegel, Willie Turnesa, Frank Stranahan,
Smiley Quick)

1949

US 10,   GB&I 2   Winged Foot

1951

GB&I 4½,   US 7½   Birkdale

(US – Sam Urzetta, Charles R Coe)

1953

US 9,   GB&I 3   Kittansett

(US – Gene Littler, Ken Venturi)

1955

GB&I 2,   US 10   St Andrews

(US – Billy Joe Patton)

1957

US 8½,   GB&I 3½   Minikahda

(US – Bill Hyndman, Hillman Robbins, Jr, Mason
Rudolph; GB – Reid Jack, Doug Sewell, Guy
Wolstenholme)

1959

GB&I 3,   US 9   Muirfield

(GB – Michael Bonallack; US – Tommy Aaron,
Deane Beman, Jack Nicklaus)

1961

US 11,   GB&I 1   Seattle

(GB – Ronnie Shade)

1963

GB&I 10, US   8   Turnberry

1965

US 12,   GB&I 12   Baltimore

(US – Dave Eichelberger; GB – Clive Clark,
Rodney Foster, Peter Townsend)

1967

GB&I 9,   US 15   Royal St George's

(US – Bob Murphy; GB – Peter Oosterhuis)

1969

US 13,   GB&I 11   Milwaukee

(US – Marvin Giles III, Bruce Fleisher, Steve
Melnyk, Lanny Wadkins; GB – Peter Tupling, Bruce
Critchley)

1971

GB&I 13,   US 11   St Andrews

(GB – Warren Humphreys, Roddy Carr; US – Tom
Kite)

1973

US 14,   GB&I 10   Brookline

(US – Gary Koch, Bill Rogers; GB – Howard Clark)

1975

GB&I 8½,   US 15½   St Andrews

(GB – Mark James, Martin Poxon; US – Jerry
Pate, Curtis Strange, George Burns, Craig Stadler)

1977

US 16,   GB&I 8   Shinnecock Hills

(US – Jay Sigel, Lindy Miller, Vance Heafner, John
Fought;
GB – Sandy Lyle, Peter McEvoy)

1979

GB&I 8½,   US 15½   Muirfield

(GB – Gordon Brand, Jr, Brian Marchbank; US –
Scott Hoch, Hal Sutton)

1981

US 15,　GB&I 9　　　　　　　Cypress Point
(US – Jodie Mudd, Corey Pavin; GB – Roger
Chapman, Philip Walton, Paul Way, Ronan
Rafferty)

1983

GB&I 10½,　US 13½　　　　Royal Liverpool
(US – Brad Faxon, Nat Crosby, Rick Fehr, Willie
Wood; GB – Andrew Oldcorn, Philip Parkin)

1985

US 13,　GB&I 11　　　　　　Pine Valley
(US – Duffy Waldorf, Scott Verplank, Sam
Randolph, Jay Haas, Davis Love III; GB – Colin
Montgomerie, Peter Baker, David Gilford)

1987

GB&I 7½,　US 16½　　　　　Sunningdale
(US – Billy Mayfair, Billy Andrade)

1989

US 11½,　GB&I 12½　　　　Peachtree
(US – Robert Gamez, Phil Mickelson; GB – Russell
Claydon)

1991 GB&I 10,　US 14　　　　　　Portmarnock
(GB – Jim Payne, Andrew Coltart, Gary Evans,
Paul McGinley; US – David Duval, Bob May. Tom
Scherrer)

1993 US 19,　GB&I 5　　　　　　Interlachen
(US – David Berganio, Tim Herron, Justin
Leonard; GB – Iain Pyman, Padraig Harrington,
Bradley Dredge, Van Phillips, Raymond Russell)

1995

GB&I 14,　US 10　　　　　Royal Porthcawl
(GB – Gordon Sherry, Stephen Gallacher, Gary
Wolstenholme; US – Notah Begay III, Tiger
Woods)

1997

US 18,　GB&I 6　　　　　　Quaker Bridge
(GB – Justin Rose, Keith Nolan, David Park)

1999

GB&I 15,　US 9　　　　　　　Nairn
(GB – Graeme Storm, Philip Rowe, Luke Donald,
Paul Casey)

Series Position

US	31 wins
GB&I	5
Tie	1

Most Points

Jay Sigel (US)	20½

Most Appearances

Joe Carr (GB&I)	10

In 1989, the creator of Ping golf equipment, the Norwegian Karsten Solheim, decided that the world now needed a Ryder Cup equivalent for which the burgeoning Ladies' Tours could compete. The timing was very shrewd, as was much in Solheim's life, for European lady golfers who could actually take on the Americans on a level playing field were now being discovered, not once in a blue moon, but in significant numbers. The format and ultra-confusing qualifying rules are similar to those begat by the competition for men. Sadly, Karsten Solheim's death has been announced as I write, aged 88, but he surely has left golf more than one legacy.

MATCH RESULTS

1990

VENUE:	Lake Nona GC
LOCATION:	Orlando, Florida
DATE:	16-18 November
CAPTAINS:	US – Kathy Whitworth (non-playing)
	Europe – Mickey Walker (non-playing)
RESULT:	US 11½, Europe 4½

Day 1 Foursomes

US 3	Europe 1

Day 2 Fourballs

US 3 (6)	Europe 1 (2)

Day 3 Singles

US 5½ (11½)	Europe 2½ (4½)

TEAMS (Scores W-L-H)

US	Europe
Pat Bradley (2-1-0)	Helen Alfredsson (0-3-0)
Beth Daniel (3-0-0)	Laura Davies (2-1-0)
Cathy Gerring (2-1-0)	Marie-Laure de Lorenzi (0-3-0)
Rosie Jones (2-1-0)	Trish Johnson (0-3-0)
Betsy King (2-0-1)	Liselotte Neumann (1-2-0)
Nancy Lopez (2-1-0)	Alison Nicholas (1-2-0)
Dottie Mochrie (2-1-0)	Dale Reid (1-2-0)
Patty Sheehan (2-1-0)	Pamela Wright (1-1-1)

1992

VENUE:	Dalmahoy Hotel G & CC
LOCATION:	Edinburgh, Scotland
DATE:	2-4 October
CAPTAINS:	US – Kathy Whitworth (non-playing)
	Europe – Mickey Walker (non-playing)
RESULT:	Europe 11½, US 6½

Day 1 Foursomes

Europe 2½	US 1½

Day 2 Fourballs

Europe 2 (4½)	US 2 (3½)

Day 3 Singles

Europe 7 (11½)	US 3 (6½)

TEAMS (Scores W-L-H)

Europe	US
Helen Alfredsson (2-0-1)	Danielle Ammaccapane (1-1-0)
Laura Davies (3-0-0)	Pat Bradley (0-2-1)
Florence Descampe (0-2-1)	Brandie Burton (0-1-1)
Kitrina Douglas (0-1-0)	Beth Daniel (1-1-0)
Trish Johnson (1-1-1)	Juli Inkster (1-1-1)
Liselotte Neumann (2-0-1)	Betsy King (1-2-0)
Alison Nicholas (2-1-0)	Meg Mallon (2-1-0)
Catrin Nilsmark (1-0-0)	Dottie Mochrie (0-2-1)
Dale Reid (1-1-1)	Deb Richard (1-1-1)
Pamela Wright (1-1-1)	Patty Sheehan (0-2-1)

1994

VENUE:	The Greenbrier
LOCATION:	White Sulphur Springs, West Virginia
DATE:	21-23 October
CAPTAINS:	US – JoAnne Carner (non-playing)
	Europe – Mickey Walker (non-playing)
RESULT:	US 13, Europe 7

Day 1 Foursomes

US 2   Europe 3

Day 2 Fourballs

US 3 (5)   Europe 2 (5)

Day 3 Singles

US 8 (13)   Europe 2 (7)

TEAMS (Scores W-L-H)

US	Europe
Donna Andrews (2-1-0)	Helen Alfredsson (2-1-0)
Brandie Burton (3-0-0)	Laura Davies (1-2-0)
Beth Daniel (2-1-0)	Lora Fairclough (2-1-0)
Tammie Green (1-2-0)	Trish Johnson (0-3-0)
Betsy King (1-2-0)	Liselotte Neumann (1-2-0)
Meg Mallon (2-1-0)	Alison Nicholas (2-1-0)
Dottie Mochrie (3-0-0)	Catrin Nilsmark (1-2-0)
Kelly Robbins (1-2-0)	Dale Reid (2-1-0)
Patty Sheehan (1-2-0)	Annika Sorenstam (1-2-0)
Sherri Steinhauer (2-1-0)	Pamela Wright (0-3-0)

1996

VENUE:	St Pierre Hotel & GC
LOCATION:	Chepstow, Wales
DATE:	20-22 September
CAPTAINS:	US – Judy Rankin (non-playing)
	Europe – Mickey Walker (non-playing)
RESULT:	Europe 11, US 17

Day 1 Foursomes and Fourballs

Europe 3   US 5

Day 2 Foursomes and Fourballs

Europe 6 (9)   US 2 (7)

Day 3 Singles

Europe 2 (11)   US 10 (17)

TEAMS (Scores W-L-H)

Europe	US
Helen Alfredsson (1-2-1)	Pat Bradley (0-2-0)
Laura Davies (3-2-0)	Brandie Burton (2-1-0)
Marie-Laure de Lorenzi (1-3-0)	Beth Daniel (1-1-2)
Lisa Hackney (1-1-0)	Jane Geddes (1-2-1)
Trish Johnson (1-1-1)	Rosie Jones (2-1-0)
Kathryn Marshall (1-1-1)	Betsy King (3-0-0)
Joanne Morley (0-2-0)	Michelle McGann (1-1-1)
Liselotte Neumann (1-2-2)	Meg Mallon (1-0-4)
Alison Nicholas (1-1-2)	Dottie (Mochrie) Pepper (3-1-0)
Catrin Nilsmark (2-2-0)	Kelly Robbins (1-2-2)
Dale Reid (0-2-0)	Patty Sheehan (2-2-0)
Annika Sorenstam (3-0-1)	Val Skinner (2-2-0)

1998

VENUE:	Muirfield Village GC
LOCATION:	Dublin, Ohio
DATE:	18-20 September
CAPTAINS:	US – Judy Rankin (non-playing)
	Europe – Pia Nilsson (non-playing)
RESULT:	US 16, Europe 12

Day 1 Foursomes and Fourballs
US 5½   Europe 2½

Day 2 Foursomes and Fourballs
US 5 (10½)   Europe 3 (5½)

Day 3 Singles
US 5½ (16)   Europe 6½ (12)

TEAMS (Scores W-L-H)

US	Europe
Donna Andrews (2-2-0)	Helen Alfredsson (1-3-0)
Brandie Burton (1-2-0)	Laura Davies (3-1-1)
Tammie Green (1-2-0)	Marie-Laure de Lorenzi (1-2-0)
Pat Hurst (3-1-0)	Sophie Gustafson (0-1-1)
Juli Inkster (3-1-0)	Lisa Hackney (2-2-0)
Chris Johnson (0-2-1)	Trish Johnson (0-2-0)
Rosie Jones (2-1-0)	Catriona Matthew (1-2-0)
Betsy King (0-2-1)	Liselotte Neumann (1-3-0)
Meg Mallon (2-1-1)	Alison Nicholas (0-2-0)
Dottie Pepper (3-0-0)	Catrin Nilsmark (1-2-0)
Kelly Robbins (3-0-0)	Annika Sorenstam (3-1-0)
Sherri Steinhauer (3-0-0)	Charlotta Sorenstam (1-2-1)

Series Position
US 4   Europe 1

Best Performances
(% of Points to Matches – min 5 points)
A/M = Appearances/Matches

	A/M	W	L	H	Pts	%
SHERRI STEINHAUER	2/6	5	1	0	5	83.3
Dottie (Mochrie) Pepper	5/16	11	4	1	11½	71.9
Annika Sorenstam	3/11	7	3	1	7½	68.2
Beth Daniel	4/12	7	3	2	8	66.7
Rosie Jones	3/9	6	3	0	6	66.7
Laura Davies	5/19	12	6	1	12½	65.8
Meg Mallon	4/14	7	3	4	9	64.3
Brandie Burton	4/9	5	3	1	5½	61.1
Kelly Robbins	3/11	5	4	2	6	54.5
Betsy King	5/15	7	6	2	8	53.3

Harriet and Margaret Curtis were two Boston sisters with more time and money than most to play at anything they wanted. As it happened they were both excellent sportswomen, with younger sister Margaret winning the US Open doubles title in tennis in 1908. Between them in golf they won the US Ladies Amateur Championship four times, with Margaret winning three, including the trouncing of her sister 7&6 in the 1907 final, and their rosy existence brought them across the Atlantic on frequent occasions. Often competing in Britain, they harboured the dream one day of setting up an international event between British and American teams, but before they could formalise anything, the Great War intervened. Margaret went to France to represent the Red Cross in quite an exalted position; she was awarded the *Legion d'Honneur* for her pains. Harriet stayed at home and involved herself in the suffragette movement. By the time they were able to put their thoughts to an international golf tourney again, the 20s had flown by. The men had already got such matches under way, courtesy of George Walker and Samuel Ryder, so Margaret had the format upon which to invest her money. This she eventually did, by guaranteeing the first few matches, and the series began in 1932. Just like their male counterparts, the British ladies were happy to take some horrendous beatings, and the obliging US gals were just as happy to dole it out; but as in the case of those competitions, somehow a degree of parity has almost been reached in latter years.

RESULTS

1932	GB&I	3½	US	5½	Wentworth
1934	US	6½	GB&I	2½	Chevy Chase
1936	GB&I	4½	US	4½	Gleneagles
1938	US	5½	GB&I	3½	Essex, Massachusetts
1940-1946			No Matches — World War Two		
1948	GB&I	2½	US	6½	Birkdale
1950	US	7½	GB&I	1½	Buffalo
1952	GB&I	5	US	4	Muirfield
1954	US	6	GB&I	3	Merion
1956	GB&I	5	US	4	Prince's
1958	US	4½	GB&I	4½	Brae Burn
1960	GB&I	2½	US	6½	Lindrick
1962	US	8	GB&I	1	Broadmoor, Colorado
1964	GB&I	7½	US	10½	Royal Porthcawl
1966	US	13	GB&I	5	Hot Springs
1968	GB&I	7½	US	10½	Royal Co Down
1970	US	11½	GB&I	6½	Brae Burn
1972	GB&I	8	US	10	Western Gailes
1974	US	13	GB&I	5	San Francisco
1976	GB&I	6½	US	11½	Royal Lytham
1978	US	12	GB&I	6	Apawamis
1980	GB&I	5	US	13	St Pierre
1982	US	14½	GB	3½	Denver
1984	GB&I	8½	US	9½	Muirfield
1986	US	5	GB&I	13	Prairie Dunes
1988	GB&I	11	US	7	Royal St George's
1990	US	14	GB&I	4	Somerset Hills
1992	GB&I	10	US	8	Royal Liverpool
1994	US	9	GB&I	9	Honor's
1996	GB&I	11½	US	6½	Killarney
1998	US	10	GB&I	8	Minikahda

Series Position

US	21 wins
GB&I	6
Ties	3

THE OFFICIAL WORLD GOLF RANKING

The first issue of the 'Sony' Ranking was published by Tony Greer of IMG in London on 6 April 1986. Tony still issues the Ranking weekly to this day, although in 1997 the association with Sony was ended when the major adminsitrators in Golf (the R&A, the USGA, the PGA of America and Augusta National); and the Tours (the PGA Tour, the European Tour, Japan PGA Tour, PGA Australasia Tour and the Southern Africa Tour), all ratified the Ranking for the first time.

These tables represent the Top 20 players at regular quarterly intervals since inception of the Ranking, and indicate movements up and down and in and out of the Ranking. The positions are based on results over previous seasons as well as current form: the criteria used have been adjusted over the course of the 15 years in an attempt to provide the fairest picture of players' form. Previous Quarter's positions are in brackets: (-) indicates previous position was outside the Top 50. Figures following nationality of newcomers to the Top 20 indicate the number of re-visits.

6 APRIL 1986

1	Bernhard Langer (Ger)
2	Seve Ballesteros (Sp)
3	Sandy Lyle (Sco)
4	Tom Watson (US)
5	Mark O'Meara (US)
6	Greg Norman (Aus)
7	Tommy Nakajima (Jap)
8	Hal Sutton (US)
9	Corey Pavin (US)
10	Calvin Peete (US)
11	Lanny Wadkins (US)
12	Curtis Strange (US)
13	Andy Bean (US)
14	Payne Stewart (US)
15	Craig Stadler (US)
16	Tom Kite (US)
17	Isao Aoki (Jap)
18	John Mahaffey (US)
19	Ray Floyd (US)
20	Fuzzy Zoeller (US)

Selected other positions in Top 50:

21 Lee Trevino; 23 Sam Torrance; 24 Nick Faldo; 32 Ian Woosnam; 33 Jack Nicklaus; 34 Howard Clark; 40 Ian Baker-Finch

OFFICIAL WORLD RANKING

END-JUNE 1986

1	(2)	Seve Ballesteros
2	(1)	Bernhard Langer
3	(6)	Greg Norman
4	(7)	Tommy Nakajima
5	(8)	Hal Sutton
6	(3)	Sandy Lyle
7	(5)	Mark O'Meara
8	(4)	Tom Watson
9	(12)	Curtis Strange
10	(10)	Calvin Peete
11	(13)	Andy Bean
12	(11)	Lanny Wadkins
13	(14)	Payne Stewart
14	(9)	Corey Pavin
15	(19)	Ray Floyd
16	(18)	John Mahaffey
17	(15)	Craig Stadler
18	(16)	Isao Aoki
19	(33)	Jack Nicklaus (US)
20	(16)	Tom Kite

Selected other positions in Top 50:
25(34) Howard Clark; 27(-) Bob Tway; 31(24) N Faldo; 32 (40) Ian Baker-Finch; 39(-) Rodger Davis; 41(-) Nick Price; 43(-) Mark McNulty; 46(-) Chip Beck

END-SEPTEMBER 1986

1	(3)	Greg Norman
2	(1)	Seve Ballesteros
3	(2)	Bernhard Langer
4	(4)	Tommy Nakajima
5	(7)	Mark O'Meara
6	(6)	Sandy Lyle
7	(5)	Hal Sutton
8	(12)	Lanny Wadkins
9=	(10)	Calvin Peete
	(8)	Tom Watson
11	(14)	Corey Pavin
12	(9)	Curtis Strange
13	(13)	Payne Stewart
14	(18)	Isao Aoki
15	(11)	Andy Bean
16	(27)	Bob Tway (US)
17	(20)	Tom Kite
18	(15)	Ray Floyd
19	(17)	Craig Stadler
20	(21)	Fuzzy Zoeller (US,1)

Selected other positions in Top 50:
23(19) Jack Nicklaus; 24(39) Rodger Davis; 27(-) Jumbo Ozaki; 30(36) Ian Woosnam; 36(46) David Frost; 42(-) Doug Tewell; 50(-) Ben Crenshaw

END-DECEMBER 1986

1	(1)	Greg Norman
2	(3)	Bernhard Langer
3	(2)	Seve Ballesteros
4	(4)	Tommy Nakajima
5	(15)	Andy Bean
6	(16)	Bob Tway
7	(7)	Hal Sutton
8	(12)	Curtis Strange
9	(13)	Payne Stewart
10	(5)	Mark O'Meara
11	(14)	Isao Aoki
12	(6)	Sandy Lyle
13	(9)	Calvin Peete
14	(18)	Ray Floyd
15	(8)	Lanny Wadkins
16	(17)	Tom Kite
17	(24)	Rodger Davis (Aus)
18	(9)	Tom Watson
19	(11)	Corey Pavin
20	(20)	Fuzzy Zoeller

Selected other positions in Top 50:

21(38) Mark McNulty; 37(45) Joe Ozaki; 43(-) Jose-Maria Olazabal; 46=(-) Gordon J Brand; 46=(32) Sam Torrance; 48(34) Nick Faldo

END-MARCH 1987

1	(1)	Greg Norman
2	(2)	Bernhard Langer
3	(3)	Seve Ballesteros
4	(4)	Tommy Nakajima
5	(9)	Payne Stewart
6	(12)	Sandy Lyle
7	(15)	Lanny Wadkins
8	(6)	Bob Tway
9	(19)	Corey Pavin
10	(7)	Hal Sutton
11	(11)	Isao Aoki
12	(8)	Curtis Strange
13	(5)	Andy Bean
14	(14)	Ray Floyd
15	(10)	Mark O'Meara
16	(17)	Rodger Davis
17	(16)	Tom Kite
18	(38)	Ben Crenshaw (US)
19	(18)	Tom Watson
20	(20)	Fuzzy Zoeller

Selected other positions in Top 50:

25(13) Calvin Peete; 26(25) Jack Nicklaus; 27(27) Howard Clark; 37(-) Scott Simpson; 38=(-) Chen Tze Chung; 49(-) Mark Calcavecchia; 50(-) Paul Azinger

END-JUNE 1987

1	(1)	Greg Norman
2	(3)	Seve Ballesteros
3	(2)	Bernhard Langer
4	(4)	Tommy Nakajima
5	(5)	Payne Stewart
6	(6)	Sandy Lyle
7	(7)	Lanny Wadkins
8	(12)	Curtis Strange
9	(11)	Isao Aoki
10	(35)	Larry Mize (US)
11	(37)	Scott Simpson (US)
12	(22)	Jumbo Ozaki (Jap)
13	(18)	Ben Crenshaw
14	(8)	Bob Tway
15	(21)	Mark McNulty (Zim)
16	(9)	Corey Pavin
17	(10)	Hal Sutton
18	(16)	Rodger Davis
19	(17)	Tom Kite
20	(50)	Paul Azinger (US)

Selected other positions in Top 50:

21(32) Ian Woosnam; 27(13) Andy Bean; 31(14) Ray Floyd; 33(49) Mark Calcavecchia; 35(-) Peter Senior; 37(20) Fuzzy Zoeller; 40(27) Howard Clark; 44(-) Nick Faldo; 49(-) Fred Couples

END-SEPTEMBER 1987

1	(1)	Greg Norman
2	(2)	Seve Ballesteros
3	(3)	Bernhard Langer
4	(8)	Curtis Strange
5	(5)	Payne Stewart
6	(4)	Tommy Nakajima
7	(15)	Mark McNulty
8	(6)	Sandy Lyle
9	(7)	Lanny Wadkins
10	(21)	Ian Woosnam (Wal)
11	(18)	Rodger Davis
12	(13)	Ben Crenshaw
13	(20)	Paul Azinger
14	(11)	Scott Simpson
15	(10)	Larry Mize
16	(9)	Isao Aoki
17	(19)	Tom Kite
18	(12)	Jumbo Ozaki
19	(16)	Corey Pavin
20	(44)	Nick Faldo (Eng)

Selected other positions in Top 50:

23(14) Bob Tway; 24(33) Scott Hoch;28(-) Larry Nelson; 39=(-)DA Weibring; 41(28) Ian Baker-Finch; 42(-) Gordon Brand Jr

END-DECEMBER 1987

1	(1)	Greg Norman
2	(3)	Seve Ballesteros
3	(2)	Bernhard Langer
4	(8)	Sandy Lyle
5	(4)	Curtis Strange
6	(10)	Ian Woosnam
7	(5)	Payne Stewart
8	(9)	Lanny Wadkins
9	(7)	Mark McNulty
10	(12)	Ben Crenshaw
11	(13)	Paul Azinger
12	(15)	Larry Mize
13	(11)	Rodger Davis
14	(20)	Nick Faldo
15	(6)	Tommy Nakajima
16	(26)	Tom Watson (US,1)
17	(14)	Scott Simpson
18	(18)	Jumbo Ozaki
19	(16)	Isao Aoki
20	(21)	Hal Sutton (US)

Selected other positions in Top 50:

22(39) David Ishii; 33(42) Gordon Brand Jr; 36(48) Chip Beck; 44(-) Sam Torrance; 49(43) Jose-Maria Olazabal

END-MARCH 1988

1	(1)	Greg Norman
2	(3)	Seve Ballesteros
3	(2)	Bernhard Langer
4	(8)	Sandy Lyle
5	(6)	Ian Woosnam
6	(5)	Curtis Strange
7	(10)	Ben Crenshaw
8	(11)	Paul Azinger
9	(7)	Payne Stewart
10	(14)	Nick Faldo
11	(8)	Lanny Wadkins
12	(13)	Rodger Davis
13	(23)	Larry Nelson (US)
14	(15)	Tommy Nakajima
15	(16)	Tom Watson
16	(21)	Tom Kite (US)
17	(36)	Chip Beck (US)
18	(22)	David Frost (RSA)
19	(18)	Jumbo Ozaki
20	(9)	Mark McNulty

Selected other positions in Top 50:

22(12) Larry Mize; 27(-) Mark McCumber; 33(40) Ian Baker-Finch; 35(-) Jay Haas; 37(-) Joey Sindelar; 38(-) Mike Reid; 42(-) Steve Pate; 46(24) Corey Pavin

END-JUNE 1988

1	(1)	Greg Norman
2	(4)	Sandy Lyle
3	(6)	Curtis Strange
4	(2)	Seve Ballesteros
5	(3)	Bernhard Langer
6	(10)	Nick Faldo
7	(5)	Ian Woosnam
8	(7)	Ben Crenshaw
9	(11)	Lanny Wadkins
10	(18)	David Frost
11	(8)	Paul Azinger
12	(17)	Chip Beck
13	(13)	Larry Nelson
14	(20)	Mark McNulty
15	(12)	Rodger Davis
16	(9)	Payne Stewart
17	(16)	Tom Kite
18	(25)	Scott Hoch (US)
19	(19)	Jumbo Ozaki
20	(25)	David Ishii (US)

Selected other positions in Top 50:

24(41) Mark Calcavecchia; 26(32) Mark O'Meara; 27(37) Joey Sindelar; 31(40) Fred Couples; 36(22) Larry Mize; 39(-) Ken Green; 48(36) Ray Floyd; 49(-) Ronan Rafferty

END-SEPTEMBER 1988

1	(1)	Greg Norman
2	(4)	Seve Ballesteros
3	(2)	Sandy Lyle
4	(6)	Nick Faldo
5	(3)	Curtis Strange
6	(7)	Ian Woosnam
7	(8)	Ben Crenshaw
8	(11)	Paul Azinger
9	(5)	Bernhard Langer
10	(9)	Lanny Wadkins
11	(12)	Chip Beck
12	(10)	David Frost
13	(14)	Mark McNulty
14	(24)	Mark Calcavecchia (US)
15	(16)	Payne Stewart
16	(13)	Larry Nelson
17	(17)	Tom Kite
18	(22)	Tommy Nakajima (Jap,1)
19	(42)	Jose-Maria Olazabal (Sp)
20	(23)	Tom Watson (US,2)

Selected other positions in Top 50:

21(27) Joey Sindelar; 27(35) Mike Reid; 34(45) Nick Price; 38(-) Jeff Sluman; 43(33) Gordon Brand Jr; 50(-) Mark James

END-DECEMBER 1988

1	(2)	Seve Ballesteros
2	(1)	Greg Norman
3	(3)	Sandy Lyle
4	(4)	Nick Faldo
5	(5)	Curtis Strange
6	(11)	Ben Crenshaw
7	(6)	Ian Woosnam
8	(12)	David Frost
9	(8)	Paul Azinger
10	(14)	Mark Calcavecchia
11	(22)	Jumbo Ozaki (Jap,1)
12	(11)	Chip Beck
13	(17)	Tom Kite
14	(10)	Lanny Wadkins
15	(9)	Bernhard Langer
16	(15)	Payne Stewart
17	(33)	Ken Green (US)
18	(13)	Mark McNulty
19	(26)	Fred Couples (US)
20	(19)	Jose-Maria Olazabal

Selected other positions in Top 50:
26(20) Tom Watson; 32(18) Tommy Nakajima; 37(28) Craig Stadler; 48(-) Bruce Lietzke; 49(-) Des Smyth

END-MARCH 1989

1	(1)	Seve Ballesteros
2	(2)	Greg Norman
3	(5)	Curtis Strange
4	(3)	Sandy Lyle
5	(4)	Nick Faldo
6	(13)	Tom Kite
7	(10)	Mark Clacavecchia
8	(12)	Chip Beck
9	(7)	Ian Woosnam
10	(9)	Paul Azinger
11	(6)	Ben Crenshaw
12	(20)	Jose-Maria Olazabal
13	(11)	Jumbo Ozaki
14	(8)	David Frost
15	(19)	Fred Couples
16	(14)	Lanny Wadkins
17	(23)	Larry Nelson (US,1)
18	(16)	Payne Stewart
19	(29)	Tom Watson (US,3)
20	(18)	Mark McNulty

Selected other positions in Top 50:
22(48) Bruce Lietzke; 23(15) Bernhard Langer; 25(41) Nick Price; 34(26) Mark McCumber; 41(30) Jeff Sluman; 43(-) Jose Rivero; 45(-) Steve Jones; 47(-) Bill Glasson

END-JUNE 1989

1	(1)	Seve Ballesteros
2	(5)	Nick Faldo
3	(2)	Greg Norman
4	(3)	Curtis Strange
5	(9)	Ian Woosnam
6	(6)	Tom Kite
7	(4)	Sandy Lyle
8	(12)	Jose-Maria Olazabal
9	(8)	Chip Beck
10	(7)	Mark Calcavecchia
11	(13)	Jumbo Ozaki
12	(10)	Paul Azinger
13	(15)	Fred Couples
14	(18)	Payne Stewart
15	(11)	Ben Crenshaw
16	(14)	Davis Frost
17	(17)	Larry Nelson
18	(34)	Mark McCumber (US)
19	(21)	Ken Green (US,1)
20	(23)	Bernhard Langer (Ger,1)

Selected other positions in Top 50:
25(40) Scott Hoch; 31(45) Steve Jones; 37(28) Larry Mize; 39(-) Ronan Rafferty; 41(-) Jodie Mudd; 45(-) Craig Parry; 47(-) Peter Jacobsen

END-SEPTEMBER 1989

1	(3)	Greg Norman
2	(1)	Seve Ballesteros
3	(2)	Nick Faldo
4	(4)	Curtis Strange
5	(10)	Mark Calcavecchia
6	(6)	Tom Kite
7	(14)	Payne Stewart
8	(5)	Ian Woosnam
9	(9)	Chip Beck
10	(8)	Jose-Maria Olazabal
11	(11)	Jumbo Ozaki
12	(12)	Paul Azinger
13	(7)	Sandy Lyle
14	(16)	David Frost
15	(15)	Ben Crenshaw
16	(13)	Fred Couples
17	(18)	Mark McCumber
18	(20)	Bernhard Langer
19	(21)	Tom Watson (US,4)
20	(17)	Larry Nelson

Selected other positions in Top 50:
21(26) Mike Reid; 24(45) Craig Parry; 27(39) Ronan Rafferty; 34(42) Mark James; 36(-) Wayne Grady; 39(33) Rodger Davis; 44(-) Graham Marsh; 48(-) Tim Simpson; 49(-) Sam Torrance

END-DECEMBER 1989		
1	(1)	Greg Norman
2	(3)	Nick Faldo
3	(2)	Seve Ballesteros
4	(4)	Curtis Strange
5	(7)	Payne Stewart
6	(6)	Tom Kite
7	(10)	Jose-Maria Olazabal
8	(5)	Mark Calcavecchia
9	(8)	Ian Woosnam
10	(12)	Paul Azinger
11	(9)	Chip Beck
12	(11)	Jumbo Ozaki
13	(14)	David Frost
14	(13)	Sandy Lyle
15	(16)	Fred Couples
16	(18)	Bernhard Langer
17	(15)	Ben Crenshaw
18	(17)	Mark McCumber
19	(33)	Larry Mize (US,1)
20	(19)	Tom Watson

Selected other positions in Top 50:

21(27) Ronan Rafferty; 26(46) Peter Senior; 33(25) Ken Green; 35(48) Tim Simpson; 45(-) Blaine McCallister; 48(-) Joe Ozaki

END-MARCH 1990		
1	(1)	Greg Norman
2	(2)	Nick Faldo
3	(3)	Seve Ballesteros
4	(4)	Curtis Strange
5	(8)	Mark Calcavecchia
6	(9)	Ian Woosnam
7	(10)	Paul Azinger
8	(5)	Payne Stewart
9	(7)	Jose-Maria Olazabal
10	(6)	Tom Kite
11	(12)	Jumbo Ozaki
12	(15)	Fred Couples
13	(11)	Chip Beck
14	(13)	David Frost
15	(16)	Bernhard Langer
16	(19)	Larry Mize
17	(14)	Sandy Lyle
18	(18)	Mark McCumber
19	(21)	Ronan Rafferty (NI)
20	(24)	Scott Hoch (US,1)

Selected other positions in Top 50:

21(27) Mark O'Meara; 26(49) Jodie Mudd; 27(46) Peter Jacobsen; 35(43) Rodger Davis; 42(-) Eduardo Romero; 45(-) Gil Morgan; 46(-) Ian Baker-Finch; 48(-) Brett Ogle; 49(-) Robert Gamez

END-JUNE 1990

1	(1)	Greg Norman
2	(2)	Nick Faldo
3	(9)	Jose-Maria Olazabal
4	(8)	Payne Stewart
5	(3)	Seve Ballesteros
6	(5)	Mark Calcavecchia
7	(4)	Curtis Strange
8	(7)	Paul Azinger
9	(6)	Ian Woosnam
10	(10)	Tom Kite
11	(12)	Fred Couples
12	(11)	Jumbo Ozaki
13	(15)	Bernhard Langer
14	(14)	David Frost
15	(16)	Larry Mize
16	(21)	Ben Crenshaw (US,1)
17	(19)	Ronan Rafferty
18	(13)	Chip Beck
19	(35)	Rodger Davis (Aus,1)
20	(-)	Hale Irwin (US)

Selected other positions in Top 50:

21(-) Wayne Levi; 29(42) Eduardo Romero; 31(20) Scott Hoch; 32(23) Larry Nelson; 33(18) Mark McCumber; 46(-) Mike Harwood; 47(-) Ray Floyd

END-SEPTEMBER 1990

1	(2)	Nick Faldo
2	(1)	Greg Norman
3	(3)	Jose-Maria Olazabal
4	(9)	Ian Woosnam
5	(4)	Payne Stewart
6	(8)	Paul Azinger
7	(10)	Tom Kite
8	(6)	Mark Calcavecchia
9	(5)	Seve Ballesteros
10	(11)	Fred Couples
11	(7)	Curtis Strange
12	(25)	Mark McNulty (Zim,1)
13	(12)	Jumbo Ozaki
14	(15)	Larry Mize
15	(18)	Chip Beck
16	(20)	Hale Irwin
17	(17)	Ronan Rafferty
18	(13)	Bernhard Langer
19	(21)	Wayne Levi (US)
20	(25)	Lanny Wadkins (US,1)

Selected other positions in Top 50:

21(14) David Frost; 22(27) Tim Simpson; 23(19) Rodger Davis; 25(42) Gil Morgan; 28(45) Wayne Grady; 30(40) Mark James; 31(22) Sandy Lyle; 38(23) Tom Watson; 40(-) Ian Baker-Finch; 46(32) Larry Nelson

END-DECEMBER 1990

1	(2)	Greg Norman
2	(1)	Nick Faldo
3	(3)	Jose-Maria Olazabal
4	(4)	Ian Woosnam
5	(5)	Payne Stewart
6	(6)	Paul Azinger
7	(9)	Seve Ballesteros
8	(7)	Tom Kite
9	(12)	Mark McNulty
10	(8)	Mark Calcavecchia
11	(10)	Fred Couples
12	(11)	Curtis Strange
13	(14)	Larry Mize
14	(18)	Bernhard Langer
15	(15)	Chip Beck
16	(16)	Hale Irwin
17	(13)	Jumbo Ozaki
18	(22)	Tim Simpson (US)
19	(17)	Ronan Rafferty
20	(19)	Wayne Levi

Selected other positions in Top 50:
21(20) Lanny Wadkins; 25(36) Jodie Mudd; 32(48) Mike Harwood; 41(31) Sandy Lyle; 44(-) Davis Love III; 45(29) Peter Senior; 46(-) David Feherty; 48(-) Ray Floyd; 50(-) Sam Torrance

END-MARCH 1991

1	(2)	Nick Faldo
2	(4)	Ian Woosnam
3	(3)	Jose-Maria Olazabal
4	(1)	Greg Norman
5	(5)	Payne Stewart
6	(6)	Paul Azinger
7	(9)	Mark McNulty
8	(12)	Curtis Strange
9	(14)	Bernhard Langer
10	(8)	Tom Kite
11	(7)	Seve Ballesteros
12	(21)	Lanny Wadkins (US,2)
13	(13)	Larry Mize
14	(11)	Fred Couples
15	(10)	Mark Calcavecchia
16	(17)	Jumbo Ozaki
17	(16)	Hale Irwin
18	(20)	Wayne Levi
19	(15)	Chip Beck
20	(18)	Tim Simpson

Selected other positions in Top 50:
25(37) Wayne Grady; 26(31) Mark James; 28(-) Corey Pavin; 32(43) Tom Watson; 33(44) Davis Love III; 36(49) Steve Pate; 42(-) Fuzzy Zoeller; 43(-) Steve Elkington; 46(30) Steve Jones

END-JUNE 1991

1	(2)	Ian Woosnam
2	(3)	Jose-Maria Olazabal
3	(2)	Nick Faldo
4	(4)	Greg Norman
5	(5)	Payne Stewart
6	(11)	Seve Ballesteros
7	(6)	Paul Azinger
8	(9)	Bernhard Langer
9	(14)	Fred Couples
10	(7)	Mark McNulty
11	(10)	Tom Kite
12	(17)	Hale Irwin
13	(12)	Lanny Wadkins
14	(13)	Larry Mize
15	(15)	Mark Calcavecchia
16	(16)	Jumbo Ozaki
17	(28)	Corey Pavin (US,1)
18	(19)	Chip Beck
19	(35)	Eduardo Romero (Arg)
20	(8)	Curtis Strange

Selected other positions in Top 50:
23(33) Davis Love III; 24(38) Ian Baker-Finch; 26(39) Craig Parry; 28(42) Fuzzy Zoeller; 30(23) Ronan Rafferty; 34(-) Sam Torrance; 38(24) David Frost; 40(27) Ben Crenshaw; 44(-) John Cook

END-SEPTEMBER 1991

1	(1)	Ian Woosnam
2	(2)	Jose-Maria Olazabal
3	(3)	Nick Faldo
4	(4)	Greg Norman
5	(6)	Seve Ballesteros
6	(5)	Payne Stewart
7	(9)	Fred Couples
8	(7)	Paul Azinger
9	(8)	Bernhard Langer
10	(24)	Ian Baker-Finch (Aus)
11	(10)	Mark McNulty
12	(12)	Hale Irwin
13	(13)	Lanny Wadkins
14	(11)	Tom Kite
15	(17)	Corey Pavin
16	(21)	Mark O'Meara (US,1)
17	(14)	Larry Mize
18	(16)	Jumbo Ozaki
19	(25)	Rodger Davis (Aus,2)
20	(26)	Craig Parry (Aus)

Selected other positions in Top 50:
22(46) Mike Harwood; 24(15) Mark Calcavecchia; 26(36) Nick Price; 27(48) Bruce Lietzke; 31(22) Tim Simpson; 33(-) Tom Purtzer; 35(-) Steven Richardson; 36(-) Colin Montgomerie; 44(-) John Cook

END-DECEMBER 1991

1	(1)	Ian Woosnam
2	(3)	Nick Faldo
3	(2)	Jose-Maria Olazabal
4	(5)	Seve Ballesteros
5	(4)	Greg Norman
6	(7)	Fred Couples
7	(9)	Bernhard Langer
8	(6)	Payne Stewart
9	(8)	Paul Azinger
10	(19)	Rodger Davis
11	(10)	Ian Baker-Finch
12	(11)	Mark McNulty
13	(12)	Hale Irwin
14	(16)	Mark O'Meara
15	(13)	Lanny Wadkins
16	(14)	Tom Kite
17	(20)	Craig Parry
18	(15)	Corey Pavin
19	(27)	Bruce Lietzke (US)
20	(24)	Mark Calcavecchia (US,1)

Selected other positions in Top 50:

21(32) Craig Stadler; 30(18) Jumbo Ozaki; 31(17) Larry Mize; 37(45) Mark James; 46(31) Tim Simpson; 47(-) John Daly; 49 Billy Andrade

END-MARCH 1992

1	(2)	Nick Faldo
2	(6)	Fred Couples
3	(3)	Jose-Maria Olazabal
4	(1)	Ian Woosnam
5	(4)	Seve Ballesteros
6	(7)	Bernhard Langer
7	(8)	Payne Stewart
8	(5)	Greg Norman
9	(9)	Paul Azinger
10	(12)	Mark McNulty
11	(11)	Ian Baker-Finch
12	(23)	Davis Love III
13	(14)	Mark O'Meara
14	(10)	Rodger Davis
15	(17)	Craig Parry
16	(13)	Hale Irwin
17	(43)	Ronan Rafferty (NI,1)
18	(33)	Tom Watson (US,5)
19	(18)	Corey Pavin
20	(38)	Ray Floyd (US,1)

Selected other positions in Top 50:

23(45) John Cook; 28(16) Tom Kite; 35(42) David Feherty; 40(29) Tom Purtzer; 41(32) Steven Richardson; 42(-) Mark Brooks; 43 (-) Jeff Sluman; 44(-) Jose Rivero; 47(-) Vijay Singh; 48(-) Gene Sauers

END-JUNE 1992

1	(2)	Fred Couples
2	(1)	Nick Faldo
3	(3)	Jose-Maria Olazabal
4	(4)	Ian Woosnam
5	(6)	Bernhard Langer
6	(5)	Seve Ballesteros
7	(8)	Greg Norman
8	(12)	Davis Love III
9	(9)	Paul Azinger
10	(28)	Tom Kite (US,1)
11	(13)	Mark O'Meara
12	(10)	Mark McNulty
13	(7)	Payne Stewart
14	(11)	Ian Baker-Finch
15	(20)	Ray Floyd
16	(29)	Bruce Lietzke (US,1)
17	(15)	Craig Parry
18	(14)	Rodger Davis
19	(24)	Chip Beck (US,1)
20	(23)	John Cook (US)

Selected other positions in Top 50:
23(30) Jumbo Ozaki; 24(-) Ronan Rafferty; 25(37) Colin Montgomerie; 26(-) Tony Johnstone; 27(43) Jeff Sluman; 30(18) Tom Watson; 32(50) Sandy Lyle; 40(13) Hale Irwin; 42(-) Jim Gallagher Jr; 48(-) David Gilford; 50(37) Mark James

END-SEPTEMBER 1992

1	(2)	Nick Faldo
2	(1)	Fred Couples
3	(5)	Bernhard Langer
4	(3)	Jose-Maria Olazabal
5	(4)	Ian Woosnam
6	(7)	Greg Norman
7	(9)	Paul Azinger
8	(6)	Seve Ballesteros
9	(22)	Nick Price (Zim)
10	(20)	John Cook
11	(8)	Davis Love III
12	(10)	Tom Kite
13	(12)	Mark O'Meara
14	(21)	Corey Pavin (US,2)
15	(16)	Bruce Lietzke
16	(15)	Ray Floyd
17	(23)	Jumbo Ozaki (Jap,2)
18	(12)	Mark McNulty
19	(18)	Rodger Davis
20	(13)	Payne Stewart

Selected other positions in Top 50:
22(14) Ian Baker-Finch; 25(37) Steve Elkington; 34(24) Ronan Rafferty; 36(-) Brad Faxon; 37(-) Anders Forsbrand; 42(-) Ben Crenshaw; 45(-) Dan Forsman; 48(39) Steven Richardson; 50(-) Andrew Magee

OFFICIAL WORLD RANKING

END-DECEMBER 1992

1	(1)	Nick Faldo
2	(2)	Fred Couples
3	(5)	Ian Woosnam
4	(3)	Jose-Maria Olazabal
5	(6)	Greg Norman
6	(3)	Bernhard Langer
7	(10)	John Cook
8	(9)	Nick Price
9	(7)	Paul Azinger
10	(11)	Davis Love III
11	(12)	Tom Kite
12	(13)	Mark O'Meara
13	(8)	Seve Ballesteros
14	(16)	Ray Floyd
15	(17)	Jumbo Ozaki
16	(14)	Corey Pavin
17	(15)	Bruce Lietzke
18	(25)	Steve Elkington (Aus)
19	(18)	Mark McNulty
20	(23)	Colin Montgomerie (Sco)

Selected other positions in Top 50:

26(-) David Frost; 40(-) Ernie Els; 46(-) Duffy Waldorf; 47(-) Joe Ozaki; 48(40) Mark Calcavecchia; 50(-) John Huston

END-MARCH 1993

1	(1)	Nick Faldo
2	(2)	Fred Couples
3	(8)	Nick Price
4	(5)	Greg Norman
5	(6)	Bernhard Langer
6	(3)	Ian Woosnam
7	(11)	Tom Kite
8	(4)	Jose-Maria Olazabal
9	(10)	Davis Love III
10	(9)	Paul Azinger
11	(7)	John Cook
12	(15)	Jumbo Ozaki
13	(19)	Mark McNulty
14	(12)	Mark O'Meara
15	(13)	Seve Ballesteros
16	(20)	Colin Montgomerie
17	(16)	Corey Pavin
18	(14)	Ray Floyd
19	(21)	Payne Stewart (US,1)
20	(17)	Bruce Lietzke

Selected other positions in Top 50:

23(29) Sandy Lyle; 28(38) Vijay Singh; 29(-) Ben Crenshaw; 31(-) David Gilford; 37(-) Frank Nobilo; 38(-) Larry Mize; 40(-) Mark James; 41(31) Lanny Wadkins; 44(34) Steve Pate; 45(-) Wayne Westner; 48(-) Lee Janzen; 49(-) Jay Haas

END-JUNE 1993

1	(1)	Nick Faldo
2	(5)	Bernhard Langer
3	(3)	Nick Price
4	(2)	Fred Couples
5	(4)	Greg Norman
6	(10)	Paul Azinger
7	(6)	Ian Woosnam
8	(8)	Jose-Maria Olazabal
9	(11)	John Cook
10	(7)	Tom Kite
11	(13)	Mark McNulty
12	(12)	Jumbo Ozaki
13	(9)	Davis Love III
14	(19)	Payne Stewart
15	(17)	Corey Pavin
16	(22)	Steve Elkington (Aus,1)
17	(14)	Mark O'Meara
18	(21)	David Frost (RSA,1)
19	(16)	Colin Montgomerie
20	(48)	Lee Janzen (US)

Selected other positions in Top 50:

21(28) Vijay Singh; 22(15) Seve Ballesteros; 28(40) Mark James; 34(-) David Edwards; 40(-) Rocco Mediate; 42(-) Tom Lehman; 44(-) Gordon Brand Jr; 45(33) Jeff Sluman; 46(-) Costantino Rocca; 48(-) Barry Lane

END-SEPTEMBER 1993

1	(1)	Nick Faldo
2	(5)	Greg Norman
3	(2)	Bernhard Langer
4	(3)	Nick Price
5	(6)	Paul Azinger
6	(4)	Fred Couples
7	(7)	Ian Woosnam
8	(10)	Tom Kite
9	(8)	Jose-Maria Olazabal
10	(18)	David Frost
11	(13)	Davis Love III
12	(14)	Payne Stewart
13	(9)	John Cook
14	(12)	Jumbo Ozaki
15	(15)	Corey Pavin
16	(19)	Colin Montgomerie
17	(16)	Steve Elkington
18	(17)	Mark O'Meara
19	(21)	Vijay Singh (Fij)
20	(11)	Mark McNulty

Selected other positions in Top 50:

21(20) Lee Janzen; 25(31) Peter Senior; 27(38) Tom Watson; 31(47) Larry Mize; 32(-) Sam Torrance; 33 (-) Ronan Rafferty; 43(-) Fuzzy Zoeller; 44(-) Scott Simpson; 48(-) Nolan Henke; 49(39) Anders Forsbrand

END-DECEMBER 1993

1	(1)	Nick Faldo
2	(2)	Greg Norman
3	(3)	Bernhard Langer
4	(4)	Nick Price
5	(6)	Fred Couples
6	(5)	Paul Azinger
7	(7)	Ian Woosnam
8	(8)	Tom Kite
9	(11)	Davis Love III
10	(15)	Corey Pavin
11	(10)	David Frost
12	(14)	Jumbo Ozaki
13	(12)	Payne Stewart
14	(16)	Colin Montgomerie
15	(9)	Jose-Maria Olazabal
16	(19)	Vijay Singh
17	(18)	Mark McNulty
18	(13)	John Cook
19	(17)	Steve Elkington
20	(29)	Ernie Els (RSA)

Selected other positions in Top 50:
21(31) Larry Mize; 28(18) Mark O'Meara; 29(44) Scott Simpson; 34(-) Jim Gallagher Jr; 40(24) Rodger Davis; 44(28) Craig Parry; 47(-) Phil Mickelson; 48(-) Tom Lehman; 50(-) Jeff Maggert

END-MARCH 1994

1	(2)	Greg Norman
2	(1)	Nick Faldo
3	(4)	Nick Price
4	(3)	Bernhard Langer
5	(5)	Fred Couples
6	(6)	Paul Azinger
7	(11)	David Frost
8	(7)	Ian Woosnam
9	(10)	Corey Pavin
10	(12)	Jumbo Ozaki
11	(15)	Jose-Maria Olazabal
12	(14)	Colin Montgomerie
13	(9)	Davis Love III
14	(8)	Tom Kite
15	(13)	Payne Stewart
16	(20)	Ernie Els
17	(16)	Vijay Singh
18	(46)	Fuzzy Zoeller (US,2)
19	(17)	Mark McNulty
20	(18)	John Cook

Selected other positions in Top 50:
23(30) Tony Johnstone; 25(44) Craig Parry; 27(47) Phil Mickelson; 28(50) Jeff Maggert; 36(-) John Huston; 40(24) Ray Floyd; 47(-) Loren Roberts; 49(35) Mark James

END-JUNE 1994

1	(1)	Greg Norman
2	(2)	Nick Faldo
3	(3)	Nick Price
4	(4)	Bernhard Langer
5	(5)	Fred Couples
6	(11)	Jose-Maria Olazabal
7	(16)	Ernie Els
8	(7)	David Frost
9	(12)	Colin Montgomerie
10	(6)	Paul Azinger
11	(8)	Ian Woosnam
12	(9)	Corey Pavin
13	(14)	Tom Kite
14	(10)	Jumbo Ozaki
15	(37)	Tom Lehman (US)
16	(13)	Davis Love III
17	(20)	John Cook
18	(17)	Vijay Singh
19	(19)	Mark McNulty
20	(26)	Larry Mize (US,2)

Selected other positions in Top 50:

22(47) Loren Roberts; 24(34) Brad Faxon; 26(41) Seve Ballesteros; 28(-) Hale Irwin; 30(43) Tommy Nakajima; 33(15) Payne Stewart; 45(-) Curtis Strange; 47(23) Tony Johnstone; 49(-) Ben Crenshaw; 50(-) Darren Clarke

END-SEPTEMBER 1994

1	(3)	Nick Price
2	(1)	Greg Norman
3	(2)	Nick Faldo
4	(4)	Bernhard Langer
5	(6)	Jose-Maria Olazabal
6	(5)	Fred Couples
7	(9)	Colin Montgomerie
8	(7)	Ernie Els
9	(12)	Corey Pavin
10	(8)	David Frost
11	(14)	Jumbo Ozaki
12	(13)	Tom Kite
13	(11)	Ian Woosnam
14	(15)	Tom Lehman
15	(18)	Vijay Singh
16	(19)	Mark McNulty
17	(16)	Davis Love III
18	(10)	Paul Azinger
19	(21)	Fuzzy Zoeller (US,3)
20	(22)	Loren Roberts (US)

Selected other positions in Top 50:

21(26) Seve Ballesteros; 30(34) Barry Lane; 33(-) David Gilford; 34(-) Jesper Parnevik; 37(-) Scott Hoch; 45(-) Miguel Jimenez; 46(-) Mark McCumber; 47(-) Mark Roe; 48(-) Eduardo Romero; 50(32) Jim Gallagher Jr

END-DECEMBER 1994

1	(1)	Nick Price
2	(2)	Greg Norman
3	(3)	Nick Faldo
4	(4)	Bernhard Langer
5	(5)	Jose-Maria Olazabal
6	(8)	Ernie Els
7	(6)	Fred Couples
8	(7)	Colin Montgomerie
9	(11)	Jumbo Ozaki
10	(9)	Corey Pavin
11	(10)	David Frost
12	(19)	Fuzzy Zoeller
13	(12)	Tom Kite
14	(21)	Seve Ballesteros (Sp,2)
15	(15)	Vijay Singh
16	(13)	Ian Woosnam
17	(14)	Tom Lehman
18	(16)	Mark McNulty
19	(46)	Mark McCumber (US,1)
20	(20)	Loren Roberts

Selected other positions in Top 50:
25(17) Davis Love III; 34(42) Ben Crenshaw; 36(-) Bill Glasson; 37(-) Bob Estes; 43(38) Steve Elkington; 48(-) Robert Allenby; 49(-) Mark Calcavecchia; 50(-) Rick Fehr

END-MARCH 1995

1	(1)	Nick Price
2	(3)	Nick Faldo
3	(2)	Greg Norman
4	(4)	Bernhard Langer
5	(6)	Ernie Els
6	(5)	Jose-Maria Olazabal
7	(7)	Fred Couples
8	(8)	Colin Montgomerie
9	(10)	Corey Pavin
10	(9)	Jumbo Ozaki
11	(14)	Seve Ballesteros
12	(16)	Ian Woosnam
13	(11)	David Frost
14	(17)	Tom Lehman
15	(18)	Mark McNulty
16	(12)	Fuzzy Zoeller
17	(20	Loren Roberts
18	(15)	Vijay Singh
19	(19)	Mark McCumber
20	(13)	Tom Kite

Selected other positions in Top 50:
24(32) Lee Janzen; 26(43) Steve Elkington; 27(-) Peter Jacobsen; 29(41) Bruce Lietzke; 30(23) Tom Watson; 35(-) Scott Simpson; 38(49) Mark Calcavecchia; 40(-) Payne Stewart; 45(31) Frank Nobilo; 47(39) Jesper Parnevik

END-JUNE 1995

1	(3)	Greg Norman
2	(1)	Nick Price
3	(2)	Nick Faldo
4	(4)	Bernhard Langer
5	(9)	Corey Pavin
6	(5)	Ernie Els
7	(7)	Fred Couples
8	(8)	Colin Montgomerie
9	(6)	Jose-Maria Olazabal
10	(10)	Jumbo Ozaki
11	(14)	Tom Lehman
12	(11)	Seve Ballesteros
13	(19)	Mark McCumber
14	(18)	Vijay Singh
15	(13)	David Frost
16	(12)	Ian Woosnam
17	(16)	Fuzzy Zoeller
18	(25)	Davis Love III (US,1)
19	(15)	Mark McNulty
20	(21)	Phil Mickelson (US)

Selected other positions in Top 50:
23(33) Ben Crenshaw; 26(38) Mark Calcavecchia; 28(-) Jim Gallagher Jr; 31(20) Tom Kite; 33(40) Payne Stewart; 36(47) Jesper Parnevik; 42=(-) David Duval; 42=(-) Brian Watts; 46(-) Costantino Rocca; 50(-) Kenny Perry

END-SEPTEMBER 1995

1	(1)	Greg Norman
2	(2)	Nick Price
3	(4)	Bernhard Langer
4	(6)	Ernie Els
5	(3)	Nick Faldo
6	(8)	Colin Montgomerie
7	(5)	Corey Pavin
8	(7)	Fred Couples
9	(10)	Jumbo Ozaki
10	(9)	Jose-Maria Olazabal
11	(22)	Steve Elkington (Aus,2)
12	(11)	Tom Lehman
13	(14)	Vijay Singh
14	(13)	Mark McCumber
15	(47)	Sam Torrance (Sco)
16	(25)	Lee Janzen (US,1)
17	(18)	Davis Love III
18	(15)	David Frost
19	(12)	Seve Ballesteros
20	(21)	Loren Roberts (US,1)

Selected other positions in Top 50:
22(32) Scott Hoch; 26(46) Costantino Rocca; 31(18) Mark McNulty; 35(16) Ian Woosnam; 38(-) Michael Campbell; 44(-) Mark O'Meara; 46(31) Tom Kite; 49(49) Barry Lane; 50(-) John Daly

END-DECEMBER 1995

1	(1)	Greg Norman
2	(2)	Nick Price
3	(4)	Ernie Els
4	(3)	Bernhard Langer
5	(7)	Corey Pavin
6	(6)	Colin Montgomerie
7	(8)	Fred Couples
8	(5)	Nick Faldo
9	(11)	Steve Elkington
10	(9)	Jumbo Ozaki
11	(12)	Tom Lehman
12	(20)	Loren Roberts
13	(10)	Jose-Maria Olazabal
14	(15)	Sam Torrance
15	(21)	Peter Jacobsen (US)
16	(13)	Vijay Singh
17	(16)	Lee Janzen
18	(14)	Mark McCumber
19	(22)	Scott Hoch (US,2)
20	(17)	Davis Love III

Selected other positions in Top 50:

21(25) Ben Crenshaw; 28(38) Michael Campbell; 30(-) Billy Mayfair; 33(39) David Duval; 35(23) Fuzzy Zoeller; 38(49) Barry Lane; 42(-) Kenny Perry; 44(34) Payne Stewart; 50(-) Peter Senior

END-MARCH 1996

1	(1)	Greg Norman
2	(6)	Colin Montgomerie
3	(2)	Nick Price
4	(3)	Ernie Els
5	(5)	Corey Pavin
6	(4)	Bernhard Langer
7	(7)	Fred Couples
8	(9)	Steve Elkington
9=	(11)	Tom Lehman
	(10)	Jumbo Ozaki
11	(8)	Nick Faldo
12	(13)	Jose-Maria Olazabal
13	(16)	Vijay Singh
14	(24)	Phil Mickelson (US,1)
15	(18)	Mark McCumber
16	(19)	Scott Hoch
17	(14)	Sam Torrance
18	(20)	Davis Love III
19	(12)	Loren Roberts
20	(17)	Lee Janzen

Selected other positions in Top 50:

21(26) Jay Haas; 23(41) Mark O'Meara; 26(-) Ian Woosnam; 35(-) Bob Tway; 36(15) Peter Jacobsen; 50(-) Justin Leonard

END-JUNE 1996

1	(1)	Greg Norman
2	(3)	Nick Price
3	(2)	Colin Montgomerie
4	(7)	Fred Couples
5	(4)	Ernie Els
6	(5)	Corey Pavin
7	(11)	Nick Faldo
8	(9)	Jumbo Ozaki
9	(6)	Bernhard Langer
10	(23)	Mark O'Meara (US,2)
11	(8)	Steve Elkington
12	(14)	Phil Mickelson
13	(9)	Tom Lehman
14	(18)	Davis Love III
15	(16)	Scott Hoch
16	(39)	David Duval (US)
17	(13)	Vijay Singh
18	(19)	Loren Roberts
19	(33)	Tom Watson (US,6)
20	(24)	Costantino Rocca (Ita)

Selected other positions in Top 50:

23(34) Jeff Maggert; 24(31) Brad Faxon; 28(50) Frank Nobilo; 30(46) Craig Parry; 33(-) Steve Jones; 36(-) Jim Furyk; 38(-) Robert Allenby; 41(30) Michael Campbell; 42(13)Jose-Maria Olazabal; 43(-) Duffy Waldorf; 49(25) Seve Ballesteros

END-SEPTEMBER 1996

1	(1)	Greg Norman
2	(5)	Ernie Els
3	(3)	Colin Montgomerie
4	(7)	Nick Faldo
5	(13)	Tom Lehman
6	(4)	Fred Couples
7	(8)	Jumbo Ozaki
8	(6)	Corey Pavin
9	(12)	Phil Mickelson
10	(10)	Mark O'Meara
11	(14)	Davis Love III
12	(11)	Steve Elkington
13	(2)	Nick Price
14	(9)	Bernhard Langer
15	(-)	Steve Stricker
16	(18)	Loren Roberts
17	(16)	David Duval
18	(22)	Mark McCumber (US,2)
19	(15)	Scott Hoch
20	(17)	Vijay Singh

Selected other positions in Top 50:

21(-) Mark Brooks; 27(48) Kenny Perry; 28(-) Justin Leonard; 41(22) Sam Torrance; 42(29) Mark Calcavecchia; 47(-) Tommy Tolles; 49(31) Jay Haas; 50(-) Fred Funk

OFFICIAL WORLD RANKING

END-DECEMBER 1996

1	(1)	Greg Norman
2	(2)	Tom Lehman
3	(3)	Colin Montgomerie
4	(2)	Ernie Els
5	(6)	Fred Couples
6	(4)	Nick Faldo
7	(9)	Phil Mickelson
8	(7)	Jumbo Ozaki
9	(11)	Davis Love III
10	(10)	Mark O'Meara
11	(8)	Corey Pavin
12	(15)	Steve Stricker
13	(13)	Nick Price
14	(12)	Steve Elkington
15	(19)	Scott Hoch
16	(14)	Bernhard Langer
17	(22)	Tom Watson (US,7)
18	(21)	Mark Brooks (US)
19	(17)	David Duval
20	(20)	Vijay Singh

Selected other positions in Top 50:

21(29) Mark McNulty; 30(18) Mark McCumber; 33(-) Tiger Woods; 34(43) Payne Stewart; 43(31) Billy Mayfair; 44(-) Michael Bradley

END-MARCH 1997

1	(1)	Greg Norman
2	(2)	Tom Lehman
3	(3)	Colin Montgomerie
4	(14)	Steve Elkington
5	(10)	Mark O'Meara
6	(4)	Ernie Els
7	(8)	Jumbo Ozaki
8	(6)	Nick Faldo
9	(7)	Phil Mickelson
10	(13)	Nick Price
11	(5)	Fred Couples
12	(15)	Scott Hoch
13	(9)	Davis Love III
14	(33)	Tiger Woods (US)
15	(11)	Corey Pavin
16	(28)	Steve Jones (US)
17	(12)	Steve Stricker
18	(19)	David Duval
19	(16)	Bernhard Langer
20	(21)	Mark McNulty (Zim,2)

Selected other positions in Top 50:

25(39) Jesper Parnevik; 29(-) Paul Stankowski; 32(42) Craig Stadler; 33(26) Ian Woosnam; 40(-) John Cook; 43(-) Jeff Sluman; 50(-) David Frost

OFFICIAL WORLD RANKING

END-JUNE 1997

1	(1)	Greg Norman
2	(6)	Ernie Els
3	(14)	Tiger Woods
4	(3)	Colin Montgomerie
5	(10)	Nick Price
6	(2)	Tom Lehman
7	(4)	Steve Elkington
8	(7)	Jumbo Ozaki
9	(5)	Mark O'Meara
10	(8)	Nick Faldo
11	(9)	Phil Mickelson
12	(12)	Scott Hoch
13	(26)	Brad Faxon (US)
14	(11)	Fred Couples
15	(25)	Jesper Parnevik (Swe)
16	(33)	Ian Woosnam (Wal,1)
17	(19)	Bernhard Langer
18	(13)	Davis Love III
19	(34)	Justin Leonard (US)
20	(23)	Vijay Singh (Fij,1)

Selected other positions in Top 50:

27(18) David Duval; 31(48) Jim Furyk; 33(-) Tommy Tolles; 36(-) Shigeki Maruyama (Jap); 37(-) Lee Westwood; 39(15) Corey Pavin; 42(31) Payne Stewart; 48(-) Darren Clarke

END-SEPTEMBER 1997

1	(1)	Greg Norman
2	(3)	Tiger Woods
3	(2)	Ernie Els
4	(5)	Nick Price
5	(6)	Tom Lehman
6	(4)	Colin Montgomerie
7	(11)	Phil Mickelson
8	(8)	Jumbo Ozaki
9	(9)	Mark O'Meara
10	(18)	Davis Love III
11	(19)	Justin Leonard
12	(12)	Scott Hoch
13	(14)	Fred Couples
14	(7)	Steve Elkington
15	(10)	Nick Faldo
16	(13)	Brad Faxon
17	(23)	Steve Jones (US,1)
18	(20)	Vijay Singh
19	(15)	Jesper Parnevik
20	(31)	Jim Furyk (US)

Selected other positions in Top 50:

21(26) Frank Nobilo; 22(17) Bernhard Langer; 24(16) Ian Woosnam; 35(-) Tom Kite; 36(24) Steve Stricker; 39(-) Scott McCarron; 43(-) Stuart Appleby; 44(-) Per-Ulrik Johannson; 45(34) Costantino Rocca; 50(-) Joe Ozaki

END-DECEMBER 1997

1	(1)	Greg Norman
2	(2)	Tiger Woods
3	(4)	Nick Price
4	(3)	Ernie Els
5	(10)	Davis Love III
6	(7)	Phil Mickelson
7	(6)	Colin Montgomerie
8	(8)	Jumbo Ozaki
9	(5)	Tom Lehman
10	(9)	Mark O'Meara
11	(11)	Justin Leonard
12	(29)	David Duval (US,1)
13	(12)	Scott Hoch
14	(16)	Brad Faxon
15	(18)	Vijay Singh
16	(14)	Steve Elkington
17	(15)	Nick Faldo
18	(19)	Jesper Parnevik
19	(25)	Tom Watson (US,8)
20	(13)	Fred Couples

Selected other positions in Top 50:
23(31) Lee Westwood; 28(34) Mark Calcavecchia; 37(48)
Brian Watts; 40(-) Craig Parry; 41(-) Bill Glasson; 42(-)
Jose-Maria Olazabal; 47(41) Payne Stewart

END-MARCH 1998

1	(2)	Tiger Woods
2	(4)	Ernie Els
3	(1)	Greg Norman
4	(5)	Davis Love III
5	(3)	Nick Price
6	(11)	Justin Leonard
7	(7)	Colin Montgomerie
8	(6)	Phil Mickelson
9	(9)	Tom Lehman
10	(8)	Jumbo Ozaki
11	(12)	David Duval
12	(15)	Vijay Singh
13	(10)	Mark O'Meara
14	(13)	Scott Hoch
15	(19)	Tom Watson
16	(18)	Jesper Parnevik
17	(14)	Brad Faxon
18	(23)	Lee Westwood (Eng)
19	(28)	Mark Calcavecchia (US,2)
20	(21)	Bernhard Langer (Ger,2)

Selected other positions in Top 50:
21(17) Nick Faldo; 27(42) Jose-Maria Olazabal; 28(20)
Fred Couples; 30(25) Ian Woosnam; 37(-) Stewart Cink;
40(34) Lee Janzen; 45(-) Michael Bradley; 50(-)
Costantino Rocca

END-JUNE 1998

1	(1)	Tiger Woods
2	(2)	Ernie Els
3	(4)	Davis Love III
4	(11)	David Duval
5	(7)	Colin Montgomerie
6	(3)	Greg Norman
7	(6)	Justin Leonard
8	(28)	Fred Couples (US,1)
9	(5)	Nick Price
10	(18)	Lee Westwood
11	(13)	Mark O'Meara
12	(8)	Phil Mickelson
13	(9)	Tom Lehman
14	(10)	Jumbo Ozaki
15	(22)	Jim Furyk (US,1)
16	(12)	Vijay Singh
17	(14)	Scott Hoch
18	(16)	Jesper Parnevik
19	(15)	Tom Watson
20	(19)	Mark Calcavecchia

Selected other positions in Top 50:
21(40) Lee Janzen; 26(32) Darren Clarke; 27(49) Payne
Stewart; 31(39) Steve Stricker; 38(-) Thomas Bjorn; 41(-)
Brandt Jobe; 42(-) Carlos Franco; 45(-) Andrew Magee;
46(-) Frankie Minoza; 48(21) Nick Faldo; 50(-) Bob Estes

END-SEPTEMBER 1998

1	(1)	Tiger Woods
2	(4)	David Duval
3	(3)	Davis Love III
4	(10)	Mark O'Meara
5	(2)	Ernie Els
6	(5)	Colin Montgomerie
7	(9)	Nick Price
8	(16)	Vijay Singh
9	(10)	Lee Westwood
10	(8)	Fred Couples
11	(12)	Phil Mickelson
12	(14)	Jumbo Ozaki
13	(6)	Greg Norman
14	(15)	Jim Furyk
15	(7)	Justin Leonard
16	(18)	Jesper Parnevik
17	(17)	Scott Hoch
18	(13)	Tom Lehman
19	(20)	Mark Calcavecchia
20	(19)	Tom Watson

Selected other positions in Top 50:
23(37) Brian Watts; 28(23) Bernhard Langer; 30(41)
Brandt Jobe; 38(-) Billy Mayfair; 43(-) Jeff Sluman; 44(32)
Loren Roberts; 45(33) Frank Nobilo; 46(-) Glen Day;
47(39) Mark McNulty; 48(-) Hal Sutton

END-DECEMBER 1998

1	(1)	Tiger Woods
2	(4)	Mark O'Meara
3	(2)	David Duval
4	(3)	Davis Love III
5	(5)	Ernie Els
6	(7)	Nick Price
7	(6)	Colin Montgomerie
8	(9)	Lee Westwood
9	(9)	Vijay Singh
10	(11)	Phil Mickelson
11	(10)	Fred Couples
12	(14)	Jim Furyk
13	(12)	Jumbo Ozaki
14	(16)	Jesper Parnevik
15	(15)	Justin Leonard
16	(25)	Steve Elkington (Aus,3)
17	(22)	Darren Clarke (NI)
18	(13)	Greg Norman
19	(23)	Brian Watts (US)
20	(17)	Scott Hoch

Selected other positions in Top 50:
29(-) John Huston; 30(35) Stuart Appleby;33(41) Bob Tway; 34(48) Hal Sutton; 37(40) Ian Woosnam; 39(-) Carlos Franco; 50(-) Scott Verplank

END-MARCH 1999

1	(3)	David Duval
2	(1)	Tiger Woods
3	(4)	Davis Love III
4	(2)	Mark O'Meara
5	(5)	Ernie Els
6	(8)	Lee Westwood
7	(9)	Vijay Singh
8	(6)	Nick Price
9	(7)	Colin Montgomerie
10	(11)	Fred Couples
11	(12)	Jim Furyk
12	(15)	Justin Leonard
13	(13)	Jumbo Ozaki
14	(10)	Phil Mickelson
15	(31)	Jeff Maggert (US)
16	(17)	Darren Clarke
17	(27)	Payne Stewart (US,2)
18	(14)	Jesper Parnevik
19	(16)	Steve Elkington
20	(22)	Tom Lehman (US,1)

Selected other positions in Top 50:
21(26) Steve Stricker; 23(34) Hal Sutton; 28(18) Greg Norman; 29(49) Bill Glasson; 30(24) Tom Watson; 33(25) Jose-Maria Olazabal; 35(48) Andrew Magee; 44(-) Fred Funk; 45(-) Miguel Jimenez; 46(-) Tim Herron; 48=(-) Craig Parry

OFFICIAL WORLD RANKING

END-JUNE 1999			**END-SEPTEMBER 1999**		
1	(1)	David Duval	1	(2)	Tiger Woods
2	(2)	Tiger Woods	2	(1)	David Duval
3	(3)	Davis Love III	3	(5)	Colin Montgomerie
4	(7)	Vijay Singh	4	(3)	Davis Love III
5	(9)	Colin Montgomerie	5	(8)	Lee Westwood
6	(4)	Mark O'Meara	6	(7)	Ernie Els
7	(5)	Ernie Els	7	(4)	Vijay Singh
8	(6)	Lee Westwood	8	(11)	Payne Stewart
9	(14)	Phil Mickelson	9	(10)	Nick Price
10	(8)	Nick Price	10	(6)	Mark O'Meara
11	(17)	Payne Stewart	11	(16)	Hal Sutton
12	(12)	Justin Leonard	12	(9)	Phil Mickelson
13	(11)	Jim Furyk	13	(12)	Justin Leonard
14	(13)	Jumbo Ozaki	14	(13)	Jim Furyk
15	(18)	Jesper Parnevik	15	(15)	Jesper Parnevik
16	(23)	Hal Sutton (US,1)	16	(20)	John Huston
17	(15)	Jeff Maggert	17	(17)	Jeff Maggert
18	(16)	Darren Clarke	18	(14)	Jumbo Ozaki
19	(10)	Fred Couples	19	(19)	Fred Couples
20	(25)	John Huston (US)	20	(26)	Carlos Franco (Par)

Selected other positions in Top 50:

23(33) Jose-Maria Olazabal; 26(42) Carlos Franco; 29(47) Loren Roberts; 31(-) Steve Pate; 32(28) Greg Norman; 34(22) Lee Janzen; 35(46) Tim Herron; 36(27) Bernhard Langer; 47(39) John Cook; 49(-) Chris Perry; 50(34) Bob Tway

Selected other positions in Top 50:

25(-) Sergio Garcia; 29(48) Craig Parry; 32(49) Chris Perry; 42(30) Scott Hoch; 46(36) Bernhard Langer; 48(-) Paul Lawrie; 50 Brent Geiberger

END-DECEMBER 1999

1	(1)	Tiger Woods
2	(2)	David Duval
3	(3)	Colin Montgomerie
4	(4)	Davis Love III
5	(6)	Ernie Els
6	(5)	Lee Westwood
7	(7)	Vijay Singh
8	(9)	Nick Price
9	(10)	Phil Mickelson
10	(10)	Mark O'Meara
11	(14)	Jim Furyk
12	(25)	Sergio Garcia (Sp)
13	(13)	Justin Leonard
14	(11)	Hal Sutton
15	(15)	Jesper Parnevik
16	(16)	John Huston
17	(17)	Jeff Maggert
18	(20)	Carlos Franco
19	(17)	Darren Clarke
20	(11)	Fred Couples

Selected other positions in Top 50:
21(43) Miguel Jimenez; 23(32) Chris Perry; 24(-) David Toms; 31(39) Tim Herron; 32(40) Stewart Cink; 33(-) Retief Goosen; 34(-) Dudley Hart; 36(18) Jumbo Ozaki; 40(26) Brian Watts; 43(-) Greg Norman; 50(-) Padraig Harrington

SUMMARY

Of course these extracts cannot tell the full story of what happens week-in, week-out. There is no space here for that, unfortunately. A quarterly review will miss out some important data: for example, Ernie Els was at number one for nine weeks over three visits in 1997 and 1998; and Tom Lehman was there briefly in April 1997, and both events were missed.

However, even taken quarterly, the World Ranking provides an unique snapshot of the relative success of the world's top golfers over the last fourteen years. Fourteen years is about a typical span for the professional golfer at least for his best years; and the Ranking throws up the performances of some great players. It's sad Tony Greer's statistics were not around earlier, when quantifiable comparisons of player performances down the years would have been most illuminating. However, we can count ourselves lucky that Jack Nicklaus' final Major win at Augusta just a few days after the inaugural Ranking elevated him into the Top 20.

At the beginning, in 1986, we capture the evergreen Langer and Norman already at the top of the sport; while Seve was still in his pomp, and Sandy Lyle was between his two Major triumphs. Langer finally disappeared (temporarily?) from the Top 50 only in December 1999; and Norman, having clung to the top spot more tenaciously than anyone else, only to dip because of his season-long injury, has already, by the close of the year, made a positive step back up the chart.

Tom Watson was already at the top for a decade and more when he appeared in the first Top 10; and it's a measure of his durability that even in a quarterly survey like this, he sprang back into the Top 20 no fewer than eight times. At 98th in the final Ranking of 1999, can Tom do it again?

No one would blame Mark O'Meara, another in the first Top 10, for thinking his best days were behind him when he disappeared out of the Top 50 back in 1995. Then after the Masters, Open Championship and the World Matchplay in 1998, he shot back up to second after the Tiger.

We can witness the rise and fall of great players over the period, and recall just how good Faldo and Woosnam were in their heyday; and is it surprising Europe did so well in the Ryder Cup when you study the Rankings, especially in the early and middle years? Others, like Nick Price, seem to go on forever. The Ranking is also fascinating, watching the players' stock rise and fall, sometimes spectacularly, sometimes, as in the case of the most consistent (Montgomerie and the stay-at-home Jumbo Ozaki come to mind), more sedately. Dips in form, self-enforced sabbaticals (for example Faldo's swing reconstruction) and long-term injury (Norman and Olazabal, for instance) can all be plotted against the Ranking.

Finally, it is exciting to monitor the progress of newcomers, and the Ranking records of Tiger Woods and Sergio Garcia are as spectacular as the golf these young tyros produce.

OFFICIAL WORLD RANKING TOP 200

*Positions at 31 December 1999 with 97/98 positions in brackets. Winners of Major Championships in **bold***

1	(1)	**Tiger Woods** (US)
2	(3)	David Duval (US)
3	(7)	Colin Montgomerie (Sco)
4	(4)	**Davis Love III** (US)
5	(5)	**Ernie Els** (RSA)
6	(8)	Lee Westwood (Eng)
7	(9)	**Vijay Singh** (Fij)
8	(6)	Nick Price (Zim)
9	(10)	Phil Mickelson (US)
10	(2)	Mark O'Meara (US)
11	(12)	Jim Furyk (US)
12	(399=)	Sergio Garcia (Sp)
13	(15)	**Justin Leonard** (US)
14	(33)	**Hal Sutton** (US)
15	(14)	Jesper Parnevik (Swe)
16	(28)	John Huston (US)
17	(30)	Jeff Maggert (US)
18	(38)	Carlos Franco (Par)
19	(17)	Darren Clarke (NI)
20	(11)	**Fred Couples** (US)
21	(53)	Miguel Jimenez (Sp)
22	(22)	**Tom Lehman** (US)
23	(92)	Chris Perry (US)
24	(70)	David Toms (US)
25	(16)	**Steve Elkington** (Aus)
26	(25)	**Jose-Maria Olazabal** (Sp)
27	(75)	Steve Pate (US)
28	(37)	**Jeff Sluman** (US)
29	(26)	Steve Stricker (US)
30	(44)	Bob Estes (US)
31	(83)	Tim Herron (US)
32	(45)	Stewart Cink (US)
33	(82)	Retief Goosen (RSA)
34	(58)	Dudley Hart (US)
35	(29)	Stuart Appleby (Aus)
36	(13)	Jumbo Ozaki (Jap)
37	(43)	Glen Day (US)
38	(40)	Thomas Bjorn (Den)
39	(23)	**Lee Janzen** (US)
40	(19)	Brian Watts (US)
41	(20)	Scott Hoch (US)
42	(52)	Craig Parry (Aus)
43	(18)	**Greg Norman** (Aus)
44	(240)	**Paul Lawrie** (Sco)
45	(32)	**Bob Tway** (US)
46	(55)	Joe Ozaki (Jap)
47	(90)	Brent Geiberger (US)
48	(54)	Fred Funk (US)
49	(46)	Loren Roberts (US)
50	(105)	Padraig Harrington (Ire)
51	(27)	**Bernhard Langer** (Ger)
52	(41)	Billy Mayfair (US)
53	(215=)	Bob May (US)
54	(172)	Ted Tryba (US)
55	(115)	Rocco Mediate (US)
56	(47)	Andrew Magee (US)
57	(306)	Mike Weir (Can)
58	(21)	**Mark Calcavecchia** (US)
59	(48)	Bill Glasson (US)
60	(154=)	Angel Cabrera (Arg)
61	(35)	Brandt Jobe (US)
62	(42)	Shigeki Maruyama (Jap)
63	(101)	Olin Browne (US)
64	(130)	Duffy Waldorf (US)
65	(617=)	Dennis Paulsen (US)
66	(31)	John Cook (US)
67	(66)	Robert Karlsson (Swe)
68	(112)	Jarmo Sandelin (Swe)
69	(71)	Jay Haas (US)
70	(88)	Skip Kendall (US)
71	(61)	**Paul Azinger** (US)
72	(36)	**Ian Woosnam** (Wal)
73	(49)	Scott Verplank (US)
74	(69)	Greg Turner (NZ)
75	(106)	Toshimitsu Izawa (Jap)
76	(208)	Scott Dunlap (US)
77	(65)	Peter O'Malley (Aus)
78	(111)	Frank Lickliter (US)
79	(60)	Eduardo Romero (Arg)
80	(80)	Kirk Triplett (US)
81	(131)	Mark James (Eng)
82	(68)	Andrew Coltart (Sco)
83	(136)	Kaz'ko Hosokawa (Jap)
84	(93)	David Frost (RSA)
85	(79)	Hidem'i Tanaka (Jap)
86	(50)	Patrik Sjoland (Swe)
87	(617=)	Notah Begay III (US)
88	(81)	Stephen Ames (T&T)

89	(57)	Stephen Leaney (Aus)
90	(215=)	Tsuy'hi Yoneyama (Jap)
91	(170)	Jean Van de Velde (Fra)
92	(200)	Greg Kraft (US)
93	(64)	**Craig Stadler** (US)
94	(124)	Alexander Cejka (Ger)
95	(78)	Brandel Chamblee (US)
96	(39)	Brad Faxon (US)
97	(73)	Steve Flesch (US)
98	(24)	**Tom Watson** (US)
99	(34)	**Steve Jones** (US)
100	(51)	Frankie Minoza (Phi)
101	(129)	Sh'o Katayama (Jap)
102	(133)	Tommy Armour III (US)
103	(174)	Tom Pernice Jr (US)
104	(109)	Phillip Price (Wal)
105	(204)	Pierre Fulke (Swe)
106	(96)	Peter Baker (Eng)
107	(617=)	Jarrod Moseley (Aus)
108	(359)	Michael Campbell (NZ)
109	(299=)	Craig Spence (Aus)
110	(138)	Kaname Yokoo (Jap)
111	(205)	Scott Gump (US)
112	(119)	David Carter (Eng)
113	(161)	David Howell (Eng)
114	(63)	Per-Ulrik Johannson (Swe)
115	(233=)	**Corey Pavin** (US)
116	(132)	Paul Goydos (US)
117	(97)	**Larry Mize** (US)
118	(617=)	Jonathan Kaye (US)
119	(114)	Kevin Sutherland (US)
120	(123)	JP Hayes (US)
121	(100)	Hajime Meshiai (Jap)
122	(143)	Toru Taniguchi (Jap)
123	(417=)	John Bickerton (Eng)
124	(156)	Gary Orr (Sco)
125	(617=)	Rich Beem (US)
126	(90)	Costantino Rocca (Ita)
127	(146)	Paul McGinley (Ire)
128	(134)	Harrison Frazar (US)
129	(611=)	Choi Kyoung-Ju (Kor)
130	(121)	Peter Senior (Aus)
131	(72)	Mark McNulty (Zim)
132	(180)	Santiago Luna (Sp)
133	(171)	Steve Webster (Eng)
134	(135)	Joey Sindelar (US)

135	(237)	Gabriel Hjertstedt (Swe)
136	(117)	Bradley Hughes (Aus)
137	(110)	Kenny Perry (US)
138	(99)	Peter Lonard (Aus)
139	(151)	Miguel Martin (Sp)
140	(267=)	Taichi Teshima (Jap)
141	(361=)	Nick O'Hern (Aus)
142	(67)	Greg Chalmers (Aus)
143	(86=)	Sam Torrance (Sco)
144 =	(98)	Eduardo Herrera (Col)
	(186)	Nob'itsu Yuhara (Jap)
146	(62)	Michael Bradley (US)
147	(77)	Billy Andrade (US)
148	(84)	Robert Allenby (Aus)
149	(258)	Hirofumi Miyase (Jap)
150	(125)	Sven Struver (Ger)
151	=(196)	Brian Henninger (US)
	(327)	Dean Robertson (Sco)
153	(178)	Kats'i Kuwabara (Jap)
154	(617=)	David Park (Wal)
155	(126)	Ignacio Garrido (Sp)
156	(108)	Russell Claydon (Eng)
157	(113)	Mathias Gronberg (Swe)
158	(202)	Yasuharu Imano (Jap)
159	(103)	Jet Ozaki (Jap)
160	(194)	Kim Jong-Duck (Kor)
161	=(301)	Chris DiMarco (US)
	(321=)	Nic Henning (RSA)
	(213)	Rodney Pampling (Aus)
164	(128)	Robert Damron (US)
165	(95)	Tommy Tolles (US)
166	(173)	Mike Reid (US)
167	(85)	Joe Durant (US)
168	(89)	Trevor Dodds (Nam)
169	(319)	Jeev Milka Singh (Ind)
170	(104)	Jay Don Blake (US)
171	(153)	Jim Carter (US)
172	(74)	Scott McCarron (US)
173	(165)	Paul Broadhurst (Eng)
174	(497=)	Geoff Ogilvy (Aus)
175	(56)	**Nick Faldo** (Eng)
176	(150)	Mark Wiebe (US)
177	(184)	Jose Coceres (Arg)
178	(254)	**Mark Brooks** (US)
179	(118)	Dan Forsman (US)
180	(140)	Tom Byrum (US)

181	(347)	Franklin Langham (US)
182	(209)	Kats'oshi Tomori (Jap)
183	=(145)	Nolan Henke (US)
	(181)	Jamie Spence (Eng)
185	=(116)	Ke'ro Fukabori (Jap)
	(191)	Jerry Kelly (US)
187	(193)	Satoshi Higashi (Jap)
188	(94)	Kats'a Miyamoto (Jap)
189	(176)	Len Mattiace (US)
190	(76)	Paul Stankowski (US)
191	(167=)	Peter Mitchell (Eng)
192	(210)	Mats Lanner (Swe)
193	(127)	Toru Suzuki (Jap)
194	(617=)	Aaron Baddeley [a] (Aus)
195	(203)	Kevin Wentworth (US)
196	(360)	Jay Delsing (US)
197	(249)	Ryoken Kawagishi (Jap)
198	(230)	JL Lewis (US)
199	(617=)	Warren Bennett (Eng)
200	(190)	Tsukasa Watanabe (Jap)

HOLDERS OF THE NO 1 POSITION APRIL 1986-DECEMBER 1999

		Weeks/Max	(Runs)
1	Greg Norman	331/715	(11)
2	Nick Faldo	97	(4)
3	Tiger Woods	*90	(7)
4	Seve Ballesteros	60	(5)
5	Ian Woosnam	50	(1)
6	Nick Price	43	(1)
7	Fred Couples	16	(2)
8	David Duval	15	(2)
9	Ernie Els	9	(3)
10	Bernhard Langer	3	(1)
11	Tom Lehman	1	(1)

*Incumbent at 31 December 1999. Norman has been at No 1 for 46% of the 715-week Ranking history, to the end of 1999

MOST CONSECUTIVE WEEKS AT NO 1 APRIL 1986-DECEMBER 1999

		No of Weeks/Max
1	Greg Norman	96/715
2	Nick Faldo	81
3	Greg Norman	62

4	Greg Norman	54
5	Ian Woosnam	50
6	Greg Norman	48
8	Nick Price	43
9	Tiger Woods	41
10	Greg Norman	27

MOST WEEKS IN THE TOP TEN:

		No of Weeks
1	Greg Norman	644/715
2	Nick Faldo	470
3	Bernhard Langer	405
4	Nick Price	350*
5	Ian Woosnam	337
6	Seve Ballesteros	336
7	Fred Couples	324
8	Jose-Maria Olazabal	313
9	Colin Montgomerie	293*
10	Paul Azinger	291
11	Ernie Els	288*
12	Payne Stewart	248**
13	Curtis Strange	221
14	Davis Love III	206*
15	Jumbo Ozaki	193
16	Mark O'Meara	190*
17	Tom Kite	175
18	Corey Pavin	167
19	Sandy Lyle	166
20	Tiger Woods	142*

*Still in the Top 10 at 31 December 1999
** Stewart was withdrawn from the Ranking four weeks after his death in 1999. He was in the Top 10 at the time of his death.
Woods' run is consecutive.